THE PAPERS OF
BENJAMIN FRANKLIN

SPONSORED BY

The American Philosophical Society

and Yale University

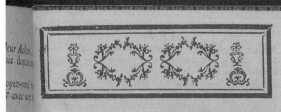

INFORMATION

TO THOSE
WHO WOULD REMOVE
TO AMERICA.

M ANY Perfons in Europe having directly or by
Letters, exprefs'd to the Writer of this, who is
well acquainted with North-America, their Defire
of tranfporting and eftablishing themfelves in that
Country; but who appear to him to have formed
thro' Ignorance, miftaken Ideas & Expectations of
what is to be obtained there; he thinks it may be
ufeful, and prevent inconvenient, expenfive & fruit-
lefs Removals and Voyages of improper Perfons, if
he gives fome clearer & truer Notions of that Part
of the World than appear to have hitherto prevailed.

He finds it is imagined by Numbers that the Inhabitants of North-America are rich, capable of
rewarding, and difpos'd to reward all forts of
Ingenuity; that they are at the fame time ignorant
of all the Sciences; & confequently that ftrangers
poffeffing Talents in the Belles-Letters, fine Arts, &c.
muft be highly efteemed, and fo well paid as to
become eafily rich themfelves; that there are alfo
abundance of profitable Offices to be difpofed of,

A

"Information to Those Who Would Remove to America"

THE PAPERS OF

Benjamin Franklin

VOLUME 41   *September 16, 1783, through February 29, 1784*

ELLEN R. COHN, *Editor*

JONATHAN R. DULL, *Senior Associate Editor*

ROBERT P. FRANKEL, JR., KATE M. OHNO, AND

PHILIPP ZIESCHE, *Associate Editors*

ALICIA K. ANDERSON, ALLEGRA DI BONAVENTURA,

ALYSIA M. CAIN, ADRINA M. GARBOOSHIAN, AND

MICHAEL SLETCHER, *Assistant Editors*

New Haven and London   YALE UNIVERSITY PRESS, 2014

As indicated in the first volume, this edition was made possible through the vision and generosity of Yale University and the American Philosophical Society and by a substantial donation from Henry R. Luce in the name of Life Magazine. Additional funds were provided by a grant from the Ford Foundation to the National Archives Trust Fund Board. Subsequent support has come from the Andrew W. Mellon Foundation. Major underwriting of the present volume has been provided by the Packard Humanities Institute through Founding Fathers Papers, Inc., the Florence Gould Foundation, the Cinco Hermanos Fund, and The Pew Charitable Trusts. We gratefully acknowledge the bequest of Raymond N. Kjellberg, which will continue to sustain our enterprise. We offer particular appreciation to Richard Gilder, Charles and Ann Johnson, Mason Willrich, the Yale Class of 1954, Claude-Anne Lopez, and the Benjamin Franklin Tercentenary for generous donations that will insure the future of the edition. We are grateful for the generous support of Candace and Stuart Karu, Richard N. Rosenfeld, Phyllis Z. and Fenmore R. Seton, Malcolm N. Smith, Ralph Gregory Elliot, and Sheldon Cohen. Gifts from many other individuals as well as donations from the American Philosophical Society, Yale University, the New York Times Foundation, the Friends of the Franklin Papers, and the Saturday Evening Post Society help to sustain the enterprise. The Papers of Benjamin Franklin is a beneficiary of the generous and long-standing support of the National Historical Publications and Records Commission under the chairmanship of the Archivist of the United States. The National Endowment for the Humanities, an independent federal agency, has provided significant support for this volume. For the assistance of all these organizations and individuals, as well as for the indispensable aid of archivists, librarians, scholars, and collectors of Franklin manuscripts, the editors are most grateful.

Library of Congress catalog card number: 59–12697
International standard book number: 978-0-300-20374-5

⊗ The paper in this book meets the guidelines for permanence and durability of the Committee on Production Guidelines for Book Longevity of the Council on Library Resources.

Printed in the U.S.A.

Administrative Board

To

DAVID BRION DAVIS

with gratitude and appreciation

Contents

Foreign-language surnames and titles of nobility often run to great length. Our practice with an untitled person is to provide all the Christian names at the first appearance, and then drop them; a chevalier or noble is given the title used at the time, and the full name is provided in the index.

*Denotes a document referred to in annotation.

CONTENTS

List of Illustrations

"Information to Those Who Would Remove to America"
Frontispiece

A twelve-page pamphlet written by Franklin during the fall and winter of 1783/84, and printed at Passy *circa* March. Franklin ostensibly composed this essay to answer the legions of "improper" Europeans who were clamoring for his financial and political assistance in emigrating to the United States. What he produced was a rich and idealistic description of American culture and values. He printed a French edition as well as this English one, both anonymous. After the English text was reprinted in London under his name, the essay circulated widely throughout Great Britain and Europe. The essay and an explanatory headnote are published below, [before March]. Reproduced by courtesy of the Yale University Library.

Edward Nairne's Patent Electrical Machine *facing page 118*

Plate 1 of Edward Nairne's *Description and Use of Nairne's Patent Electrical Machine: with the Addition of Some Philosophical Experiments and Medical Observations* (London, 1783). Nairne sent Franklin a machine and a copy of this book in August. When acknowledging their receipt in a letter of October 18, Franklin praised the machine as "very ingeniously contrived indeed." The plate shows the machine fully assembled. A glass cylinder (A) and two metal cylinders (G and R) are supported by four insulating glass rods (B B and D D) attached to a wooden stand. The man in the picture holds one of the many possible attachments: a metal ball (h) connected to a metal tube (f). Reproduced by courtesy of Houghton Library, Harvard University.

The First Manned Balloon Flight, as Seen from Franklin's Terrace *facing page 217*

Engraving by Nicolas Delaunay (*DBF*) based on a drawing by the chevalier de Lorimier, an amateur artist. The legend reads "Premier Voyage Aërien En présence de Mgr. le Dauphin. / Experience faite dans le Jardin de la Muette. / Sous la Direction de Mr. Montgolfier. / Par Mr. le Marquis d'Arlandes et Mr. Pilatre du Rosier, le 21. 9bre. 1783. / Vüe de la Terrasse de Mr. Franklin à Passi." The engraving was the frontispiece for Barthélemy Faujas de Saint-Fond's *Premiere Suite de la description des expériences aérostatiques de MM. de Montgolfier* ... (Paris, 1784). Faujas noted that it was drawn from nature by Lorimier expressly for his book, as were most of the other illustrations (p. [i].) This was the only drawing made from Franklin's terrace. Franklin was not on it at the time; he viewed the launch from La Muette as a commissioner of the Académie des sciences. (See Franklin to Joseph Banks, Nov. 21 [*i.e.*, 22–25].) Another version of this engraving was subsequently issued in which the balloon appears closer to the viewer and is much larger (Gillispie, *Montgolfier Brothers*, p. 54). Reproduced by courtesy of the Library of Congress.

Franklin's Sketches of a Fire-Grate   *facing page 257*

These preliminary sketches of Franklin's coal-burning grate were drawn on the verso of one of the pages of his draft of "Information to Those Who Would Remove to America." In these early sketches, the grate is supported by two legs. Franklin improved the design by the summer of 1785, when he described the grate in the course of his essay, "Description of a New Stove for Burning of Pitcoal, and Consuming all its Smoke," written at sea. In the engraved plate that accompanied the publication of that essay, the grate was supported by a single stem rather than two legs. This allowed the user to rotate the grate horizontally in order to control the direction of the heat: APS *Transactions*, 11 (1786), 72–3, plate 11 (figures 18 and 19). Reproduced by courtesy of the Yale University Library.

Benjamin Franklin Bache's First Broadside   *facing page 353*

Printed at Passy *c.* December 27, 1783, the day Benny wrote a letter to his father Richard Bache enclosing a copy. Answering his father's letter of November 5, Benny wrote "you seem to be afraid that I shall not know how to speak english before I return home, Perhaps I shall not talk it very correctly, but I shall know enough to understand, and be understood, for since I have left Geneva I have made already considerable progress in it; I learn to print, and I send you a Copy of my first Printing. . . . My Grandpapa longs to go to America which gives me hopes to see you and all my Freinds there, sooner than I expected" (APS). The poem featured in this broadside, "An Ode in Imitation of Alcæus," is by Sir William Jones, but is here incomplete. The young printer had no room to include the final eight lines of verse. Reproduced by courtesy of the American Philosophical Society.

Franklinia alatamaha   *facing page 381*

Watercolor illustration (1788) by William Bartram of the flowering tree that William and his father John Bartram, Sr., discovered in 1765. Seeds of the tree were first offered for sale in the Bartrams' 1783 broadside catalogue. They named the tree for Franklin the following year; see the annotation of the letter from the abbé de la Roche to Franklin,

[December, 1783?]. This illustration was the frontispiece to an album of botanical specimens made by William Bartram for Robert Barclay. The line of text at the bottom of the plate reads, "A beautiful flowering Tree discoverd growing near the banks of the R. Alatamaha in Georgia." For more information on the album and the text that accompanied this illustration, and for a color reproduction of this watercolor, see Joseph Ewan, ed., *William Bartram, Botanical and Zoological Drawings, 1756–1788* (Philadelphia, 1968), frontispiece and pp. 151–2, 154, 164. Reproduced by courtesy of the Natural History Museum, London.

Sketch of a "Flying Machine" *facing page 390*

Undated ink drawing with captions by Franklin: "Umbrella of Quill Feathers," "Flying Machine," "Ring for Hands," "Stirrups," "Body of Man girt to the long Handle/his Feet in Stirrups" (top to bottom). It is hard to know exactly what Franklin had in mind, or when he made this sketch. It appears to envision either a parachute-like device or, perhaps, a fanciful kind of glider. Around the time of the first manned balloon ascents, Franklin and others became highly concerned for the safety of the aeronauts; see Franklin's letter to Joseph Banks of Dec. 1[–2]. In late November, Louis-Sebastien Le Normand in Montpellier experimented with what he called a *parachute* by jumping from a moderate height holding two large parasols. Further experiments were conducted over the next several months by Le Normand, Joseph Montgolfier, and the abbé Bertholon. The accident that befell Montgolfier's *Le Flesselles* balloon launched at Lyon in early 1784, in which the fabric ripped and the passengers (thankfully unharmed) descended gently to earth, made the issue of safety devices that much more urgent. For the *Le Flesselles* balloon see Le Roy to Franklin, [Jan. 7]. In the annotation to that letter, we also explain that the Académie des sciences appointed a new commission in December, 1783, to conduct further research on balloons, including the need to find lighter and more resilient fabric. If Franklin ever thought seriously of quill feathers as a practical substitute for oiled silk or paper, he certainly never wrote about it. For a brief history of the early parachute experiments see Gillispie, *Montgolfier Brothers*, pp. 85–7. Reproduced by courtesy of the American Philosophical Society.

Society of the Cincinnati Eagle Insignia, Obverse *facing page 503*

The May, 1783, institution, or charter, of the Society of the Cincinnati stipulated that members should receive a gold medal suspended by a blue ribbon edged with white, symbolizing the Franco-American alliance. Pierre L'Enfant appealed to the society that, in order to gain respect in Europe as a military order, it should adopt instead a distinctive badge. The society accepted his proposal of a double-sided bald eagle featuring the designs and inscriptions originally intended for the medal. L'Enfant volunteered to travel to France to have artisans execute the insignia. After his arrival in Paris in mid-December, he commissioned Duval and Francastel and possibly other firms to manufacture the first batch of 45 eagles. L'Enfant distributed them at the first meeting of the French branch of the society in mid-January. We have no record of when Franklin saw one, but he discussed the badge in his January 26 letter to Sarah Bache. The eagle in gold and enamel pictured here belonged to the naval officer François-Aymar, baron de Monteil (XL, 55). The society believes it to be one of the earliest made in France: information kindly provided by Emily Schulz of the Society of the Cincinnati; Minor Myers, Jr., *Liberty without Anarchy: a History of the Society of the Cincinnati* (Charlottesville, 1983), pp. 26–7, 32–4, 149–50; Myers, *The Insignia of The Society of the Cincinnati* (Washington, D.C., 1998), pp. 14–17; W. W. Abbot *et al.*, eds., *The Papers of George Washington*, Confederation Series (6 vols., Charlottesville and London, 1992–97), I, 26. Reproduced by permission of the Society of the Cincinnati, Washington, D.C.

Contributors to Volume 41

The ownership of each manuscript, or the location of the particular copy used by the editors of each rare contemporary pamphlet or similar printed work, is indicated where the document appears in the text. The sponsors and editors are deeply grateful to the following institutions and individuals for permission to print or otherwise use in the present volume manuscripts and other materials which they own.

INSTITUTIONS

American Philosophical Society
Archives Départementales de la
  Gironde
Archives du Ministère des affaires
  étrangères, Paris
Archives Nationales, Paris
Bibliothèque Municipale, Nantes
British Library
William L. Clements Library,
  University of Michigan
Columbia University Library
Dartmouth College Library
Harvard University Library
Haus-, Hof- und Staatsarchiv,
  Vienna
Historical Society of Pennsylvania
Hobart College Library

Henry E. Huntington Library
Johns Hopkins University Library
Library of Congress
Massachusetts Historical Society
National Archives
New-York Historical Society
New York Public Library
Princeton University Library
Royal Society, London
South Carolina Historical Society
Staatsbibliothek zu Berlin
University of Pennsylvania
  Library
University of South Carolina
  Library
Yale University Library

INDIVIDUALS

Mrs. Marion Brawley, Oakley, South Carolina
Mrs. Frances V. Finletter, Philadelphia, Pennsylvania

Statement of Methodology

Arrangement of Materials

The documents are printed in chronological sequence according to their dates when these are given, or according to the date of publication in cases of contemporary printed materials. Records such as diaries, journals, and account books that cover substantial periods of time appear according to the dates of their earliest entries. When no date appears on the document itself, one is editorially supplied and an explanation provided. When no day within a month is given, the document is placed at the end of all specifically dated documents of that month; those dated only by year are placed at the end of that year. If no date is given, we use internal and external evidence to assign one whenever possible, providing our explanation in annotation. Documents which cannot be assigned a date more definite than the entire length of Franklin's stay in France (1777–85) will be published at the end of this period. Those for which we are unable to provide even a tentative date will be published at the conclusion of the series.

When two or more documents have the same date, they are arranged in the following order:

1. Those by a group of which Franklin was a member (*e.g.*, the American Commissioners in Paris)
2. Those by Franklin individually
3. Those to a group of which Franklin was a member
4. Those to Franklin individually
5. "Third-party" and unaddressed miscellaneous writings by others than Franklin.

In the first two categories letters are arranged alphabetically by the name of the addressee; in the last three, by the name of the signatory. An exception to this practice occurs when a letter to Franklin and his answer were written on the same day: in such cases the first letter precedes the reply. The same rules apply to documents lacking precise dates printed together at the end of any month or year.

Form of Presentation

The document and its accompanying editorial apparatus are presented in the following order:

1. *Title.* Essays and formal papers are headed by their titles, except in the case of pamphlets with very long titles, when a short form is substituted. Where previous editors supplied a title to a piece that had none, and this title has become familiar, we use it; otherwise we devise a suitable one.

Letters written by Franklin individually are entitled "To" the person or body addressed, as: To John Adams; To John Adams and Arthur Lee; To the Royal Society.

Letters to Franklin individually are entitled "From" the person or body who wrote them, as: From John Adams; From John Adams and Arthur Lee; From the Committee of Secret Correspondence.

Letters of which Franklin was a joint author or joint recipient are titled with the names of all concerned, as: Franklin and Silas Deane to Arthur Lee; Arthur Lee to Franklin and Silas Deane. "Third-party" letters or those by or to a body of which Franklin was a member are titled with the names of both writers and addressees, as: Arthur Lee to John Adams; The American Commissioners to John Paul Jones.

Documents not fitting into any of these categories are given brief descriptive headings, as: Extract from Franklin's Journal.

If the name in the title has been supplied from external evidence it appears in brackets, with a question mark when we are uncertain. If a letter is unsigned, or signed with initials or an alias, but is from a correspondent whose handwriting we know, the name appears without brackets.

2. *Source Identification.* This gives the nature of the printed or manuscript version of the document, and, in the case of a manuscript or a rare printed work, the ownership and location of the original.

Printed sources of three different classes are distinguished. First, a contemporary pamphlet, which is given its full title, place and date of publication, and the location of the copy the editors have used. Second, an essay or letter appearing originally in a *contemporary* publication, which is introduced by the words "Printed in," followed by the title, date, and inclusive page numbers, if necessary, of the publication. Third, a document, the manuscript or contemporary printed version of which is now lost, but which was printed at a later date, is identified by the words "Reprinted from," followed by the name of the work from which the editors have reproduced it. The following examples illustrate the distinction:

Printed in *The Pennsylvania Gazette*, October 2, 1729.
Reprinted from William Temple Franklin, ed., *Memoirs of the Life and Writings of Benjamin Franklin* . . . (3 vols., 4to, London, 1817–18), II, 244.

The Source Identification of a manuscript consists of a term or symbol (all of which are listed in the Short Title List) indicating the character of the manuscript version, followed by the name of the holder of the manuscript, as: ALS: American Philosophical Society. Because press copies replicate the manuscripts from which they were made, we indicate the character of the original manuscript, as: press copy of L. Since manuscripts belonging to individuals have a tendency to migrate, we indicate the year in which each private owner gave permission to publish, as: Morris Duane, Philadelphia, 1957. When two or more manuscript versions survive, the one listed first in the Source Identification is the one from which we print.

3. An editorial *Headnote* precedes some documents in this edition; it appears between the Source Identification and the actual text. Such a headnote is designed to supply the background of the composition of the document, its relation to events or other writings, and any other information which may be useful to the reader and is not obtainable from the document itself.

4. The *Text* of the document follows the Source Identification, or Headnote, if any. When multiple copies of a document are extant, the editors observe the following order of priority in determining which of the available versions to use in printing a text: ALS or ADS, LS or DS, AL or AD, L or D, and copy. An AL (draft) normally takes precedence over a contemporary copy

based on the recipient's copy. If we deviate from the order set forth here, we explain our decision in the annotation. In those instances where multiple texts are available, the texts are collated, and significant variations reported in the annotation. In selecting the publication text from among several copies of official French correspondence (*e.g.*, from Vergennes or Sartine) we use the version which is written in the best French, on the presumption that the French ministers used standard eighteenth-century spelling, grammar, and punctuation.

The form of presentation of the texts of letters is as follows:

The place and date of composition are set at the top, regardless of their location in the original manuscript.

The signature, set in capitals and small capitals, is placed at the right of the last line of the text if there is room; if not, then on the line below.

Addresses, endorsements, and notations are so labelled and printed at the end of the letter. An endorsement is, to the best of our belief, by the recipient, and a notation by someone else. When the writer of the notation has misread the date or the signature of the correspondent, we let the error stand without comment. Line breaks in addresses are marked by slashes. Different notations are separated by slashes; when they are by different individuals, we so indicate.

5. *Footnotes* to the Heading, Source Identification, Headnote, and Text appear on the pages to which they pertain. References to documents not printed or to be printed in later volumes are by date and repository, as: Jan. 17, 1785, APS.

Method of Textual Reproduction

1. *Spelling* of all words, including proper names, is retained. If it is abnormal enough to obscure the meaning we follow the word immediately with the current spelling in brackets.

2. *Capitalization and Punctuation* are retained. There is such variety in the size of initial letters, often in the same manuscript, that it is sometimes unclear whether the writer intended an upper or lower case letter. In such cases we make a decision on the basis of the correspondent's customary usage. We supply a capital letter when an immediately preceding period, colon, question mark, exclamation point, or dash indicates that a new

sentence is intended. If a capital letter clearly indicates the beginning of a new thought, but no mark of punctuation precedes it, we insert a period. If neither punctuation nor capital letter indicates a sentence break, we do not supply them unless their absence renders comprehension of the document nearly impossible. In that case we provide them and so indicate in a footnote.

Dashes were used for a variety of purposes in eighteenth-century personal and public letters. A dash within a sentence, used to indicate a break in thought, is represented as an em dash. A dash that follows a period or serves as a closing mark of punctuation for a sentence is represented as an em dash followed by a space. Occasionally correspondents used long dashes that continue to the end of a line and indicate a significant break in thought. We do not reproduce the dash, but treat it as indicating the start of a new paragraph.

When there is an initial quotation mark or parenthesis, but no closing one, we silently complete the pair.

3. *Contractions and abbreviations* are retained. Abbreviations such as "wd", "honble", "servt", "exclly", are used so frequently in Franklin's correspondence that they are readily comprehensible to the users of these volumes. Abbreviations, particularly of French words, that may be unclear are followed by an expanded version in brackets, as: nre [navire]. Superscript letters are brought down to the line. Where a period or colon is a part of the abbreviation, or indicates that letters were written above the line, we print it at the end of the word, as: 4th. for 4.th. In those few cases where superscript letters brought down to the line result in a confusing abbreviation ("Made" for "Mad^e"), we follow the abbreviation by an expanded version in brackets, as: Made [Madame].

The ampersand by itself and the "&c." are retained. Letters represented by the "y" are printed, as: "the" and "that". The tailed "p" is spelled out, as: "per", "pre", or "pro". Symbols of weights, measures, and money are converted to modern forms, as: *l.t.* instead of ₶ for *livres tournois*.

4. *Omissions, mutilations, and illegible words* are treated as follows:

If we are certain of the reading of letters missing in a word because of a torn or taped manuscript or tightly bound copy-book, we supply the letters silently.

If we cannot be sure of the word, or of how the author spelled it, but we can make a reasonable guess, we supply the missing letters in brackets.

When the writer has omitted a word absolutely required for clarity, we insert it in italics within brackets.

5. *Interlineations* by the author are silently incorporated into the text. If they are significant enough to require comment a footnote is provided.

Textual Conventions

/	denotes line break in addresses; separates multiple endorsements and notations.
⟨roman⟩	denotes a résumé of a letter or document.
[*italic*]	editorial insertion explaining something about the manuscript, as: [*one line illegible*]; or supplying a word to make the meaning clear, as: [*to*].
[roman]	editorial insertion clarifying the immediately preceding word or abbreviation; supplies letters missing because of a mutilated manuscript.
(?)	indicates a questionable reading.

Abbreviations and Short Titles

AAE	Archives du Ministère des affaires étrangères.
AD	Autograph document.
Adams Correspondence	Lyman H. Butterfield, Richard A. Ryerson *et al.*, eds., *Adams Family Correspondence* (10 vols. to date, Cambridge, Mass., 1963–).
Adams Papers	Robert J. Taylor, Gregg L. Lint *et al.*, eds., *Papers of John Adams* (16 vols. to date, Cambridge, Mass., 1977–).
ADB	*Allgemeine Deutsche Biographie* (56 vols., Berlin, 1967–71).
Adm.	Admiral.
ADS	Autograph document signed.
AL	Autograph letter.
Almanach des marchands	*Almanach général des marchands, négocians, armateurs, et fabricans de France et de l'Europe et autres parties du monde* ... (Paris, 1779).
Almanach royal	*Almanach royal* (91 vols., Paris, 1700– 92). Cited by year.
Almanach de Versailles	*Almanach de Versailles* (Versailles, various years). Cited by year.
Alphabetical List of Escaped Prisoners	Alphabetical List of the Americans who having escap'd from the Prisons of England, were furnish'd with Money by the Commissrs. of the U.S. at the Court of France, to return to America. A manuscript in the APS, dated 1784, and covering the period January, 1777, to November, 1784.
ALS	Autograph letter signed.

xl

Amiable, *Une Loge Maçonnique* — Louis Amiable, *Une Loge maçonnique d'avant 1789* . . . (1897; reprint, followed by an introduction, commentary, and notes, separately paginated, by Charles Porset, Paris, 1989).

ANB — John A. Garraty and Mark C. Carnes, eds., *American National Biography* (24 vols., New York and Oxford, 1999).

APS — American Philosophical Society.

Archaeol. — Archaeological.

Assn. — Association.

Auphan, "Communications" — P. Auphan, "Les communications entre la France et ses colonies d'Amérique pendant la guerre de l'indépendance Américaine," *Revue Maritime*, new series, no. LXIII and LXIV (1925), 331–48, 497–517.

Autobiog. — Leonard W. Labaree, Ralph L. Ketcham, Helen C. Boatfield, and Helene H. Fineman, eds., *The Autobiography of Benjamin Franklin* (New Haven, 1964).

Bachaumont, *Mémoires secrets* — [Louis Petit de Bachaumont *et al.*], *Mémoires secrets pour servir à l'histoire de la république des lettres en France, depuis MDCCLXII jusqu'à nos jours; ou, Journal d'un observateur* . . . (36 vols. in 12, London, 1784–89). Bachaumont died in 1771. The first six vols. (1762–71) are his; Mathieu-François Pidansat de Mairobert edited them and wrote the next nine (1771–79); the remainder (1779–87) are by Barthélemy-François Mouffle d'Angerville.

Balch, *French in America*   Thomas Balch, *The French in America during the War of Independence of the United States, 1777–1783* (trans. by Thomas Willing Balch *et al.;* 2 vols., Philadelphia, 1891–95).

BF   Benjamin Franklin.

BF's accounts as commissioner   Those described above, XXIII, 20.

BF's journal of the peace negotiations   Described in XXXVII, 291–346. This refers to the copy in Josiah Flagg's hand with corrections by BF, at the Library of Congress.

BFB   Benjamin Franklin Bache.

BFB's journal   Described above, XXXVII, 682n.

Bigelow, *Works*   John Bigelow, ed., *The Works of Benjamin Franklin* (12 vols., New York and London, 1887–88).

Biographie universelle   *Biographie universelle, ancienne et moderne, ou histoire, par ordre alphabétique, de la vie publique et privée de tous les hommes qui se sont fait remarquer* ... (85 vols., Paris, 1811–62).

Bodinier   From information kindly furnished us by Cdt. Gilbert Bodinier, Section études, Service historique de l'Armée de Terre, Vincennes.

Bodinier, *Dictionnaire*   Gilbert Bodinier, *Dictionnaire des officiers de l'armée royale qui ont combattu aux Etats-Unis pendant la guerre d'Indépendance* (Château de Vincennes, 1982).

Bradford, *Jones Papers*   James C. Bradford, ed., *The Microfilm Edition of the Papers of John Paul Jones, 1747–1792* (10 reels of microfilm, Alexandria, Va., 1986).

Burke's Peerage	Sir Bernard Burke, *Burke's Genealogical and Heraldic History of the Peerage Baronetage and Knightage with War Gazette and Corrigenda* (98th ed., London, 1940). References in exceptional cases to other editions are so indicated.
Burnett, *Letters*	Edmund C. Burnett, ed., *Letters of Members of the Continental Congress* (8 vols., Washington, 1921–36).
Butterfield, *John Adams Diary*	Lyman H. Butterfield *et al.*, eds., *Diary and Autobiography of John Adams* (4 vols., Cambridge, Mass., 1961).
Cash Book	BF's accounts described above, XXVI, 3.
Chron.	*Chronicle.*
Claghorn, *Naval Officers*	Charles E. Claghorn, *Naval Officers of the American Revolution: a Concise Biographical Dictionary* (Metuchen, N.J., and London, 1988).
Cobbett, *Parliamentary History*	William Cobbett and Thomas C. Hansard, eds., *The Parliamentary History of England from the Earliest Period to 1803* (36 vols., London, 1806–20).
Col.	Column.
Coll.	*Collections.*
comp.	compiler.
d.	*denier.*
D	Document unsigned.
DAB	*Dictionary of American Biography.*
DBF	*Dictionnaire de biographie française* (20 vols. to date, Paris, 1933–).
Dictionary of Scientific Biography	Charles C. Gillispie, ed., *Dictionary of Scientific Biography* (18 vols., New York, 1970–90).

Deane Papers	*The Deane Papers, 1774–90* (5 vols.; New-York Historical Society *Collections*, XIX–XXIII, New York, 1887–91).
DF	Deborah Franklin.
Dictionnaire de la noblesse	François-Alexandre Aubert de La Chesnaye-Dubois and M. Badier, *Dictionnaire de la noblesse contenant les généalogies, l'histoire & la chronologie des familles nobles de la France . . .* (3rd ed.; 19 vols., Paris, 1863–76).
Dictionnaire historique de la Suisse	*Dictionnaire historique & biographique de la Suisse* (7 vols. and supplement, Neuchâtel, 1921–34).
Diplomatic Correspondence of the United States	*The Diplomatic Correspondence of the United States of America, from the Signing of the Definitive Treaty of Peace, 10th September, 1783, to the Adoption of the Constitution, March 4, 1789* (7 vols., Washington, D.C., 1833–34).
DNB	*Dictionary of National Biography.*
Doniol, *Histoire*	Henri Doniol, *Histoire de la participation de la France à l'établissement des Etats-Unis d'Amérique. Correspondance diplomatique et documents* (5 vols., Paris, 1886–99).
DS	Document signed.
Dubourg, *Œuvres*	Jacques Barbeu-Dubourg, ed., *Œuvres de M. Franklin . . .* (2 vols., Paris, 1773).
Ed.	Edition or editor.
Edler, *Dutch Republic*	Friedrich Edler, *The Dutch Republic and the American Revolution* (*Johns Hopkins University Studies in Historical and Political Science,* ser. XXIX, no. 2; Baltimore, 1911).

xliv

Etat militaire	*Etat militaire de France, pour l'année . . .* (36 vols., Paris, 1758–93). Cited by year.
Exper. and Obser.	*Experiments and Observations on Electricity, made at Philadelphia in America, by Mr. Benjamin Franklin* . . . (London, 1751). Revised and enlarged editions were published in 1754, 1760, 1769, and 1774 with slightly varying titles. In each case the edition cited will be indicated, *e.g., Exper. and Obser.* (1751).
f.	florins.
Ferguson, *Power of the Purse*	E. James Ferguson, *The Power of the Purse: a History of American Public Finance* . . . (Chapel Hill, N.C., 1961).
Fitzpatrick, *Writings of Washington*	John C. Fitzpatrick, ed., *The Writings of George Washington* . . . (39 vols., Washington, D.C., 1931–44).
Fortescue, *Correspondence of George Third*	Sir John William Fortescue, ed., *The Correspondence of King George the Third from 1760 to December 1783* . . . (6 vols., London, 1927–28).
France ecclésiastique	*La France ecclésiastique pour l'année . . .* (15 vols., Paris, 1774–90). Cited by year.
Freeman, *Washington*	Douglas S. Freeman (completed by John A. Carroll and Mary W. Ashworth), *George Washington: a Biography* (7 vols., New York, 1948–57).
Gaz.	*Gazette.*
Gaz. de Leyde	*Nouvelles extraordinaires de divers endroits,* commonly known as *Gazette de Leyde.* Each issue is in two parts; we indicate the second as "sup."

Gen.	General.
Geneal.	*Genealogical.*
Gent. Mag.	*The Gentleman's Magazine, and Historical Chronicle.*
Gillispie, *Montgolfier Brothers*	Charles C. Gillispie, *The Montgolfier Brothers and the Invention of Aviation, 1783–1784* (Princeton, 1983).
Giunta, *Emerging Nation*	Mary A. Giunta *et al.*, eds., *The Emerging Nation: a Documentary History of the Foreign Relations of the United States under the Articles of the Confederation, 1780–1789* (3 vols., Washington, D.C., 1996).
GW	George Washington.
Harlow, *Second British Empire*	Vincent T. Harlow, *The Founding of the Second British Empire, 1763–1793* (2 vols., London and New York, 1952–64).
Hays, *Calendar*	I. Minis Hays, *Calendar of the Papers of Benjamin Franklin in the Library of the American Philosophical Society* (5 vols., Philadelphia, 1908).
Heitman, *Register of Officers*	Francis B. Heitman, *Historical Register of Officers in the War of the Revolution . . .* (Washington, D.C., 1893).
Hillairet, *Rues de Paris*	Jacques Hillairet, pseud. of Auguste A. Coussillan, *Dictionnaire historique des rues de Paris* (2nd ed.; 2 vols., [Paris, 1964]).
Hist.	Historic or Historical.
Hoffman and Albert, eds., *Peace and the Peacemakers*	Ronald Hoffman and Peter J. Albert, eds., *Peace and the Peacemakers: the Treaty of 1783* (Charlottesville, Va., 1986).
Idzerda, *Lafayette Papers*	Stanley J. Idzerda *et al.*, eds., *Lafayette in the Age of the American Revolution:*

	Selected Letters and Papers, 1776–1790 (5 vols. to date, Ithaca, N.Y., and London, 1977–).
JA	John Adams.
Jay Papers	Elizabeth M. Nuxoll *et al.*, eds, *The Selected Papers of John Jay* (3 vols. to date, Charlottesville and London, 2010–).
JCC	Worthington Chauncey Ford *et al.*, eds., *Journals of the Continental Congress, 1744–1789* (34 vols., Washington, D.C., 1904–37).
Jefferson Papers	Julian P. Boyd, Charles T. Cullen, John Catanzariti, Barbara B. Oberg, *et al.*, eds., *The Papers of Thomas Jefferson* (39 vols. to date, Princeton, 1950–).
Jour.	*Journal.*
JQA	John Quincy Adams
JW	Jonathan Williams, Jr.
Kaminkow, *Mariners*	Marion and Jack Kaminkow, *Mariners of the American Revolution* (Baltimore, 1967).
L	Letter unsigned.
Larousse	Pierre Larousse, *Grand dictionnaire universel du XIXe siècle* . . . (17 vols., Paris, [n.d.]).
Lasseray, *Les Français*	André Lasseray, *Les Français sous les treize étoiles, 1775–1783* (2 vols., Paris, 1935).
Laurens Papers	Philip M. Hamer, George C. Rogers, Jr., David R. Chestnutt, *et al.*, eds., *The Papers of Henry Laurens* (16 vols., Columbia, S.C., 1968–2003).
Le Bihan, *Francs-maçons parisiens*	Alain Le Bihan, *Francs-maçons parisiens du Grand Orient de France* . . . (Commission d'histoire économique

et sociale de la révolution française, *Mémoires et documents*, XIX, Paris, 1966).

Lewis, *Walpole Correspondence* Wilmarth S. Lewis *et al.*, eds., *The Yale Edition of Horace Walpole's Correspondence* (48 vols., New Haven, 1939–83).

Lopez, *Mon Cher Papa* Claude-Anne Lopez, *Mon Cher Papa: Franklin and the Ladies of Paris* (rev. ed., New Haven and London, 1990).

Lopez and Herbert, *The Private Franklin* Claude-Anne Lopez and Eugenia W. Herbert, *The Private Franklin: the Man and His Family* (New York, 1975).

LS Letter or letters signed.

l.t. *livres tournois.*

Lüthy, *Banque protestante* Herbert Lüthy, *La Banque protestante en France de la Révocation de l'Edit de Nantes à la Révolution* (2 vols., Paris, 1959–61).

Mackesy, *War for America* Piers Mackesy, *The War for America, 1775–1783* (Cambridge, Mass., 1965).

Madariaga, *Harris's Mission* Isabel de Madariaga, *Britain, Russia, and the Armed Neutrality of 1780: Sir James Harris's Mission to St. Petersburg during the American Revolution* (New Haven, 1962).

Mag. *Magazine.*

Mass. Arch. Massachusetts Archives, State House, Boston.

Mazas, *Ordre de Saint-Louis* Alexandre Mazas and Théodore Anne, *Histoire de l'ordre royal et militaire de Saint-Louis depuis son institution en 1693 jusqu'en 1830* (2nd ed.; 3 vols., Paris, 1860–61).

Medlin, *Morellet* Dorothy Medlin, Jean-Claude David, Paul LeClerc, eds., *Lettres d'André Morellet* (3 vols., Oxford, 1991–96).

Métra, *Correspondance secrète* [François Métra *et al.*], *Correspondance secrète, politique & littéraire, ou Mémoires pour servir à l'histoire des cours, des sociétés & de la littérature en France, depuis la mort de Louis XV* (18 vols., London, 1787–90).

Meyer, *Armement nantais* Jean Meyer, *L'Armement nantais dans la deuxième moitié du XVIIIe siècle* (Paris, 1969).

Meyer, *Noblesse bretonne* Jean Meyer, *La Noblesse bretonne au XVIIIe siècle* (2 vols., Paris, 1966).

Morison, *Jones* Samuel E. Morison, *John Paul Jones: a Sailor's Biography* (Boston and Toronto, 1959).

Morris, *Jay: Peace* Richard B. Morris *et al.*, eds., *John Jay, the Winning of the Peace: Unpublished Papers, 1780–1784* (New York, Cambridge, London, 1980).

Morris, *Jay: Revolutionary* Richard B. Morris *et al.*, eds., *John Jay, the Making of a Revolutionary: Unpublished Papers, 1743–1780* (New York, Evanston, San Francisco, 1975).

Morris Papers E. James Ferguson, John Catanzariti, Mary A. Gallagher, Elizabeth M. Nuxoll, *et al.*, eds., *The Papers of Robert Morris, 1781–1784* (9 vols., Pittsburgh, Pa., 1973–99).

Morton, *Beaumarchais Correspondance* Brian N. Morton and Donald C. Spinelli, eds., *Beaumarchais Correspondance* (4 vols. to date, Paris, 1969–).

MS, MSS Manuscript, manuscripts.

Namier and Brooke,
House of Commons

Sir Lewis Namier and John Brooke, *The History of Parliament. The House of Commons 1754–1790* (3 vols., London and New York, 1964).

NNBW

Nieuw Nederlandsch Biografisch Woordenboek (10 vols. and index, Amsterdam, 1974).

Nouvelle biographie

Nouvelle biographie générale depuis les temps les plus reculés jusqu'à nos jours . . . (46 vols., Paris, 1855–66).

p.

pence.

Pa.

Pennsylvania.

Pa. Arch.

Samuel Hazard *et al.*, eds., *Pennsylvania Archives* (9 series, Philadelphia and Harrisburg, 1852–1935).

Palmer, *Loyalists*

Gregory Palmer, ed., *Biographical Sketches of Loyalists of the American Revolution* (Westport, Conn., 1984).

Parry, *Consolidated Treaty Series*

Clive Parry, comp., *The Consolidated Treaty* Series (243 vols., Dobbs Ferry, N. Y., 1969–86).

Phil. Trans.

The Royal Society, *Philosophical Transactions.*

PMHB

Pennsylvania Magazine of History and Biography.

Price, *France and the Chesapeake*

Jacob M. Price, *France and the Chesapeake: a History of the French Tobacco Monopoly, 1674–1791, and of Its Relationship to the British and American Tobacco Trade* (2 vols., Ann Arbor, Mich., 1973).

Proc.

Proceedings.

Pub.

Publications.

Quérard, *France littéraire*

Joseph Marie Quérard, *La France littéraire ou Dictionnaire bibliographique des savants, historiens, et gens de lettres de la*

France, ainsi que des littérateurs étrangers qui ont écrit en français, plus particulièrement pendant les XVIIIe et XIXe siècles . . . (10 vols., Paris, 1827–64).

RB   Richard Bache.

Repertorium der diplomatischen Vertreter   Ludwig Bittner *et al.*, eds., *Repertorium der diplomatischen Vertreter aller Länder seit dem Westfälischen Frieden (1648)* (3 vols., Oldenburg, etc., 1936–65).

Rev.   *Review.*

Rice and Brown, eds., *Rochambeau's Army*   Howard C. Rice, Jr., and Anne S. K. Brown, eds., *The American Campaigns of Rochambeau's Army, 1780, 1781, 1782, 1783* (2 vols., Princeton and Providence, 1972).

Roberts and Roberts, *Thomas Barclay*   Priscilla H. Roberts and Richard S. Roberts, *Thomas Barclay (1728–1793): Consul in France, Diplomat in Barbary* (Bethlehem, Pa., 2008).

s.   *sou.*

s.   shilling.

Sabine, *Loyalists*   Lorenzo Sabine, *Biographical Sketches of Loyalists of the American Revolution* . . . (2 vols., Boston, 1864).

SB   Sarah Bache.

Schulte Nordholt, *Dutch Republic*   J. W. Schulte Nordholt, *The Dutch Republic and American Independence* (trans. Herbert M. Rowen; Chapel Hill, N.C., 1982).

Sellers, *Franklin in Portraiture*   Charles C. Sellers, *Benjamin Franklin in Portraiture* (New Haven and London, 1962).

Sibley's Harvard Graduates   John L. Sibley, *Biographical Sketches of Graduates of Harvard University* (18 vols. to date, Cambridge, Mass.,

	1873–). Continued from Volume IV by Clifford K. Shipton.
Six, *Dictionnaire biographique*	Georges Six, *Dictionnaire biographique des généraux et amiraux français de la Révolution et de l'Empire (1792–1814)* (2 vols., Paris, 1934).
Smith, *Letters*	Paul H. Smith *et al.*, eds., *Letters of Delegates to Congress* (26 vols., Washington, D.C., 1976–2000).
Smyth, *Writings*	Albert H. Smyth, ed., *The Writings of Benjamin Franklin . . .* (10 vols., New York, 1905–7).
Soc.	Society.
Sparks, *Works*	Jared Sparks, ed., *The Works of Benjamin Franklin . . .* (10 vols., Boston, 1836–40).
Taylor, *J. Q. Adams Diary*	Robert J. Taylor *et al.*, eds., *Diary of John Quincy Adams* (2 vols. to date, Cambridge, Mass., and London, 1981–).
TJ	Thomas Jefferson.
Tourneux, *Correspondance littéraire*	Maurice Tourneux, *Correspondance littéraire, philosophique et critique par Grimm, Diderot, Raynal, Meister, etc. revue sur les textes originaux comprenant outre ce qui a été publié à diverses époques les fragments supprimés en 1813 par la censure les parties inédites conservées à la Bibliothèque Ducale de Gotha et l'Arsenal à Paris* (16 vols., Paris, 1877–82).
Trans.	Translator or translated.
Trans.	*Transactions.*
Van Doren, *Franklin*	Carl Van Doren, *Benjamin Franklin* (New York, 1938).

Van Doren, *Franklin-Mecom*	Carl Van Doren, ed., *The Letters of Benjamin Franklin & Jane Mecom* (American Philosophical Society *Memoirs*, XXVII, Princeton, 1950).
Villiers, *Commerce colonial*	Patrick Villiers, *Le Commerce colonial atlantique et la guerre d'indépendance des Etats-Unis d'Amérique, 1778–1783* (New York, 1977).
W&MQ	*William and Mary Quarterly*, first or third series as indicated.
Waste Book	BF's accounts described above, XXIII, 19.
WF	William Franklin.
Wharton, *Diplomatic Correspondence*	Francis Wharton, ed., *The Revolutionary Diplomatic Correspondence of the United States* (6 vols., Washington, D.C., 1889).
Wolf and Hayes, *Library of Benjamin Franklin*	Edwin Wolf 2nd and Kevin J. Hayes, eds., *The Library of Benjamin Franklin* (Philadelphia, 2006).
WTF	William Temple Franklin.
WTF, *Memoirs*	William Temple Franklin, ed., *Memoirs of the Life and Writings of Benjamin Franklin, L.L.D., F.R.S., &c . . .* (3 vols., 4to, London, 1817–18).
WTF's accounts	Those described above, XXIII, 19.

Note by the Editors and the Administrative Board

As we noted in volume 23 (pp. xlvi–xlviii), the period of Franklin's mission to France brings with it roughly two and a half times as many documents as those for the other seventy years of his life. In the present volume once again we summarize a portion of his incoming correspondence in collective descriptions; they appear in the index under the following headings: consulship seekers; emigrants, would-be; favor seekers; offerers of goods and schemes.

As first noted in volume 30 (p. lx), Franklin's French secretary Jean L'Air de Lamotte made letterbook copies of official correspondence. Many of these copies contain errors that could not have been present in Franklin's originals. Regrettably, they are in many cases the only extant versions. We publish them as they stand, pointing out and correcting errors only when they threaten to obscure Franklin's meaning.

A revised statement of textual methodology appeared in volume 28 and is repeated here. The original statement of method is found in the Introduction to the first volume, pp. xxiv–xlvii. The various developments in policy are explained in xv, xxiv; xxi, xxxiv; xxiii, xlvi–xlviii.

As noted in volume 39 (p. liv), the digital edition of *The Papers of Benjamin Franklin,* conceived and sponsored by the Packard Humanities Institute, is freely accessible at www .franklinpapers.org. It contains texts of all the documents in our archive up to Franklin's death, including those that are only summarized or mentioned in the letterpress edition, as well as biographical sketches of Franklin's correspondents and an introduction by Edmund S. Morgan. Transcriptions of documents that will be included in future volumes are preliminary, and will be replaced as the letterpress edition proceeds.

All volumes of the Franklin Papers build on the work of earlier editors and assistants. Our predecessors collected and transcribed thousands of manuscripts, identified correspondents, supplied dates for undated documents, and left us the benefit of their research notes and proposed annotation. We acknowledge here with special appreciation the work of Claude-Anne Lopez, who died in 2011 at the age of ninety-one. Claude joined the Franklin Papers at its inception, and spent more than thirty years transcribing, proofreading, researching, dating, and annotating documents from the eight and a half years of Franklin's residence in France. Her name appeared on the title pages of twenty-five volumes, beginning with Volume 15. She was Editor of Volume 28, and thereafter continued her association as a Consulting Editor. Claude's research notes and draft annotation remain invaluable to the current editors. We shall always miss her expertise, judgment, and wit. We also gratefully acknowledge the work of Karen Duval, an associate editor who left the project in 2006. Karen drafted preliminary annotation for some twenty documents that fall within the time period of this volume.

Assistant editors Alicia Anderson, Adrina Garbooshian, and Allegra di Bonaventura left the project as work on Volume 41 was under way. We thank them for their many contributions and wish them well. Assistant editors Ellen Pawelczak and John Huffman joined our team after the manuscript had been completed. They contributed as much as any of us to the final corrections, and we are extremely grateful. Lesley Kent provided much-needed temporary assistance with skill and good cheer. Kate Woodford, our current editorial assistant, joined us in time to assist with page proofs; we thank her for all her help. Michael Hattem, a graduate student in the Yale History Department, assisted with proofreading and research.

Finally, and with a sense of profound loss, we note that Volume 41 will be the last to bear the name of Edmund S. Morgan, who died in 2013 at the age of ninety-seven. Ed joined the Administrative Board in 1969, served as its Chairman from 1992 until 2004, and remained an active member until his retirement in 2012. No one was more committed to the success of this project than he, or more aware and appreciative of the work that went into every page. His counsel was invaluable, his wisdom irreplaceable. This edition is immeasurably richer on account of his association with it.

Introduction

In the months following the signing of the definitive peace treaty on September 3, 1783, Franklin's diplomatic activities diminished and he found himself with the kind of leisure time that he had not experienced since before the outbreak of the war. In September, he and the British negotiator David Hartley began corresponding about the trade agreement that had been postponed during the peace negotiations. Their expectations of settling that agreement gradually evaporated, however, as on Hartley's side the British ministry let his proposals languish, and on Franklin's side Congress never sent the American peace commissioners the authority to conclude such a convention. Congress failed to act on the two draft treaties with Portugal and Denmark that Franklin had sent the previous summer. The instructions that Congress passed on October 29 made no mention of the treaties and gave the commissioners no powers to conclude any others. Even the simple act of ratifying the peace treaty with England proved difficult for Congress, causing the commissioners to worry that they would miss the deadline. When writing to friends, Franklin made light of English newspaper reports on American disunity and congressional impotence. In fact, he was deeply concerned about Congress' inability to raise funds, pay its debts, and impose its will on the states, and about the damage such reports did to the new republic's standing in Europe. Apart from warning his colleagues at home, however, there was little he could do.

In October, Franklin's fellow commissioners John Jay and John Adams each left Paris for England. Jay returned to Paris at the end of January, rejoining his family, while Adams went on to Holland. (Henry Laurens had left for England the previous summer and was making plans to return to the United States.) Franklin found himself once again the sole American commissioner in Paris. This had its advantages: in mid-December, a letter from then-president of Congress Elias Boudinot allowed Franklin to consider himself authorized to move forward with the consular convention that he and Vergennes had long been discussing. The two ministers settled the draft convention be-tween themselves in late December, unfettered by the need to consult colleagues. (In Vergennes' case, his recent elevation to *chef du conseil royal des finances* gave him the power to wrest the final decisions from his longtime rival, the marquis de Castries.) Though they would not sign the final consular convention be-tween France and the United States until the following July, the text they approved in December remained substantially intact.[1] This draft convention was Franklin's only official accomplish-ment of these months.

By Christmastime, when all hope of negotiating a commer-cial treaty with England had dissolved, Franklin begged Con-gress to allow him to return home, to "enjoy the little left me of the Evening of Life in Repose and in the Sweet Society of my Friends and Family."[2] His reasons for this poignant appeal were age and poor health. In early December, Franklin's blad-der stone became so painful that he found it excruciating to ride in a carriage. He ceased all travel, deputizing his grandson Wil-liam Temple Franklin to take his place at the weekly meetings of the diplomatic corps at Versailles.[3]

His afflictions did not prevent him from following the diz-zying progress being made in the field of aeronautics. At the time the present volume opens, Franklin was writing to Richard Price of the balloon experiment that was to be staged by the famous Montgolfier. Throughout the fall he kept Joseph Banks apprised of the balloon experiments being conducted by Mont-golfier and by the Robert brothers. In September, Montgolfier would send up into the air a trio of barnyard animals, followed in November by a pair of men. A popular print depicted the latter flight as seen from Franklin's balcony, though the doc-tor himself witnessed the ascension with fellow members of the Academy of Sciences at the launching stage on the grounds of La Muette.[4]

1. Draft Consular Convention between France and the United States, [before Dec. 24].
2. BF to Thomas Mifflin, Dec. 26, letter I.
3. See BF to Vergennes, Dec. 6.
4. A famous engraving of a balloon was made from the vantage of BF's terrace; see the illustration facing p. 217.

Scientific and social improvements continued to fascinate Franklin, and he was consulted on numerous projects. His approval was solicited for a new clinic using electroshock therapy and for an improved oil lamp whose design resembled an idea he had proposed years earlier. During the unusually severe winter, one of the coldest on record for Europe and North America, the French government asked for his design of a coal-burning stove. The co-director of the royal baking school solicited his advice on how to make nutritious bread from cornmeal. Franklin sent detailed instructions for making cornbread.[5]

Making alliances, mending fences, and perpetuating the peace were very much on Franklin's mind during these months. He continued to work with Anthony Todd on a cooperative transatlantic postal service that would share costs and responsibilites among Great Britain, France, and the United States. In mid-October, when still optimistic about negotiating commercial articles with Britain, he wondered about creating a "family compact" among the three countries. "America would be as happy as the Sabine Girls," he wrote David Hartley, "if she could be the means of uniting in perpetual peace her father and her husband. (What repeated follies are these repeated Wars! You do not want to conquer and govern one another, why then should you continually be employed in injuring and destroying one another?)" He went on to suggest what "excellent things" might be done with the resources expended in waging war: building bridges, roads, canals, and institutions devoted to the common good. "You are near Neighbours and each have very respectable qualities," he wrote. "Learn to be quiet and to respect each others rights. You are all Christians. One is the most Christian King, and the other defender of the faith. Manifest the propriety of these titles by your future conduct. By this says Christ shall all men know that ye are my Disciples if ye Love one another. Seek peace and ensure it."[6]

While waiting for his recall—vainly, as it would happen—Franklin began to reflect on unfinished business[7] and think about taking his leave of the people who had shown him such

5. The recipe is published below, [c. Feb. 5].
6. BF to Hartley, Oct. 16; we expand the contractions.
7. See the List of Letters to Write, [c. Jan. 1?].

hospitality. In December he hired a compositor to help him print essays and bagatelles, which he would distribute as keepsakes.

Leave-taking, in combination with his mission to publicize the virtues of the United States, inspired Franklin during the late fall and winter to write three of his most remarkable pieces: essays, very different in kind, that contrasted the New World with the Old. One of them, couched as a letter to his daughter, was a pointed rejection of the Society of the Cincinnati and hereditary privilege, which he decided against making public. The other two were printed as pamphlets and distributed: "Remarks concerning the Savages of North America" and "Information to Those Who Would Remove to America."[8] In these two pieces, Franklin told the world what America was and what he wished it to be. He had already explained his concept of personal industry as being central to success and morality to a visiting Englishman, John Baynes, in September. (Baynes recorded that conversation and subsequent ones in his diary.)[9] Those same thoughts were incorporated in "Information to Those Who Would Remove to America," a description, analysis, and warning to everyone considering emigration. In America, Franklin wrote, aristocratic lineage is irrelevant. People do not inquire of a stranger, "*What* IS *he?*" but "*What can he* DO?"

8. The essays are published under [before Jan. 7] and [before March], respectively. The letter is BF to Sarah Bache, Jan. 26.
9. Extracts of John Baynes's Diary, [Sept. 23–Oct. 17].

Chronology

1783

c. September 21: Henry Laurens returns to Paris for a brief stay on his way to visit his brother in Le Vigan.

September 22: After falling ill in mid-September, John Adams moves in with Thomas Barclay in Auteuil.

c. September 22: Jonathan Williams leaves for Nantes.

October 9–January 22: John Jay visits England.

October 20–January 2: John Adams takes a trip to England for his health.

October 31: Congress ratifies February 25, 1783, contract for repayment of French loans, negotiated by Franklin.

Early November: The Jay family leave their lodgings with Franklin at the Hôtel Valentinois and move to Chaillot.

November 3: Thomas Mifflin elected president of Congress.

November 4–7: Henry Laurens visits Paris on his way from Le Vigan to London.

November 19: John Thaxter arrives in New York, carrying a copy of the definitive peace treaty.

November 21: First manned flight in an untethered balloon conducted by Etienne Montgolfier at the château de la Muette.

November 30: The Dutch banking consortium notifies Franklin that Robert Morris' bills are in danger of being protested; over the next four months, John Adams and Franklin engage in negotiations to secure funds to cover the overdraft.

December 1: Charles and Robert ascend in a hydrogen balloon before thousands of spectators at the Tuileries.

December 6: Franklin informs Vergennes that his health prevents him from traveling to Versailles; William Temple Franklin will go in his place.

December 13: A new session of Congress begins; the definitive peace treaty is officially laid before Congress.

December 19: William Pitt is appointed prime minister of England.

December 26: Franklin makes a personal appeal to the president of Congress, requesting to be relieved of his duties.

1784

January 2–early August: John Adams' trip to the Netherlands.

January 14: Definitive peace treaty ratified by Congress.

February 6: Franklin exchanges ratified commercial treaty with Swedish minister.

c. February 8: Jonathan Williams leaves Nantes to establish himself in Saint-Germain.

February 20: John Adams announces that he has negotiated a new loan in Holland.

THE PAPERS OF
BENJAMIN FRANKLIN

VOLUME 41

September 16, 1783, through February 29, 1784

Editorial Note on Franklin's Accounts

The following accounts, identified in earlier volumes, continue to apply to the current period: VI and VII (XXIII, 21); XVII (XXVI, 3); XIX and XXII (XXVIII, 3–4); XXV, XXVII (XXXII, 3–4); XXX (XXXVI, 3); XXXI (XXXVIII, 3). We offer here a summary of entries that have not found a place elsewhere in our annotation but provide insights into Franklin's private and public life.

Account XVII (Franklin's Private Accounts with Ferdinand Grand, XXVI, 3). M. Durandy, from whom the Franklins were now leasing horses, had evidently been engaged in the summer of 1783, when Franklin bought a carriage. His first two bills were paid on September 25 and January 19.[1] William Temple Franklin received 1,200 *l.t.* on December 30. On February 13 the Paris banking firm of Tourton & Ravel was paid 960 *l.t.;* next to this entry Franklin wrote "Bourdeaux wine".[2]

Account XXV (Account of Postage and Errands, XXXII, 3). Franklin's secretary Jean L'Air de Lamotte continued to keep these records during the months covered by this volume. They include the monthly accounts submitted by the postman Berthelot and reflect the errands (unspecified) performed by Bonnefoÿ, Franklin's domestic. There is also a payment on November 21 of 1 *l.t.* 4 *s.* to the Duke of Manchester's *commissionnaire*, and on March 4 a certain Memain ran errands in Paris. On December 27, L'Air de Lamotte himself was dispatched on an errand of great importance: delivering Franklin's dispatches to Captain Joshua Barney in Le Havre. L'Air de Lamotte submitted a memorandum of his expenses for the six-day journey, which totaled 272 *l.t.* In addition to the usual costs of renting a cabriolet and post horses, with their accoutrements, he was obliged to pay for repairs to the carriage and hire extra horses on account of the severe weather. The postage accounts mainly reflect the unspecified activities of the Franklin household, but they occasionally include

1. Durandy is listed by name only in the account; his profession is revealed in letters written to WTF by L'Air de Lamotte on Aug. 30 and Sept. 5 and 15, 1784 (all at the APS). For the purchase of a carriage see XL, 3.

2. JW had ordered 500 bottles of the "best old Claret" for BF in September from the Bordeaux merchants V. & P. French & Nephew. They shipped eight cases (480 bottles) to Robert and Anthony Garvey in Rouen, who received the wine on Dec. 15. French & Nephew requested that their bill be settled with Tourton & Ravel (XXXIX, 304n). WTF, who handled such matters, acknowledged French & Nephew's letters on Feb. 9 and ordered the payment: French & Nephew to WTF, Sept. 13 and Dec. 27, 1783, and Feb. 24, 1784 (all at the APS).

letters for others. On September 21 L'Air de Lamotte accepted letters addressed to Jonathan Williams, Jr., who was staying in Saint-Germain.[3] On October 13 he received a letter directed to Colonel Jeremiah Wadsworth.[4] On November 15 he recorded 2 *l.t.* 2 *s.* received from the Jays for the carriage of letters, doubtless from the time they lived at the Hôtel Valentinois.[5] He sent a letter on behalf of John Paul Jones on January 14.

Account XXVII (Accounts of the Public Agents in Europe, XXXII, 4). On October 28 Franklin, William Temple Franklin, and L'Air de Lamotte received their salaries. Franklin received 14,583 *l.t.* 6 *s.* 8 *d.*, Temple received 1,811 *l.t.* 5 *s.*, and L'Air de Lamotte received 420 *l.t.* Temple received another quarter's salary on January 12. L'Air de Lamotte was paid the postage expenses he itemized in Account XXV on November 11 and December 10. Dumas' draft for his salary was paid on November 10. John Bondfield's bills of 1,000 *l.t.* and 670 *l.t.* 12 *s.* were paid on January 14 and February 29, respectively. The largest expenditure was the payment on December 10 of 237,200 *l.t.* for bills of exchange drawn on the American commissioners for interest.[6]

Account XXX (Franklin's Account with Congress, XXXVI, 3). On January 1 Franklin paid 282 *l.t.* in New Year's gratifications to the ministers' servants and others at Versailles. He was also credited with a 99 *l.t.* outlay for newspapers and periodicals sent to Congress during 1784.

3. See XL, 506n.
4. A Conn. merchant who had supplied Rochambeau's army. He arrived in France on Aug. 27 seeking payment from the French government, but left for England after about a month. He returned to Paris from London at the end of October: XXXVIII, 546; *Morris Papers*, VIII, 566; *Jay Papers*, III, 407–8, 450–1, 498–9.
5. The Jays moved to Passy around the beginning of June. After John Jay went to England on Oct. 9, Sarah Jay, their two young daughters, John Jay's nephew Peter Jay Munro (XXX, 556n), and their servants continued to live with the Franklins until early November, when the house they had leased in Chaillot was ready: XL, lviii, 180–1n; *Jay Papers*, III, 494, 496, 509–10.
6. Robert Morris had promised BF that he would no longer be responsible for payment of interest on loan office certificates after April 1, 1782. On July 1, 1782, Congress resolved to pay the interest bills out of the revenues of the impost, and the following September forbade issuing bills on American ministers in Europe for the interest. The interest bills must have been sent to Europe for payment when the impost failed to go into effect: XXXVI, 155, 673; XXXVII, 570; XXXVIII, 197n, 489n.

Account XXXI (Jacques Finck's Accounts of Household Expenditures, XXXVIII, 3) is complete through the end of January, when Finck's arrangement with Franklin changed and he no longer itemized monthly expenses.[7] The food items include the customary array of meats, fish, fruit, and vegetables, including 50 dozen oysters for a dinner in November. On October 24 the maître d'hôtel purchased lacquer as well as pigments in green, amber, Prussian blue, carmine, and vermilion; we assume that painting was being done. In November he paid 48 *l.t.* 10 *s.* to the *maréchaussée* of the Marais. In January, Finck paid the wet cooper's account for extending the stovepipe in the print shop. He laid in stores of coal in September, November, December, and January. On January 14 he purchased ingredients for a *tisane*. The Jay family's stay in the Valentinois is reflected in two "extraordinary" expenses: in October Finck purchased 12 blue porcelain dishes and four bowls worth 29 *l.t.* to replace the ones belonging to Sarah Jay that had been broken, and in November he replaced two of her place settings, said to have been lost.

Finally, we describe an account that is not Benjamin Franklin's but reflects the life of his household: Sarah Jay's account with William Temple Franklin for the Jay family's expenses incurred between September and November (one page, Columbia University Library). It acknowledges responsibility for half the household expenses for September and October and lists sums that were lent or paid on the family's behalf: 6 *l.t.* "for the subscription for a medal", 111 *l.t.* 4 *s.* for three months of fencing lessons (presumably for Peter Munro), 72 *l.t.* that Munro had borrowed from L'Air de Lamotte, and 60 *l.t.* that Temple paid on November 4 on account of "Abbe" (a slave who had run away).[8] From the subtotal Sarah Jay deducted the 1,200 *l.t.*

7. See Finck's proposal of Feb. 1, below. One additional expense was not recorded on Finck's accounts: BF's share of the candles that Veuve Leleu & Cie., of the Manufacture Royale de Bougies on rue St.-Martin, sent to the Hôtel Valentinois on Nov. 28. BF received the invoice, totalling 72 *l.t.* 10 *s.*, for 25 *livres* of candles. Le Ray de Chaumont paid the bill but did not settle with BF for his share (28 *l.t.*) until May 22, 1785, when he noted BF's payment on the original invoice (APS).

8. Abby, a black slave, ran away near the end of October. On Oct. 30 Lenoir, the lieutenant of police, informed WTF that she had been arrested, according to WTF's and Mrs. Jay's wishes. Because she refused to return to her mistress, Lenoir was obliged to confine her, and he requested that Mrs. Jay pay for her board. Sarah Jay agreed, and sent Peter Munro to visit the young woman. Abby insisted on staying in prison (happy at having nothing to do, she allegedly said) until either John Jay returned or she was sent to

that she had paid to Temple on October 9, and on December 19 she recorded that she wrote an order to L'Air de Lamotte on Ferdinand Grand for the balance, 1,270 *l.t.* 6 *s.* 3 *d.*

To Richard Price

Press copy of ALS: Library of Congress

My dear Friend,   Passy near Paris, Sept. 16. 1783.

Having this Opportunity by Mr Bingham,[9] who has the Honour of being known to you, I seize it to thank you for your excellent Book[1] and other Favours, and to let you know that I continue well, except a little Gout, which perhaps is not more a Disease than a Remedy. Mr Petrie[2] inform'd me of your being also well with Mrs Price lately at Brighthelmstone, which gave me great Pleasure: Please to present my affectionate Respects to that good Lady.—

All the Conversation here at present turns upon the Balloons fill'd with light inflammable Air; and the means of managing them so as to give Men the Advantage of Flying. One is to be let off on Friday next at Versailles, which it is said will be able to carry up a 1000 pounds weight,[3] I know not whether inclusive or exclusive of its own. I have sent an Account of the former to Sir Joseph Banks,[4] our President, and shall be glad to hear if

America. BF evidently recommended leaving her where she was for a while, and John Jay agreed. When Abby became ill, she asked to be returned to the Jays. Peter Munro brought her home on Dec. 6; she died a week later. Lenoir to WTF, Oct. 30, 1783; WTF to Lenoir, Oct. 31, 1783 (both at the APS); *Jay Papers*, III, 509–10, 513, 516, 520, 527, 528–9, 529, 532, 537.

9. William Bingham.

1. *Observations on Reversionary Payments* . . . (4th ed.; 2 vols., London, 1783), which Benjamin Vaughan forwarded in June: XL, 41–2n; Vaughan to WTF, June 6, 1783 (APS).

2. Samuel Petrie.

3. Montgolfier's official demonstration before the royal family was scheduled for Sept. 19. The secret gas he would use to fill his balloon was heated air, not "inflammable air" or hydrogen: XL, 393–8, 609–10. For BF's account of this demonstration see his Oct. 8 letter to Joseph Banks.

4. The first public balloon demonstration in Paris was Charles's Aug. 27 experiment using hydrogen: XL, 547–52.

the Experiment is repeated with Success in England. Please to forward to him the enclosed Print.—[5]

Inflammable Air puts me in mind of a little jocular Paper I wrote some Years since in ridicule of a Prize Question given out by a certain Academy on this side the Water, and I enclose it for your Amusement.—[6] On second Thoughts, as it is a mathematical Question, and perhaps I think it more trifling than it really is, and you are a Mathematician, I am afraid I have judg'd wrong in sending it to you. Our Friend Dr. Priestly, however, who is *apt* to give himself *Airs,* i.e. fix'd, deflogisticated, &c &c., and has a kind of Right to every thing his Friends *produce* upon that Subject, may perhaps like to see it, and you can send it to him without reading it.

We have at length sign'd our Preliminary Articles as definitive; all the Additions we have been so long discussing, being referr'd to a future Treaty of Commerce. I have now a little Leisure and long to see and be merry with the Club, but doubt I cannot undertake the Journey before Spring. Adieu, and believe me ever, my dear Friend, Yours most affectionately

B Franklin

They make small Balloons now of the same materials with what is call'd Gold-beaten Leaf. Inclos'd I send one which being fill'd with inflammable Air by my Grandson, went up last Night to the Cieling in my Chamber, and remained rolling about there for some time.— Please to give it also to Sir Joseph Banks.[7] If

5. The engraving depicting Charles's experiment is reproduced in XL, facing p. 543. The legend identified it as Montgolfier's experiment, repeated with a balloon filled with inflammable air and executed by the Robert brothers under the direction of Faujas de Saint-Fond. BF added Charles's name in pen: XL, xxix–xxx.

6. The paper was "To the Royal Academy of Brussels." BF suppressed the name "Brussels" (which was present in his draft and the one surviving AL) when he later printed it for his collection of bagatelles: XXXII, 396–400. The copy he sent to Price evidently identified the academy as "B———"; see Price's response of April 6, 1784 (APS). That response also indicates that the essay was not enclosed in the present letter, but was delivered by a brother of Henry Dagge. BF arranged for that conveyance around Sept. 26; see the letters of that date from John Baynes and Henry Dagge.

7. In the interval between Charles's experiment of Aug. 27 and Montgolfier's demonstration on Sept. 19, amateur physicists began to

a Man should go up with one of the large ones, might there not be some mechanical Contrivance to compress the Globe at pleasure and thusly incline it to descend, and let it expand when he inclines to rise again?——

From Prince Bariatinskii, with Franklin's Draft of a Reply

AL: American Philosophical Society

Ce 16. 7bre. mardÿ

Le Prince Bariatinskoÿ prie monsieur Francklein de lui faire L'honneur de venir diner chez lui aprés demain jeudi Le 18. du Courant.

R:S:V:P:

Addressed: à Monsieur / Monsieur Francklein / ministre plenipotentiaire des / Etats Unis de l'Amerique / près S:M:T:C: / à Passÿ

Endorsed: Mr Franklin presents his respectful Compliments to Prince Baritinsky, with Thanks for his obliging Invitation,

---

manufacture small-size balloons. On Sept. 11 the baron de Beaumanoir exhibited a hydrogen balloon with a diameter of about 18 inches, made of *peau de baudruche* (goldbeater's skin). Three days later M. Blondy advertised eight-inch balloons of the same material for 6 *l.t.* apiece: *Jour. de Paris,* Sept. 11 and 14, 1783; Barthélemy Faujas de Saint-Fond, *Description des expériences de la machine aérostatique de MM. de Montgolfier* . . . (Paris, 1783), pp. 22–8. On Sept. 22 JQA noted in his diary that the balloons could be purchased empty or, for an additional 2 *l.t.,* filled with hydrogen, but that "several accidents have happened to persons who have attempted to make inflammable air, which is a dangerous operation, so that government have prohibited them": Taylor, *J. Q. Adams Diary,* 1, 194. On the same day JW asked WTF to buy him one or two balloons at 6 *l.t.* and send them to Nantes (APS).

Replicating WTF's experiment was not easy. According to Charles Blagden, who himself had trouble with a similar balloon, Price forwarded BF's balloon to Banks after failing to "make it light enough" to rise in his home: Neil Chambers, ed., *Scientific Correspondence of Sir Joseph Banks, 1765–1820* (6 vols., London, 2007), II, 192.

which Mr F. would accept with Pleasure but that he happens to be pre-engaged.

Passy, Sept. 17. 83

Translate this, & let me see the Translation[8]

From Sir Edward Newenham

ALS: American Philosophical Society

Dear Sir   Dublin 16 Sept: 1783

With every Sentiment of Respect & Esteem, I have the Honour to Congratulate you on the final completion of American Independance— To you, thou Virtuous Patriot, they owe much—to your illustrious Character, words are wanting to pay due respect— I shall sum up all in a few, thou ar't great, thou hast proved faithfull & honest in the Day of Tryal— Though not an American born, My Villa will be honoured with a pillar, to remind Posterity of *thy* transcendant Virtues—it is partly finished;—

I arrived here only 15 Days prior to the General Election,[9] and when all the Kingdom had been canvassing for 8 months during my Absence, yet I had *& am returned*, by a large Majority, in opposition to Government, Lawn Sleeves[1] & an AMAZING EXPENDITURE OF MONEY—& I did not *one* Guinea—[2]

In 1781 I moved for a bill for the more Equal Representation

---

8. This note may have been intended for BFB, who had returned from Geneva in July and was relearning English (a language he had almost entirely forgotten during the four years he was in boarding school). BF normally relied on either his French secretary Jean L'Air de Lamotte or WTF for translations; the latter's French, by this time, was excellent.

9. The election began on Aug. 13: XL, 205n.

1. Bishops.

2. Newenham won the second seat in his constituency of County Dublin by a substantial margin. Although he had been in France for nearly a year and had not campaigned in person, he and his supporters at home made sure that his name and political platform appeared regularly in the Dublin newspapers: XXXVIII, 187–8; James Kelly, *Sir Edward Newenham MP, 1734–1814: Defender of the Protestant Constitution* (Dublin, 2004), pp. 193–5.

9

of the People— I obtained leave—the Ministry opposed the reading of it—*but now they dare not*— I think that measure MUST now succeed—& all other Subordinate Measures of Trade will follow of Course—

Permit me now—to ask you as a private Man—whether it will not be necessary to have Some Law or Declaration from the Parliament of this Country, in order to fix a Trade with America, or whether *we* are deemed to be included in the late Treaty.[3]

Lady Newenham, who reveres you—who never Ceases wishing for your prosperity & happiness desires her sincerest respects to you— My son joins me in every sentiment of respect & Esteem—

I have the Honor, to be, my Dear Sir with respect & Esteem your Excellencys Most obt: & most Humble st

EDWD NEWENHAM

No Time can Obliterate our Gratefull Remembrance of yr worthy Grandson, to whom we request our best regards— I shall Count the Days with the Greatest Impatence, untill I have the Honor of an Answer—

Addressed: To / His Excellency Dr: B: Franklin / Minister Pleniopotentiary / of America— / Paris—

From James Bennet
ADS: American Philosophical Society

Paris 17th sepr 1783

The Petition and Representation of James Bennet native of Philadelphia.

Humbly Sheweth:

That whereas in the month of January last past the Petitioner Shiped himself as Clk & Steward on Board a Scooner of Balti-

---

3. Newenham had asked BF the same question the previous November, when the preliminary peace treaty was being negotiated. He feared that unless the treaty made provisions for Irish-American trade, Ireland would be forced to adhere to restrictive English trade policies: XXXVIII, 301.

more in Maryland bound wt. a Cargo of Tobaccoe to Gothen-
burgh in Swedland; But being intercepted in our course, had not
the good fortune to Land our Cargo conform to expectation,
Being taken by the Argo 44. a British man of War[4] On board
of which ship the Petr. [Petitioner] has been closely confined
since, untill her Arivall at Plymouth about a month ago where
the men were sett at Large— That the Petr. finding no Opportunity there to Emigrate to his native Country he concluded, he
would take a passage in a Dunkirque fishing: boat thinking a
favourable Opportunity might offer there, But being frusterated
in this he was constrained to depart Dunkirque and sett off for
Paris in a very disasterous situation with an intention to go from
thence to Burdeaux or some other Seaport in France where he
should have an Opportunity of Embarqueing for *America*.

That the Petr. arived last night in the sd. City of Paris, poor
in purse and person, after a very long & tedious Journey and as
he is totally destitute in a Country very exotic to him, and unacquainted Also he is of necessity constrained to Apply to Your
Honour for relief in this undressed manner, in order the poor
Representer may be enabled to proceed immediately to Burdeaux and Afterwards Obtain a sight once more of Philadelphia
which is long wished for.

May it Please your Honour to Consider the Premisses & out
of your extream goodness & wantoned Clemency to confer
upon the Petr. what seemeth meet to your Honour which shall
be refunded by the Almity of the poor & rich if not otherways
& the Petr shall as in duty bound Pray[5]   JAS: BENNET

Unto The Honble. Doctor Franklain Ambassadore for the
Honble. Congress for the Unitted Provinces in America.

4. Launched in 1781: David Lyon, comp., *The Sailing Navy List: All
the Ships of the Royal Navy—Built, Purchased and Captured—1688–1860*
(London, 1993), p. 80.
5. BF granted Bennet 72 *l.t.* on Sept. 19, when the sailor signed a set
of triplicate promissory notes. The only other promissory note from the
period covered by this volume was issued on Feb. 19, 1784, to the illiter-
ate Giraud Pegasse, who signed with an X. L'Air de Lamotte filled in the
date and identified the recipient, but no amount was indicated. Grand gave
the Frenchman 24 *l.t.* on Feb. 21: Account XXVII (XXXII, 4).

Petition & Representation of James Bennet of Philadelphia
1783.

Notation: Bennet 17. 7bre. 1783.——

From Robert Morris   ALS: American Philosophical Society

Dear Sir   Philada Septr. 17th. 1783

You have above an extract of a letter from the Honble
Mr. Jefferson, to me[6] by which you will perceive that he wants
one of your late invented Machines for Copying Writings, he
desires me to write to England but if I am not much mistaken
France is the place.[7] You however will know where his order
can be best executed, and give orders accordingly, shou'd it be
shipped from France Messrs LeCouteulx & Co will supply the
Money to pay Cost on my acct. If you think it best to order it
from London Messrs Herries & Company of that place will pay
for it,[8] or in either case if it will suit you to draw on Mr. Jefferson
or me payable in America for the Cost the bill shall be punctually acquitted. You will excuse this trouble it is occasioned by
the opinion which I entertain, that this is the most likely way to

6. The extract, copied by a secretary at the top of Morris' sheet, is the
only surviving record of TJ's letter. Dated Aug. 15 from Monticello, it begins, "Being desirous of getting from England as soon as possible one of
those copying Machines invented there not long since, and of which I dare
say you have seen Specimens of it's Execution in Doct. Franklin's Letters, I
take the Liberty of asking the favor of you to write thither for one for me,
with half a dozen Reams of the Paper proper for it." TJ asked that Morris
order it as soon as possible and have the machine shipped to Philadelphia,
"as I shall be there in November to continue some Time." The extract and
Morris' brief reply of Sept. 9 are in *Jefferson Papers*, xv, 608–9.

7. BF had ordered three copy presses from James Watt, the inventor,
in 1780. The following year, when Congress asked him to send some to
America, he had them replicated in Paris: XXXIII, 115–18; XXXIV, 371n;
XXXV, 174, 249–50, 476; XXXVI, 5. We have not found any record of their
having been shipped nor of their having arrived, but Morris seemed to
know that such presses could be obtained in France.

8. Morris had longstanding relationships with both banking firms:
XXXV, 136; *Morris Papers*, I, 124n; VIII, 613n.

have our Friend Jefferson well Served.[9] With sincere Attachment I ever am Dear Sir Your most Obedient & Most humble
servant   ROBT MORRIS

His Excy Benjn. Franklin Esqr Minister Plenipy a Passy—

From Patrick Murphy *et al.*

ALS: American Philosophical Society

Sir,   Bourdox September the 17th. 1783
    I hope Yr. Honr. will look into the Affair As Our Case is
Verry hard at present and take it into Yr. Serious Considration
As Wee Are Strangers here And Cant Get abirth too Any part
Likewise to let Yr. Honr. know that Wee have Been in his Majesties Service All this War We Want to Go home Or To the
West indies As Wee Are Determined Not to Go to England
But Willing To Serve in the Merchant Service as Usual So Wee
hope Yr. honr. will Relieve us in Our poor. & low Situation
the Number of Us is 26. Running in Debt And Expect to Go
to Goal Except Yr. Hr. Does Something in Our Behalf in So
Doing Youl Oblige And Serve Yr. humble & faithful Servants
till Death Wee Humbly Beg And Request of Yr. Honour To
Write A few lines in Our Behalf to Mr. Bunfill[1] in Bourdeaux
Yr. Verry humble Servants—   PATRICK MURPHY
                                               JOSEPH MITCHEL
                                               MATHEW JACKSON
                                               WM. BRIEN

Notation: Brien. 17 Sept. 1783.

9. It was WTF who took care of this order. In a now-missing letter of
April 3, 1784, he sent Herries & Co. a copy of Morris' letter and asked
the firm to ship the requested machine and paper to TJ, debiting Morris'
account. They answered on April 13 that they would do so "by the first Opportunity to Virginia": APS. (WTF had obviously neglected to mention TJ's
request that it be sent elsewhere.) The copy press had still not arrived by the
time TJ left for Europe in early July: *Jefferson Papers,* VII, 362.
    1. John Bondfield, the American agent at Bordeaux.

To Benjamin Rush[2]

ALS: Yale University Library

Dear Doctor,   Passy, Sept. 18. 1783.——

M. du Trône,[3] who will have the Honour of presenting you this Line, is recommended to me by very respectable Persons, as a young Gentleman of excellent Character, who goes to America with Views of residing there some Years, and practising Chemistry. I beg leave to recommend him to your Protection and good Counsels, and to those Civilities you delight in showing to Strangers of Merit. With great Esteem, I am ever, my dear Friend, Yours most affectionately   B FRANKLIN

Dr Benja. Rush

2. This letter of introduction and the one to RB of Sept. 23 were written at the request of an unnamed woman acting on behalf of a certain Le Roy whose letter to her, unsigned as well as undated, is now among BF's papers. (We identified him by the handwriting, which matches that of the Nov. 29 letter on the same subject written by Le Roy to BF.) In this letter, dated only "ce dimanche," Le Roy sends regrets that an important meeting will prevent his seeing the woman on Wednesday, and asks her to solicit from BF a letter of recommendation to someone in Philadelphia for a young doctor of his acquaintance, an honest, well-educated man named du Trône who plans to spend "une dixaine d'années en Amerique pour y exercer un employ de chimiste." This doctor does not ask for favors, only a letter that will allow him to be received in good company. APS.

3. This was probably Jacques-François Dutrône de La Couture (1749–1814), the *docteur en médecine* who went to Saint-Domingue in 1784 to study the sugar-cane industry, evidently at the request of Minister of the Marine Castries, and devised an improved method of processing cane based on extensive chemical analyses. In 1788 he sent his treatise on sugar cane and his processing method to Castries' successor, César-Henri de La Luzerne, who submitted it to the Academy of Sciences for examination. The work was published with their enthusiastic approbation the following year, and went through several editions: *DBF;* Dutrône de La Couture, *Précis sur la canne et sur les moyens d'en extraire le sel essentiel . . .* (Paris, 1789); Académie des sciences, *Procès-verbaux,* CVII (1788), 136. Dutrône's methods are summarized in Joseph Needham *et al., Science and Civilisation in China* (7 vols. to date, Cambridge, 1954–), VI, part III, 473.

From Samuel Chase[4]   LS: American Philosophical Society

Dear Sir   London, 18th. Septr. 1783.

Your letter of the 15th. of July last by Captain Barney, came to my Hands the 18th. of March, but I have never had the pleasure of seeing Mr. Jones, or Mr. Paradise.[5] It was very unfortunate for Mr. Russell that your recommendation of him did not arrive sooner; the Character and Conduct of this Gentleman entitle him to every favour. His property was ordered to be sold by Law, and the Money appropiated to the Officers and Soldiers of our State. On representing his Case to the Governor, the sale has been postponed, and I hope something will still be done in his favour.[6]

4. This prominent Md. statesman met BF in 1776 when they served as co-commissioners to Canada: XXII, 148–9, 380–6, 438–40. Thereafter, to the best of our knowledge, they had no further contact until BF sent the letters acknowledged here. Chase sailed for England in August, 1783, commissioned by Maryland to recover its investment in Bank of England stock (as he explains below). He arrived in London on Sept. 7: James Haw et al., *Stormy Patriot: the Life of Samuel Chase* (Baltimore, 1980), pp. 121–2; Jacob M. Price, "The Maryland Bank Stock Case: British-American Financial and Political Relations before and after the American Revolution," in Aubrey C. Land et al., eds., *Law, Society, and Politics in Early Maryland* (Baltimore and London, 1977), pp. 10–11.

5. BF's letter to Chase is missing, but three other letters of recommendation for William Jones and John Paradise, all written to eminent Americans on July 15, 1782, are in XXXVII, 630–2. The pair had the letters with them in Nantes, their port of embarkation, but after Jones returned to London and canceled his trip, he sent the letters back to BF: XXXVII, 629, 704–5; XXXVIII, 311. BF evidently gave them to Capt. Joshua Barney, who at that time was preparing to return to America. Barney arrived in Philadelphia in March, 1783: XXXVIII, 560n. Paradise, meanwhile, also returned to London and decided against making the voyage: XXXVII, 704n.

6. BF wrote on behalf of William Russell at the request of Joseph Priestley; see XXXVII, 532. Russell's property was seized and scheduled to be sold under Maryland's confiscation act of 1780. In the spring of 1782, when the amnesty period ended (see XXXV, 179), it was clear that the petitions filed by William's brother Thomas, a citizen of Maryland, had failed to win him an exemption. The brothers then solicited letters from prominent Americans who could attest to William's relief efforts for the American prisoners at Forton. (Henry Laurens agreed to write at the urging of Thomas Wren: *Laurens Papers*, XV, 497.) Thomas included these letters with the new petition he submitted to the Md. legislature in November, 1783. On

I requested Mr. Laurens to present you with my best wishes, and to inform you of my arrival in this City, where I am come from the Legislature of our State to receive their Stock in the Bank of England. From the Conduct of two of the trustees, I expect to meet with some Difficulties, if not an absolute Refusal to make the transfer.[7]

I am considerably interested in a matter in which I beg leave to solicit your advice and Assistance. The state of the Case is briefly this. A Company of Merchants in Baltimore Town; known by the firm of Dorsey, Wheeler & Co. (of which Company I am one) were owners of a Ship called the Matilda, carrying sixteen nine, and four four pounders, manned with 90 men, and loaded with 1800 Barrels of flour, which sailed from Baltimore Town, on the 2d. September 1782, bound for the Havana. A few days before the Ship sailed, at the Request of the Merchants of Baltimore to his Excellency, Count De Rochambeau, he wrote to the Chevalier De Quèmÿ, Commander of the frigate Emraude,[8] to convoy the vessells of the Baltimore Merchants off the Coast of America. The owners of the Matilda for a variety of Reasons instructed James Belt[9] the Master of their Ship before he left

---

the basis of these "authentic testimonials," the committee recommended compensation, but the award did not pass a vote: *Votes and Proceedings of the House of Delegates of the State of Maryland, November 1783 Session* (Annapolis, 1784), pp. 20, 22–3, 27, 29, 33, 91; *Votes and Proceedings of the House of Delegates of the State of Maryland, November 1798 Session* (Annapolis, 1799), pp. 23, 27–30, 130; S. H. Jeyes, *The Russells of Birmingham in the French Revolution and in America, 1791–1814* (London, 1911), p. 255.

7. BF already knew something of this matter, having assisted the governor of Maryland in 1780 by writing to James Russell, Silvanus Grove, and Osgood Hanbury, the three London trustees appointed by the state to sell its stock. They refused to do so: XXXI, 336–8; XXXII, 401; XXXIII, 254–5. The trustees did not agree to negotiate with Chase until February, 1784, by which time Hanbury had died; see the annotation of Chase to BF, Jan. 19, below.

8. Louis-Alexandre Macquerel, chevalier de Quemy, commander of the *Emeraude*, would later transport Rochambeau and his officers back to France: XXXVIII, 537n, 539; Christian de La Jonquière, *Les Marins français sous Louis XVI: Guerre d'indépendance américaine* (Issy-les-Moulineaux, France, 1996), p. 199.

9. Capt. James Belt of Philadelphia was commissioned to command the *Matilda* on Feb. 21, 1782: Claghorn, *Naval Officers*, p. 21.

Baltimore, to sail with, or without the Convoy, as he should in his descretion think proper, on his arrival near the Capes. On the 9th. of September the Ship arrived at Mobjack Bay, and Captain Belt determined to sail without Convoy, the first fair Wind. On the 10th. the frigate Emraude came to anchor in the Bay. On the 13th, the Wind was fair, and Captain Belt weighed Anchor, but was prevented by the Chevalier De Quèmÿ from passing him, and detained by force from the 13 to 26th. of September; though the Wind was fair on several different Days within that time; and the Chevalier was acquainted with the descretionary orders to Captain Belt, to sail with, or without Convoy, and repeated applications were made to him by Captain Belt to permit the Ship to proceed on her Voyage, and during the time several flags of truce were allowed by the Chevalier to put to sea. On the 26th. of September, the fleet went out of the Capes, under Convoy of the Chevalier De Quèmÿ in the frigate Emraude which carried 36 Guns. On the 27th. a British frigate called the Jason of 32 guns appearing in sight, the said Chevalier called on the Master of the Matilda, and on the master of another Ship, called the Jolly Tar,[1] carrying sixteen sixes to Assist him in Engaging the Enemy, which they promised and prepared to perform; but in about half an hour afterwards, the Enemy being within about four miles, and cleerly to be distinguished to be a frigate, the said Chevalier made a signal; for the fleet to run, and each to shift for himself; and immedietly crowded all his sail and fled as fast as he could, and deserted the fleet, which he had delayed by his Signal to heave to, and prepare for action, and during which time instead of preparing for Action the Chevalier employed himself in Rigging out steering Sail Booms, and getting Steering sails ready to set. The Ship Matilda Steered the same Course with the frigate and thereby went greatly out of the Course of her Voyage to the Havana. On the 28th. the Chevalier left the Ship Matilda, and returned to the Capes of Chesepeak, and on the 29th. the Matilda was taken by a British frigate, called the

1. The *Jolly Tar*, commanded by Capt. Charles Harrison, was soon captured by the *Jason:* Claghorn, *Naval Officers*, p. 141; *Pa. Packet or, the Gen. Advertiser*, Oct. 12, 1782.

persaverance.[2] The Ship Matilda and her Cargo cost 9000 Sterling. All the fleet except one or two were taken to the Value of 100,000 Sterling. Dorsey, Wheeler & Co. proposed to apply to his most Christian Majesty for Redress against the Chevalier De Quèmÿ his Subject and Commander of his Ship; and they intend to ground their application on the seisure and detaining of their Ship, by the said Chevalier for 13 days from the 13th. to the 26th. of September; without any lawful cause; and on his cowardice, and desertion of the Matilda, whom he had compelled to accept of his protection and Convoy. By the 15th. Article of the treaty between france and America;[3] it is provided that if any commander of any Ship of his most Christian Majesty shall do any damage or injury to any of the subjects of the United States he shall be punished; and moreover make satisfaction for all matter of damage and the interest thereof by reparation under the pain and Obligation of his person and goods. If you can spare time to peruse the protest of Captain Belt,[4] you will see how greatly Dorsey, Wheeler & Co. have been injured by the Chevalier De Quèmÿ, I cannot believe that the Justice and Honour of the Monarch of france will permit such a wanton Violation of American property to be unredressed. I beg the favour of you My Dear Sir to give me your Opinion, whether there is a probability of Obtaining Compensation for the loss of the Ship and Cargo, from the property of the Chevalier, or from the generosity of his Royal Master, if there is I will come to Paris immediatly, otherwise I will delay the pleasure of seeing you untill I have Compleated my Business here, which will probably be about the begining of November.

I am now to entreat your kind Offices on behalf of a Worthy Lady of the City of Annapolis. In the year 1777 Monsr. Jean Le Vachè de Vaubrun, whose father was ancient treasurer of the Marine at Breast, entered as a Volunteer in the Artiliry of our

2. H.M.S. *Perseverance*, 36: David Lyon, *The Sailing Navy List: All the Ships of the Royal Navy—Built, Purchased and Captured—1688–1860* (London, 1993), pp. 81–2.

3. This is Article 17 of the original Treaty of Amity and Commerce: XXV, 611–12; two articles were subsequently dropped.

4. James Belt's protest of Oct. 28, 1782, was ten pages long (APS). Chase's description of events is based on Belt's account.

State, and for his Military services was afterwards promoted to the Rank of Captain in the Army of the United States.[5] On the 4th. September 1781 he Married Miss Ann Howard of the City of Annapolis. On the 4th of August 1782 he sailed from Annapolis for Nantz on board the Ship called the favourite, commanded by Mr. James Buchanan;[6] the Vessell has never since been heard of, and was undoubtedly lost, and all on board perished. Monsr. Sanè, chief Engineer at Brest,[7] wrote a letter of the 30th. March 1782, to Madame Le Vachè enquiring after Monsr. Jean Le Vachè which her Brother[8] answered the 7th. of June last. I am enclined to think from the Terms of the letter of Monsr. Sanè to Mrs. Le Vachè that he was doubtful, whether she was married to Monsr. Le Vachè. Mr. Carroll, your fellow Traveller to Canada, in August last, wrote to his Excellency Count De Rochambeau, and requested, that he would communicate the Contents of his letter to Monsr. Sanè at Brest. Inclosed is

5. Jean Le Vacher de Vaubrun, a native of Brest, was the son of the late Jean-Baptiste Le Vacher de Vaubrun, *trésorier de la marine* in that port: Eugène Giboin, "Un Eminent Ingénieur du génie maritime: Jacques Noël Sané, 1740–1831," in *Etudes d'histoire maritime* (Paris, 1984), p. 213. (The first names of Le Vacher *père* were kindly confirmed by the Archives départementales du Finistère.) He was commissioned in the 4th Md. Regiment on March 10, 1777: *Records of Service of Maryland Troops in the American Revolution* (Baltimore, 1900), XVII, 364, 380, 481.

6. Le Vacher de Vaubrun had requested a furlough to visit his dying father and was granted a ten-month leave: Le Vacher de Vaubrun to John Hanson, June 5, 1782 (National Archives); *JCC*, XXII, 323. Buchanan had been a naval officer since 1779: XXXVI, 556; Claghorn, *Naval Officers*, pp. 39–40.

7. Jacques-Noël Sané (1740–1831), one of the premier naval architects of the eighteenth century, was appointed chief engineer of the port of Brest in 1774. On April 29, 1783, he married one of Le Vacher de Vaubrun's sisters, Marie-Louise: Eugène Giboin, "Un Eminent Ingénieur du génie maritime," pp. 213–19; Philippe Henwood, "Jacques-Noël Sané (1740–1831): un ingénieur constructeur de la Marine au service de la nation," in *La Bretagne des savants et des ingénieurs, 1750–1825*, ed. Jean Dhombres (Rennes, France, 1991), pp. 263–6.

8. Most likely Samuel Harvey Howard (b. 1750), her eldest brother, a well-established merchant: Harry W. Newman, *Anne Arundel Gentry* (1971; reprint, 3 vols., Westminster, Md., 1996), II, 238–41; Eric C. Papenfuse, *In Pursuit of Profit: the Annapolis Merchants in the Era of the American Revolution, 1763–1805* (Baltimore and London, 1975), pp. 33, 81, 151.

a duplicate of Mr. Carrolls letter; which I beg you to convey to Count Rochambeau, and a Copy of Mr. Carrolls letter is presented to you for your Perusal.[9] The Marriage is as well known in Annapolis, as almost any fact which ever happened there, and the Young Lady, bears an unspotted Reputation. I have taken the liberty to send you authenticated depositions of the Clergyman who performed the Marriage; and of three Witnesses who were present.[1] If Count Rochambeau is in Paris woud you condescend so far as to request him to take the trouble of writing to Monsr. Sanè at Brest; and will you be so kind as also to write, and if proper, transmit the proof of the Marriage to Monsr. Sanè, or some other Gentleman of that City? The Parents of Monsr. Le Vachè died before he was lost, and it is said he was entitled to an Estate by his Mother. Mrs. Le Vachè has been informed by some french Gentlemen from Brest, that the father of her Husband was a Gentleman of very considerable fortune, and that he and his Lady (who survived) made a provision for her Husband in their Wills. You, Sir, can inform Me, whether, by the laws or Custom of france, an American, the wife of a french Man, is entitled to any part of his property.[2] If Mrs. Le Vachè is not

9. BF's copy has not been located.

1. These depositions were sworn on July 25, 1783, before Annapolis mayor James Brice (later Md. governor), who added and signed his own attestation and affixed the seal of the city. Rev. Thomas Gates affirmed that he performed the marriage on Sept. 4, 1781, at the home of Abraham Claude, in the presence of Claude and his wife, and Elizabeth Quynn. The three witnesses together affirmed that they had attended the wedding and knew the couple to have lived together as man and wife. Finally, the clerk of the Anne Arundel county court, Nicholas Harwood, affirmed that he had granted the marriage license to Rev. Gates. APS.

2. According to the customary law of Brittany, Jean Le Vacher and his two sisters were each entitled to share in the estates of their deceased parents, regardless of the existence of a will. As a widow, Ann Le Vacher de Vaubrun was able to claim a life-interest in a portion of her husband's estate through her dower rights under both Breton custom and Md. law: Jean Brissaud, *A History of French Private Law* (Boston, 1912), pp. 771–7; Suzanne Desan, "'War between Brothers and Sisters': Inheritance Law and Gender Politics in Revolutionary France," *French Historical Studies*, XX (1997), 604. The outcome of any French claim is not known, but she later received a war widow's pension from the state of Maryland: Aubrey C. Land, ed. *Archives of Maryland: Journal and Correspondence of the State Council of Maryland* (Baltimore, 1970), LXXI, 106–7, 137, 303.

entitled by law, I hope the Sisters of her Husband, from their Affection to him, will afford her some Assistance, which her circumstances require. If Monsr. Sanè, or the sisters of Monsr. Le Vachè, will write to me, or to their sister in America, under Cover to Mr. Joshua Johnson Merchant here, their letters will come safe.

I request the favour of you to present my most respectful Compliments to Mr. Jay and his Lady. If Mr. Laurens is in Paris be so Obliging when you see him as to remember me to him and Miss Laurens.

I beg you to accept of my sincere Wishes for your Health and every other felicity in life, and beleive me to be, with the most perfect Esteem & Respect Dear Sir Your Affectionate Friend and Obedt. Servt   SAML. CHASE

Notation: Mr Chace's Letter to Dr Franklin 18 Sep. 1783

From Anthony Todd

LS: American Philosophical Society; copy: Royal Mail Archive

Dear Sir,   General Post Office. September 19th. 1783.

I had the pleasure of writing to you on the 22nd. past, and since that time a great deal of Sorrow has fallen to my Share by the unexpected Death of my beloved Nephew Mr. George Maddison, who is also an heavy loss to me and others in a public Capacity, and particularly as he was so well informed in the Negotiations going forward between this and the French Post Office, as also with yourself, respecting the Conveyance of Letters both English and French by Packet Boats to and from New York.[3] That part however, with your usual good Abilities and your Willingness to oblige me on all Occasions, you can easily supply, and even settle between this post Office and that of

3. Todd and BF were arranging the resumption of postal service between England and New York; see their correspondence in vol. 40. Todd informed BF on Aug. 22 that George Maddison would be negotiating with French postal officials for the coordination of services, but the young man died on Aug. 27: XL, 502.

Paris without any person going from hence, in whatsoever may relate to the Conveyance of Letters to or from New York by the way of England or France.

I am therefore in My Lord Foley's and Mr. Carteret's Names,[4] and with Their best Compliments, to acknowledge the one you were pleased to write me on the 31st. past,[5] which agrees so generally with their Sentiments, that I have little more than to recapitulate the Substance of it.

In the first place, an Agent on our part, to reside at New York, appears to be necessary, and it will be offered to your old Colleague Mr Foxcroft, whose Business it will chiefly be to take care that the Packets arrive and sail with their proper Compliment of Hands, and do not delay their Departure at the stated Times, the first Wednesday of every Month.

On their Arrival at New York, he should, as you justly observe, receive the Mail from the Captain, and deliver the Letters with a Bill to the American Postmaster, who must give a Receipt for the Value, and pay the Amount of postage every three Months, deducting Dead, Returned and Missent Letters, but it will by no means answer the Intention of the Writers, to send all Letters from thence for Europe by the first Packet, English or French, that offers; People in general are too careless and inattentive to say on the outsides of Letters, what they wish should be done with them, and therefore I rather recommend such an Advertisement as the inclosed from hence, signifying that all Letters for Great Britain and Ireland are to be conveyed from New York by our Packet Boats, unless directed viâ France, and if in America you should approve of an Advertisement in the same Manner, it would be of great Use, and in such a Case, I know you will not be offended with me for now inclosing the Project of one for your Approbation.[6]

It was once a favorite Idea of yours and mine to leave it to the Option of the Writer to pay or not beforehand, to prevent the opening and sending back of Letters for the postage, yet that Idea must now be renounced, and in Great Britain and Ireland

4. The joint postmasters general.
5. Though the letter has not been located, BF's notes for it are in XL, 558–9.
6. His proposals for those two advertisements are below.

the Postage must be paid to London, and in North America in the same Manner to New York. As to the Packet postage, which we will call it, to and from London and New York, at one Shilling per Letter and so in proportion, it may yet be paid or not beforehand at Option.

The foregoing is nearly all that concerns this Office and the United States of America, the rest is respecting the Conveyance of American Letters, through France and England, which I should think, you could easily settle between us, as the Matter is quite reciprocal, and though the Post Office at Paris may not like to exchange all such without taking any Account, yet they cannot object to exchange them at some certain equal moderate Rate, for Single, Double & Ounce Weight, and the best Policy in all Cases is for the Postage to be low and reasonable, and you may remember in the Act of the 5th of the present King,[7] although the Rates of Letters in America were thereby reduced, we thought them yet too high, and that too, instead of 2 d. [pence] for every 100 Miles after a certain accumulated postage of 2/. shgs. [shillings] or less for a single Letter, there should be no higher rate for the greatest Distances throughout America.

I remember no more at present, but that for mere Curiosity I should wish to know the Tonnage and Number of Men in the French Packet Boats.

Mr Hartley drank your Health here with me last Monday as well as today again and is well. I am sorry my Nephew John Maddison[8] did not pay his Respects to you on his late melancholy Excursion to Paris, but he had not Spirits to see any body, so you will I am sure excuse it, and requesting your speedy Answer to believe me with sincere and true Esteem and Respect, Dear Sir, Your most faithful and most obedient Servant

ANTH TODD Secy

To His Excellency Dr Franklin

7. For this act (5 Geo. III, c. 25), enacted on May 10, 1765, see XI, 535–6; XII, 268n.

8. John Maddison (1742–1808), deputy receiver general at the post office, was George Maddison's older brother: Kenneth Ellis, *The Post Office in the Eighteenth Century: a Study in Administrative History* (London, New York, Toronto, 1958), pp. 90, 93–4, 143.

General Post Office September [*blank*] 1783.[9]
A sufficient Number of Packet Boats of about 200 Tons and 30 Hands are established between Falmouth and New York to support a monthly Correspondence, and the Mails will continue to be dispatched as at present from London and from New York upon the first Wednesday in every Month.

All Persons are however to take notice that instead of its being any longer left to the Option of the Writer to pay or not the Postage beforehand, there is now a necessity for the postage on all Letters from any Part of Great Britain or Ireland for North America to be paid up to London, without which they must be opened and returned to the Writers, but the Packet Postage of one Shilling for a single Letter, and so in proportion between London & New York may or not be paid at each Place beforehand.

And all Persons upon the Continents of Europe and of North America corresponding by these Packet Boats are to take particular Notice that they are to put them under Cover to their Friends in London.

By Command.

New York October [*blank*] 1783.
Five Packet Boats of 200 Tons and 30 Hands are established between Falmouth and New York to sail from each side on the first Wednesday of every Month as at present. There are also five Packets established between Port Louis & New York to sail from those Ports on the 3rd. Wednesday of every Month.

The Letters from North America for Great Britain and Ireland will be sent by way of Falmouth unless directed viâ France, and the Letters for France will be sent by Port Louis unless directed viâ England, and all Persons are to take notice that it is now become necessary [*that*] the Postage of Letters from all Parts of North-America for Great Britain and Ireland as also for France should be paid up to New York without which they must be opened and returned to the Writers.

---

9. The versions that Todd enclosed of this text and the one that follows are missing; we publish them from his letterbook (Royal Mail Archive), where they follow the present letter.

John Thaxter, Jr.,[1] to the American Peace Commissioners

Copies: Library of Congress, Massachusetts Historical Society

Gentlemen,   L'Orient 20 Septr. 1783

I have the honour to acquaint you that I arrived here in the morning of the 18th Inst. and had the Mortification of finding that the Packet in which I was to have taken Passage for America had sailed four hours before my Arrival, after having been detained two Days for me— I was dispatched upon the Presumption that she was to sail the 20th. and arrived two days before the time notwithstanding very long detentions on the Road by Reason of fatigued Horses and oftentimes for want of Horses— Being thus disappointed and much embarassed what Course to take, I waited on the Commandant de la Marine Monsr. Thevenard who was extremely chagrined at the disappointment & thought it necessary that a Vessel should be dispatched as soon as possible to carry me over. He instantly gave Orders that a Vessel should be prepared for that purpose, & in six and thirty hours his Orders were completely executed— The Ship was Victualled, manned and had a new Deck laid on in that time and nothing but the Prevalence of Westerly Winds which absolutely prevent a Ship from going out of this Harbour, has impeded my sailing.

The enclosed Paper, Gentlemen, will shew the Nature of the Request which the commandant thought it necessary to make. I acquainted him that I could make no Request, or take any step in the Business, which would involve the United States in the least Expence, without consulting & taking the Advice of the Ministers for Peace. He asked me if I did not think it important that the Treaty should be sent? I answered that I thought it was but could not pretend to say that it was necessary to send a Vessel on purpose, as it would be attended with considerable Expence. He replied he thought the matter very Important. And then having received an Assurance that the United States would incur no Expence in the fitting out or sending the Vessel, I de-

---

1. JA's secretary, whom the American peace commissioners had chosen to carry the definitive peace treaty to America: XL, 600. He left Paris on Sept. 14: Butterfield, *John Adams Diary*, III, 143.

livered in the inclosed Paper,[2] which I hope will meet with your Approbation, Gentlemen.

Nothing could have exceeded the Zeal and Activity of the Commandant in the Preparation of this Vessel, and I am under the highest Obligations to him for his repeated Attentions & Civilities, as well as those of Mr. L'oreilhe.[3]

As every thing is ready the moment the Wind changes I shall embark, & hope to arrive as soon as the Packet Boat, which must have been retarded by the Westerly Winds.

With the highest Respect I have the honor to be Gentlemen, Your most obedt. & most hble. Servant

(signed) JOHN THAXTER

Their Excellencies John Adams, B Franklin & John Jay Esqrs. &ca. &ca. &ca.

From Henry Laurens

Copy: University of South Carolina Library

Sir.   Paris 21st Sept. 1783.

I have with much concern perused your address of the 10th. Inst,[4] which you did me the honor of delivering this Afternoon, intimating that you had received a Letter from a very respectable Person in America containing the following words vizt.

"It is confidently reported, propagated, & believed by some among us, that the Court of France, was at the Bottom against

2. The enclosure, transcribed on the copies, was a Sept. 18 note from Thaxter to Commandant Thévenard. It was important that the peace treaty arrive in the United States as soon as possible, Thaxter wrote; he therefore asked Thévenard to procure for him the earliest opportunity to sail to Philadelphia or to any other port the commandant deemed preferable.

3. Zachariah (Zacharie) Loreilhe or Loreilhé, had served as acting American consul in Lorient: *Morris Papers*, VIII, 662; *Jefferson Papers*, XIV, 60. He was married to Barclay's sister: Matthew Ridley's Journal (Mass. Hist. Soc.), entry of May 30, 1782.

4. Nearly identical to the ones BF addressed to JA and John Jay. We publish the one to JA: XL, 606–7.

our obtaining the Fishery & Territory in that great extent, in which both are secured to us by the Treaty; that our Minister at that Court favored, or did not oppose the design against us; & that it was entirely owing to the firmness, sagacity, & disinterestedness of Mr Adams, with whom Mr Jay united, that we have obtained those important advantages." and appealing to me "as a Witness of your Conduct in that Affair." That such a report may have been propagated and believed by some, is far from improbable, Those who were industrious in Attempts to poison our Minds with Prejudices against out best Friends, & against each other, on this side the Atlantic, have unquestionably been busy on both sides, nor have they yet ceased from their Labors, but unless we could trace the report to its source, & know who the Believers are, the Calumny of Rumor might with Propriety & Safety be disregarded by Doctor Franklin, whose whole Conduct from the beginning of the late Disputes of Great Britain with the Colonies might be referred to, as a sufficient Refutation. However Sir, as you have condescended to appeal to me, I will afford you all the Satisfaction in my Power, but I feel it necessary first to take Caution, inasmuch, as I have neither received nor heard of any Proof "that the Court of France at Bottom was against our obtaining the Fishery & Territory in that great Extent in which both are secured to us." & that the charge is of too serious a Nature to be reasoned upon without evidence, would too deeply affect the Honor & Interest of our Country, were we to take it for granted.

Touching your particular Conduct, respecting the Fishery Territory, & every other Article, coming within my Cognizance I have from the moment I came in as an acting Commissioner observed in you that Sagacity, Penetration, & Perspicuity which denote the able Minister, that Zeal & Attention to the Business of the United States of America, which mark Fidelity.— Your Country Sir & Posterity will do you Justice; as a Colleague & a Fellow Citizen(?) I should be ungrateful in witholding my Acknowledgements.

I believe by this time it is pretty well known I am un-addicted to Flattery, in the present Case, I am sure, there can be no motive for commencing the Art.

With most fervent Wishes that the Evening of your Day may be blessed with Tranquillity equal to your well-earned Honors, & with the highest Esteem & Veneration. I am Sir your obedt. hum. Servt.

Dr. Franklin. Passy

From Robert Pigott   AL: American Philosophical Society

Geneva 21 Septemr 1783—
Mr Pigott presents his Respects to Dr. Franklyn & begs the favour to have forwarded the two inclosed Letters for America[5] hoping He will excuse the liberty as not Knowing any other so certain conveyance.

Addressed: A Son Excellence Dr: Franklyn / Ministre Plenipotentiaire des Etats / Unis d'Amerique / a / Paris

To Richard Bache   LS:[6] Yale University Library

Dear Son,   Passy, 23. Sept. 1783.
    The Bearer Mr. Du Trône, is extreamly well recommended to me here, by Persons of the first Distinction & Character.[7] He is a Physician by Profession, but goes over to America with other Views. I beg you will introduce him to some of my Friends, & that you will shew him every Civility & Attention in your Power.—
    My Love to Sally and the Children, & believe me ever, Your affectionate Father.   B FRANKLIN

R. Bache Esqr—

5. It is possible that these letters were addressed to Albert Gallatin or his companion, Henri Serre; see XXXVI, 555; XXXVIII, 360.
6. In the hand of WTF.
7. See the recommendation that BF wrote to Benjamin Rush on Sept. 18.

From James Bowdoin

ALS: American Philosophical Society

Dear Sir   Boston Sept. 23. 1783

I beg leave to congratulate you on the return of peace, and the conspicuous part You had in bringing it about: especially as the terms of it are So advantageous to the united States.

Though the late contending powers appear disposed to peace, we greatly wish the confirmation of it by the completion of the definitive treaty: wch. notwithstanding reports, that have been circulated, we do not know has yet taken place.

I have received a Letter from the Comtee. of Falmouth in Casco Bay: whose inhabitants in Octo 1775, had the greater part of their houses and Effects destroyed by the merciless orders of Adml. Graves. They have written a Letter to you on that occasion, which, with an Address to the people of France, accompanied with an authenticated certificate concerning the appointment of the Comtee. & their right of agency will be enclosed.[8]

There is delivered to the french Consul, Monsr. Le Tombe, at his request, a copy of that address, wch. he told me he would send, with a letter of his own, to the minister at Versailles: and in the course of the conversation, he supposed it probable you would consult that minister, in order to obtain his favr. in this business.[9]

8. The committee's letter to BF was dated Sept. 3; it is in XL, 576–8. Their address to the French people is described in annotation there (p. 576n). Bowdoin enclosed two certificates with the present letter: one, signed on Sept. 13 by Falmouth's notary public John Frothingham, attested to the committee's authority; the other, signed by Gov. John Hancock on Sept. 24, authenticated Frothingham's official status. All these documents are at the APS. The committee's cover letter to Bowdoin was dated Sept. 15: William Willis, *The History of Portland, from 1632 to 1864* ... (2nd ed., Portland, Me., 1865), p. 902.

9. Létombe was the French consul for the New England states: XXXVI, 463n. The committee also composed an appeal to the English people, which Bowdoin forwarded to Thomas Pownall under cover of a letter similar to this one, dated Sept. 23. Pownall was not optimistic about its outcome: Willis, *History of Portland*, pp. 902–4. We have not found evidence of any action by BF or Vergennes, though BF did have BFB make an extract of the relevant portion of the present letter, beginning with the third paragraph (APS).

A Gentleman of your known philanthropy, especially as it respects your countrymen, will not be displeased with an opportunity of befriending a worthy people, greatly embarrassed by the losses they have So unmeritedly, and So unrighteously suffered; and which could not have been brought upon them, but by those, who had lost the feelings of humanity. I have the honour to be, with the most perfect regard, my dear friend, Yr most affectionate & very hble Servant   JAMES BOWDOIN

His Excy. Benja. Franklin Esqr.

From Jean Zinner[1]   ALS: Library of Congress

Monsieur   Vienne le 23 Sept 1783.

C'est eté ces jours ci que M. de Banck ci devant Major et Aide de Camp chez Mons. General Major de Gates[2] m'inspiré tant de respect pour la nouvelle Republique de l'Amerique Septemtrionale, que je me suis resolu de dedier mon ouvrage latin, intitulé: Notitia Historica Coloniarum Americæ Septemtrionalis ab earum origine usque ad nostra tempora[3] au tres Honorable Congrès des États Unis.

Monsieur, si Vous croyez, que cet ouvrage soit digne, de venir au publique, ayez la bonté d'envoyer ma petition en Amerique au Congrés, et de m'en instruir. C'est pour recommander la bravour, et le courage des Vos heros, et la dignité de vos Congrès.

1. When he last wrote to BF, in 1778, Zinner mentioned having written the history of the American colonies that is the subject of the present letter: XXVII, 646–8. See also XXXII, 146–7, where a compatriot referred to him as an abbé.

2. John Valentine Bancke left Europe in 1776 to join the American army but was taken prisoner the following year with the marquis de Brétigney. Gen. Gates described him to John Jay in March, 1779, as a "respectable German Officer." On July 10 of that year, Congress resolved to pay Bancke $3,000 for his services and encouraged him to return home, as they found it "impracticable under our present circumstances to employ him in the Army": *Jay Papers*, I, 611–12; *JCC*, XIV, 811, 816, 847.

3. As we noted in XXVII, 646n, there is no evidence that this work was ever published.

On n'a que m'en avertir, qu'on accepte ma bonne intention, je ferai avec plaisir tout a mes frais.[4]

Voila Monsieur des preuves de Veneration et d'atachement, avec lequel Je serai toute ma vie Monsieur Votre tres humble Serviteur   JEAN ZINNER
                                          Professeur de l'Hist. Universel dans
                                          l'Academie Royal a Cassau.

A l'ordinair je demeure a Cassau en Hongrie

Extracts of John Baynes's Journal[5]

Reprinted from *The Life of Sir Samuel Romilly, Written by Himself. With a Selection from His Correspondence. Edited by His Sons.* (3rd ed.; 2 vols., London, 1842), I, 452–8.

[September 23–October 17, 1783]

Tuesday, September 23. Walked to Passy to see Dr. Franklin, but took care to make the servant announce me regularly. Found him with some American gentlemen and ladies, who were conversing upon American commerce, in which the ladies joined. On their departure I was much pleased to see the old man attend them down stairs and hand the ladies to their carriage. On his return I expressed my pleasure in hearing the Americans, and even the ladies, converse entirely upon commerce. He said that it was so throughout the country: not an idle man, and consequently not a poor man, was to be found.

In speaking of American politics, I mentioned Dr. Jebb's sen-

4. Zinner's petition, in Latin and still among BF's papers, congratulated Congress on the victory of the new republic and expressed his wish to dedicate his work to them. Library of Congress.

5. John Baynes, the political reformer, was in Paris from late August through late October, 1783, and kept an account of several conversations with BF. We publish here the final portion of his journal entries. The first portion is in XL, 525–34; see the annotation there for background on the journal, its author, and its publication. As noted there, rows of asterisks are original to the 1842 publication. Ellipses indicate where we deleted text that was not related to BF.

timents on the famous vote of the House of Commons which put an end to the American war; that he disapproved of the terms of the resolution,[6] which was, on the face of it, founded on our being the better able to combat France, and which therefore could not be very agreeable to America. "Certainly not," said he; "I trust we shall never forget our obligations to France, or prove ungrateful." "You are at so great a distance," said I, "from the European powers, that there does not seem much probability of your quarrelling with any of them unless on account of Canada or the West Indies." He said that he hoped they would keep themselves out of European politics as much as possible, and that they should make a point of adhering to their treaties.

In the course of this conversation, I mentioned the shameful neglect of treaties which so much prevailed at present; the great injustice of several of our own wars, and the triviality of the avowed cause of others. I likewise mentioned Dr. Price's plan for a general peace in Europe.[7] He observed that nothing could be more disgraceful than the scandalous inattention to treaties, which appeared in almost every manifesto; and that he thought the world would grow wiser, and wars become less frequent. But he observed that the plans which he had seen for this purpose were in general impracticable in this respect, viz. that they supposed a general agreement among the sovereigns of Europe to send delegates to a particular place. Now though perhaps two or three of them might be willing to come into this measure, it is improbable and next to impossible that all, or even a majority of them, would do it. "But," said he, "if they would have patience, I think they might accomplish it, some way in this manner:— Two or three sovereigns might agree upon an alliance against all aggressors, and agree to refer all disputes between each other to some third person or set of men, or power. Other nations, seeing the advantage of this, would gradually accede; and, perhaps, in 150 or 200 years, all Europe would be included. I will, however," continued he, "mention one plan to you, which came to me in rather an extraordinary manner, and which seems to

6. Passed by the House of Commons on Feb. 28, 1782. It called for an end to all offensives on the North American continent: xxxvi, 621–2.

7. Outlined in Price's *Observations on the Nature of Civil Liberty* . . . (London, 1776), pp. 8–9.

me to contain some very sensible remarks. In the course of last year, a man very shabbily dressed—all his dress together was not worth 5*s*.—came and desired to see me. He was admitted, and, on asking his business, he told me that he had walked from one of the remotest provinces in France, for the purpose of seeing me and showing me a plan which he had formed for a universal and perpetual peace. I took his plan and read it, and found it to contain much good sense. I desired him to print it. He said he had no money: so I printed it for him. He took as many copies as he wished for, and gave several away; but no notice whatever was taken of it."[8] He then went into a closet and brought a copy of this plan, which he gave me. I took the liberty to remind him of his list of books, which he promised not to forget, saying the *Abbé* was now with Lord Shelburne in Holland.[9]

N.B.—He this day expressed his opinion that in England the executive power might be maintained without all the expense which at present seems to be esteemed so necessary for its establishment.

* * * * * * *

Thursday, Oct. 2. Walked with M. Hernon to Passy. Called upon Dr. Franklin, who showed me an Irish newspaper he had just received, containing the noble and spirited resolutions of the delegates of the Ulster volunteers at Dungannon, in which they appointed a grand national convention at Dublin.[1] He expressed his sentiments very strongly that they would carry their point;

8. For the visit of Pierre-André Gargaz in 1782 and the printing of his *Conciliateur de toutes les nations d'Europe* see XXXVII, 611–14. For a fuller treatment see Ellen R. Cohn, "The Printer and the 'Peasant': Benjamin Franklin and Pierre-André Gargaz, Two Philosophers in Search of Peace," *Early American Studies*, VIII (2010), 146–72.

9. BF had told Baynes that the abbé Morellet could supply him with a list of pamphlets written by both the physiocrats and their opponents: XL, 533–4. However, the abbé was at Spa, with Shelburne, in August and September and did not get back to Paris until about Oct. 8: Medlin, *Morellet*, I, 492–6.

1. The resolves of the Dungannon Convention were published in the *Dublin Evening Post*, Sept. 13, 1783. Sir Edward Newenham probably enclosed them in his Sept. 16 letter to BF; see also BF's answer to Newenham of Oct. 2.

and that, if parliament would not execute their plan of reform, they would drop the parliament and execute it of themselves. On my asking his opinion of our hopes of success in England,[2] he said he feared we were too corrupt a nation to carry the point. "I have not patience," said he, "to read even your newspapers; they are full of nothing but robberies, murders, and executions: and when a nation once comes to that, nothing short of absolute government can keep it in order."

In speaking of the Irish volunteers I took the liberty of mentioning (what seemed to me an omission in the constitution of America) the want of any sufficient armed force. He said they had a militia who met and exercised five or six days in a year. I objected the smallness of the time, and their serving by substitutes, and in support of personal service mentioned Andrew Fletcher's opinion.[3]

He seemed to think the objections of no great weight, "for," said he, "America is not, like any European power, surrounded by others, every one of which keeps an immense standing army; therefore she is not liable to attacks from her neighbours—at least, if attacked she is on an equal footing with the aggressor; and if attacked by any distant power, she will always have time to form an army. Could she possibly be in a worse situation than at the beginning of this war, and could we have had better success?"

Insensibly we began to converse on standing armies, and he seeming to express an opinion that this system might some time or other be abolished, I took the liberty to ask him in what manner he thought it could be abolished; that at present a compact among the powers of Europe seemed the only way, for one or two powers singly and without the rest would never do it; and that even a compact did not seem likely ever to take place, be-

2. As one of the founding members of the Society for Constitutional Information, Baynes was an advocate of parliamentary reform: *ODNB*.

3. Scottish political theorist Andrew Fletcher argued against military service by substitutes, who would resent having to defend the lives and property of their masters. He proposed the establishment of compulsory militia camps for all young men, regardless of rank or means. They would enter at age 22 and spend two years at their own expense; those who could not afford it would spend one year, supported by public taxes: *A Discourse of Government with Relations to Militia's* (Edinburgh, 1698), pp. 47–57.

cause a standing army seemed necessary to support an absolute government, of which there were many in Europe. "That is very true," said he; "I admit that if one power singly were to reduce their standing army, it would be instantly overrun by other nations; but yet I think that there is one effect of a standing army, which must in time be felt in such a manner as to bring about the total abolition of the system." On my asking what the effect was to which he alluded, he said he thought they diminished not only the population, but even the breed and the size of the human species. "For," said he, "the army in this and every other country is in fact the flower of the nation—all the most vigorous, stout, and well-made men in a kingdom are to be found in the army. These men in general never marry."

I mentioned to him that in England, our military establishment not being so large, we did not as yet feel these effects, but that the multiplication of the species was dreadfully retarded by other causes, viz.:—1. Our habits of luxury, which make us fancy that a young man is ruined if he marry early, nobody ever thinking of retrenching their expenses; and 2. Our absurd laws, *e. g.* the Marriage Act and the law of descents, which gives all to the eldest son, whereby younger sons are generally excluded.[4]

"Yes," said he, "I have observed that myself in England. I remember dining at a nobleman's house where they were speaking of a distant relation of his who was prevented from marrying a lady, whom he loved, by the smallness of their fortunes: everybody was lamenting their hard situation, when I took the liberty to ask the amount of their fortunes. 'Why,' said a gentleman near me, 'all they can raise between them will scarce be 40,000*l.*' I was astonished: however, on recollecting myself, I suggested that 40,000*l.* was a pretty handsome fortune; that it would, by being vested in the Three per Cents., bring in 1200*l.* a year. 'And pray, Sir, consider, what is 1200*l.* a year? There is my lord's carriage and my lady's carriage, &c. &c.' So he ran up 1200*l.* in a moment. I did not attempt to confute him; but only added, that notwithstanding all he had said, if he would give me the 40,000*l.*, I would endow 400 American girls with it, every one of whom should be esteemed a fortune in her own

4. The medieval law of primogeniture.

country. As to the custom of giving the eldest son more than the others, we have not actually been able to get entirely rid of it in America. The eldest son in Massachusetts has, without either rhyme or reason, a share more than any of the rest. I remember before I was a member of the Assembly, when I was clerk to it,[5] the question was fully agitated. Some were for having the eldest son to have the extraordinary share; others were for giving it to the youngest son, which seemed indeed the most reasonable, as he was the most likely to want his education, which the others might probably have already had from their father. After three days' debate, it was left as it stood before, viz. that the eldest son should have a share more.

I observed that this was the Jewish law of descent. He asked if it was to be found among Moses' laws? I answered that it was.[6] Upon which he said, it was remarkable that he had not seen or heard of it before; "but," said he, "the mention of Moses' laws reminds me of one which always struck me as very extraordinary; and I do not remember an instance where it appears to have been carried into execution—I mean the law prohibiting the alienation of land for a longer time than from Jubilee to Jubilee, *i. e.*, for 50 years.[7] This must evidently have been intended to prevent accumulation of landed property, but it seems very difficult to execute; indeed, in one respect, it is perhaps impolitic, for it must necessarily follow that the land will be run out at the end of the term."

"That," said I, "will always be the case even at the end of a fourteen or seven years' lease, and it seems a difficult thing to determine how long a lease in prudence and justice ought to be;

5. BF was clerk of the Pa. Assembly from 1736 to 1751: II, xxv; IV, 155.

6. Deuteronomy 21:15–17, where in the case of a husband having two wives, a double share of the patrimony must go to the eldest son. Most of New England and the middle colonies followed Mosaic law, granting a double portion to the eldest son: Lee J. Alston and Morton O. Schapiro, "Inheritance Laws Across Colonies: Causes and Consequences," *The Journal of Economic History*, XLIV (1984), 278.

7. Leviticus 25:11–34. According to the Jubilee laws, the seller of farmland could reclaim his property every 50 years. As BF remarks in the text, there is no evidence that these laws were ever executed: Richard H. Hiers, "Transfer of Property by Inheritance and Bequest in Biblical Law and Tradition," *Journal of Law and Religion*, X (1993), 139–40.

these long leases throw too much into the power of the tenant, and in leases from year to year the tenant is too dependent." "That very thing," replied he, "convinces me that no man should cultivate any land but his own. I rather am of opinion that land at present is of too high a value throughout these parts of the world. I was reading the other day some accounts of China, sent over by two young Chinese, who were educated here at the expense of government, and sent into their own country again. They were desired to send over minute accounts of every thing relative to that country, and several volumes have been published already.[8] In the last of these I find that they allow a very high interest on money, (about 30 per cent.,)[9] and it struck me that it was a politic measure, for the consequence would be that no person would be desirous of having a large quantity of land, which therefore must be the more equally divided. All laws for keeping the landed property exactly equal are impracticable on account of the fluctuating state of population; and where at the first the property is equal, if alienation be allowed it will very soon be unequal again. Antigua was at first divided into lots of

8. Kao Lei-Ssu and Yang Te-Wang, young Jesuits at the French mission in Peking, were sent to Paris in 1751 to complete the lengthy training for the priesthood. They did so, adopting the western names Áloys (Louis) Kao and Etienne Yang, after which the French government sponsored their further education. Members of the Academy of Sciences taught them physics, natural history, and chemistry, and they received instruction in French manufacturing methods, drawing, engraving, and printing. The king bestowed on them an annual income and financed their return to China at the end of 1765 on the understanding that they would send back reports on various aspects of Chinese history and culture. After several reports arrived (most of them written by the missionaries) and were published in different forms, the government issued them as a series: *Mémoires concernant l'histoire, les sciences, les arts, les moeurs, les usages, &c., des chinois* (17 vols., Paris, [1776–1814]). BF bought the first six volumes in July, 1780: XXXIII, 5. We have no record of when BF acquired vols. 7 and 8 (pub. 1782), vol. 9 (pub. 1783), and vol. 10 (pub. 1784). By 1789 he had secured the 14 volumes published to that time: BF to Grand & Cie., Sept. 5, 1789 (Library of Congress). See *Mémoires concernant . . . des chinois*, I, i–xv; Camille de Rochemonteix, *Joseph Amiot et les Derniers Survivants de la Mission Française* (Paris, 1915), pp. 102–14; Basil Guy, *The French Image of China before and after Voltaire*, Studies on Voltaire and the Eighteenth Century (Geneva, 1963), pp. 354–6.

9. *Mémoires concernant . . . des chinois*, IV, 336–91.

37

ten acres; it is not an ancient colony. I remember hearing one who was a very old man when I was a very young one, observe that he recollected there being a great number of ten-acre men in the island, and yet that when he spoke there was hardly a ten-acre man to be met with. At this time I do not believe there is one remaining." I mentioned to him my intention of leaving Paris in ten days: he said he expected his Abbé in less than that time. . . .

* * * * * * *

Sunday, October 12. Walked to Passy to call on Dr. Franklin. Found him with two French gentlemen, conversing on the subject of the *ballon.* Dr. Franklin said he had subscribed to another *ballon,* and that one of the conditions of the subscription was that a man should be sent up along with it.[1] The gentlemen did not stay long. After they were gone our conversation turned chiefly on the state of the arts here and in other countries, particularly printing and engraving. He admitted that we had one or two artists superior to any French engravers, but he seemed to think the art in much higher perfection here than in England. He showed some engravings (coloured in the engraving) of birds, &c., for Buffon's Natural History, which were wonderfully finely executed.[2] I cannot, however, think that they can execute a large print so finely as we do in England. I have never seen a large print engraved here which had not a sort of coarseness not to be found in Bartolozzi.[3] Their small designs, vignettes, &c., are beautiful, both in design and execution.

He showed me, among other specimens of printing, the Spanish Don Quixote, in 5 vols. 4to., which for elegance of ty-

1. The experiment proposed by Charles and the Robert brothers; see BF to Sir Joseph Banks, Oct. 8.

2. Some were undoubtedly plates for the comte de Buffon's *Histoire naturelle des oiseaux:* XX, 219n. The great naturalist met BF soon after the latter arrived in France, and they remained good friends. See XXV, 138–9; XL, 270.

3. The Italian engraver Francesco Bartolozzi (*ODNB*), who settled in England in 1764 and was a founding member of the Royal Academy of Arts.

pography and engraving equals anything I ever saw except the translation of Sallust by Don Gabriel, the second son of the King of Spain.[4]

* * * * * * *

I mentioned to him Howard's book on Prisons,[5] as one of our best printed books. He said he had never seen it; I promised to send it to him.

In the course of conversation he again expressed his doubts of our success in accomplishing a parliamentary reform, and repeated his opinion that we had been too tender of places and pensions:[6] he said that these were in general, either directly or indirectly, the objects of coming into Parliament. This he confirmed by an instance taken from America, where he said that he had sat in the Assembly 12 years and had never solicited a single vote; that this was not peculiar to him—hundreds had done the same; that the office of an Assembly-man was looked upon as an office of trouble, and that you perpetually saw the papers filled with advertisements requesting to decline the honour.[7] And to show that the salary is the thing which makes the office desirable, the Sheriff's place is always sought for by a number of candidates. Anciently when the office of sheriff was instituted in America, the fees were fixed at rather too small a rate to make a sufficient salary, there being then very few writs: the fees were therefore increased; but since that time the number of lawsuits having increased, the salary is increased so much as to make the office an object of desire. He seemed to express a fear that the spirit of the Pennsylvania constitution was not in this instance perfectly kept up;[8] however, he said if he ever went into

4. BF owned both, and had earlier expressed a similar opinion: XXXVI, 193, 339. The printer was Joaquín Ibarra.

5. John Howard, *The State of the Prisons in England and Wales* ... (London, 1777), printed by William Eyres.

6. For their earlier conversation on this topic see XL, 526–7.

7. BF served in the Pa. Assembly from 1751 to 1764. He was also elected in October, 1775, but did not take his seat and resigned from the assembly in February, 1776: IV, 154–80; XXII, 35, 367–8.

8. As provided in Article 36 of the Pa. Constitution; see XL, 527n, where the article is quoted.

America, he would endeavour to diminish the sheriff's salary. He therefore strongly recommended us to persist in the present economical reform, as that would at all events save us from ruin, by taking away the object at which most men at present aim who seek a seat in Parliament.

I asked if the *Abbé* was yet arrived. "Upon my word," said he, "I had actually forgot your list. The *Abbé* is arrived, and he was one of the gentlemen who were with me when you came in. But I will write him a note to request he will send you the list of books you wish to have." I promised to send him word when I intended to set off, as he wished to send a letter or two by me to England.

Wednesday, Oct. 15. Not being able to get a place for Rouen sooner, engaged one for Friday night. Dr. Franklin having expressed a wish to read *Mason's English Garden*, I sent it to him to-day, with a letter of thanks for his politeness.[9] He returned a most obliging answer.[1]

Thursday, Oct. 16. Called on M. l'Abbé Morellet, at Dr. Franklin's instance, to get my list, but he was in the country.

Oct. 17. Called again, but he was still in the country; therefore I was at last disappointed of my list.

* * * * * * *

From David Hartley[2]   ALS: William L. Clements Library

My Dear friend   Bath Septr 24 1783
    I am at present at Bath with my Dearest Sister, whom I have found as well as I cd have expected, and I hope with reasonable

---

9. That letter is below, Oct. 15. See the annotation there for William Mason's poem.

1. Missing, but see Baynes's reply of Oct. 17.

2. This is the British negotiator's first letter since he left Paris for London on Sept. 8 carrying the definitive peace treaty. He arrived in London on the night of Sept. 12: XL, 586; Fortescue, *Correspondence of George Third*, VI, 445–6.

hope of recovery in time.[3] I have seen in London the ministry and hope things will go well with them. I am sure all is right & firm. The chief part of the cabinet ministers are out of town, but there will be a full cabinet held in a few days, in wch a specific proposition in the nature of a temporary convention will be given in instructions to me, I imagine nearly upon the ground of my memorial of 19 May 1783 wch I delivered to the American Ministers viz Amern. ships not to bring foreign manufactures into G Britain nor to trade directly between the British West Indies & G Britain. All the rest to be as before the war.[4] I imagine that something to this effect will be their determination. And if it shd be so I should hope not to meet with difficulty on your parts. I want to see some specific beginning. As to my farther proposition respecting the trade between Gt Britain & the british West Indies, I doubt whether any such can be discussed before the meeting of Parlt.— I wish to look forward not only to the continuation of peace between our two Countries but to the improvement of reconciliation into Alliance, & therefore I wish the two parties to be disposed to accommodate each other without the strict measure by weights & scales as between aliens & strangers actuated towards each other by no other principle but cold and equalizing indifference.[5] Friendly dispositions presumed have the fairest chance of being realized but if we set out presuming against them The good wch might have happened may be prevented. Pray remember me to your three collegues & all friends I am &c   D HARTLEY

To Dr Franklin &c &c &c

3. During Hartley's stay in Paris, his half sister Mary suffered a severe illness that left her partially disabled: George H. Guttridge, *David Hartley, M. P.: an Advocate of Conciliation, 1774–1783* (Berkeley and London, 1926), p. 323.

4. Hartley gave this memoir to the American commissioners on May 21: XL, 33–9.

5. He had made more detailed arguments against complete reciprocity in Anglo-American trade relations in the memoir cited above and in his letter to the commissioners of June 14: XL, 165–72.

From the Comte de Mercy-Argenteau

L: American Philosophical Society

Ce Mercredi 24. Septembre [1783][6]
L'Ambassadeur de l'Empereur a l'honneur d'envoyer à Monsieur Franklin une lettre de M. Ingenhouze,[7] qu'il vient de recevoir de Vienne; il le prie en même temps d'agréer les assurances de son parfait et sincere attachement.[8]

From Joseph (Jean) Dupas de Iden de Valnais and Eunice Quincy de Valnais[9]

AL: American Philosophical Society

Paris the 25th. [September?] 1783—
Mr. & Mrs. De Valnais present their Respects to Dr. Franklin and will do themselves the honour to wait on his Excellency agreable to the invitation they have Received today

Addressed: His Excellency Dr. Franklin. / Minister plenipotentiary from the / united States of N. America to the / Court of France / Passy—

6. The only possible year before 1785, after Mercy-Argenteau offered to convey letters between BF and Ingenhousz (XXXV, 549).

7. Ingenhousz wrote on Aug. 15 and Sept. 1: XL, 475–84, 562–3.

8. Occasionally, Mercy-Argenteau used Francesco Favi to deliver papers or packages to BF; see XXXVIII, 483. Among BF's papers at the APS is an undated statement written by Favi for BF's signature, concerning papers he had handled: "M. franklin a envoyé à Leur destination Les Lettres, que M. favi Lui a fait passer de la part de Monsieur Le Comte de Mercy, et a recomandè L'affaire que contenoit La Lettre pour L'Amerique, et pour La quelle ce Ministre s'interessoit." BF signed this statement. We cannot identify the "affaire," nor can we explain why this DS was not delivered to its intended recipient.

9. For this couple, who had been recommended to BF by John Hancock, see XL, 261. We place this undated acceptance at its earliest possible date. Valnais and his family arrived in Paris by mid-September, and by Oct. 3 BF had written at least one letter of recommendation for him; see Genet to BF of that date.

From François-Antoine de Flandre de Brunville[1]

LS: American Philosophical Society

Monsieur, Paris ce 25. septembre 1783.

Je fais instruire le procès à ma requête de L'ordonnance de
M. le Lieutenant Criminel, contre le Noé. [nommé] Jean Robert
Schaffer et autres,[2] prévenus de s'être annoncés dans le Public
comme tenans Banque et maison de Commerce,[3] et à la faveur
de ces titres et de billets souscrits de Correspondans à eux af-
fidés, avoir abusé de la Confiance de différens marchands, et en
conséquence excroqué leurs marchandises. Il a paru nécessaire
d'entendre en déposition dans l'information que j'ai requis être
faite devant le Commissaire Chénon fils,[4] Monsieur votre petit
fils, annoncé pour être en état de procurer des renseignemens

---

1. *Procureur du roi* (chief prosecutor) at the Châtelet since 1780: Christine Favre-Lejeune, *Les Secrétaires du Roi de la grande chancellerie de France:
Dictionnaire biographique et généalogique (1672–1789)* (2 vols., Paris, 1986),
1, 555–6.

2. Under the Criminal Ordinance of 1670, which governed criminal
procedure, this investigation was likely initiated in one of two ways: by a
written victim complaint to a judge, a police commissioner, or a *lieutenant
criminel* (the second-highest officer at the Châtelet); or by a formal denunciation to a prosecutor, who officially registered the denunciation—signed
by the denouncer and kept confidential—and referred the case to the presiding judge. Once judicial action was initiated, a preparatory instruction
phase of investigation began, usually conducted by the presiding judge,
who at the Châtelet was often the *lieutenant criminel*. During this phase,
the judge deposed each witness and interrogated the suspect, often multiple times. Suspects who did not speak French were provided with interpreters: Richard M. Andrews, *Law, magistracy, and crime in Old Regime
Paris, 1735–1789* (1 vol. to date, Cambridge and New York, 1994–), 1, 60,
422–31.
The *lieutenant criminel* was Charles-Simon Bachois de Villefort: *Almanach royal* for 1783, p. 394.

3. For background on this most recent arrest of Shaffer's see XL, 618–
20. The firm of "John Shaffer & Compagnie, Commissionnaires des Etats
Unis de l'Amérique" was listed among the bankers in the *Almanach royal*
for 1782 and 1783 (pp. 468 and 474, respectively). The address listed for the
firm was Shaffer's own address on the rue des fossés Saint-Marcel.

4. Chénon fils, on the rue Saint-Honoré, shared with his father the jurisdiction of the department of the Louvre, or Saint-Germain l'Auxerrois:
Almanach royal for 1783, p. 400.

sur cette affaire.[5] J'ai crû ne pas devoir lui faire remettre une assignation pour se rendre chez le commissaire qui recevra sa déposition, sans avoir eû l'honneur de vous en prévenir. C'est une considération dont je m'acquitte avec d'autant plus de plaisir, qu'elle est duë tant à votre mérite personnel qu'au caractère dont vous êtes revêtu.

J'ai l'honneur d'être très respectueusement, Monsieur, Votre très humble et très obéissant serviteur,

DE FLANDRE DE BRUNVILLE
Procureur du Roy au châtelet

M. Francklin, ministre Plenipotentiaire des Etats unis de L'amerique

Notation: De Flandre de Breunville Paris 25 Sept. 1783.

From John Baynes   ALS: American Philosophical Society

Sir   Friday—Septr. 26th. [1783]
I have not till this morning been able to find any gentleman who was going to England— Mr. Dagge[6] however has this moment informed me, that he has an opportunity of conveying a letter by an acquaintance, the son of General Dalling,[7] who will set off tomorrow. I fear you will by this time have sent by some other conveyance the letter you mentioned—however, lest you shod. not, I take the liberty of informing you that if it be sent to Mr. Dagge today, it will certainly be forwarded.

I am, with all respect, Sir, Your most obedt. & obliged humble Servt.   JOHN BAYNES.

Chez Mr. Boulnois,[8] Ruë Neuve Ste. Généviéve.

5. WTF had been named in the deposition that, according to Shaffer, was responsible for his arrest; see the annotation of Shaffer to BF, [Oct. 9?].

6. Henry Dagge; see his letter immediately below.

7. Possibly Lt. Gen. John Dalling (*ODNB*), former governor of Jamaica, though his eldest son, John Windham Dalling, was 14 years old at this time: information kindly confirmed by the Norfolk Record Office, England.

8. Boulnois was a language instructor who advertised French courses in the *Jour. de Paris* (*e.g.*, May 6, 1783). He and his wife also rented apartments,

Mr. Dagge is at the hôtel d'Hamburgh, Ruë Jacobe.

Addressed: A Monsieur / Monsieur Franklin / Ambassadeur pour les Américains en son / Hôtel / à Passy.

From Henry Dagge[9]

ALS: American Philosophical Society

My dear Sir　　　　Friday Morning [September 26, 1783][1]

I find by Mr. Baynes that you wish to convey a Letter to London as soon as you can. I have an Oppertunity of sending to morrow Morning in a Letter to my Bror.[2] who will send it immediately where it is directed. I hope to have the honour of paying my respects to you some Morning the beginng. of next week & am always D Sir, Yrs sincerely　　　　　H DAGGE

From Charles Thomson

ALS: American Philosophical Society; AL (draft): Library of Congress

Dear Sir,　　　　　Philada. 26 Sept 1783.

Mr Isaac Norris is the son of our ancient and worthy friend Mr Charles Norris.[3] Though I am confident this would be a sufficient recommendation of him to you, yet as he thinks a letter

---

with or without board, and catered to the British tourist trade. By 1787, when they moved to a better location, they were advertising in English newspapers, adding that they taught French, English, Latin, and Greek: *World and Fashionable Advertiser,* Aug. 31, 1787. Boulnois was the author of *Principes raisonnés de la langue françoise* (Paris, 1788).

9. BF had known this London solicitor since the 1760s through their mutual involvement in the Walpole Company land syndicate: XVI, 166–7; XX, 310–11. While in Paris, Dagge delivered Benjamin West's Sept. 7 letter to BF: XL, 592.

1. This letter was probably written the same Friday as was John Baynes's letter (immediately above).

2. Either John or James Dagge: XVI, 167n; XX, 310n.

3. Twenty-three-year-old Isaac Norris (1760–1802) was the eldest son of Philadelphia merchant Charles Norris, who died in 1766 (II, 376n): Elaine F. Crane *et al.,* eds., *The Diary of Elizabeth Drinker* (3 vols., Boston, 1991),

from me will be of some advantage, I cannot refuse it, especially as he is a young man of an amiable disposition, sober, modest, of good principles and good morals.

I could have wished he had seen and known more of his own country before he went abroad. But the war has confined him much at home. On the return of peace, he was persuaded to visit England, but I find by his letters, it has no charms for him. He therefore proposes to make but a short stay in that country and to spend the greatest part of his time abroad in visiting the low countries and France. You will confer an Obligation on me by taking him under your protection, pointing him to objects worthy his notice and by giving him reason to find that this letter proved advantageous to him.

I am with the greatest respect your most Obedient And most humble Servt   CHA THOMSON

Honble. Doct Franklin

Notation: Cha. Thomson 26 sept. 1783—

To Elias Boudinot   ALS and transcript: National Archives

Sir,   Passy, Sept. 27. 1783—

Mr Thaxter late Secretary of Mr Adams, who is charg'd with all our Dispatches that were intended to go by the French Pacquet-Boat, writes from L'Orient, that tho' he arriv'd there two Days before the time appointed for her Sailing, he miss'd reaching her by four Hours; but another light Vessel was fitting and would sail the 21st. Inst. in which he hop'd to arrive at New York nearly as soon as the Pacquet.[4] We shall send Duplicates

---

III, 2192; William W. Hinshaw, *Encyclopedia of American Quaker Genealogy* (6 vols., Ann Arbor, 1936–50), II, 400.

4. See Thaxter to the Commissioners, Sept. 20. Thaxter reached New York with the treaty on Nov. 19, and Boudinot, in New Jersey, had it two days later. No longer president of Congress, he forwarded it to Thomas Mifflin in Philadelphia. Though the intention was to keep the text private until Congress reviewed it, the treaty was soon

by the next from hence. In the mean time I inclose a printed Copy of the Definitive Treaty,[5] which I hear is ratify'd. Indeed we have already the Ratification of the Preliminaries.[6]

Mr Hartley when he left us, expected to return in three Weeks, in order to proceed with us in forming a Treaty of Commerce. The new Commission that was intended for us is not yet come to hand.[7] With great Respect, I have the Honour to be, Sir, Your Excellency's most obedient & most humble Servant

B FRANKLIN

His Excelly. Elias Boudinot, Presidt of Congress

Notation: Letter 27 Sept 1783 B. Franklin with printed copy of definitive treaty.

To [Anthony Todd]

Press copy of ALS: American Philosophical Society

Sir,   Passy, Sept. 27. 1783.

I receiv'd last Night your Favour of the 19th. Inst. and have this Day sent to propose a Meeting on the Subject with Mr. Cou-

---

published, reprinted from English newspapers: Edwin Wolf 2nd, "The American Printings of the Definitive Treaty of Peace of 1783 Freed of Obfuscation," Bibliographical Soc. of America *Papers*, LXV (1971), 274–5.

5. BF had the treaty printed by Philippe-Denis Pierres. The title page, displaying the Great Seal of the United States, is reproduced as the frontispiece to vol. 40. Pierres sent BF proofs to review on Sept. 9 (XL, 599), but the present letter is the first indication of the pamphlet's having been issued. On Sept. 17, the chevalier de Kéralio wrote to WTF requesting a copy, whenever it was ready; WTF sent it on Oct. 7. (Both letters are at the APS). For a bibliographic description of the imprint see Wolf, "American Printings," p. 273; Luther S. Livingston, *Franklin and his Press at Passy* (New York, 1914), pp. 188–9.

6. BF had first informed Boudinot that the British had ratified the preliminary treaty in his letter of Sept. 13: XL, 621.

7. BF and his colleagues had as yet received only the congressional resolution of May 1 authorizing a new commission to make a commercial treaty with Great Britain; see XL, 604.

teulx;[8] but he was not in Town. I shall do what you desire of me as soon as may be.

Be so good as to forward the enclos'd,[9] if not too late, by your next Wednesday's Mail, and let me Know by a Line if it was in time.

With great Esteem, I have the honour to be, Sir, Your most obedient humble Servant   B FRANKLIN

From Richard Champion[1]   ALS: American Philosophical Society

Sir,   Whitehall Sepr. 27. 1783.

I cannot suffer a pacquet which Mr. Chase has put under my Care (and which will go by the next Messenger) to pass through my hands, without making use of the opportunity of expressing the pleasure I felt at being introduced to the honour of your Acquaintance; at the same time I lament the particular Circumstances which obliged me to leave Paris so very suddenly, that I was prevented from profiting by an Introduction I very earnestly desired.

It is now only left to me to request the favour of being permitted to repeat to you, the very sincere respect I feel for your Character, and the fervent hope, that the late unhappy Events which have separated the two Countries may be wholly forgotten, and one desire prevail to obliterate the past by the Interchange of future good Offices; as essential to the happiness of both Nations, as the ties of Religion, Manners and Language are

8. Undoubtedly Barthélémy-Jean-Louis Le Couteulx de la Noraye (1752–1799), the partner in Le Couteulx & Cie. who took charge of administering the French packet boat service: XL, 400n; Geneviève Daridan, *MM. Le Couteulx et Cie., banquiers à Paris: un clan familial dans la crise du XVIIIe siècle* (Paris, 1994), pp. 53, 66, 329.

9. BF to Boudinot, Sept. 27; see Todd's answer of Oct. 3, below.

1. The Bristol ceramics manufacturer whose elaborate porcelain portrait of BF is illustrated in XXXIII, facing p. 207. During the summer of 1783, Champion was studying American trade and seeking a consulship in the United States. In late August and early September he visited Paris with a letter of introduction to BF from Edmund Burke; see XL, 515n.

natural ones to them. It is far from me to attempt to travel over a Road big with so many Calamities. I would willingly draw a Veil over it: But it should be a Veil composed of the purest Materials of friendship and affection, covering from the View the latter Pages of our History, and recalling the happy friendly Union of former years.

I shall trouble you no farther than to express my very earnest prayers for the happiness and prosperity of the United States of America; and that you, Sir, may receive in the Bosom of your Country, the well earned Recompence of high Desert, in its affectionate and reverential Regard.

I have the honour to be with the most perfect Sentiments of Esteem and Respect Sir Your most obedient and faithful Servant   RICH CHAMPION

Notation: Champion 27 Sept. 1783.—

From Jean-Charles-Pierre Lenoir   LS: Library of Congress

A Paris Ce 27. 7bre. 1783.

J'ai reçu Monsieur, le bel exemplaire des *Constitutions des États unis de L'Amérique,*[2] que vous avez bien voulu m'envoyer. Je vous prie d'agréer le témoignage de ma reconnoissance, et les nouvelles assurances du respectueux attachement, avec lequel j'ai L'honneur d'être Monsieur, votre très humble et très obéissant Serviteur.   LENOIR

M. Franklin, ministre. plenipre. des Etats unis.

2. This French edition of the American state constitutions, translated by La Rochefoucauld under BF's direction, was published in July. Lenoir may have received one of the elegant, bound editions; see XL, 149–50, 376–7n.

From Benjamin Putnam[3]

ALS: American Philosophical Society

Honble. Sir,   Portsmouth Virga. 1783. Sept. 27th.

I cannot, cease to trouble you while my All is at stake, my Mind at the highest Reach of Pain & Anxiety, & only to be determined & reliev'd by your Excellency's Interference without which of what Consequence to me, are Resolutions of Congress, however favorable to my Interest, they may have been past?[4] I am Sir, without your Assistance in these two Cases, all but ruin'd—

Mr. Ridley who politely offer'd his Assistance in my absence has never let me hear from him. I am therefore totally ignorant how my Affairs stand. I have thro' my Corespondent at Boston deposited Mony with Mr. Jona. Williams at Nantes, should it be wanted, & to be drawn for, by Mr. Ridley. The Amt. of this Acct. is to me very Considerable & its Consequence nearly my Existence.—

We were unfortunately taken on our Passage by a British Man of War & consequently I became a large sufferer— By a Recapture we were bro't into this Place where as an Owner I am involv'd in a Lawsuit, the End of which, Courts in this Country being so dilitory in giving Judgment, I am unable to assertain. I have till then, settled in my Profession, & where I beg your Excellency to address for me.

I am Your Excellency's most Obed. & most Hble Servant.[5]

BENJ. PUTNAM

His Excelly Dr. B. Franklin.—

3. The Massachusetts shipowner who was pursuing two prize claims that had yet to be decided by the *Conseil des finances pour les prises en mer.* Unable to obtain a settlement during a visit to Paris at the end of 1782, Putnam engaged Matthew Ridley to be his agent; see XXXIX, 401–2, and the references cited there. Putnam sent BF two letters during the summer of 1783 that BF forwarded to Ridley. Now missing, they were dated July 2 and Aug. 9: Ridley to Putnam, Oct. 9, 1783 (Mass. Hist. Soc.).

4. Congress resolved in Putnam's favor in the first case, concerning a sloop taken in 1779: XXXIX, 402n. In the second case, however, dating from 1781 and concerning the *Terrible*, Congress tabled consideration indefinitely: *JCC*, XXI, 945.

5. On the same day as the present letter, Putnam wrote to WTF, asking him to intervene and telling him that he had renewed his pleas to BF. Desperate for news, as he had received no letters from Ridley, Putnam wrote

Addressed: A Monsieur / Monsur. Doct. B. Franklin / Minr. Plenipotentiare / A la Court de France / a Paris— / Per Post, via, Dunkirk. Capt. Duccroÿ.—

Notation: Putnam Mr. Benjn. 27 Sept. 1783.—

From the Prince de Soubise[6]

ALS: American Philosophical Society

27. 7bre. 1783

C'est avec grand plaisir, Monsieur, que j'ai l'honneur de vous envoier une permission de chasse pour Monsieur votre petit fils, et je la renouvellerai dans quelque tems, quoique l'année soit bien peu favorable.[7]

J'ai l'honneur d'etre avec les sentiments les plus distingues, Monsieur, Votre tres humble et tres obeissant Serviteur

LE M. P. DE SOUBISE

Notation: Le M. P. de Soubise 17 7bre '83

From Mary Hewson

ALS: American Philosophical Society

Dear Sir   Cheam Sepr. 28. 1783

Many thanks to you for your kind packet[8] which I was favoured with by Mr Hartley. As some time was taken up by his writing to

---

twice more to WTF before the end of the year: Putnam to WTF, [Sept.] 27, Nov. 25, and Dec. 29, 1783, all at the APS. Ridley did, in fact, write to Putnam on Oct. 9 (cited above). Responding to the shipowner's letter of July 20, he explained that he had hired a lawyer, but had learned that the council would not meet again before Christmas.

6. The governor of the hunting preserve at the Tuileries and the Bois de Boulogne, who had sent hunting permits for WTF two years earlier: XXXVI, 57.

7. Evidently WTF concurred, for the enclosed permit was not used. Dated Sept. 27 and signed by the prince, it reads: "Les Gardes du Canton de Pantin laisseront chasser M. Franklin avec un ami, et raporteront la permission a Paris." APS.

8. BF's Sept. 7 letter, which enclosed monthly installments of Berquin's *L'ami des enfans:* XL, 588–90.

51

me & waiting for my answer it did not arrive here till last thursday night. I tell you this to account for your not having a more speedy reply about your Grandson. I shall be happy to do every thing in my power for him if you trust him to my care, and my boys will have a peculiar pleasure in introducing him to their comrades, some of whom are two or three years older than Bache, tho the greatest part of the school consists at present of boys under his age. But how will my young Friend like to lay aside his powder and curls, and return to the simplicity of a rustic school-boy? I fear he will think us all so unpolished he will scarcely be able to endure us, but if English cordiality will make amends for French refinement we may have some chance for making him happy. Mr Gilpin has the good fortune to have some boys at the head of his school[9] who are an honour to the society, so I hope I may say in return to you that yours will have no bad example set him.

The subject of the latter part of your letter I hope to talk over with you next spring, as I chuse to infer, from what you say that you will then pay us a visit.

I am, Dear Sir, Your faithful & affectionate   MARY HEWSON

Addressed: A Monsieur / Monsieur Franklin / á Passy / pres de / Paris[1]

Notation: Hewson Mary Sept. 28. 1783.—

From Lewis Boudinot[2]   ALS: American Philosophical Society

Sir   Falmouth Septr 29th 1783

I have done myself the Honor this Day to Transmitt to London the Dispatches herewith, by the desire of my Brother who ordered me in Case I should not have the honor of delivering

---

9. William Gilpin was headmaster of the Cheam School: XXXVII, 259n.
   1. Other notations on the address sheet indicate that postage was paid to London.
   2. Lewis Carré Boudinot (1753–1789?), the youngest brother of Elias Boudinot, was entrusted with carrying the latter's July 15 letter to the commissioners (XL, 301–8): George A. Boyd, *Elias Boudinot, Patriot and Statesman, 1740–1821* (Princeton, 1952), pp. 10, 18, 128, 289.

them myself in person to transmitt them to the French Ambassador—[3] And as the Weather seems very turbulent And my Passage round like to be long I have sent them Accordingly and hope there is no doubt but they will Come safe to hand.— And with wishing You every Happiness the present Sunshine is possible to Afford And Your Virtues so richly deserve Have the Honor to subscribe myself Your mos Ob' & very Hble Servt

LEWIS BOUDINOT

Honble Benj Franklin Esqe

Addressed: The Honble. / Benjamin Franklin Esqe / Minister Plenipotentiary &c &c / Paris

Notation: L. Boudinot 29 Sepr 1783

From Jean-François-Paul Grand[4]

L: University of Pennsylvania Library

Sir   Paris the. 29th of 7bre. 1783./.

I beg leave to acknowledge receipt of the honour of your Esteemed favour from the 26 Int. Covering your remittance of £1900.—.— on Denis Rougemont[5] from the 8th. August at 2/m date. The value of which shall be received by me & for which produce Your particular account shall be Credited agreable to your desire of the abovesaid sum.—[6]

With great regard I have the honour to remain Sir! Your most humble & most obedient servant

3. The current ambassador was Jean-Balthazar, comte d'Adhémar de Montfalcon: *DBF; Repertorium der diplomatischen Vertreter*, III, 118.

4. Writing on behalf of his father, Ferdinand Grand. Jean-François-Paul wrote two versions of this letter: one in French, which he signed, and this English translation on the verso.

5. Who by 1792 was a managing partner of the London banking firm of Agassiz, Rougemont & Co.: Lüthy, *Banque protestante*, II, 725–6.

6. BF's letter has not been found, but the bill of exchange, for £82 15 s. 11 p. (equivalent to approximately 1,900 *l.t.*), had been sent to WTF by William Vaughan on Aug. 8, 1783 (APS). The money was a reimbursement for funds BF had advanced to Samuel Vaughan, Jr.; see XL, 96, 443n. BF's private account was credited on Oct. 18: Account XVII (XXVI, 3).

Mr. B: Franklin at Passy./.

Addressed: A / Monsieur / Monsieur Benjamin / Franklin / à Passy

From Robert Morris

Copy: Library of Congress

Sir,   Office of Finance 30 Septem: 1783.

I am to acknowlege the Receipt of your Favors of the seventh of March and twenty seventh of July.[7] For both of them accept my Thanks. You express an Apprehension lest the Union between France and America should be diminished by Accounts from your Side of the Water. This Apprehension does you equal Honor as a Statesman and as a Man. Every Principle which ought to actuate the Councils of a Nation requires from us an affectionate Conduct towards France and I very sincerely lament those Misapprehensions which have indisposed some worthy Men towards that Nation whose Treasure and Blood have been so freely expended for us. I believe the Truth with respect to some to be this. A warm Attachment to America has prevented them from making due Allowances in those Cases where there Country was concerned. Under certain Prepossession it was natural for them to think that the french Ministry might do more for us, and it was quite as natural for the Ministers to think that we ought to have done more for ourselves. The Moment of Treaty with England was of Course the Moment of Profession with english Ministers. I fear that the Impressions made by these were for a little while rather more deep than was quite necessary. But the same Love of America which had raised such strong Irritability where her Interests were concerned, will of Course stimulate it to an equal Degree when those Interests are assailed from another Quarter. I think I may venture to assure you that the Esteem of this Country for France is not diminished and that the late Representations have not been so unfavorable as you fear.

Our Commerce is flowing very fast towards Great Britain

7. XXXIX, 301–2; XL, 399–402.

and that from Causes which must for ever influence the commercial Part of Society. Some Articles are furnished by Britain cheaper many as cheap and all on a long Credit. Her Merchants are attentive and punctual. In her Ports our Vessels always meet with Dispatch. I say Nothing of Language and Manners because I do not think they influence so strongly on Commerce as many People suppose but what is of no little Importance is that the English having formed our Taste are more in a Capacity to gratify that Taste by the Nature and fashion of their Manufactures. There is another Circumstance also which must not be forgotten. The great Demand for french Manufactures during the War increased the Price of many and some Time will be required before it can by a fair Competition be discovered which of the two Countries france or England can supply us cheapest. The Delays in the public Bills[8] is a further Circumstance which militates (a momentary Obstacle) against the Trade with France. I must therefore mention to you also a Matter which is of great Effect. Until we can navigate the Mediteranean in Safety we cannot trade in our own Bottoms with the Ports of france or Spain which are on that Sea. And we certainly will not Trade there in foreign Bottoms because we do not find the same Convenience and Advantage in so doing as in our own Vessels. Unless indeed it be on Board of English Ships. This may be a disagreable Fact but it is not the less a Fact. I beleive that Informations are transmitted from hence to the Court which they ought not to rely on. Their Servants doubtless do their Duty in transmitting such Informations but I am perswaded that they are themselves not well informed. Indeed it is quite natural that Men should mistake when they examine and treat of a Subject with which they are unacquainted. And it cannot well be supposed that political Characters are competent to decide on the Advantages and Disadvantages of allowing to or witholding from us a share in the carrying Trade—[9] On this Subject I will make a further Observation and you may rely on it that I speak to you with Candor and Sincerity not with a View to making any Im-

8. The French government had suspended payment of bills of exchange issued in America: XXXIX, 289–90, 301, 340–1.

9. La Luzerne and Barbé-Marbois had both reported to Versailles on the subject of Franco-American trade: *Morris Papers*, VIII, 560n, 683–5.

pressions on the Court. You may communicate or withold what
I say and they may or may not apply it to their own Purposes. If
any thing will totally ruin the Commerce of England with this
Country it is her blind Attachment to her Navigation Act. This
Act which never was the real Foundation of her naval Superi-
ority may and perhaps will be the Cause of its Destruction. If
france possesses commercial Wisdom she will take Care not to
imitate the Conduct of her Rival. The West India Islands can be
supplied twenty per Cent cheaper in american than in french or
british Bottoms I will not trouble you with the Reasons but you
may rely on the Fact. The Price of the Produce of any Country
must materially depend on the Cheapness of Subsistence. The
Price at which that Produce can be vended abroad must depend
on the Facility of Conveyance. Now admitting for a Moment
(which by the bye is not true) that France might by Something
like a british Navigation Act, increase her Ships and her Seamen
these Things would necessarily follow. 1st. Her Islands would
be less wealthy and therefore less able to consume and pay for
her Manufactures 2ly. The Produce of those Islands would be
less cheap and therefore less able to sustain the weight of Duties
and support a Competition in foreign Markets. 3ly. The Commerce with this Country would be greatly lessened because that
every American Ship which finds herself in a french or english
or other Port will naturally seek a freight there rather than go
elswhere to look for it because in many Commodities the Difference of Price in different Parts will not compensate the Time
and Cost of going from Place to Place to look after them. To
these Principal Reasons might be added many others of lesser
weight tho not of little Influence such as the probable Increase
of commercial Intercourse by increasing the Connections and
Acquaintances of Individuals. To this and to every Thing else
which can be said on the Subject by an American I know there
is one short Answer always ready. viz: That we seek to encrease
our own Wealth. So far from denying that this is among my Motives I place it as the foremost and (setting aside that Gratitude
which I feel for France) I do not scruple to declare that a Regard to the Interests of America is with Respect to all Nations
of the World my political Compass. But the different Nations
of Europe should consider that in Proportion to the Wealth of

this Country will be her Ability to pay for those Commodities which all of them are pressing us to buy.

The People of this Country still continue as remiss as ever in the Payment of Taxes. Much of this (as you justly observe) arises from the Difficulties of Collection. But those Difficulties are much owing to an ignorance of proper Modes and an Unwillingness to adopt them. In short tho all are content to acknowlege that there is a certain Burthen of Taxation which ought to be borne Yet each is desirous of Shifting it off of his own Shoulders on those of his Neighbors. Time will I hope produce a Remedy to the Evils under which we labor but it may also increase them.

Your Applications to the Court for Aid are certainly well calculated to obtain it, but I am not much surprized at your ill Success indeed I should have been much surprized if you had been more fortunate— Of all Men I was placed in the Situation to take a deep Concern in the Event but I cannot disapprove of the Refusal for we certainly ought to do more for ourselves before we ask the Aid of others— Copies of your Letters to the Court were laid before Congress and also the Copy of the new Contract.[1] I will enclose with this a further Copy of the Ratification of the old if I can obtain it in Season from Princeton where the Congress now are.[2]

I have written also on the Subject of the Debt due to the farmer's general[3] and should Congress give me any Orders about it I shall attend carefully to the Execution. The Conduct they have maintained with regard to us has been generous and will demand a Return of Gratitude as well as of Justice. This I hope my Countrymen will always be disposed to Pay. I shall take some proper Opportunity of writing to the farmer's General but will wait a while to Know what may be the Determination of Congress on their Affairs.

1. BF enclosed that Feb. 25, 1783, contract (XXXIX, 201–6) in his letter of March 7.
2. He sent it under cover of his Nov. 4 letter, below.
3. In his July 27 letter, BF enclosed a copy of the July 17 letter he had received from the farmers general. Morris forwarded a copy to President of Congress Boudinot on Sept. 15. On Nov. 1 Congress promised to remit the interest to the farmers and to pay the balance as soon as possible: *Morris Papers*, VIII, 519–20, 705–6; *JCC*, XXV, 792–3.

It gives me much Pleasure to find that by the proposed Establishment of Packetts we shall shortly be in Condition to maintain more regular and connected Correspondence for altho I shall not myself be much longer in public Office I feel for those who are or will be charged with the Affairs of our Country both at Home and abroad.— It will naturally occur however that a good Cypher must be made use of not unfrequently when Dispatches are trusted to foreigners. They have no Regard either to Propriety or even Decency where Letters are concerned.

With very sincere Esteem and Respect I am Sir your Excellency's most obedient and humble Servant   RM.

His Excelly. Benja. Franklin

From Anne-Catherine de Ligniville Helvétius

L: American Philosophical Society

mercredy matin [September, 1783?][4]

Si Messieurs franklin ne sont pas Engagés pour aujourdhuy, madame Helvétius Les prie de venir dîner Chez elle en famille. Comme hier elle voulait être seule, elle avait fait défendre sa

---

4. This is one of several undated letters from Mme Helvétius that I. Minis Hays catalogued for the APS as [1782]. When the present editors examined the manuscript in preparation for vol. 38, we saw that the sealing wax was black, indicating that the note was written during a period of mourning. Mme Helvétius observed three such periods during BF's stay in Paris, none of which were in 1782.

The first possible date for this letter is c. August, 1779, when one of Mme Helvétius' brothers-in-law died: XXX, 192n. An argument for 1779 is that the letter is in the hand of Cabanis, who wrote most of her letters during the initial period of her friendship with BF; see XXX, 278–9, 373. Because we did not publish the letter at the earliest possible time, we now place it during the second mourning period, after the death of her other brother-in-law on Aug. 11, 1783. Mourning for siblings customarily lasted two months (*Jour. de Paris* for Dec. 31, 1783, p. 1508). BF's ailments would have prevented him from traveling in mid-August, but by Sept. 12 he accepted a dinner invitation in Chaillot (XL, 615–16); hence, our tentative attribution of September. The third mourning period was in March, 1784, when her sister died: David Smith *et al.*, eds., *Correspondance générale d'Helvétius* (5 vols., Toronto, Buffalo, and Oxford, 1981–2004), IV, 48n, 49n.

porte; et Lorsqu'ils s'y présenterent, elle Etait renfermée dans sa petite maison de bains: ils doivent juger que La défense n'etant pas pour eux, Elle à été bien fâchée de ce Contretems.

Addressed: a Monsieur / Monsieur franklin / a Passy

From the Marquise de Lafayette

L: American Philosophical Society

[September, 1783?][5]

Mde. De la fayette offre son hommage, a monsieur franklin, et Le supplie de vouloir bien Lui mander, et si mr Edward newnham, est a paris, ou quand il doit y venir, et s'il y est ou il demeure;[6] mr De La fayette, qui est toujours en Lorrainne, La chargée de sen informer, et Lui a fait esperer que mr franklin, voudroit bien L'instruire de sa marche. Elle profite avec bien du plaisir de cette occasion, pour lui renouveller Lassurance de ses sentimens.

Addressed: A Monsieur / Monsieur franklin, ministre plenipotentiaire / des Etats unis De L'amerique, / A Passy

John Jay: Account of Conversation with Franklin[7]

AD: Columbia University Library

Sep. 1783

Dr. Franklin lived at Pha. in the Neighbourhood of Mr Boudinot the Father of Elias Boudinot the present Presidt. of Con-

5. Dated by her reference to her husband's absence. Lafayette was in Nancy attending an ill friend from no later than Sept. 7 through the end of the month: Idzerda, *Lafayette Papers*, V, 148, 154–5.
6. Newenham had left France at the end of June: XL, 205–6.
7. This is the second of four casual conversations with BF that Jay recorded in a small quire. The first took place on July 19, about six weeks after the Jay family moved into the Hôtel Valentinois: XL, 342–6. The final two conversations took place the following March and will be published in our next volume. All entries are in *Jay Papers*, III, 436–42.

gress—the Father was a Silver Smith who had come from NYork to settle at Pha., a man much devoted to Whitfield, by whom his Son was baptized *Elias* after the Prophet of that Name— Dr. Franklin remembers Elias coming to his Father's Door with half a Water Melon & a Spoon in his Hand—several of the neighboring Boys gathered round in hopes of sharing in the Melon— Elias observd their Intention, but told them as they came up, that those who asked shd recieve nothing, & went on eating his Melon— The others imagining he meant to Share with them, & fearing to ask lest they shd. as he threatned be refused, silently waited his Motions—he went on however eating his Melon, & finished it— He was 8 or nine Yrs. old— He had a Sister who was a sensible Girl—she wrote Verses & had Wit— Mr. Stockton of Printon married her—& took Elias into his Office & taught him Law, which he practiced at Eliz. Town until the War, with the Reputation of Integrity & fairness—[8]

From the Duc and Duchesse de Crillon et de Mahon[9]

AL: American Philosophical Society

[before October 1, 1783]

Le duc et La duchesse de crillon et de mahon sont venus pour avoir l'honneur de voir Monsieur franklin ministre plenipotentiaire des ettats unis damerique Le prier de Leur faire celuy De venir Souper mercredi prochain a passi et de vouloir bien y etre rendu a Sept heures du Soir pour y prendre part a un Divertisse-

8. Annis Boudinot Stockton (1736–1801) was a renowned poet and hostess in Princeton. She married Richard Stockton, a signer of the Declaration of Independence, in the winter of 1757–58. Four years later, his sister Hannah wed Elias Boudinot: Carla Mulford, ed., *Only for the Eye of a Friend: the Poems of Annis Boudinot Stockton* (Charlottesville, 1995), pp. 8–9, 12, 15, 19, 26–8, 187n.

9. Louis de Berton, duc de Crillon, and his third wife, Josepha-Athanase-Roman Gusman d'Espinoza de Los Monteros. In recognition of Crillon's capture of Minorca from Great Britain, Charles III of Spain had bestowed on him the hereditary title of duc de Mahon: XXXIII, 454n; *DBF*, under Crillon; *Courier de l'Europe*, XIII (1783), 362–3.

ment de Campagne occasioné par La joye De La naissance Dès deux infants d'espagne.[1]

On trouvera a La porte de passi qui entre dans Le bois de boulogne, un Suisse qui indiquera Le Lieu ou il faut mettre pied a terre.[2]

Notation: Le Duc & la Desse. de Crillon

From Maximilien de Robespierre

ALS: University of Pennsylvania Library

Monsieur a arras ce 1 8bre 1783

Une sentence de proscription rendue par les échevins de st. omer contre Les conducteurs électriques m'a présenté l'occasion de plaider au conseil d'artois la cause d'une découverte sublime, dont le genre humain vous est redevable. Le désir de contribuer a déraciner les préjugés qui s'opposoient à ses progrès dans notre province m'a porté à faire imprimer le plaidoyer que j'ai prononcé dans cette affaire.[3] J'ose espérer, Mon-

1. Carlos and Felipe, the twin sons of the prince and princess of Asturias, were born on Sept. 5. They died the following year: Germán Bleiberg, ed., *Diccionario de Historia de España* (3 vols., Madrid, 1979), 1, 709; *Almanach royal* for 1784, p. 35.

2. The elaborate feast and entertainment on the evening of Oct. 1 began in the Salle de la Comédie with several symphonic and theatrical performances. The distinguished company then proceeded to an enormous tent for a show of fireworks and *danses champêtres*, accompanied by two orchestras, after which they dined in the Ranelagh by the light of chandeliers and candelabra. A highlight of the evening was the launch of a small balloon, which BF described in his letter to Joseph Banks of Oct. 8, below. This was followed by more music and dancing, walks in the illuminated parts of the Bois de Boulogne, and a ball in the Ranelagh that lasted until three in the morning: *Jour. de Paris*, Oct. 10, 1783.

3. Praised by his client Vyssery de Bois-Valée as "un des plus Eloquent plaideur à Arras," the 25-year-old Robespierre argued on May 17 and 31 Vyssery's appeal against the removal of his lightning rod in Saint-Omer; see XXXVIII, 435–8. While the brief of his senior colleague Buissart had relied on the expert testimony of scientists, Robespierre declared that the benefits and benign character of lightning rods were proven by experience

sieur, que vous daignerez recevoir avec bonté un éxemplaire de cet ouvrage,[4] dont l'objet étoit d'engager mes concitoiens à accepter un de vos bienfaits: heureux d'avoir pu etre utile à mon pays, en déterminant ses premiers magistrats à accueillir cette importante découverte; plus heureux encore si je puis joindre à cet avantage l'honneur d'obtenir le suffrage d'un homme dont le moindre mèrite est d'etre le plus illustre sçavant de l'Univers.

J'ai l'honneur d'etre avec respect Monsieur votre tres humble et tres obéissant serviteur   DE ROBESPIERRE,

avocat au conseil d'artois

From Philippe-Denis Pierres

ALS: American Philosophical Society

Monsieur,   [before October 2, 1783][5]

J'ai l'honneur de vous envoyer

Constitutions 8°. brochée	350. Ex. [Exemplaires]
remis précedemment	
50 Reliés	50
50. demie reliure	50
50. brochés	50.
Total	500. Ex.

---

and readily apparent to everyone. He dismissed the prosecution's claims about the potential dangers of Vyssery's particular rod as unwarranted speculation. On May 31 the court ruled that Vyssery would be allowed to reinstall the rod but that he had to pay for the installation and for the appeal: Jessica Riskin, *Science in the Age of Sensibility: the Sentimental Empiricists of the French Enlightenment* (Chicago and London, 2002), pp. 176–84.

4. Robespierre's pleas received a favorable mention in the *Mercure de France (Jour. politique de Bruxelles)* of June 21, 1783, pp. 135–7. He persuaded Vyssery to finance the printing of 500 copies of them, some of which he and Buissart sent to prominent scientists in Paris: Riskin, *Science in the Age of Sensibility*, pp. 184–5. BF's copy of *Plaidoyers pour le sieur de Vissery de Bois-Valé* . . . (Paris, 1783) is at the Hist. Soc. of Pa.

5. The date that Pierres sent BF most of the 60 quarto copies of *Constitutions des treize Etats-Unis de l'Amérique* mentioned here; see his letter of Oct. 2. For the book's publication see XL, 139, 149–50, 249, 376–7n.

plus 4 Ex. in 4°. qui avec les 36. remis précedemment font 40 J'ai à votre disposition 60. in 4°.

Je crois, monsieur, que nous avons oublié le stathouder de hollande, ainsi que les États Généraux.[6] Au reste je ferai de ces 60 Ex. l'usage qu'il vous plaira m'indiquer. Si même vous jugez à propos que je vous les envoye, je vous les enverrai en feuilles.

Je suis avec un profond respect, Monsieur Votre très humble & très obeissant serviteur   PIERRES

M. franklin.

Endorsed: Pierre

To Sir Edward Newenham

Reprinted from William Temple Franklin, ed., *Memoirs of the Life and Writings of Benjamin Franklin* . . . (3 vols., 4to, London, 1817–18), II, 226–7.

DEAR SIR,   *Passy, Oct. 2, 1783.*

I have just received your very kind letter of the 16th past. I rejoice sincerely to hear of your safe return to your own country, family and friends, and of the success of your election.

It is a pleasing reflection arising from the contemplation of our successful struggle and the manly, spirited, and unanimous resolves at Dungannon,[7] that liberty, which some years since

6. BF had sent a copy to Berkenrode, the Dutch ambassador to the French court, which was acknowledged on July 25: XL, 380. We have found no record of his sending presentation copies to the stadholder, William V, Prince of Orange, or to the States General of the Netherlands.

7. On Sept. 8, a meeting at Dungannon of over 500 delegates from the Ulster Volunteer companies passed resolutions demanding reforms of the parliamentary election system. It also called a Grand National Convention of Volunteers, to be held in Dublin on Nov. 10, which would discuss a plan for parliamentary reform drawn up by the Ulster Volunteer Corps Committee of Correspondence (for whom see XL, 337–42) and would outline a course of action. An account of the Dungannon meeting and a complete list of the resolutions were published in the *Dublin Evening Post*, Sept. 13, 1783. Newenham probably enclosed that paper in his Sept. 16 letter, since BF received the account of Dungannon on Oct. 2; see the Oct. 2 entry in Extracts of John Baynes's Journal, Sept. 23–Oct. 17, above.

appeared in danger of extinction, is now regaining the ground she had lost, that arbitrary governments are likely to become more mild, and reasonable, and to expire by degrees, giving place to more equitable forms; one of the effects this of the art of printing which diffuses so general a light, augmenting with the growing day, and of so penetrating a nature, that all the window shutters despotism and priestcraft can oppose to keep it out, prove insufficient.

In answer to your question respecting what may be necessary to fix a trade between Ireland and America, I may acquaint you between ourselves, that there is some truth in the report you may have heard, of our desiring to know of Mr. Hartley whether he was empowered or instructed to include Ireland in the treaty of commerce proposed to us, and of his sending for instructions on that head, which never arrived.[8] That treaty is yet open, may possibly be soon resumed, and it seems proper that something should be contained in it to prevent the doubts and misunderstandings that may hereafter arise on the subject, and secure to Ireland the same advantages in trade that England may obtain. You can best judge whether some law or resolution of your parliament may not be of use towards gaining that point.

My grandson joins me in wishes of every kind of felicity for you, Lady Newenham and all your amiable family. God bless you and give success to your constant endeavours for the welfare of your country. With true and great respect and esteem, I have the honour to be &c.   B. FRANKLIN

8. The American commissioners had raised the issue of Irish-American trade in discussions with Fitzherbert about the American Intercourse Bill in March, 1783, before bringing it up again with Hartley during the negotiations for a British-American commercial treaty later that spring. In both cases, the British negotiators did not feel authorized to give a response: XL, 52n, 173n, 601.

From Robert Morris   ALS: Hobart College Library

Dear Sir   Philada. October 2d. 1783

This Letter will either be delivered or forwarded to you by a most Worthy Gentn. Nathl. Gorham Esqr. of Boston[9] for whose Public & private Character I have the highest respect, This Gentn has served as Member & Speaker of the Massachusetts assembly. & lately he had a pretty long Campaigne in Congress where I had that opportunity of knowing the integrity of his Conduct & the Soundness of his judgement that did not fail to inspire me with Strong personal Attachment it is probable that he will make some proposals to the Court for supplying their Marine with Masts & Spars & in this business he is associated with Thos. Russell & Wm Burgess Esqrs of Boston[1] and John Langdon Esqr of Portsmouth in New Hampshire[2] all Gentn of that Character & Solidity which ought to give Weight to what they offer.

They were kind enough to invite me to join them, but not suiting my situation & Views I declined it, I am however equally desirous of promoting their Interest and hope what I have Said may procure them your favourable aid. I will engage the Chevr La Luzerne to write in their favour. You always have my best Wishes for I am very Sincerely Dear Sir Your Affectionate Friend & Obedt. humble servt.   ROBT MORRIS

His Excy Benjn. Franklin Esqr Minister de Passy

9. Nathaniel Gorham (1738–1796), a Charlestown, Mass., merchant and politician. He served in the colonial and state legislature for much of the 1770s and 1780s, was elected to the Continental Congress in 1782, and left Congress in June 1783, presumably to pursue the business interests outlined in the present letter. He was reelected as a delegate in November, 1784, was elected president of Congress in 1786, and served as a delegate to the Constitutional Convention of 1787: *ODNB*.

1. Thomas Russell was a wealthy merchant of Charlestown: XXXVI, 160n; *Morris Papers*, 1, 247n. William Burgess, a London merchant, migrated to Boston in late 1782: XXXVII, 702; XXXVIII, 332–3.

2. Langdon had made an unsuccessful attempt to supply the French navy with masts in 1778: XXVII, 582; XXVIII, 278–9, 357–8.

Addressed: His Excy / Benjn. Franklin Esqr. / Minister Plenipy at the Court of Versailles

Notation: R Morris

From Pierres

ALS: American Philosophical Society

Monsieur, Paris, le 2 8bre. 1783.

J'ai l'honneur de vous envoyer cinquante-trois Exemplaires des Constitutions de l'Amérique in-4°. Papier d'Annonay. Il en reste trois entre les mains du Relieur; ces trois Exemplaires sont avancés à la reliure & prêts à couvrir.

Vous en avez reçu déja . . . . 42 Ex.
Au Relieur . . . . 3.
Que j'envoye aujourd'hui . . . . 53.
un Exemplaire imparfait ici . . . . 1.
Un, que je garde suivant les Regle-
    mens de la Librairie . . . . . .   1.
                      Total 100 Ex.

Le Relieur m'a fait demander si vous trouviez bon qu'il allât vous porter le mémoire de ses reliures, Il me paroit qu'il a besoin d'argent.[3] Je vous prie de vouloir bien me faire savoir quel est le jour que vous voulez que je lui assigne.

Quant aux brochures elles me regardent & entreront dans le compte de mon Impression.[4]

Je suis avec autant d'attachement que de respect, Monsieur, Votre Très-humble & très-obéissant serviteur[5]   PIERRES

M. Franklin

3. The bookbinder Pierre-Etienne Janet (*DBF*) was paid 552 *l.t.* 10 *s.* on Oct. 5: Account XXVII (XXXII, 4).

4. Pierres was paid in two installments for printing *Constitutions des treize Etats-Unis de l'Amérique*. He received 1,200 *l.t.* on Oct. 27 and 1,722 *l.t.* on Nov. 6: Account XXVII.

5. Around this time, Pierres was printing for the publisher and bookseller Jean-Baptiste Cussac the first volume of *Œuvres de Plutarque*, translated from the Greek by Jacques Amyot and annotated by the abbé Brotier. Cussac had sent BF several copies of the prospectus (printed by Pierres), asking him to forward them to America; his undated letter announced that the edition would run to 24 volumes and be dedicated to Lafayette

From Charles Stamitz,[6] with Franklin's Note for a Reply

ALS: American Philosophical Society

Monsieur!   à Spa çe 2 octobre 1783.

Pardonnez la liberté que je prends de vous Ecrire sans avoir l'honneur d'être Connû de vous; je viens d'apprendre trés positivement que Messieurs les Amériquains, voulant faire refleurir les beaux arts chez Eûx. Sont sur le point d'avoir une troupe française, dont Monsieur Clerval, ancien Comédien de Provinçe doit en être le Regiseur, qui pour cet Effect est actuéllement en Amerique.[7]

J'ai L'honneur de me proposer pour en être maitre de Musique. Je suis Connû dans toutes les Cours de L'Europe, par mes Ouvrages, je ne vous Cacherai pas, que je suis sur le point de me fixer dans une, mais je donnerai la préférençe à L'Amerique. Je me trouverai trop recompensé, si par les soins que je me donnerai, je puis faire des Elèves digne de grand Maitre.— Je joins à la Composition, celui de jouér du Violon, La Quinte, La Viole d'amour, et une nouvel instrument, que j'ai inventé nommée Violetton!

J'osse me flatter Monsieur, de votre Protection après avoir pris des renseignements sur mes talents.

J'ai L'honneur de vous offrir trois bons sujets, qui dessir-

(APS). Cussac's letter was probably sent c. December, 1782, soon after the prospectus was issued. Vol. 1 was announced for sale in the *Jour. de Paris* on Oct. 24, 1783, and reviewed favorably in the issue of Oct. 29. The review praised Pierres's typography and reported that Lafayette's portrait and the dedication had been removed because, as the volume explained (pp. vii–viii), the "jeune & illustre Guerrier" declined the honor out of modesty. For the date of the prospectus and an overview of the story see George B. Watts, *Philippe-Denis Pierres, First Printer Ordinary of Louis XVI* (Charlotte, N.C., 1966), pp. 23–4.

6. Charles (Carolus, Carl) Stamitz (1745–1808) was a composer, conductor, and virtuoso on violin and viola who served as court conductor for the duc de Noailles in the 1770s and between 1782 and 1784 was in The Hague, performing frequently at the court of the Prince of Orange. See Stanley Sadie, ed., *The New Grove Dictionary of Music and Musicians* (20 vols., Washington, D.C., 1980); Peter Gradenwitz, "The Stamitz Family: Some Errors, Omissions, and Falsifications Corrected," *Notes*, 2nd ser., VII (1949), 61.

7. We have found no evidence of Clairval's having gone to America; for his petition to BF see XL, 27.

eraient Comme moi de passer dans çe pays, qui sont Messrs. Laubertie *Basse Taile,* Villeneuve *Haute Contre* et julien *pour les la Ruétte,*[8] çes trois sujets sont attaché au Spectacle de la Prinçipauté de Liége, et ils en font tous les Plaisirs, c'est une très bonne aquisition à faire pour Messieurs Les Ameriquains, je reponds de Leurs Talents, & de Leurs Conduites. J'osse me flatter Monsieur! que vous me ferez la grâce de me repondre à la Haÿe, où je dois me rendre au premier jour.

J'ai l'honneur d'être avec le plus profond Respect Monsieur! Votre trés hble: et trés obt: serviteur

CHARLES STAMITZ
Compositeur de Musique de la
Cour de Vienne, & celle de la Haÿe

N.B. Personne mieux que Monsieur de Sartinne Ministre, ne peut vous donner de r'enseignements sur mes talents. En l'anné 1771. j'ai eû l'honneur de reçevoir une letre de remerciment de sa part, pour des Pièces que j'ai Composé, et Executé au Concert gratuite de l'Ecole de Dessins, à Paris.

Endorsed: That the Beaux Arts are much better encourag'd in Europe than in America where the People are not so rich. That I cannot therefore advise him to go there. That I doubt the Success of M. Clerval's Project: our Country not being yet ripe for such Amusements.

Notation: Stamitz 2. Oct 1783.

From Jacques-Joseph Ducarne de Blangy[9]

ALS: University of Pennsylvania Library

Monsieur   hirson en thierache ce 3. 8bre 1783.

Je commence par vous avoüer que j'ai presque juré hier contre vous, en voyant La reponse que vous vous contentés de faire à ceux, ou au public qui Demande à quoi bon La Découverte

8. Named for Jean-Louis Laruette of the *Opéra comique,* this came to be known as an old man's role sung in a high tenor voice: Sadie, ed., *The New Grove Dictionary of Music.*

9. An agronomist and inventor (1728–c. 1803) best known for designing a rocket-propelled lifeline that could reach a distressed vessel within

importante De m. mongolfier. C'est, Dites vous, Monsieur, un enfant qui vient de naitre, et qui peut Devenir celebre, ou rester Dans L'obscurité.[1] Et voila Donc, Monsieur, tout ce que vous paroissez vouloir accorder aujourdhui à m. mongolfier?

Quoique je ne sois qu'n tres petit sujet vis-avis De m. franklin, j'ose L'assurer que je vois clairement plusieurs objets importans où cette Dècouverte sera D'un tres grand service, et je ne peux m'empecher de lui avouer que je suis Dans une tres grande sur-prise qu'on ait pû faire cette question aujourdhui que Depuis sa pre. épreuve qui a si bien reussi on a eû Le temps dela reflexion.

L'art De La guerre sera, selon moi, celui oú on en fera Le plus D'usage. Et si cette Decouverte eût été faîte 12. ou 15. mois plu-tot je ne Doute pas que gibraltar n'eut été pris, n'y eut-il eû que moi seul au monde pour Le faire prendre.[2]

L'electricité sera un second objet oú Les balons seront encore D'une grande utilité, et personne ne pourra mieux que vous, Monsieur, en tirer tous Les avantages possibles.

Une Connoissance plus particulier, De La formation, De La nature et Des effets De La foudre sera un 3e. objet oú cette De-couverte sera encore D'une grande utilité.

Enfin Monsieur, je parierois presque, qu'avant Dix oú Douze mois, on aura fait par cette voie Le trajet De calais à Douvres, ou celui de Douvres à calais.

Si vous etiez curieux, Monsieur, de voir Les idées un peu plus étendues D'un homme qui est si peu de chose vis à vis De vous, vous pourrez Les voir Dans un mèmoire que j'ai été forcé

---

650 feet of shore. He advertised his invention to President Jefferson in 1801, when his pamphlet on the subject was published: *DBF*, under Ducarne; *Jefferson Papers*, XXXIV, 495–6.

1. Later in this letter Ducarne de Blangy identifies his source as the *Jour. de Genève,* issue of Sept. 27, p. 609. There, BF's response was quoted as: "c'est un enfant qui vient de naitre; peut-être sera-t-il un imbécille ou un homme de beaucoup d'esprit; attendons pour le juger que son éducation soit achevée." This was a distortion of what by then had become a widely known *bon mot.* For a discussion of the original quip and its circulation in print see XL, 543–7.

2. Joseph Montgolfier later claimed that the possibility of conquering Gibraltar by air had inspired him to pursue his observations of the levitating powers of hot air in November, 1782: Gillispie, *Montgolfier Brothers,* p. 16.

D'abreger beaucoup, et que j'adresse aujourdhui par Le meme ordinnaire à mrs. Les auteurs Du journal De geneve, ou j'ai vû hier, page 609. no. 39. La reponse que vous faites à ceux qui sont assez peu èclairés pour faire La question que j'y ai vû.

J'ai crû, Monsieur, qu'il etoit De mon Devoir De vous en prevenir; j'aurois eû L'honneur De vous en envoyer Copie ci jointe si Le temps me L'eut permis.[3]

J'ai L'honneur D'etre avec toute L'estime respectueuse que vous meritez à tant de titres, Monsieur votre tres humble et ts. obeiss. serviteur   DUCARNE DE BLANGŸ

From Edmond-Charles-Edouard Genet

ALS: American Philosophical Society

Monsieur   Versailles Le 3 8bre 1783

Mr de Valnais m'a remis la lettre que vous avés pris la peine de m'écrire.[4] J'ai été on ne peut pas plus flatté de cette marque de votre souvenir et J'ai fait tout ce qui a dépendu de moi pour donner à Mr de Valnais des preuves de l'Interêt qu'une recommandation telle que la votre devoit faire prendre à ses affaires.

J'ai l'honneur d'être avec respect Monsieur Votre tres humble et tres obeissant serviteur   GENET

Mr franklin

Notation: Genet 3 Decr. 1783.

3. Ducarne did not enclose a memoir, but on Oct. 7 wrote a ten-page letter providing details about the potential applications of the balloon. If attached to ships, balloons could prevent them from sinking and increase their speed. Balloons could be used to cross the Channel or for short trips over land. He reiterates the balloon's utility in warfare. Dismissing the Parisian savants who failed to recognize these advantages as quickly as he did, he tells BF that he is about to launch an air-filled vessel on a local river, where it should float as on air. He asks BF to keep all these ideas secret to guard against plagiarists. APS.

4. Not found, but doubtless it echoed John Hancock's recommendation; see the letter from Joseph Dupas de Iden de Valnais and his wife, [Sept.?] 25, above.

From Anthony Todd, with Franklin's Note for a Reply

ALS: Historical Society of Pennsylvania

Dear Sir,   General Post Office London 3 Octr. 1783.

This very morning I had the Pleasure to receive Your Letter of the 27th. past inclosing one for the President of Congress, which was so exactly in Time that I forwarded it along with Lord Norths Dispatches this Evening to Falmouth with Orders for the three several Packet Boats for New York Jamaica and the Lewards Islands to sail immediately. These Boats have been so much delayed from day to day that they carry the Mails of September also. I shall be very happy indeed to hear from you on the Subject of my last Letter to you,[5] and desire to say what I have hitherto forgot that you may always depend on my Care of any Letters You inclose to me and that I am Dear Sir Yours most truly   ANTH TODD

To B. Franklin Esq

Addressed: To His Excellency / Benjamin Franklin Esqr. / &c. &c. / at Passy. / Franche S. V. P. / Antoine Todd.

Endorsed:[6] I wish you to write a Letter for Mr Todd, acquainting him with the Agreement I propos'd respecting the Post Office, and what pass'd between you & Mr. le Couteulx &c

From David Hartley

Reprinted from William Temple Franklin, ed., *The Private Correspondence of Benjamin Franklin, LL.D., F.R.S., &c.* (2nd ed.; 2 vols., London, 1817), II, 440–1.

My Dear Friend,   Bath, October 4, 1783.

I only write one line to you to let you know that I am not forgetful of you, or of our common concerns. I have not heard any thing from the ministry yet: I believe it is a kind of vacation

---

5. Above, Sept. 19.
6. This note was intended for WTF, who drafted BF's Oct. 9 letter to Todd, below.

with them before the meeting of parliament.[7] I have told you of a proposition which I have had some thoughts to make as a kind of co-partnership in commerce. I send you a purposed temporary convention, which I have drawn up. You are to consider it only as one I recommend. The words underlined are grafted upon the proposition of my memorial, dated May 21, 1783.[8] You will see the principle which I have in my thoughts to extend for the purpose of restoring our ancient co-partnership generally. I cannot tell you what event things may take, but my thoughts are always employed in endeavouring to arrange that system upon which the *China Vase,* lately shattered,[9] may be cemented together, upon principles of compact and connection, instead of dependence. I have met with a sentiment in this country which gives some alarm, viz. lest the unity of government in America should be uncertain, and the States reject the authority of Congress. Some passages in General Washington's letter have given weight to these doubts.[1] I don't hear of any tendency to

7. The fourth session of the 15th Parliament convened on Nov. 11: Cobbett, *Parliamentary History,* XXIII, 1122–3.

8. BF's copy of Hartley's temporary convention is missing, but Hartley sent a copy dated "September 1783" to Fox on Oct. 29, with a 23-page memoir that summarized his views on "the present state of the negotiation" with the American commissioners (Clements Library). His convention is a rephrased version of the May 19 proposed agreement that he gave the commissioners on May 21: XL, 39. The section he mentions as having been underlined was in a new paragraph stating that American ships would be excluded from the trade between the United States and the British West Indies (as was stipulated by the Order in Council of July 2: XL, 289n), "*unless one half of the property of such Ships belong to some British owner or owners & that such Ships shall be navigated by an equal number of British & American Seamen.*" The convention was limited to one year.

9. "That fine and noble China Vase the British Empire," which BF told Lord Howe he had long endeavored to preserve: XXII, 520.

1. In a circular letter sent in June to the state governors (Fitzpatrick, *Writings of Washington,* XXVI, 483–96), GW warned that in order to avoid the dissolution of the union, the states had to submit to the powers bestowed on Congress by the Articles of Confederation. In particular, the states needed to comply with the demand Congress made in its own circular letter of April, 1783 (XXXIX, 579n), that each state contribute to the payment of the national debt. Elias Boudinot sent the American peace commissioners a newspaper containing the circular letter in July: XL, 308. It was reprinted in

this opinion; *that the American States will break to pieces, and then we may still conquer them.* I believe all that folly is extinguished. But many serious and well disposed persons are alarmed lest *this should be the ill-fated moment for relaxing the powers of the union, and annihilating the cement of confederation*[2] (vide Washington's letter), and that Great Britain should thereby lose her best and wisest hope of being re-connected with the American States *unitedly.* I should for one, think it the greatest misfortune. Pray give me some opinion upon this.[3] You see there is likewise another turn which may be given to this sentiment by intemperate and disappointed people, who may indulge a passionate revenge for their own disappointments, by endeavouring to excite general distrust, discord, and dis-union. I wish to be prepared and guarded at all points. I beg my best compliments to your colleagues; be so good as to show this letter to them. I beg particularly my condolence (and I hope congratulation) to Mr. Adams; I hear that he has been very dangerously ill, but that he is again recovered.[4] I hope the latter part is true, and that we shall all

---

England in the Aug. 9–12 issue of the *London Chronicle,* and by the beginning of September had been issued as a pamphlet by at least two publishers; see *St. James's Chronicle,* Aug. 23–26, 1783; *Whitehall Evening Post,* Sept. 2–4, 1783.

2. Fitzpatrick, *Writings of Washington,* XXVI, 486.

3. BF did not respond until Oct. 22. Before receiving that reply, Hartley on Oct. 27 forwarded to Fox the letter BF had written to him on Sept. 6, which may have been drafted with the British ministry in mind. In it, BF praised Fox as "a *Great* Man" and argued that British expectations of benefitting from alleged American disunity were misguided and would destroy any chances for reconciliation: XL, 582–3. Hartley added an explanation of his own of how further delaying negotiations of a temporary commercial convention was contrary to British interests. On Nov. 1 and 6, Hartley sent Fox two more lengthy memoranda discussing unresolved issues from the peace negotiations and proposing a naval alliance between the United States and Great Britain. All three letters are at the Clements Library.

4. For several weeks after the signing of the definitive treaty, JA was ill with a fever that left him emaciated and fatigued. On Sept. 22, he moved to Thomas Barclay's house in Auteuil to recover: XXXV, 556; Butterfield, *John Adams Diary,* III, 143–4; John Ferling and Lewis E. Braverman, "John Adams's Health Reconsidered," *W&MQ,* 3rd ser., LV (1998), 88–97.

survive to set our hands to some future compacts of common interest, and common affection, between our two countries. Your ever affectionate, 　　　　　　　　　　　　　　　　　　D. HARTLEY

From Madame ——— His[5]

al: American Philosophical Society

ce 4 8bre 1783

Mde his s'est chargée bien volontier des Comissions de Mde La Comtesse d'houdetot pour monsieur francklin. Elle desire avoir des nouvelles de sa santé, elle veut lui marquer son impatience de Le Voir a sanois, et Lui fait quelques reproches dêtre privée d'une Reponse a la lettre qu'elle a eu lhonneur de lui ecrire touchant un matelot americain.[6] Mde his ajoute a linteret dêtre utile a mde La Ctesse dhoudetot, Celuy de pouvoir assurer mr francklin des Respectueux sentimens qui lui sont accordé, par Ceux meme qui Nont pas lhonneur de Le Conoitre personelment.

5. Probably the wife of Pierre-François His, née Marie-Anne Demaris Dumoustier de Vastre, best known for having been sculpted by Houdon. Another possibility is his mother, née Louise-Magdeleine Chaunel (1707–1786); both women were resident in Paris at this time. Pierre-François was director of the merchant banking firm Pierre His & fils and the agent of the Danish king at Hamburg: Georges Giacometti, *La Vie et l'œuvre de Houdon* (2 vols., Paris, [1929]), II, 72; Albert Besnard, *La Tour: la vie et l'œuvre de l'artiste* (Paris, 1928), p. 144; *Dictionnaire historique de la Suisse*, IV, 108; Lüthy, *Banque protestante*, II, 622–3.
6. Her letter of Sept. 6: XL, 584–5.

To Thomas Brand Hollis[7]   Transcript:[8] Library of Congress

Sir   Passy, near Paris, Octor 5th. 1783.

I received but lately (tho' sent in June) your most valuable present of the Memoirs of Thomas Hollis Esqr.[9] who was truly as you describe him in your letter, a good "Citizen of the World and a faithful Friend of America." America too is extremely sensible of his Benevolence and great Beneficence towards her, and will ever revere his Memory.— These Volumes are a Proof of what I have sometimes had occasion to say, in Encouraging People to undertake difficult Public Services, that it is prodigious the quantity of Good that may be done by one Man, *if he will make a Business of it.* It is equally surprizing to think of the

7. This letter, answering one that is now missing, is the first appearance in BF's papers of a political reformer, dissenter, and fellow member of the Royal Society and the Society of Arts, Manufactures, and Commerce whom BF had known in London. On the eve of the American Revolution, Thomas Brand Hollis (1719–1804) was part of the circle that included Price and Priestley. BF dined with them at Brand Hollis' home on at least two occasions in the winter of 1774/1775: "Journal of Josiah Quincy, Jun. . . . ," Mass. Hist. Soc. *Proc.*, 3rd ser., L (1916–17), 456, 482.

Born Thomas Brand, Brand Hollis took the surname of his longtime friend Thomas Hollis—the subject of the present letter—when he unexpectedly inherited Hollis' estate at the beginning of 1774. He continued his friend's tradition of charitable contributions, though at lower levels; more of his fortune (it is said) went to his personal collection of antiquities. He was elected an honorary foreign member of the American Academy of Arts and Sciences in 1782: *ODNB;* Caroline Robbins, "Thomas Brand Hollis (1719–1804), English Admirer of Franklin and Intimate of John Adams," APS *Proc.*, XCVII (1953), 239–47; *Sibley's Harvard Graduates*, XI, 551–5; American Academy of Arts & Sciences, *Book of Members, 1780–2010* (Cambridge, Mass., 2010).

8. In the hand of a secretary whom WTF employed *c.* 1817 to copy the papers he intended to include in his edition of BF's writings. WTF gave these copies to the printer, often marked with his own title lines, commentary, or directions. (All known examples are at the Library of Congress.) In some cases, including the present one, the original MSS were subsequently lost. This text is in WTF, *Memoirs*, II, 44.

9. [Francis Blackburne], *Memoirs of Thomas Hollis, Esq. . . .* (2 vols., London, 1780). The work was sponsored by Brand Hollis, who sent copies to various "friends of liberty": [John Disney], *Memoirs of Thomas Brand-Hollis . . .* (London, 1808), p. 8.

very little that is done by many; for such is the general Frivolity of the Employments and Amusements of the Rank we call Gentlemen, that every Century may have seen three successions of a Set of a thousand each in every Kingdom of Europe (Gentlemen too, of equal or superior Fortune) no one of which Set in the Course of their Lives have done the good effected by this Man alone! Good, not only to his own Nation, and to his Cotemporaries, but to distant Countries, and to late Posterity: for such must be the effect of his multiplying and distributing Copies of the Works of our best English Writers on Subjects the most important to the Welfare of Society.[1]

I knew him personally but little. I sometimes met with him at the Royal Society and the Society of Arts, but he appeared shy of my acquaintance, tho' he often sent me valuable Presents, such as Hamilton's Works, Sydney's Works, &c. which are now among the most precious Ornaments of my Library.[2] We might possibly, if we had been more intimate, have concerted some useful Operations together; but he loved to do his good alone and secretly, and I find besides, in perusing these Memoirs, that

1. Thomas Hollis (1720–1774) was an early supporter of America, a critic of repressive regimes, and an active promoter of liberty. As the *Memoirs* show, he generously donated books, money, and scientific instruments to institutions and individuals throughout England, the colonies, and Europe, often anonymously. He was an important benefactor of Harvard College, continuing a family tradition. *ODNB*.

2. Hollis was known for the handsomely bound books he sponsored and donated. He had been sending copies of Sidney's writings to libraries for decades before he commissioned the expanded and corrected edition printed by William Strahan, Jr.: [J. Robertson, ed.], *The Works of Algernon Sydney* (London, 1772). See Bernhard Knollenberg, "Thomas Hollis and Jonathan Mayhew, Their Correspondence, 1759–1766," Mass. Hist. Soc. *Proc.*, 3rd ser., LXIX (1947–50), 102; W. H. Bond, *Thomas Hollis of Lincoln's Inn: a Whig and His Books* (Cambridge, 1990), pp. 18, 29–33, 84–88, 103, 108–9. Whichever edition BF received from Hollis, it was most likely not with him in France, as he purchased Sidney's *Discourses Concerning Government* in 1779: XXXVI, 332. We are unable to identify "Hamilton's Works" and wonder, as previous BF editors have, whether the copyist mistranscribed the name. Hollis revered John Milton, and frequently gave custom-bound copies of Milton's works as part of his plan to distribute "liberty texts": W. H. Bond, *Thomas Hollis*, pp. 46–7.

I was a doubtful Character with him.[3] I do not respect him less for his Error; and I am obliged to the Editors for the Justice they have done me.[4] They have made a little mistake in page 400. where a Letter which appeared in a London Paper, Jany: 7th. 1768, is said to have been written by Mr. Adams. It was written by me, and is reprinted in Mr. Vaughan's Collection of my political Pieces P. 231.[5] This Eratum is of no great importance, but may be corrected in a future Edition.

I see Mr. Hollis had a Collection of curious Medals. If he had been still living, I should certainly have sent him one of the Medals that I have caused to be struck here. I think the countenance of my *Liberty* would have pleased him.——[6] I suppose

3. The *Memoirs* reprinted Hollis' answer to a letter from Jonathan Mayhew (quoted above, XII, 423n) concerning the possibility that BF had recommended a certain undeserving Boston clergyman for an honorary degree at a Scottish university. It included the following passage: "What share Dr. F———n might have in obtaining the degree, I am ignorant. He is certainly a man of knowledge, ability; wishes well to what is right, loves his country, North America, even to partiality; and yet, according to old observings, to me he is a trimmer. His card too, which came forth in such numbers, appeared not, if I am well informed, till after the death of the D. of C. [Duke of Cumberland] and till the spring, that the leaders in the ministry had taken party, and resolved to repeal the stamp-act": [Blackburne], *Memoirs*, I, 333, 335–6.

4. Blackburne's comment on p. 336 reads: "We confess here to want some explanation; we are strangers to the facts here alluded to, which, in order to prove Dr. F———n a trimmer, should be clear and evident, beyond the possibility of a doubt. Had Mr. Hollis lived to see the present day, we are firmly of opinion, he would freely have relinquished every idea of Dr. F———n's duplicity."

5. Hollis published BF's pseudonymous essay "Causes of the American Discontents before 1768" (XV, 3–13) in *The True Sentiments of America of 1768:* XXI, 139. Benjamin Vaughan included it in 1779 in *Political, Miscellaneous, and Philosophical Pieces:* XXXI, 216.

6. Blackburne described Hollis as beginning early in life to "collect books and medals for the purpose of illustrating and upholding liberty, and preserving the memory of its champions." Hollis even favored the symbols of Liberty and the liberty cap for his book bindings. Included in the *Memoirs* is a catalogue of Hollis' renowned numismatic collection: [Blackburne], *Memoirs*, I, 59–61; II, 808–39; Bond, *Thomas Hollis*, pp. 62–4. BF refers here to his own recently struck medal, *Libertas Americana*, illustrated as the frontispiece to vol. 39.

you possess the Collection, and have the same Taste. I beg you therefore to accept of one of these Medals as a Mark of my Respect, and believe me to be with sincere esteem, &c.   B.F.

To Brand Hollis Esqr. on receiving from him the Memoirs of Thos. Hollis Esq

From the Comtesse d'Houdetot

LS: American Philosophical Society

a Sanois Le 6. 8bre. 1783.
Je Crains que Mon Cher Et Venerable Docteur n'ait pas Reçu une Lettre que j'ay Eû L'honneur De Luy Adresser il y a quelque tems au Sujet D'un Matelot Americain pour Lequel je Luy Demandais Sa protection avec Des papiers Relatifs a Cette Affaire;[7] je Luy Rapelle aussi la promesse qu'il M'avait faitte De me Venir Voir Encore une fois Cet Automne, je Le Suplie D'En Choisir Le jour S'il me Conserve Sa Bonne Volonté, Madame Iss, m'a assurée qu'il Etait instruit De La perte que j'ay faitte. J'ay Autour De Moy quelques Amis Et la presence De Mon Aimable Et Venerable Docteur Et Celle De Son petit fils Serait une Consolation De plus pour Moy   LA CTESSE DHOUDETOT

Notation: La Cesse. d'Houdetot 6 Oct. 1783.

From Dorcas Montgomery

AL: American Philosophical Society

Paris, Octr. 6th: 1783—
Mrs. Montgomery & Son,[8] will have the Honor of Dining with Doctr. Franklin, on Friday next.—[9]

7. He had indeed received her letter of Sept. 6 requesting his intervention on behalf of John Hammon (XL, 584–5), and only two days earlier had been reminded of the fact by the Mme "Iss" mentioned below: Mme His to BF, Oct. 4. The present letter, finally, spurred him into action; see her acknowledgment of Oct. 14.

8. Thirteen-year-old Robert: XXXV, 481n.

9. Oct. 10. Decades later, TJ told a story he had heard about a gathering of English and French speakers at BF's house at which Dorcas Montgomery

Addressed: A Son Excellence. / Monsieur Franklin / en Son Hotel / A Passy

From Thomas Pownall   ALS: American Philosophical Society

My Old Friend—   Richmond Surrey Octr 6—83—

Permitt me thus to address you—for, however I may have been rejected by the Govt of my own Country, I am vain enough to think it will be no dishonor to You—to be known, that We were unchangeable friends for more than twenty Years.—

Our Govt Officers are buisy this day at London Proclaiming Peace—[1] I wish, (I hope that it is not a wish in Vain) That events of warr & the uncorresponding issue of peace may at length teach the civilized part of the World that *Warr is a bad way* of adjusting claims and rights & that Treaties must settle them at last. I will hope at least that the Rights of the two Branches of the English Nation, now two seperate Dominions & Governments, are settled in a permanent Peace— Our holy book says, blessed are the peace makers but referrs them for their reward to heaven—[2] You must feel the Reward in the heaven, you are in possession of, Your own Mind.

In your last letter to me dated Passey March 23—83—[3] You was so kind to say—that "You would carefully forward my

---

made herself "ridiculous" by repeatedly correcting BF's French, though hers was not much better. (TJ characterized BF's French as "wretched.") When she took it upon herself to answer a question that BF had addressed to Sarah Jay, she made an elementary French mistake—to the amusement of the crowd—that turned an innocuous statement into something off-color: John C. Van Horne and Lee W. Formwalt, eds., *The Correspondence and Miscellaneous Papers of Benjamin Henry Latrobe* (3 vols., New Haven, 1984–88), I, 234–6. This incident had to have taken place before May, 1784, when the Jays left France.

1. On Oct. 6 local officials took part in a procession that stopped at various points around the city for the public reading of the proclamation of peace: [London] *Public Advertiser,* Oct. 6, 1783.

2. Matthew 5:9.

3. Not found.

Letters to Mr Bowdoin & Dr Cooper enclosing my power of Attorney to them." I have not as yet received any Answer— I am anxious to know whether arrived or whether the conveyance by which You sent them has miscarried— I shall be much obliged to You if You can inform me, because if they have I will send Duplicates.—[4]

From the Moment I receiv'd your letter I made every inquiry in my power after Mr Williams of Boston both in West end of the town as well as in the City—but cou'd not obtain any information of him—

I took the Liberty to send to You & beg your acceptance of a Copy of my *Memorial to the Sovereigns of America*. I hope you receiv'd it— I took a like liberty in sending a Copy to each of Your Colleagues begging also their acceptance—[5]

I have the honor to be Sir Yr Excellency, most Obedt & most humble Servt   T POWNALL

His Excellency Benj Franklin Esqr &c &c &c—

Addressed: A Son Excellency / Benjn: Franklin &c &c / Minister Plenipotentiar Des / Etats Unies Americaines &c / a Passy / via / Paris—

4. Pownall had already conveyed this concern to BF through George Hobart, who came to Paris in September; see XL, 617–18. When Pownall wrote again to James Bowdoin on Dec. 9 (Mass. Hist. Soc.), renewing his offer of land to Harvard College, he mentioned that BF had sent him a note (now missing) confirming that he had forwarded Pownall's letters and that the ship carrying them had arrived. Meanwhile, Bowdoin had responded on Nov. 20, saying that although the land had been alienated for non-payment of taxes, he would lay the deed before the corporation of the college: "Letters of Bowdoin and Pownall," Mass. Hist. Soc. *Proc.*, V (1860–62), 245–6.

5. He sent them through George Hobart; see XL, 618.

To Joseph Banks

ls:[6] Royal Society; al (draft): University of Pennsylvania Library; press copy of ls: Massachusetts Historical Society; copy: Library of Congress

After heavy winds and rain had marred the demonstration of his hot-air balloon at the Réveillon manufactory on September 12,[7] Etienne Montgolfier and his collaborators had just one week to prepare a new balloon to be launched before the royal family at Versailles. The new vessel was somewhat smaller than its predecessor (57 feet tall and 41 feet in diameter), and its taffeta bag was coated with varnish rather than lined with paper. The most spectacular innovation was that the balloon would lift a wicker cage containing the first three aeronauts, a sheep, a duck, and a rooster. The balloon was completed with just enough time left for one successful trial before it was transported to Versailles, where an octagonal stage had been erected for the launch in the palace courtyard. On September 19 at one o'clock, after the royal family inspected the balloon and listened to Montgolfier's explanation of the experiment, the burner underneath the stage was lighted, fueled by damp straw and shredded wool. The balloon, which had been spread out over the stage, slowly took shape and rose before a large crowd of spectators. After it left the ground, a gust of wind almost caused the balloon to capsize, and the resultant loss of hot air meant that it rose to a height of only about 1,500 feet and traveled about two miles in eight minutes, before landing in the woods of Vaucresson. Although there were reports that the rooster had broken its head in the fall,[8] these were vehemently denied by Faujas de Saint-Fond, who assured the public that the rooster suffered only a scratch on his wing, inflicted by the hoof of the sheep before takeoff.[9]

Sir   Passy, Oct: 8. 1783.

The Publick were promised a printed particular Account of the Rise and Progress of the Balloon Invention, to be published

---

6. Written, we believe, by BFB. BF added the last seven words of the complimentary close before signing.

7. See XL, 609–10.

8. *E.g.*, in Bachaumont, *Mémoires secrets*, XXIII (1783), 162–3, and the *Mercure de France* (*Jour. politique de Bruxelles*) for Sept. 27, 1783, pp. 177–8.

9. Gillispie, *Montgolfier Brothers*, pp. 39–43; Faujas de Saint-Fond, *Description des expériences de la machine aérostatique de MM. de Montgolfier . . .* (Paris, 1783), pp. 36–48.

about the End of last month.[1] I waited for it to send it to you, expecting it would be more satisfactory than any thing I could write; but it does not appear. We have only at present the enclosed Pamphlet, which does not answer the expectation given us. I send you with it some prints.[2] That of the Balloon raised at Versailles is said to be an exact representation. I was not present, but am told it was filled in about ten minutes by means of burning Straw. Some say Water was thrown into the flame, others that it was Spirits of Sal Volatile. It was supposed to have risen about 200 Toises: But did not continue long at that height, was carried horizontally by the Wind, and descended gently as the Air within grew cooler— So vast a Bulk when it began to rise so majestically in the air, struck the spectators with surprize and Admiration. The Basket contained a sheep, a duck, and a Cock, who, except the Cock, received no hurt by the Fall.

The Duke de Crillon made a feast last week in the Bois de Boulogne just by my habitation, on Occasion of the Birth of two Spanish Princes;[3] after the Fireworks we had a Balloon of about 5 feet Diameter filled with permanent inflammable Air. It was dismissed about One a Clock in the Morning. It carried under it a large Lanthorn with inscriptions on its sides. The Night was quite calm and clear, so that it went right up. The appearance of the light diminished gradually till it appeared no bigger than one of the Stars, and in about twenty minutes I lost sight of it entirely. It fell the next Day on the other side of the same Wood near the Village Boulogne, about half after twelve, having been suspended in the Air eleven hours and a half. It lodged in a tree, and was torn in getting it down; so that it cannot be

1. In the *Jour. de Paris* of Sept. 18, Faujas de Saint-Fond announced that an account of all balloon experiments, including Montgolfier's upcoming demonstration at Versailles, would be published at the end of the month. His *Description des expériences de la machine aérostatique* did not appear until late November; see BF to Banks, Nov. 21 [*i.e.*, 22–25].

2. The pamphlet may have been the anonymous *Considérations sur le globe aérostatique, par M. D . . .* (Paris, 1783), which was approved for publication by Lenoir on Sept. 17 and advertised in the *Jour. de Paris* on Oct. 10. The "book and prints" were forwarded to Banks by Edward Nairne, who received them from Ami Argand: Nairne to BF, Dec. 2.

3. See the letter from the duc and duchesse de Crillon, [before Oct. 1].

ascertained whether it burst when above, or not, tho' that is supposed. Smaller Repetitions of the Experiment are making every day in all quarters. Some of the larger Balloons that have been up are preparing to be sent up again in a few Days; but I do not hear of any material improvements yet made either in the mechanical or Chemical parts of the Operation. Most is expected from the new one undertaken upon subscription by Messieurs Charles and Robert, who are Men of Science and mechanic Dexterity. It is to carry up a Man. I send you enclosed the Proposals, which it is said are already subscribed to by a considerable number, and likely to be carried into execution.[4] If I am well at the Time, I purpose to be present, being a subscriber myself, and shall send you an exact Account of Particulars.

With great esteem and respect, for yourself and the Society; I have the honour to be, Sir, Your most obedient & most humble Servant, B FRANKLIN

To David Hartley

Press copy of ALS and transcript: Library of Congress; copy: William L. Clements Library

My dear Friend, Passy, Oct. 8. 1783.
I received your favour of the 24th past, and rejoice that you have a reasonable Prospect of the Recovery of your dear Sister in time.

4. The enclosure has not been found. The copy of the present letter at the Library of Congress, in the hand of Charles Blagden, includes a section marked "Extract of the Proposals": the new balloon will be made of gummed silk, 26 feet in diameter, and launched sometime in November. One hundred subscribers are needed at 4 *louis* apiece; this sum will entitle them to watch the ascension from a special enclosed viewing area, and they will each receive 30 tickets to distribute for admission to another enclosed area. If the subscription is not filled by Oct. 20, all money will be refunded.
According to the Robert brothers' letter in the Nov. 19 *Jour. de Paris*, it had been six weeks since they announced their subscription (*i.e.*, they advertised it around Oct. 8). By Nov. 19 they had received subscriptions from only "quelques amis," not nearly enough to cover the balloon's estimated cost of 10,000 *l.t.* While preserving the privileges of the subscribers, they were now offering "amateurs" the opportunity to buy pairs of tickets for 6 *l.t.*

I join with you most cordially in "Wishes to forward, not only the Continuance of Peace between the two Countries, but the Improvement of Reconciliation"; and I "presume" as much as I can that the same "Friendly Dispositions" are in your Ministers, tho' their Dilatoriness respecting the Treaty of Commerce & the Evacuations of New York, &c: sometimes occasion Doubts.— Our Commission[5] is not yet arriv'd, but we expect it daily. Mr Jay, who will deliver this Line to you, goes to England on some particular Business of his own:[6] I am sure you will render him any Service he may have occasion for. My best Wishes attend you, being ever, with sincerest Esteem, my dear Friend, Yours most affectionately   B FRANKLIN

D. Hartley Esqr

To Benjamin Vaughan

ALS: Mrs. Frances V. Finletter, Philadelphia (1956)

My very dear Friend,   Passy, Oct. 8. 1783.
    I cannot let this Opportunity of Mr. Jay's going to London, pass without Dropping a Line to you, to say that I am tolerably well and love you as much as ever; and that I wish to hear from you oftner, tho' I am so bad a Correspondent as not to deserve it.
    I find I have, left, four of my Vols. on Electricity, and none of your Collection. If Mr Johnson does not think I have already had too many Copies, and will send me four more, I shall be oblig'd to him.[7] Mr Jay will be kind enough to bring them.[8] I am

    5. To negotiate a commercial treaty with Great Britain. The American commissioners learned of this commission, and informed Hartley, just before he left Paris: XL, 586–7.
    6. Jay left for England on Oct. 9, and stayed until late January, 1784. He visited London, where he stayed with William Bingham, as well as Bristol and Bath: *Jay Papers*, III, 489–93, 495–6.
    7. Joseph Johnson was the publisher of Vaughan's edition of BF's *Political, Miscellaneous, and Philosophical Pieces* (XXXI, 210–18). BF's volumes on electricity presumably were the fifth edition of his *Experiments and Observations on Electricity*: IV, 125–30; XXI, 292–7.
    8. By the time Vaughan decided to give Jay the four requested volumes, he learned that Jay had already left London: Benjamin Vaughan to John Jay, Jan. 20, 1784 (Columbia University Library).

long in your Debt: when will you send me your Account?—
Have you receiv'd News of your good Father & Family's Arrival?[9] My Love to your Brother William, & let me know how
you, your Spouse, & Children do; for I suppose you have now
more than one.[1] My Grandson presents his respectful Compliments, and I am ever Yours most affectionately   B FRANKLIN

Benjn Vaughan Esqr

Endorsed: Dr. Franklin 8 Octr: 1783.

Franklin: Proposed Plan of Agreement for Packet Boat Service[2]

AD (draft): American Philosophical Society

[before October 9, 1783]

Plan of Agreement

The Packet Boats from England to America & from France
to America, both departing once a Month, the English in the
Beginning & the French in the Middle of each Month, afford
Opportunities to the Merchants of each Nation of Writing every Fortnight; and this it is thought will induce the English to
write often by the French Pacquet Boats, and the French by the
English Boats.

9. The family sailed to Philadelphia in July and were staying with the
Baches: XL, 175, 185, 236, 597.
1. Sarah Vaughan gave birth to their second child, William Oliver
(1783–1826), on Nov. 5. Their daughter, Harriet (1782–1798), celebrated
her first birthday six days later: John H. Sheppard, "Reminiscences and
Genealogy of the Vaughan Family," *New England Hist. and Geneal. Register,* XIX (1865), 348, 355.
2. On the bottom of Anthony Todd's letter of Oct. 3, BF instructed
WTF to compose a letter informing Todd of the plan of agreement BF had
"propos'd" to the French. (That letter, dated Oct. 9, is immediately below.)
BF's use of the past tense implies that this proposal had already been delivered to the bureau of the French postal service, undoubtedly in translation.
BF's Oct. 9 letter to Todd enclosed the plan. The fair copy of that letter and
its enclosure have not been located, but Todd's reply of Oct. 17 makes clear
that what BF enclosed was the French translation. Todd returned a copy of
it with his letter of Oct. 17, crossing out a passage he wanted deleted (APS).
We publish here the English version as BF drafted it; the translation does
not vary in any substantive way.

For the more convenient Receipt of the respective Postages it is proposed in England

That all Letters[3] from any Part of the Continent of Europe for North America, intended to go by the English Pacquet Boat, should be sent by the Writers under Cover to their Friends in London.

In like manner it may be required that all Letters from any Part of Great Britain or Ireland intended to go by the French Pacquet Boats, should be sent by the Writers under Cover to their Friends in Paris.

Thus these Letters will have no Postage to be demanded on them when they arrive in America but the Pacquet Postage only.

It is supposed that a similar Regulation will take place in America, and that the Postages from different Parts of that Continent being all paid to New York, there will be only the Pacquet Postage charg'd upon them when they arrive at *London* or *Paris*—

As there may probably arrive a Number of Letters for England by the French Pacquet Boats, nearly equal to that of Letters for France by the English Pacquet Boats, it is proposed to exchange them without Account, leaving the respective Offices in France & England to charge & receive the Pacquet Postage together with the Postage between London & Paris.

Or Accounts may be kept of the Letters so exchanged, and the Ballance paid quarterly as it shall become due.

To [Anthony Todd]   L (draft):[4] American Philosophical Society

Dear Sir,   Passy, 9 Oct. 1783.

I have not as yet been able to settle any thing in Consequence of the Power you have vested me with. The Person I am to treat

---

3. At this point BF drafted and crossed out: "from any Part of Great Britain or Ireland for North America, should have their Postage paid to London; and that all Letters".

4. Written by WTF, as instructed by BF; see BF's note for a reply on Todd's Oct. 3 letter.

with is in the Country but is expected soon to be in Town.[5] I am told he is likewise authorized to treat with me relative to the Arrangement necessary between the American & french Post Offices. & that he has already drawn out a Plan of Agreement for that purpose.— I have likewise done so with regard to the Arrangement you propose—[6] Inclosed I send you a Copy of it;[7]—if you chuse any Alterations to be made in it let me know it as early as possible—

My Grandson has had some Conversation on the Subject with the Entreprenneur of the French Pacquet boats,[8] who thought some Difficulties might arise, if it was settled as you propose "That all Letters from Any Part of America directed to England should go by the English Paquet boats unless *Via France* was put on the Cover & so *vice versa.*" These Words, he sd might be added by Persons interrested in the respective Boats—& that the Proposal did not stipulate for Letters directed out of France & England. As for Hambourgh &ca. He thought it would be better to agree that all Letters that arrived at N. York from any Part of the United States, from the 1st. to the 15th. of each Month, should go by the French Boats—& those that arrived from the 15th. to the End of the Month should go by the English Boats,—and so settle the Departure of the respective Boats from New York Accordingly.— What is your Opinion of this?—

I have just now recd. your Favour of the 3d Inst & return you many Thanks for your kind Care of the Letter I sent you for the Presdt. of Congress—

I am Dear Sir, with great Truth & Esteem Your most obedt and most humble Sert.

---

5. The "Person" was Claude-Jean Rigoley, baron d'Ogny (1725–1793), *intendant général des postes, relais, et messageries:* BF to Todd, Oct. 29, below; *Almanach royal* for 1783, p. 633; Didier Ozanam and Michel Antoine, eds., *Correspondance secrète du comte de Broglie avec Louis XV (1756–1774)* (2 vols., Paris, 1956–61), II, 299n.

6. WTF originally wrote here but deleted, "between your Country & this".

7. See the document immediately above.

8. Le Couteulx de la Noraye.

From James Jay[9]   ALS: American Philosophical Society

Sir   Paris Octobr. 9. 1783.
I expect to set out for England in a day or two, and propose
to go by the way of Calais. I beg therefore you will send me a
passport sometime to morrow by the petit Post. I have the honour, Sir, to be, Your Most Obt: & hble: Servt: JAMES JAY

Hotel de Chatillon Rue du Petit Bourbon prés St: Sulpice.—

His Excelly. Benjn: Franklin

Addressed: A Son Excellence / Monsieur Franklin / Ministre
Plenipotentiare des Etats Unis / de L'Amerique &c.— / a /
Passy

Notation: James Jay. Oct. 9. 1783.

From Lorenzo Manini[1]   ALS: American Philosophical Society

⟨Cremona, October 9, 1783, in Italian: The illustrious name
of Doctor Franklin is venerated and held in the highest esteem
throughout Italy and especially in Lombardy. In testimony
of this admiration, I have dedicated to you a fine work I just
printed, the *Lettere Americane* by the famous President Carli.[2]

9. This is the last known letter to BF from John Jay's estranged older
brother James, who was returning to England after unsuccessful business
negotiations in France: *Jay Papers,* III, 275–7, 490–1. James eventually
moved to Springfield, N.J., and died there in 1815: *DAB.*
    1. Prominent bookseller, printer, and freemason in Cremona (*c.* 1757–
1821): Alice Pizzocaro, "Lorenzo Manini: Libraio e stampatore a Cremona
fra Ancien Régime ed età Napoleonica," *Storia in Lombardia,* XII (1993),
5–6, 16–17, 36.
    2. *Le Lettere americane* (3 vols., Cremona, 1781–83) was published
anonymously by Count Gian Rinaldo Carli (1720–1795), a versatile
scholar who also served as president of the Supremo consiglio di eco-
nomica in Milan: *Dizionario biografico degli Italiani* (73 vols. to date, Rome,
1960–). The work was intended to refute Cornelius de Pauw's and Buffon's notions of American degeneracy. The first volume, published in
1781, opened with an undated dedicatory letter addressed to BF by Isidoro
Bianchi, a professor of ethics at Cremona. Bianchi praised the unnamed

I humbly submit to you by post two copies of this book and beg
you to accept them as a sincere tribute.³⟩

From John Shaffer⁴   ALS: American Philosophical Society

Sir   [October 9, 1783?]⁵

As an unfortunate Countryman I take the liberty onst more
to adress my Self to you Knowing That you have a heart that
Sincerly feals the Sorrow of anothers boosom, the Judges of my

---

author as the first Italian to rival other great European philosophers, and
declared that only BF was competent to decide which European scholar
had rendered the best account of American history. In rhetorically asking
for BF's permission to dedicate the work to him, Bianchi claimed to follow the example of Regnier, who had prefaced *Recueil des loix constitutives
des colonies angloises* . . . (Philadelphia [*i.e.*, Paris], 1778) with a dedicatory letter (XXVI, 529–30). For a detailed discussion of *Le Lettere americane* see Antonio Pace, *Benjamin Franklin and Italy* (Philadelphia, 1958),
pp. 135–40.

3. BF kept one set, now at the Library Company of Philadelphia: Wolf
and Hayes, *Library of Benjamin Franklin,* p. 176. He donated the other set
to the APS, inscribing the first and second volumes as being from Manini
"to the Society". The first volume of both sets had been altered in two
places, for reasons we cannot explain. On the title page, the publication
date (printed in roman numerals) was subtly changed from 1781 to 1782 by
the addition of a final I that appears to have been either stamped or sten-
ciled. Moreover, the final page of the dedication was replaced by a reprinted
sheet whose only change was in the typeset signature: Manini's name was
substituted for that of Bianchi.

Having heard nothing from BF, Manini wrote again on March 8, 1784,
saying that he had just learned that the volumes had been delivered (APS).

4. Shaffer had sent BF a somewhat shorter and more confused version
of this letter on Oct. 7. The following day, Oct. 8, he wrote a plea to WTF
that added one detail: a man named Cuture had stated in a deposition that
WTF, to whom he had applied for information, said that Shaffer was "a bad
subject and an imposter." It was this statement that caused Shaffer to be arrested. Being certain that WTF had never said any such thing, he asked for
WTF's assistance in proving his citizenship. Shaffer sent a near-duplicate of
that letter to WTF on Oct. 11, this time claiming that the deposition alleged
that WTF had called him a "duplicte Rober and a bad Subject." (All at APS.)

5. Dated on the basis of Shaffer's allusion on Oct. 10, below, to his letter
of "yesterday."

affair Demands that I prove that I am a Native of Amerique if your Exelency will be Kind Enough as you Know I am Realy a Native of Philadelphia to Certify that I am from Philaa. and belong to a good honest fameley and Suported in that Country a good Carracter as you Know I wallways have Done, you will Rilive me from the greatest Pain in Life if your Exelency Should Refuse me this feavour I am Lost Lost for Ever—this is the most unhappest affair in Life I do Not Know for what I am arrested the accused me of being a Partner of a Certain Saintyver[6] but as I have Proved to the Conturrary they Know Say I am an imposter and that I never was in that Country that if I Realy was that my ambasedeuer would Not Refuse me to Certify that I am from that Country my liberty Depends upon the Goodness of your Exelency in Righting those few fowloing Lines— Sir you have arrested a Subject of the united Stats of amereca Named John Shaffer a Son of David Shaffer a good honest famely and who allways Suported a good Carracter in that Country I beg that you will Render him the Justis that he merets—you See by my Request the inosance of my Cause.

If you Do Not Clame me in this unhappe affair I am Loost for Ever, I am very senceble that I do Not Merite your Protection owing to my bad Conduct but hope you will Pardon me for my Past Conduct, thinck of my good honest fameley my God what I have brought my Self to by my imprudence if it is only for the Sake of my famely Do Not Refuse me the feavour I ask and beleve me I Ever Shall look upon you as my Salvateur and acnoledge my Self to be with Respect Sir your Most obedent and very humble Servant   J SCHAFFER

The few Lines that you will be Kind Enough to Right in my feavour, one to Monr. Gude Consillier au Chattlet[7] one to Monr. Bachois Lieutenant Criminel, and the other to the Procureur du Roy[8] it will be sufecent to give me my liberty, for Heaven Sake

6. Menier de Saint Yver; see XL, 619.
7. Judde de Neuville, whose name he spells correctly in a Nov. 19 letter to WTF (APS), had been *conseiller au Châtelet* since 1772: *Almanach royal* for 1783, p. 395.
8. For Bachois de Villefort, *lieutenant criminel*, and Flandre de Brunville, *procureur du roi*, see the latter's letter above, Sept. 25.

Donot Refuse me this feavour I therw my Self Down upon my Knees before you and Pray you will Not abandon me. I am sick in bed and am without the Lest Reserve if you would only be Kind Enough to Send me a Small Sum of money as I have Not a farthing to Subsist— enclose I Send you a Small bill upon my father who will pay it at Sight if your Exelency will be Kind Enough to put this Small bill into the hands of Mr Barclay As he Knoes my famely he will procure you the amount by the first opertunety I have Still a Small bill of your acceptation but is Since with all my affairs I owe a Small Sum to Mr Balon, the Governeur of the Prison if I Do Not Pay him he will turn me upon the Straw[9] my god waht an unhappe Situation the letter that you will be Kind Enough to Right I beg you will Send them by the bearrer as I have No time to loose I have the honour to be Your Exelency Most obedent and very humble Servant

J. SCHAFFER

His Exelency Doctor Franklin

From Graf von Brühl

ALS: American Philosophical Society

Sir   Petwirth Oct: 10th. 1783.

I was very much flattered with the Letter I had the pleasure to receive from your Excellency by the Means of the ingenious Mr de Kempelen's Arrival in this Country.[1] The favourable Opinion you entertain of his talents is alone sufficient to convince me of their Intent & usefullness. I cannot find Words to express the gratitude I feel for the honour of your Remembrance. I shall therefore only beg Leave to assure you that it will be the pride of my Life to have been noticed by one of the most distinguished

---

9. Prisoners negotiated their lodging with the prison's director. Those who were not able to pay were put in common rooms, where they slept on straw pallets, sometimes in shifts, and were given a daily ration of bread and water: Richard M. Andrews, *Law, magistracy, and crime in Old Regime Paris, 1735–1789* (1 vol. to date, Cambridge and New York, 1994–), I, 377.

1. BF's letter of Aug. 22 introduced Wolfgang von Kempelen, inventor of a chess-playing automaton and a speaking machine: XL, 497–8.

Characters of the Age & that I shall endeavour upon all occasions to contribute my small mite of admiration to the universal Applause your eminent qualities as a Philosopher & a Politician are so well entitled to. I have the honour to be with great respect, Sir Your Excellency's Most obedient humble Servant.

THE COUNT DE BRÜHL

Addressed: To / His Excellency / Dr. Franklin, Ministre Plenipoten / tiary of the United States of North / America to His Most Christian / Majesty, / Passy

Endorsed: From the Minister of the Elector of Saxony to the Court of Great Britain.

From Horace-Bénédict de Saussure

ALS: University of Pennsylvania Library

Monsieur,   Genève ce 10: Octbre. 1783.

J'ai été infiniment sensible à la marque obligeante de souvenir dont vous m'avés honoré en m'envoyant un Exemplaire des Constitutions des Etats unis de l'Amérique.[2] C'est un monument bien curieux & bien intéressant de cette grande & mémorable rèvolution à la quelle vous avés, Monsieur, si puissamment coopéré. Je souhaite pour le bonheur de l'Amérique que vous conserviés toujours sur son Gouvernement l'influence que meritent vos rares talents, vos vertus & votre patriotisme, & que vous viviés assez longtems pour voir solidement affermir & prospérer cette République qui vous doit en grande partie son existence.

Comme je suis persuadé, Monsieur, que vos occupations politiques n'ont point éteint chez vous le gout des sciences physiques dans les quelles vous vous êtes acquis une si grande gloire, je prends la liberté de vous envoyer par la Messagerie un exemplaire des Essais sur l'Hygromètrie que je viens de publier.[3] Cet

2. Which BF sent on Aug. 23: XL, 503.
3. *Essais sur l'hygrométrie* (Neuchâtel, 1783), one of the founding works of meteorology. The first essay describes Saussure's invention of the hair hygrometer, which measured atmospheric humidity with far more precision than hitherto possible. Subsequent essays deal with its application and

ouvrage est trop long & trop détaillé pour que vous ayés le tems de le lire, mais vous le parcourrés du moins & vous en saisirés les principaux résultats: heureux s'il pouvait obtenir un suffrage aussi flatteur que le votre.

J'aurois encore, Monsieur, une grace à vous demander. Un de mes amis, le Chevalier Landriani Professeur de Physique à Milan a reçu du Gouvernement l'ordre de faire ériger des Conducteurs sur tous les édifices publics de la Lombardie Autrichienne & de publier en même tems un mèmoire raisonné pour éclairer le peuple sur l'utilité de ce préservatif.[4] Il desireroit extrèmement de savoir & de pouvoir dire dans son mèmoire quel est actuellement en Amérique le sort de cette utile invention; si elle a été génèralement adoptèe dans toutes les Provinces & par le Public et par les Particuliers; à quoi l'on pourroit porter le nombre des conducteurs actuellement existans en Amèrique; si l'on en fait usage dans la marine; & enfin s'il n'existe aucun exemple d'un conducteur qui ait ète funeste à la maison qui en ètoit armée.[5]

Si vous aviès la complaisance, Monsieur, de rèpondre aussi laconiquement que vous le voudrès, mais un peu promptement si cela vous est possible, vous nous rendrès à mon ami & à moi un vèritable service & vous contribuerès ainsi au soutien de

---

describe new experiments and theories concerning meteorology, some of which refer to BF's writings (*e.g.*, on pp. 274, 279). The work was announced and highly praised in the *Jour. de Paris* of Oct. 12. For an assessment of the work see also René Sigrist, "Les *Essais sur l'hygrométrie* (1783) ou l'art de la mesure précise," in *H.-B. de Saussure (1740–1799): un regard sur la terre,* ed. René Sigrist (Geneva and Paris, 2001), pp. 109–40.

4. Marsilio Landriani (XL, 430) had befriended Saussure in Geneva in 1782 while on an assignment for the Milanese government to study local manufacturing. For his new project, Landriani again turned to Saussure for help. The Genevan contributed two letters, dated Oct. 11 and 13, responding to Landriani's queries; a general statement about the importance of conductors and lightning rods; and a March 26, 1784, letter to the editor from the *Jour. de Paris* of April 10, which Landriani included without date: *Dizionario biografico degli Italiani* (73 vols. to date, Rome, 1960–); Landriani, *Dell'Utilità dei conduttori elettrici. Dissertazione* (Milan, 1784), pp. 190–201, 274–84.

5. BF had addressed these same issues in his letter to Saussure of Oct. 8, 1772: XIX, 325.

cette théorie dont le genre humain vous a, Monsieur, l'obligation toute entiére.[6]

J'ai l'honneur d'etre avec le devouement le plus respectueux, Monsieur, Votre très humble & très obeissant serviteur

DE SAUSSURE

From John Shaffer

ALS: American Philosophical Society

Sir   Paris ce 10 8bre 83

Your answer[7] to my letter of yesterday has threwn me in the most unhappe Situation,—if you will Not do aney thing for me to Relive me from my Pain—for god Sake have Pitte upon my unhappe Situation I have No bread Even to Eat and Not a far-thing in my Pocket if you will Lend me Ever so Small a Sum it will confer the greatest obligations upon me if you Refuse me this feavour I shall perrish for want of Nessisarys—it is 8 days that I have Not Eat aney thing but the black bread of the Prison, and I am Sick in bead— Belive me Sir that the bill I inclose upon my father will be paid wech will Reimburs the money that you was Kind Enough to Lend me it will be the Greatest obligation Confered upon an unhappe Country man do Not Refuse me let me intreat you to Send if it is Ever So Small Sum by the bearrer as it will prevent me from Pireshing.

I hae the honour to be with Respect Your Exelenceys Most Obedient and Very humble Servant   J SCHAFFER

if you Exelency Should be disposed To Render me the Service I ask—if it is Ever so Samall a Sum you will be Kind Enough to Send it by the bearrer

6. BF was reminded of this request at some unknown time by Ferdinand Grand, who passed along an undated letter he had received from Louis Necker de Germany (XXIV, 401) asking him to tell BF that Saussure would be greatly obliged if he would send the information on lightning rods in America: APS. Saussure and Germany had known one another for decades; their children (daughter and son, respectively) married in 1785: Lüthy, *Banque protestante*, II, 235–6. Landriani, anxious for a response, wrote an appeal of his own on Nov. 9; see that letter for details of his project.

7. Missing.

His Exelency Docter Franklin

Addressed: A Monsieur / Monsieur Frankline / Ambasedeuer a la Cour de france / a Son Lhotel / A Passy

From Francis Coffyn

ALS: American Philosophical Society

Hond. Sir. Dunkerque 11th. Octor. 1783.

I had the honnor of addressing your Excellency on the 15. ulta. an abstract of the general account of my disbursments for the relief of the american prisonners during the war, ballanced by £.361. 12. 8. [*i.e., l.t.*] in my favour[8] and to inform your Excellency that I remitted a copy of the same to M. Barclay in order to convince him that Since the commencement of the war the Honnorable Commissionners had intrusted me with the American business at this port, in hopes that in consequence he would have departed from the promise he made to M. Grand to appoint a M. Morel Dufaux, Consul or agent for the united States at this port. By the enclosed copy of M. Barclays answer dated Nantes the 4th. ins't, your Excellency will observe that instead of having produced the desired effect, this Gentleman tells me plainly that his voice will go for M. Morel.[9]

If I could have thought that my Zealous and uninterrupted Services during a Series of years, could have less weight on the mind of M. Barclay then the Sollicitation of the Gentlemen he mentions in his letter, I might have claim'd the recommendation of my friends, but I shall let my actions and my pass'd conduct Speak for me, and claim no other testimony then your Excellency's, on whose Justice and protection I have too great reasons to rely, to think your Excellency would Suffer an other to re-

8. Coffyn's letter and enclosure are missing.

9. Barclay's Oct. 4 letter explained that he could not deviate from the assurance he had given to Morel Dufaux, whom he did not know personally but who was highly recommended by "Mr. Grand" (presumably Georges), Isaac Hazelhurst, and Daniel Crommelin & fils, in Amsterdam. At the time he gave his word, he was unaware that any other qualified candidate existed. He would never appoint a consul against the wishes of the American ministers at Paris, however, and if Coffyn should be their choice, he would be pleased to work with him. APS.

ceive the recompence due to my Zealous exertions in all matters concerning America, which have been committed to my care by your Excellency, and which I have allways conducted with the Strictest honnor and regularity. I beg leave to assure your Excellency, that the Same Sentiments will ever guide me, in order to merit the recommendation your Excellency has been pleased to promise in my behalf, when the appointment of a Consul should take place. Interim I have the honnor to remain with the Sincerest gratitude and respect.

Your Excellency's most obedient & most humble Servant

F COFFYN

From David Hartley

ALS: Library of Congress

Dear Sir   London October 11 1783
I beg leave to introduce to you by this letter the Revd Dr Scrope[1] a Gentleman of a very respectable character & family in Wiltshire bordering upon Glo'stershire. He has likewise the honour of being one of his Majesty's Chaplains. He is in an infirm state of health and is going in to France for change of climate. The State of his health makes it uncertain at what time he may be able to avail himself of an introduction to you. In these circumstances he has desired me to make him known to you. The very polite attention wch you always show to every English Gentleman makes it unnecessary for me to do any thing farther than to present to you the name and character of Dr Scrope & his request.[2]

I am Dear Sir with the greatest respect Your Most obedt humble Servt.   D HARTLEY

To Dr Franklin &c. &c. &c.

1. Richard Scrope (c. 1729–1787), D.D. Oxford University (1764), was a chaplain to George III from 1777 until his death: Joseph Foster, *Alumni Oxonienses: the Members of the University of Oxford, 1715–1886* . . . (4 vols., London, 1887–88), IV, 1268.

2. On Oct. 24, writing from the Hôtel d'York, Scrope accepted BF's invitation to dinner the following Sunday on behalf of himself, his wife, and his daughter (APS). His wife was Anne Lambert Scrope and their daughter was Harriet: *Gent. Mag.*, LVII (1787), 644; LXXXIX (1819), 588.

From Benjamin Morel Dufaux

ALS: American Philosophical Society

My Lord.   Dunkirk the 11 8br 1783

For a while past Messieurs Veuve Dque. Morel & Self had the honor of writing to your Highness.[3] Tho' not honoured with an answer, yet I make it bold Humbly to beg of your Highness to accept my petition with regard to obtaining a prefference for the Consular office in Dunkirk.[4] Thro' the Channel of Mr Grand Banker in Paris we had occasion to render Important Services to the Americans in the most Critical times. Those Services I have related in my petition, they seem to Justiffy my Claims. I am favored with M Thos Barclay's protection, & shall Esteem myself happy to be honored with that of your Highness.[5] Shou'd I not be Sufficiently Known, I flatter myself I might yet merit Authentical Certifficates of a good Conduct & shou'd furnish them when Needfull.

I Remain with Sincere Respect of Your Highness The most Humble & most Obedient Servant[6]   MOREL DUFAUX

My Lord

---

3. Morel Dufaux, his mother, and his brother were partners in the firm Veuve Dominique Morel & fils. The firm's first application for Morel Dufaux to become the American consul in Dunkirk dates back to November, 1778: XXVIII, 87–8. In January, 1780, they reminded BF of their attachment to the United States: XXXI, 338–9.

4. Titled "Memoirs," the 14-page undated petition, in English, details the firm's exertions and sacrifices on behalf of American captains dating back to February, 1777. This account "proves" that Morel & fils was the first firm in Dunkirk to help the Americans and that they therefore deserve preference. Morel Dufaux, who speaks and writes English, asked Silas Deane and Thomas Barclay for a consular appointment; both promised to "remember him in Case there Was any Named in the ports of france."

5. See Coffyn's Oct. 11 letter, above.

6. Morel Dufaux wrote again on Dec. 31, offering New Year's greetings and reminding BF of his application (Hist. Soc. of Pa.).

From Graf von Schönfeld[7]   AL: American Philosophical Society

ce Lundy 13. d'Octobre 1783

Le Baron de Schönfeld a l'honneur d'assurer de ses hommages Monsieur Franklin et de Le prier de vouloir bien faire passer par son Paquet à Philadelphie, la lettre ci jointe pour le Sr. Thieriot.[8] Il Le prie d'agréer ses excuses et ses remercimens.

From Nicolas Albert[9]   ALS: American Philosophical Society

Monsieur   Paris ce 14 8bre. 1783

Vous m'avez fait L'honneur de me faire Entrévoir que l'appartement audessus de mes Bains pouroit Vous Convenir;[1] si Je pouvois compter être assès hureux de Vous avoir dans ma

7. The Saxon minister, who roughly a month earlier had sent BF an undated invitation to dinner on Thursday, Sept. 18 (APS).

8. For Thieriot, a Saxon charged with establishing commercial relations with the United States, whom Schönfeld had introduced to BF in July, see XL, 270, 350–1, 375–6, 555.

9. The proprietor of a new bathing establishment located on the quai d'Orsay, across from the jardin des Tuileries. With separate wings for men and women, it offered what had never been available in Paris: every variety of ordinary and medicinal bath (including sauna, steam, aromatic, mineral, and friction) and hot and cold showers whose various jets sprayed water from above, below, and horizontally. Prices ranged from 2 *l.t.* 8 *s.* to 12 *l.t.*, with two rooms reserved for the poor at no charge. Albert had conceived the project in 1769, and received encouragement from both the Faculté de médecine and the Société royale de médecine. The Faculté approved the establishment at the end of July, 1783, whereupon Albert sent an announcement to the *Jour. de Paris*. Later in the summer the paper described the baths and encouraged the public to visit: *Jour. de Paris,* July 30, Aug. 26, 1783. The Académie royale de chirurgie gave its approval on Nov. 6, and in the spring of 1784 the Société royale de médecine appointed an investigatory commission that included BF; their report will be covered in vol. 42. Albert died in 1801: Claude Pris, ed., *Documents du minutier central des notaires de Paris concernant l'histoire économique et sociale (1800–1830)* (Paris, 1999), p. 286. Our thanks to Marie Davaine of the library at the Académie nationale de médecine for assistance with this research.

1. No reply from BF has been found, and it is unclear whether he was interested in using this apartment when taking the baths or more generally during visits to Paris.

maison, n'importe dans quelque tems que ce fut, Je me hâterai de le mêtre en Etât de Vous recevoir.

J'ai L'honneur dêtre avec respect Monsieur Votre tres humble et trés Obeissant Serviteur   ALBERT

From Pierre Dessin[2]   LS: American Philosophical Society

Monsieur   Calais le 14 8bre. 1783

Conformement à la lettre dont vous m'avés honoré le 9 court: [courrant][3] J'ai pris note de la paire de roues de Carosse qui doivent me venir de Londres sous votre adresse pour vous les expédier du moment de leur arrivée.[4] En vous priant de vous reposer entierement sur mes soins à cet Egard, Permettés moi de vous faire mon remerciment de la confiance dont vous daignés m'honorer; C'est avec le desir de la mériter de plus en plus, que J'aime à me protester avec le plus profond respect Monsieur Votre très humble & très dévoué serviteur   PIERRE DESSIN

Notation: Dessein 14 Oct. 1783

From the Comtesse d'Houdetot

LS: American Philosophical Society

a Sanois Le 14. 8bre. 1783.

J'aprend avec Bien Du Chagrin que Mon Respectable Amy a Eté Malade il Est plus triste Encore D'Estre privée De Le Voir pour une Si fascheuse Raison, je le Remercie De la Lettre qu'il

2. The Calais innkeeper who had forwarded boxes arriving from England; see XL, 176–7.

3. Not found.

4. BF had ordered these wheels from John Viny in a now-missing letter of Oct. 9; see Viny's answer, [after Nov. 28]. Also on Oct. 9, BF wrote a now-missing letter to Hodgson asking him to pay Viny's bill and arrange for sending the shipment, which he must have suggested directing to Calais. See Hodgson's answer of Oct. 30, which proposed sending the wheels by Rouen.

m'a Envoyée pour Le Malheureux Matelot[5] il a dû Voir par Les papiers que j'avais Envoyé qu'on avait pris touttes Les precautions possibles pour n'estre pas trompés sur L'objet De nôtre Commiseration, jay mandé qu'on Les renouvellat Encore Et Ce ne sera qu'apres s'Estre Bien assuré qu'on s'Employe En Effet pour un objet qui Le Merite qu'on fera usage de La Lettre De mon Respectable Amy. Je Suis attachée Encore a Ma Campagne jusqu'au mois De Decembre[6] par Le Besoin qu'en ont mon Corps et mon Ame apres la perte que j'ay faitte. Je prie Mon Respectable Amy De Reçevoir Les tendres assurances de tous mes sentimens pour Luy. Oserai-je Le Suplier De vouloir Bien M'informer du Succés Des Remedes qu'il fait

La Ctesse dhoudetot

From John Shaffer

ALS: American Philosophical Society

Sir   Paris th 14 8br 83

The few lines that your Exelency was Kind Enough to honour me with[7] you Reproch me in Saing that if I had my liberty I would do Somthing that would bring me to the weelle or gallos— No Sir Notwith Standing my unhappy Situation I Niver diviated from the presinplas of honour. No doubt but your Exelency has bean informed that I have Contracted a Numbre of Depts in Paris belive me Sir that I Niver Contracted for one farthing personaley but unfortunately trusted my Signeture to a Person who Niver gave me one [Sum?]. Not only that he Dressed up a man Saing that it was Mr Shaffer in order to impose upon the Merchants— I am allso informed that a Numbre of Complaints have bean made against me to you belive me Sir it is without Ever Knowing me, and I defy all Paris to prove that

5. It was dated Oct. 8 and addressed to the *intendant* of Caen; see her previous letter of Oct. 6, and the response to BF from Charles-François-Hyacinthe Esmangart, dated Nov. 6.

6. She was back in Paris by Dec. 14, when she wrote to WTF announcing her return, conveying sympathy for BF's sufferings from his "maladie cruelle et douloureuse," and asking whether she could visit. APS.

7. Not found.

I Ever Contracted for a farthing—but unfortunately trusted my Signeture without having Recved the valour.

If the fealing of humanety will Not urge you to do Somthing in my feavour After being Convinced of my inosance I Shall be the most unfortunate of Mankind— The Avocat who interesst him Self Without interest[8] will Explain to your Exelency the inosance of my Cause you will See that I do Not impose upon you and affter Knowing my Positeon will Not Refuse to Reclame an unfortunate Countryman As you accuse me with Not telling the truth the Gentelman who is a man Very Respactable will Prove what I say to be true if I Should have the good fortune onst more to be Relived from my Confin[?]ment if I Should be oblidged to walek afoot to the first See Port in order to go To my Native home I will live Paris th moment I get out of Prison you Depend upon it.

If your Exelency will Not Refuse the Request that my Avocat will ask you the Justise will Return me what the have Sised wich is my waches buckels 1800 Livers in good bills one of wich is upon you wich I will Return you in Payments as it is Near the Sum I owe you. I have No other Person in this Country whom I can Claim to be of Servise to me. Theirefore hope you will Not Refuse me the feavour and belive me to be with Respect your Exelencys Most Obedent and very humble Servant   J SCHAFFER

His Exelency le Doctre Frankline

From ———   AL: American Philosophical Society

Monsieur   [on or after October 14, 1783][9]
Je crois devoir vous prévenir que Confiér les affaires de Mr Chaffert a de Baumont C'est a proprement dire donner la

8. Beaumont, who would advocate for Shaffer in personal as well as legal affairs, does not appear among the *avocats au parlement* in the *Almanach royal*. A brief, undated letter from Shaffer introducing him—still without naming him—may have accompanied the present letter. It tells BF that the bearer, his *avocat*, would explain both the circumstances of his detention and his "Malheurs" (APS). Shaffer first names him in his letter of Nov. 5, below.

9. This anonymous tip can be dated only in conjunction with the letter immediately above, in which John Shaffer introduces his *avocat*.

Brebis a garder au Loup ce dernier ayant fait cent Coquinneries dont quatre l'ont conduit en prison la derniére a la fin de juillet sans compter le courant Et notament des billets quil s'est fait faire par Chaffert soit disant pour Nouriture.

Mr le procureur de Roy du chatellet en expliquera davantage. Je suis avec Respect

From John Baynes

ALS: American Philosophical Society

Hôtel de Luxembourg—Ruë des Petits Augustins.
Wedn. Morning. [October 15, 1783][1]

Sir

I take the liberty of informing your Excellency, that I shall sett off for England either tomorrow Evening or Friday. Not having my own servant with me just now, I send this by a Messenger who will either wait for any letters with which you may wish to favor me, or will call for them tomorrow, as shall be most agreeable. If you have been able to procure the list of books,[2] I will request the favor to send it at the same time.

Having lent Grays Poems sometime ago to a gentleman in this town, I have not yet been able to get them returned, but will leave such directions as may ensure their being forwarded to Passy: I have however sent Mr. Masons poem[3]—& I send it with a firm confidence that it will be read with pleasure, when you are informed that the author is an independent man & a sincere friend to civil & religious liberty.

Permit me now to make my sincere acknowlegemts. for the great honor done me by Your Excellency in condescending to declare your sentiments so freely upon so many interesting subjects to one in every respect so little intitled to that attention as myself. The great distance between your Excellency & myself in age, rank, ability & consideration, make me feel so forcibly the favor I have received that I am at a loss how to express my

1. The Wednesday before Baynes left Paris; see Extracts of John Baynes's Journal (published under Sept. 23, above), entry of Oct. 15.

2. See Baynes's journal, above, entry of Oct. 12.

3. Baynes had evidently discussed with BF both publications: Thomas Gray, *Poems* (London, 1768), and William Mason, *The English Garden: a Poem* (4 vols., London, 1772–81). See Baynes's journal, above, entry of Oct. 15.

sentiments. I can only say that I value the instruction & pleasure I have received from your Excellency's conversation at too high a rate ever to forget the obligation conferred in permitting me to enjoy it. Wishing that your Excellency may enjoy many years of health and happiness, I remain, with all respect, Your Excellencys most obedient & obliged humble Servant,

JOHN BAYNES.[4]

Addressed: To / His Excellency Dr. Franklin.

Louis-Guillaume Le Veillard: Notes on the Life of Franklin[5]

Reprinted from Carl Van Doren, ed., *Benjamin Franklin's Autobiographical Writings* (New York, 1945), pp. 634–6.

[before October 16, 1783?]

Josias [Josiah] Franklin born in England, established in Boston in 1680 [1683], had seven children by a first wife and ten by a second. Benjamin is the eighth of the latter.

4. Beneath the signature BF added, "of Gray's Inn London".
5. Le Veillard's undated biographical sketch of BF has puzzled generations of editors. It survives in only one MS version: a copy in the original French made in 1786 by TJ's secretary, William Short. TJ endorsed it "Notes of Dr. Franklin's life taken from himself by Mons. Le Veillard of Passy." Because the notes loosely follow the order of elements in BF's outline of his autobiography (which he had received from Abel James at the end of 1782: XXXVIII, 425–8), and because when Short copied these notes he also copied Le Veillard's copy of that outline, it has been supposed that the two manuscripts might have been part of the same general project. That supposition is not altogether convincing, however; much in the outline is left out, and other information is added. These notes have the feel of being transcribed from a conversation during which BF may have simply referred to his outline as Le Veillard posed questions. (Le Veillard undoubtedly asked the name of BF's father, for example, which he misspelled.)
We believe that Le Veillard may have been asked by Brissot de Warville or Brissot's colleague Villar to write a biography of BF for publication; if so, these notes are what Le Veillard refers to in his letter to WTF of Oct. 16, below, when he promises that "ces nottes" would never be published without BF's approval.
Short's copy of Le Veillard's MS is published and discussed in *Jefferson Papers*, IX, 495–8. We reprint here the translation by Carl Van Doren,

At the age of twelve years Benjamin is apprenticed to one of his brothers aged twenty-two [twenty-one] years, printer at Boston, of a harsh and overbearing character. Benjamin, intelligent, skillful, and active, is very useful to his brother. He quarrels with him five years after going into his printing house. Leaves him. Finds no other place with the other printers of Boston, forewarned by his brother. Comes to New York. There was then only one printer, who cannot give him work and who advises him to go to Philadelphia where there are two of them. He sets off on foot. Arrives some days later at nine o'clock in the evening [morning, *according to the Autobiography*], having only two or three shillings and knowing nobody. He is received the next day into the house of Mr. Bradford. Quickly wins his friendship and that of his fellow-workmen. One may suspect that he was more clever than they.

Benjamin pleases M. William Keith, vice-governor, who desires him to establish himself at Philadelphia and promises him that he shall be printer to the government. He sends him to Boston to ask for assistance from his father, who finds him too young and refuses. He returns to New York and to Philadelphia and to London, where he [*blank space*] in his art. After staying there eighteen [nineteen] months he comes back with Mr. Denham, a merchant, and works in his business. He was then twenty years old. Mr. Denham dies after six months and leaves him a small legacy. He returns to printing, and forms a partnership with Hugh Meredith. It goes badly. Mr. Meredith leaves and goes to Carolina to cultivate his land [to buy cheap land there]. Benjamin receives assistance from two friends, establishes himself [*blank space*] works with the greatest assiduity for twenty years, and prospers.

In the month of October 1728 [1729] he founds [buys] and prints the *Pennsylvania Gazette*. It has the greatest success even among the people and is still continued by Benjamin's successors. He proposes and finds the means to set up by subscriptions a great number of useful establishments: a public library, a University, an insurance company for houses, an Academy of

---

retaining the corrections and supplemental information that he supplied in brackets.

Sciences, etc., etc. The date of his experiments in physics and of his writings may be found in his collected works.

In the same year 1728 [1729] Benjamin produces a pamphlet in favour of the increase of paper money because of the scarcity of specie. This work brings him much honour. The project succeeds. The State of Pennsylvania issues the paper money as a loan. The interest derived from it in time defrays the expenses of the government. Benjamin is appointed printer to the Assembly. In 1736 he becomes clerk of the Assembly and [in 1737] postmaster of Philadelphia. In 1741 [1747] he enlists the people in a defense of the province. He is in charge of the projects. Ten thousand men are trained in Pennsylvania, a thousand in Philadelphia. He is offered the command of the latter. He refuses. Proposes M. Laurent [Lawrence], who is accepted, and Benjamin serves as a private soldier. Batteries and new forts built by a lottery projected and directed by him.

In 1752 [1751] he is, without having asked for it, chosen to represent the city in the Assembly, and gives up the clerkship to his son William Franklin. He is continued in office to 1764, although he was sent as envoy to England in 1757.

In 1753 he is made postmaster general [joint deputy postmaster general] for [North] America. The Royal Society gives him a gold medal and elects him to membership without his having asked for it. He has received the same honour from a great many academies in Europe.

In 1754 [1753] he is employed by the government as plenipotentiary [one of three commissioners] to treat at Carlisle with the Shawnee and other savage nations from the Ohio; with the Delaware at [blank space for Easton, 1756]. He is sent in the same year [1754] to Albany as member of the first Congress convened by the king, and to treat with the Iroquois. He proposes the first Plan of Union of the colonies.

He receives in the war of 1755 the commission of lieutenant general [colonel] to defend the northwest frontiers of the province. He raises the troops and builds [blank space for forts or stockades]. The same year he gives great assistance to General Braddock. In 1757 he is put in charge of the affairs of Pennsylvania in London.

Benjamin returns to Philadelphia in 1762. His son is made royal governor of New Jersey.

Benjamin is sent by the Assembly of Pennsylvania to the Court of Great Britain to oppose the Stamp Act [primarily in 1764 to petition the Crown to take over the government of the province]. His examination in Parliament in 1766. His replies particularly contribute to the repeal of the Act. He remains in England till 1775, having been appointed by five [four] provinces as their agent. He opposes without success the tax on tea. The act passes in spite of him. The tea is burnt [thrown into the water] in Boston. Parliament, incensed, closes the port, and by various acts takes away privileges, forbids fishing, etc. Benjamin fears unpleasant consequences, and to prevent them offers to pay for the tea out of his own private fortune if Parliament will withdraw these acts. His offer is refused. He gives excellent advice to the minister and shows in several of his writings the bad policy of the administration, which is angry with him. It mistreats him, takes away his place as postmaster general in America, stops the payment of his fees as colony agent, and harasses him with a suit in Chancery.

He returns in 1775 to America. Encourages the colonies to defend themselves. The day after his return to Philadelphia the Assembly chooses him its delegate to Congress. He is at the same time chairman of the Committee of Safety for the defense of the city. He designs cheveaux de frise to hinder the approach of warships. This is a new invention which may serve to close ports. It has great effect. The English are held up by it for seven weeks. He is sent to confer on the army with General Washington.

In 1776 he is elected by Philadelphia to the [Pennsylvania] legislative Convention, and the Convention makes him its president. Congress sends him with two other members to Canada to regulate the affairs of the Army in that province. In the same year he is assigned with two others to parley with Lord Howe in September. In October of the same year he is sent to France on a vessel so frail that it was lost on its return. Takes two prizes on the voyage over. Arrives at the end of November 1776 at Nantes. Participates with his colleagues in the negotiations with France and England. A signer of the treaty of commerce and alliance with France, finally of that of peace with England on the most favourable conditions, stating and establishing, irrevocably and absolutely, the independence of his country.

He has since made [*blank space*] a treaty with Sweden. He had already come twice to France, in 1767 and in 1769.

To David Hartley   Copy:[6] William L. Clements Library

My Dear friend   Passy Oct 16 1783

I have nothing material to write to you respecting public affairs, but I cannot let Mr Adams who will see you[7] go without a line, to enquire after your welfare, to inform you of mine, & to assure you of my constant respect and attachment.

I think with you that our quaker article is a good one & that men will in time have sense enough to adopt it, but I fear that time is not yet come.[8]

What wd you think of a proposition, if I shd make it of a family compact between England France & America? America wd be as happy as the Sabine Girls, if she cd be the means of

6. In Hartley's hand and retained among his papers.

7. JA left Auteuil on Oct. 20 for what proved to be a two-month visit to England. He arrived in London on Oct. 26, was introduced by Hartley to the Duke of Portland, Edmund Burke, and Charles James Fox, and then proceeded to Bath in hopes of recovering his health: Butterfield, *John Adams Diary*, III, 146–52.

8. BF is referring to the article that he wished to see incorporated into the Law of Nations, guaranteeing protection during wartime for unarmed civilians "who labour for the common Subsistence and Benefit of Mankind"; see XXXVII, 610; XXXVIII, 444–5. He sent it to Hartley as soon as the latter arrived in Paris for the final round of peace negotiations the previous spring, and the American commissioners included it among the new articles they proposed, unsuccessfully, for the definitive treaty with Great Britain: XXXIX, 569–70; XL, 257–8, 438. In 1786, when writing to TJ, Hartley quoted from this article (which by that time had been codified in the 1785 Prussian-American treaty of commerce), using it to invoke a fundamental American principle of benevolence. He called it "our Quaker article, yours as first proposing; mine as first adopting": *Jefferson Papers*, IX, 316. His "adopting" of the article was not entirely apparent when he sent it to Fox in July, 1783; see XL, 257n.

uniting in perpetual peace her father & her husband.[9] (What repeated follies are these repeated Wars! You do not want to conquer & govern one another, why then shd you continually be employed in injuring & destroying one another)? How many excellent things might have been done to promote the internal welfare of each Country; What Bridges roads canals & other usefull public works, & institutions tending to the common felicity might have been made and established with the Money & Men foolishly spent during the last seven centuries by our mad wars in doing one another mischief. You are near Neighbours & each have very respectable qualities. Learn to be quiet & to respect each others rights. You are all Christians. One is the most Christian King, and the other defender of the faith. Manifest the propriety of these titles by your future conduct. By this says Christ shall all men know that ye are my Disciples if ye Love one another.[1] Seek peace and ensue it.[2]

Adieu yours most affectely   B FRANKLIN

To D Hartley Esqr.

From Samuel Cooper   ALS: American Philosophical Society

Sir,   Octobr. 16. 1783.

The Consul General of France[3] kindly informing me that a Vessel was on the Point of sailing for Brest, I have only a Moment to inform you that the House of Representatives for this State have this Moment passed an Act for a Duty of 5 pr Cent on all Goods imported for paying the Interest of our National Debt, according to the Requisition of Congress.[4] This

9. In the myth as told in Plutarch's *Romulus*, 14–19, Hersilia and the other Sabine women who had been carried off to Rome interposed themselves between the Roman and Sabine armies and brought about a reconciliation between their Sabine fathers and Roman husbands.

1. John 13:35.

2. 1 Peter 3:11.

3. Létombe, who was based in Boston.

4. Congress' resolution of April 18; see XL, 65n. The Mass. House of Representatives did not actually pass the bill until Oct. 17, though it had

Measure has met with uncommon Opposition here. Congress having voted to the Officers of the Army 5 Years whole Pay after the War instead of half pay for Life, a great popular Disgust took place in the N. England States. At the Beginning of the present Session of the Genl. Court, a great Majority of the lower House were warmly determined against granting the Impost to Congress, knowing that part of it would be applied to the Payment of the Officers. Near 40 Towns in this State had expressly instructed their Representatives against such an Impost. The Senate, however, judging more wisely, were almost unanimous in Favor of it. Both Houses remained firm in their Opinion, and it was concluded Nothing could be done on this Business, at least in the present Session— At this Juncture, the Governor who had before in his Speech to both Houses at the Meeting of the Court, endeavor'd to impress them with the Importance of supporting public Credit, made a second Address to them of the same Import. It produced a Conference between both Houses, and the Effect of all has been a Decision in the House of Representatives in Favor of the Impost— The Senate will no doubt concur & the Governor give his Consent immediately. The Struggle has been hard; 75 against 68.[5] I hope the other States will come into the same Measure, and lay a Foundation for the Support of our National Credit.

We have yet no Account of the Conclusion of the Definitive Treaty.

I hope my Grandson is now on his Passage to us— His Father assures me he has wrote to France and made Provision for his Return. His Affairs have been embarrassed, and I have not seen or received a Line from him for several Months— I am

---

voted approval of each paragraph the day before: Stephen E. Patterson, "After Newburgh: the Struggle for the Impost in Massachusetts," in *The Human Dimensions of Nation Making: Essays on Colonial and Revolutionary America*, ed. James K. Martin (Madison, Wis., 1976), pp. 232–5.

5. The final vote of the House was 72 to 65. On Oct. 20 the Senate concurred, and the impost bill became law. It would not go into effect until all the states had passed similar bills: Patterson, "Struggle for the Impost in Massachusetts," p. 235. The Mass. governor was John Hancock.

anxious about my dear Boy, and most earnestly wish his immediate Return.[6]

The Vessel waiting for this Letter, I have only to subscribe myself most respectfully & Affectionately Your's

SAML: COOPER.

His Excellency Benjn. Franklin Esqr.

Notation: Cooper Mr. Saml. Oct. 16 1783.—

From Louis-Pierre Dufourny de Villiers[7]

ALS: American Philosophical Society

Votre Excéllence   A Paris le 16— 8bre 1783.

L'Ingénieur françois qui a commandé au siége d'York-town, pour lequel je vous avois demandé audience,[8] n'a pu profitter de la faveur que vous luy avies accordeé, les lettres par lesquelles je luy en faisois part ne luy etant point parvenües, soit qu'il m'aie mal indiqué sa demeure, soit qu'il soit parti de Paris dans le même tems, ce qui me paroit le plus vraisemblable. Je vous fais mes remerciements de l'attention que vous aves eu pour ma priére et pour l'empressement qu'avoit cet officier de satisfaire à touttes les informations que vous auries jugés convenable de prendre de luy.

Je sollicitte encor aujourdhuy vos bontés, pour un Négotiant en draps, établi à Paris, lequel muni des Passeports et lettres de

6. Samuel Cooper Johonnot left France on Sept. 16. Gabriel Johonnot had asked BF to procure a passage for his son, which BF underwrote, along with his other travel expenses: XL, 59–60, 468–9, 507–8.

7. This is the final extant letter to BF from the sculptor and engineer. By 1789 Villiers was chief engineer of the city of Paris and continued in that capacity through the French Revolution, becoming president of the *département* of Paris in 1793. He was arrested during both the Terror and the Thermidorian reaction: Harvey Chisick, "An Intellectual Portrait of a Jacobin Activist: the Morality and Politics of Dufourny de Villiers (1789–1796)," in *Visions and Revisions of Eighteenth-Century France*, ed. Christine Adams, Jack R. Censer, and Lisa Jane Graham (University Park, Pa., 1997), pp. 105–33; Sellers, *Franklin in Portraiture*, p. 243.

8. His letter of March 29 recommending Querenet de La Combe: XXXIX, 407–8.

notre Gouvernement, se prépare à faire un voyage à Philadelphie, tant pour speculer sur diverses branches de son commerçe
que pour compter avec un correspondant. Ce Negotiant qui doit
avoir L'honneur de vous remettre la présente, sentant tout le
prix de votre protection, désire vivement qu'apres l'exposé qu'il
aura l'honneur de vous faire de ses motifs, vous luy accordies
tout l'appuy que votre caractére public et la vénération que l'on
vous porte peuvent luy assurer dans toutte l'etendue du térritoire
des États-unis. Je vous supplie d'avoir égard à sa priére. Je suis
avec le plus profond respect Votre Excellence Votre tres humble
et tres obeissant serviteur[9]   Dufourny de Villiers

From Hope & Co.[1]   ALS: American Philosophical Society

Sir   Amsterdam the 16 October 1783—
We presume on the Strength of the personal Acquaintance
we have the honour of & the Sentiments of Esteem inseper-
able from this advantage to present to You our estimable friend
William French Esqr., prior of the Firm of French Crawford &
Co. one of the most opulent & respectable Houses at Glasgow,[2]
who with Peter Spiers Esqr. a Young Gentlemen of Family
there are on a tour to Paris,[3] the former to Join his Son lately

9. On the verso of the signature page are two pencil sketches, presumably by BF, of devices we cannot identify. Whether BF assisted the unnamed
textile merchant is not known.
    1. This is the first extant letter from the firm since 1779 (XXVIII, 342–4).
The Hopes had first entertained BF at Amsterdam in 1761: IX, 367.
    2. William French (1732–1802), a tobacco merchant, was involved in
the Chesapeake trade through multiple firms, most notably the preemi-
nent Speirs syndicate discussed below. He was provost of Glasgow between 1778 and 1780 and a director of the Chamber of Commerce for
1783: T. M. Devine, *The Tobacco Lords: a Study of the Tobacco Merchants of
Glasgow and their Trading Activities, c. 1740-90* (Edinburgh, 1975), pp. 74,
115, 164, 180; *Plan for the Chamber of Commerce and Manufactures in the City
of Glasgow* . . . (Glasgow, 1783), p. 13.
    3. Peter Speirs was the son of French's late partner Alexander Speirs
(1714–1782), who began his career as a Va. plantation owner, returned to
Glasgow in the 1740s, and built several tobacco syndicates that made him
one of the wealthiest merchants in that city. Peter had been educated to the

returned from India & farther with the View of Soliciting your powerfull Assistance & Protection in a matter Depending in America which he will crave leave to lay before you.[4] We Shall esteem ourselves particularly happy if our Recommendation of Mr. French be an additional Motive to your Attention to his Concerns from the Interest we take in what regards him & from the flattering proof it will afford that we retain a place in Your remembrance.—

We Shall be proud on every Occasion of your Commands here to convince you of the particular and respectful Sentiments of Esteem & Attachment with which we have the honour to be.— Sir.— Your most Obedient humble Servants

HOPE & CO:

The Honble. Benjamin Franklin Esqr.—

Endorsements:[5] Mr James French / Mercht at Petersburg / James River Virginia / Lands in Prince Edward / Property

---

trade in France, Holland, and London, and after his father's death became a member of the Merchants House of Glasgow: Devine, *Tobacco Lords*, pp. 7–8, 26, 183; *Plan for the Chamber of Commerce*, p. 14.

4. The only clues to their conversation, which undoubtedly concerned how to reclaim sequestered property in America, are the notes BF jotted on the verso of this letter, published below as the first endorsement. Alexander Speirs, John Bowman, and William French were partners in various trading firms that imported tobacco from Virginia and Maryland. Speirs, Bowman & Co., of which French was a controlling partner, held numerous stores along the James River. In 1783, their attempts to recover property seized during the war were unsuccessful. Land belonging to "Spiers and company" in Prince Edward County, Va., was likewise litigated, as was French, Crawford & Co.'s property in Richmond: Devine, *Tobacco Lords*, pp. 71, 74, 76, 187; Memorial of Speirs, Bowman & Co., n.d. (Public Record Office); William W. Hening, ed., *The Statutes at Large; Being A Collection of All the Laws of Virginia* . . . (13 vols., Richmond and Philadelphia, 1810–23), XI, 392–3; *Sundry Resolutions and Proceedings, in Cases Before the Board of Commissioners* . . . (Philadelphia, 1799), pp. 90–2; Isaac S. Harrell, *Loyalism in Virginia: Chapters in the Economic History of the Revolution* (Durham, N.C., 1926), pp. 99–100, 161–2.

5. We indicate the line breaks in BF's first endorsement by means of single slashes and use a double slash to separate the first and second endorsements, which were written on different sections of the same sheet.

of Alexr Spears, John Bowman[6] & Compa.— // Hotel de York

Le Veillard to William Temple Franklin

ALS: American Philosophical Society

Dreux 16 8bre 1783

Sérieusement, Monsieur, vous avez cru que jallois faire imprimer ces nottes comme elles sont?[7] Sans doute il faut les etendre et les mettre en style, mais ce n'est pas mon affaire, cette besogne regarde mr. de Villars[8] amy de mr. de Condorcét qui ma vivement sollicité pour avoir ces renseignements; mon intention est d'éxiger qu'il ne fasse rien imprimer sans nous l'avoir communiqué j'en causerai avéc Le Grand pere de monsieur W. T. franklin et avéc monsieur W. T. franklin luymeme s'il veut bien avoir cette complaisance. Je retourne par cet éffet a Passy ou je compte les embrasser tous deux dimanche   LE VEILLARD

Voules vous bien dire a monsieur Benjamin autre petit fils de monsieur franklin que je le verrai avéc grand plaisir Le Lundy 20 le matin.

6. The former provost of Glasgow whose son, a Ga. planter, presumably met BF in 1777 and received a passport from him in 1780: XXV, 45–6; XXXIII, 230–1, 508; Devine, *Tobacco Lords*, p. 178.

7. Le Veillard is probably referring to his notes on BF's life that, based on this letter, we publish as [before Oct. 16?], above.

8. Noël-Gabriel-Luce de Villar was a professor of rhetoric at the Collège de La Flèche and friend to many *philosophes*, including Condorcet. Villar's interest in these notes may stem from his involvement in two of Brissot de Warville's literary endeavors: *Correspondance universelle sur ce qui peut intéresser le bonheur de l'Homme et de la Société*, which published its first issue in January, 1783, and the *Jour. du Licée de Londres*, which first appeared in January, 1784. Despite Villar's efforts to promote the *Correspondance universelle* in France, the journal ceased publication after November, 1783. The *Jour. du Licée de Londres* ran for a year. Though no biography of BF ever appeared in its pages, the *Licée* did publish its own French translations of BF's "Remarks concerning the Savages of North America" and "Information to Those Who Would Remove to America" (for which see [before Jan. 7] and [before March]): *Biographie universelle;* Claude Perroud, ed., *J.-P. Brissot:*

Addressed: A Monsieur / Monsieur William Temple / franklin secretaire de la commission / pour la paix ches monsieur / son grand pere / A Passy près Paris

Notation: Le Veillard Dreux 16 8bre 83

From John Baynes

ALS: American Philosophical Society

Sir—   Paris Octr. 17th. 1783.

I waited on M. l'Abbé Morellet both yesterday & today, but he was in the country—therefore I cod. not get the list which your Excellency was so kind as to write to him about—perhaps he will be obliging enough to favor me with it by the post to England.[9]

I shall certainly with great pleasure on my arrival in London communicate your message to the bishop of St Asaph.[10] Every friend to liberty & humanity must venerate his character.

A gentleman who sets off on Monday from the hôtel de Luxembourg for England has promised to bring any letters left there for me. If your Excellency have any letters, they will certainly arrive safe, if sent thither on Sunday Night, under cover to me at Greys Inn, *by favor of Mr. Smith.*

I have only one more favor to ask—which is that your Excellency will honor me so much as to keep the two books (Masons *English Garden* & Greys Poems)[1] as a small testimony of the regard, with which I am, Sir, Your Excellencys most obedt. & obliged humble Servant,   JOHN BAYNES.

Notation: Baynes Mr. John Oct. 17 1783.

Correspondance et papiers (Paris, [1912]), pp. xxi, 46–50, 74–7; Jean Sgard, ed., *Dictionnaire des journaux, 1600–1789* (2 vols., Paris, 1991), I, 265–6; II, 659–60.

9. For background on this note see Extracts of John Baynes's Journal (published under Sept. 23, above), entries of Oct. 12–17.

10. Jonathan Shipley.

1. See Baynes's letter above, Oct. 15.

From Mary Ann Davies

ALS: American Philosophical Society

Dear Sir.   Florence Octbr the 17th. 1783.

I took the liberty of writing You a Letter last April[2] to enquire after your Health. At the same time (not doubting the continuation of your friendship) I made so free as to trouble You with some account of my present Situation, entreating your Advice, but I am so unfortunate as never to have had any Answer. I have been and am still in the greatest Anxiety imaginable on this account and can only conclude that either the said Letter or your Answer must have miscarried: for surely had You received it, you would have favour'd me with a Line before now. I am doubly unhappy about this affair, between the disapointment of not hearing from You, and the fear of my Letter having fallen into other Hands. If You receive this as I hope you will, I beg most earnestly you will not retard writing that I may know as soon as possible if my former Letter went safe: and You will oblige me much by informing me if I have directed this quite right. I have thought of a method by which it appears to me I cannot fail receiving Yours, which is, if you will be so obliging to enclose your Letter (Seal'd and Directed for me) in a Blank Cover with the underwritten Direction on it. Excuse Dear Sir my being so troublesome and believe me to be with the greatest Gratitude and Respect Your most oblig'd & most humble Servant

MARY ANN DAVIES

A Monsieur
Monsieur Filippo
Mingoni
Firenze
Toscana.

ps— MY Sister does not know of this Letter no more than of that I troubled You with last April for the Reason I explain'd in the said Letter: therefore I must beg you will not mention to any one in Paris having heard from me.[3]

2. XXXIX, 504–9.
3. We know that BF intended to answer this (see his list of letters to write, printed under [c. Jan. 1, 1784?]), though no response has been found. Mary Ann and her sister Cecilia were still at Florence in 1784 or early 1785,

Addressed: A Son Excellence / Monsieur Benjamin Franklin / Ministre Plénipotentiaire des / Etats-unis de l'Amérique / Septentrionale prés S.M.T.Ch. / A Paris. / per la Francia

From Anthony Todd

LS: American Philosophical Society; copy: Royal Mail Archive

Dear Sir, General Post Office October 17th. 1783

I received on Tuesday Night last[4] at 12. the Letter you were pleased to write me the 9th: Instant, and consequently too late to thank you for it by that Post.

My Lord Foley and Mr Carteret are both in the Country at present, but I have not a doubt of their approving the plan d'Arrangement which you have put into French, exactly as you have drawn it out, and yet perhaps the latter part of it after the Words, sans tenir de Comptes, may be as well omitted,[5] and I have added a few Words to the proposed Advertisement from this Office, that Letters from hence for North America are to be put under Cover to Paris,[6] which must of course be approved,

---

when the English community there sponsored a private concert at which they performed. They seem to have been back in London by the middle of 1785, and despite favorable reviews they continued to struggle to support themselves and died in obscurity: [Richard Edgcumbe, Earl of Mount Edgcumbe], *Musical Reminiscences of an Old Amateur, for Fifty Years, from 1773 to 1823* (London, 1824), pp. 17–18, 41–54; [London] *Gazetteer and New Daily Advertiser,* July 2, 1785; *ODNB,* under Mary Ann Davies.

4. Oct. 14.

5. In the copy that Todd enclosed, he marked for deletion everything after "sans tenir de Comptes." In the English draft published above ([before Oct. 9]), the equivalent phrase "without Account" occurs in the middle of the penultimate paragraph.

6. Todd enclosed this new version of the advertisement he had sent on Sept. 19 with the additional paragraph inserted at the end: "Likewise all persons in Great Britain or Ireland desirous of sending any Letters for the United States of North America by the French Packet Boats are to cause them to be put under Cover to some Correspondent at Paris." BF lined through the word "North" and made several other changes, which he details in his response of Oct. 29.

and that you may the easier comprehend these small Alterations I inclose a Copy of both the Plan d'Arrangement and of the Advertisement as now proposed, and should be obliged to you for your Approbation of the Advertisement as soon as it may be in your Power, to be circulated in these Kingdoms in time for the November Mail from hence.

The Entrepreneur of the French Packet Boats seems very much to mistake the two Points upon which your Grand Son has had a Conversation with him; That of Persons interested in the respective Packet Boats writing viâ France or viâ England upon the Letters for Europe, which Letters can fall into no Hands except the Postmaster of New York and of other Places of the United States, but I cannot have an Idea of any thing so corrupt in them, and am however sure that nobody is or can be interested at New York in the postage of Letters for these Kingdoms, and therefore that Matter must stand as I have put it, without which almost half the Letters both for France and for England will be sent through the Channels they were not intended.

With respect to our Proposal, that it did not stipulate for Letters directed out of France and England, as for Hamburgh &ca. we can by our Situation have nothing to do with any such Letters, they must all belong to the French Conveyance, unless such as are put under Cover to London in both going and coming to or from Hamburgh and all such Places, for no Letter comes hither from thence nor goes from hence thither, for which we do not each way from the Situation pay a certain rate per Letter to the Post Offices of either Amsterdam, Brussels or Paris, all which is so perfectly well understood by the Baron D'Ogny, that if you should have an Opportunity to converse with him upon the Subject, you will be perfectly satisfied therewith, and that France by her Situation avails herself of this, which we cannot.

I shall be happy to hear your Indisposition is removed, for with true Respect, I am, Dear Sir, Your most obedient and most humble Servant.   ANTH TODD Secy

His Excellency Dr. Franklin at Paris.

To Edward Nairne

Reprinted from William Temple Franklin, ed., *Memoirs of the Life and Writings of Benjamin Franklin* ... (3 vols., 4to, London, 1817–18), III, 459.

DEAR SIR,   Passy, Oct. 18, 1783.

I received your favor of August 14,[7] by Mr. Sykes, with the book of directions for using your patent electric machine. The machine itself is also come to hand in good order, after some delay on the road;[8] and I think it very ingeniously contrived indeed: I wish your success in the sale may be equal to its merits. The experiments in your pamphlet gave me pleasure, and I shall be glad to see the account you mention of the shortening of wires by lightning.

What you have heard of the eyes of sheep forced out by a stroke of lightning which killed them, puts me in mind of having formerly seen at Philadelphia six horses all killed by lightning in a stable, every one of whom appeared to have bled at the eyes, nose, and mouth; though I do not recollect that any of their eyes were out.

You are so good as to consider how much my time has been and is taken up, and to excuse on that account my being a bad correspondent. Near three years ago I began a letter to you on the subject of hygrometers. I had written three folio pages of it when I was interrupted by some business; and before I had time to finish it I had mislaid it. I have now found it, and having added what I suppose I had intended to add, I enclose it.[9] You can judge better than myself whether my idea of such an instrument is practicable and may be useful.

If you favor me with another line, let me know how Mrs. Nairne does, and your amiable children.[1] With great esteem, &c. I am,   B. FRANKLIN

7. XL, 470–1.

8. This was the second machine shipped by Benjamin Vaughan, as the first had been damaged: XL, 176n, 235, 470.

9. Though the letter was not finished and copied until October, 1783, BF retained his original dateline of Nov. 13, 1780; see XXXIII, 518–23. It appeared under that date in the APS *Transactions* for 1786, and in WTF, *Memoirs*, where it is published as the enclosure to the present letter.

1. His daughters, Polly and Fanny, named in Nairne's reply of Dec. 2.

Edward Nairne's Patent Electrical Machine

From John Shaffer: Two Letters

(I) and (II) LS: American Philosophical Society

I.

Monsieur   Paris 18 Octobre 1783

Mr. L'avocat[2] qui a eu la bonté d'aller voir votre Excellence pour moi, m'a dit que vous vouliez bien avoir la bonté de m'avancer quelques secours pour mes alimens en attendant l'arrivée de Monsieur Barkely. Les obligations que je vous ai deja pour pareil service que vous avez bien voulu me rendre précedement, me fait espérer que vous ne me refuserez pas cette grace dans le cas pressent où je me trouve, malade et denué de tout, jusques à ce que mes effets sont dégagés, Vous pouvez compter Monsieur sur mon exactitude a vous rembourser ce que je vous dois. Je prendrai au reste ensuite avec vous tels arrangemens que vous croirez le plus convenable pour mon retour, ne desirant rien de plus que de vous donner les preuves de ma déference pour vos avis.[3]

Pardonnez moi, Monsieur, si me trouvant incommodé j'emprunte une main etrangère pour vous ecrire, et agreez les Sentimens respectueux avec lesquels j'ai l'honneur d'etre Monsieur De Votre Excellence Le très humble et très Obeissant Serviteur.   J. SCHAFFER

II.

                                    Paris le 18 Octr 1783

Si S. Excellence Monsieur le Dr. Franklin veut bien me remettre quelques deniers je le prie de le faire par la dame qui se charge de cette lettre, et qui a ma confiance.   J SCHAFFER

Addressed: A Son Excellence / Monsieur le Dr. Franklin / Ministre plenipotentiaire des Etats / Unis / à Passy.

---

2. Beaumont.

3. On Oct. 22 Shaffer reiterated in stronger terms his promise to leave Paris, as BF desired, as soon as he was released from prison. The letter is in French and written in an unknown hand (APS).

From Antoine-Alexis-François Cadet de Vaux

ALS: American Philosophical Society

Monsieur   ce 19 8bre. 1783

M. le lieutenant Général de Police fera mercredi 22 l'Installation du traitement Electrique, au couvent des célestins, près l'arsenal.[4] Je l'ai flatté du plaisir de S'y rencontrer avec vous, et ce magistrat Jouira de la double Satisfaction de réunir la cause et les effets c'est a dire l'auteur immortel de la découverte de l'Electricité et les Infortunés qui lui doivent le bonheur de leur Existence.[5]

En conséquence Permettés, monsieur, que Je vous propose le rendès vous pour mercredi 22 à 11 heures très précises aux celestins près l'arsenal. Le magistrat S'y rendra à cette heure là et il est communement fort èxact. De là nous irons à la halle au blé. Les architectes Sont prévenus et placeront le model et les dessins;[6] de là nous reviendrons diner chès moi, et Si M. de

---

4. Lenoir had just arranged for Nicolas-Philippe Ledru, known popularly as "Comus" (xx, 519–20), and one of his sons to open a government-sponsored clinic for electroshock therapy in the hospital of the former couvent des Célestins. In 1782 Ledru had asked the Faculté de médecine to examine his method of using electricity to treat epilepsy and other nervous disorders. They did so, encouraged by the duc d'Orléans, Vergennes, and Lenoir, and the report they published in June, 1783 (summarized at length in the *Jour. de Paris*), was overwhelmingly enthusiastic. Ledru was made a member of the Faculté with the title *physicien du roi*, and Lenoir provided him with a house where he could treat patients free of charge once they obtained the proper permissions. This experiment was deemed such a success that Lenoir arranged for Ledru to move to the couvent des Célestins in the fall: *Nouvelle biographie;* Geoffrey Sutton, "Electric Medicine and Mesmerism," *Isis*, LXXII (1981), 375–6, 380–1, 387–90; *Jour. de Paris*, June 8, 23, and 25; Nov. 28, 1783. By the following spring, however, when Ledru's results proved disappointing, the Faculté fought to regain control of the hospital: Bachaumont, *Mémoires secrets*, XXV, 219 (entry of April 9, 1784).

5. BF did attend this installation and demonstration, and was acknowledged for both his discovery of electricity and his early applications of it for medical purposes: *Jour. de Paris*, Nov. 28, 1783; Bachaumont, *Mémoires secrets*, XXIV, 48–9.

6. Architects Jacques-Guillaume Legrand and Jacques Molinos had only the previous month completed work on the dome, the largest in France, covering the municipal grain market, the Halle au Blé. Based on a carpentry technique invented in the sixteenth century, the dome consisted

Montgolfier à qui J'en Ecris peut disposer Sa machine,[7] nous irons apres midi.

Je Suis avec un profond respect Monsieur Votre très humble et très obéissant Serviteur   CADET DE VAUX

Rue des Gravilliers N° 16

From Silas Deane   ALS: University of Pennsylvania Library

Sir   London Octr. 19th: 1783

I am informed by Col Wadsworth,[8] and others lately from Paris, that it was currently reported of Me that I was intimate with Genl Arnold, and that a Pamphlet, lately published by Lord Sheffeild, owed to Me most of the Facts and Observations contained in it.[9] I have found by experience that from the Moment a Man becomes unpopular, every report which any way tends to his prejudice, is but too readily credited without the least examination, or proof, and that for him to attempt to contradict them in public is like An Attack on the hydra, for every falsehood detected, and calumny obviated, several new ones of the same Family come forward, this has well nigh rendered Me callous to the Attacks made on Me in this Way, yet it is impossible for Me, not To wish to stand fair

---

entirely of wooden beams and 25 large glass panels. The combination of the dome's size and its airiness and transparency fascinated contemporaries, including BF, who reportedly offered to install a lightning rod on its iron lantern. His concern about the dome's inflammability was well founded. In 1802 an accidental fire completely destroyed the edifice: Bachaumont, *Mémoires secrets*, XXIII, 277–8; Mark K. Deming, *La Halle au Blé de Paris, 1762–1813: "Cheval de Troie" de l'abondance dans la capitale des Lumières* (Brussels, 1984), pp. 175–88.

7. Etienne Montgolfier staged a series of manned balloon experiments—on Oct. 15, 17, and 19—at Réveillon's paper factory: see Le Roy to BF, [Oct. 19?].

8. Jeremiah Wadsworth (XXXVIII, 546) was a business associate of Silas Deane's brother Barnabas: *Deane Papers*, V, 172. During the war Wadsworth was an American agent in charge of supplying French troops, and in that capacity he went to Paris the previous July: XL, 263–4.

9. Nathaniel Falconer, who saw Deane in London, reported to BF that Deane had admitted writing part of Baron Sheffield's *Observations on the Commerce of the American States:* XL, 331–2.

in the Opinion, of those with whom I formerly acted, and with whose confidence, and Freindship, I have been more particulary honored, and this occasions my troubling You with this Letter. Though You have condemned Me of having been guilty of great imprudence, (and that justly) yet I have the satisfaction to know that You are still convinced of my Integrity, and fidelity whilst in The service of my Country, and whilst I had the honor of being Your Colleague;[1] and I wish to remove from Your Mind, if possible, every Idea of my having acted an unfreindly part, Toward the Interest of my Country, or of my having countenanced so notorious an Enemy as Genl Arnold by Associating with him, since my Arrival in this City. The next day after my being in London when I had no reason to suspect, that any one knew any thing of Me, save those, to whom I had sent Notice, of my being in Town, and of my Lodgings, I was surprized to find Genl. Arnold introduced into my Chamber, without being announced, by my Landlord untill he opened the Door, (my Circumstances, do not permit Me to keep a Servant.) Several Gentlemen were with Me, and among others Mr. Hodge[2] of Philada., I can most sincerely say, that I never was more embarrassed, and after a few questions on either part, and as cold a civility as I could use, consistent with common decency he took his leave,[3] You well know, that he is one, who never wanted for Assurance, or address, and as if We had been on Our former footing, he urged Me at parting to dine with him, which I civilly declined. The next Day I changed my Lodgings, and received from him, repeatedly, Cards of Invitation to his House, which I declined Accepting and in a few Days, he again called on Me, at my New Lodgings, in the same unceremonious manner as before, a Gentleman from America was then with Me, and remained in my Chamber, untill he left Me, on my parting with him on the stairs I told him very freely, that his Visits were disagreeable to Me, and could be of no service to him, that

1. See XXXVII, 172–3; XXXVIII, 468–9.

2. The merchant William Hodge, whose assistance to the privateer captain Gustavus Conyngham in 1777 had landed him in the Bastille: XXIV, 414–15.

3. In a July 25 letter Deane had told his brother Barnabas, "A remembrance of past personal civilities and of hospitality would not permit me to shut the door in his face": *Deane Papers*, V, 176.

I could not return them, except that I might call with Mr Sebor,[4] some Evening to pay Our respects to Mrs Arnold, from whom I had received, so many Civilities, in Philada., This We did, a few Evenings after, and from that Time, now more than five Months since, I have not seen him, except in his Carriage passing Me in the street.— I accidentally became acquainted with Lord Sheffeild, a few Days after my being in Town, I had no previous knowledge of his political Character, nor was I interested, To enquire what it was, I had no knowledge of his intention, (if in reality he then had any,) of writing on American Commerce, and of course I answered his queries, on the Subject, without reserve, there could be no ground for any, for the Answers which I gave, afforded no kind of information, not to be had from Thousands of Persons, as well or better informed on the subject, or even from the Custom house Books; I had but little acquaintance with any one in London and his Lordships polite Attention to Me, a stranger, naturally led Me to Visit him often, and without ceremony, and to form an intimate Acquaintance, in his Family, when he informed Me, of his design of writing, on the Subject. We had many Conversations on it, & in presence of Persons of Note, particularly of Sir Robt. Herries,[5] who with his Lordship, can testify, what my sentiments and mode of Reasoning was, & that I differed materially from those contained in the Pamphlet, yet such has been my Fate, that simply from my Acquaintance, and known Intimacy, with his Lordship, I have had Those Arguments, & principles, which I opposed, attributed To Me; his Object is, to secure to this Country the Carrying Trade, & to preserve the Navigation Act, from being in any degree altered, my Arguments have been to shew, that the Carrying Trade, beyond a certain degree, cannot be retained by this Country, that it is in Fact, already in great part, irrecoverably gone into other hands, and that the Navigation Act, though wisely formed for The Period, when it passed, wants many alterations, to adapt it to the present Times, and that like all other Acts, which respect Commerce, that it ought To be made Conformable, to the present Circumstances. This Sir, is a true state, of every thing that gives the least foundation, for those

4. Deane's secretary Jacob Sebor; see *Morris Papers*, VIII, 609, 613.
5. Whom Deane was using as a forwarding address: *Morris Papers*, VIII, 609.

Reports, and I have been the more particular that You, from a knowledge of the whole, may judge if I have merited the censures past on Me on their Account. I know none of the Ministers of this Country, unless it be by sight, I have not, or ever had any Connection with any of them, yet the Papers have mentioned My frequenting their Levies, dining with Them, &c[6] it would be endless To take notice of every report, of this kind, and therefore I let them pass, but whenever a Report to my disadantage, is likely to make an impression on one for whose good Opinion, I am so sollicitous, as for Yours, & one whom I think disposed, to do Me Justice, it becomes a duty to him, as well as to Myself, to place the whole in its True point of Light. I most sincerely thank You, for Your Wishes that my conduct may in future, be such as To regain That Esteem, and Confidence, of my Countrymen, which I once enjoyed.[7] But such new, & groundless Reports, daily arising, and so easily gaining Credit, make me almost despair of it, but of this You may be assured, that Nothing shall ever force Me, to be what these Reports would represent Me, to be, unfriendly to The Interests & prosperity of my Country. You will excuse the Length of this Letter; by Col Wadsworth on his return to France, I hope to put every objection to the Settlement of my Accts., out of the Way, and To obtain a final Settlement, in the meantime I have the honor to be, with great Respect Sir Your Most Obedt Huml Sert

S DEANE

His Excelly. Benja: Franklin Esqr

From Jean-Baptiste Le Roy   AL: American Philosophical Society

[October 19?, 1783][8]

J'ai lhonneur de vous souhaiter le bon Jour mon Illustre Docteur et de vous demander votre Ultimatum et celui de Monsieur votre

6. Deane was more specific about the allegations in his letter to his brother Barnabas—that he had attended a levee of the Duke of Portland and had dined with Fox, etc.: *Deane Papers*, v, 176.

7. XL, 423–4.

8. We date this letter based on two clues: Le Roy's suggestion that if BF wishes to witness Montgolfier's experiment he should leave Passy around

petit-Fils au sujet de Lexperience de M De Montgolfier.[9] Le tems ne s'annonce pas d'une manière trop favorable mais comme Le Brouillard tombe il pourra faire beau vers les midy. Si Monsieur votre petit fils vous mene il faudra partir à trois heures Car c'est encore plus loin que M. De Montalembert.[1]

---

3 P.M., and the allusion to fog. Among the six occasions on which Montgolfier launched balloons in Paris, three of them—the trials on Sept. 12 and 19 and on Nov. 21—took place earlier in the day. The much-anticipated experiment of Oct. 19, based on semiprivate, preliminary trials conducted on Oct. 15 and 17 (whose times are unknown), was scheduled for 4:30 P.M. According to the *Jour. de Paris*, the day was foggy, as the previous several days had been. Contemporary accounts, however, reported that the skies were clear at the time of the launch: Gillispie, *Montgolfier Brothers*, p. 47.

9. Montgolfier's October trials were the first manned balloon ascensions, designed to perfect techniques for controlling altitude and landing. His balloon was similar in size and design to the one destroyed on Sept. 12. Below the base he added a wicker gallery from which passengers could feed a burner suspended inside the balloon. The vessel remained tied to the ground with ropes. The passenger during the first tests was Jean-François Pilatre de Rozier, who had applied unsuccessfully to the Académie des sciences in August for permission to fly in Montgolfier's balloon at Versailles (XL, 550).

Réveillon was inundated with requests from the public to observe these experiments. As the date approached, he announced that the first trials could be attended only by the principals and scientists. His courtyard was small, and he would notify his correspondents as to when they could come: *Jour. de Paris*, Oct. 11, 1783. After the first trial on Oct. 15, however, news of the first-ever manned flight spread, partly through the efforts of Pilatre himself. Large crowds gathered for the following two experiments. On Oct. 19, before more than 2,000 spectators, Pilatre flew four times, twice with a co-pilot, ascending and descending at will and finally remaining at a height of 324 feet for at least nine minutes: Gillispie, *Montgolfier Brothers*, pp. 45–8; Barthélemy Faujas de Saint-Fond, *Description des expériences de la machine aérostatique de MM. de Montgolfier . . .* (Paris, 1783), pp. 268–78. We have found no evidence that BF attended any of the October trials.

1. Marc-René, marquis de Montalembert (1714–1800), military engineer, general, and member of the Académie des sciences, owned a house at 136 rue de la Roquette, where his wife hosted a popular salon: Larousse; Hillairet, *Rues de Paris*, II, 365. The residence was in the same faubourg as Réveillon's manufactory but northwest of it and therefore somewhat closer to Passy.

From Cadet de Vaux

AL: American Philosophical Society

ce 20 8bre 1783

Monsieur Brunier premier Médecin de Monseigneur le dauphin[2] est Venu avec M. Cadet de Vaux pour Se procurer l'honneur de Voir Monsieur franklin. M. Brunier desirant connaitre la maniere d'Electriser de M. Comus Se dispose à y Venir Mercredi.[3] Je lui ai proposé d'accompagner Monsieur franklin, dans le cas où cet arrangement pourait lui convenir.

En consequence M. Brunier qui est actuellement à la muette Envoyera Savoir demain mardi, Sil peut venir prendre Monsieur franklin Mercredi Sur les 10 heures du matin./.

M. Cadet de Vaux présente l'assurance de Son très humble respect a Monsieur franklin.[4]

Addressed: a Monsieur / Monsieur franklin Ministre / Plenipotentiaire des Etats unis / à Passy

From Francis Childs[5]

ALS: American Philosophical Society

Honored Sir.   New York October 20th 1783—

In addition to that Happiness which resulted from being honored with a Letter from Mr. Jay was that of perceiving myself

2. Pierre-Edouard Brunyer (1729–1811) had served as the personal physician to the royal children since 1775. In 1783 he married Antoinette Chappuis, the first lady-in-waiting to Marie-Thérèse-Charlotte, *Madame Royale.* The following year he became *conseiller d'état:* Danielle Gallet, ed., *Dans l'ombre de Marie-Antoinette: le journal de Madame Brunyer* (Paris, 2003), pp. 11–13.

3. The day that "Comus" would give a demonstration at his new clinic; see Cadet de Vaux to BF, Oct. 19.

4. A few weeks later, on Nov. 8, Cadet de Vaux asked WTF to remind BF that he was invited to dinner on Nov. 12, before the public session of the Académie des sciences (APS). BF's name does not appear in the academy's minutes for that session, but the *Mémoires secrets,* XXIII, 261–3, reported that Condorcet acknowledged BF during a eulogy for Sir John Pringle and congratulated him "de n'être plus Anglois."

5. This aspiring printer (1763–1830), born in Philadelphia to a family named Child, was known as Francis Child until February, 1785, when he added an "s" to his last name as he prepared to launch his first independent

noticed by you— Permit me to return you my most sincere thanks for your generosity shewn to me—[6]

I feel a pleasure in informing you that by application of Col. Smith to Sir Guy Carleton[7] the Press alluded to in Mr. Jay's Letter—your property, is now in my possession— I shall endeavour to make use of it in such manner as shall convince you that your condescending to favor me is not unmeritted— My ambition to shew myself as grateful as I sincerely am will always prompt me to make every return in my power—

---

venture, the *New-York Daily Advertiser.* John Jay had been Francis' sponsor ever since the boy's father died, providing for his education and arranging for an apprenticeship under Philadelphia printer John Dunlap. With Jay's encouragement, Childs moved to New York in 1783 (see the following note) and found employment with the printer John Holt. After Holt died in January, 1784, Childs continued to work for his widow, Elizabeth, until establishing his own printing house the following year. In the early 1790s Childs became the printer to the state of New York, and with his partner, John Swaine, he opened an office in Philadelphia and printed for the United States government: obituary in [Washington] *Daily National Intelligencer,* Oct. 27, 1830; *Morris Papers,* I, 113, 114n; Francis Childs to John Pierce, Feb. 11, 1784 (National Archives); Douglas C. McMurtrie, *A History of Printing in the United States* . . . (New York, 1936), pp. 161, 166–9, 297–9; *New-York Journal, and the General Advertiser,* Feb. 24, March 10 and 17, 1785.

6. Jay's letter of May 11 answered a now-missing appeal from Childs dated Jan. 1, proposing to establish his own press in New York after the British evacuated. Jay approved this plan, and assured Childs of his continued "aid and protection." BF was willing to lend the young man a printing press that had been confiscated by the British and taken to New York— where it was now "in the possession of one Robinson, a printer"—providing that Childs could reclaim it under the terms of the preliminary treaty. Jay would draw up a letter of attorney for that purpose, as BF had suggested. Furthermore, Jay pledged to furnish Childs with type, and added that BF had "promised his assistance." Details would be forthcoming, but in the meantime, Childs should write BF and thank him: Henry P. Johnston, ed., *The Correspondence and Public Papers of John Jay* . . . (4 vols., New York and London, [1890–93]), III, 45–6. For the confiscation of BF's presses by James Robertson, see XXIX, 598; XXX, 363–4.

7. Col. William Stephens Smith (*ANB*) was appointed by GW on May 8, 1783, to be one of three commissioners who would oversee the British evacuation of New York and the return of property belonging to citizens of the United States, pursuant to Art. 7 of the preliminary treaty (XXXVIII, 386): Fitzpatrick, *Writings of Washington,* XXVI, 412–14.

Be pleased to accept together with my best respects—my
most Sincere Wishes for your Happiness— I am Honored Sir,
Your Most obliged, & Obedient Humble Servant

FRANCIS CHILD—

Benj. Franklin Esqr.

Addressed: His Excellency / Benjamin Franklin Esqr. / Paris—

From the Marquis de Lafayette

ALS: American Philosophical Society

My dear Sir   Paris Monday Morning [October 20, 1783][8]
The famous William Pitt is just Arrived in Paris, and is just
Returning to London— He Has Expressed a warm desire to
Get Acquainted with You, and As I Hoped You would Come to
day to the American dinner, I Have invited Him together with
Lord Camden's, duke of Grafton's Sons, and two other of His
friends—it is Possible You will be Glad to know a Young Man
Whose Abilities and Circumstances are So Uncommon— So
that, Unless the Going Very Gently in a Carriage Hurts you,
You will do me an extreme pleasure to dine with us, as You
are the Center Upon Which Moves the Whole Party—[9] Butt I

8. The date of one of the most remarkable of the marquis and marquise
de Lafayette's Monday night dinners (for which see XL, 118n). The 18 at table included BF, WTF, Lewis Littlepage (XL, 563–4), the vicomte de Noailles
(XXVIII, 188n), the comtesse de Boufflers (XXXV, 20n), William Pitt the
younger, who was making his first and only visit to the continent (*ODNB*),
and four of Pitt's friends. These friends were William Wilberforce (XXXIII,
320n), George Henry Fitzroy, the future fourth Duke of Grafton (*ODNB*),
John Jeffreys Pratt, the future second Earl and later first Marquess Camden
(*ODNB*), and Edward James Eliot (Namier and Brooke, *House of Commons*, II, 390): Idzerda, *Lafayette Papers*, V, 158–9; Robert I. Wilberforce
and Samuel Wilberforce, *The Life of William Wilberforce* (5 vols., London,
1838), I, 41; Louis Gottschalk, *Lafayette between the American and the French
Revolution (1783–1789)* (Chicago, 1950), pp. 34–7.
9. Lafayette had sent BF an invitation to this dinner on Oct. 17; it was
an engraved form identical to the one published in XL, 118. Eight similar
engraved invitations to Monday dinners survive among BF's papers; seven
are addressed to BF and one is to WTF. Of the former, six have firm dates:

would not Have You do Yourself Any Harm on that Account—
Most Respectfully and Affectionately Yours   LAFAYETTE

From Jonathan Nesbitt & Co.

LS: American Philosophical Society

Sir   L'Orient. 20 October 1783—
    In consequence of orders received last winter from Philadel-
phia we desired our Correspondents at Nantes Messrs. David
Gallwey & Co.[1] to make Insurance on the Ship Nancy: Capt.
Shewell[2] to the Amount of One hundred and Seventy thousand Livres. They not being able to compleat the whole Sum,
gave orders to Mr. Richard Gallwey of Bordeaux[3] to Insure the
residue, which he effected: to the amount of Fifty one thousand
Eight hundred Livres a 25 ¼ per Ct. "in case she sailed before
the Cessation of Hostilities & 5 ¼. per Ct. only if after, or with
passports." Capt Shewell was detained in the Delaware by the
frost & contrary winds until the 20th March at which time he
sailed and arrived here the 1st May. We wrote immediately after
his arrival to our Correspondents both at Nantes & Bordeaux
informing them that as the Nancy did not sail until fifteen days

---

Dec. 18, 1783; Jan. 3 and 8, Feb. 10 and 26, and March 9, 1784. The seventh is dated only "*the 18 1784*", and must have been issued before the end
of June, when Lafayette left for America. The final example, addressed to
WTF, is dated March 30, 1784. All are at the APS except the one of March 9,
1784 (Columbia University Library).

    1. The firm is first mentioned as such in XXXVIII, 62, where we suggest it
consisted of David and his brother Andrew. In the spring of 1783, Barclay
had used them to ship supplies to America on the public account: Robert
Morris to Thomas Barclay, Feb. 12, 1784, *Morris Papers*, IX, 101–4.

    2. Robert Shewell of Philadelphia, owner and commander of the *Nancy:*
Robert Shewell to Congress, May 23, 1784 (National Archives). His ex-
tended family included merchants and shipowners: Richard K. Murdoch,
"Benedict Arnold and the Owners of the *Charming Nancy*," *PMHB*,
LXXXIV (1960), 31n.

    3. Richard Gallwey has been identified as the nephew of Andrew Gall-
wey, who had an interest in his firm: Paul Butel, *Les Négociants bordelais:
L'Europe et les îles au XVIIIe siècle* (Paris, 1974), pp. 174, 179.

after the cessation of hostilities, the Underwriters were entitled to 5 ¼ per Ct. only. Thus the matter lay until the latter end of last month when the Insurers at Bordeaux brought their Action on the Court of Admiralty against Mr. Richard Gallwey for the full premium of 25 ¼. per Ct. who was cast immediately without being allowed time to make a proper defence, or the adverse party producing any papers whatever in support of their claim, as you will perceive by the inclosed copy of Mr. Richard Gallwey's Letter on that subject, to which we request your attention, as it sets that matter, in our opinion in a very clear & proper light—[4] We should be sorry to trouble your Excellency in trivial matters but this we apprehend is an affair of consequence, not only to the persons in America by whose orders we made the Insurance (who if the cause is finally determined against us will lose unjustly about Forty thousand Livres) but to the Americans in general residing in this Kingdom against whom the Courts of Justice in all causes whatever are too ready to decide with great precipitation & in our opinion with some degree of partiality; but when it is *quite* evident that the Sentence when given *must* be in their favor, the Adverse party may train the cause to Eternity, a proof of which we have in the Court of Admiralty of Dunkirk, where a Cause of Insurance of the utmost consequence to us has been depending for upwards of Six Months, and our friend there writes us that he finds it impossible to obtain a sentence.— Thus cruelly situated it is to your Excellency alone that we can apply for redress; which no doubt we shall obtain immediately on your application to the Comte de Vergennes, before whom we request you will lay Mr Gallwey's letter. We took the liberty to write him the 29. Ulto. requesting an explanation of the

4. Gallwey's letter to Nesbitt & Co. is dated Oct. 11, 1783. The court, he complains, rendered their decision precipitately and with partiality. He requested a delay so that he could procure BF's opinion on the subject of captures and a certificate from Messrs. Arnoux of Nantes, who had had a ship captured around the same time as the *Nancy* sailed that was taken into Bermuda and released. This request was denied. Gallwey has just received an Oct. 3 letter from Nesbitt enclosing a copy of BF's statement. He intends to appeal to the *parlement*. If Vergennes' response to Nesbitt is favorable, their success is assured. If not, it will be too expensive to proceed. If Vergennes says nothing, BF's "declaration" will be important, but Gallwey would need the original, "as a Copy can be of no use." APS.

22nd. article of the preliminary treaty between France & Great Britain but have not yet been honored with an answer. We beg that in your first conference with him you will point out the necessity of his granting a Certificate similar to that which you gave to Mr. J. Williams,[5] which in our opinion will at once settle the dispute subsisting between us & the Insurers at Bordeaux relative to the Nancy. We have the honor to remain with sentiments of the greatest respect Your Excellency's most obedt humb servts.

JONATN: NESBITT & CO:

P.S. Perhaps your Excellency may think it improper to lay the latter part of Mr Gallwey's letter before the Comte de Vergennes

His Excellency Benj: Franklin Esqr.

Addressed: Son Excellence / Benjamin Franklin Ecuyer ministre / plénipotentiaire des Etats Unis de L'Amerique / à La Cour de France, à Son hôtel / à Passy—

Endorsed: Mr Nesbit's Affair respecting Capture after the Peace—

From Sir Edward Newenham

ALS: American Philosophical Society

Dear Sir   20th October 1783

Every hour of my Life induces me most Gratefully to commemorate the Æra, that first made me acquainted with the Virtuous Heir of ancient Roman Patriotism; this day I had the honor of your Excellencys of the 2d Inst: at the same time that I

---

5. On July 2 JW requested from BF a signed certificate declaring that vessels captured in any longitude north of the Canary Islands were protected according to the timetable stipulated in Article 22 of the preliminary treaty. He needed it to settle an insurance dispute concerning a ship that sailed from Philadelphia on March 10: JW to WTF, July 2, 1783 (APS). JW had first requested clarification of Article 22 in February, shortly after the preliminaries were signed, and BF prepared what appears to have been a circular letter: XXXIX, 171–2.

had one from Philadelphia, mentioning a *hope* that this Independant Kingdom would be included in the Commercial Treaty—[6]

I had determined on the first day of the meeting of our Parliament to have introduced that Subject, but a dangerous disorder in my bowels has Obliged me to Keep my room untill this
day, when I ventured down stairs; the late rains have been so
incessant, & the air so damp & foggy, that this disorder in the
Bowels has Carried off great Numbers, particularily my ever to
be lamented friend Mr Baron Burgh; He was the mover of the
Amendment—a Free Trade—he was my Second in Stopping
more troops being sent to America—he was a warm friend to a
Parliament Reform, & he would have proved a Valuable acquisition to the house of Lords, as Appeals are now to be tried before
them; for I am Sorry to Say, we have not ten Lords fit, competent or proper to Judge Appeals; I would rather (if our Constitution could permit it) have our appeals tried in any Country
than this,—Mr Burgh pleaded my Cause against the Crown for
8 years & finaly cast them, but never accepted of a fee—he first
encouraged the Cotton Manufacture, which is now well Established—he died, almost a Pauper—but Parliament have recommended his Orphan Children to Government; he was a faithfull
friend & a Virtuous Citizen; Pardon this digression!—[7]

6. The letter, from an unknown correspondent and dated Sept. 4,
urged Newenham to call for the explicit inclusion of Ireland in an Anglo-
American commercial treaty and for the appointment of Irish consuls in
American ports. Newenham presented it to the Irish Parliament on Oct. 27,
characterizing its author as a "gentleman . . . of the first consequence in
the state of Virginia." He also paraphrased the third paragraph of BF's
Oct. 2 letter, calling its author "a nobleman of exalted rank and character in
France": *The Parliamentary Register: or, History of the Proceedings and De-
bates of the House of Commons of Ireland . . .* (17 vols., Dublin, 1784–1801),
II, 27–8.

7. Walter Hussey Burgh (1742–1783) served as M.P. for Athy (1769–76)
and Trinity College, Dublin (1776–82), and was an outspoken advocate
for the repeal of English restrictions on Irish trade and for Irish legislative independence. In November, 1775, Burgh and Newenham voted in the
minority against the deployment of Irish troops to America. Despite his
prominence as a reformer, Burgh was appointed chief baron of the exchequer in 1782. After his death on Sept. 29, 1783, his five children received
an annual pension of £2,000: *ODNB;* Homer L. Calkin, "American Influence in Ireland, 1760 to 1800," *PMHB,* LXXI (1947), 108–9.

Our Linnens have had a Quicker & better sale than last year, & Larger returns in Specie; and a good deal have been sent to Different parts of america; our Manufacturers are more carefull and more Exact in their work, than formerly; but the Trade of this City in Woollens is very Low, many hundreds are starving, & thousands out of Employment; as the Shops are overstocked; however I hope a very Short Time will releive them; I shall move a Clubb that I am in, to give a grand Maskqued Ball to 5 or 600 persons; this will circulate 2 or 3000 pound;[8] a Number are gone and others going to America, but they complain very much of the Cruelty of the Captains of the Ships; this hinders some of the Better Sort of People from going; In Leiu of those we are getting some Germans & some Genevans—

Should the Roman Catholics obtain Votes here, Even those worth £50 a year, they would out-poll the Protestants by such considerable Majorities, that no Protestant Candidate could Carry a Single County or free City in Ireland, & Should they have a parlement of their own, they would soon revise the acts of Settlements & *forfeitures;* they would serve us, as the Scotch & American Rebels intended to have served the friends of Liberty in america, had Tyranny prevaild over Virtue— In Some Counties the Papists of £100 a year, outnumber *all* ranks of Protestant Electors; they have every other Freedom; however, this Important Subject has not been publickly agitated; nor will it untill the Grand Convention meets on the 10th,[9] when I think it will be warmly & *Closely* contested, but if it should pass there, I do not think it will pass Either house of Parliament, as the Commons will not readily pass a Law to prevent their Heirs from Sitting in Parliament;—we have a new Sight here—a Bishop preaching in favour of Popery—Clad in Military array—& accepting of a Commission as General & Delegate—his address to his Corps is bad English & very poor; I Expected something

8. There is no evidence that this benefit masquerade ball took place: James Kelly, *Sir Edward Newenham, M. P.* . . . (Dublin, 2004), p. 200.

9. The delegates to the Sept. 8 Dungannon convention of Ulster Volunteers had debated whether to include Catholic enfranchisement in a plan for parliamentary reform. They deferred a decision to the Grand National Convention in Dublin: Patrick Rogers, *The Irish Volunteers and Catholic Emancipation (1778–1793)* . . . (London, 1934), pp. 96–8.

Grand & sensible from him, but alass, Parturiunt Montes nas-
cetur ridiculus mus[1]—one Earl of Bristol was Vice-roy, & this
Bishop wants to succeed his Brother—[2]

I find my Daughter, at Marsailles, is near having a French
Newenham; the Consulship would be Very acceptable to that
house—[3] She intends to pay us a Visit in the Spring, & to pass
through Paris—

Permit me most Earnestly (as a friend to the Welfare of Ireland which I am convinced you are) to Entreat you will give
me any Instructions for the benefit of the Irish Trade that may
occur to you—and also, that you will (if the treaty is not finaly
concluded) acquaint the Ministers who are to Sign, that I have
assured you, *that Measure* will be mentioned in the Irish Parliament on the 27th Instant, & therefore hope they will wait the
result of it; I mean to agitate it myself; the Issue of which I shall
immediatly have the Honor of communicating to your Excellency— Permit me also to Enquire if it is not necessary, that we
should have Consuls in some one or two Towns in America, &
whether it is not intended that the United states should have one
or more in Ireland? because I would wish to have that done by
us before the Adjournment of this Session; a Friend of Mine at
Philadelphia urged this matter to me.

Lady Newenham, with Every sentiment of the warmest respect & Esteem, most thankfully acknowledges your obliging

1. Mountains will labor, to birth will come a laughter-rousing mouse:
Horace, *Ars Poetica*, line 139, in *Satires, Epistles and Ars Poetica*, trans.
H. Rushton Fairclough (Cambridge, Mass., and London, 1961), pp. 462–3.

2. Frederick Augustus Hervey, fourth Earl of Bristol and Bishop of
Derry (XXX, 319; *ODNB*), was a colonel of the Londonderry corps of the
Volunteers and served as one of its delegates to the Dungannon meeting,
which he addressed in a combination of military and ecclesiastical attire,
and later to the Grand National Convention. He was a longtime proponent
of religious toleration and one of the most prominent advocates of Catholic
emancipation within the Volunteer movement. His enemies accused him of
trying to succeed his brother George William as lord lieutenant of Ireland
or even using the Catholics to set himself up as king of Ireland: Rogers,
The Irish Volunteers and Catholic Emancipation, pp. 95, 105–12.

3. This is the fourth time that Newenham recommended Jean-Christophe
Hornbostel, the business partner of his son-in-law François-Philippe
Fölsch, as the American consul in Marseille: XXXVIII, 306–7; XXXIX, 356.

remembrance of her; and entreats your Acceptance of her sincere wishes for your perfect Enjoyment of Every happiness; I may possibly be partial, but I must say, I adore her as a friend & Companion—all my family join me in respects to your Excellency, & best wishes to your Grandson—

I have the Honor, to be, with due Respect your Excellencys most Obliged & most obt Hble: Servt   EDWARD NEWENHAM

PS: we are anxious for the Treasure of THE Bust—[4] Galway Election has lasted 5o days, 5oo has polled for 2 Candidates & 4oo for the other two. Such an Election was never heard of—[5]

Addressed: His Excellency B: Franklin / Passy / Paris

4. BF evidently promised Newenham and his wife a bust of himself after they met in the fall of 1782; see XXXVIII, 303. Writing to WTF three days before the date of the present letter, Newenham mentioned that his wife longed to place the bust in the couple's new study and that it could be shipped on a merchant vessel sailing out of Bordeaux. A plaster cast after the bust that Caffiéri had fashioned in 1777 was ready for shipment by mid-November. It never arrived at its destination, and in the fall of 1784 Newenham renewed his appeals, which were ignored until BF began making plans to return to America. L'Air de Lamotte placed an order for another plaster cast on March 12, 1785, and it had been shipped by month's end. Newenham acknowledged its receipt in early June: XXV, 266–7 and illustration facing p. 266; Newenham to WTF, Oct. 17, 1783 (APS); Caffiéri to WTF, Nov. 16, 1783 (University of Pa. Library); Newenham to WTF, Oct. 28, 1783; Newenham to BF, Sept. 29, 1784, [Oct. 9, 1784], Dec. 14, 1784; Lamotte to Caffiéri, March 12, 1785; Caffiéri to WTF, March 31, 1785; Newenham to BF, June 4, 1785 (all at the APS).

5. Supporters of parliamentary reform in County Galway nominated two candidates to challenge the incumbents, William Power Keating Trench and Denis Daly, who were well-known opponents of the Volunteer movement. After 52 days of voting, the local sheriff called the election in favor of Trench and Daly: Edith M. Johnston-Liik, ed., *History of the Irish Parliament, 1692–1800* . . . (6 vols., Belfast, 2002), IV, 7–8; VI, 439–40; James Kelly, "The Politics of 'Protestant Ascendancy': County Galway, 1650–1832," in *Galway: History & Society,* ed. Gerard Moran (Dublin, 1996), pp. 252–3.

From Anne-Louise Boivin d'Hardancourt Brillon de Jouy

AL: American Philosophical Society

ce lundi avant de partir [after October 20, 1783?][6]
Adieu mon bon papa, en Vérité il m'en coutte presqu'autant
d'aller á paris que d'aller a Nice;[7] pourtant je viendrai vous voir,
le coeur me dit que vous pourrés venir aussi; pourqu'oi donc estre si beste? C'est que j'aime beaucoup le bon papa et que quand
on aime Si fort, on est toujours un peu beste au moment de se
quittés:

Mille tendrésses de tous les miens; amitiés aussi pour le petit
fils qui n'ayant pas la goutte est instamant priés de venir nous
donner des nouvélles de la vostre le plus souvent qu'il pourra:

Le bon papa veut il se chargér d'embrassér la jolie mde caillot[8]
pour lui et pour moi, toutes les fois qu'il la vérra:

Addressed: A Monsieur / Monsieur Franklin / [In another hand:]
A Passy

---

6. This letter signals Mme Brillon's move from Passy to Paris, where the
previous March she and her husband had purchased the elegant Hôtel de
Mailly on the rue des Vieilles Haudriettes in the Marais. The date of their
move is not known. It was probably after Oct. 20, when their daughter
Cunégonde married Lt. Col. Antoine-Marie Paris d'Illins; the marriage
contract, signed on Oct. 13 (Archives nationales), lists both mother and
daughter as living at Passy. The young couple also moved into the Hôtel
de Mailly, and Mme Brillon established it as her main residence, though
she continued to visit her other homes: Bruce Gustafson, "Madame Brillon
et son salon," *Revue de Musicologie*, LXXXV (1999), 301, 315; information
on the purchase of the hôtel and the addresses on the marriage contract
were kindly provided by Professor Gustafson. Paris d'Illins is identified in
Jacques and Noel Charavay, *Les Généraux morts pour la patrie, 1792–1871*
(2 vols., Paris, 1893–1908), II, 61–2.

The Brillons sent BF a printed wedding announcement (undated, APS)
on which BF wrote, "They were married Monday Oct. 20, 1783". In 1781
BF had proposed that Cunégonde marry WTF, but the Brillons rejected the
idea: XXXIV, 560–3.

7. Where she had gone in September, 1781, to recover her health:
XXXV, 513.

8. Blanchette Caillot.

From Jean-Baptiste Le Roy

AL: American Philosophical Society

Mon Illustre Docteur   Mardy matin [October 21, 1783][9]

J'ai passe hier chez vous et j'ai èté bien fache de ne vous y avoir pas trouvé car malheureusement J'ai poussé de là Jusqu'à Paris d'ou je suis revenu trop tard pour vous aller défier aux èchecs. M. Argand m'a dit hier que M. De Montgolfier avoit appris que vous désiriez voir une Expérience de Son ballon tout à votre aise et avec peu de monde et m'a chargé de vous demander ce qui en est et Si L'avis est vrai quel Jour vous conviendroit par Exemple demain parcequ'il a appris en même tems que vous alliez dîner chez M. Cadet de Vaux ruë des Gravilliers ce qui n'est pas très loin de la ruë de Montreuil[1] un mot de réponse Mon Illustre Docteur Sur vos intentions a ce Sujet afin que je puisse en faire part à M. De Montgolfier ou à M Argand qui doit envoyer ce matin.

Je compte Si vous êtes chez vous ce Soir Mon Illustre Docteur aller me dédommager de ce que Jai perdu ces deux Jours cy.

Addressed: a Monsieur / Monsieur Franklin

To David Hartley

Reprinted from William Temple Franklin, ed., *Memoirs of the Life and Writings of Benjamin Franklin* ... (3 vols., 4to, London, 1817–18), II, 439.

Passy, Oct. 22, 1783.

I received my dear friend's kind letter of the 4th instant from Bath, with your proposed temporary convention which you desire me to shew to my colleagues. They are both by this time

---

9. Dated in part by the allusion to BF's dining the next day with Cadet de Vaux, who had invited BF for Wednesday, Oct. 22: Cadet de Vaux to BF, Oct. 19. The other clue concerns Montgolfier's test flights of his balloon in Réveillon's courtyard, which were concluded on Oct. 19 before a huge crowd; see Le Roy to BF, [Oct. 19].

1. Cadet de Vaux lived at 16, rue des Gravilliers. No. 31, rue de Montreuil was the location of the Réveillon manufactory, in whose courtyard Montgolfier constructed and tested his balloon: Hillairet, *Rues de Paris*, I, 604; II, 161.

in London, where you will undoubtedly see and converse with
them on the subject. The apprehension you mention that the
cement of the confederation may be annihilated, &c. has not
I think any foundation. There is sense enough in America to
take care of their own china vase. I see much in your papers
about our divisions and distractions, but I hear little of them
from America; and I know that most of the letters said to come
from there with such accounts are mere London fictions. I will
consider attentively the proposition above mentioned against
the return of my colleagues, when I hope our commission will
be arrived. I rejoice to hear that your dear sister's recovery advances, and that your brother is well:[2] please to present my affectionate respects to them, and believe me ever, yours &c.

B. FRANKLIN

From Geneviève-Elisabeth Belamy Le Veillard

L:[3] American Philosophical Society

mercredy 22 8bre 1783

Me. Le Veillard souhaite le bonjour a monsieur franklin et le
prie de venir ce soir prendre le Thé avéc elle.

From John Curwen[4]

ALS: American Philosophical Society

Honourd Sir—   Little Broughton Octr. 23d. 1783—
You may truely be surprized at the Receipt of a Letter from
a Stranger (a Person in a remote Corner in England, a Coun-

2. His half brother, Winchcombe Henry (XXXVI, 624n). BF may have
heard this news from Richard Scrope, who had recently arrived bearing an
introduction from Hartley (above, Oct. 11).
3. In her husband's hand.
4. We have found no record of a response from BF, but Curwen (1749–
1825) was the kind of emigrant he would have encouraged. The "ploughman" did liquidate his property, as he proposed to do in this letter, and
sailed to Philadelphia in mid-1784, sending for his wife and children the following year, when he purchased a farm outside the city. He signed an oath

try with which you have been at War) & one who is not ambitious of aspiring above the humble Rank of a Ploughman.
I have often of late had a great Desire to write to you, & as
often suppress'd it, for when I compared my own Insignificancy
with your justly admired Abilities, & exalted Station I thought
I shou'd be deemed a Fool & a Madman. But, Sir, Your well
known Humanity, & liberal Sentiments, & the Want of Satisfactory Information which I cou'd wish to obtain relative to
America have at last induced me to take up the Resolution of
Queen Esther, & shou'd I like her obtain my Request I wou'd
esteem it the greatest Favour ever conferred upon me. I have
always been an Advocate for equal & universal Liberty, consequently one of that Rebellious Crue who wish'd well to the
Americans in the late noble Strugle, that Contest being ended
through the Blessing of Providence, & to your imortal Honour. I wish for Nothing more ardently than to become a Citizen
amongst you. But the late Accounts from America relative to
the Treatment of the Loyalists (though I'm not surprised at that)
that the English indiscriminately will suffer the same Fate, &
that there is Nothing but Anarchy & Confusion amongst the
Americans themselves furnish my Friends with fresh Arguments to disuade me from going; what better Treatment, say
they, do you expet, how will they know you were a Friend to
them &c. &c. As I look upon these Accounts to be greatly exaggerated, if at all true, they have made very little Impression
upon me, but when a good Oppinion is once entertained, it is
possible one may be a little Partial, & shou'd I dispose of my
small landed Property here (wch. before the War wou'd have

---

of allegiance on Aug. 15, 1785, and joined the Philadelphia Society for Promoting Agriculture, becoming friends with Charles Thomson, a neighbor
and fellow member of the Society, and John Vaughan. He subsequently purchased other lands, built roads, became a captain of the militia, was named
superintendent of the turnpike, and became a justice of the peace and president of his church. When sending Curwen a copy of his *Notes on Farming*
in 1788, Charles Thomson wrote that he hoped Curwen would keep notes
and "favour this country which you have adopted for your own . . . with an
account of your experiments & success." Patricia Talbot Davis, *A Family
Tapestry, Five Generations of the Curwens of Walnut Hill . . .* (Wynnewood,
Pa., 1972), pp. 3–4, 8–10, 13–14, 16–17, 20; Smith, *Letters*, XXV, 434.

sold for £2000) & emigrate to America with my Wife & Family (we have been married six Years) & there meet with the dismal Reception which is painted out to us, the mortification wou'd be inexpressible.— If Hond. Sir, from the great national Concerns in which you are engaged, you cou'd spare a few Moments, & condesend to give me the necessary Information for so great an undertaking (for I thought of going next Spring & shou'd be preparing for it) & inform me how Land sells &c.— If the Accts. prove favourable, it wou'd have a great tendency to reconcile my Wife (whose Timourousness is one Reason for my presuming to trouble you in this manner) confer the greatest Obligation upon me, & perhaps the only & best Return I may ever be able to make, shall be my fervent Prayers for your present & future Wellfare.

I am Hond. Sir Your most obedient & hble. Servt.

JOHN CURWEN

P.S. Please, direct to me at Little Broughton near Cockermouth Cumberland.— Many of my Neighbours tell me if I send them a good Acct. of America after I get there, they'll follow me.

Notation: Curwen Oct 23. 1783—

From the Comtesse de Golowkin: Two Letters

(I) and (II) ALS: American Philosophical Society

[after October 23, 1783][5]

I.

à Paris, rue Basse du Rempart. Nro. 15.

Je ne suis arriveè à Paris, mon cher et bon Papa, qu'avant hier au soir, j'ai fait un sèjour de trois Semaines à St. Germain, ou je me suis plû extremement, nous avons bien parlè de vous, mon Papa, et vous avès là, comme partout ailleurs de bons amis, et de Zélès

5. The publication date of part I of the *Phil. Trans.*, LXXIII (1783), which the comtesse requests here: *Public Advertiser*, Oct. 18, 1783. These are the comtesse's final extant letters to BF.

admirateurs. Au premier jour, vous me verrès arriver chez vous, *en Globe,* à moins que je ne prefère de marcher sur la rivière, sans me mouiller les Souliers, c'est le Siècle des miracles, il ne faut plus douter de rien.

Je vous suplie, mon cher Papa, de vouloir bien me prêter pour 24 heures, le dernier Volume des Transactions Philosophiques, de l'academie de Londres, ou il y à le Mèmoire du Chevalier Hamilton sur le tremblement de Terre, de la Calabre,[6] je vous en aurai la plus grande obligation, et vous le rapport[erai][7] tout de suite, car je compte au plutôt venir vous embrasser et [vous] dire que je vous aime [avec(?)] tout mon Coeur.   LA [*torn*]

Addressed: à Monsieur / Monsieur le Docteur Francklin / à Passÿ

II.

Vous êtes bien aimable, mon cher Papa et je vous remercie un million de fois de vos bontès, vous voÿès mon exactitude à vous renvoÿer le Livre, malheureusement ce n'est point celui que je dèsire d'avoir, et que je vous suplie mon bon Papa, de vouloir bien me renvoÿer en place de celui ci; c'est à dire

Philoso: Trans: Vol. LXXIII. for the Year 1783. Part. 1.[8]

Aÿès la bontè mon aimable et cher Papa de faire remettre le susdit Volume, à la personne qui rapporte celui ci— Je suis bien impatiante d'aller vous embrasser et de vous dire que je vous aime bien tendrement.   C. GOLOFKIN

Addressed: à Monsieur / Monsieur le Docteur Francklin / a Passy

6. Sir William Hamilton, "An Account of the Earthquakes which happened in Italy, from February to May 1783," *Phil. Trans.,* LXXIII (1783), 169–208.

7. The lower right corner of the manuscript, including most of the comtesse's signature, is torn off. We supply missing text in brackets.

8. It appears that BF, following the comtesse's request for "le dernier Volume," sent her part II for 1782, which he had received in September, 1783, without checking whether it contained Hamilton's paper: XL, 617n.

From the Comte de Vergennes[9]

LS: Library of Congress; L (draft): Archives du Ministère des affaires étrangères

A Fontainebleau le 24 8bre. 1783

Je crois, Monsieur, devoir vous adresser la copie de la réponse que j'ai reçue de M. le Maal. [Maréchal] de Castries, ainsi que de la piéce qu'il y a jointe relativement à la Saisie faite à l'Orient par le Sr. Pachelberg d'armes et de munitions dont le Sr. Barclay demande la mainlevée.[1] Vous y verrez, Monsieur, les raisons que le Sr. Puchelberg allégue pour prouver l'impossibilité où il est de se prêter à cette réquisition. Je vous prie de communiquer le tout au S. Barclay. C'est à lui à faire connoitre les motifs qu'il peut avoir à alléguer pour détruire ceux sur les quels on fonde le refus de la mainlevée qu'il sollicite.

J'ai l'honneur d'être très sincerement Monsieur, votre très humble et très obéissant serviteur   DE VERGENNES

M. Franklin

From David Hartley

ALS: Library of Congress

My Dear friend   Golden Square Oct 25 1783

As short days & winter weather approach I have sent you the 12 yards of Scarlet Welsh flannel wch you requested me to bring

9. This letter finally answers the letters that Thomas Barclay and BF had written to Vergennes in July concerning the attachment of American arms in the arsenal at Nantes by Puchelberg & Cie. Vergennes forwarded their letters to Castries on Aug. 15, underscoring the merits of their case: XL, 407–9. Castries answered Vergennes on Aug. 31: he was instructing Clouet, the *commissaire de marine* at Lorient, to send him an account and to direct Puchelberg to lift the attachment. (A notation on this letter says that an extract was sent to BF. AAE.) Puchelberg, however, refused to comply. On Sept. 26, Castries ordered Clouet to send Puchelberg's explanation as soon as possible, whereupon the king would surely order him to comply: Castries to Clouet, Sept. 26, 1783 (AAE).

1. Castries' Oct. 16 letter enclosed a memoir by Puchelberg dated Oct. 1. Puchelberg refused to lift the attachment because it would make him solely responsible for the outfit totaling 31,668 *l.t.* 12 *s.* 3 *d.* that he had furnished to the *Alliance* at the request of the ship's captain and on the order of his

with me at my return, because as the meeting of Parlt. is now so near at hand, I imagine that my return to Paris will be postponed till after that time. I wd not make you wait during Cold weather for the confortable scarlet waistcoat.[2] Mr Jay is arrived, and is now very well, he has been a little out of order but is entirely recovered. I am going to Bath again to see my Dear Sister who goes on very well, and I expect Mr Jay to go likewise to Bath, and then we shall be very sociable together. My Brother & Sister desire to be kindly remembered to you. Pray give my best compts to Mr Adams & all friends in your own house particularly. Your ever affecte friend   D HARTLEY

Addressed: A Son Excellence / Monsr Franklin / M P des E U A / á Passy / proche Paris / France

Endorsed: D Hartley to B F. Oct 25. 83

From Jean-Baptiste Le Roy

ALS: American Philosophical Society

ce Dimanche matin [October 26?, 1783][3]
Permettez vous Mon Illustre Docteur que Je vous rappelle la promesse que vous avez bien voulu faire au Jeune M. Argant

---

associate, Schweighauser of Nantes. Schweighauser's firm had been designated to furnish all American ships in the ports of Brittany; these orders had come from American agent William Lee, ministers BF, JA, and Arthur Lee, and the naval offices of both Boston and Philadelphia. On Aug. 23, 1781, Congress resolved that its auditor, Johnson, should settle the accounts of the *Alliance* and arrange for BF to pay. This has not yet been done, though BF himself ordered Schweighauser to furnish whatever was necessary to the *Alliance*.

2. Hartley's secretary, George Hammond, who did not leave Paris for England until Oct. 25, discovered the packet of flannel in Dover when he arrived there. It was addressed by Hartley to BF. Hammond sent it to Pierre Dessin in Calais, with orders to forward it to Passy. When writing to WTF to inform him, Hammond cautioned that the importation of flannel into France was prohibited, and that there might be difficulties at customs: Hammond to WTF, Oct. 23 and 31, 1783, APS. See also Dessin to BF, Nov. 4.

3. Le Roy had spoken with Ami Argand the day before writing his previous letter, most likely dated Oct. 21 (above). If this date is accurate, then Argand was still in Paris on Oct. 20. In his letter of Dec. 2, Edward Nairne

d'une lettre pour Londres[4] et dont J'ai eu l'honneur de vous parler avant-hier il part demain à dix heures du matin je compte le
voir ce Soir et Je Serois bien Glorieux de pouvoir lui porter cette
lettre que vous lui avez promise. J'ai lhonneur de vous Souhaiter
bien le bon Jour. Si vous avez le tems de l'ecrire je l'enverrai
chercher avant une heure.   LE ROY

M. Franklin

---

reported that Argand had delivered a book and prints that BF had intended
for Joseph Banks. These were very likely the pamphlet and prints enclosed
in BF's letter to Banks of Oct. 8. Banks acknowledged receipt of that letter
on Nov. 7. The only two Sundays between Oct. 20 and Nov. 7 were Oct. 26
and Nov. 2, of which we choose the earlier date.

4. Where Argand hoped to find the materials and skilled artisans for the
manufacture of an improved oil lamp of his design, and to obtain a patent:
John J. Wolfe, *Brandy, Balloons, & Lamps: Ami Argand, 1750–1803* (Carbondale and Edwardsville, Ill., 1999), pp. 8, 23–5. No letter of introduction
for Argand from BF has been found. Nairne would have been a suitable
addressee because of both his expertise as an instrument maker and his connections in the British scientific community.

It appears that Argand's lamp was similar in principle to one that BF
had worked on intermittently for more than a decade. In a letter written
in 1801, Johann Sebastian Clais remembered that in 1772 he had brought
home from England a lamp designed by BF and manufactured by their mutual friend Matthew Boulton. When Clais visited BF in Paris in 1781, BF
showed him "an addition" to this lamp. Clais claimed to have given his
prototype of BF's lamp to Argand in 1782 and said that Argand later added
a glass chimney. Argand's associates in London, Samuel More and glassmaker William Parker, remarked on the similarity between Argand's con-
ception and a lamp that Boulton had produced earlier: XXXV, lxii; Wolfe,
Brandy, Balloons, & Lamps, pp. 12–20, 81. According to TJ's description in
1784, Argand's lamp produced a much brighter light than a candle because
it formed "the wick into a hollow cylinder so that there is a passage for the
air through the hollow. The idea had occurred to Dr. Franklin a year or two
before: but he tried his experiment with a rush, which not succeeding he did
not prosecute it. The fact was that the rush formed too small a cylinder":
Jefferson Papers, VII, 518.

Elias Boudinot to the American Peace Commissioners

Reprinted from J. J. Boudinot, ed., *The Life, Public Services, Addresses and Letters of Elias Boudinot* . . . (2 vols., Boston, 1896), I, 410–13.

GENTLEMEN   PRINCETOWN Oct. 27th[–November 3,] 1783

Previous to my leaving the Chair of Congress,[5] I take the liberty again to address you, merely as an individual that you may not be left totally without Information until the Choice of a Minister for foreign Affairs shall take place.[6] I have pressed Congress much on this subject, and am fully convinced of the difficult Situation you must be in for want of Information from this important Office— I have the honor of acknowledging the rect of your several favours of the ————[7] My last addressed to you, was on the 15th of July giving you a minute account of the Mutiny of the Soldiers in Philadelphia and of our subsequent removal to this Place[8]—since which we have remained here tho. in but indifferent Circumstances of accommodation— Congress lately have determined to fix their place of Residence at the Head of the Delaware over the Falls of Trenton— They take in contemplation to fix another place the Falls of Potomack near Georgetown and to sit alternately at each Place year about— They have also determined to adjourn on the 8th Novr to Annapolis for their temporary residence—[9] They have also

5. With his year as president of Congress ending, Boudinot wrote the N.J. legislature on Oct. 27 to ask that he not be reelected as a delegate: George A. Boyd, *Elias Boudinot, Patriot and Statesman, 1740–1821* (Princeton, 1952), p. 136.

6. Boudinot was handling Congress' foreign correspondence until a new secretary for foreign affairs was elected to replace Robert R. Livingston, who had resigned the office: XL, 179.

7. Boudinot had not yet seen the peace commissioners' Sept. 10 letter announcing the signing of the definitive treaty (XL, 600–6). The most recent letters from the commissioners read in Congress were those of July 18 and 27 (XL, 325–30, 388–9), read on Sept. 12. Since that date many letters from individual commissioners to Livingston had also been received, including a June 12 letter from BF (XL, 150–2): *JCC*, XXV, 587–8; Smith, *Letters*, XX, 670n; XXI, 120n.

8. XL, 301–8.

9. On Oct. 21 Congress resolved to meet alternately in Trenton and Annapolis until buildings were erected for its use on the banks of the Delaware and Potomac. It also voted to adjourn on Nov. 12 and reconvene at Annapolis two weeks later: *JCC*, XXV, 711–14; *Morris Papers*, VIII, 662–5.

passed several important Acts lately, which you will see by the several Proclamations contained in the Newspapers which I do myself the honor of transmitting herewith from the month of Sept 2d— Congress have not yet taken the Appointment of a minister for foreign Affairs under Consideration, as their Time is principally taken up with previous measures of a Peace arrangement both Civil & Military— It will now be put off till the removal to Annapolis— I shall add to this Letter (I believe) several Acts of Congress. In consequence of a Report on your last Official Letter we have been most Anxiously (looking(?)) for the Definitive Treaty which is really a matter of much more importance in this Country than it is in Europe— The States at best cannot be convinced that Peace is made to any Purpose without this welcome Act, and the Conduct of the British in these States has confirmed them in the Opinion— We lately sent Baron Steuben to Canada to settle with Genl Waldenson[1] the Time and manner of delivering up & receiving the Posts and fortifications on the Frontiers whenever that Genl should be ready so to do— He was refused even a conference on the subject— Genl Waldenson declaring that he knew of no Peace between Britain and America, that his orders were to cease Hostilities which he had carefully done but could go no further—[2] The Baron thinks they are planning their schemes in Canada for holding the Frontier Posts for a year or two longer which would prove ruinous to these States rendition of them must be urged without delay. The Minister from Holland[3] is arrived and to receive his public Audience on Friday next.

1. A mistranscription. The British commander-in-chief in Canada was Sir Frederick Haldimand (XXVI, 337n).

2. Steuben had been ordered by GW to meet with Haldimand and to inspect the nine posts on the frontier still held by the British. When he inquired when the United States could expect the posts to be delivered, Haldimand, who had not received orders on the subject, declined to answer: Fitzpatrick, *Writings of Washington*, XXVII, 39–40, 61–5, 124; Charles R. Ritcheson, *Aftermath of Revolution: British Policy Toward the United States, 1783–1795* (Dallas, 1969), pp. 62, 75; Freeman, *Washington*, v, 448.

3. Pieter Johan van Berckel (XXXVII, 564n; XL, 155n) arrived in Philadelphia on Oct. 11: *Morris Papers*, VIII, 615n.

The Effects of the Mutiny in Philadelphia are all done away— The Sergeants who were condemned to die, recd Pardon from Congress in the very last moment of despair[4] this has had a good Effect and the Army have been disbanded without any bad consequences but unhappily without Money.[5]

Nov. 1st— Yesterday we gave public audience to Mr Van Berckel— Just before the Ceremony began Col Ogden arrived with the News of the completion of the Definitive Treaty,[6] this gave a large addition to the general Joy that was already great on the occasion of the Day— Mr Van Berckel appears to be a person very much suited to the Manners of our People and I am very much mistaken if he does not do great honor to his Commission— I shall endeavour to enclose his address and our answer—[7] Novr 3d— This Morning Congress met & made choice of a new President for the ensuing Year. General Mifflin was unanimously chosen, tho' absent I suppose he will take the Chair in a day or two—[8] I feel myself very happy in having filled up my year and that after having devoted myself altogether to the Public Service for near eight years, I am like

4. For the mutiny and the Sept. 13 pardon see XL, 301–8, 598n.

5. Boudinot had recently informed Robert Morris that the army would be disbanded except for garrisons at West Point and Fort Pitt: *Morris Papers*, VIII, 666. GW and Alexander Hamilton had urged the retention of a 2,600-man regular army: Richard H. Kohn, *Eagle and Sword: the Federalists and the Creation of the Military Establishment in America, 1783–1802* (New York and London, 1975), pp. 40–53. By the end of the year, the soldiers received promissory notes for outstanding balances of pay: *Morris Papers*, VII, 579–84; VIII, 205–6, 256, 260.

6. Ogden, who had left Paris on Sept. 10, reported that John Thaxter, Jr., would bring a copy of the treaty: Smith, *Letters*, XXI, 137.

7. On Oct. 31 Van Berckel made a formal address to Congress and delivered a letter from the States General of the Netherlands (*JCC*, XXV, 780–5). The enclosed copy of his address, translated from French into English, is in the hand of Charles Thomson (APS). The enclosed copy of Congress' response of the same day (*JCC*, XXV, 785–6) is in Boudinot's hand (Library of Congress). BF had his secretary L'Air de Lamotte make an extract of the Nov. 1 section of the present letter, followed by the texts of both enclosures. A press copy of that document is at the Library of Congress.

8. *JCC*, XXV, 799. Thomas Mifflin called on Robert Morris on Nov. 13 to announce his acceptance: *Morris Papers*, VIII, 761.

to retire to private Life under the blessings of so glorious a Peace— My Presidentship has also been honored by the Signature of both Preliminary Articles & Definitive Treaty which has greatly compensated for all my other Sacrifices.   E B.

To The Honble Commissioners

Commissioners Private

From Gaetano Filangieri

ALS:[9] Historical Society of Pennsylvania

⟨La Cava,[1] October 27, 1783, in Italian: I wish to thank you for the honor you do me in sending the code of the American Constitutions,[2] a worthy product of the country, the times, the circumstances, and its authors. I would like to express my respect and admiration by sending you the fourth volume of my Works, which includes the second part of the Criminal Law.[3] In it, I considered all the legislations of all peoples and of all times. I adopted what seemed reasonable and rejected, without partiality, what seemed useless or pernicious. My procedural approach required a new system which I propose under the Penal Code. I hope this work will meet with your approval, which would be the highest recognition for me.⟩

9. The Italian text is published in Antonio Pace, *Benjamin Franklin and Italy* (Philadelphia, 1958), p. 401, and in Eugenio Lo Sardo, ed., *Il mondo nuovo e le virtù civili: l'epistolario di Gaetano Filangieri (1772–1788)* (Naples, 1999), pp. 248–9 (where it is misdated Nov. 27). The editors express their thanks to Graziano Kratli of the Yale University Library for his translation.

1. Cava dei Tirreni, a town outside Naples. For Filangieri's move to the country see XL, 298n.

2. *Constitutions des treize Etats-Unis de l'Amérique*, which BF forwarded to Filangieri in July, through Luigi Pio: XL, 379.

3. Filangieri had sent the third volume in July, advising BF that the fourth would follow within a few days and cautioning him to read both together. The two volumes make up Book III of *La scienza della legislazione*. See XL, 297–8.

From Jonathan Nesbitt & Co.

LS:[4] American Philosophical Society

Sir   L'Orient. 27 Octob: 1783

We took the liberty to write your Excellency the 20th. Inst: relative to the Insurance on the Ship Nancy Capt Shewell, & the Sentence given by the court of Admiralty of Bordeaux in that affair, since which we have received an answer from the Comte de Vergennes of which we have the honor to annex you a Copy.—[5] We must confess ourselves extremely surprised to find his sentiments regarding the 22nd. Article of the Preliminary Treaty so diametrically opposite to those of your Excellency; & it appears likewise that they do not in any manner correspond with those of the British Ministry, for it is well known that many Vessels taken on the Coast of the United States during the month of March were released without difficulty— The Importance of the present affair we hope will plead our excuse for the trouble we have already given your Excellency, & requesting that you will further Interest yourself in our behalf by speaking to the Comte De Vergennes on the Subject, who perhaps has not maturely considered the matter; if he persists in his opinion it will be most prudent in us to give up the dispute with the Underwriters rather than incur further Expence.— We have the honor to remain with the greatest Respect.— Your Excellencys most Obedt. humble Servts.—   JONATN: NESBITT & CO:

His Excelly. Benjn. Franklin Esqr—

---

4. Jonathan Nesbitt added the complimentary close before signing.

5. Vergennes' response, dated Oct. 20 from Fontainebleau, acknowledges receipt of the firm's letter of Sept. 29. If they reread Article 22, Vergennes writes, they will see that the term of one month applies only to the area of the Canaries themselves, and extends to the southernmost island. The article refers to distance, not latitude.

From Jonathan Williams, Jr.

ALS: American Philosophical Society

Dear & hond Sir.   Nantes Octor 27. 1783.

The inclosed is just come to hand from Phila. Capt Cunningham arrived the [*torn*] of Septemr last,[6] I suppose you have other Letters which will give you all the news if there is any.—

I am as ever most dutifully & affectionately Yours.

JONA WILLIAMS J

Addressed: A Son Excellence / Monsieur Franklin / Ministre Plenipotentiaire des Etats / Unis de l'amerique Septentrionale / en son Hotel A Passy / prés Paris.

Notation: Jona. Williams Oct. 27. 1783.—

From ——— Birckel[7]   ALS: American Philosophical Society

Monsieur   strasbourg ce 28. 8bre. 1783.

Dans la lettre, que vous m'avez fait l'honneur de m'ecrire[8] vous parles d'une metode. C'este metode est gravé dans votre ame, et dans l'ame du meilleur patriote en france, en angletere, et en amerique. Reclaméz les degrés de bonté, et les degrés de forces d'ames, que vous trouverez dans ces trois cabinets, l'union de ces ames sensibles se soumettant a l'intantion du tres haut ces trois cabinets feront le bonheur de l'univers.

Je suis avec un profond respect, Monsieur, votres tres humble et tres obeïssent serviteur   BIRCKEL

chev: au m: militaire[9]

Notation: Birkel— 28 Oct: 1783.—

6. The *Hannibal*, Capt. Conyngham, had sailed for Philadelphia on July 13: XL, 140n.

7. This is the last extant letter from this former captain in the La Marck regiment and the only one since February, 1782: XXXVI, 56n.

8. Not found.

9. The *Ordre du mérite militaire* was instituted by Louis XV for officers born in Protestant countries: *Almanach royal* for 1784, pp. 210–11.

From Sir Edward Newenham

ALS: American Philosophical Society

Dear Sir   Dublin 28 octr: 1783

Your Excellency will see by the Enclosed how delicately I mentioned the affair of the treaty;[1] the Very post that brought me your Letter[2] brought me several from America; I MOST EARNESTLY entreat you will inform me by RETURN OF THE POST whether Ireland is mentiond, & if it is, at what Period; it is incumbent on me, to be precise in that point, as I have pledged myself to the House, to state, from Time to Time, the progress of that Treaty—the Public Expectations are high, & this City is in a state of the Greatest anxiety—do, my Dear & much respected friend, assist *my* Country as I & my friends assisted Virtue when oppressed by the hand of Power—*all* in this affair depends on your Excellency— Parliament seems determined to Support me in any motion, that may appear requisite; my Object is the Honor of Ireland, & that the states of North America & Ireland may Ever be friends to Each other— I am in the Strictest Sence of the word, a Citizen of the world— I adore Virtue where ever I find it—whether on this or the other side of the Atlantic—

By the Secretarys reply, he seems to think that the Treaty will not Speedily be concluded;[3] You have now the public Debates of the Irish Parliament to warrant your Excellency in *demanding* of M Hartly whether Ireland is to be included by Name or

1. Newenham most likely enclosed a copy of that day's *Dublin Evening Post*, which published a summary of the Oct. 27 debates in the Irish House of Commons, including a full account of Newenham's speech on the inclusion of Ireland in a commercial treaty between Great Britain and the United States.

2. Of Oct. 2, above.

3. Thomas Pelham (*ODNB*) was chief secretary of the Irish administration (Dublin Castle). His response to Newenham's address, briefly summarized in the *Dublin Evening Post*, cast doubt on Newenham's optimistic belief that the treaty was close to being concluded. Pelham promised, however, to "inform his Majesty's ministers that a doubt had arisen that the interests of Ireland would not be attended to, and urge them to demonstrate the contrary, which they were well inclined to do": *The Parliamentary Register: or, History of the Proceedings and Debates of the House of Commons of Ireland* . . . (17 vols., Dublin, 1784–1801), II, 28–9.

Not—the British Ministry will find various ways of evading this buisiness, if they Can— Your Excellency will see, that in pursuance of my agitating the Question, Mr: Forster one of the Ministry, moved for a Bill to facilitate the Commercial interscourse between Ireland & America,[4] I wish I had a Copy of the British treaty, as far as it is gone, that I might take Care to have Matters rightly Settled on the discussing of Mr: Forsters Bill—

The Protecting Duties as taken up by Mr Gardiner[5] will occasion much contest, we call them Protecting Duties, Government stiles them prohibitory Duties, & therefore will Support the English Woollen & silken Trade—and the English Breweries—

I Know not how to apologize for this trouble; it is in your own breast I claim my pardon.—

Lady Newenham, still anxious for the Bust, desires her best & Sincerest respects to your Excellency & your Grandson—

I have the Honor, to be, with the most perfect respect & Esteem your Excellencys Most Obt: & Most Humble sert

EDWARD NEWENHAM

Mr Flood & Mr Grattan have had a most Violent Altercation— it is imagined they cannot part untill one falls;[6] I shall send

4. John Foster (*ODNB*), M.P. for County Louth, had acted as the chancellor of the Irish exchequer since 1777 even though he did not officially obtain that position until 1784. After Newenham's address he requested and received permission to prepare the bill mentioned here: A. P. W. Malcolmson, *John Foster: the Politics of the Anglo-Irish Ascendancy* (Oxford and New York, 1978), pp. 43–9; *Parliamentary Register*, II, 29; *The Journals of the House of Commons of the Kingdom of Ireland* . . . (31 vols., Dublin, 1782–94), XXI, 115.

5. The popularity of protective tariffs, such as those proposed by Luke Gardiner, M.P. for County Dublin (*ODNB*), induced Newenham to support them, even though he remained unconvinced that they would alleviate the high unemployment in the Dublin textile trade: James Kelly, *Sir Edward Newenham MP, 1734–1814* . . . (Dublin, 2004), p. 200.

6. The rivalry between prominent reformers Henry Flood and Henry Grattan (*ODNB*) came to a head in the Irish House of Commons on Oct. 28, Flood's second day as an M.P. During a debate on financial policy, Grattan called Flood an apostate who had supported sending "4000 men to butcher our brethren in America." Flood responded by challenging Grattan to a duel and denouncing him as a "mendicant patriot who was bought

the result next post—they are not half full in the present publication—

Addressed: His Excellency B: Franklin / Minister Plenipotentiary / from the United States / Passy

To Anthony Todd

Press copy of ALS: American Philosophical Society

Dear Sir, Passy, Oct. 29. 1783—

I have been in hopes of being able to answer sooner yours of the 17th. but am at last inform'd that tho' M. D'Ogny is come to Town, he can enter into no Agreement till he has receiv'd his Instructions, which he cannot have till after the Return of the Court from Fontainbleau to Versailles. So I can only say at present, that the Reasonings in your Letter appear to me clear, and such as should be satisfactory to this Office. I approve likewise of the Advertisement as you have drawn it, proposing only that in the last Paragraph but one, you would add, if you think fit, after the Word *corresponding,* the Words, *with each other;* and change the Word *them,* for the Words, *their Letters:* these Alterations are not very necessary, but may serve methinks to make the Sense more immediately clear, and prevent a Person on the Continent of North America who would correspond with his Friend in Yorkshire, from imagining that he is to inclose his Letter to a Friend in London.— The Word *North* also, in the last Paragraph, may if you please be omitted, as it is not used in the Title of the United States.—[7]

---

by my country for a sum of money, and then sold my country for prompt payment." In turn, Grattan charged that Flood's career so far had consisted of an "intemperate," a "corrupt," and now a "seditious" stage. A duel on Oct. 30 was prevented only when the police detained Flood and Grattan on their way to the meeting ground: *Parliamentary Register,* II, 39–43; James Kelly, *Henry Flood: Patriots and Politics in Eighteenth-Century England* (Dublin, 1998), pp. 349–53.

7. BF marked these changes on the text he received from Todd. L'Air de Lamotte then prepared a copy that incorporated them. Both documents are at the APS.

With great Esteem, I am, Dear Sir, Your most obedient & most humble Servant   B FRANKLIN

Anthy Todd Esqr

Continental Congress to the American Peace Commissioners: Instructions[8]

DS: Library of Congress; draft,[9] two copies, and incomplete copy: National Archives; copy: Massachusetts Historical Society

October 29th. 1783.

BY THE UNITED STATES IN CONGRESS ASSEMBLED

To the Ministers Plenipotentiary of the United States of America at the Court of Versailles empowered to negociate a Peace or to any one or more of them.

FIRST. You are instructed and authorised to announce to his Imperial Majesty the Emperor of Germany[1] or to his Ministers the high sense which the United States in Congress Assembled entertain of his exalted character and eminent virtues

---

8. These instructions were prepared by a committee appointed on Sept. 29 to respond to letters Congress had received from individual American commissioners, including BF's long letter to Livingston, July 22[–26] (XL, 355–70). The committee, consisting of Samuel Huntington, Arthur Lee, and James Duane, delivered its report on Oct. 22 (see the following note). The instructions were approved on Oct. 29: *JCC*, XXV, 630–1, 636–7, 753–7. Boudinot enclosed them in his Nov. 1 letter to the American commissioners. Congress also ordered that the fifth instruction be sent to Francis Dana, along with "a copy of the other instructions for his information": *JCC*, XXV, 757.

9. In the hand of James Duane, and marked by Charles Thomson as having been delivered on Oct. 22. This draft bears emendations and notations indicating which articles were passed. The committee's third article was rejected: "You are instructed to put a Stop to all Loans for money which are negotiating, or authorized, on behalf of the United States, in any part of Europe." The seventh article of the final version, published here, was added during debate.

1. Emperor Joseph II, who was also archduke of Austria and ruler of the possessions of the House of Habsburg. For his overtures to the United States see XXXIX, 188–9, 445; XL, 368.

and their earnest desire to cultivate his friendship and to enter into a Treaty of Amity and Commerce for the mutual advantage of the Subjects of his Imperial Majesty & the Citizens of these United States.

SECONDLY. You are instructed to meet the advances and encourage the disposition of the other Commercial Powers of Europe for entering into Treaties of Amity and Commerce with these United States. In negociations on this subject you will lay it down as a principle in no case to be deviated from that they shall respectively have for their basis the mutual advantage of the contracting Parties on terms of the most perfect equality and reciprocity and not to be repugnant to any of the Treaties already entered into by the United States with France and other Foreign Powers. That such Treaties shall in the first instance be proposed for a term not exceeding fifteen Years, and shall not be finally conclusive until they shall respectively have been transmitted to the United States in Congress Assembled for their examination and final direction; and that with the draughts or propositions for such Treaties shall be transmitted all the information which shall come within the knowledge of the said Ministers respecting the same and their observations after the most mature enquiry on the probable advantages or disadvantages & effects of such Treaties respectively.

THIRDLY. You are instructed to continue to press upon the Ministers of his Danish Majesty[2] the justice of causing satisfaction to be made for the value of the Ships and Goods Captured by the Alliance Frigate and sent into Bergen, and how essentially it concerns the honor of the United States that their gallant Citizens should not be deprived of any part of those Prizes, which they had so justly acquired by their valour. That as far as Congress have been informed, the estimate of those Prizes at fifty thousand pounds sterling is not immoderate; that no more however is desired than their true value, after every deduction which shall be thought equitable. That Congress have a sincere disposition to cultivate the friendship of his Danish Majesty and to promote a commercial intercourse between his Subjects and the Citizens of the United States on terms which shall promise

2. Christian VII.

mutual advantage to both Nations. That it is therefore the wish of Congress that this claim should still be referred to the equitable disposition of his Danish Majesty in full confidence that the reasonable expectations of the Parties interested will be fully answered; accordingly you are fully authorised and directed after exerting your best endeavours to enforce the said claim to the extent it shall appear to you to be well founded, to make abatements if necessary and ultimately to accept such compensation as his Danish Majesty can be prevailed on to grant.[3]

FOURTHLY. You are further instructed to enquire and report to Congress the reasons why the expedition of the Alliance and Bon homme Richard and the Squadron which accompanied them was carried on at the expence and on account of the Court of France?[4] Whether any part of the profit arising therefrom accrued to the United States; or any of the expence thereof hath been placed to their Account? Whether the proceeds of any of the Prizes taken in that expedition and which is due to the American Officers and Seamen employed therein is deposited in Europe, and what amount; where; and in whose hands?

FIFTHLY. The acquisition of support to the Independence of the United States having been the primary object of the instructions to our Ministers respecting the Convention of the neutral Maritime Powers for maintaining the freedom of Commerce, You will observe that the necessity of such support is superceded by the Treaties lately entered into for restoring peace. And although Congress approve of the principles of that Convention as it was founded on the liberal basis of maintainance of the rights of neutral nations and of the Privileges of Commerce; yet they are unwilling at this juncture to become a party to a Confederacy which may hereafter too far complicate the interests of the United States with the Politics of Europe; and therefore if such a progress is not already made in this busi-

3. This article is a response to BF's explanation of his negotiations with Denmark: XL, 361–2.

4. See XL, 364–5. Such royally financed expeditions had a long history. In the present case, Louis apparently acted from a combination of financial, military, and altruistic motives: Jonathan R. Dull, *American Naval History, 1607–1865: Overcoming the Colonial Legacy* (Lincoln, Nebr. and London, 2012), pp. 24–5.

ness as may render it dishonorable to recede, it is the desire of Congress and their instruction to each of the Ministers of the United States at the respective Courts in Europe, that no further measures be taken at present towards the admission of the United States into that Confederacy.[5]

SIXTHLY. The Ministers of these United States for negociating a Peace with Great Britain are hereby instructed, authorised & directed to urge forward the definitive Treaty to a speedy conclusion and unless there shall be an immediate prospect of obtaining Articles or explanations beneficial to the United States in addition to the provisional Articles, that they shall agree to adopt the provisional Articles as the substance of a definitive Treaty of Peace.[6]

SEVENTHLY. The Minister or Ministers of these United States for negociating a Peace are hereby instructed to negociate an explanation of the following paragraph of the declaration acceded to by them on the 20th. of January 1783 relative to Captures Viz: "That the term should be one month from the Channel and North Sea as far as the Canary Islands inclusively whether in the Ocean or the Mediterranean."[7]

EIGHTHLY. Mr. Jay is hereby authorised to direct Mr. Car-

5. In 1780 Congress had agreed to the principles of Empress Catherine II's League of Armed Neutrality and had designated Francis Dana as minister to the Russian court. It also had authorized its ministers in Europe to accept an invitation to join the league: XXXIV, 188–9, 244n, 532; *JCC*, XVIII, 905. See also XL, 88–9, where Livingston foretold what these instructions might say.

6. The American peace commissioners had already done so. They adopted the preliminary articles as the basis for the definitive peace signed on Sept. 3 (XL, 566–75).

7. This article, added by Congress during the final days of discussion, had been drafted the previous August. It was in response to an Aug. 18 petition from a group of Boston merchants whose ships were taken by the British after March 3, the day they believed the armistice should have taken effect on the east coast of the United States: *JCC*, XXIV, 518; *Adams Papers*, XVI, 107n. For the declaration of the cessation of hostilities, which included the timetable of the armistice, see XXVIII, 605–8; XXXIX, 7n. As soon as it was signed, BF had had to issue a memorandum clarifying the reference to the Canary Islands for American merchants in France. Livingston had written for clarification in April, and the American commissioners had responded on July 18: XXXIX, 171–2, 487–8; XL, 330.

michael to repair to Paris should Mr. Jay be of opinion that the interest of the United States at the Court of Madrid may not be injured by Mr. Carmichael's absence;[8] and that Mr. Carmichael carry with him the Books and Vouchers necessary to make a final and compleat settlement of the account of public monies which have passed through the hands of Mr. Jay and himself and that Mr. Barclay attend Mr. Jay and Mr. Carmichael to adjust those Accounts.[9]

NINTHLY. Mr. Jay has leave to go to Bath should he find it necessary for the benefit of his health.[1] CHA THOMSON
secy.

Endorsements: [*in John Adams' hand:*] Instructions / [*in Franklin's hand:*] Oct. 29. 83—

Notation: For the Ministers plenipo &c

8. William Carmichael had been received by the Spanish court as American chargé d'affaires in late August. He gave the date variously as Aug. 22 (in a letter to Jay: *Jay Papers*, III, 459) and Aug. 23 (in a letter to Livingston; see XXXIX, 464n).

9. This eighth instruction had been approved as a resolution on Oct. 1 (*JCC*, XXV, 636). Congress wrote the resolution in response to Jay's letters to Livingston of May 30 and June 1, complaining that Carmichael had not responded to his repeated requests to send a complete set of accounts relating to the Spanish mission, and asking Congress to order Carmichael to come to Paris and settle the accounts with Barclay. Without such an order, Jay feared that Carmichael would never do so: *Jay Papers*, III, 369, 372. Jay was correct. On July 1 he informed Carmichael of Barclay's commission to settle the American public accounts in Europe and instructed him to bring all relevant documentation to Paris as soon as possible. Carmichael refused on July 29, claiming he was obligated to remain in Madrid unless he was instructed otherwise by Congress. The two men continued to argue until Jay forwarded the congressional resolution to Carmichael on Jan. 28, 1784. (All these letters between Jay and Carmichael are at the Columbia University Library.) For background on the relationship between Jay and Carmichael and the settling of the Spanish accounts see *Jay Papers*, II, 168–74; III, 550–4, 555–6.

1. This instruction had also been resolved by Congress on Oct. 1: *JCC*, XXV, 636.

From Jean-Jacques Caffiéri

ALS: American Philosophical Society

Monsieur   Paris ce 29 octobre 1783

En Lisant La Gazette Dernier j'ay vû que Les Etats Unis de Lamerique etoit dans Lintention de faire Elevé une Statue au General De Wanchinton et quel Doit se faire a Paris.[2] Si La chose est vraie je vous prie Monsieur de vouloir bien vous Resouvenire de moy, j'ay quel que Droit pour obtenire votre chois, L'ancienté sur Les personnes qui peuve vous faire La même Demende, votre Portrait et Le tombeau De Montgomerie, vous ons du prouver mon zele et mon Savoire.[3]

Je sui avec Respet Monsieur Votre tres humble et tres obeissant Serviteur   CAFFIERI

2. The Oct. 24 supplement of the *Gaz. de Leyde* reprinted a congressional resolution of Aug. 7 directing that a commission for a bronze equestrian statue of GW be awarded to the best artist in Europe. The statue was to be set on a marble pedestal engraved with scenes of the general's major victories and placed "where the residence of Congress shall be established." GW was to be in Roman dress and crowned with laurel. The resolution further directed that BF should supervise the work, and ordered the secretary of Congress to send him an excellent likeness of GW and a description of the events to be carved in bas relief on the pedestal: *JCC*, XXIV, 494–5. This resolution was widely reprinted in the American press, including the Sept. 3 issue of the *Pa. Gaz.*, but we have found no record of BF's having been notified. The idea was revived after BF returned to Philadelphia, at which time he recommended Houdon: John Jay to Richard Henry Lee, Oct. 29, 1785 (National Archives). The commission, however, was never awarded.

3. Caffiéri had not received an American commission since 1777, when he completed the marble monument to Gen. Montgomery and the terracotta bust of BF (XXIV, 160–1; XXV, 266–7), but he persisted in soliciting such work: XXXII, 474; XXXVII, 84; XXXIX, 9, 386; XL, 561. On the same day as the present letter he also sent a solicitation to WTF (APS).

From William Hodgson

ALS: American Philosophical Society

Dear sir   London 30 Octr. 1783

I recd your kind Letter of the 9th[4] per Mr Jay, who has been somewhat indisposed since his arrival, you may be assured if it lies in my Power to be in the least usefull to him I shall have great Pleasure therein— I shall pay Mr Vinys Bill for your Chariot Wheels & know of no better mode of Conveyance for them than by Rouen—[5] Inclosed you have your Acct with me ballance due to you £49..7.6—[6] In a former Letter[7] I quoted the Ballance wrong having taken it from the Expenditure after receipt of Mr Vaughans money, without adverting to what I had advanced before that Time— There is an Article of £21. to Mr Cooke[8] that I do not consider myself as quite warranted to charge you with. I was in hopes Mr Cook wou'd himself have repaid me, but I have not heard a Word from him alltho now a year & half ago, I therefore submit it entirely to your Generosity, hoping you will think this a pardonable stretch of my Instructions— Some of my Friends have suggested to me that if Congress appointed a Consul for G Brittain, I had some Pretensions to offer them my Services in that Capacity— I just submit the Idea to your friendship & Consideration, if you approve the thought you will favor me with your Advice &

4. Not found.

5. See Dessin to BF, Oct. 14, and John Viny to BF, [after Nov. 28].

6. This account, the final extant one submitted by Hodgson, was completed by him on Oct. 24 (APS). The debit side includes payments relating to American prisoners and BF's private concerns; some of these are specified in XXXVII, 31n. He credited BF for cash received at Paris in November, 1782 (XXXVIII, 441n) and a bill of exchange on Benjamin Vaughan of February, 1783 (XXXIX, 209). At some later time BF tried to bring the account up to date, adding entries in pencil. Hodgson had paid Dr. Withering £5.5 and paid Viny "for Wheels"; the amount of the latter was left blank. He noted that all the money dispersed by Hodgson (£275 15 s.) was furnished out of his own private account with Ferdinand Grand. The final balance due him was £248 9s.

7. XXXIX, 479–80.

8. See XXXVII, 31n.

Assistance I am very truly Dr sr Your much Obliged Friend & servt   WILLIAM HODGSON

His Excellency B. Franklin Esqr

Addressed: To / His Excellency / Benj. Franklin Esqr. / Paris

From John Shaffer

ALS: American Philosophical Society

Sir   Paris ce 30 8bre 83

My avocat informed me that you have the Goodness for me, to imploy Mr Barclay to do what will be Nessesary to Render me justis. When I was arrested the inspecter of the Polize[9] Put a gardien in to my house to garde my goods and gard de Robe, two days ago I was informed that the Person Stole all that was left in to his Care but Very fortunate we have got him arrested and is in the Same Prison hear.

My Avocat will Explain to you the unjust maner in wich I am Treated the Robe me of What I have got and do Not Know what maner to Recover my Property—if your Exelency will Not interrest your Self for me to Procure my liberty I hope you will Not Refuse to Render me Justis in order to Prosecute the Villen who has Stole my Cloths and goods or Pay me for them if you will be So Kind as to Right a few lines to the Lt Creminel in order that he may Render me Justis it will be an adition upon the many obligations Confered upon your Exelencys Most Obedent and Very humble Servant[1]   J. SCHAFFER

His Exelency Docter Frankline

---

9. M. Quidor was *inspecteur de police* in charge of Shaffer's department: *Almanach royal* for 1783, p. 431.

1. The following day, Oct. 31, Shaffer wrote again, promising to repay BF's advance and begging for another 2 *louis* "to make the nessary Pursuit a gainst the Person who has taken my Goods and Clothes." APS.

From Bernard Rufin and Moritz Chretien Meyer[2]

ALS: American Philosophical Society

Monsieur,   Passi le 31 8bre 1783

Deux Étrangers, Allemands de nation, L'un Prussien, et Interprete des langues Allemande, Francoise, Italienne, et parlant un peu d'anglais, en Outre Officier de Cuisine, et d'office, capable de Gouverner le detail d'une Maison telles Consequentes qu'elles Soient, et à même d'en donner des preuves dès que vous l'ordonnerez; L'autre Saxon de Nation, et Compositeur des Lettres, Connaissant à fond L'imprimerie, et Capable d'être Censeur de la langue francoise, et latine, Suplient instament Monsieur Le Docteur Francklin, Ministre Plenipotentiaire du Congrés de l'amerique d'avoir la bonté de leurs indiquer les Moyens dont on pourrait se Servir pour Captivér l'honneur de votre Bienvaillance, et pour offrir leurs faibles Talens au Continent de l'amerique. Encouragés par vos Soins paternels, et se flattant d'avance de pouvoir un jour Augmenter le nombre des Illustrès déffenseur de votre Patrie, ils ne manqueront pas de faire des Progrès rapides, Surtout si l'on Seconde leurs Envies, et ils ont l'honneur d'être avec la Soumission, et la reconnaissance la plus parfaite, Monsieur, Vos très, humbles Serviteurs

BERNARD RUFIN, Prussien
MORITZ CHRETIEN MEYER, Saxon

P.S. Les deux Etrangers, se sont presentés chez vous, Monsieur, il y à environ deux heures; mais privés de l'honneur de vous Voir, ils sont au Grand Vainquer où ils attendent une réponse de votre part, fut-elle même Verbale

Notation: Meyer, & Rufin. 31 Oct. 1783.

---

2. These would-be emigrants did not go to America, to the best of our knowledge, but BF hired Meyer (whom he called "Maurice") to work for him. On May 8, 1784, Meyer received 395 *l.t.* in wages, and that same day BF recommended him to William Strahan in London, saying that he had been a member of his Passy household for five months, was a good compositor, understood Latin, French, and German, and had "the Character of an honest Man": Account XVII (XXVI, 3); BF to Strahan, May 8, 1784 (Morgan Library and Museum, New York).

From William Vaughan

ALS: American Philosophical Society

Dear Sir   London Oct 31 1783

From the friendly concern with which you have so frequently interested yourself respecting our family, it will give you some pleasure to learn of their safe arrival at Phia— My father landed severely afflicted with the Gout, the rest of the family were all well and experiencing Mrs. Beache's hospitality.[3] They had been under her roof for some days, but were in a day or two to remove to their own habitation. My sisters write me that Mrs. Beache's maners & spirits resembled very much Mrs. Priestleys and were their conversation committed to writing that Dr. P. would be sometimes puzzled to find which was not his wife. I shall feel now an additional pleasure whenever I pay Birmingham a visit.

I have been favored with a line from Miss Beckworth which I have been remiss in not communicating sooner to you it is dated July 26th. "If you write to Dr. Franklin I beg my compts. I have two of his grand daughters here tho too young to be on any other footing than as my guests."[4] She had then fourteen young ladies under her care, and expected to compleat her numbers before winter.

My letters from Philadelphia of 14 Sepr advise that "our late proclomation of July 2d[5] has given much displeasure, but the supposed injury will be to ourselves." The history of that Proclomation is well known, and I lament that the Coalition here has given a check to that system which would have followed the peace had the same Administration continued: France seems to have adopted a more liberal policy with respect to her islands.[6]

---

3. The Vaughans arrived in Philadelphia on Sept. 8 and lodged with the Baches: XL, 596, 597.

4. Deborah and Elizabeth Bache were aged two and six, respectively: I, lxiv. For their visit to Sally Beckwith's school in Mount Airy, see SB to BF, Nov. 5.

5. The king's Order in Council prohibiting trade between the British West Indies and the United States in American ships: XL, 289n.

6. This may be a reference to the July 23 proclamation by the acting governor of the Windward Islands and the *intendant* of Martinique granting Americans full privileges in French ports in the West Indies: *Courier de l'Europe*, XIV (1783), 283.

Could we in England overcome our narrow ideas on Commerce and open our doors by taking off those fetters to industry we shod: have little to fear from rivalship or petty jealousies. Payne I think says time makes more converts than reason.[7]

I duly recd Mr W. T. Franklins letter of 26 Sepr. the bill I remitted was intended to have been at Sight had not a mistake been committed by the person who negociated the bill. My brother Saml still continues in Germany.[8] Benj: is well and about expecting an addition to his family.[9]

It is with pleasure I inform you that Dr Price yesterday communicated your description of the Air Balloons to the Club who hope one day or other to see you amongst them again.[1] I am to give him a meeting with Mr Jay & Mr Adams. I wish I could form the compleat body of the Corps diplomatique; but as we cannot have your company in person we must be contented with your Portrait[2] as our President. Beleive me with the greatest respect & esteem to be Dear Sir Your sincere & obedient humble Servant   WM VAUGHAN

Addressed: Dr. B. Franklin / Passy / Paris

Notation: Vaughan Oct. 31. 1783

---

7. Vaughan is quoting the final sentence of the first paragraph of Thomas Paine's introduction to *Common Sense* (Philadelphia, 1776).

8. The bill of exchange was payment for BF's advances to Samuel Vaughan, Jr., who left Paris for Germany around the beginning of June bearing a letter of recommendation from BF and possibly also a passport. William Vaughan sent the bill of exchange to WTF on Aug. 8; see Grand to BF, Sept. 29, above.

9. The wife of William's brother Benjamin gave birth on Nov. 5; see BF to Benjamin Vaughan, Oct. 8.

1. The previous day was a Thursday, when the fortnightly meetings of the Club of Honest Whigs took place: Verner W. Crane, "The Club of Honest Whigs: Friends of Science and Liberty," *W&MQ*, 3rd. ser., XXIII (1966), 210. Price may have read BF's letter of Sept. 16.

2. William Vaughan owned the portrait of BF described in Sellers, *Franklin in Portraiture*, p. 422. It is thought to have been painted by Joseph Wright.

To Elias Boudinot

LS[3] and transcript: National Archives; press copy of LS and transcript: Library of Congress

Sir,   Passy, Nov. 1. 1783

Inclos'd is a Copy of my last, which went by the English Pacquet.[4] I heard after I wrote it, that the French Pacquet putting back by contrary Winds, Mr. Thaxter had an Opportunity of getting on board her and that She sail'd the 26th. of September. The mentioned new Commission is not yet come to hand. Mr. Hartley is not returned, and I hear will stay for the meeting of Parliament, which is to be the 11th. Instant, and not come hither till the Recess for the Christmas Holidays.[5] Mr. Jay went to England about three Weeks since on some personal affairs, and Mr Adams follow'd last Week to see that Country and take some Exercise during this Vacancy of Business. This Court is now at Fontainbleau but will return to Versailles in a few Days. Its good Disposition towards us continues. The late Failure of Payment in the Caisse d'Escompte, an Institution similar to the Bank of England, occasioned partly by its having gone too far in assisting the Government with Money, and the Inability of the Government to support their Credit, tho' extreamly desirous of doing it, is a fresh Proof that our not obtaining a farther Loan was not occasioned by want of Good will to assist us, as some have unjustly supposed, but by a real Want of the Means. Money is at present unaccountably scarce here, what is arrived and expected in Spain since the Peace, it is thought will set Things to rights. The Government has proposed a second Lottery for this Year by which they borrow 24 Millions, and is fill'd readily. This helps; and the Caisse d'Escompte goes on again with its operations, but it is said the Interest paid by the lottery Plan is near 7 per Ct.[6]

3. In the hand of L'Air de Lamotte, as is the now-missing LS from which the press copy was made. The one we publish is marked "duplicate." In both cases BF completed the complimentary close before signing.

4. BF to Boudinot, Sept. 27.

5. See Hartley to BF, Oct. 25.

6. Established in 1776 as a bank for bankers, the *caisse d'escompte* had become involved in the financial crisis caused by the government's shortage of specie. The crisis had been alleviated by giving notes of the *caisse d'escompte* the status of currency, but the political standing of Controller

I have received the Duplicate of your Excellency's Letter of the 15th. July to the Commissioners,[7] which is very satisfactory; tho' it came to hand but lately. The first sent, via N. York has not yet appeared. I have sent Copies of it to the Hague and Madrid. The Substance is published in several Papers.

I have acquainted the Minister of Sweden, that I have received the Ratification of the Treaty,[8] and he has written to me that he shall be in Town in a few Days, when he will make the Exchange.[9] The Conclusion of the Danish Treaty waits only for the Commission & Instructions from Congress. The Ambassador of Portugal inform'd me lately, that his Court had our proposed Plan under Consideration and that we should soon hear from them. I sent it to Congress by Barney, and hear the Ship is arrived. A Commission & Instructions will be wanting for that also, should the Congress be disposed to conclude a Treaty with that Nation.[1]

I see by the Public Prints, that the Congress have ratified the contract I made with the Minister here respecting the Loans and Aids we had received; but the Ratification itself, tho' directed to be sent me, has never come to hand, and I am often asked for it. I beg it may be forwarded by the first Opportunity.[2]

There has been with me lately Mr. Pierre du Calvet, a Merchant of Montreal, who when our Army was in Canada, furnished our Generals & Officers with many things they wanted, taking their Receipts and promisory Notes for Payment; and when the English repossess'd the Country, he was imprisoned

---

General Lefèvre d'Ormesson was ruined. He was dismissed on Nov. 2: J. F. Bosher, *French Finances, 1770–1795: From Business to Bureaucracy* (Cambridge, 1970), p. 257; Munro Price, *Preserving the Monarchy: the Comte de Vergennes, 1774–1787* (Cambridge, 1995), pp. 94–114. BF owned shares in the *caisse d'escompte:* XXX, 4; XXXVI, 434; XXXIX, 3.

7. XL, 301–8.

8. Congress ratified the treaty on July 29. Boudinot sent it to BF on Aug. 15: XL, 474.

9. That letter is missing. The ratifications were not exchanged until the following February; see the Baron Staël von Holstein to BF, Jan. 29.

1. For the proposed Portuguese-American treaty of commerce see XL, 122–32, 360–1. Capt. Joshua Barney's packet boat, the *General Washington,* reached Philadelphia on Sept. 9: XL, 444n.

2. Morris sent it on Nov. 4; see his letter of that date.

and his Estate seized, on Account of the Services he had rendered us. He has shown me the Originals of his Papers, which I think are genuine. He produced also a Quantity of Congress Paper which he says he receiv'd in Payment for some of the Supplies, and which appear'd to me of our first Emissions, and yet all fresh and clean, as having passed thro' no other hands. When he was discharg'd from Prison, he could not obtain Permission to go into the United States to claim the Debt, but was allow'd to go to England; and from thence he came hither to solicit Payment from me. Having no Authority to meddle with such Debts, and the Sum being considerable, I refus'd and advised him to take Passage for America, and make his Application to Congress. He said he was grown old, much broken and weakned by near 3 Years Imprisonment, and that the Voyage from Canada to London had like to have been too much for him, he being sick all the Way; so that he could not think of another, tho' distressed for want of his Money. He appears an honest Man, and his Case a hard one. I have therefore undertaken to forward his Papers, and I beg leave to recommend them to the speedy Consideration of Congress,[3] To whom I request you would be pleased to present my dutiful Respects, and assure them of my most faithful Services. With great Esteem & Regard, I have the Honour to be Sir, Your Excellency's most obedient & most humble Servant   B. FRANKLIN

His Excelly. Elias Boudinot Esqr. President of Congress

---

3. Du Calvet (1735–1786), French by birth, immigrated to Canada in 1758, becoming a merchant. The supplies he provided to the American army in 1775 and 1776 amounted to 56,394 *l.t.*, by his later account, and his incarceration at the hands of the British governor Haldimand lasted from September, 1780, until May, 1783. He sailed for London in August, 1783, seeking justice for what he considered an illegitimate imprisonment, and met with BF in Passy on Oct. 17 and 20: *JCC*, XXVI, 260; Du Calvet to BF, July 20, 1784 (APS). On April 21, 1784, Congress resolved to honor its debt to Du Calvet and to instruct BF to forward the "papers and vouchers in support of said account," after making duplicates that could serve if the originals were lost: *JCC*, XXVI, 261. If that resolution was ever sent to Passy, it has left no trace. See the *Dictionary of Canadian Biography* (15 vols. to date, Toronto, 1966–), IV, 227–32.

Duplicate.

Elias Boudinot to the American Peace Commissioners

Copy: National Archives

Gentlemen, Princeton 1. Nov. 1783

I am honored by the commands of Congress to transmit you a set of instructions in consequence of your joint and seperate letters of the months of June and July last, by Captain Barney, which I do myself the honor to enclose.[4] These were not finished till the 29th. ult. after having undergone the most mature deliberation and fullest discussion in Congress.

Yesterday we received from Colo. Ogden the news of the signature of the definitive Treaty on the 3d. of September, and that Mr. Thaxter was on the way with the official news. We long for his arrival tho' we have no doubt of the fact, which is also announced by the post this day from Boston.

I do most sincerely congratulate you, Gentlemen, on this most important and happy event, which has diffused the sincerest Joy throughout these States, and the terms of which must necessarily hand down the names of its American Negociators to Posterity with the highest possible honor. May the Gratitude of your Country ever be the fair reward of all your labours.

New York is not yet evacuated, but Sir Guy Carleton has informed our Commander in Chief, that he shall get clear of it in all this month, tho' I think they will not dare to stay much beyond the 15th. instant.[5]

Your &c. E B

4. The instructions are above, Oct. 29.
5. Carleton sent word to GW in mid-October that he would evacuate New York City in November. On Nov. 12 he sent his intended timetable. British troops left the city on Nov. 25 and the surrounding areas by Dec. 4, on which day GW bid farewell to his officers: Smith, *Letters*, XXI, 66, 71,

The Honorable The Ministers Plenipotentiary of the United
States of America Paris—

From Elias Boudinot

LS: American Philosophical Society; AL (draft): Library of Congress;
copy: Princeton University Library

Sir   Princeton 1st. November 1783

My last letters to you, were on the 15th. of August and 9th.
of September,[6] on the same subject, enclosing the ratification of
the Treaty with Sweden and duplicate, with an act of Congress
for your altering a few words in it—striking out the word *North*
before *America* in the title of the United States; and changing
the title of Delaware from *the three lower Counties on Delaware* to
the *Delaware State.*

I have the honor of acknowledging the receipt of your favours of the 12th. of June and from the 22d to the 25th. of July,[7]
by Capt. Barney.

By the present opportunity I forward public instructions, on
the subjects of your several letters, in an official letter directed
to the Commissioners jointly.[8]

Since the receipt of yours The Baron de Beelen Bertholf arrived here from Germany, who has given us some farther information relative to that Empire.[9] A Mr. De Boor has also arrived from the City of Hamburgh with Credentials from the
Government, who seem to wish a connection with us. I enclose
our answer, which I must beg the favour of your forwarding

157n; Jared Sparks, ed., *The Writings of George Washington* . . . (12 vols.,
Boston, 1834–37), VIII, 545–7; Freeman, *Washington,* V, 458–68.

6. XL, 474–5, 598.

7. These letters (XL, 150–2, 355–70) were written to former secretary for
foreign affairs Robert R. Livingston.

8. Boudinot's Nov. 1 letter to the American commissioners, and letters
to the individual commissioners, were entrusted to John Paul Jones, who
delivered them to JA in London. JA forwarded the present letter to BF on
Dec. 5 (below).

9. For the mission of the Baron Beelen de Bertholff see XXXIX, 445n, 491.

through the proper Channel. A copy of it you have enclosed for your information.[1]

The plan of the peace establishment is not yet so far digested with certainty that I can give you any answer to your request of dismission or relating to your Grandson.[2] Of this you may however be assured, that it is the prevailing disposition of Congress to do every thing for you or your Grandson that they can, consistent with the general plan they shall establish. Tho' perhaps you are not without your enemies, yet they are so few, that I am sure they never can prevent, or even unnecessarily delay, the gratitude of your Country, which is acknowledged your just due by even the few who are suspected to be not altogether your friends. As far as I can judge of the peace establishment, it will be to employ but two or three Ministers in Europe and those not higher in Character than Residents, or simply Ministers—The business in other places to be done by Consuls. Our Finances are so very low as to require every œconomical measure.

I have received the additional number of Medals, which, not having any particular directions from you, I distributed among the Members of Congress; presented one to the Governor of each State, and the Ministers round Congress. The compliment to the Grand Master of Malta,[3] I doubt not, will produce good effects, and for which the commercial interests of this Country will be much indebted to you.

Your approbation of the Revd. Mr. Wren's conduct has produced the enclosed vote of thanks to that Gentleman. I send for

1. BF's copy is missing, but the text is published in Smith, *Letters*, XXI, 133. Dated Nov. 1, it is addressed to the burgomasters and senate of Hamburg, responding to their letter of March 29 (Giunta, *Emerging Nation*, II, 77–9), which had been delivered by Johann Abraham de Boor. Boudinot quoted from an Oct. 29 congressional resolution promising to encourage trade between the United States and Hamburg (*JCC*, XXV, 757–8).

BF himself had forwarded a copy of the March 29 letter to Congress, as the city officials of Hamburg had asked him to do, though he waited until Sept. 13: XXXIX, 417–18; XL, 622.

2. In his letter of July 22[–26]; see XL, 364, 366.

3. To whom BF had sent a *Libertas Americana* medal. BF sent Congress a copy of his letter to Rohan, the grand master of the Knights of Malta, and a copy of the reply: XXXIX, 436; XL, 209, 369, 623.

your perusal my letter to Dr. Wren, with a Diploma I obtained for him from the University in this place, which I beg you will seal and forward.[4]

I shall leave the Chair of Congress next Monday and return to private life at Elizabeth Town, where however I shall always think myself honored by hearing of your health & happiness.

I have the honor to be, with the sincerest sentiments of respect and esteem, Sir, Your most obedient & very humb. Servt.

ELIAS BOUDINOT

P.S. If Mr. Dana has probably left Petersburgh you will be so good as to obtain the letter addressed to him,[5] and the large Packett only containing News Papers, I submit to your Judgment whether to send on or not—

The Treaty with Denmark is under Consideration,[6] but for want of 9 States could not be finished in Time for this Opportunity—

(Private)

The honble Benj. Franklin, Esq.

Endorsed: From the President to B Franklin Nov. 1. 1783

4. BF had suggested that Congress recognize Wren and that some American university award him an honorary degree: XL, 369–70. Boudinot's Nov. 1 letter to Wren expressed the thanks of Congress (pursuant to a Sept. 29 resolution) and enclosed a degree of doctor of divinity from the College of New Jersey: Smith, *Letters*, XXI, 136–7.

5. Boudinot to Dana, Nov. 1: Smith, *Letters*, XXI, 130–1. The recipient's copy is among Dana's papers at the Mass. Hist. Soc.

6. BF had enclosed the proposed treaty in his letter of July 22[–26]: XL, 367. On Oct. 22, a congressional committee suggested alterations to it: *JCC*, XXV, 720–2.

From Jan Ingenhousz: Dedication[7]

Printed in *Nouvelles Expériences et observations sur divers objects de physique* (Paris, 1785), pp. iii-iv; ADS (draft): Teylers Museum

Vienne en Autriche, ce 1re de novembre 1783.

A SON EXCELLENCE
MONSIEUR
BENJAMIN FRANKLIN,

Ministre Plénipotentiaire des Etats-Unis de l'Amérique auprès de la Cour de France, Membre de l'Académie royale des Sciences de Paris, de la Société royale de Londres, &c. &c. Président de la Société Philosophique de Philadelphie, &c.

MONSIEUR,

En faisant paroître cet Ouvrage sous vos auspices, je m'honore de votre amitié & de votre correspondance devant le public, qui connoît vos grands talens & vos succès dans les sciences physiques, & a conçu les plus hautes idées de votre caractère moral.

Agréez, je vous prie, MONSIEUR, cette preuve de la vénération singulière que je vous porte, & des sentimens d'une estime distinguée, qui me sont communs avec vos compatriotes, que vous avez si bien servi; avec les physiciens, qui vous doivent des idées, des expériences & des découvertes importantes, par lesquelles les bornes de leur science sont reculées; & j'ose dire avec la génération présente que vous illustrez. Je desire que le public voie dans cet hommage, la reconnoissance dont je suis pénétré, pour l'intérêt que vous ne cessez, depuis près de vingt ans, de prendre à mes travaux physiques, les conseils dont vous m'avez aidé dans mes recherches, & l'affection particulière que vous m'avez toujours portée, & qui vous a fait dire que vous trouviez de la satisfaction à être connu comme l'ami de l'Auteur.

Je suis, avec la plus grande estime, DE VOTRE EXCELLENCE, Le très-humble & très-obéissant serviteur & ami,

JEAN INGEN-HOUSZ

---

7. On May 16 BF had granted Ingenhousz permission to dedicate *Nouvelles Expériences et observations sur divers objects de physique* to him, considering it an honor (as he wrote) to have their friendship so acknowledged. Ingenhousz dated this dedication Nov. 1, 1783, but the work was not issued until 1785. See XL, 8, and the references there.

From Pierres   ALS: American Philosophical Society

Monsieur   Paris 3 9bre. 1783.
J'ai l'honneur de vous adresser les Essais dont je vous ai parlé
& que j'avois oublié de vous faire passer par ma derniere Lettre.[8]
Vous voudrez bien les faire rendre au porteur sous envelope.

J'y joins un Essai d'Impression en Or que je viens de faire
les fêtes. Je vais faire un second Essai & j'espere que je réussirai
mieux.

Je m'empresserai de vous faire part de mes differens pas dans
la Carriere que je parcours; c'est un hommage que je vous dois
& que je me feroi un plaisir de vous rendre.

Je suis avec un respect infini, Monsieur, Votre très humble &
très obeissant serviteur   PIERRES

M. franklin.

To Pierres

LS: Yale University Library; AL (draft): American Philosophical Society

Monsieur,   à Passy ce 3 Nov. 1783,
Je vous renvoïe cy inclus les Essais que vous avez bien voulu
me montrer. Je vous en remercie. J'ai vû avec plaisir le Progrès
que vous avez fait, dans une maniere qui differe de la mienne,
quoique peut être meilleure. Je serai bien aise de vous voir,
quand vous en aurez le Loisir, afin de finir notre Compte

Je suis avec beaucoup d'estime, Monsieur, Votre très humble
et très obeissant Serviteur./.   B FRANKLIN

M. Pierres.—

8. Presumably the "Essais" in stereotyping that Pierres made at BF's suggestion, and sent to him: entry for 1783 in Philippe-Denis Pierres, "Auto-
biographie" (MS, Newberry Library). See also George B. Watts, *Philippe-
Denis Pierres, First Printer Ordinary of Louis XVI* (Charlotte, N.C.,
1966), p. 28.

From John Bondfield   ALS: American Philosophical Society

Sir—   Bordeaux 4 Novr 1783
   I am Honord with your Confidential Letter of the 22 Ulto
(sans signature).[9]
   A fall from my Horse by which I have my left arm Broken
confines to my room and will prevent for some days longer applying to the Contents of your Enquiries wch I shall do so soon
as able and transmit you every information I can obtain from the
most Inteligent & impartial of our friends at this City. The Subject has already been 'descuted' in the Chamber of Commerce
our Merchants do not conclude that an admission into their Islands of American Traders ought to be forbid but they cannot
trace out a line but what will bring great Injury to their Trade.[1]
The Line that appeard most equitable was a Duty on Tonage
say a certain stipulated Sum on every Ton burthen of every vessel inwards & outwards that should unload or (&) Load in any
of the Islands belonging to France which Duty should be calculated so that the Economy of the American Navigation should
be cloggd with a burthen equal or even some little more than the
rate at which the National Navigation can be carried on.
   They are greatly jealous of their Sugar Trade deriving so
many various advantages that to burthen The Exportation to

9. Not found.
1. Since early 1783 the French government had been trying to formulate
a policy for the West Indies that balanced liberalized trade with America
and the established mercantile interests of French ports like Bordeaux. As
a temporary measure, France returned to the restrictions on American access to the islands that had been in place before the 1778 Treaty of Amity
and Commerce. At the end of August, 1783, Castries consulted Barclay,
Matthew Ridley, and Lafayette on the issue. Barclay probably conveyed
to BF his impression that the status quo was going to prevail. On Oct. 23,
Castries wrote a letter to the Chamber of Commerce of Guienne, urging
the expansion of Franco-American commerce and explaining why previous ventures had failed. Perhaps aware of this initiative, BF may have asked
Bondfield for information about its likely reception: XL, 360n; Roberts and
Roberts, *Thomas Barclay*, p. 129; Marvin MacCord Lowes, "Les Premières
Relations commerciales entre Bordeaux et les Etats-Unis d'Amérique
(1775–1789)," *Revue historique de Bordeaux et du département de la Gironde*,
XXI (1928), 87–9, 131.

compensate them would be laying a prohibition refering to the report I may make in virtue of the different sentiments that I may occasionally gather I have the Honor to be respectfully Sir your most Obedient Humble Servant   JOHN BONDFIELD

His Excellency D B Franklin Esqr

Notation: Bondfield 4 Nov. 1783.

From Dessin
LS: American Philosophical Society

Monsieur   Calais le 4 Novbre. 1783.

J'ai L'honneur de vous informer que d'ordre & d'Envoi de Mr. Hartley, Je viens de vous expédier par la Diligence qui partira demain pour arriver samedi prochain à Paris, *un paquet plombé* accompagné d'un acquit à Caution du Bureau en destination pour la Douane de Paris.[2] Vous avés d'autre part la note de mes frais & débours à cette expédition, Elle porte *douze francs* que J'ai fait suivre, & qui vous seront demandés avec le port.[3]

Je n'ai point encore de nouvelles des roues qui doivent me venir D'angleterre.[4] J'aurai grand soin de vous les acheminer citot leur arrivée, Entretems J'ai L'honneur de me protester avec le plus profond respect, Monsieur Votre très humble & tres dévoué serviteur   PIERRE DESSIN

Notation: Dessein 4 Decbre. 1783.

From Flandre de Brunville   LS: American Philosophical Society

Monsieur   Paris ce 4. 9bre. 1783.

J'ai reçu la lettre que vous m'avez fait l'honneur de m'ecrire[5] pour me demander de retarder le Jugement de l'affaire du

2. It contained Welsh flannel; see Hartley to BF, Oct. 25.

3. That note is on the verso of the sheet. It lists various expenses that total 12 *l.t.*

4. For which see Dessin's Oct. 14 letter.

5. Not found. Beaumont had asked BF to do this favor; see the annotation of Shaffer to BF, Nov. 9.

S. Scheffer détenu dans les Prisons du Chatelet jusqu'à ce que M. Barclay consul des Etats unis Soit de retour de Nantes.[6] Quoique cette affaire Soit actuellement totalement instruite, je suis trop jaloux de faire quelque chose qui puisse Vous être agreable pour ne pas differer à donner mes conclusions pendant quelques jours ainsi que Vous le desirez.

J'ai l'honneur d'être très respectueusement Monsieur, Votre très humble, et très obeissant Serviteur

DE FLANDRE DE BRUNVILLE

M. franklin ministre Plenipotentiaire des Etats unis à Passy

From Robert Morris

LS: American Philosophical Society; copy: Library of Congress

Sir,   Office of Finance 4th. Novr. 1783

I do myself the Honor to enclose another Copy of the Ratification of Congress to the Contract with the french Court of the sixteenth of July 1782 which is dated the twenty second Day of January last also the Ratification of the Contract of the twenty fifth of February last which is dated on the last Day of October—[7] These Pieces will go by the Washington Packet and I hope that you may receive them safely and soon.[8]

I am Sir Your most Obedient and Humble Servant

ROBT MORRIS

His Excellency Benjamin Franklin Esqr.—

6. Barclay, who was visiting Nantes and Lorient, would not return to Paris for another month; see the annotation of Barclay to BF, Dec. 16.

7. For the July 16, 1782, contract, ratified on Jan. 22, 1783, see XXXVII, 633–9. Congress had ratified the Feb. 25, 1783, contract on Oct. 31: XXXIX, 301n.

8. The *General Washington*, Capt. Joshua Barney, sailed *c.* Nov. 10. Among the passengers were John Paul Jones, William Jackson, Pierre-Charles L'Enfant (XXVI, 144n), and Louis Lebègue de Presle Duportail (XXIII, 93–4): Jackson to BF, Dec. 3 (below); *Morris Papers*, VIII, 646n.

From Richard Bache   ALS: American Philosophical Society

Dear & Hond. Sir   Philadelphia Novr. 5th. 1783.

I have put on board the Washington packet, Captain Barney, by whom this goes, two Barrels of Newton pippins, one Barrel of Chestnuts, a Box of Seeds, and a small Box of Grafts, put up as you directed; the cost of the Box of Seeds is five Guineas, you will herewith receive a Catalogue of them— I should have sent you a Barrel of Hiccory Nuts, could they have been procured, but none have come to Market yet.[9] Perhaps another opportunity may present itself soon, either from this place or Newyork when I shall not fail availing myself of it.

Sally has wrote you a long Letter, and given you the history of our little family.[1] I need not therefore add on that subject—

You will herewith receive the Newspapers wch will inform you of the unsettled state of our great Folks, who have been resolving & re-resolving for Six Months past on places for their permanent residence,[2] and this is almost all that has been done; they have lowered themselves much in the opinions of the people on this side the Atlantic, I wish it may not be the case in Europe—

With the Duty and Affections of the Family, I remain ever Dear sir Your affectionate Son   RICH: BACHE

Addressed: Dr. Franklin

From Sarah Bache   ALS: Yale University Library

Dear and Honoured Sir   Philadelphia Nov. 5th. 1783

Most earnestly have I wished for the Definitive Treaty to arrive, and Congress to find a resting place, that they might then

---

9. BF requested these items on July 27: XL, 390–1. On Oct. 27, RB recorded BF's debt to him of £5.8.0 for "Apples & Nuts to send to France": Penrose R. Hoopes, "Cash Dr to Benjamin Franklin," *PMHB*, LXXX (1956), 64.

1. Immediately below.

2. For Congress' decision see Boudinot to the American peace commissioners, Oct. 27.

have time to recall you, and our little Family be once more joined, the Treaty I am told is come, but when Congress will settle no one can say, they have lost much of the Confidence of the People since they began to wander, your old Friend General Gates, told me they were all splitting and seperateing, that no man in the world could hoop the Barrel but you,[3] and that you were much wanted here: Your Old Friends the Vaughans are here, and have taken a house in Our Neighbourhood, I promise myself great pleasure in their Society this Winter, the time they stay'd with us on their first coming, with your recommendation of them[4] has made me quite their Friend, I never knew altogether a more amiable Family. The dear little Children are all perfectly well and lively, tho they suffered in the summer heat particularly the youngest, which I expect will allways be the case till I am happy enough to have a retreat for them at that Season, it is true Deby was in the Country at Miss Beckwiths, but there I could not be with her, and I look upon a Mothers care to be as necessary as the fresh air, they want a great deal of attention the two or three first Summers of their lives, and some times even that does not do. You would be much pleased with Deborah the rest you know very well by description, tho she has black eyes, her skin is remarkably Fair, she talks plainer than Louis who is four years old, and about ten times as much, she calls herself her Papa's black eyed Boy, all this day has she been abroad, a Friend of mine that has no Children is quite in love with her, when I sent for her home this evening she was set up at the teatable with the Ladies and absolutely refused returning home, I would give a great deal that you were half an hour in Company with the dear little Soul that you might be perfectly convinced I am not partial when I say she is the loveliest little Creture in the world. To oblige Miss Beckwith and do her a service I let Betsy go with her out of town, but do not think I shall permit her to return, as I think her too young to be from under a

3. An anonymous pamphlet written in February, 1783, had claimed that a confederation of states without a sovereign authority was like "a cask without hoops": [Pelatiah Webster], *A Dissertation on the Political Union and Constitution of the Thirteen United States* . . . (Philadelphia, 1783), pp. 3–4.

4. For the Vaughans' arrival see William Vaughan to BF, Oct. 31. BF's recommendation has not been found.

Mothers wing, and what she can learn now very immaterial, her temper at present I wish to attend to as the most important thing, Miss B. too has a Number of young Ladies with her and cannot Miss such a Fairy, she has already made me a shift body, and done it very well but hates reading to a great degree, and never happy without work, Will if he had good masters would make a fine Fellow, he has a quick Memory, remarkable so, tho I do not think it a retentive one but time making him more steady, would make great alteration, he never thought it a trouble to learn any thing, and seems to be without dificulty when employ'd about his exercises, he loves play to his soul, and almost kill'd himself last Summer with Swimming, in which he excells but going too frequently and in the heat he was much weakened, the holidays are now given in August, and to a Boy that is to stay in the town it is rather an injury, than an advantage, I intended only to have talked to you about Our little stranger, and have some how or other introduced almost all the party, but you will not think it tedious to hear old acquaintance talked off, and I must not forget little Louis, among the Group, he is a lovely fellow, by far the most active of them all, has a great share of drollery, and is famous for dancing, loveing Custards, and hateing a Womans School. They wish to see Benjamin much, Mr Lardner a Friend of ours goes in a few days by whom I shall again write,[5] the Children join in duty with your Afectionate Daughter

S BACHE

Addressed: Dr: Franklin

From John Shaffer

ALS: American Philosophical Society

Sir　　　　　　　　　　　　　Paris le 5 9bre 1783

Mr Beaumont avocat whas Kind Enough to inform me that you are disposed to make me a Small Advane from time to time for my Subsistance during My Confingment, Blive me what Ever Advance your Exelency Should be Kind Enough to make me will be Returned with Gratitude before my departure from

5. For John Lardner and the letters he carried see RB to BF, Nov. 9, letter (II).

this Country, If I have Justis Rendered me and the Only Return to me what the have taken from me when I was arrested, and what has bean Stole from me Since I have bean Arrested amounts to £5400 *Livre* And, As to my falts impresinment it depends upon the Discretion of the Justis, what Sum the thinck Proper to give me, theirfore have No great hopes, I desire No More then what is Just beteen man and man—

I am allso informed that you was Kind Enough to Right a few lines to the Kings Attorney[6] wherin you have desired that he would Render me Justis wich I asure your Exelency is a great Consolation for wich I Ever Shall acnoladeg my Self to be with Profound Respect your Exelencys Most Obedent and Veriy humble Servant   J. SCHAFFER

P.S. the bearrer of this letter is a fidel Commisiariere

His Exelency Docter Franklin

From William Alexander[7]   ALS: American Philosophical Society

My Dear Sir   Nantes 6 November 1783
  I left St Germains Sunday Morning & got here on Tuesday.[8]
The post since come in, brought me your most acceptable let-

---

6. The *procureur du roi* Flandre de Brunville; see his letter to BF of Nov. 4.
  7. In early September, Alexander proposed to the farmers general a plan whereby he and JW would supply France with American tobacco: Alexander would establish himself in Virginia and arrange for the shipments, while JW would remain in France and receive them. The farmers general drew up a nonexclusive contract that did not preclude the arrangement they had proposed to Robert Morris in July, whereby the United States would repay its debt through tobacco shipments. Vergennes approved the Alexander-Williams contract on Oct. 3. For detailed overviews of this plan, which eventually included Morris as a partner, see Price, *France and the Chesapeake*, II, 741–6; *Morris Papers*, VIII, 739–41; IX, 150–9. JW's letter to WTF of Sept. 1, 1783 (APS), asking for names of farmers to whom they could address their proposal, helps establish the chronology.
  8. Nov. 4. In preparation for emigrating, Alexander swore an oath of allegiance to the United States before BF at Passy on Oct. 30 (APS). The oath, in the hand of BFB, is essentially identical to that published in XXXIV,

ter of the 2d which Cover'd a packet for the President of the Congress, to be forwarded immediatly on my arrival—[9] You also hand me two letters from a Woman calling herself widow to Mr Sprowl of Norfolk—In fact she was widow to his nephew James Hunter, whose Children are one of the three families, to whom he bequested his Estate. She herself is a very bad Woman, with I am assured no Mean talents of Insinuation & address—[1] I leave the letters with Mr Williams, to be returnd to you, if Called for— I most heartily thank you for your recommendations to your friends, & will be obliged to you for mentioning me to *Mr Morris* when you write Him—[2] I expect to Sail in two days,[3] & quit Europe without reluctance, in Hopes that my absence may be of Some benefit to my Family, a Consideration to which It is no great Compliment to them, to say I am willing to devote my remaining days— I beg my Compliments to your Son—and That you will believe me with unvaried Attachment My Dear Sir Your most Devoted humble Ser,

W: ALEXANDER

Addressed: A Son Excellence / Le Docteur Franklin / Ministre plenipo: des Etats / Unies de L'amerique / a Passy / pres / Paris

Notation: W. Alexander 6 Nov. 1783

581–2, except that it lacks the final sentence, "So help me God." Once in Nantes, Alexander signed articles of agreement with JW on behalf of their respective firms, William Alexander & Co. and Jonathan Williams & Co. The text of that agreement is in *Morris Papers*, IX, 156–7.

9. BF's letter of Nov. 2 is missing. It undoubtedly enclosed BF to Boudinot, Nov. 1.

1. Alexander was obviously among those who did not believe that Katherine Sproule Douglas had been legally married to Andrew Sprowle (Sproule). It is possible that Alexander knew of her first husband, James Hunter, in Scotland. For Mrs. Douglas' marriages, allegiances, and claims, see her letter to BF of Nov. 28 and the annotation there. The letters BF forwarded have not been located.

2. Among the now-missing letters of recommendation was one to RB dated Nov. 2, which asked him to introduce Alexander to Robert Morris: RB to BF, March 7, 1784 (Yale University Library). BF's letter to Morris of Dec. 25 includes an explanation of Alexander's mission and a recommendation.

3. Contrary winds delayed his departure until Nov. 22. He sailed aboard JW's ship *Mariamne:* JW to Alexander J. Alexander, Dec. 6, 1783 (Yale University Library).

From Charles-François-Hyacinthe Esmangart[4]

LS: American Philosophical Society

Monsieur   A Paris le 6. 9bre. 1783.

Ce n'est que depuis peu de jours que la lettre que vous m'avés fait lhonneur de m'écrire le 8. 8bre.[5] m'est parvenue. Dès Sa réception j'ai pris, Monsieur, Sur le compte du nommé John Hammon, les éclaircissements que vous desiriés. L'Amérique n'est point la patrie de ce Matelot. Il est né en Irlande; mais en 1773 il S'est rendu à Philadelphie et a passé Successivement dans plusieurs Isles. Il prétend que, Sur la fin de la derniere guerre, il a été pris par les Anglois et envoyé au Havre pour y être échangé; mais qu'il a perdu Ses papiers, S'est égaré en route, et n'a pu obtenir Son renvoi. Vous trouverés peutêtre, Monsieur, que cette partie de Sa déclaration laisse quelque chose de louche et de peu Satisfaisant. Aureste cet homme a été trouvé Sans passeport et mendiant. On l'a arrêté et il a été conduit dans la maison de force de Beaulieu près Caen.[6] Depuis le 13 Juillet que cet homme y est détenu, personne ne l'a réclamé; mais je dois, Monsieur, vous prévenir qu'il S'y est toujours bien conduit. Il paroit qu'il est d'un caractére doux et tranquile, et il Seroit à desirer que l'on lui procurât les moyens de Se livrer à Son premier état. Son desir Seroit de retourner dans le Sein des Etats unis, et Si vous avés la bonté de vous intéresser à son Sort, et de lui procurer les moyens de Se rendre à l'Orient ou dans un autre port de mer, je lui ferai rendre l'usage de la liberté, et il recevra un passeport pour qu'il puisse Se rendre à sa destination Sans être inquiétté.

Je Suis avec respect Monsieur Votre très humble et très obéissant Serviteur./.   Esmangart

M. Franklin

Notation: Esmangare 6 Nov. 1783.

4. The *intendant* of Caen: XL, 585n.
5. BF sent this now-missing letter under cover to Mme d'Houdetot; see her acknowledgment of Oct. 14.
6. The workhouse was erected between 1765 and 1768: Gabriel Désert, ed., *Histoire de Caen* (Toulouse, 1981), p. 331.

From Joseph Banks   ALS: University of Pennsylvania Library

Dear Sir   Soho Square Nov. 7. 1783
    Yesterday Evening I opend the Session of the Royal Society
by reading to them your two Communications upon the subject
of the Aerostatique Machines lately executed in France[7] & I can
Assure you without Flattery that an Evident pleasure was visible in the manner in which they receivd your return (as they
Considerd it) to Philosophical amusements after having so long
being detaind from them by business so inimical to Science.
    Whether you would chuse to have these Essays printed in
the Philosophical transactions is a Question to which I should
be much obligd to you for an answer the reason against it is that
during the Long Vacation of the Society the business is much
more developd than it was when you Communicated the reason
why they should be printed is that as far as they go they are distinctly & well written in short unless you intend to amuse your
Leisure by giving some more general detail of what has been
done on this subject I should have no doubt of the propriety of
Printing them & will answer for the readyness of the Committee of Papers to give their approbation.
    Beleive me there are many here who would rejoice to see you
again in your old haunts to which I do not doubt you feel some
inclination to return & none more than Your Faithfull Servant
                                                Jos: Banks

We are told by the newspapers that a Ballon has been let fly from
London[8] I know nothing relative to the particulars but I think
I see an inclination in the more respectable part of the R. S. to
guard against the Ballomania which has prevaild in & not to
patronize Ballons merely on account of their rising in the atmo-

---

    7. bf's letters to Banks of Aug. 30[–Sept. 2] (xl, 543–52) and Oct. 8,
above.
    8. Banks may be referring to the Nov. 4 release of a balloon, five feet in
diameter, by the Italians Count Francesco Zambeccari and Michael Biaggini: J. E. Hodgson, *The History of Aeronautics in Great Britain* . . . (London, 1924), pp. 101–2.

sphere till some experiment likely to prove beneficial either to
Society or Science is proposd to be annext to them[9]

From Jacques-Aimée de Bourzeis[1]

LS: American Philosophical Society

Monsieur   [c. November 7, 1783]
Des faits vrais, et simplement exposés dans cette brochure,
offriront les procédes de l'art de guerir en opposition aux effets
de L'Empirisme.[2]
Je suis avec le plus profond Respect de Votre excellence.
Monsieur Le très humble et tres obeïssant serviteur.

DE BOURZEIS D. M. P.[3]

9. Among those arguing against any involvement of the Royal Society
in balloon experiments was Charles Blagden. During Banks's absence from
London in the fall (he was at his Lincolnshire estate from mid-September
to early November), Blagden frequently sent him scientific news, including
regular updates on French balloons. Noting the heated arguments among
French scientists, Blagden gloated that "during all the heat & enthusiasm
of our neighbours we retained in this country a true philosophical tranquillity," and he counseled against "the folly of simple imitation" until balloons
could be used in "some capital experiment": Neil Chambers, ed., *Scientific
Correspondence of Sir Joseph Banks, 1765–1820* (6 vols., London, 2007), II,
133, 164–5, 174–5, 204.

1. The physician for the *Cent-Suisses*, one of the Swiss guard companies
at the French court, and a privy councillor of the margrave of Branden-
burg: *Almanach royal* for 1783, p. 603.

2. Bourzeis enclosed a copy of *Observation très-importante sur les effets
du magnétisme animal* (Paris, 1783), which was first advertised in the *Jour.
de Paris* on Nov. 7. The book criticized the treatment Franz Anton Mesmer
(identified only as "M. M. . . .") applied to one of Bourzais's patients, who
suffered from pulmonary edema (*hydropisie de poitrine*) and ultimately died.
BF's copy is at the Hist. Soc. of Pa.: Wolf and Hayes, *Library of Benjamin
Franklin*, p. 144. For a detailed discussion of the relationship between mesmerism and empiricism see Jessica Riskin, *Science in the Age of Sensibility:
the Sentimental Empiricists of the French Enlightenment* (Chicago and London, 2002), pp. 190–209.

3. Docteur-Médecin de la Faculté de Paris.

From Silas Deane

ALS: University of Pennsylvania Library

Sir,   London Novr: 7th: 1783

I took the Liberty a few Days since To write You on the subject of certain reports lately propagated to my disadvantage,[4] I hope that the Letter came safe to Your hands, and I have only to add, that I have both before, & since my writing, improved every Opportunity, in my power, To serve the Commerce of Our Country, particularly to have the restraint, on Our West India Trade taken off; but my acquaintance, & influence do not extend, beyond a small private Circle, though what I have said, and wrote on that subject, may possibly have reached farther, I believe it has, and have some reason to hope, that those and some other restraints, will be removed, or moderated, whither they are, or not, I have done my duty, as a private Volunteer, in the service. I have wrote a long Letter to Mr. Barclay, and one to Col Wadsworth, on the subject of my Accts.,[5] and hope that what I have said, and the documents which I have Transmitted, will facilitate a settlement for which I am extremely impatient. I propose to send Mr sebor to Paris, if I can have any prospect of closing by that means my Accts. I have the honor To be with much respect Your most Obedt & Very huml: servt.

S DEANE

P.S. I have taken the Liberty to enclose my Letter To Col Wadsworth to Your Care— My Compliments To Your Grandson Mr W T Franklin.

His Excelly. Benja: Franklin Esqr.

Addressed: His Excelly. / Benjn Franklin Esqr. / Minister Plenipoty. for the United / States of America in France

---

4. Above, Oct. 19.
5. His letters to Thomas Barclay and Jeremiah Wadsworth were both dated Nov. 7: *Deane Papers*, v, 228–32, 233–4.

From Richard Bache: Two Letters

(I) ALS: New York Public Library; (II) ALS: American Philosophical Society

I.

Dear & Hond: Sir   Philadelphia Novr. 9th. 1783

Permit me to introduce to you Mr. Rucker, who tho' a native of England, has formerly resided in France; and having spent a few Months in this Country, I have had the pleasure of his acquaintance; and have formed a favorable opinion of him— I wish to recommend him to your notice & Civilities, as a Gentleman very deserving of them—[6] I wrote to you & Benny per Capt. Barney who sailed this day with a fair Wind;[7] I have put on board of him, the Seeds, Grafts, Apples & Nuts you wrote for, & wish them safe to your hands.

I am ever Dear Sir Your affectionate Son.   RICH: BACHE

Dr. Franklin.

Addressed: His Excellency / Dr. Benjamin Franklin / at / Passy. / Favored by Mr. Rucker.[8]

II.

Dear & Hond: Sir   Philadelphia November 9th. 1783.

This I hope will be handed you by my very particular & worthy Friend Mr. John Lardner, Son of the late Mr. Linford Lardner of this City—[9] I take the liberty of introducing him, not

6. John Rucker had written to BF from Lorient in 1782, acting on behalf of Jonathan Nesbitt & Co.: XXXVI, 560–1. For more background on Rucker and his mercantile family see *Morris Papers*, IX, 418. On this return trip to France, he took charge of the squirrel skins that SB was sending to WTF: SB to WTF, Nov. 10, 1783 (APS).

7. RB's letters to BF and BFB were written on Nov. 5. The former is above. To BFB, RB wrote that he was enclosing a letter from the boy's mother and one from his younger brother William, despite its being "scratched and blotted." He hoped that BFB's health was perfectly restored, instructed him to be dutiful, and advised him to relearn English before returning to America so that his parents would be able to converse with him (Musée de Blérancourt).

8. At the top of the present letter WTF wrote "Hotel de Vauban, Rue de Richelieu", which may have been Rucker's local address.

9. Lardner carried letters of introduction from SB and RB to WTF as well. SB wanted BF to know that Lardner was also a grandson of "Old

only as my particular Friend, but as a Gentleman highly deserving your notice & Esteem— Should he at any time require your advice in any matters, or your assistance in monied matters, you may rely on his faith & integrity— Your giving full Credence to this recommendation, will ever oblige Dear Sir Your affectionate Son

RICH BACHE

Dr. Franklin

Addressed: His Excellency / Dr. Benjamin Franklin / at / Passy / favored by Mr. Lardner.

From Marsilio Landriani[1]

ALS:[2] Historical Society of Pennsylvania

⟨Milan, November 9, 1783, in Italian: I would fail in the commission given to me by the Imperial Court of publishing a *mé-*

Mr Branson's." For William Branson, see XIX, 57n. Lynford Lardner (III, 12n) had been a member of the APS and a director of the Library Company. His son John Lardner (1752–1825) was an active member of the Philadelphia City Cavalry throughout the war; at the end of 1782 he was elected to the Friendly Sons of St. Patrick, of which Bache was a member. He sailed to Europe at the end of 1783, returning in September, 1784. He was elected to the Pa. legislature in 1791: SB to WTF, [Nov. 6, 1783], APS; RB to WTF, Nov. 9, 1783, APS; Charles P. Keith, *The Provincial Councillors of Pennsylvania* . . . (Philadelphia, 1883), pp. 315–19; John H. Campbell, *History of the Friendly Sons of St. Patrick* (Philadelphia, 1892), pp. 55, 144; *Pa. Gaz.*, Sept. 15, 1784.

1. The Milanese professor of experimental physics whose project, the subject of the present letter, had been introduced to BF by Saussure on Oct. 10. Landriani was an early supporter of lightning rods and in 1780 published an article about the effects of a lightning strike at a monastery in Milan. Three years later the Austrian government commissioned him to oversee the protection of all public buildings in the region and produce a dissertation that would help dispel popular misconceptions about lightning rods and encourage their widespread use. The book, published by order of the government, was *Dell' Utilità dei conduttori elettrici* (Milan, 1784). See Antonio Pace, *Benjamin Franklin and Italy* (Philadelphia, 1958), pp. 26, 39–41; *Dizionario biografico degli Italiani* (73 vols. to date, Rome, 1960–).

2. The existence of a contemporary French translation, filed with the original at the Hist. Soc. of Pa., suggests that BF did not share Landriani's

moire raisonné on the utility of conductors, in order to make their use more common among us, if before its publication I did not write to you, the illustrious and celebrated gentleman to whom we owe this great discovery. Not knowing you personally, I asked my dear friend Monsieur de Saussure to request from you all the information you have about the use of conductors and those that have been erected in the United States, because I seek to persuade a people for whom this carries more authority than all philosophical arguments. I will include at the end of my memoir a list of conductors that have been installed in different parts of Europe. To this end I have contacted friends in Germany, France, and England, etc. who have provided the relevant information.[3]

At present I am only lacking information regarding the United States, which I consider crucial because it is rumored that in America there have been many cases in which conductors proved dangerous. Any communication from you will be sufficient to remove this prejudice, which prevents the public from adopting conductors.[4]

Count di Wilzeck, who succeeded Count di Firmian as imperial commissioner and minister plenipotentiary in Austrian

---

confidence in his Italian reading skills (expressed in the postscript). The Italian original is printed in Pace, *Benjamin Franklin and Italy,* pp. 369–71.

3. Landriani continued to receive replies for several months after writing this letter; they came from as far north as Copenhagen. He printed many of them, including those from Magellan, Saussure, Bertholon, Toaldo, and Buffon, and concluded with a catalogue listing the locations of more than 300 conductors. The main body of the book recounted the lightning rod's development, provided additional information gleaned from correspondents, and instructed readers on how to construct and set up a conductor.

4. On p. 170 of *Dell' Utilità dei conduttori elettrici,* Landriani noted that he had written BF for information on the current usage of lightning rods in America and still hoped to receive a reply before the printing of the book was completed. If BF ever sent a reply, that letter has been lost. He did not receive a copy of Landriani's book until long after he had returned to Philadelphia; at that time he thanked the author and reported on how a conductor on his own house had saved it from destruction while he had been away in France: BF to Landriani, Oct. 14, 1787 (Österreichische Nationalbibliothek).

Lombardy,[5] asked me to offer you his services and assure you of his highest esteem. I lent him the Constitutions of the United States, which M. de Saussure sent me, and he would like to have a copy in English. He would have asked this himself but did not dare, not being known to you. If you can grant him this favor, please send the book to the following address [*which he provides*].

P.S. I wrote to you in Italian because I know that you understand it very well. However, your reply can be in English, which I understand fairly well.⟩

From Sir Edward Newenham

ALS: American Philosophical Society

Dear Sir   Sunday Novr: the 9th[-15][6] 1783

The Importance of Mr: Floods defence, & the Statement of his Conduct having been so plainly & truly Expressed, that I imagine the enclosed paper will prove agreable to you—it has entirely overthrown his Antagonist Mr Grattan in the public estimation—[7]

5. Johann Joseph Graf von Wilczek (1738–1819) succeeded Karl Gotthard Graf zu Firmian (1718–1782) as Austrian minister plenipotentiary in Lombardy in 1782: Constant von Wurzbach, ed., *Biographisches Lexikon des Kaiserthums Oesterreich* (60 vols., Vienna, 1856–91), under Wilczek; Rudolf Vierhaus, ed., *Deutsche Biographische Enzyklopädie* (2nd ed.; 12 vols., Munich, 2005–8), under Firmian; *Repertorium der diplomatischen Vertreter*, III, 83.

6. Newenham must have misdated his postscript, whose subject is the committee on the Portugal trade. Parliament appointed that committee on Nov. 15: *The Parliamentary Register: or, History of the Proceedings and Debates of the House of Commons of Ireland* . . . (17 vols., Dublin, 1784–1801), II, 141; *The Journals of the House of Commons of the Kingdom of Ireland* . . . (31 vols., Dublin, 1782–94), XXI, 272.

7. On Nov. 1, against customary practice, Henry Flood was given the opportunity in the House of Commons to respond at length to Henry Grattan's accusations of Oct. 28 (for which see the annotation to Newenham's letter of that date). Grattan rose to reply, but Newenham declared the dispute resolved and successfully moved for the House to adjourn: *Parliamentary Register*, II, 61–70; James Kelly, *Henry Flood: Patriots and Politics in Eighteenth-Century England* (Dublin, 1998), p. 354. The Nov. 1 proceedings

Tomorrow "is the Day, the Important Day"; the Grand National Convention meet at the Royal Exchange at 12 oClock; what the result of it may be, I cannot Say, but on thursday last, the State Trumpeter of Corruption (Mr John Forster) at a late hour, & a thin house, moved & Carried the Question of adjournment for to *morrow*, to avoid any Attempts that might be made to direct our Representatives to Limit the Bill of Supplies to 6 months; as was our Intention, in order to Obtain the Royal assent to a bill for a Parliamentary reform;[8] No man can be excused attending the House of Commons on Monday without being put under arrest, agreable to act of Parliament, whenever a Contested Election is to be tried;[9] we have Committees Sitting, how to parry off the deadly blow—my plan is to Keep as many Members off, so as to reduce the Number of Attendants below Sixty, if that should be Obtained the House cannot proceed upon any buisiness untill the Day following; before which time, we shall have resolved that no money bill should pass for a longer Term—

10th Novr: My plan for having a thin house did not take, for administration had 72 present, & the Supplies passed for 15 months,[1] so that they have absolutely declared hostility against

---

of the House were published in the *Dublin Evening Post* on Nov. 4. The same issue also contained an open letter to Grattan severely criticizing his conduct, written by Newenham under the pseudonym Leonidas. On Nov. 8, the *Dublin Evening Post* printed a full transcript of Flood's Nov. 1 speech.

   8. It was on Friday, Nov. 7, that Foster successfully moved to have the House consider the spending bill on the following Monday, the first day of the Grand National Convention. The convention responded by adjourning early that day to allow M.P.s to attend the debates in the House: *Parliamentary Register*, II, 91; *The History of the Proceedings and Debates of the Volunteer Delegates of Ireland, on the Subject of a Parliamentary Reform . . .* (Dublin, 1784), pp. 27–9.

   9. On Monday, Nov. 10, the House appointed a committee for the trial of the disputed election in the borough of Baltinglass, County Wicklow, and noted the names of absent M.P.s, following the regulations in the Act to Regulate Trials of Controverted Elections or Returns of Members to Serve in Parliament: *Parliamentary Register*, II, 91; *Journals of the House of Commons of the Kingdom of Ireland*, XXI, 238–9.

   1. The Bill of Supply was considered by the Committee of Supply on Nov. 10. Newenham's attempt to limit the bill to six months was rejected 92 to 32, and the Supply Committee resolved to propose the bill for 15 months: *Parliamentary Register*, II, 109–10, 126.

the County Freeholders & the whole Volunteer Army; This morning we mett, of which the papers will give you an Account of;[2] I shall only add, that it was one of the most Solemn & Grand Processions I ever saw; 219 Volunteer Delegates with a General[3] at their head, who wore the Ensignes he was lately honoured with by his Peers I mean the Starr & Ribband of St: Patrick;[4] the Volunteers lined the streets; Such Crowds of People were never seen; Peals of Applause ecchoed from Every Quarter; After some Necessary Forms being Established, we adjourned untill to morrow, first having appointed a Committee of 45 to prepare a Plan of Reform, & who are to deliver it on Friday or saturday; all the Delegates are Obliged to Sign the roll before they can Speak or Vote; instead of fines, every Member absent at roll Call, is to [be] censurd from the Chair in the most pointed Manner—[5] The Roman Catholics finding that 20 to one were against them have Dropt all Pretensions for the Present to obtaining Votes—[6]

2. The opening of the convention was reported in the *Dublin Evening Post*, Nov. 11, 1783.

3. The commander-in-chief of the Irish Volunteers was James Caulfield, first Earl of Charlemont (1728–1799), who was elected as president of the convention at its opening session: *ODNB;* Patrick Rogers, *The Irish Volunteers and Catholic Emancipation (1778–1793)* . . . (London, 1934), p. 115.

4. The British government had created the Most Illustrious Order of St. Patrick the previous February as an Irish equivalent to the English and Scottish orders of knighthood. The lord lieutenant of Ireland, Earl Temple, selected the 15 peers who were knighted either to reward their attachment to the crown or to secure their future loyalty. In the case of Charlemont, Temple hoped that the honor would make him suspect among reformers: Peter Galloway, *The Most Illustrious Order: the Order of St Patrick and its Knights* (London, 1999), pp. 11–25.

5. The convention actually passed these measures on its second day, Tuesday, Nov. 11. It formed a committee to present a plan for parliamentary reform to the convention. The committee in turn appointed a subcommittee consisting of one delegate from each county (including Newenham) to examine existing reform proposals and to draft a plan. Earlier, the convention had passed a motion to censure absent delegates: *History of the Proceedings and Debates of the Volunteer Delegates of Ireland*, pp. 30–2, 40–2.

6. On Nov. 11 and 14 the delegates debated at length whether to take up the issue of Catholic enfranchisement. However, when the subcommittee formed to devise a reform plan met on Nov. 13, only two of its 40 members

I shall impatiently expect the honor of your Excellencys Answer in regard to *this Island* being enserted in the Treaty, as I wish to have my Country fixed upon the firmest foundation of *mutual* regard with America; you will considerably Add to the other obligations I owe you by your friendship to my *Injured* Country—

I like not the beginning of this administration;[7] they are inimical to Every Extension of Liberty and they are prodigal of the public money; I cannot give them a Single Vote;—

When your Excellency has read the Enclosed papers, I request you will send them to the truly worthy & Patriotic Marquiss Le Fayette—

All my family join me in most respectfull wishes for your Excellencys health & happiness— Lady Newenham always remembers you with every warm sentiment of Sincere regard & respect—

I have the Honor to be with Every sentiment of Regard & respect Dear Sir your Excellencys Most Obl: & Most Obt: Hble Sert   EDWD NEWENHAM

14 Novr 1783

There is a Committee now sitting upon the Portugal Trade— I wish to Lower the Duties on French wines & rize those of Portugal—of the two I would give France the Preference—[8]

---

favored voting rights for Catholics. The subcommittee's plan, written largely by Henry Flood and submitted to the committee on Nov. 21, explicitly limited extensions of the franchise to Protestant freeholders and leaseholders. The committee passed these provisions on Nov. 24 and 25: *History of the Proceedings and Debates of the Volunteer Delegates of Ireland*, pp. 30, 33–7, 42–52, 77, 79–90 ; Rogers, *Irish Volunteers and Catholic Emancipation*, pp. 117–27.

7. The first session of the Irish parliament under the new lord lieutenant, Robert Henley, second Earl of Northington (who had assumed the position on April 30), began on Oct. 14. Chief Secretary Thomas Pelham had been in office since August: *ODNB*.

8. The long-standing trade dispute between Britain and Portugal was behind Newenham's repeated requests to BF for information about the British-American commercial treaty and his suggestion that Ireland should appoint consuls in America (see his letter of Oct. 20 and the annotation there). Since 1780 Portugal had closed its ports first to some Irish textiles

Addressed: His Excellency Dr: Franklin / Passy / Paris / under Cover to Mr Dupont

From John Shaffer   ALS: American Philosophical Society

Sir   Paris ce 9 9bre 1783

As my avocat has Just informed me affter the information He has made that in Justis to my Self it will be the Shortest way to bring my Cause to a Conclution. The Partis has Even made a Proposition to arange the affair but Knowing my inosance am determend to bring on my trial as Soon as Possible in order to Convince to the world of my inosance.

Theirfore as thiere is Seaverl trials Comming on in a few days Should be happe to be on of the first, but as your Exelency was Kind Enough to Right a few lines to the Kings atterney in order Not to bring on my trial untill the arrival of Mr Barclay, theirfore will prevent him from Giving in his Conclutions untill he hears further from you, Mr Beaumont will Explain to you my Reason for bringing on the Conclution of my affair.

Theirefore if your Exelency will be Kind Enough only to Right a few lines to the Kings Attoney in order to give his Conclution as Soon as *Possible* it will be an adetion upon the maney Obligations Confered upon your Exelenys Most Obedent & Very humble Servant[9]   J SCHAFFER

His Exelency Docter Franklin

---

and later to all Irish commodities in order to force Britain to negotiate a new commercial treaty. The failure of successive British governments to resolve this dispute at a time of economic crisis reinforced resentments among Irish reformers against British control over their nation's commerce. Their demands included trade sanctions against Portugal (like the one mentioned here) as well as greater autonomy for Ireland in conducting its commercial relations: James Kelly, "The Irish Trade Dispute with Portugal, 1780–87," *Studia Hibernica,* XXV (1990), 7–48.

9. Shaffer sent another letter to BF the following day (this in French, written by Menier de Saint Yver), explaining that Beaumont had made a mistake when asking BF to request a postponement. He now begged BF to write to the *procureur du roi* and the *lieutenant criminel* requesting that the

From Thomas Collinson[1]

ALS: American Philosophical Society

Southgate. Middlesex Nov. 12th— 1783—

My dear Friend,

At length the lenient hand of Time, hath in part effected, what was refused to Philosephy and Reason; I therefore find myself enabled to indulge my Wish of addressg. a Line to you; affectionately to inquire after your Welfare, both in Body and Mind— This I cannot well do, to so particular a Friend, without touching on my late Calamities; but as such Subjects are never agreeable; I will be as brief as possible— The Seeds of that Harvest of Sorrow, which I have lived to reap, were not sown by myself— On the Decease of my Partner and Brother in law, J B,[2] I found, when his Papers came into my Hands; that by his easy Belief, and deficiency in those Abilities and Knowledge of Mankind, which were so conspicuous in his Father; he had involved Affairs so deeply—that tho' I did not despair; yet I trembled, when I beheld it. The Times that succeeded were remarkably Adverse to the Banking Business— Money became very scarce—its high Value induced every Body to employ it; at large Interest in Discounts, Loans and other Governmt. Securities— Under these additional Disadvantages and Pressures; the House, consisting of myself, and my Nephew Tritton,[3] still subsisted, and from our constant Attendance, and unremitting Exertions, we flattered ourselves, that gradually all Difficulties

---

trial take place that week. Otherwise, Shaffer explained, he would have to remain in prison until February or March, which his health would not permit. Shaffer wrote his own letter to WTF (in English) the same day, asking him to remind BF to write to the *procureur du roi*. Shaffer to BF and WTF, Nov. 10, 1783, APS.

BF must have complied, as the trial was scheduled for Nov. 20: Shaffer to BF, Nov. 19, below.

1. BF's former banker (a partner in Brown, Collinson & Tritton) and the nephew of BF's old friend Peter Collinson. BF had last corresponded with the banking firm in 1780; it failed in 1782: XXXI, 360n; XXXVII, 175–6.

2. James Brown (IX, 218n), the son of BF's old friend Henton Brown.

3. John Henry Tritton (XXXVII, 175n).

would be finally surmounted—but, alas! the sudden Demands for Money, for the then New Loan—where so great; that in the [sh]ort⁴ Space of two Days; the Cash of the House sunk so rapidly—that we almost lost all Spirit and Courage. However we thought it our Duty, as well as our Interest; to continue the House if possible— Accordingly, we made one great Effort; on which we had plac'd no inconsiderable Reliance; but which was only adviseable from the suddenness of the Emergency— We convened late at Night such Bankers, as could immediately be found in the City—and made known to them our Situation— They replied; that for the Support of Publick Credit; for their own sakes, and for ours, they truly wished to support us—but, that they perceiv'd no small Sum could do us any service; and that the Times did not render it prudent to advance a very large one— This fatal Moment was decisive— All our Hopes immediately vanish'd— Therefore (that all our Connections might fare alike) we came to the afflicting Conclusion, not to open the Bank next Morning; either to receive, or pay— A Week, or even four Days, before this dreadful Night, we did not see any Reason, why we should be compelld to stop more than we had done at any other Period for a Year before. The Event, tho with Pain I contemplate it, as a Loss to many; has fallen with the most ruinous Force on myself— I have worse than fruitlessly consumed sixteen Years of my Life, and by coming into the House, have lost all my own private Fortune, towards Thirty Thousand Pounds, besides Twenty Thousand Pounds more the House owed me, on my Partnership Claim; so that, at five and fifty, after handling Millions; I found myself strippd of every thing—had no Provision for my Wife & Son, but what I now owe to the Humanity and Liberality of my Friends—just sufficient to enable me to live in a small but decent House in the Village from whence this is written;⁵ I mean not however to convey to my Friend an Idea, that I am destitute of every Consolation,

---

4. The MS is torn in several places; we supply those readings in brackets.
5. Collinson's friends raised a subscription to purchase him an annuity; see XXXVIII, 45.

since I have not lost in my present Situation, those wise and virtuous Friends which form so considerable a Part of my Happiness in the midst of my apparent Prosperity; they kindly visit me here; as all the best Families do around us— This Testimony of the Worlds Discrimination between Misfortune, and intentional Evil, affords me no small Comfort; and the more so—as my own Conscience acquits me of ever forming any Design to injure any Man— Pardon this Detail; it will never be repeated.

By residing in the Country I now sit down at the George and Vulture⁶ only as I happen to be occasionally in Town, and from having spent great part of the Summer amongst my old Banking-Connections at Bath and Bristol I am not furnished with any new philosophical Subject meriting your Notice—except one derived from your Letter to Sr Jos. Banks on the Air Balloons—which a Friend of mine had the pleasure of hearing read at the R. S last Thursday⁷—several Experiments of the like nature are making here—tho' they are checked a little by the cui bono?— A Consideration which (in my Opinion) ought not to have so much force, as is frequently given to it. Who for Instance, who first observ'd the Magnet attract Iron, could foresee that so simple an Effect—would lead us to discover new Worlds.

Your friend Mitchell has I hear, succeeded at length, in his large Speculum—and I weekly expect a Letter with Particulars— Herschell has also effected one, I apprehend about 2 feet diamr. and intends proceeding from larger to larger—⁸ When I paid him a Visit and lodged at his House at Datchet last Spring, he shew'd me the Mould for casting one, I think of 38 ins. diamr, but having mislaid the Memorandum of it, am not quite

6. An inn and tavern in London that served as the meeting place for the Monday Club, of which BF had been a member: x, 250.

7. On Nov. 6 Joseph Banks read BF's letters of Aug. 30 and Oct. 8 at the meeting of the Royal Society: Banks to BF, Nov. 7, above.

8. William Herschel (XL, 78–9n) began to use the 20-foot reflecting telescope with an 18-inch mirror of his own construction in October, 1783: *ODNB*. John Michell (VII, 357n; XI, 480n) was also interested in the fabrication of mirrors for telescopes: Sir Archibald Geikie, *Memoir of John Michell* (Cambridge, 1918), pp. 91–3; Clyde L. Hardin, "The Scientific Work of the Reverend John Michell," *Annals of Science*, XXII (1966), 43–4.

certain. By this means we may reasonably hope that a sufficient quantity of Light will be gained to sustain a distinct magnifying Power of 2. or even 3000; perhaps more—since it is possible to see with Herschell's 6000. As several of the Stars, which I look'd at thro' his largest Telescope, illuminated the Tube with such vivid azure, topaz, and garnet colour'd Rays; I suggested to him, whether it might not be worth while to make some Experiments on them with the Prism, and [see?] whether he could not analyze the Light of those distant Suns, [as?] we do that of ours—some new Colours perhaps might arise; [at worst?] it might be discover'd whether the Stars afford the same original Colours as our Sun—whether aranged in the like Order &—Indeed Light is of so wonderful a nature, that I have ever most earnestly wish'd to make further Discoveries; for I well recollect what you once said to me, "That there was nothing in which you was more in the Dark about; than Light"— My long Absence from Town renders me a Stranger to what Hers[chell] has done in this affair—and also whether it is settled, that the [per]iodical Occultation of Algol, is occasioned by a [large?] Spot on its Surface, or by a large Planet revolving round it.[9] [*Torn: word or words missing*] his attempt to determine whether the fix'd Stars have any observable Parallax—ingenious as his Method is—it must require much Time.

Now my worthy Friend; if such a Writer as Horace could say he sinned against the Publick-Weal by the Length of his Address to [Mae]cenas;[1] what is to become of me?— However I cannot avoid adding, that I have had the Satisfaction of hearing of your Welfare from Time to Time by our worthy and mutual Friend D Barclay;[2] and am likely to have further opportunities this Winter of having that Satisfaction repeated in my morn-

9. This question was examined in a paper that was read by John Goodricke before the Royal Society on May 15, 1783, and that was subsequently published as "A Series of Observations on, and a Discovery of, the Period of the Variation of the Light of the bright Star in the Head of Medusa, Called Algol . . . ," *Phil. Trans.*, LXXIII (1783), 474–82.

1. Horace, *Epistles*, book 2, epistle 1, lines 1–6.

2. David Barclay, Jr., (IX, 190–1n) was the half brother of Collinson's mother: Hubert F. Barclay and Alice Wilson-Fox, *A History of the Barclay Family* (3 vols., London, 1934), III, 234, 248.

ing visits to Sr Jo. Banks, who kindly lamenting to me, that my select & valuable Library, consisting of more than eight Thousand Vols. was now [Sc]atterd abroad; most genteely and liberally invited me to use his, as my own, to be equally open to me, whether he was in Town or out—

When I consider the weighty and important Affairs that daily solicit your Attention, I can scarce venture to indulge myself in the Hope of being favourd with a Line from you—yet knowing your long & steady Friendship to my Family & to myself, I am unwilling utterly to despair; and therefore have added such an Address at Foot, as will find its way to the Habitation of your ever faithful and truly affectionate Friend—

THOS. COLLINSON.

P.S. Since our Calamities my late Partner, my Nephew Tritton, has been taken into Partnership into the very respectable House of Messrs. Barclay, Bevan & Co. Bankers in Lombard Street;[3] and a few months since, has married our Frd. D. Barclay's Neice,[4] the eldest Daughter of his Brother Jno. Barclay— Therefore any Letter directed to that House, for me, will be taken all due Care of—

Addressed: Pour son Excellence / Monr. le Docteur Franklin / a Passy / pres Paris.

From Lenoir   LS: American Philosophical Society

Ce 13 9bre. 1783
J'ai L'honneur de vous Envoyer, Monsieur, la permission nécessaire, pour que la Caisse de Livres arrivée à la Douanne, Soit délivrée au S. Desaint[5] à qui elle est adressée, ou a toute autre

3. The Barclay in question was David Barclay, Jr.: XXVII, 580n.
4. Mary Barclay: Jacob M. Price, "The Great Quaker Business Families of Eighteenth-Century London: the Rise and Fall of a Sectarian Patriciate," in *The World of William Penn*, ed. Richard S. Dunn and Mary M. Dunn (Philadelphia, 1986), p. 371.
5. Probably Pierre Dessin in Calais, who often received shipments from England and forwarded them to BF; see, for example, his letters of Oct. 14 and Nov. 4.

personne, que vous chargerez de la retirer, Sans passer à la Chambre Syndicale.

Je Suis avec un respectueux attachement, Monsieur, votre très Obeissant Serviteur.   LENOIR

M francklin.

Notation: Le Noir 13. 9bre. 1783

From Samuel Mather[6]   ALS: American Philosophical Society

Honoured Sir,   Boston. Novr. 13th. 1783.

As I am far advanced in Life, You know, being now in my 78th. Year, I was thinking some Time ago, what I could do, before I quitted the World, for the Benefit and Comfort of my Countrey and People: And it came into my Head and Heart to write *the dying Legacy,*[7] which I now send You, as a small Token of my Regard and Esteem for You. It has met with a better Reception than I imagined: And I have the Comfort to inform You, that his Excellency the President of Congress has seen fit in a very complaisant and respectful Manner to thank me for it.[8]

I rejoice with You, that You have been so successfull in your prudent, unwearied and faithful Endeavours to serve your Countrey and People: And I wish your last Days and Comforts may be your best. And, commending You to the special Care, Protection and Blessing of the Everlasting Parent and the

6. The Congregational minister who last wrote to BF in 1778: XXVI, 681–3.

7. *The Dying Legacy of an Aged Minister of the Everlasting Gospel, to the United States of North-America* (Boston, 1783) was an essay in which Mather exhorted Americans to preserve peace and independence through righteous conduct, and argued against the United States' intervening in European affairs. He sent a copy to JA under cover of a more detailed letter; see *Adams Papers,* XV, 362–3.

8. In his Aug. 20 letter, Elias Boudinot agreed with Mather that divine intervention, rather than the Americans' strength or wisdom, was responsible for the success of the Revolution: Smith, *Letters,* XX, 565–6.

wonderful Counsellour; I am, with cordial Regard and Esteem, Your aged and obliged Friend, and very humble Servant

SAMUEL MATHER

Dr Franklin.

Notation: Mather Mr. Samuel, Boston Nov. 13 1783.

From Anthony Todd
LS: American Philosophical Society

Dear Sir,— General Post Office Novr. 18. 1783.

I beg leave to send you inclosed a Copy of the Advertisement, which will be published in this Night's Gazette and in all the London, Dublin and Edinburgh News Papers, relative to the Packet Boats established to support a Monthly Correspondence between Falmouth and New York, corrected according to the judicious alterations you proposed in the Letter you were pleased to write me the 29th. past.[9]

I shall send a few Copies of it to your old Colleague Mr. Foxcroft, for his Government, who is to remain as Agent for the Packet Boats at New York; and if you should approve of the Sketch of the Advertisement, calculated for the United States, which I submitted to your better Judgement the 19th. of September last for your Corrections or Alterations, I could wish you would send it to America for publication, either by the French Packet Boats, or ours, or both, and I shall be happy to forward it or any Letters you may have to write upon this occasion, or any other, being with true Respect, Dear Sir, Your most obedient and most humble Servant ANTH TODD Secy

His Excellency Dr. Franklin

9. Two printed broadsides of the advertisement, dated Nov. 18, are at the APS; the one Todd enclosed is filed with the present letter. The advertisement did indeed appear in the Nov. 18–22 issue of the *London Gazette*.

From Edward Nathaniel Bancroft[1]

ALS: American Philosophical Society

Cher Docteur   Chiswick ce 19 Novr. 1783

J'ai attendu longtemps à vous écrire & je pense que vous vous étes bien impatienté tout le temps que nous avons été séparés. Je vous eus écris plutôt, mais je voulois un peu connoitre l'Angleterre. Nous fumes dix jours dans notre voyage, nous nous embarquames à Dunkerque, débarquames à Chatham, & arrivames à Londres le lendemain matin tous en bonne santé, Dieu merci. Un mois & demi après notre arrivée à Londres, mon Papa partit pour Philadelphie[2] après nous avoir mis en pension chez le Dr. Rose à Chiswick.[3] J'aime Londres c'est une belle ville, très propre de la grandeur de Paris, on prétend même que le nombre d'habitants est égal. Je m'accoutume aux mets des Anglois dont les François ont si mauvaise opinion; leur grosse viande, leur Pudding en gateau sont excellents. Faites mes compliments à Mr Puech & a Mde Montgommery.[4]

Je suis avec le plus profond respect, Cher Docteur, Votre très humble & très obéissant serviteur

EDWRD. NATHL. BANCROFT

Répondez moi le plutôt qu'il vous sera possible./.

Addressed: A Monsieur / Monsieur le Dr. Franklin à / Passy près Paris / En France.

---

1. Edward Nathaniel Bancroft (1772–1842) was the eldest child of Edward Bancroft and Penelope Fellows Bancroft. After graduating from Cambridge in 1794, he became a celebrated physician and author: *ODNB*.

2. Bancroft left Paris with his family in mid-June; he sailed to America on Aug. 13: XL, 161n, 331n.

3. Schoolmaster William Rose was an old friend of BF's: XI, 98n, 100n. Bancroft wrote to WTF on July 11 that his sons would begin school at Dr. Rose's in Chiswick the next day. He had rented a furnished house for the rest of the family and would soon be ready to depart (APS).

4. Dorcas Montgomery, the mother of Robert Montgomery, a contemporary of young Bancroft and of BFB: XXXV, 481.

From Ingenhousz ALS: American Philosophical Society

Dear friend. Vienna Nov. 19. 1783.

I recieved your favour dated Passy Sept. 2. 1783,[5] with an inclosed of Mr. Samuel Lewis Wharton,[6] which Contained a bill of exchange of 8000 L. tournois. He refers to a lettre which mr. Sam. Wharton wrote to me on the 14 of April by the Way of France and on the 29 of may by the way of France, of which letters none came to right, which is probably owing to the want of paying the postage to the frontiers of Germany or from Holland to Frankford. As there will probably go regular paquets from America to France and Holland, you would Doe a service to your country and to all Europe now greately interested in the Correspondence with America, if you ordred to be publish'd through your Country, that all lettres directed to any place beyond France or Holland must first be payed for to Frankford and that they can not be recieved at the post office without this postage being payed, and that, for security's Sake, such letters will be marked at the post office in America *postage payed to Frankford*. Without a similar precaution the most part of letters Send from America will only be thrown in the post office of the place where the ship arrives, and there they will remain for ever.

I found in your lettre inclosed also a print of the allarm of the peasants at Goness and a copy of your lettre to Sir joseph Banks on that subject,[7] for which both recieve my harty thanks. I was in hopes of recieving a copy of the next lettre you probably have or will write to him on that Subjects. I think the aerial ballons a object of great importance and should very much like to See one going up. I should be glad to know accurately in which way they are filled with inflammable air. As much as I can gess by the account of news papers, they only burn coals or straw in the middel of the ballon or under it, by which means the air within is become lighter by heat and mixed also with a miphitic air lighter than Common air and remaining therefor within the ballon. You would oblige me to give me some light in this

5. XL, 565.
6. Samuel Wharton's son, to whom Ingenhousz had written in 1782: XXXVIII, 178n.
7. See XL, 565n.

affaire— I hope you have recieved my lettre Dated Aug. 15th
and one afterwards[8] containing a bill of exchange on Amsterdam to be Send to a nursery Man or Gardener in America on
account of our vice-chancelour of Bohemia. I should be glad
to know, whether you forwarded it, as Count Choteck should
like to know it—[9] As to the different questions of the former
letter, never mind whether you answer on all of them or only on
Som— I employed the 8000 Livr. sent me by mr. Wharton in
the mercantil undertaking, which is a goying on in king's ships
from france to China, for private concerns by why of actions.

If I may trust on what mr. le Begue writes me, my book now
allready two years in the press will soon come out.[1] I have matter enough ready for a second volum of my book on Vegetables,[2] but am at a loss how to get it printed as I am afrayed of its
remaining, just as the present book, some years in the press by
avarice and want of faith of the bookseller. A second Volum of
the Collection of Detached opuscula, of which you have a Copy
in the German language, will soon be printed here.[3] Mr. Molitor, how [who] translated the first volum from my manuscripts,[4]
is busy with it— Mr. le Begue has sent me a pamphlet of mr.
Lavoisier on heat Containing experiments made by order of the
Royal academie:[5] but I See they have nothing similar to what
you will find in my book now printing— I should be proud of
the honour of being made a membre of your Philosophical Society of Philadelphia. If you still keep Connection with it, as

8. Aug. 15 and Sept. 1: XL, 475–84, 562–3.
9. For the count's request, see XL, 562.
1. Lebègue de Presle was overseeing the printing of Ingenhousz' *Nouvelles expériences et observations sur divers objets de physique,* which was not
published until 1785; see XXXV, 548n, 549–50n; XXXVI, 221.
2. *Experiments upon Vegetables* . . . (London, 1779) included Ingenhousz'
discovery of photosynthesis. The copy he sent BF in November, 1779
(XXXI, 122) is at the APS.
3. *Vermischte Schriften physisch-medicinischen Inhalts* (2nd ed.; 2 vols.,
Vienna, 1784).
4. See XXXV, 549n. Nicolaus Karl Molitor (1754–1826) was a former student of Ingenhousz': *ADB.*
5. Antoine-Laurent Lavoisier and Pierre-Simon, marquis de Laplace,
Mémoire sur la chaleur. Lu à l'Académie royale des sciences, le 28 juin 1783
(Paris, 1783). BF's copy is at the Hist. Soc. of Pa.

President, I should be obliged to you to propose me— I have not seen mr. Vynbrenner and doe not know whether you forwarded to him the introductory letters you promish'd to send him for his commissary whose name I mentioned to you—[6] I am sorry to see that your old masters, after being humbled by you more than any nation was ever before, exert the small remains of their usual pride and haughtiness against my Country, where they are now generaly hated as much as in America.[7] I trust however, that the Dutch will no more submit their necks under the yoke of that Corrupted nation.

I hope you will find some leasure hour to let me know Some news from you.

I begg the favour of forwarding the inclosed packet containing M.S. for the press, to Mr. le Begue, and the others to America. Have you some fresh American news papers to spare?

I am with the greatest estime Dear friend Your most obedient humble servant   J. INGEN HOUSZ

I am informed that Mr. Sam. Wharton is in som difficulty about an immense tract of land he baught from the indians, and that the affaire is braught in Congress to be decided, and that there is good hoop of his Succeeding.[8]

to his Exc. Benjam. Franklin at Passy

6. Ingenhousz informed BF of the agent's name (Joseph Donath) on June 23: XL, 216. For background on this request from Viennese merchant Weinbrenner see XXXIX, 444; XL, 10, 475.

7. Ingenhousz is probably referring to the protracted peace negotiations between Great Britain and the Dutch Republic. These were hampered by numerous factors, including the British government's attempts to restore its own influence in Dutch politics: H. M. Scott, *British Foreign Policy in the Age of the American Revolution* (Oxford, 1990), pp. 335–7.

8. In 1768 a group of land speculators, including Wharton and BF, acquired a large tract of land from the Six Nations in what is today West Virginia. BF and others tried to gain British sanction for the venture, called at different times the Indiana, Grand Ohio, Walpole, or Vandalia Company. With the outbreak of the Revolution efforts shifted to obtaining confirmation of the title from Congress, a goal that Wharton still pursued as a delegate from Delaware in 1782 and 1783. Virginia's cession of its far western land claims to Congress in 1784 in exchange for a guarantee of its territorial integrity put an end to all competing claims of private land companies: XXXI, 525–48; *DAB;* James D. Anderson, "Samuel Wharton and the

From John Shaffer   ALS: American Philosophical Society

Sir   Paris ce 19 9bre 83
My Avocat has informed me that it is Nessesary that your Son
Wm Temple, Should Right a line to the Letn Creminel, to Convince him that he has Not Said that I am a bad Subject &&&,[9]
    If he Realy has Not Said what I am acused of he Canot Re-
fuse me my Request,
    My trial Comes On to morrow without fail. Thierefore you
Canot Consistant with Reason Refuse me what I ask you.
    Mr Temple has Refused me and Sais he will Not medle with
my affairs, wich is a Proof that he has indeavored to ingure me
as much as Posible but hope in the Course of life will meat for
an Explanation wich will be a Sattisfaction,
    I am without a farthing of Money if you will be Kind Enough
to make me a Small advance belive me Sir it will be Returned
with gratitude,[1]
    One line from Mr Temple your Son will be Of Great Servise
to me.
    I have the honour to be with Respect Sir your most Obedent
and Very humble Servent   J. SCHAFFER

Addressed: A Son Exelance / Monsieur le Docteuer / franklin
En Son Lhotel / A Passy

Indians' Rights to Sell Their Land: an Eighteenth-Century View," *Western
Pa. Hist. Mag.*, LXIII (1980), 139–40; Peter S. Onuf, *The Origins of the
Federal Republic: Jurisdictional Controversies in the United States, 1775–1787*
(Philadelphia, 1983), pp. 78–102.
    9. Shaffer had written to WTF twice in October to convince him to re-
tract this statement; see the annotation of Shaffer's letter to BF of [Oct. 9].
He sent a new appeal to WTF along with the present letter; it is in French, in
the hand of Menier de Saint Yver, and is dated Nov. 19 (APS).
    1. Five days earlier BF had received an appeal from an angry creditor
who had just heard that BF was taking an interest in Shaffer's affairs out of
consideration for the prisoner's father (and in spite of his "mauvaise con-
duite"). M. Pecoul had lent Shaffer 960 *l.t.* to cover his linens and the fees
required for his release from prison. He asks BF's help in obtaining payment: Pecoul to BF, Nov. 14, 1783, APS.

From [Louis-Valentin Goëzmann] de Thurn[2]

AL: University of Pennsylvania Library

[*c.* November 19, 1783][3]

Memoire

M. de Thurn, de la Societé Roiale de Metz, issû d'une trés ancienne famille d'Allemagne, Etablie depuis Deux siecles dans la province d'Alsace, aujourd'huy sous la domination de la france, et allie aux meilleures maisons de cette province, réclame la bienveillance et l'appui du ministre plenipotentiaire des Etats-unis de L'Amerique, pour le sucçés du projet qu'il a formé d'aller S'Etablir sous leur domination, avec le Seul Enfant qui lui reste, et d'y transporter toute sa fortune.

Il est d'un pays, où la culture de la vigne forme une des grandes occupations des gens de la Campagne; mais comme on n'y a trouvé jusqu'à present des débouchés qu'en Suisse, une tres grande quantité de vignerons, dont la subsistence est devenue si difficile dans un pays accablé d'impots, et qui manque de Commerce, se determineroient aisément à le quitter, pour adopter une patrie plus heureuse.

Il a le désir le plus ardent de Contribuer, suivant tous ses moiens, à la prosperité des Etats-unis en General, et de celle des Colonies en particulier, qui voudra l'adopter.

Mais pour rassembler ces moiens, et pouvoir offrir aux Etats-unis Sa personne et Sa fortune, il a besoin de L'Entremise et de L'appui de leur ministre plenipotentiaire.

Il ne jouit quant à present que de 4000 Liv. de pension, dont 2000 sur le trésor Roial, et 2000 sur les fonds des affaires Etrangeres, que M. Le Comte de Vergennes lui a fait accorder dernierement à son retour de Londres.

---

2. Goëzmann (1729–1794), who appended de Thurn to his name, began his career as a magistrate of the Maupeou Parlement. He was forced to resign in 1774 after Beaumarchais accused him of corruption in a series of celebrated pamphlets. In late 1780 or thereabouts, the French government hired him as a spy. He operated in London under several aliases until July, 1783, though his work was criticized and he was accused of various indiscretions: *DBF*, under Goezmann; Richard B. Morris, *The Peacemakers: the Great Powers and American Independence* (New York, 1965), pp. 136–46.

3. The date of Castries' certification of de Thurn's *bon du Roi*, which was enclosed with the present letter.

Mais il a une créance Considerable sur le domaine d'Alsace, pour raison de la quelle, et d'un traitement dont il jouissoit cy-devant sur la finance, il lui a eté promis, de la part du Roi, une indemnité.

C'est pour l'obtention de cette indemnité qui le mettroit à meme d'offrir aux Etats-unis Des services réelement utiles, en Cooperant de sa fortune à l'avancement de la Culture, de la population, et de L'industrie De la Colonie où il S'Etabliroit, qu'il réclame les secours et l'appui de leur ministre plenipotentiaire auprès de la Cour de france.

Il Espere que ce ministre s'y prêtera d'autant plus facilement, qu'il ne s'agit que de l'exécution litterale Des titres les plus respectables qui existent parmi les hommes, et des promesses Contenues dans un *Bon* signé de la main du Roi.

A L'Effet de quoi il a l'honneur de joindre à ce mémoire une copie Certifiée de celui Sur le quel ce *Bon du Roi*[4] est intervenu, et qui fera voir au ministre des Etats-unis, que c'est pour avoir secondé leur Cause et leurs interets autant qu'il a Dépendu de lui, Durant le Guerre et dans un pays ennemi, que le Roi lui a fait ces promesses.

Et afin de manifester dèz à present qu'il n'est occupé que de ce qui peut Contribuer au plus Grand interêt des Etats-unis, il a l'honneur de joindre ici un memoire sur un projet de Commerce de vin,[5] qui peut promettre les plus grands avantages à la Compagnie Ameriquaine qui L'Entreprendroit.

4. The enclosure is de Thurn's copy of a memoir presented by Sartine to the king in September, 1780. Sartine explains the need to send a spy to London to discover the intentions of the enemy fleet. He recommends de Thurn as a man who would be capable of such work and who could assume the guise of a malcontent. He proposes to pay him and his son, an officer in the Bavarian regiment, 12,000 *l.t.* for their joint efforts. Before agreeing to the assignment, de Thurn requests 200 *louis* to cover debts that he claims to have acquired in the service of the government. Below this text, de Thurn copied the certification that Castries had written on Nov. 19, 1783, confirming that the memoir was presented to the king by Sartine and that the king had approved it.

5. Missing.

From Samuel Cooper   ALS: American Philosophical Society

My dear Sir,   Boston Novr 20th. 1783
    I never in all my Life wrote a Letter with half the Difficulty
of this— Sick in my Chamber, attended by two Physicians &c.
But I could not allow the Chevr. de Bonne leave without bringing to you my warmest Thanks for introducing to the Acqain-
tance of a Gentleman of such fine Talents & promising Abilities.[6] You seem to speak of him as designed for the Service of
his Country in America somehow in the Consular Line.
    This is an important Line indeed; and upon many Accounts.
I can write no more at present, but as soon as my Health is restored I will write and do all in my Power to aid the Views of
the Chevr, and His Friends who appear so very respectable, as
far as Prudence will allow. Pray write me what you think proper
on the Subject.
    Your's in every Sense   SAML. COOPER

His Excellency Benjn. Franklin Esqr.

Endorsed: The last Letter from my dear Friend Dr Cooper, who
dy'd in January following[7]

Notation: Saml. Cooper, Nov. 20 1783.—

From Charles-Guillaume-Frédéric Dumas
                    ALS: Library of Congress; AL (draft): Nationaal Archief

Monsieur   Lahaie 20e. Nov. 1783
    J'ai reçu la faveur du 10e.,[8] que m'a faite de votre part
Mr. Votre Petit-fils, auquel vous voudrez bien permettre que
j'en témoigne ici ma reconnoissance, en me recommandant

    6. BF had spelled his name "Bannes": XL, 42–3.
    7. After a six-week illness, Cooper died on Dec. 29, 1783, at the age of
58: Charles W. Akers, *The Divine Politician: Samuel Cooper and the American Revolution in Boston* (Boston, 1982), pp. 4, 355. BF had known him for at
least 33 years: IV, 64, 69.
    8. Not found.

toujours à une bonne part dans son amitié, qui m'est précieuse. J'ai envoyé tout de suite les Papiers concernant la translation du Congrès à Princeton, à mon ami à Leide, pour qu'il en soit fait usage dans son papier & dans les papiers hollandois; ce qu'il m'a promis.[9] Cela est très à propos, depuis trois mois sur-tout, que les Anglomanes n'ont cessé d'abuser le public sur cette affaire, en la représentant au désavantage du Congrès & de la Confédération Américaine, pour ébranler la confiance des Rentiers.

L'incluse pour le Congrès[1] vous apprendra Monsieur ce qui se passe ici de plus nouveau. Vous voudrez bien avoir la bonté de la fermer & faire acheminer par L'Orient ou Port-Louis. Je fais bien des voeux pour votre bonne santé, & suis avec tout le respectueux attachement qui vous est voué, De Votre Excellence Le très-humble & très obeissant serviteur,   C. W. F. DUMAS

Paris à Son Excellence Mr. Franklin

Addressed:[2] à Son Excellence / Monsieur Franklin, Esqr. / Mine. Plenipo: des Etats-Unis / d'Amérique, / à Passy./.

9. No doubt the friend was Jean Luzac, editor of the *Ga*ʒ. *de Leyde;* see XXVI, 20; XXVIII, 617. In the supplements to its Nov. 21, 25, and 28 and Dec. 5, 9, 12, and 16 issues, the *Ga*ʒ. *de Leyde* printed a French translation of Boudinot's July 15 letter to the American commissioners and its enclosures (XL, 301–8) describing the soldiers' mutiny that had caused Congress to adjourn to Princeton.

1. Not found.

2. Above the address, in an unknown hand, is the name "Grand."

Franklin et al.: Procès-verbal of Montgolfier Balloon Experiment[3]

DS: Staatsbibliothek zu Berlin; copies: California State Library, University of Pennsylvania Library; press copy of copy: Massachusetts Historical Society[4]

aujourd'hui 21 novembre 1783 au chateau de la muette.[5] L'on à procedé à une expérience de la machine aerostatique de m. de montgolfier

Le Ciel etant Couvert de nuages dans plusieurs parties, clair dans D'autres, le vent nordouest. à midy. 8 minutte lon à tiré une Boitte, qui a Servi de Signal pour annoncer qu'on Commencoit à remplir la machine. En 8 minutte malgré le vent, elle a êté développée dans tous les points, et prette à partir m. le marquis d'arlandes,[6] et m. pilatre de rozier etant dans la Gallerie.

La 1ere intention etoit de faire enlever la machine et de la re-

---

3. Immediately after conducting trials on Oct. 15, 17, and 19 (for which see Le Roy to BF, [Oct. 19?]), Etienne Montgolfier was invited to use the château de la Muette, a residence of the royal family, as the staging ground for his experiment in manned flight. One full month elapsed before he did so. On Nov. 15 he delivered an address to the Académie des sciences, and made plans to conduct the experiment before members of the academy on Nov. 20. Wind and rain forced a postponement until Nov. 21, when the weather was fine. Despite Montgolfier's insistence that there be no public announcement, a large crowd gathered. The best-known engraving of the flight, reproduced here, is from the vantage of BF's terrace in Passy; see the List of Illustrations. BF, however, watched the ascension at the château with his colleagues: Barthélemy Faujas de Saint-Fond, *Premiere suite de la description des expériences aérostatiques* ... (Paris, 1784), pp. 12–14, 19; Gillispie, *Montgolfier Brothers*, pp. 50–6, 185n; see also BF to Joseph Banks, Nov. 21 [*i.e.*, 22–25].

4. The DS is in the hand of Faujas de Saint-Fond. The two copies were written by L'Air de Lamotte and BFB, respectively. The press copy was made from the former, and is filed with a press copy of BF to Banks, Nov. [22–25]. This *procès-verbal* was published in the *Jour. de Paris*, Nov. 22, 1783.

5. According to Faujas de Saint-Fond, the duchesse de Polignac (XXXV, 543–4n) was the one who suggested the castle grounds for the experiment: *Premiere suite de la description des expériences aérostatiques*, pp. 11–12.

6. François-Laurent, marquis d'Arlandes de Salton (1742–1809), major of infantry: *DBF*. His firsthand account of the flight is in Faujas de Saint-Fond, *Premiere suite de la description des expériences aérostatiques*, pp. 23–30.

tennir avec des Cordes, pour la metre à lepreuve, etudier les poids exacts quelle pouvoit porter, et voir si tout etoit Convenablement disposé pour l'expérience importante qu'on alloit tenter.

Mais la machine poussée par le vent loin de s'èlever verticalement, s'est dirigée Sur une des allées du jardin et les Cordes qui la retennoient agissant avec trop de force ont occasionné plusieur dechirures dont une de plus de six pieds de longeur. La machine ramenée Sur lestrade, a été rèparée en moins de deux heures.

Ayant été remplie de nouveau, elle est partie à une heure 54 minuttes portant les mêmes personnes. On l'a vue S'èlever de la maniere la plus majestueuse et lorsquelle a été parvenue, a environ deux cent Cinquante pieds de hauteur, les intrepides voyageurs, Baissant leur chapeau, ont Salué les specteurs. L'on n'a pu S'empecher d'eprouver alors un espece de Sentiment, melé de crainte et d'admiration.

Bientot les navigateurs aeriens on été perdu de vue, mais la machine plannant sur l'horizon et étalant la plus Belle forme a monté au moins à trois mille pieds de hauteur ou elle est toujours restée visible; elle a traversé la *Seine* au dessous de la Bariere de la *Conférence,* et passant de la entre l'ecole militaire et l'hotel royal des invalides, elle a été à portée d'etre vue de tout paris.

Les voyageurs Satisfait de cette expérience, et ne voulant pas faire une plus grande Cource Se Sont Concerté pour descendre, mais voyant que le vent les portoit Sur les maisons de la rue de Seve fauxbourg st Germain, ils ont Conservé leur Sang froid, et developpant du gaz, ils Se Sont elevès de nouveau, et ont Continué leur route dans lair jusqu'a ce quils aient eu depassé paris.

Ils Sont descendu alors tranquillement dans la Campagne au dela du nouveau Boulevard vis a vis le moulin de *Croulebarbe* Sans avoir eprouvé la plus legere incommodité, ayant encore dan leur Gallerie les deux tiers de leur approvisionement, ils pouvoient donc franchir S'ils leussent desiré une espace triple de Celui qu'ils ont parcouru.

Leur route a été de quatre a cinq mille toises et le tems qu'ils y employé de 20 a vingt cinq minuttes.

Fait au chateau de la muette a Cinq heures du soir.

Cette machine avoit 70 pieds de hauteur 46 pied de diametre, elle Contennoit 60 000 pieds Cubes, et le poid quelle a enlevè etoit d'environ 16 a 17 Cent livres.

> LE DUC DE POLIGNAC[7]
> D'HUNAUD[8]
> LE D. DE GUINES[9]
> B FRANKLIN
> LE CTE. DE POLASTRON[1]
> LE CTE. DE VAUDREUIL[2]
> FAUJAS DE SAINT FOND
> DELISLE
> LE ROY
> de L'Acad des Sciences

From the Baron von Blome

LS: Library of Congress; two copies, press copy of copy:[3] National Archives

à Paris, ce 21. Novbre. 1783.

Le Soussigné Envoyé Extraordinaire de Sa Majesté Danoise près Sa Majesté Très-Chretienne est chargé par ordre exprès de Sa Cour d'exposer à Monsieur Franklin, Ministre Plénipotentiaire des Etats-Unis de L'Amérique près Sa Majesté Très-Chretienne, le Fait suivant:

Le Vaisseau Danois la *Providentia,* Cape. André Brun, appartenant à Erasmus Dybevad à Christiania en Norvège, avoit

7. Jules, duc de Polignac: XXXV, 543n.

8. A comte d'Hunnaud was the cousin of François-Antoine-Henri d'Andlau (for whom see the *DBF*): David Smith *et al.*, eds., *Correspondance générale d'Helvétius* (5 vols., Toronto and Oxford, 1981–2004), III, 418n.

9. Adrien-Louis de Bonnières de Souastre, now duc de Guines: XIX, 305n.

1. Jean-François-Gabriel, comte de Polastron, governor of Castillon and Castillonnès: *Dictionnaire de la noblesse.*

2. Joseph-François de Paule, comte de Vaudreuil (1740–1817), army general: Larousse. Faujas de Saint-Fond dedicated *Description des expériences de la machine aérostatique de MM. de Montgolfier* . . . (Paris, 1783) to him.

3. One of the copies, in L'Air de Lamotte's hand, was the source of the press copy. They were probably sent by different conveyances, enclosed in BF's Dec. 25 letter to Thomas Mifflin.

été fretté à Londres en Juillet 1781, pour aller avec une Cargaison consistant en marchandises Sèches à L'Isle de Saint-Thomas en Amérique; Le 27. Octobre, étant à la hauteur de l'Isle Téneriffe, il fut rencontré par le Corsaire Américain the Henrick, Cape. Thomas Benson, ou Bentzon, portant Pavillon Anglois, qui sans aucun égard pour le Pavillon Danois S'en empara et L'envoya à Salem, où il n'est arrivé que le 7. Janvier Suivant, après avoir été mené dans cet intervalle le long des Côtes, dont il a été fort endommagé.

Par le Jugement d'une Cour maritime tenue à Boston en Fevrier 1782, ce Batiment a été remis en liberté, en lui payant à peu près la moitié du Fret, sans aucun autre Dédommagement; et quant à la Cargaison, elle a été confisquée au profit des Capteurs, sous prétexte qu'elle étoit de propriété Angloise.

Sans s'arrèter à ce qu'il y a eù d'irrégulier dans la Procédure, les Proprietaires et Intéressés tant du Vaisseau que de la Cargaison sont en droit de reclamer la Réstitution entiere avec une Indemnité proportionnée aux Dommages qu'ils ont soufferts par cette Saisie illégale.[4]

Les Piéces cy-jointes no. 6-12, contenant les Déclarations, Factures et Comptes, produits dans la forme requise, constatent que la perte pour les Proprietaires du Batiment monte

à £726:17.

et celle de la Cargaison . . . . a £24567. 8. 2

faisant en total la Somme de 25294: 5. 2

Livres Sterling, qu'ils réclament justement avec les Interèts à 5. pour Cent â compter du 1r. Janvier 1782.

La Cour de Dannemarc ne peut qu'appuyer leur Réclamation, parcequ'elle est fondée sur les principes de la Liberté et de la Sureté du Pavillon Neutre, principes que les Etats-Unis de L'Amérique ont temoigné de reconnoitre pour justes et con-

---

4. The Danish court first protested this matter in April, 1782. BF sent the complaint to Congress, and was still waiting to receive from America a copy of the admiralty court's proceedings: XXXVII, 204, 538; XXXIX, 395–6; XL, 362–3. At least part of the *Providentia*'s cargo was English property belonging to English-born Richard Vaux, a Loyalist who left Philadelphia during the war but eventually returned there. Vaux loaded his goods aboard the ship in London. In 1782 Vaux affirmed his allegiance to the United States before BF: XXXVII, 632; XXXIX, 395n.

formes au Droit des Nations libres et indépendantes, et qui ont été déclarés par la Convention maritime des Neutres aux Puissances Belligérantes. Les Circonstances n'avoient pas permis jusqu'ici de demander au Congrès des Etats-Unis la Satisfaction duë au Pavillon de Sa Majesté Danoise; Mais après les preuves multipliées et non équivoques que Sa Majesté lui a données de Son Amitié et de Son Affection Sincères, Elle espere avec une entiere confiance dans les Sentiments de Justice et d'Equité du Congrès, qu'Il ne se refusera pas à faire Droit à cette Demande légitime.   DE BLOME

Monsieur Franklin est prié de vouloir bien renvoyer les Pièces cy-jointes no. 6-12, aprés en avoir fait usage.[5]

Endorsed: Minister of Denmark

From Ignaz Edler von Born[6]

ALS: American Philosophical Society

Monsieur!   Vienne ce 21 Novr 1783.
    Les bontés, avec lesquelles Vous avés accueilli Mr. le Professeur Märter pendant Son Sejour a Paris, avant Son depart pour l'Amerique Septentrionale,[7] m'encourage a Vous prier de lui faire parvenir la lettre ci jointe. Ce Märter est mon Eleve, mon disciple, mon ami. Je l'ai proposé a l'Empereur pour le voyage en Amerique, et j'espere, que les decouvertes, qu'il fera en Histoire naturelle justifieront le choix, que j'en ai fait. Ce petit paquet contient les instructions ulterieures pour ce Märter. Il

5. BF returned the enclosures with his response of Jan. 12, below.
    6. The mineralogist (1742–1791) whose survey of the mines of Hungary and Transylvania had been sent to BF in English translation: XXIX, 430 (and see XL, 432). In 1776 Empress Maria Theresa appointed Born keeper of the natural history collection in Vienna, and in 1779 he became court counselor in the department of mines and the mint. He was also a leading freemason in Vienna: *Dictionary of Scientific Biography.*
    7. BF had provided Franz Joseph Märter with a letter of recommendation to Gov. John Dickinson. The Austrian naturalist was part of a scientific expedition sponsored by Joseph II to collect plant and animal specimens in the Americas: XXXIX, 474–5, 490–1.

m'interesse beaucoup qu'elles lui parviennent pendant Son Sejour a Philadelphie. La part que Vous prennés aux progrés des
Sciences, qui Vous doivent tant, me fait esperer, que Vous me
pardonnerés d'avoir osé m'addresser la dessus a Vous.

S'il est flatteur aux Souverains de recevoir des hommages
des peuples Sauvages, dont le nom meme leur est inconnu, je
crois que Vous dont le nom regnera eternellement dans le monde
politique et literaire, ne dedaignerés pas d'accepter les hommages d'un homme dont le nom ne peut jamais etre parvenu
jusqu'a Vous.

Le porteur de cette lettre est Mr. Stratmann, envoyé par S.M.
l'Empereur pour acheter une partie des livres de la bibliotheque
du Duc de la Valiere.[8] Je lui envie le bonheur de Vous presenter
Ses respects.

Je suis avec la veneration et le respect le plus vrai Monsieur
Votre tres humble et trés obeissant Serviteur

IGNACE CHVR. BORN
Conseiller aulique de S.M. l'Empereur.

Endorsed: Nov 21. 83

Notation: Ignace Cher. Born 21 Nov 83[9]

8. The duc de La Vallière (*DBF*), who had entertained BF on at least
one occasion before his death in 1780 (XXXI, 317), was renowned for his
vast collection of rare books and manuscripts, which were sold at auction
posthumously. Austrian bibliographer and librarian Paul Strattmann, one
of the keepers of the Court Library in Vienna, was authorized to spend
around 4,000 ducats at the December, 1783, sale. Strattmann acquired
many items, exceeding his budget by 1,060 ducats: Josef Stummvoll, ed.,
Geschichte der Österreichischen Nationalbibliothek (2 vols., Vienna, 1968–
73), I, 276–7, 298–9.

9. On the verso of the letter, BF wrote an unrelated note: "Hotel
d'Orleans / Rue St. Anne."

To Joseph Banks

LS:[1] Library of Congress; incomplete AL (draft):[2] University of Pennsylvania Library; press copy of LS: Massachusetts Historical Society

Dear Sir,   Passy, Novr. 21st. [*i.e.*, 22–25][3] 1783

I received your friendly Letter of the 7th. Inst. I am glad my Letters respecting the Aerostatic Experiment were not unacceptable. But as more perfect Accounts of the Construction and Management of that Machine have been and will be published before your Transactions, and from which Extracts may be made that will be more particular and therefore more satisfactory, I think it best not to print those letters. I say this in answer to your Question: for I did not indeed write them with a view of their being inserted. Mr. Faujas de St. Fond acquainted me yesterday, that a Book on the Subject which has been long expected, will be publish'd in a few Days,[4] and I shall send you one of them. Enclosed is a Copy of the *Procés verbal*[5] taken of the Experiment made yesterday in the Garden of the Queen's Palace *la Muette*, where the Dauphin now resides, which being near my House I was present. This Paper was drawn up hastily, and may in some Places appear to you obscure; therefore I shall add a few explanatory Observations.

This Balloon was larger than that which went up from Versailles and carried the Sheep &c.[6] Its bottom was open, and in the middle of the Opening was fixed a kind of Basket Grate in

1. In BFB's hand. BF signed and added the postscript after the press copy was made.

2. Only the first four pages survive, written on the recto and verso of a single folded sheet. The draft ends with the paragraph concluding "and the Balloon was very little damaged."

3. The experiment that BF describes here took place on Nov. 21; see the annotation to the *procès-verbal* of that date. BF wrote this letter the following day, *i.e.*, Nov. 22, and added a postscript on Nov. 25.

4. Barthélemy Faujas de Saint-Fond, *Description des expériences de la machine aérostatique de MM. de Montgolfier* . . . (Paris, 1783), was first advertised in the *Jour. de Paris* on Nov. 27.

5. Above, Nov. 21. BF sent it immediately, as he explains in the postscript, but delayed sending the present letter.

6. The Sept. 19 experiment that BF described to Banks in his letter of Oct. 8.

The First Manned Balloon Flight, as Seen from Franklin's Terrace

which Faggots and Sheaves of Straw were burnt. The Air rarified in passing thro' this Flame rose in the Balloon, swell'd out its sides and fill'd it.

The Persons who were plac'd in the Gallery made of Wicker, and attached to the Outside near the Bottom, had each of them a Port thro' which they could pass Sheaves of Straw into the Grate to keep up the Flame, & thereby keep the Balloon full. When it went over our Heads, we could see the Fire which was very considerable. As the Flame slackens, the rarified Air cools and condenses, the Bulk of the Balloon diminishes and it begins to descend. If those in the Gallery see it likely to descend in an improper Place, they can by throwing on more Straw, & renewing the Flame, make it rise again, and the Wind carries it farther.

La Machine poussée par le Vent s'est dirigée sur une des Allées du Jardin.[7] That is against the Trees of one of the Walks. The Gallery hitched among the top Boughs of those Trees which had been cut and were stiff, while the Body of the Balloon lean'd beyond and seemed likely to overset. I was then in great Pain for the Men, thinking them in danger of being thrown out, or burnt, for I expected that the Balloon being no longer upright, the Flame would have laid hold of the inside that leaned over it. But by means of some Cords that were still attach'd to it, it was soon brought upright again, made to descend, & carried back to its place. It was however much damaged.

Planant sur l'Horizon. When they were as high as they chose to be, they made less Flame and suffered the Machine to drive Horizontally with the Wind, of which however they felt very little, as they went with it, and as fast. They say they had a charming View of Paris & its Environs, the Course of the River, &c but that they were once lost, not knowing what Part they were over, till they saw the Dome of the Invalids which rectified their Ideas. Probably while they were employed in keeping up the Fire, the Machine might turn, and by that means they were *desorientés* as the French call it.

There was a vast Concourse of Gentry in the Garden, who had great Pleasure in seeing the Adventurers go off so chear-

7. This and the other underlined passages in French are quotations from the *procès-verbal*.

fully, & applauded them by clapping, &c. but there was at the same time a good deal of Anxiety for their Safety. Multitudes in Paris saw the Balloon passing, but did not know there were Men with it, it being then so high that they could not see them.

Developpant du Gaz. That is, in plain English, *burning more straw;* for tho' there is a little Mystery made, concerning the kind of Air with which the Balloon is filled, I conceive it to be nothing more than hot Smoke or common Air rarify'd, tho' in this I may be mistaken.

Aiant encore dans leur Galerie le deux tiers de leur Approvisionement. That is their Provision of Straw, of which they carried up a great Quantity. It was well that in the hurry of so hazardous an Experiment, the Flame did not happen by any accidental Mismanagement to lay hold of this Straw; tho' each had a Bucket of Water by him, by Way of Precaution.

One of these courageous Philosophers, the Marquis d'Arlandes, did me the honour to call upon me in the Evening after the Experiment with Mr. Montgolfier the very ingenious Inventor. I was happy to see him safe. He informed me they lit gently without the least Shock, and the Balloon was very little damaged.

This Method of filling the Balloon with hot Air is cheap and expeditious, and it is suppos'd may be sufficient for certain purposes, such as elevating an Engineer to take a View of an Enemy's Army, Works, &c. conveying Intelligence into, or out of a besieged Town, giving Signals to distant Places, or the like.

The other Method of filling a Balloon with permanently elastic inflammable Air, and then closing it, is a tedious Operation, and very expensive. Yet we are to have one of that kind sent up in a few Days. It is a Globe of 26 feet diameter. The Gores that compose it are red and white Silk so that it makes a beautiful appearance. A very handsome triumphal Car will be suspended to it, in which Messrs. Robert, two Brothers, very ingenious Men, who have made it in concert with Mr. Charles, propose to go up. There is room in this Car for a little Table to be placed between them, on which they can write and keep their Journal, that is, take Notes of every thing they observe, the State of their Thermometer, Barometer, Hygrometer &c which they will have more leisure to do than the others, having no fire to take Care of. They say they have a contrivance which will enable them to descend at Pleasure I know not what it is. But the Expence of this Machine, Filling included, will exceed it is said, 10,000 Livres.[8]

This Balloon of only 26 feet diameter being filled with Air ten times lighter than common Air, will carry up a greater Weight than the other, which tho' vastly bigger was filled with an Air that could scarcely be more than twice as light— Thus the great Bulk of one of these Machines, with the short duration of its Power; & the great Expence of filling the other will prevent the Invention's being of so much Use, as some may expect, till Chemistry can invent a cheaper light Air producible with more Expedition.

But the Emulation between the two Parties running high; the Improvement in the Construction and Management of the Balloons has already made a rapid Progress; and one cannot say how far it may go. A few Months since the Idea of Witches riding thro' the Air upon a Broomstick; and that of Philosophers upon a Bag of Smoke, would have appear'd equally impossible and ridiculous.

These Machines must always be subject to be driven by the Winds. Perhaps Mechanic Art may find easy means to give them progressive Motion in a Calm, and to slant them a little in the Wind.

I am sorry this Experiment is totally neglected in England where mechanic Genius is so strong. I wish I could see the same Emulation between the two Nations as I see between the two Parties here: Your Philosophy seems to be too bashful. In this Country we are not so much afraid of being laught at. If we do a foolish Thing, we are the first to laugh at it ourselves, and are almost as much pleased with a *Bon Mot* or a good *Chanson*, that ridicules well the Disappointment of a Project, as we might have been with its Success. It does not seem to me a good reason to decline prosecuting a new Experiment which apparently increases the Power of Man over Matter, till we can see to what

8. Some of this information was contained in the Robert brothers' prospectus of the upcoming experiment, published in the *Jour. de Paris* on Nov. 19. They announced that the experiment would take place between Nov. 26 and 30, weather permitting.

Use that Power may be applied. When we have learnt to manage it, we may hope some time or other to find Uses for it, as Men have done for Magnetism and Electricity, of which the first Experiments were mere Matters of Amusement.

This Experiment is by no means a trifling one. It may be attended with important Consequences that no one can foresee. We should not suffer Pride to prevent our progress in Science. Beings of a Rank and Nature far Superior to ours have not disdained to amuse themselves with making and launching Balloons, otherwise we should never have enjoyed the Light of those glorious Objects that rule our Day & Night, nor have had the Pleasure of riding round the Sun ourselves upon the Balloon we now inhabit.

With great and sincere Esteem, I am, Dear Sir, Your most obedt. & most humble Servant　　　　　　　　　B FRANKLIN

P.S. Nov. 25. The *Procés verbal* to which this Letter relates, went by last Post. I have now got the within mentioned Book; but it being too bulky to send by Post, I shall try to get it forwarded to you by the Duke of Manchester's Courier, who goes usually on Thursdays. I inclose one of the Plates of it, which gives a perfect Representation of the last great Balloon.[9] You can put it in its Place when you receive the Book BF

Sir Joseph Banks

Addressed: To / Sir Joseph Banks, Bart. / President of the Royal Society / London.

Endorsed: Dr. Franklin Explanation of the proces verbal./.

9. Plate No. 8, facing p. 268 in Faujas's *Description*, depicts the highly decorated balloon that Montgolfier and his associates demonstrated on Oct. 19.

From the Chevalier de Saint-Olympe[1]

LS:[2] American Philosophical Society

Monsieur L'ambassadeur   au havre le 24. 9bre. 1783.

Permettés que je consacre le dernier moment de mon Séjour en france a vous renouveller l'hommage de tous les Sentimens de respect, de veneration, et de reconnoissance que je vous dois a tant d'egards; vos bontés me Seront toujours presentes, et je Saisirai avec le plus vif empressement toutes les occasions qui pouront Se presenter pour vous renouveller l'hommage des sentimens avec les quels je Suis Monsieur L'ambassadeur Votre tres humble et tres obeissant serviteur   st. olympe

Voulés vous bien permettre que Monsieur votre fils recois ici l'assurance de mon attachement. Mde. de st. olympe sera fort aise de le voir dans mon absence et à mon retour je serai fort empressé a l'aller chercher et à avoir L'honneur de vous faire ma Cour[3]

Notation: St. Olympe 24 9bre. 1783

From Antoine Court de Gébelin[4]

ALS: American Philosophical Society

Monsieur   Au Musée de Paris Rue Dauphine 25. Nov. 83

J'ai l'honneur de vous envoyer quelques billets pour la seance du Musée du 4 Decembre: Toute notre Societé serait très

1. The recently married chevalier, whose wedding contract was witnessed by BF and WTF, was leaving for Martinique; see XL, 487n, 496–7, and his letter of Feb. 15, below.

2. Saint-Olympe himself added the postscript.

3. The newlyweds had become part of the social circle that included BF, WTF, the Jays, and the Le Roys: Le Roy to WTF, [Oct. 26 and 31, 1783]; Mme de Saint-Olympe to Sarah Jay, [Oct.] 26, [1783]; the chevalier de Saint-Olympe to WTF, Oct. 29, 1783; all at the APS.

4. This is his last letter to BF. Court de Gébelin had been ill for the past year, suffering from the stone and other ailments. Though in July, 1783, he had proclaimed himself cured by Mesmer's animal magnetism, his condition worsened in December, and he died on May 12, 1784, in Mesmer's apartment: Paul Schmidt, *Court de Gébelin à Paris (1763–1784)* (St.-Blaise,

flattée que vous en pussiez profiter: vous ne reconnoitriez pas nos Salles agrandies & embellies.[5] Nos Seances publiques sont actuellement de 12. par an; les Dames admises à toutes. Nous esperons donner cet hyver un volume de Memoires: nous serions bien satisfaits si vous vouliez bien nous en fournir pour enrichir ce 1°. volume.[6]

Permettez que j'aie l'honneur de vous recommander en meme tems un de mes excellens amis, M. Dupuis Architecte:[7] il vient de composer en VI. grandes feuilles grandeur d'Atlas une Salle de Spectacle de la plus grande beauté & infiniment plus commode qu'aucune de celles qui existent: il seroit très jaloux de la dedier à la Reine, & nous osons en consequence vous prier de vouloir bien vous interesser pour cela [one word illegible] en sa faveur auprès de M. Le Comte de Vaudreuil à qui j'ai eu l'honneur d'en ecrire.

M. Dupuis est d'ailleurs un membre distingué du musée & connu très avantageusement par d'excellens ouvrages, entr'autres par un en 2 vol in 4to. qui paroit depuis peu sur l'Architecture, la Perspective &c(?) qui lui fait beaucoup d'honneur par les grandes vues qui y regnent.

Il est egalement connu très avantageusement d'un grand nombre de Seigneurs.

Je suis respectueusement Monsieur Votre très humble & très obeissant Serviteur   COURT DE GEBELIN

Switzerland, and Roubaix, France, [1900]), pp. 174–7; Frank A. Pattie, *Mesmer and Animal Magnetism: a Chapter in the History of Medicine* (Hamilton, N.Y., 1994), pp. 185–90.

5. In early 1783 the Musée de Paris (XXXV, 32n) had moved into sumptuous new quarters on the rue Dauphine: Anne-Marie Mercier-Faivre, *Une Supplément à l'"encyclopédie": le "Monde primitif" d'Antoine Court de Gébelin . . .* (Paris, 1999), pp. 65–6.

6. The Musée began publishing its short-lived journal *Mémoires du Musée de Paris* in 1784: Michael R. Lynn, "Enlightenment in the Public Sphere: the Musée de Monsieur and Scientific Culture in Late Eighteenth-Century Paris," *Eighteenth-Century Studies*, XXXII (1999), 466.

7. Charles Dupuis, an architect at Versailles: Michel Gallet, *Les Architectes parisiens du XVIIIe siècle: dictionnaire biographique et critique* (Paris, 1995), p. 203. His publications included *Traité (nouv.) d'architecture avec un sixième ordre nommé ordre français* (2 vols., Paris, 1782), presumably the work mentioned in the next paragraph.

From Giacomo Francisco Crocco

Press copy of copy,[8] two copies: National Archives

Sir,   [November 25, 1783]

On the 15th. July last[9] I had the honor to acquaint your Excellency of my arrival in Europe and that I was appointed by his Majesty the Emperor of Marroco Bearer of the Answer to the Congress Sovereign of the Thirteen United States of North America and that according to my Instructions I was to meet at Paris the Ambassador that would be appointed by the Congress to Sign at the Court of Marroco the Treaty of Peace and Commerce agreable to the proposals made to his Imperial Majesty by Robert Montgomery Esqr. per his Letter dated at Alicant the 4th. January 1783. Since I have been at the Court of Madrid[1] where I had some Commissions from the Emperor and to see the Execution of them I came to this Place from whence I intend to embark in three or four Months for Barbary, unless that in the mean while I should receive an Answer from your Excellency with orders that Richard Harrison Esqr. should give me for my traveling Charge fifteen hundred hard Dollars, although the Courts of Europe are accustom'd to allow the ministers of My Master at the rate of ten Pounds Sterling per day while they are in Europe to defray their Expences, besides Presents for their good Offices on those important Affairs. His Imperial Majesty was graciously pleased at my Sollicitation to agree at the Request of the Congress to grant them a Treaty of Peace (which other Powers in Europe could not obtain but after many Years) and my return without the full Execution of his Commands I apprehend with just Motif may forever indispose him against the United Provinces.

I remain most truly, Sir, Your most obedient & humble Servant.   (signed) GIACOMO FRANCO. CROCCO

Copy of a Letter from Giacomo Franco Crocco to B. Franklin Esqr. dated Caidiz 25th. November 1783.—

---

8. In the hand of L'Air de Lamotte. This was one of the three letters relating to Morocco that BF enclosed in his Dec. 25 letter to Mifflin.

9. XL, 310–12.

1. See his letter cited above.

From Armand-Benoît-Joseph Guffroy[2]

ALS: American Philosophical Society

Monsieur   d'arras le 25 9bre 1783.

Demander justice à un homme juste c'est lui faire plaisir; je ne crains donc pas de vous importuner en vous adressant les reclamations fondées d'un marin qui a eté emploié en qualité De Capitaine dans la division du Commodore paul-jones.

Le sr jean charles igonnem Chevalier De Richebourg, aiant ete emploié Dans L'escadre du Commodore paul-jones en 1779 sur le vaissaeau la vengeance Capitaine Ricot,[3] Languit encore Depuis Ce tems après la recompense de ses services.

Le Chevalier De Richebourg ne resta cependant pas dans L'inaction; a peine eut on Desarmé qu'il sollicita son payement; il ecrivit à Mr Ray De Chaumont,[4] il le vit même a passy en mars 1780: Sur les observations que fit le Ch. De Richebourg, qu'il esperoit avoir au moins *huit parts des prises* faites par la Division De jones, Mr Ray De chaumont lui repondit qu'il devoit être mieux partagé que Cela, et il eut la Complaisance de Communiquer alors une liquidation qu'il avoit faite lui même d'après laquelle 37500 *l.t.* Devoient etre partagées entre 17 officiers du Rang Du sr chr De Richebourg.[5]

Mais alors il y avoit procès au Conseil sur les pretentions du proprietaire du vaisseau Corsaire Lagranville,[6] il fallut attendre; et Mr De Chaumont a Cette epoque indemnisa même le sr chr De Richebourg Des Depenses De voiage et sejour, qu'il avoit eté obligè De faire a paris et a passy pour reclamer ses droits.

En 1781 le sr chr De Richebourg fut renvoié par une lettre De Mr De chaumont, a Mr Montigny de-Monplaisir a L'orient

2. Lawyer from Arras who rose to prominence during the French Revolution as deputy to the National Convention and member of the Comité de Sûreté Générale: *DBF*.

3. XXIX, 494n.

4. The French government had appointed Chaumont as paymaster for Jones's squadron: XXIX, 240n.

5. The distribution of prizes was the subject of much debate between Jones and Capt. Ricot, and Jones later blamed Chaumont for imposing the final terms: XXX, 223; XXXI, 95n.

6. The French privateer *Grandville*: XXX, 284n.

(Lettre du 17 janv: 1781, jointe.);[7] il s'y adressa: celui cy repondit qu'il ne sçavoit s'il seroit chargé de cette repartition.

Le Chr De Richebourg eut De nouveau recours à M Ray De chaumont qui assura qu'on ne pouvoit proceder a une répartition à Cause des prétentions du Corsaire Lagranville et que le Ministre n'avoit pas encore fait remettre le prix du Serapis (Lettre du 12 juillet 1781).

En 1782 Mr Ray De Chaumont eut L'attention De Donner avis au sr. chr. De Richebourg que pour obtenir ce qui lui etoit dû il falloit qu'il s'adressa au ministre a qui il avoit rendu ses Comptes (Lettre de fev: 1782 remise depuis a Mr De chardon),[8] et par une seconde lettre il disoit que si le ministre lui donnoit des ordres pour faire la repartition il s'empresseroit de les executer et d'en donner avis au chr De Richebourg, mais que Depuis ses Comptes il ne sçavoit ou en etoit cette affaire.[9] (autre lettre remise a M. De chardon).

En juillet 1782 Mr De chardon aiant eté envoié a Dunkerque pour obliger les armateurs à liquider les Comptes des marins qui avoient eté en Course, Le sr chr De Richebourg Crut pouvoir s'adresser à lui, il lui presenta un memoire avec les Deux lettres De Mr Ray De chaumont dont je viens de parler; mais ce fut encore infructueusement: Mr De chardon ne fit rendre justice ni pour ce qui concerne les droits que le sr chevalier avoit a repeter à dunkerque, ni pour L'objet qui L'oblige d'avoir recours a vous.

Toutes ces demarches infructueuses avoient Decouragé le sr chr De Richebourg lorsque le hazard me le fit Connoitre à dunkerque au moment ou il avoit fait une requette adressée a Mr *De Castries* ministre De nôtre marine. J'avois quelqu'un auprès de ce Ministre a qui je L'adressai avec le mémoire explicatif.

Ce Ministre vit le memoire et la requette, il me fit dire qu'il ne vouloit pas se mèler de ces affaires qui concernoient

7. The enclosures to the present letter are missing. Monplaisir (XXIV, 278n) was Chaumont's agent at Lorient: XXXII, 204.

8. Chardon was *procureur général* of the *conseil des finances pour les prises en mer:* XXIX, 164n.

9. In response to the numerous claims for outstanding prize money he received in 1780 and 1781, Castries ordered Chaumont to turn over all his accounts to officials in the naval ministry: XXXVI, 529–30.

L'administration des etats unis de L'amerique, qu'il falloit s'adresser a Mr Ray de chaumont, ou a vous, Monsieur.

D'après Cette reponse, Comme Mr Ray de chaumont Connoissoit Deja les reclamations du chr De richebourg je lui ecrivis le 25 juillet Dernier, et je n'ai pas eu de reponse.

Non seulement je me flatte que vous daignerez, Monsieur, m'honnorer De la vôtre, mais encore que vous ferez enfin rendre justice a un brave homme qui reclame ce qui lui est Si legitîmement Dû.

J'ai la Confiance de vous adresser les requette et Memoire, qui ont eté presentés au Ministre De france, avec Copie authentique des lettres que le sr chevalier produit à L'appuy De ses Demandes.

Je suis avec le plus profond Respect Monsieur Vôtre très humble et très obeissant serviteur

GUFFROY
Avocat au conseil d'artois ancien echevin
des Ville et Cité d'arras rue des agaches

Notation: Guffroy 25. 9bre. 1783

From Sir Edward Newenham

ALS: American Philosophical Society

Dear Sir—   25 Novr 1783—
You will see by the enclosed,[1] what has been done in the Grand National Convention; The Variety of Sentiment & Contending Interests are Objects almost unsurmountable objections to any Plan; the Speeches are not fully enserted, but the Substance is—In my private opinion—all will end in a just & Equitable place Bill, which in a few sessions will prove a real reform—and to which there cannot be so many Objections—
I Still keep up the Idea of our entering into a Treaty Seperately

1. Newenham probably enclosed one or more issues of the *Dublin Evening Post*, which the Grand National Convention had appointed on Nov. 14 to publish its proceedings: *The History of the Proceedings and Debates of the Volunteer Delegates of Ireland, on the Subject of a Parliamentary Reform . . .* (Dublin, 1784), p. 44.

& distinctly with the united States of North America, but I cannot do it without your Excellencys Assistance & Advice; I hope, therefore, (on the part of a Nation), who always Supported the Just Claims of the United States to be honoured with your Advice; I am anxious to unite both Countries in the bonds of friendship & Commerce; America never had a more Sincere or warmer advocate & friend than I & my friends here, were—when the Very mention of our Principles were deemed Treason—

Our Parliament is dayly sinking in the Estimation of the public; Prodigality & Profusion—Venality & its attendant consequences, direct *its* proceeding—the People will be Drove to Violent resolutions; Such Conduct cannot long be endured, it must—be resisted—from Vice to Vice they are dayly running, & every hour adds new distress to the People— I wish we were a thousand Leagues removed from a Selfish Wicked Ministry, whose sole View is the Slavery of the People & the Aggrandising of themselves—[2]

So much was their own friends ashamed of them, that the Prime [*Serjeant*] (who hourly expects to be made a Judge) left them on my motion for Supporting the City Petition— Leinsters Corrupted Duke, & Shannons profligacy gave way to truth, & their Squadrons joined us on that division— At 8 oClock, the house was Cleared & Kept Shut for two Days; Such violent Speeches never occurred in any Parliament; the People have been grosly insulted—[3]

2. Three days earlier, Newenham had been in the minority when he opposed addressing the king to increase the salaries of the lord lieutenant and his secretary: *The Parliamentary Register: or, History of the Proceedings and Debates of the House of Commons of Ireland* . . . (17 vols., Dublin, 1784–1801), II, 197–204.

3. On Nov. 24, Travers Hartley, M.P. for Dublin City, introduced a petition on behalf of the Council of the Chamber of Commerce of Dublin, calling for more equitable commercial relations between Ireland and England. Several members objected that the House could accept petitions only from individuals, not from a "self-erected body" unauthorized by the government. Newenham protested that refusal to receive the petition would "absolutely dissolve the bonds of the governing and governed." Prime Serjeant Thomas Kelly spoke in favor of receiving the petition and declared he would support the government "in every honourable measure, and in none but honourable measures." This statement received loud applause from the gallery, which was thereupon cleared of visitors, and the House voted to

I am obliged to make this a Short Note—but am desired to assure your Excellency & your Worthy Grandson of Lady Newenhams & my Constant wishes for your health & Prosperity; I entreat the honor of a few Lines from you—when convenient—

I have the Honor to be with Every sentiment of Respect & Esteem your Excellencys Most Obt & Humble st

EDWD NEWENHAM

you will please, when read, to Send the papers to my *much respected* friend, the Marquiss Le Fayette—

Addressed: His Excellency Dr Franklin / Passy / Paris—

From Jean Rousseau[4]   ALS: American Philosophical Society

Monsieur   Londres le 25: 9bre: 1783.

Je demande pardon à Vôtre Excellence si je viens encore l'interrompre: mais m'etant depuis peu trouvé en Compagnie de quelques Messieurs du Nord de l'Amerique; & Sur quelques questions que je pris la liberté de leur faire au Sujet de leur Pays: ils me témoignèrent qu'il y avoit quelque jalousie au Sujet de l'endroit oû Siégeroit le Congrès: tout d'un coup l'idée me vint & qui en même tems fut ma réponse: C'est que le Congrès ne devoit point être fixe ou permanent dans un endroit; mais Siéger alternativement & Successivement dans chacune des treize Provinces unies.

Y ayant depuis refléchi murement: je me Suis confirmé dans mon opinion, & ai cru être de mon devoir de le communiquer à Vôtre Excellence qui Sans doute y a pensé long tems avant moy. Etant un des premiers moyens de bannir la jalousie & de conserver l'union & l'egalité.

---

ban all spectators. William Robert Fitzgerald, 2nd Duke of Leinster, and Richard Boyle, 2nd Earl of Shannon, were leading supporters of the Irish administration in Parliament: *Parliamentary Register,* II, 205–10; Edith M. Johnston-Liik, *History of the Irish Parliament, 1692–1800* . . . (6 vols., Belfast, 2002), III, 248–51; IV, 159–62, 374–5; V, 15.

4. The Genevan merchant, long established in London, who three years earlier had sent BF a memoir on American independence and, more recently, congratulated him on winning it: XXXII, 152–3; XL, 157–8.

Il me naitroit Sans doute bien d'autres idées, Si elles n'etoient pas absorbées, par l'ouvrage monotone d'un comptoir, & par une espéce de malaise Sur ma Situation future.

Je Suis avec un profond respect Monsieur De Vôtre Excellence Le très humble & très obeissant Serviteur

JEAN ROUSSEAU

Notation: Rousscecault Mr. Jean 25 Nov. 1783.—

From Joseph Banks

ALS: American Philosophical Society

Dear Sir　　　　　　　　　　　Soho Square Novr. 28 1783

I am in truth much indebted to you for the favor you have done me in transmitting the Copy of the Procès verbal on Mr Montgolfiers experiment,[5] which I have this moment receivd. The Experiment becomes now interesting in no small degree. I laught when Ballons of scarce more importance than Soap bubbles occupied the attention of France but when men Can with Safety pass & do pass more than 5 miles in the first Experiment I begin to fancy that I espy the hand of the master in the Education of the infant of Knowledge who so speedily attains such a degree of maturity & do not scruple to guess that My old Friend who usd to assist me when I was Younger has had some share in the success of this Enterprise.

On Tuesday last a miserable Taffeta Ballon was let loose here under the direction of a Mr. Zambeccari an Italian Nobleman[6] as I hear it was 10 feet in diameter & filld with inflammable air made from the filings of Iron & Vitriolic acid the silk was oild the seams coverd with Tar & the outside Gilt it had been shewn for several days floating about in a public room at a shilling for

5. Enclosed in his letter of Nov. 21 [*i.e.*, 22–25].

6. After exhibiting their balloon at the Lyceum in the Strand, Francesco Zambeccari and Michael Biaggini (for whom see Banks to BF, Nov. 7) staged their experiment on the Artillery Ground at Moorfields on Nov. 25 before a vast crowd. It was the first public demonstration of a balloon ascension in England: *Gent. Mag.*, LIII (1783), 977; J. E. Hodgson, *The History of Aeronautics in Great Britain* ... (London, 1924), p. 102.

the sight & half a Crown for the Admission when it should be let loose.

The day was fine to Excess the wind a gentle breeze from the North at a few minutes after one it set out & before night fell at Grafham a small village near Pelworth in Sussex having ran over about 48 miles of Countrey the Countreyman who first saw it observd it in its descent it appeard at first small & increasing fast surprizd him so much that he ran away he returnd however & found it burst by the expansion of the Containd fluid.

I wish I had somewhat more interesting to tell you of but I am this moment risen from the dinner which I annualy give to the auditors of the treasurers accounts. I would not delay my thanks to you and I trust you will make some allowance for the Effects of the festivity of the day which has I fear Crampd my Accuracy but I can assure You has not diminishd the real gratitude with which I declare myself Your Obligd & Faithfull Servant

Jos: Banks

Addressed: Dr. Franklin / Passy / near / Paris / France

From Katherine Sproule Douglas[7]

ALS: American Philosophical Society

Geore Street No 3 Adelphi London Novr 28th 1783

May it Please your Excellency

To accept my *unbounded* thanks for the *Honor* you did my freind Miss Maxwell when in Paris which I *Sincerly* Charge to

7. A woman with a complicated past. The seven children mentioned in this letter were fathered by her first husband, James Hunter, who died in 1774. A year later she married Hunter's uncle Andrew Sprowle (Sproule), a wealthy Loyalist merchant of Norfolk, Va., who established the shipyard in Gosport and owned a plantation and several residences. When fighting broke out in Norfolk, the family was evacuated to Lord Dunmore's fleet, and Sprowle's properties were burned and his stores consumed. He died on board ship in May, 1776, whereupon his widow, plagued by accusations that she had not been legally married and had been a spy, went to London to petition for her inheritance and a pension. The Loyalist board ruled in

my acct of *Gratitude!* & thanks to almighty God! for puting in my *Heart* to *presume* on Such an application;[8] which I again most Gratefully imbrace on the Permission *Graciously* & bountifully granted by your Excellency to miss Maxwell! which I *humbly* flatter myself *will* under almighty God Reinstate *me* & my Seven *poor indigent* Children in their *Just* Claims of Virginia Property; which the Herewith sent Coppies of Correspondence[9] will *authenticate to us all* your Excellencys *Gracious* & *Humane* answewer will Lay an *Everlasting* obligation on your Devoted & obliged humble Sert   KATH SPROULE
                                                    Now DOUGLAS

Miss Maxwell begs to be *humbly* remembred to your Excellency your Son Govr Frankland is well Paiys His Duty Sorry to hear you are Indisposd Hopes in God to hear you are better

Addressed: His Excellency / Doctor Franklin / Paris

---

her favor on March 6, 1783, confirming her marriage and praising her husband's efforts on behalf of the British government, but granting a smaller pension than she expected. She then petitioned Parliament for compensation for Sprowle's Va. holdings, married Francis Douglas (her husband at the time of this letter), and by November, 1783, was petitioning the state of Virginia for permission to return. In 1785, when asking TJ to intercede on her behalf, she denied that her husband and her son (who fought with a British regiment in Virginia) had been loyal to the crown: Peter W. Coldham, *American Loyalist Claims* (1 vol. to date, Washington, D.C., 1980–), I, 461; William P. Palmer *et al.*, eds., *Calendar of Virginia State Papers* . . . (11 vols., Richmond, 1875–93), III, 542; Isaac S. Harrell, *Loyalism in Virginia: Chapters in the Economic History of the Revolution* (Durham, N.C., 1926), pp. 44–5, 96–8; William B. Clark *et al.*, eds., *Naval Documents of the American Revolution* (11 vols. to date, Washington, D.C., 1964–), V, 776–7, 793–4; Memorial of Katherine Sproule, Oct. 14, 1783 (Public Record Office); Alan Flanders, "Andrew Sproule's Widow Lost It All," *Virginian-Pilot* (Norfolk, Va.), Feb. 10, 2002; *Jefferson Papers*, VIII, 243–4, 259–60, 329–30, 364.

8. The visit of Miss Maxwell has left no other trace, but she presumably delivered the letters or petitions from Mrs. Douglas that BF in turn forwarded to William Alexander to carry to Virginia; see Alexander to BF, Nov. 6.

9. Not located.

From Henry Knox   ALS (draft): New-York Historical Society[1]

Sir   New-York 28th Novr 1783
    I take the liberty to introduce to your acquaintance and ci-
vilities Jeremiah Platt, a gentleman of this City, who has just
returned from a long exile of seven years, in which period he
has in every instance approved himself a zealous and upright
citizen of the republick, a warm asserter of its liberties and ever
ready to contribute his full proportion for its defence. Any attentions which You may have an opportunity of affording him
& Mrs Platt who accompanies him will be gratefuly ackn[owl-
edge]d by me.[2]
    In this auspicious moment America has the opportunity of
rising to greatness and empire— The troops who have long
been hostile to the liberty we have been seeking, at length are
withdrawing from a country too stubborn to be conquered,
& whose independence & sovereignty are acknowledged,
and confirmed by solemn treaties— If in this happy conjunction of Affairs we should possess true wisdom & unbiassed
Justice our natural Character will be Completely formed, and
posterity will experience the good effects of their fathers virtues. Mr Platt will be able to give you the details of politicks
in America which will render it unnecessary on my part. I cannot Conclude without expressing my earnest wishes that you
enjoy the felicity which you have so Ardently endevored to obtain for others, and that You may return to America to receive
the ineffable pleasures arising from the gratitude of a free and
enlightned people.

    1. We obtained this draft from the Mass. Hist. Soc.; it is now part of the
Gilder Lehrman Collection. Filed with it is the draft of a letter to JA of the
same date, introducing the bearer, Jeremiah Platt. For the recipient's copy
of the latter see *Adams Papers*, XV, 484.
    2. Platt, a merchant, had spent the war years in Hartford and was in-
volved in financing several Conn. privateers. In 1780 he married Abigail
Pynchon of Springfield, Mass.: Frederic Gregory Mather, *The Refugees of
1776 from Long Island to Connecticut* (Albany, 1913), pp. 509, 680; Louis F.
Middlebrook, *History of Maritime Connecticut during the American Revolution, 1775–1783* (2 vols., Salem, Mass., 1925), II, 49, 97, 100; Willard S.
Allen, "Longmeadow (Mass.) Families," *New England Hist. and Geneal.
Register*, XXXVIII (1884), 47.

I have the honor to be Sir with perfect respect Your most obedient humble Servant[3]   H Knox

To his Excellency Doctr Franklin 28 Novr 1783

His Excellency Benja Franklin Esqr.

To his Excellency Doctor Franklin

From Henry Laurens

Dear Sir,   Leister Square London 28th. Novem 1783—
This will be accompanied by a Letter of equal date accounting for my Reciepts of public Money to which I beg leave to refer.[5]
Since my arrival in London I have been rather too much hurried by Visits & returns to enquire minutely into News, I learn however that Mr. Fox's (Lord North's) Bill for changing the system of Government of East India Affairs passed a second reading last night & was committed between 4 & 5 oClock this morning—hard work—tis said an opposition will appear strong in the House of Lords, but that it will finally pass.[6]

3. Platt also carried a letter of introduction from GW, written on Dec. 1 and addressed to both Lafayette and BF. The two-sentence letter stated that Platt and his wife were going to England, and "probably to France." The ALS has not been located, but a letterbook copy is at the Library of Congress.
4. In the hand of Henry Laurens, Jr.
5. Laurens had just arrived in London with his daughter Martha. In the enclosed letter he apologized for the delay in sending his accounts, explaining that storms had kept him at Calais for nine days and the Channel crossing had been "perilous." His financial statement, titled "Receipts of Money from the United States of America by Henry Laurens," listed four sums totalling 60,416.13 *l.t.* that he had received from Ferdinand Grand as part of his salary. Because he did not know what salary Congress had approved, he could not "state an Account and strike a Balance" (University of S.C. Library).
6. The Fox-North administration's bill for reforming the East India Company was defeated in the House of Lords on Dec. 15 and 17. The coalition ministry was dismissed as a result: *Laurens Papers*, XVI, 356–7n; L. G. Mitchell, *Charles James Fox and the Disintegration of the Whig Party, 1782–1794* (London, Glasgow, and New York, 1971), pp. 64–75.

Mr B Vaughan may give you an Acct. of the Moorfield's Ba-loon,[7] he could not persuade me to shove into an English Mob & I saved my Watch by staying at home.

I find my good friend Mr. Adams strongly countenances Jenings who visits him and rides in the job Coach, altho' he skulks away from his ancient acquaintance & they I am as-sured by some of themselves avoid him. Three Gentlemen have informed me Mr Adams has told them, & I doubt not he has told it to thirty others, "Mr. Laurens is wrong in all that affair, Mr. Jenings was not the writer of the anonymous Letter It was the work of a banker's clerk in Amsterdam."[8] This is very pretty, Mr. A. takes two labouring Oars & has got himself into a worse hobble than Mr L was in, who had never charged Jenings with being the Writer, he had only in compliance with Jenings's press-ing desire told him, who, from circumstances he believed was; but there are charges which Mr L. has actually exhibited upon which the Chronies are hitherto silent, tho' Jennings says an an-swer is soon to come forth, the labor of three Months for telling a plain tale must produce somewhat uncommonly clever[9]—he says also there has been an inspection into the anonymous Paper in Dr. Franklin's hands by the Doctor, Mr Barclay, Mr Ridley & a comparison made with that & the one called in question, & that the Gentlemen have pronounced Mr Jenings innocent in all appearance, this may or may not be, if it be the survey must have happened since I left Passy, but be it so, tis not of moment. You promised me that Letter dated Amsterdam having the Post Mark Bruxelles without, & amendments within I forgot to ask for it when I was coming from Passy will you be so good Sir as to send it by an early Post directed for me to the care of Wm Manning Esqr.

7. The balloon of Count Francesco Zambeccari and Michael Biaggini, for which see Banks to BF of this date.

8. Laurens suspected Jenings of writing three anonymous letters attack-ing JA; see XXXVI, 499–501; XXXVII, 289–91; *Laurens Papers*, XVI, 280–1. JA assured Jenings that he did not believe him responsible: *Adams Papers*, XVI, 213.

9. Edmund Jenings, *A Full Manifestation of what Mr. Henry Laurens Falsely Denominates as Candor in Himself, and Tricks in Mr. Edmund Jenings* (London, 1783).

The protection of Mr. Adams to his very dejected associate cannot juandice my Eye, since my friend recieved *me* with an open hand and kind Salute in a very large company strengthening my assurance of his sincerity, by an audible affectionate Enquiry, "how did you leave Doctor Franklin?"

To morrow my Daughter and I go to Bath where Mr. Jay & Mr. Chace[1] are, the young Lady joins in the most respectful Salutes to yourself & Mr. Franklin with Dear Sir, your affectionate & most obedt. Servant

His Excellency B. Franklin Esqr. Passy near Paris.

From ———— Menier de Saint Yver[2]

ALS: American Philosophical Society

Monsieur   Paris ce 28. 9bre. 1783./.

Votre Excellence en refusant sa protection au S. Schaffer, qui dans cette occasion est plus malheureux que coupable, ignore qu'en l'abandonnant elle fait le malheur d'une autre famille. La chambre assemblée a reproché a M. Schaffer qu'il n'avoit point été reclamé par vous, Monsieur, l'on a meme argué de là que vous aviés lieu de vous plaindre directement et que nous avions abusé de votre confiance, enfin j'ose le dire votre silence la fait regarder comme un vagabond et a prévalu sur la recommandation de differentes personnes de merite qui s'interessent à moi, notament de M. Delaborde fermier Général du Roy[3] qui me connoissant depuis nombre d'années ainsi que ma famille veut bien prendre à moi le plus grand intéret. Je ne connois M. Schaffer que depuis le mois de Juin dernier et malgré le malheur dans lequel il m'entraine, je lui dois la Justice de dire qu'il est lui même la Victime de deux intrigants nommés Dautun et

1. Samuel Chase, who wrote BF on Sept. 18, above.

2. The former roommate and alleged partner of John Shaffer; see XL, 619n.

3. Jean-Benjamin de Laborde (or La Borde) (1734–1794), a farmer general since 1756: *DBF;* Yves Durand, *Les fermiers généraux au XVIIIe siècle* (Paris, 1971), pp. 521–2.

Eveline[4] qui l'ont perdu; Le premier est en quelque façon la cause du malheur dans lequel nous nous trouvons plongés. Je peux même assurer votre Excellence, que c'est lui qui a fait inscrire M Schaffer sur l'almanach Royal comme Banquier des Etats unis à son insçu, pour tromper le public sous son nom que l'on a contrefait plusieurs fois.

J'entre dans ces differents details non pas pour etre le deffenseur de M. Schaffer, puisque j'ai moi même lieu de regretter de le connoitre, mais parceque son malheur entraine necessairement le mien et qu'il seroit intéressant pour moi que votre animosité contre lui cesse, et que si votre Excellence ne se joint a mes protections je suis un homme perdu, et un seul mot de vous Monsieur suffira pour nous tirer du precipice où votre silence nous a plongé. Veuillés donc bien, Monsieur, ne pas me refuser la grace que je vous demande, si vous ne le faites pour M. Schaffer que ce soit au moins pour ma famille. Nous ne sommes pas aussi heureux qu'en Angleterre, où le malheur n'est que personnel; Votre ame bienfaisante sentira tout le prix de ma demande et votre humanité vous portera sans doute a me l'accorder.

Je suis avec le plus profond respect de Votre Excellence Monsieur Le tres humble et très obeissant serviteur[5]

MENIER DE SAINTYVER

Notation: Mesnier De Saintyver 28 Nov. 1783.

4. D'Autun and Edeline had been involved in the fraud leading to Shaffer's arrest in 1781: XXXV, 440–2.

5. An undated letter from Saint Yver, written around this time to an unknown recipient—a pastor—is among BF's papers at the APS. He writes on behalf of himself and Shaffer. They had been judged last Saturday, and though still ignorant of the decision, they had heard that the *procureur du roi* had appealed. They beseech the recipient to call on the *procureur* and seek an *ordre du roi* to send them to Shaffer's home in America. Saint Yver presumes that BF will not object to this request. Had he known earlier that the recipient had already called on BF (presumably about Shaffer), he would have sought his protection long before this.

From John Viny, with a Note by Mary Hewson

LS:[6] American Philosophical Society

[after November 28, 1783][7]

I am favour'd with yours of the third of Octobr,[8] in about ten days, the contents of which, does me the highest Honor as it is demonstrative of your desire to serve me and my Family, from the Impulse of Affection, the Evidence of which is so like your Self, most Indearingly conveyed; but no more, let it Suffice that we love, honor, and Revere you, and wait with anxious hope for that happy day when we may again injoy your Presance— As yours did not contain any discription of the particulars of the Wheels you was pleas'd to order I have sent two sets of different hight, and strength, in hopes that one of them may be applicable to your Carriage the other to be dispos'd of in the manner which your kind postscrip set forth; these wheels sent are such as I make in common, and Equal to any in point of durability for the different Carriages for which they are intended, the lighist for Post Chaise, or light Perch Charriots, the Other for Heavy Craneneck Charriots or Coach at Eight & nine guineas pr set, with an allowance of Eleven Shillings for finnishing them with paint, boxes &c but if for Traveling, as (Monsuier Duchateaus)[9] ten guineas or as much Stronger as shall be wish'd for, from Fifteen, to twenty guineas, for Carriages of Burden, as I have now by me a pr of Cart or Waggon Wheels which by the most Competant Judges are pronounc'd to be the strongest three Inch Wheels that Ever was made; my dear Friend if my reasoning shou'd not be Value'd in your mind with regard to the not sending the Wheels with whole rims of wood, I hope you will Acquit me of any want of regard to you, I having in a

6. Mostly in the hand of Viny's daughter Elizabeth, whom he identifies near the end of the letter as "Bettsum," BF's name for her; see XL, 48n. As an afterthought, Viny inserted a final sentence before signing.

7. The date on which Viny shipped the two sets of wheels described at the beginning of this letter; see his final sentence.

8. Missing, but clearly a response to the Viny family's letter of May 21: XL, 48–50.

9. Du Chateau, a customer who brought to France Viny's May 21 letter (cited above) and who is mentioned in that letter.

former Instance of Orders for the Prince of Condé, and others Experience'd their wish for Whole wood rims, but as that is not to be done alltogether in sets more then one in five Hundred I feard your Exhibting such would naturely be productive of such a desire, and there not being so would be risquing the favour and approbation of those for whom they may be design'd, but I will make a point of keeping them in as few piecis as possible; in answer to your wish for an Investigation of the Nature of the Subscription for my Support, its as follows; being obliged to commit an Act of Bancruptcy in order to procure a releace from Jos Jacob a Bancrupt two months before, and to give the proper claims on our Joint Cridditors, I was there by Totally divested of all property; in this state and on the day of my resignation thereof Mr. Saml Smith steptd forward and Assured me of his Assistance; accordingly he drew Up my case and opend a subcription for raising the sum of three thousand pounds, for seven Years, at one hundred Each on my bond[1] Sml Smith, Benjn Smith, his Elder Brother, Willm Smith, S Son, Jos Nash, and Jos Goss, Nephews to B, and S. Smith, Mr. Bull [Bell], and Mr. Jon Thontin [Thornton], making together seven, with wich I went forth, and where so happy as to have the following Duke of Montague, Duke of Newcatle, Duke of Dorset, the Honbl Stewart McKenzie, the Revnd Doctr Willson, now Bishop of Bristol, his Bro Mr. Thos Willson, Gent Jno Phillimore, George Jeffery, Jno Eddows, and Danl Morgan, one of my assignees, making eighteen and on my being at a stand Mr. B Smith Vollunturyly began again with a second hundred, with which I have, with our savings been enabled to go on with pleasure and profit, and for which honor, and happiness, I hope we shall ever give testamony of a due sense by exerting all diligence [*torn:* and] prudence in our several capacity; my Brother [*torn:* at(?) Ten]-terden[2] disirted me in my difficulties, and have hardly had any intercorse with him since, but he and Family are all well, and your Bettsum is grown a Jolly and harty Young Woman, and is happy in having the honor of pening these lines to her much

1. The subscription list that Viny had sent BF in May, to the amount of £1,800, included all but two of the 17 subscribers who follow, Eddows and Morgan here replacing the Duke of Buccleuch and G. Rooke. See XL, 49n.
2. Thomas Viny: XVII, 26–7.

Esteemd and kind friend, [*Added by John Viny:*] The two sets of Wheels where ship'd the 28 of Novbr on Board the Friendship for Roen and hope thay will come safe and in due time and believe me to be with Since Gratitude yours moste Affactionately

JNO. VINY

[*In Mary Hewson's hand:*] I have begged this corner to say a few words to you my dear Sir. I wrote to you immediately upon receiving the letter and the books you favoured me with by Mr Hartley.[3] I sent my letter by the post that you might not remain in doubt whether it would be *now* convenient for me to take charge of your Grandson, but as I have not heard from you since I take this opportunity of repeating that I am ready & shall be happy to receive him, and do every thing in my power for him, if you still think of sending him. I have a favour to ask of you which I hope will not give you much trouble in granting— My son's Frenchmaster, findg: the grammars published here very defective, asked me to apply for one approved at Paris as a standard. If you can send me such a one you will oblige her who is your ever obliged and affectionate   M. H.

Addressed: A Monsieur / Monsieur Franklin / a Passy / pres de / Paris

Notation: Viny

Notes on the Journey from Boston to Philadelphia in 1723   AD: American Philosophical Society

This list of days, numbers, and abbreviated words was scrawled on the verso of Ferdinand Grand's letter of November 29. They show Franklin reconstructing his flight from Boston at the age of seventeen, which he had described in Part I of his autobiography, written in 1771.[4] He did not have that text with him in France, but in December, 1782, he had received a copy of his outline from Abel James.[5] Encouraged by James and others to complete the narrative, Franklin

3. Her letter is above, Sept. 28.
4. *Autobiog.*, pp. 70–5.
5. See XXXVIII, 425–9.

began what he called the "Continuation of the Account of my Life" at Passy in 1784; his note at the top of that section, now known as Part II, is no more specific than that.[6] The table published below indicates that he was already thinking about the details of his early life at the end of 1783.

These jottings, decoded in 1980 by one of our editors, establish the date of Franklin's entrance into Philadelphia as October 6, 1723.[7] In the autobiography, Franklin said only that he arrived on a Sunday morning, mentioning that the month was October. The key to understanding this cryptic list lay in recognizing that the words and abbreviations in the left column were shorthand for places in a southward sequence through New Jersey to the Delaware River.

Franklin's journey was as follows:[8] he fled from his brother's shop in Boston on September 23. On September 25 he took passage on Arnout Schermerhoorn's boat bound for New York, arriving there on the twenty-seventh. He left New York on October 1 and landed at Perth Amboy the following day. On October 3 he took a ferry across Raritan Bay and walked through New Jersey, stopping for the night in the region known as the Pines. On October 4 he got as far as Dr. John Browne's inn at Bordentown. The following day he walked to Burlington and, finding that a small boat was sailing down the Delaware ("River D") to Philadelphia that evening, joined the crew. Around midnight they came ashore and made camp. Setting off early the next morning, they soon landed at the Market Street wharf in Philadelphia. It was Sunday, October 6.

[*c.* November 29, 1783]

Monday Sept	23
T———	24
W———	25
T———	26
F———	27

6. *Autobiog.*, p. 141.

7. Claude-Anne Lopez solved the mystery when transcribing the Grand letter. Her discovery was reported in the *Philadelphia Inquirer*, Aug. 27, 1980. The discovery is also described in J. A. Leo Lemay and P. M. Zall, eds., *Benjamin Franklin's Autobiography* (New York and London, 1986), pp. 166–8; Claude-Anne Lopez, *My Life with Benjamin Franklin* (New Haven and London, 2000), pp. xviii–xx.

8. This brief reconstruction is based on the autobiography itself, supplemented by details about the boat from Boston to New York in Lemay and Zall, *Benjamin Franklin's Autobiography*, p. 167.

	S—————	28	
	Sund————	29	
	Monday————	30	
Bay	Tuesd————	1	Oct
Amboy———	Wednes————	2	Water
Pines	Thursd————	3	Amb.
Brown's———	Friday————	4	
River D———	Sat————	5	
Philad———	Sund————	6	

From Rodolphe-Ferdinand Grand

AL: American Philosophical Society

Ce Samedy [November 29, 1783]
Dans Lincertitude Si Monsieur Franklin a Connoissance d'un arrest du Conseil concernant La Caisse dEscompte Mr Grand a Lhonneur de lui en Envoyer un Exemplaire,[9] Il y verra que les anciens actionaires ont le droit de participer pour ¼ dans les nouvelles actions & que par Consequent Monsieur franklin ayant 40 actions anciennes peut en demander 10 nouvelles S'il les desire en les payant le 15 decembre prochain, a 3500 *l.t.* chaque ce qui feroit 35000 *l.t.* a debourcer en argent.[1]

Il Conviendra que Monsieur Franklin en faisant part de Ses Intentions a ce Sujet a Mr Grand lui envoye Les Numeros de touttes Ses actions. Mr Grand regrete beaucoup quil ne lui soit

9. The *arrêt du conseil* of Nov. 23: *Arrêt . . . qui, en faisant cesser l'effet de ce qui avoit été ordonné pour un temps, par les arrêts des 27 & 30 septembre dernier, concernant le cours des Billets de la Caisse d'Escompte, affranchit leur circulation de toute contrainte, & déclare leur acceptation purement volontaire: Autorise la création de mille Actions nouvelles . . .* ([Paris], [1783]). It was designed to restore public confidence in the *caisse d'escompte* after it suspended payment on Oct. 3: Bachaumont, *Mémoires secrets*, XXIII, 184–7, 295–6. The enclosure has not been located.

1. The current shareholders had, until Dec. 1, the right of first refusal for the 1,000 new shares that were to be issued. BF bought five new shares; his private account with Grand was debited on Dec. 22 for the purchase: Robert Bigo, *La Caisse d'escompte (1776–1793) et les origines de la banque de France* (Paris, 1927), p. 85; Account XVII (XXVI, 3).

pas possible d'aller lui meme a Passy asseurer de bouche Monsieur Franklin de tous Ses Sentiments & prendre Ses ordres aujourdhui n'etant plus temps demain.

Endorsed: Nov. 29. 1783—

From [Adrien-Jean-Baptiste?] Le Roy[2]

ALS: American Philosophical Society

Monsieur   a versailles ce 29 novembre 1783
J'ay L'honneur de vous addresser Mr. du Trône, Jeune medecin pour Lequel vous m'avés déja donné deux Lettres de recommandation auprès de deux de vos amis à philadelphie.[3] C'est un Jeune homme fort honnête, fort modeste, et fort instruit. Il va partir pour nos Isles, où il a de L'employ. Mais il compte profiter de Ses Loisirs pour aller chez vous jouir du Spectacle d'un peuple devenu Libre. Avant de passer dans cet autre hemisphere, il voudroit bien avoir vû celuy qui a tant contribué à cette Liberté. Je crois aussi qu'il voudroit vous entretenir de quelques vües qui pourroient être utiles à L'Amerique et à vous. Vous m'avés toujours marqué, Monsieur, tant de bonté que je n'hesite point à vous prier de vouloir bien Le recevoir comme un homme que j'estime et que j'aime beaucoup. C'est de plus une occasion de vous renouveller L'assurance des Sentiments pleins de respect, et même d'une profonde vénération avec Lesquels j'ay L'honneur d'être Monsieur Votre très humble et très obeissant Serviteur

LE ROY

2. This signed letter and the unsigned one described in annotation of BF to Rush, Sept. 18, are in a hand that does not resemble that of any of the Le Roys with whom BF regularly corresponded. We speculate that this Le Roy was Adrien-Jean-Baptiste (1738–1846), who came from a prominent family, traveled widely as a *commissaire de la marine*, and after retiring from the naval service *c.* 1780 became an author and a poet. A frequent guest at many salons, including that of the comtesse d'Houdetot, Adrien Le Roy was a friend of Morellet's and reportedly met BF. A biographical sketch written when he was 102 reported him still in fine health and of sound mind: Bajot and Poirré, *Annales maritimes et coloniales . . . ,* 2nd series, II (Paris, 1841), pp. 497–514; Medlin, *Morellet,* III, 19, 403.
3. BF to Benjamin Rush, Sept. 18, and to RB, Sept. 23, above.

To Joseph Banks

ALS: British Library; press copy of ALS: Harvard University Library

Dear Sir,   Passy, Nov. 30. 1783—

I did myself the honour of writing to you the Beginning of last Week, and I sent you by the Courier, M. Faujas's Book upon the Balloons, which I hope you have receiv'd.[4] I did hope to have given you to day an Account of Mr Charles's grand Balloon, which was to have gone up yesterday; but the filling it with inflammable Air having taken more time than had been calculated, it is deferr'd till to-morrow. I send you herewith a Paper in which you will see what was propos'd by Messrs. Robert who constructed the Machine; and some other Papers relative to the same Subject, the last of which is curious, as containing the Journal of the first Aerial Voyage perform'd by Men.—[5] I purpose being present to-morrow at the Experiment, and shall give you an Acct of it by the Wednesday's Post. With sincere & great Esteem, I have the honour to be, Sir, Your most obedt humble Servt.   B FRANKLIN

Sir Jos. Banks Bart.

4. See BF to Banks, Nov. 21 [*i.e.*, 22–25].

5. The enclosures are lost, but among them must have been at least three issues of the *Jour. de Paris:* the Nov. 19 issue containing the Robert brothers' prospectus, the Nov. 27 issue containing a long poem and several letters in praise of the Montgolfier experiment of Nov. 21 (including one from Le Roy suggesting that the aeronauts be awarded gold medals), and the Nov. 29 issue containing the journal BF mentions here, "Lettre de M. le Marquis D'Arlandes à M. Faujas de St. Fond." Other issues included announcements by the Robert brothers of their plans for what BF here calls "Mr Charles's grand Balloon." In letters to the editor published on Nov. 26 and 28, the brothers, still trying to sell tickets, set the date of their experiment for Saturday, Nov. 29. That day they issued a brief announcement that the experiment was postponed until Monday, Dec. 1. As BF knew, they had underestimated the time and effort required to fill the balloon, even with the help of an improved hydrogen generator: Faujas de Saint-Fond, *Premiere suite de la description des expériences aérostatiques* . . . (Paris, 1784), pp. 37–9.

From the Chevalier de Kéralio

ALS: American Philosophical Society

Forbach, le 30e. 9bre. 1783.

L'officier qui vous remettra cette Lettre, Mon respectable ami, est Mr. de gourdon[6] qui a Servi avec moi à L'école Militaire, et qui ainsi que moi, a pris le parti de quitter cette Maison. Actuellement établi à passy, il desire fort voir de près le grand homme que tout bon françois doit cherir et Admirer, et à ce titre avoir l'honneur de Vous présenter son hommage: j'aime à croire que Vous en serés content: il est facheux pour le bien de la chose qu'il ait abandonné la Carriere qu'il suivoit. Son ton, sa maniere d'être le rendoient très propre à Suivre et à conduire l'éducation de la jeunesse. Il ne veut pas moins à d'autres égards; en un mot c'est un françois comme Vous les aimés.

Depuis notre Départ de paris, j'ai eu quelquefois de vos nouvelles par M. Votre petit-fils et M. Mac Mahon, et toujours elles ont fort intéressé notre digne amie qui vous fait les plus tendres amitiés;[7] sa santé se soutient assés bien, malgré les inquiétudes qu'elle a eues à l'occasion de sa fille[8] qu'une fievre opiniatre tourmentoit depuis plus d'un an; elle en est heureusement quitte depuis trois semaines et sa convalescence a ramené la joie dans la Colonie. Vous étes bien desiré pour en être le chef; un espoir aussi doux ne peut nous être permis; il faut vous aller retrouver, mais ce ne sera pas pour cet hiver, et peut-être l'année prochaine . . . éloignons l'idée d'une séparation sans doute éternelle.

Il est bien décidé que d'ici à l'année prochaine, il ne se

6. A captain in the French army: *État militaire* for 1784, p. 456. On Feb. 10, 1784, Gourdon accepted BF's invitation for the following Thursday on behalf of himself and his wife (APS).

7. Kéralio and the duchesse de Deux-Ponts ("notre digne amie") left Paris around Aug. 8: XL, 439. On Oct. 27, Kéralio thanked WTF for a letter dated Oct. 7 and its enclosure, a copy of the definitive peace treaty (APS). The physician John MacMahon was a close friend of Kéralio's; the two men invited BF to dine with them on at least one occasion (XXXIV, 487).

8. Elisabeth Friederike de Forbach de Deux-Ponts (1766–1790): Adalbert Prinz von Bayern, *Der Herzog und die Tänzerin: die merkwürdige Geschichte Christians IV. von Pfalz-Zweibrücken und seiner Familie* (Neustadt, 1966), genealogical table facing p. 204.

pasera rien dans le levant.[9] Voici à ce sujet ce que l'on mande de Saint-petersbourg— "on regarde toujours la guerre inévitable avec la porte; mais comme on a six mois pour y penser, il faut espérer que les fumées guerrieres se dissiperont d'ici au printemps. D'ailleurs le prince potemkin est à toute extremité; s'il meurt, il y a apparence que l'impératrice ouvrira les yeux et verra que la paix seule peut faire le bonheur de l'empire; personne n'y ignore que son favori est le seul à Souffler le feu de la guerre et en effet il est le seul qui puisse y gagner." Cette lettre sur laquelle vous pouvés compter prouve que la nation russe est fort éloignée de la guerre: ainsi d'après ce qui s'est passé et ce qui se passe, d'après les négociations entamées, on peut conclure que l'impératrice de Russie gardera la Crimée et les deserts du cuban; que les pauvres Turcs feront quelques sacrifices en faveur de l'empereur, et que la tranquillité de l'Europe ne sera point Troublée.

Recevés, mon Digne ami, les tendres et Respectueux hommages de toute la colonie, le chef à la tête, et vous trouverés à la queue l'homme du monde qui se fera le plus gloire d'être votre fidelle et dévoué Serviteur.[1]   LE CHR. DE KERALIO

Notation: Le Chr. de Keralio 30 Nov. 1783.

9. In a letter to WTF of Sept. 17 (APS), Kéralio had already predicted that despite their much-publicized mobilizations, Russia, Austria, and the Ottoman Empire were unlikely to go to war over Russia's annexation of the Crimea. (The brewing conflict had caused concern throughout Europe since 1782: XXXVIII, 98n, 585; XL, 480, 605.) Kéralio enclosed an extract of a letter from Warsaw written by a source he described only as "un homme qui par état est obligé d'en savoir et d'en fournir." In his letter to WTF of Oct. 27 Kéralio added that due to France's weakness after the war with Britain, it would be unable to help the Turks regain their lost territories.

1. Although this letter and one written to WTF on Jan. 31, 1784 (APS) are the last extant letters from Kéralio, the friendship continued for years. Among BF's papers at the APS is an undated document in French, in an unknown hand, on which WTF noted "Given me by the Chevr de Keralio." It details the qualities of Virginian bird grass, which the author wanted to cultivate in France to use as fodder.

From Wilhem & Jan Willink, Nicolaas & Jacob van Staphorst, and De la Lande & Fynje[2]

Copy: Massachusetts Historical Society

Sir   [November 30, 1783][3]

A Letter received of His Excellencÿ Robt. Morris Esqr. induced us to apply to your Excelly., Since we Satisfyed all the demands of Mr. Grand in consequence of the order of Said Mr. Morris, who was pleased to Say that he Should make no further disposal on us till he received our advice.[4]

We received a Letter of him dated 5 augt.[5] that the armey being disbanded the occasion he had for money induced him to draw two Hundred thousand Guilders as he Expected the wants of Mr. Grand Should not be verÿ great he intended he augment his drafts till half a million of Guilders but to day we receive an other Letter of His Excellencÿ dated 1 8ber.[6] that he had augmented his drafts to one million to be disposed of daÿlÿ desiring our acceptance and when we Should not be in Cash his Excellencÿ would make us the Needfull remittances. Abt. [About] ƒ. 525.000—are presented alreadÿ to us and the remainder maÿ dailÿ appear whilst we are and Shall be only the Cash the produce of a Cargo of Tabacco included abt. ƒ. 400.000—[7] Whilst the further distribution of obligations by the Scarcitÿ of Mony and concurrency of other Loans makes it impossible to gather a Sufficient Sum in the Space of time the bills Drawn at 90/ds. [days] become due and at the Same moment impossible to expect or desire the remittances of Mr. Morris we are to Conscious not to penetrate the fatal consequences in Case we are not

2. The consortium of bankers underwriting JA's Dutch loan. In July, they transferred money to Grand in Paris: XL, 53, 82–4, 284n, 401. The consortium wrote to Morris on Dec. 1 and to JA on Dec. 2, enclosing copies of the present letter and notifying JA that 170,000 ƒ. worth of bills already had been protested: *Morris Papers*, VIII, 391; *Adams Papers*, XV, 382–5.

3. The date is provided by BF's reply of Dec. 3, below.

4. Morris made this promise in an April 29 letter to them (*Morris Papers*, VII, 758–60).

5. *Morris Papers*, VIII, 393–7; see also the headnote on pp. 387–93.

6. *Morris Papers*, VIII, 564. Guilders and florins (ƒ.) were equivalent.

7. The *Sally* brought them about 500 hogsheads of tobacco, but it fetched less than 100,000 florins: *Morris Papers*, VIII, 90–1, 396n.

able to give acceptance to Said amount of one Million of Guilders drafts as this Should not onlÿ ruin the Loan but prove verÿ detrimental to the american Credit, we desirous to prevent Such a Mis fortune accept the mentioned *f.* 525000—not with Standing we Can not force to be in Cash but are at the Same time in a disagreable Situation for the remainder *f.* 475,000—which Can daily bee presented to us and as his Excellency J Adams is in London and an other Expeditions Left to us, than your Excelly. consult abt. the matter we have resolved to Send an Express to pray your answer if Mr. Grand his cach left of the remitte. of upward two Millions of Livre we made to him Since Mr. Morris Seems to think his wants must have been Less because his Excellency Should not have drawn Such Large Sums if he had been conscious wed have been Short of Such an amount.[8]

And as we are not in the possibilitÿ to face all those drafts which perhaps may yet be augmented & we Should however be sorry to find Such a disapointment in the financiers direction to be occasioned we request instantly your Excelly. answer that if we accept these Drafts to the amount of a Million and when due and not in Cash (where to is no probabilitÿ) if your Excellencÿ *is pleased to furnish the difficient money to us or permises* [promises] *on his word of honour to accept and pay for acct.* of the United States our drafts at 2 or 3 use. [usages] we Shall be obliged to make on you towards the payment of the accepted Sums when due and paye [payable].

We are too much persuaded of your Excelly. well wishes for your country that we Should have the least doubt of your readely complying in the promotion and preservation of its Credit bÿ which being animated we have applyed to your Excellency whose answer which we humbly beg in return with the Express Shall fix our resolution of accepting or not accepting the further drafts, the consequences of which not doing how fatal then Can never be imputed to us.

To His Exclly. B Franklin Paris / Copie

8. When Morris wrote the consortium on Sept. 18, he mistakenly expected Grand's account with the consortium to be in balance by the end of June, so that subsequent loan receipts would be available to cover his drafts. Moreover, subscriptions to the Dutch loan were lower than anticipated: *Morris Papers*, VIII, 387–91, 394–5n, 529–31.

To Joseph Banks

ALS: Yale University Library; press copy of ALS: Harvard University Library

Dear Sir,   Passy, Dec. 1.[–2] 1783—

In mine of yesterday, I promis'd to give you an Account of Messrs Charles & Robert's Experiment, which was to have been made on this Day, and at which I intended to be present. Being a little indispos'd, & the Air cool, and the Ground damp, I declin'd going into the Garden of the Tuilleries where the Balloon was plac'd, not knowing how long I might be oblig'd to wait there before it was ready to depart; and chose to stay in my Carriage near the Statue of Louis XV.[9] from whence I could well see it rise, & have an extensive View of the Region of Air thro' which, as the Wind sat, it was likely to pass. The Morning was foggy, but about One aClock, the Air became tolerably clear, to the great Satisfaction of the Spectators, who were infinite, Notice having been given of the intended Experiment several Days before in the Papers, so that all Paris was out, either about the Tuilleries, or the Quays & Bridges, in the Fields, the Streets, at the Windows, or on the Tops of Houses, besides the Inhabitants of all the Towns & Villages of the Environs. Never before was a philosophical Experiment so magnificently attended. Some Guns were fired to give Notice, that the Departure of the great Balloon was near, and a small one was discharg'd which went to an amazing Height,[1] there being but little Wind to make it deviate from its perpendicular Course, and, at length the Sight of it

9. Until 1792 the statue of Louis XV stood on the place Louis XV, today the place de la Concorde: Hillairet, *Rues de Paris*, I, 375. BF would have been eligible to observe the launch from a central enclosure at the basin of the Tuileries garden, which was reserved for royals, ministers, academicians, and subscribers. Ticket holders flooded the park, and all others were kept outside the garden by a heavy security force: Bachaumont, *Mémoires secrets*, XXIV, 54. For an account of the entire event, see Gillispie, *Montgolfier Brothers*, pp. 56–64.

1. Etienne Montgolfier, Charles's rival, was given the honor of releasing the trial balloon, which measured five and a half feet in diameter. In the same spirit of amity, BF was quoted on Dec. 5 as saying that "le machine aérostatique étoit un enfant dont M. Montgolfier étoit le pere & M. Charles la mere nourrice": Barthélemy Faujas de Saint-Fond, *Premiere suite de la description des expériences aérostatiques* . . . (Paris, 1784), p. 41; Bachaumont,

was lost. Means were used, I am told, to prevent the great Balloon's rising so high as might indanger its Bursting. Several Bags of Sand were taken on board before the Cord that held it down was cut; and the whole Weight being then too much to be lifted, such a Quantity was discharg'd as to permit its Rising slowly. Thus it would sooner arrive at that Region where it would be in Equilibrio with the surrounding Air, and by discharging more Sand afterwards, it might go higher if desired.[2] Between One & Two a Clock, all Eyes were gratified with seeing it rise majestically from among the Trees, and ascend gradually above the Buildings. A most beautiful Spectacle! When it was about 200 feet high, the brave Adventurers held out and wav'd a little white Pennant, on both Sides their Carr, to salute the Spectators, who return'd loud Claps of Applause. The Wind was very little, so that the Object, tho' moving to the Northward, continued long in View; and it was a great while before the admiring People began to disperse. The Persons embark'd were Mr Charles, Professor of Experimental Philosophy, & a zealous Promoter of that Science, and One of the Messieurs Robert, the very ingenious Constructors of the Machine.[3] When it arriv'd at its height, which I suppose might be 3 or 400 Toises,[4] it appear'd to have only horisontal Motion. I had a Pocket Glass, with which I follow'd it, till I lost Sight, first of the Men, then of the Car, and when I last saw the Balloon, it appear'd no bigger than a Walnut. I write this at 7 in the Evening. What became of them is not yet known here. I hope they descended by Day-light, so

---

Mémoires secrets, XXIV, 58, 65. This was an elaboration on his widely known comparison of a balloon to a newborn baby; see XL, 545–7.

2. In addition to discharging ballast, the passengers could maintain constant pressure inside the balloon and control altitude by releasing hydrogen through a valve at the top of the globe or through another opening near the bottom that could be operated by hand: Gillispie, *Montgolfier Brothers*, p. 58.

3. The initial plan had been for Charles to make the first ascent, with the balloon tethered to the ground, and take various scientific measurements; the Robert brothers would then embark on an aerial voyage. The first part of the experiment was canceled, however, and Charles accompanied the younger Robert in the balloon: *Jour. de Paris*, Nov. 19 and Dec. 2, 1783.

4. The balloon rose to an altitude of 300 *toises*, about 1,800 feet: Faujas de Saint-Fond, *Premiere suite de la description*, p. 42.

as to see & avoid falling among Trees or on Houses, and that the Experiment was compleated without any mischievous Accident which the Novelty of it & the want of Experience might well occasion. I am the more anxious for the Event, because I am not well inform'd of the Means provided for letting themselves gently down, and the Loss of these very ingenious Men, would not only be a Discouragement to the Progress of the Art, but be a sensible Loss to Science & Society.

I shall inclose one of the Tickets of Admission, on which the Globe was represented, as originally intended, but is altered by the Pen to show its real State when it went off.[5] When the Tickets were engraved, the Car was to have been hung to the Neck of the Globe, as represented by a little Drawing I have made in the Corner A. I suppose it may have been an Apprehension of Danger in straining too much the Balloon or tearing the Silk, that induc'd the Constructors to throw a Net over it, fix'd to a Hoop which went round its Middle, and to hang the Car to that Hoop, as you see in Fig. B.—

Tuesday Morning, Dec 2. I am reliev'd from my Anxiety, by hearing that the Adventurers descended well near l'Isle Adam, before Sunset. This Place is near 7 Leagues from Paris.— Had the Wind blown fresh, they might have gone much farther.—

If I receive any farther Particulars of Importance I shall communicate them hereafter.

With great Esteem, I am, Dear Sir, Your most obedient & most humble Servant   B FRANKLIN

P.S. Tuesday Evening.

Since writing the above, I have receiv'd the printed Paper & the Manuscript, containing some Particulars of the Experi-

5. The ticket has not been found. A ticket of admission is reproduced in François-Louis Bruel, *Histoire Aeronautique par les monuments peints, sculptés, dessinés et gravés des origines à 1830* (Paris, 1909), plate 47.

As a subscriber to the experiment, BF received 30 additional tickets; see our annotation to his letter to Banks of Oct. 8. Through WTF, he gave away two of them to visiting American merchants William Smith and Eliphalet Fitch. On Aug. 19 Fitch had sent JA a book for BF, whom he had probably encountered on a trip to Paris the previous spring: *Adams Papers*, XIV, 430n; XV, 233–4, 367n; Charles Storer to WTF, Nov. 17, 1783 (APS); WTF to Smith and Fitch, Nov. 26, 1783 (Mass. Hist. Soc.).

ment, which I enclose.—⁶ I hear farther, that the Travellers had
perfect Command of their Carriage, descending as they pleas'd
by letting some of the inflammable Air escape, and rising again
by discharging some Sand: that they descended over a Field so
low as to talk with the Labourers in passing, and mounted again
to pass a Hill. The little Balloon falling at Vincennes, shows
that mounting higher it met with a Current of Air in a contrary
Direction: An Observation that may be of use to future aerial
Voyagers.—

Sir Joseph Banks, Bart.

From Edward Nairne
ALS: American Philosophical Society

Dear Sir   Lond Decr 2: 1783
I received your favours.⁷ The book & prints which Mr Argand
was so obliging as to deliver I have since sent to Sir Joseph Banks
agreable to your request.⁸ I am very much obliged to you for your
observations on the alteration of the wood of the box belonging
to the magnets. Since I received your favour have been endeavouring to make as simple an instrument as possible, a drawing of

6. The "printed paper" was most likely the Dec. 2 issue of the *Jour.
de Paris*, which contained a description of the launch and a short *procès-
verbal* attesting to the time and place of the balloon's landing. The "manuscript" was a copy in L'Air de Lamotte's hand of a communication that
was evidently sent to BF. It is in two sections. The first relates an eyewit-
ness account given by the chevalier de Cubières, who was present at the
balloon's landing and returned to Paris late that night, when he recounted
events to the people gathered at Charles's residence. (Charles himself
did not return until the next day.) After the landing, Cubières explained,
Charles ascended by himself to make scientific observations, and set down
again four and a half miles away. The second section of the manuscript
reports that the test balloon was discovered by children in Vincennes.
(A press copy of this manuscript is filed with the press copy of the present
letter. The text was published in Abbott L. Roth, "Benjamin Franklin and
the First Balloons," *Proc. of the American Antiquarian Soc.*, XVIII (1907),
272–3. Charles's account was published in the *Jour. de Paris* on Dec. 3.)
7. BF's letter of Oct. 18 and its enclosure, a letter on hygrometers.
8. Argand may have carried a letter of introduction from BF to Nairne,
as well as material for Banks; see Le Roy to BF, [Oct. 26?], above.

which I have here sent. If you should at your leisure consider it & if you find that its not adequate to the purpose wanted should esteem it as a great favour if you'd inform me of it or if any Alterations or additions can be added to it. I was the day before yesterday at Windsor where Mr De Luc shewed me an Hygrometer it was made of a thin peice of whale bone about nine inches long was kept strait by a line fasten'd to it going over a pulley the other end of which line was fastned to a spiral spring. He observed that it was the only substance he had ever met with that would always return to the same length when soaked in water. It altered in its length about one inch from extreame Moisture to extream dryness.[9] A Day or two ago Mrs Clark called on me. She desired her duty to you when I wrote & desired I would inform you she had lost her only Brother in the Ville de Paris.[1]

Mrs Nairne Polly & Fanny desire to be particularly remembred to you. Hope you enjoy a good state of health as they at present do, they were not a little flattered that you mentioned them in your letter. I sent you sometime ago the account of shortning wire by Lightning which I hope you have received. Mr Magellan under took to have it sent to you.[2]

I am Dear Sir Your most obliged Hble servt

EDWD: NAIRNE

The explanation of the under drawing.[3] Fig 1 A a peice of wood about 12 Inches long & 2 inches broad cut cross wise the grain of the wood which slides freely between the two peices of wood

9. The whalebone hygrometer of Jean-André Deluc (xx, 78n) rivaled that of Saussure, which the latter described in the work he sent BF on Oct. 10 (above); see *Dictionary of Scientific Biography* under Deluc. For a description of the instrument see J. A. De Luc, "A Second Paper on Hygrometry," *Phil. Trans.*, LXXXI (1791), 389–[423].

1. Anne Johnson Clarke, BF's grandniece, informed him herself on March 2, 1784 (APS). The *Ville de Paris* sank in 1782.

2. If it arrived, BF's copy has not been located. This was most likely Nairne's letter to Sir Joseph Banks, for which see XL, 470n.

3. Nairne's drawings of figures 1 and 2 are no longer with the letter. We suspect that he sketched them below this legend, as the bottom third of this sheet has been largely cut away. Copies of them, however, are reproduced in *Jefferson Papers*, XI, 76–7, with a nearly identical legend: Nairne had made copies for Benjamin Vaughan, who in turn sent copies to TJ in 1787 when explaining his own realization of BF's proposed hygrometer.

BB forming groves for it. C Is a screw [for adj]usting[4] the peice of wood A so that the index [may] point to the proper division when first made. In Fig 2. *a.* Is a slit to admit the pin *e* to move [freely,] which pin by being fast in the peice of wood A moves with it as it shortens or lengthens and by pressing against the short end of the Index D causes it to move up or down according as the weather is moist or dry which is shewn on the Divided arch at the end of the instrument.

Addressed: A Monsr / Son Excellence le Dr. F[ranklin] / a Passy / pres / Paris

From Jonathan Williams, Jr.

ALS: American Philosophical Society; copy: Yale University Library

Dear & hond Sir.   Nantes Decr 2. 1783.

Mr Barclay in consequence of his Commission from Congress as Auditor General of Accounts,[5] has applied to me for all my public Accounts to be lodged in the Consular Office. As I have already lodged with you the originals of my public Accounts from the beginning to the End of my being in the public Service,[6] I have referred him to you for those Originals, and I doubt not you will agree to the propriety of delivering them to Mr Barclay. I have in the mean time furnished him with Copies of those Settled by Arbitration, having two by me, & one of the Receipts you gave me per quadruplicata for the Balance of two thousand & Sixty Livres one Sol & Seven deniers dated Augt 26. 1779.[7]

I am as ever most dutifully & affectionately Yours.—

JONA WILLIAMS J

Addressed: His Excellency Doctor Franklin, / Passy

4. The right margin of the MS has a tear affecting three lines of text. We supply our readings from the legend published in Vaughan's letter to TJ cited above.

5. Barclay was appointed on Nov. 18, 1782: XXXIX, 174.

6. For accounts that JW presented to the American commissioners between 1778 and 1781, see XXVII, 117n, 449; XXX, 263; Account XXIV (XXXI, 3).

7. The arbitrators approved JW's accounts on Aug. 17, 1779; BF certified those accounts and a subsequent one on Aug. 26: XXX, 263. JW sent the

To Wilhem & Jan Willink, Nicolaas & Jacob van Staphorst, and De la Lande & Fynje

Copy:[8] Massachusetts Historical Society

Gentlemen! Passy decmr. 3. 1783.

I: Received the letter you did me the honour of writing to me the 30: past, and am very Sensible of your zeal for Supporting the Credit of the united States, and the difficulties you must be exposed to in accepting all the drafts of Mr. Morris of which you have advice. I Communicated your letter to our Banker Mr. Grand, and desired immediate Conference with him on the Subject. He has brought with him a Sketch of Mr. Morris's Account, by which it appears that the means of assisting us are not in his hands.[9] As to the proposition of mÿ accepting bills drawn on me at three Months, I do not See the least Probality of my having more money to command at that time than I have at present, so that the Expedient would be inëffèctual. Mr. Grand will him Self write to you on this occasion. I hope that the demand for bills in America, being for the present Supplied bÿ those Mr. Morris has already Disposed of there will not be many more issued before he is informed of the Difficiency of Funds on this Side the Water, when he will certainly hold his hand. With great Esteem, I have the honour to be, Gentlemen, Your most obediënt & most humb Servt.

(:Signd:) B. Franklin.

Copia

---

present letter under cover of his to Thomas Barclay of Dec. 3, 1783 (Yale University Library).

8. Made by the consortium and sent to JA on Dec. 23, along with Grand's letter to them (mentioned in the text): *Adams Papers*, XV, 432.

9. We have not found the "Sketch," but Grand informed Morris that his accounts payable as of Nov. 5 totaled 1,600,000 *l.t.*: *Morris Papers*, IX, 191.

From William Jackson[1]   AL: American Philosophical Society

On board the Washington[2] Decemr. 3rd. 1783
Major Jackson begs leave to present his most respectful compliments to Doctor Franklin— He regrets that particular business obliges him to debark in England, as it will delay the happiness which he hopes to enjoy in the honor of renewing his acquaintance with his Excellency.

Major Jackson presents himself with respect and affection to Mr. W. T. Franklin.

Mr. Bache and his family were in perfect health when Major J. left Philadelphia on the 10th. of November.

From Vergennes

LS: Library of Congress; L (draft): Archives du Ministère des affaires étrangères

A Versailles le 3. Xbre. 1783.
Vous etes instruit, Monsieur, de tout ce qui est relatif à l'évocation faite au Conseil du Roy de la discution qui s'est élevée au sujet des oppositions formées sur une partie de la Cargaison de la frégate l'Alliance.[3] M. Chardon Procureur Général du Conseil des

1. After returning to Philadelphia in February, 1782 (XXXVI, 48n), Jackson was made assistant secretary of war. He resigned that post at the end of October, 1783, and sailed to England, intending to pursue a business venture for which Robert Morris and John Vaughan provided him credit: Charles W. Littell, "Major William Jackson, Secretary of the Federal Convention," *PMHB*, II (1878), 361–2; *Morris Papers*, VIII, 736–7. GW gave him a letter of recommendation to BF dated Nov. 1, 1783, but—as Jackson noted on that ALS—he did not deliver it, as he did not go to France: Hist. Soc. of Pa.

2. The *General Washington* landed in England before continuing to France, to accommodate the mission of John Paul Jones; see JA to BF, Dec. 5.

3. On June 6, the king overturned a previous ruling concerning Forster frères and their attachment of the proceeds of a sale of prizes taken by the *Alliance*, and referred the case to the *conseil du roi*; see XL, 207–8. In this affair, Barclay was an interested party; his firm Barclay, Moylan & Co. had handled the sale of the *Alliance*'s prizes in Lorient, and was contesting the attachment: XXXIX, 423; Chardon to Vergennes, Nov. 13, 1783 (described

Prises vient de m'écrire à ce sujet une lettre que je crois devoir vous communiquer et dont je joins ici la copie.[4] Vous y verrez, Monsieur, que c'est par le fait même du Sr. Barclay que cette affaire reste indécise. Je vous prie de vouloir bien lui transmettre toutes les réflexions détaillées dans la lettre de M. Chardon, et lui faire connoitre qu'il ne peut imputer qu'à lui même et au défaut de s'être mis en régle, si le Conseil n'a pas encore prononcé sur la mainlevée qu'il se croit fondé à réclamer. Vous voudrez bien aussi me faire part de ses intentions définitives à cet égard, afin que je puisse en informer M. Chardon.

J'ai l'honneur d'être très sincerement Monsieur, votre très humble et très obéissant serviteur   DE VERGENNES

M. Franklin.

From Lenoir
LS: American Philosophical Society

Paris le 4. Xbre. 1783.

Vous avés eu la bonté, Monsieur, de remettre à M. Cadet Deveaux la planche du Poele Cheminée, dont l'invention vous est due, et vous lui en avés fait esperer la Description.[5] Je vous prie,

below); Account XXVII (XXXII, 4), fol. 136; and for the firm, see Roberts and Roberts, *Thomas Barclay*, p. 77.

4. In this letter of Nov. 13, Chardon complains that Barclay has been sending an endless stream of letters asking for a lifting of the different attachments made by Forster frères, Puchelberg, and others on part of the prize cargo taken by the *Alliance*. He reminds Vergennes that after looking into the affair more closely, the minister had admitted that the case was irregular and should be referred to the *conseil*. BF had agreed to this. Chardon told Barclay about the case being transferred six months ago; two months ago, Barclay announced that he would not plead before the *conseil*, as he and Moylan had done in Lorient. Moylan, who also petitioned for the attachment to be lifted, never even hired a lawyer. Chardon tells Vergennes to inform Barclay that in order to move forward, he and Moylan must hire a lawyer and be prepared to plead their case. If they refuse, they must cease to send him letters.

5. Cadet de Vaux had sent BF's engraving of a vase-shaped coal stove to Vergennes on March 28. Vergennes replied on April 8: seeing the stove's advantages, he urged Cadet to obtain from BF a description and suggested that BF might even supervise the construction of one. Cast iron was not

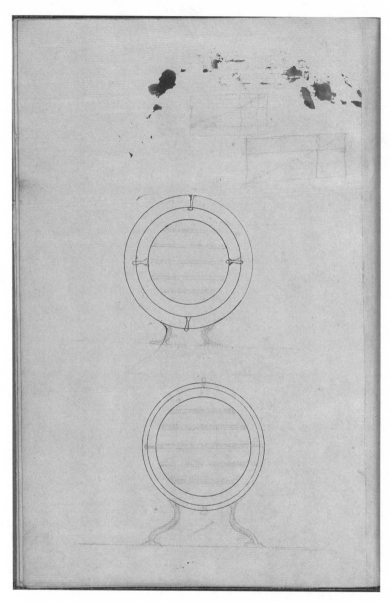

Franklin's Sketches of a Fire-Grate

Monsieur, de vouloir bien la lui procurer le plutôt possible, et je me chargerai de la rendre publique. On S'occupera aussitôt de la construction d'un Poele d'après vos principes: M. Cadet Se flatte que vous voudrés bien en diriger l'Execution.

J'ecris à Mrs. Perrier,[6] pour qu'ils vous fassent parvenir du Charbon en roche. Je vous Serai très obligé de joindre à la description du Poele, celle de la grille que vous êtes dans l'intention de faire construire, pour l'Emploi de ce Combustible dans les Cheminées; détruire ainsi que vous le faites, Monsieur, la fumée du Charbon de terre et la faire tourner au profit de la chaleur:[7]

---

available in France but was easily obtained in England: Vergennes to Cadet de Vaux, April 8, 1783 (AAE). For the engraving of the stove design see xx, facing p. 251. (We can now identify the engraver as Thomas Bonner: *ODNB*.) BF had sent it to Dubourg in 1773, to Morand in 1778, and to the Marquis Turgot in 1781: xxxv, 8–9, and the references cited there.

BF did not write a description until the summer of 1785: "Description of a New Stove for Burning of Pitcoal, and Consuming all its Smoke," Smyth, *Writings*, IX, 443–62. In the spring of 1783, however, an article describing and illustrating the vase stove and specifying the dimensions of its parts was published in *Bibliothèque physico-économique, instructive et amusante, année 1782* (Paris, 1783), pp. 137–49, under the title "Description & usage du Poêle de M. Franklin, pour brûler de la braise de Charbon de terre." The unnamed author explained (p. 138) that BF himself was too busy to write a description; the article was based on BF's engraving, personal conversations, and M. Morand's book on coal. *Bibliothèque physico-économique* was announced in the May, 1783, issue of the *Jour. des sçavans*. It proved so popular that at least five more editions were issued in subsequent years.

6. Engineer Jacques-Constantin Périer and his younger brother Augustin-Charles. In addition to running the Paris waterworks at Chaillot, the elder Périer was a partner in the immense coke-iron works based on English technology that had been under construction at Le Creusot since 1782. This attempt by the French government to establish coal as the chief fuel for industry was unsuccessful, in part because of the shortage of coal itself: xxxiv, 175–6n; Jacques Payen, *Capital et machine à vapeur au XVIIIe siècle: les frères Périer et l'introduction en France de la machine à vapeur de Watt* (Paris, 1969), pp. 11–13, 41, 137–41; Christian Devillers and Bernard Huet, *Le Creusot: naissance et développement . . .* (Mâcon, France, 1981), pp. 18–19, 24; J. R. Harris, *Industrial Espionage and Technology Transfer: Britain and France in the Eighteenth Century* (Aldershot, Eng., and Brookfield, Vt., 1998), pp. 255–60.

7. BF described this coal-burning fire grate in "Description of a New Stove for Burning of Pitcoal . . . ," Smyth, *Writings*, IX, 460–1, and figs. 18 and 19 facing p. 444. It sat in a fireplace and, in addition to warming the

c'est un Service éssentiel que vous avés rendu à l'Economie et c'est une véritable obligation que vous aura le Gouvernement qui S'occupe dans ce moment ci, de la perfection des moyens Faits pour Substituer le charbon de terre au bois.[8]

J'ai l'honneur d'être avec un respectueux attachement, Monsieur, Vôtre três humble et três obeissant Serviteur./. LENOIR

M. Franklin à Passy.

Endorsed: M. Le Noir

From Sir Edward Newenham

ALS: American Philosophical Society

Dear Sir   4th Decr: 1783

The very important Affairs now agitating in this Kingdom, may render the Enclosed papers agreable to you;—[9] Parliament, contrary to Precedent, refused us leave to Introduce a Bill for the more representation—because it came from the Volunteers; I sent you the Debates under Cover to Monsieur Dupont,[1]

---

room when in the vertical position, could also be turned horizontally to heat a tea kettle. BF's preliminary sketches are reproduced here. For more information see the List of Illustrations.

8. During this period of exceptional cold and severe wood shortages, Lenoir, who had helped establish the Ecole gratuite de boulangerie (XXXII, 481–2), must also have been interested in the use of coal as an alternate fuel for baking. An article in the December, 1783, *Jour. de physique* attributed many advantages to coal-fired ovens as compared to conventional, wood-fired ones: *Jour. de physique*, XXIII (1783), 433–47. Bakers at this time had to be given special privileges for buying wood so as not to disrupt the bread supply: Steven L. Kaplan, *The Bakers of Paris and the Bread Question, 1700–1775* (Durham, N.C., and London, 1996), pp. 53–8, 76–7.

9. Newenham probably enclosed the *Dublin Evening Post* of Dec. 2, 1783, which published excerpts from the Nov. 29 debate in the House of Commons about the parliamentary reform bill introduced by Newenham and Henry Flood, as well as the Grand National Convention proceedings.

1. Newenham had an account with the Paris banking firm Dupont et fils, and used them as the receiving address for packets to BF. Two cover letters survive: Sir Edward Newenham to Dupont et fils, Sept. 30 and Oct. 12, 1784, both at the APS.

where-in you will see the Arguments on each side; the Conduct of Government has doubled the Ardor of the Volunteers,
& every Parish in Ireland will have a meeting in order to memorial Parliament for a Reform in a reasonable degree, we will
have; we have lost the first Question by 152 to 77,[2] but that 77
would purchase the 152 five or Even Six times over; there never
was in any public Assembly that I have frequented more regularity, firmness, unanimity or Spirit; we sat in the great Rotunda, in a Circle of 200 feet on Elevated Benches covered with
Green bays, our General[3] Seated in a Superb Chair mounted
on 4 Steps covered with Capeting; Centries with fixed Bayonets
at Each Entrance to the seats; a Captain's Guard at the Door,
but Every Person was admitted on the second Day without
Tickets; the hindmost Benches were for the Members of both
houses of Parliament; the Audience was generaly 5 or 600, but
no person Admitted into the Rotunda untill the Delegates had
taken their seats & the Roll was called over; the Names of those
Present & absent were published in printed Votes every Day,
& also how they Voted upon Each Question; Every Delegate
(except the Clerical ones) were in full uniform; Each paid two
Guineas, as a present to the Lying-in-Hospital to whom the Rotunda belongs.[4]

I have the Honor of yours of the 16th of last month,[5] & it
gives the fullest Support to my Declaration, that the Commercial Treaty was not concluded, though the Contrary was solemnly asserted this day in full Parliament;—but we Cannot
cary even a turnpike bill against the present Corrupted Majority
of the Irish Parricides & the English Corruptors; no age furnished a more Obsequious set of mean time-Serving Members;— I am tired of this Nation— I wish my property was in
one Bank Note, & Even at this Time of Life, I would Change

2. The Dec. 2 issue of the *Dublin Evening Post* cited the parliamentary
vote as 157 to 77; other sources give different numbers.

3. James Caulfield; see Newenham's letter of Nov. 9[–15].

4. The Dublin Lying-in (later the Rotunda) Hospital, founded in 1745,
was the first maternity hospital in the British Isles: Ian Campbell Ross, ed.,
Public Virtue, Public Love: the Early Years of the Dublin Lying-in Hospital
(Dublin, 1986), p. 9.

5. Missing.

my Residence—my family are of my opinion; I view this Nation, as a privy purse for the British Minister; formerly England controuled us, & now an English secretary Taxes us, for his, Ipse dixit, carries every point—*this day* in the act for—Facilitating the Trade of the united States of North America with this Kingdom—I moved an Amendment after the word America—Viz—& the territories thereunto belonging—this Amendment was defended by Several, but negatived without any Support but the Book of Numbers—[6]

Lady Newenham, with every Sentiment of *real* Respect desires to be Gratefully remembred to you—In which, my Son joins;[7] he is well educated, & therefore (as heir to a Good Estate) I am proud to find, his public declarations are acceptable to the friends of Ireland—last Night Colonel Grattan was *not* Elected Colonel of the Dublin Independants—how! how! are the mighty fallen—a tolerable Share of his £50000 was distributed, but it would not do—he Voted for the Vote of Censure against the Volunteers, & they resented it— Mr Smith is Elected in his Room—it was Debated to send one pair of the Colours back; but as they were the work & present of Mrs: Grattan, it was deemed rather *ungenteel;* I wish the Corps had not been so precipitate as it may drive him into opposition on the Reform Bill—& furnish him with arguments of Dissention—[8]

6. The legislation was published as *An Act for Facilitating the Trade and Intercourse between this Kingdom and the United States of America* (Dublin, 1784). On Dec. 4, the House passed four amendments to the act and rejected one, presumably Newenham's: *Journals of the House of Commons of the Kingdom of Ireland* (31 vols., Dublin, 1782–94), XXI, 372–3.

7. Newenham's eldest son, Edward.

8. On Dec. 2 the Dublin Independent Volunteer Corps chose William Smyth to replace Grattan as its commander: *Dublin Evening Post*, Dec. 4, 1783. During the struggle for Irish legislative independence, Grattan had become an icon of the Volunteer movement, and in May, 1782, the House of Commons had awarded him £50,000 for his service to Ireland. Although he supported parliamentary reform in principle, Grattan disapproved of the involvement of the Volunteers in domestic politics. He refused to attend the Grand National Convention, and although he spoke in favor of the reform bill presented on Nov. 29, it is possible (as Newenham claims here) that Grattan also voted that day for a resolution condemning "encroachments" on parliamentary autonomy, further antagonizing his former Volunteer supporters: *Parliamentary Register*, I, 383; II, 259, 264; Maurice R.

I hope soon to hear of your Excellency good health, & the same pleasing account of your most amiable Grandson—
I have the Honor, to be, with Every sentiment of Respect & the Most unfeigned regard Your Excellencys Most Obt: & Humble Servt— EDWARD NEWENHAM

Addressed: His Excellency B: Franklin / Minister Pleniopten-tiary / from the United States / of North America

From John Adams Copy: Massachusetts Historical Society

Sir London Dec. 5. 1783.
Commodore Jones is just arrived from Philadelphia with Dispatches. Those directed to the Ministers I opened. One contained nothing but Newspapers and Proclamations. The other contained a Letter to "the Commissioners" and a Sett of Instructions. The Letter bears Date the 1. of November the Instructions the 29 of Octr.— A remaining Packet is directed to you alone, but probably contains a Commission to Us all to treat of Commerce with Great Britain.[9]
Mr Jay and Mr Laurens are at Bath, and the Bearer is inclined to go on to Paris.[1] I shall Send on the Dispatches and depend upon your Sending Us, the earliest Intelligence, if you find a Commission (in the Packet to you,) in Pursuance of the Resolution of the first of May last,[2] because that Parliament must do Something before they rise respecting the Trade, and their

---

O'Connell, *Irish Politics and Social Conflict in the Age of the American Revolution* (Philadelphia, 1965), pp. 331–2, 377–8.
9. John Paul Jones sailed on the *General Washington.* Capt. Joshua Barney had orders to put him ashore wherever he wished before continuing to France: Morison, *Jones,* p. 337; Hulbert Footner, *Sailor of Fortune: the Life and Adventures of Commodore Barney, U.S.N.* (New York and London, 1940), pp. 151–2. JA was mistaken about the packet addressed to BF; it contained not the commission, but rather Boudinot's private letter to BF of Nov. 1 (above) with its enclosures. See BF's reply to JA of Dec. 10.
1. Jones proceeded immediately to France, hoping to obtain prize money owed the officers and crews of his former ships. He would remain there for more than three years: Morison, *Jones,* pp. 336–8.
2. For the resolution see XL, 178–80.

Proceedings may probably be Somewhat the less evil, for knowing beforehand that there is in Europe a Power to treat.

I Shall wait with Some Impatience to hear from you because, if there is no Commission under Cover to you, in which I am named, I Shall go to the Hague, and there take up my abode for some time. I have just recd a Letter from Willink & Co which Shews that Money is exhausted & Credit too. He incloses me his Letter to you,[3] but I fear you will not be able to assist him. With great respect &c

Dr Franklin

From François-Pierre de Séqueville

Printed announcement with MS insertions: American Philosophical Society

[after December 5, 1783][4]

La Cour prendra le Deuil le *neuf* de ce mois, à l'occasion de la mort de *Mademoiselle.*

Sa Majesté le portera *21* jours.

> DE MAUROY[5]
> *pr Mr De séqueville*
> Secrétaire ordinaire du Roi, à la conduite de Mrs. les Ambassadeurs.

Addressed: a Monsieur / Monsieur francklin / Ministre Plenipore des Etats Unis / de l'Amerique Septentrionale / a Passy / vers Paris ./. De séqueville

3. Above, [Nov. 30]. The letter to JA from the consortium of Dutch bankers was dated Dec. 2: *Adams Papers,* XV, 382–5.

4. The date of death of Sophie, known as "Mademoiselle" (b. Aug. 5, 1776), the second child of the king's brother Charles-Philippe, comte d'Artois, and his wife, Marie-Thérèse de Savoie: Patrick Van Kerrebrouck, *La Maison de Bourbon, 1256–1987* (Villeneuve d'Ascq, France, 1987), pp. 292–4. The mourning period was announced in the *Jour. de Paris,* Dec. 7, 1783.

5. Norbert de Mauroy, Séqueville's assistant: *Almanach de Versailles* for 1781, p. 96.

To Henry Laurens

LS:[6] South Carolina Historical Society; AL (draft) and copy: Library of Congress

Dear Sir,   Passy, Decr. 6. 1783.

I received your kind Letter of the 28th. past, and I send you herewith the anonymous Brussels Letter, as you desire. When I had last the Pleasure of seeing you at Passy, I forgot to mention to you that Mr. Ridley soon after your Departure for the South of France, call'd upon me with a Request that I would let him see that Letter, and then that I would let him take it home with him, which I comply'd with, understanding it was to show it to Mr. Adams. Some Days after he acquainted me that the Handwriting was like that of M. de Neufville's Clerk, and proposed to have it compar'd with some of Neufville's Letters in my Possession, which at his Desire I lent him. When he return'd them he remark'd some Similarities, which I did not think very striking; what appeared most so to me at the time was the very long Stroke or Dash of the Pen across the Top of the small t, thus t,[7] tho' I did not think that conclusive; and I have since observed it to be a more general Practice in writing than I imagin'd. I indeed seldom make that marke to my t's, except when they are double, yet I find when I do make it, it is nearly as long as in the Brussels Letter; and I see in your last that you do the same, the Dash sometimes passing over the whole Word in which the t is plac'd. I saw neither Mr. Barclay nor Mr. Adams on that occasion, but Mr. Ridley only. I suppose the Opinion you mention as pronounc'd might be by them at Auteuil. I enclose the other anonymous, and the two Letters of Neufville, that you may compare them and judge for yourself.[8]

---

6. In the hand of L'Air de Lamotte, except for the postscript.

7. Here L'Air de Lamotte crossed the t with a very long stroke.

8. The two anonymous letters, both written to BF in 1782, were one from "W.R." of Jan. 31, and an unsigned letter of May 8: XXXVI, 499–501; XXXVII, 289–91. The two letters from Jean de Neufville & fils were dated July 23, 1781, and Jan. 21, 1782: XXXV, 307–8; XXXVI, 459–60. All four are in different hands. Edmund Jenings' pamphlet *A Full Manifestation* (for which see Laurens' Nov. 28 letter, above) reported on Matthew Ridley and JA's examination of the letters. That could have taken place

We think of nothing here at present but of Flying; the Ballons engross all Conversation. Messrs. Charles and Robert, made a Trip last Monday thro' the Air to a Place farther distant than Dover is from Calais, and would have gone much farther if there had been more Wind and Daylight. They have perfect Command of the machine, descending & rising again at pleasure.[9] The Progress made in the Management of it has been rapid, yet I fear it will hardly become a common Carriage in my time, tho' being the easiest of all Voitures it would be extreamly convenient to me, now that my Malady forbids the use of the old ones over a Pavement.

The kind Enquiry made respecting me by the Person you mention, does not much surprize me. He is so unequal in his Temper & so different from himself on different Occasions, that I should not wonder if he sometimes loved me.[1]

The promised Commission is not yet come to my hands, nor have I any Advices from the Congress later than the 9th. of September.[2]

My Grandson joins me in affectionate Respects to you & Miss Laurens, and best Wishes for your Health and Prosperity. With great & sincere Esteem, I am ever, Dear Sir, Your most obedient and most humble Servant,   B FRANKLIN

[*In Franklin's hand:*] I see my Clerk makes those long Dashes too. Vide the Word affectionate above.

Be so good as to present my Compliments to Mr Chase. I shall write to him per next Post.—

Honble. M. Laurens.

Addressed: To his Excellency / Henry Laurens Esqr[3] / Bath

---

when JA and Ridley were living in Auteuil with Thomas Barclay in late September, 1783: Roberts and Roberts, *Thomas Barclay*, pp. 126, 130.

9. See BF to Banks, Dec. 1.

1. BF had recently questioned JA's mental stability in a letter to Congress: XL, 357–8.

2. XL, 179. The commission, promised but never sent, was for negotiating a commercial treaty with Great Britain.

3. BF wrote the address thus far, originally adding, "In the care of Wm Manning / Esqr / London". A hand we do not recognize crossed out that phrase and substituted "Bath".

AFTER DECEMBER 6, 1783

Endorsed: Doctr Franklin 6th. Decem 1783 Recd 14th. Answd.
3d Febry— 1784— / Doctr Franklin inclosed are his Letter of
6th. Decem 1783 together with the two anonom & two from de
Neufvilles refered to in his Letter all received 14th.—

Notation: Dr Franklin Decr 6th. recd. 14th.

To Vergennes   ʟѕ:[4] Archives du Ministère des affaires étrangères

Sir   Passy Decr. 6th. 1783
Being now disabled by the Stone, which in the easiest Carriage gives me Pain, wounds my Bladder & occasions me to
make bloody Urine, I find I can no longer pay my Devoirs personally at Versailles, which I hope will be excused. I have yet
received from Congress no Answer to my Request of being
recalled. In the mean time I must beg your Excellency to receive my Respects by my Grandson, with such Matters as I may
occasionally have to communicate, he being Secretary of the
Legation. I am, with great and sincere Respect, Sir, Your Excellency's most obedient & most humble Servant   B Franklin

His Excellency Count de Vergennes

Endorsed: M. de R[5]

Notation: Rep. le 11 Xbre.[6]

From Félix Nogaret   ᴀʟѕ: American Philosophical Society

Monsieur   Versailles [after December 6, 1783][7]
Comme nous Sommes privés du plaisir de vous voir, je vous
Suppose un mal, peutetre apocryphé, Mais qui vous va bien

---

4. In ʙꜰʙ's hand. ʙꜰ added the complimentary close before signing.
5. Rayneval. Joseph-Mathias Gérard de Rayneval was the *premier commis* responsible for handling Vergennes' American correspondence.
6. Vergennes' reply has not been located.
7. The day ʙꜰ informed Vergennes that he was not well enough to continue his regular visits to Versailles; his letter is immediately above.

dans la circonstance où vous vous derobés aux acclamations de tout Paris.[8]

Tu fais la Paix, tu faix la guerre!
Un Septre est à tes piés, la foudre est dans tes mains.
L'encens fume, pour toi, Sur le double hémisphere;
  On t'y rend les honneurs divins!
Montre toi. Tu ne peux! Quoi! tes efforts sont vains
  Comme nos voeux et ma priere!
Qui peut donc arrêter, qui derobe, à nos yeux,
Ce Politique utile et ce rival des Dieux
Que revere L'Olympe et qu'adore la Terre?
Faibles humains!..helas! la goutte, dans Passy,
Sert les Enfers jaloux;..et l'enchaine aujourdhuy.

Felix Nogaret

From Cadet de Vaux

AL: American Philosophical Society

Ce 8 Xbre 1783

M. Cadet de Vaux présente l'assurance de Son très humble respect a Monsieur franklin et a l'honneur de lui Envoyer une lettre de Monsieur le lieutenant Général de Police,[9] et deux billets que M.M. le Grand et Molinos[1] l'ont chargé de faire accepter à Monsieur franklin./.

Notation: Cadet de Vaux 8 Xbre 83

---

8. The following poem is a variant of the one Nogaret recited at the inauguration of the Loge du Patriotisme's new Temple at Versailles in May, 1783: XXXIX, 578n. The first four lines of the two poems are identical. From there, the original continued, "Et tu viens, parmi nous, offrir à tous un frère." In this case, BF cannot present himself in person.

9. Lenoir's letter of Dec. 4.

1. The architects of the spectacular new dome for the Halle au Blé; see Cadet de Vaux to BF, Oct. 19. The tickets may have been for the public celebration of the peace held at the Halle au Blé on Sunday, Dec. 14, the largest of the celebrations that took place all over the city that day. In anticipation of the crowds, the government issued orders concerning the routes by which carriages and people on foot were to arrive: *Jour. de Paris*, Dec. 11, 12, 14, 1783; Bachaumont, *Mémoires secrets*, XXIV, 78–80. BF's own

From Wilhem & Jan Willink, Nicolaas & Jacob van Staphorst, and De la Lande & Fynje

LS: Library of Congress

Sir   Amsterdam 8 Decbr. 1783

We are favoured by the Express with the honour of your Excellencies esteemed Letter of the 3 inst, by whch. we are Sorry to observe the Stocks in your hands Cannot afford to your Excellencÿ the means to provide us with the necessary Sums for the amount of the drafts his Excellency Robt. Morris Esqr. has been pleased to furnish on us beyond, what we Can be in Cash, nor that even you have no prospect to become in Cash towards the time, our drafts at three month in rembursement of our advance on your Excellency may become due.

The abstract your Excellency intended to inclose of Mr. Grand's acct. has not been in the packet, however we learn by his letter, that it is also impossible for him to assist us, Since all our remittances are not only absorbed but his wants yet extended beyond that Considerable amount.[2]

We are on this occasion much at a loss how to prevent the final protest of the bills, when the Same become due.

We have the honour to remain with great esteem Sir Your Excellency's most Obedient Servants

WILHEM & JAN WILLINK
NICHS. & JACOB VAN STAPHORST
DE LA LANDE & FYNJE

To his Excellency Benj. Franklin Esqr. in Paris.

From Joseph Banks

ALS: American Philosophical Society

Dear Sir   Soho Square Decr. 9 1783

The Friendship which I have Experiencd from you in your so speedily sending me Accounts of the Progress of the new Art of

---

residence was illuminated on Dec. 14, at a cost of 254 *l.t.:* Account XXXI (XXXVIII, 3); Finck's bill, [after Jan. 1, 1784]. APS.

2. During 1783 the consortium remitted Grand at least 944,131 *f.* (2,042,874 *l.t.*): *Morris Papers*, VIII, 736n.

Flying which makes such rapid advances in the Countrey you now inhabit I beg to acknowledge with real gratitude. I wish I had more than gratitude something(?) to Communicate in return but times must Come when I shall be able to repay the debt which you have accumulated upon me with so much Friendly perseverance & beleive me I shall do it with a grateful pleasure.

Charles's Experiment seems decisive & must be performd here in its full extent. I have hitherto been of Opinion that it is unwise to struggle for the honor of an invention which is absultely(?) Effected. Practical Flying we must allow to our rivals. Theoretical Flying We claim ourselves. Bishop Wilkins in his Mechanical magic has as I am informd (for I have not yet got the book) a proposal for flying by means of a vessel filld with rarefied Air[3] & Mr. Cavendish when he blew Soap bubbles of his Inflammable air[4] Evidently performd the Experiment Which Carried Charles the memorable flight of the 1st. instant. When our Friends on your side of the water are coold a little however they shall see that we will visit the repositories of starrs & Meteors & try if we cannot derive as much Knowledge by application of Theory to what we find in the Armories of heaven as they can do.

Mr. Mitchel has given us a very curious paper in which he considers light as subject to the power of gravitation,[5] like all other bodies if so says he should there be any material difference in the magnitude of the Fixd Stars the light of the Large ones

3. John Wilkins, bishop of Chester and a founding member of the Royal Society, was one of the first scientists to seriously consider the problem of flight. He speculated on how a vessel filled with ethereal or rarefied air could fly to the moon in *A Discourse Concerning a New World & Another Planet: in 2 Bookes* (London, 1640), pp. 203–39. In *Mathematical Magick, or, The Wonders that may be Performed by Mechanical Geometry* (London, 1648), he proposed various kinds of flying machines but referred readers to his earlier work for an explanation of how rarefied air could be used to defy gravity. See also Barbara J. Shapiro, *John Wilkins, 1614–1672: an Intellectual Biography* (Berkeley and Los Angeles, 1969), pp. 39–45; J. E. Hodgson, *The History of Aeronautics in Great Britain* . . . (London, 1924), pp. 70–5.

4. In a series of celebrated experiments, Henry Cavendish discovered that inflammable air (hydrogen) is about 11 times lighter than common air: "Three Papers, Containing Experiments on Factitious Air," *Phil. Trans.*, LVI (1766), 141–84.

5. John Michell's "On the Means of discovering the Distance, Magnitude, &c. of the Fixed Stars, in consequence of the Diminution of the

would move more slowly & in consequence be liable to a different refraction from that of the smaller ones but no such thing being Observd with our best Telescopes we have here a right to judge them not varying from each other in any immense quantity of magnitude for was any one to be 100 times larger than another the difference would be discernable.

A miserable Comet made his Appearance to Mr. Nathan Pigot in his Observatory at yorkshire on the 19[6] & the weather has been so hazy in the Evenings that it has scarce been Observd since it was on the

	Right Ascen	North declen
19 at 11h:15'	41:0:0	3°:10'
20 10 :54'	40:0:0	4:32
21 it was seen in the place where it was expected		

but the night was too hazy to observe it.

It appears like a Nebula, with a diameter of About 2 minutes of a degree the nucleus faint it is seen with difficulty when the wires of the instrument are illuminated but is not visible with an opera glass.　　　　　　　　　　　　　　　　　　　Mr. Pigot

Novr. 29 it was seen near the Chin of Aries & appeard like a nebulous Star as there was some moon light it was dificult to find it.

Decr. 1 it was removd near the preceeding Eye of Aries but conceiving other astronomers who have fixd instruments have noted its place he has not calculated the distance from any Known star.　　　　　　　　　　　　　　　　　　Mr. Herscell[7]

We are told that a Man has prepard Wings at a very considerable expence indeed they say £1000 that the models upon which they

Velocity of their Light . . ." was read before the Royal Society on Nov. 27, 1783: *Phil. Trans.*, LXXIV (1784), 35–57.

6. It was Edward Pigott, not his father, Nathaniel, who discovered this comet on Nov. 19, 1783. He described his observations in a Nov. 22 letter to Jean-Hyacinthe de Magellan, an extract of which was read before the Royal Society on Nov. 27, 1783: *Phil. Trans.*, LXXIV (1784), 20. Banks reproduces here the information in that extract.

7. Sir William Herschel.

are Constructed have flown & that the reality now in London but packd up in a Box should by a comparative calculation carry 150 lb. more than the man. The Machine consists of 4 wings two of which beat while the other two are drawn back some people whose opinion in Mechanics is lookd upon as Authority have said that they must succeed. Credat Judeus say I. I must see it before I beleive it.[8]

I am dear Sir with real gratitude & sincere thanks Yours Faithfully   JOS: BANKS

I open this to thank you for Mr. Faujas's book[9] which I receivd this moment on my return home from dinner

Addressed: Dr. Franklin / Passy / near / Paris

From George Washington   Copy:[1] Library of Congress

⟨Philadelphia, December 9, 1783: Dr. Witherspoon, whom you know, is going to Great Britain on business and may possibly travel to France.[2] I recommend him to your civility and attention.⟩

8. As the wings were said to have been made in Birmingham, Banks wrote to Matthew Boulton for more information. Boulton had no firsthand information as yet, having just returned from several months away, but had heard that the wings, their supporting steel rods, "a great number of Springs 8 ft. long," and "a great many Wheels & pineons" had been made under the direction of a man named Miller, who had not revealed their purpose. Some people said they were intended for swimming, while others said they were for flying: Neil Chambers, ed., *Scientific Correspondence of Sir Joseph Banks, 1765–1820* (6 vols., London, 2007), II, 229, 231–2.

9. Barthélemy Faujas de Saint-Fond, *Description des expériences de la machine aérostatique de MM. de Montgolfier . . .* (Paris, 1783).

1. In the hand of GW's clerk Tobias Lear. There is no evidence that Witherspoon ever delivered the letter (now missing).

2. John Witherspoon, president of the College of New Jersey, had served in Congress with BF: XXII, 538n, 663–4. In October, the trustees of the college commissioned him and Joseph Reed, former president of the Pa. Supreme Executive Council, to raise funds in Europe. The two sailed in December and reached London at the end of January: Varnum L. Collins, *President Witherspoon: a Biography* (2 vols., Princeton, 1925), II, 138–9; Reed to JA, Jan. 30, 1784, in William B. Reed, ed., *Life and Correspondence*

To John Adams   ALS: Massachusetts Historical Society

Sir,   Passy, Dec. 10. 1783.
I received the Letter you did me the honour of writing to
me the 5th. Instant by Commo. Jones, with the Dispatches he
brought. The Packet directed to me alone, contain'd only a Letter to the Magistrates of Hambourg, and a Diploma of Doctor
of Divinity from the College at Princetown for the Reverend
Mr Wren: No Commission, nor any Mention of it; so that it
seems to have been forgotten or dropt.[3] Perhaps our Letter which
went with the Definitive Treaty[4] may remind the Congress of it.
    I received the Letter you mention from Messrs Willink &
Compa.[5] I immediately consulted Mr Grand, who brought me
a Sketch of his Account with Mr Morris, by which it appeared
that it was not in our Power to give Relief. I hope your Presence
in Holland may be of Service.
    With great Respect I have the honour to be Sir Your most
obedient humble Servant   B FRANKLIN

Honble John Adams Esqe

To William Hodgson   AL (draft): American Philosophical Society

Dear Sir   Passy Dec. 10. 1783
    Having represented to Congress the Services rendered to our
Prisoners by the Revd Mr Wren, I have the Pleasure of transmitting their Thanks, together with a Diploma from the College at Princetown, which I beg you would forward to him with
my Respects.[6] I shall not fail to recommend my Friend[7] for the
Consulship, being with unalterable Esteem & Affection Dear
Sir Your most o. & m h. S.   B FRANKLIN

---

of Joseph Reed . . . (2 vols., Philadelphia, 1847), II, 401–2; Ruth L. Wood-
ward and Wesley F. Craven, *Princetonians, 1784–1790: a Biographical Dictionary* (Princeton, N.J., 1991), pp. xxvi-xxvii.
    3. See Boudinot to BF, Nov. 1.
    4. XL, 600–606.
    5. Above, [Nov. 30].
    6. See Boudinot to BF, Nov. 1.
    7. Hodgson himself; see his Oct. 30 letter.

Charge me with this Postage & that to Portsmouth[8]
Mr Wm Hodgson London

From J. Nebon[9]   ALS: American Philosophical Society

Monseigneur   St. Malo. 10e. Xbre 1783.
J'ai l'honneur d'envoyer ci joint à votre Excellence une lettre
que Mr Le Doctr. cooper m'avoit chargé de remettre En main
propre;[1] mes [mais] mes affaires ne me permettant point de me
rendre immédiatement à Paris, je crois qu'il Est nécessaire de
Vous L'acheminer: aussi profitte je du premier courier.
J ai Lhonneur d'Etre avec le plus profond Respect, Monseigneur, De Vôtre Excellence, Le plus humble & le plus humble
serviteur   J. NEBON

J'avois, Monseigneur, apporté quelques papiers publics de Bos-
ton que je croyois pouvoir Vous *Remettre* mais présumant qu'ils
Seroient de trop Vieille date avant que je Sois á Paris, j'ose les
Expedier a vôtre Excellence, & la Supplier de croire que je les
Expedie par le Courier ne trouvant de meilleure occasion./.

Notation: J Vebon, 10 Dec. 1783.

8. Where the letter and diploma for Wren were to be sent.
9. Though the initial letter of his last name is ambiguous in the signature (L'Air de Lamotte recorded it as "Vebon" in the notation), we assume
that this is James Nebon, a French merchant living in Boston who notified
the public on Sept. 24, 1783, that he would soon sail for France. He was
French vice-consul at Newport by the early 1790s: [Boston] *Independent
Chronicle and the Universal Advertiser*, Sept. 25, 1783; [Boston] *Herald of
Freedom*, June 9, 1789; Abraham P. Nasatir and Gary E. Monell, *French
Consuls in the United States* ... (Washington, D.C., 1967), pp. 55–6.
1. This must be Cooper's letter of Oct. 16, which BF acknowledged on
Dec. 26.

From Dumas

ALS: Library of Congress; AL (draft): Nationaal Archief

Monsieur,   Lahaie 11e. Dec. 1783.

L'incluse vous apprendra la suite des affaires ici.[2] Je crois pouvoir vous dire de plus, d'avance, que cette semaine la proposition de la Gr. Br. pour finir la paix ici ou à Londres,[3] sera rejettée aux Etats d'holle. par tous les Membres, excepté le Corps des Nobles, c'est-à-dire le Str. [Stadhouder]— Il retardera tant qu'il pourra la même résolution dans les autres Provinces; mais sans y rien gagner; au contraire.

Quant aux voies de fait, sur les frontieres, de la part des Autrichiens, on ne s'en inquiete guere ici;[4] & les Patriotes regardent cela comme une tentative imaginée & excitée par le parti Anglomane, pour appuyer la derniere proposition Brite. [Britannique] tendante à conclure le Traité définitif ici ou à Londres. Aussi fit-on le lendemain de l'arrivée du Courier un Vaudeville là-dessus, qui se chante partout, & dont voici une copie, avec mes complimens pour Mr. Wm. Franklin, qui pourra vous le chanter & en amuser ses amis. J'espere d'apprendre que vous jouissez d'une santé complete, & suis avec grand respect De Votre Excellence Le très-humble & très-obeissant Serviteur

C. W. F. DUMAS

Paris à Son Exce. Mr. B. Franklin M.P.

Addressed: à Son Excellence / Monsieur Franklin, Esqr., / Min. Plenipo: des Etats Unis / Passy./. / près Paris.

2. Neither of the two enclosures mentioned in this letter has been located.

3. Fox attempted to prevent negotiations for a final Dutch-British peace treaty from taking place in Paris so as to counter French influence; the Dutch resisted. Once Fox left office, the British agreed to hold the negotiations in Paris: Nicholas Tarling, *Anglo-Dutch Rivalry in the Malay World, 1780–1824* (Cambridge and St. Lucia, Australia, 1962), pp. 10–11.

4. Using a minor dispute between the Dutch Republic and the Austrian Netherlands in October as a pretext, Joseph II had ordered the occupation of several Dutch border posts, with the ultimate goal of forcing the Dutch to reopen the river Scheldt to Austrian shipping: Walter W. Davis, *Joseph II: an Imperial Reformer for the Austrian Netherlands* (The Hague, 1974), pp. 126–7.

From ———— Bouttret Durivault fils and Other Favor Seekers

ALS: American Philosophical Society

Whether they are asking for information, advice, personal assistance, or money, many of the favor seekers who contact Franklin during the five and a half months covered by this volume preface their requests with congratulations on the hard-won independence of the United States.[5] But some of those Frenchmen who had risked the most for the American victory began to protest that they were not being properly rewarded, including Bouttret Durivault fils, whose letter we print below. The demands of unpaid and increasingly impatient French soldiers and officers would continue to embarrass both Franklin and his successor Thomas Jefferson.

Paris merchant J.-B. Grimoult sends a copy on April 6, 1782, of a bill of exchange for 500 *l.t.* drawn by Franklin on Richard Bache in favor of M. Malide, a French soldier.[6] Malide never received the bill. Now that Malide has returned from America with his regiment, Grimoult asks that he be paid in France. His letter is dated October 9.[7]

A request on behalf of a French veteran comes from the abbé Berage on November 17, writing from Nîmes, where he is a canon. He sends Franklin an unsealed letter to forward to Henry Laurens, whom he had met when Laurens passed through his city. Berage had given Laurens a *mémoire* pertaining to his brother, "Delaboyere," a captain in the Soissonnais regiment.[8] Laurens had agreed to support the favor solicited in the *mémoire*, and assured Berage that he would ask Franklin to do likewise. Berage asks Franklin to read the enclosed letter before forwarding it.[9]

---

5. Unless otherwise indicated, all the documents summarized here are in French, are at the APS, and elicited no extant response.

6. Grimoult made a request for another soldier in 1782: XXXVI, 307.

7. Jacques Malide served at Yorktown in the Soissonnais regiment and embarked for France in March, 1783: Ministère des affaires étrangères, *Les Combattants français de la guerre américaine, 1778–1783* (Paris, 1903), pp. 238, 245. BF endorsed this letter "Mr Grimoulte," and evidently honored the request. In a now-missing letter of June 17, 1784, he instructed RB to refuse payment if a bill of exchange in favor of Malide should be presented: RB to BF, Aug. 28, 1784 (Musée de Blérancourt).

8. Jean-Pierre Berage de la Boyère (b. 1736) fought with Rochambeau's forces in America: Bodinier, *Dictionnaire*.

9. Two months later, Laurens sent word to the abbé (through an intermediary) that BF had declined acting in the matter, saying that "it was a Business in which he could not with propriety interfere." Laurens then turned

The end of the war threatens the livelihood of two demobilized military men. In an undated *mémoire*, Prugné (or Pugné, as he also spells it) claims to have served in the French army for twenty-four years, the last four in America. In 1780 he accompanied Rochambeau's corps as an unpaid commissary charged with protecting the army's cattle from Tories. Since then all his personal possessions have been stolen or otherwise lost, the war's end deprived him of an income, his son was killed in battle, and his daughters were forced to join a convent. Now living in Paris without family or resources, he seeks compensation for both his service and his losses as well as the status of a disabled officer. De Montréal (as he signs himself), a former clerk to a notary, also followed Rochambeau's army to America, as director of military hospitals. Now that the army is being disbanded, he fears that he will lose his commission and be without work. In an undated note, he asks Franklin for letters of recommendation to a commercial house or another employer in America.[1]

A statement by a French sailor, which appears to have been written during a visit to Passy, implies a request for a favor, though the nature of the favor is unknown. He says that he sailed from Bordeaux on February 17 on the *Boussole*, bound for the coast of Guinea, and returned on a different ship, the first one having been lost in the straits around Saint-Domingue. He arrived back in France on October 6, 1783. William Temple Franklin noted his name at the top of the sheet: Laneufville de St. Firmin.

Three correspondents ask Franklin to forward mail. On October 28, the comtesse de La Brosse, writing from the château d'Hérouville near Void, Lorraine, asks Franklin to forward a second letter to her brother in Virginia, from whom her family has not heard for more than two years.[2] Similarly, J. Tahon, a canon from Armentières, near Lille, apologizes on January 17 for troubling Franklin for the second but what he promises will be the last time with forwarding an important letter to his brother in Boston.[3] Now that he finally

---

to Lafayette, who promised to deliver Berage's memoir to Vergennes and discuss it with him: *Laurens Papers*, XVI, 372–3.

1. Among BF's papers at the APS is an almost identical letter from Montréal to the comte d'Estaing. He is listed as one of two *directeurs des comptes* of the military hospital of Rochambeau's army. He had only arrived in Philadelphia on Dec. 28, 1782: M. Bouvet, *Le Service de santé français pendant la guerre d'indépendance des Etats-Unis, (1777–1782)* (Paris, 1933), p. 33.

2. For her first request see XXXVIII, 473.

3. His earlier letter is summarized in XXXVIII, 473–4.

knows his brother's address, he is sure that this letter will reach him. In a note of December 22, an *avocat* from Paris named Giraud hopes that the United States of America will accept the homage paid to it in the dedication of his almanac. He asks that Franklin forward the enclosed copy, presumably to Congress.

Three correspondents seek information from or about America. Krazeisen, secretary of legation for the duchy of Deux-Ponts at the court of Versailles, writes on September 27 on behalf of M. de Pachelbel, minister plenipotentiary for the duchy and chargé d'affaires for the Landgrave of Hesse-Darmstadt.[4] They have received an inquiry from Hyeronime Sommerlad, a teacher at Leihgestern in Hesse-Darmstadt, regarding his two brothers, Gottfried and Philippe Jacques, who emigrated to America in 1748 and established themselves in "Germando" near Philadelphia (Germantown) as manufacturers of hose.[5] Sommerlad has heard nothing from them since they left, but as they have property in their native land, it is important to know if they are still alive. Would Franklin please find out?

On December 9, writing from Ducey in Normandy, the chevalier d'Osmont and his sister[6] relate a convoluted story of their inheritance problems. Their brother Jacques-Charles d'Osmont had gone to Petersburg, Virginia, to be a tobacco factor. Another brother had gone with him, but returned after one year. As both parents have now died, they need confirmation of whether Jacques-Charles is still alive, and if he is not (as is rumored), they seek Franklin's help in procuring a death certificate. Having previously believed Franklin to be in America, they had written to him there, and enclose a copy of their 1777 letter. They also enclose an explanation of their situation that they wish to be circulated first in Virginia and then in Carolina, where their brother may have settled.[7]

4. In 1782, Pachelbel had asked BF to forward a letter to America: XXXVII, 34, 41. He died on Oct. 5, 1784; BF received a printed announcement from his son, Heinrich Christian Friedrich von Pachelbel-Gehag (*ADB*): University of Pa. Library.

5. Johann Gottfried and Philip Jacob Sommerlad arrived in Philadelphia and took an oath of allegiance to the British crown in September, 1748: Ralph B. Strassburger, "Pennsylvania German Pioneers: a Publication of the Original Lists of Arrivals In the Port of Philadelphia From 1727 to 1808," Pa. German Soc. *Proc.*, XLII (1934), 377.

6. She signs simply "d'Osmont." They are probably Jean and Marie-Anne-Jeanne d'Osmont, whose brothers' names were Jacques-Charles and François-Clément: *Dictionnaire de la noblesse*, XV, 274–5.

7. The enclosed letter to BF is missing. The letter they hoped would be forwarded to America remains filed with the present appeal.

The abbé de Fonténai[8] writes on February 24 from his address at 47, rue St. Hyacinthe in Paris. He has received an inquiry from a French officer who served with distinction in America and is at the moment in Provence; this officer needs the current titles and address of General Washington as well as the name and address of the first president of Congress. Knowing that newspapers are too often inaccurate, the abbé sought this information from several people who all advised him to consult Franklin.[9]

Several correspondents seek Franklin's advice or intervention. Retired officer Rouzier from Montargis inquires on November 15 if Franklin could recommend a cure for the gout. Rouzier has suffered from this affliction for several years, but in the past fifteen months it has moved up his legs and into his groin. Purging relieved the symptoms but did not remove the cause. Friends finally convinced him to turn to Franklin for help.

A widow with a large family who signs her name as Tonnelier Diannyere writes from Moulins on December 18, asking for Franklin's protection. Based on her description, her late husband must have been Jean Diannyère, a physician in Moulins.[1] In order to compensate for his small income as a doctor, he had accepted the position of supervisor of the local springs, which allowed his family to benefit from a tax exemption. Could Franklin help her keep this exemption or perhaps obtain a royal pension or anything that would help her raise her children?

Since his family is of American descent and they share the same name, asks Charles Benjamin, a painter from Valenciennes in northern France, would Franklin be interested in obtaining for him a place in one of the kingdom's art schools, or at least a position as a draftsman at the Ecole royale du génie in Mézières?[2] His letter is written from Mézières-sur-Meuse on January 12.

8. The pen name of Louis-Abel Bonafous (1736–1806), a former Jesuit, a man of letters, and the founder and editor of the journal *Affiches, annonces et avis divers* (later called *Journal général de France*): *DBF* under Fontenai.

9. On a blank leaf of the abbé's letter WTF wrote the titles and addresses of GW and Thomas Mifflin, the current president of Congress. This information was presumably sent in a letter now lost.

1. Diannyère (1701–1782) devoted his practice to prisoners and the poor: *DBF*.

2. Founded in 1748, this highly selective school trained the officers of the corps of engineers of the royal army: Anne Blanchard, *Les Ingénieurs du "roy" de Louis XIV à Louis XVI: étude du corps des fortifications* (Montpellier, 1979), pp. 188–212.

Joseph-Antoine Hédouin de Pons-Ludon[3] has been a freemason since 1766, though not a permanent member of a particular lodge. He writes on January 26 from Epernay because Marchal de Saincy,[4] a fellow Mason, is appointing a new agent to the diocese of Reims. Hédouin has applied for the position but hears that Marchal prefers someone else. Hédouin calls on Franklin as the *vénérable* of the Neuf Sœurs[5] to notify Marchal that, all things being equal, a Masonic brother should always be preferred to a layman. He also asks Franklin to inform the duc de Chartres, who doubtless would also demand Hédouin's appointment.

On February 21 a sieur de la Porte writes on behalf of the baronne de Bissy, who has for the past two years been the sole provider for her six children. For their education she depends on the charity of kind souls. She asks Franklin's help in placing one of her children in the merchant marine. The child's father served with distinction as a navy officer.[6] Péchigny[7] can also speak in the child's favor.

Undated, but clearly written after the end of the war, is the request from Nicolas Pachot, a cook from Canada. He needs help to return to Montreal and his wife and children, whom he has not seen for six years. During his absence he served as a cook for Governor "Winthoise" and for Daniel and Samuel Sherburne in Portsmouth, New Hampshire.[8] He mentions two other military officers whom

---

3. Poet and author (1739–1817) who served as *conseiller raporteur du point d'honneur* at the Tribunal des maréchaux de France, which, among other duties, adjudicated disputes between nobles: *Nouvelle Biographie;* Lucien Bély, ed., *Dictionnaire de l'Ancien Régime: royaume de France, XVIe–XVIIIe siècle* (Paris, 1996), p. 795.

4. The *receveur général des économats:* Le Bihan, *Francs-maçons parisiens.*

5. BF's two-year term as *vénérable* ended in May, 1781: XXIX, 528–30; XXXV, 88n.

6. The father is undoubtedly the baron de Bissy who in 1777 presented BF with a bizarre plan involving a secret weapon: XXIII, 166–7.

7. The proprietor of the Passy boarding school that JA's sons attended: XXXII, 46.

8. He may be referring to John Wentworth, governor of New Hampshire from 1767 to 1775: John W. Raimo, *Biographical Directory of American Colonial and Revolutionary Governors, 1607–1789* (Westport, Conn., 1980), pp. 176–7. Col. Samuel Sherburne was a member of the N.H. House of Representatives in 1776, and that same year became captain in the Independent Company of Militia of Portsmouth: XVII, 48n; *Sibley's Harvard Graduates,* XVI, 231–4. Daniel and Samuel Sherburne were co-owners of the privateer *McClary: Jefferson Papers,* VI, 448–52.

he served: General "Lyéborne" in Grenada, and "Major Ethering-
tonne," of the Royal American Regiment.[9]

Two undated requests for help with publication projects were
probably written after the definitive peace treaty was signed in
September, 1783. Philippe de Delleville[1] from Fontenay-sous-Bois
announces his intention of undertaking a comprehensive history of
the American Revolution. He cannot think of anyone better qualified
than Franklin to help him sort fact from fiction. Baron de Favagnac
explains that he is compiling an almanac of all foreign courts. For
this he needs the assistance of all foreign ministers in Paris. Would
Franklin please send him the names of the ministers and ambassadors
that his "Couronne" has sent to the princes of Europe?[2]

Many supplicants send desperate pleas for money. On November 27, Guyon, a sixty-one-year-old former employee of a *receveur-
général*, informs Franklin that he lost his job. This misfortune was
followed by the death of his wife, after a long illness, and now he
alone cares for their ten-year-old daughter, who is afflicted with "im-
bécilité." All his efforts to find new employment have been fruitless.
He encloses a two-page memoir on his daughter's medical history
and hopes that Franklin will come to their aid. He sends a second appeal on December 3, hoping to speak to Franklin in person.

In a short note written around the beginning of the new year,
the abbesse Marie du Saint Esprit of L'Avé Maria de Paris implores
Franklin to continue his generous contributions to the convent.[3]

Longchamps,[4] a Parisian cartographer in desperate need of cash,
writes on January 26 to offer Franklin a manuscript that a former cavalry colonel and chevalier de Saint Louis had given Longchamps' son as

9. Brigadier General Leybourne had governed Grenada and surrounding islands since 1771: E. Gittens Knight, comp., *The Grenada Handbook
and Directory* (Bridgetown, Barbados, 1946), pp. 24–5. Major George
Etherington served as lieutenant colonel of the 2nd Battalion of the 60th
Royal American Regiment of Foot: W. W. Abbot *et al.*, eds., *The Papers of
George Washington*, Revolutionary War Series (21 vols. to date, Charlottesville and London, 1985–), IX, 366n.

BF endorsed the letter "Nicholas Pachot Canadien."

1. Lieutenant general of the admiralty who corresponded with BF in
1780: XXXII, 233, 255.

2. His letter is at the University of Pa. Library.

3. For her most recent appeal, see XXXVIII, 528–9.

4. He is listed in Josephine French *et al.*, eds., *Tooley's Dictionary of
Mapmakers* (rev. ed.; 4 vols., Tring, Eng., and Riverside, Conn., 1999–
2004), III, 150.

payment for tutoring the colonel's son. It is entitled "L'esprit des Etats, ou des conditions que lhomme peut Embrasser." Everyone to whom he has shown it, including several booksellers and the rector of the Collège Mazarin, has pronounced it to be good, but no one is in a position to acquire it. Despite his urgent need of money, Longchamps will offer Franklin a fair price. Longchamps writes again on January 30 hoping that the manuscript, which his son delivered to Passy, has met with Franklin's approval. Even if Franklin should not be interested, Longchamps hopes he will be his "ange tutelaire" and help him out of his financial straits. The marquis d'Amezaga[5] can tell Franklin more about his situation. Finally, on February 6, Longchamps expresses his regret at Franklin's negative reply, but informs him that he has already followed the minister's advice to offer the manuscript to military schools and scholars. While awaiting their response, Longchamps asks Franklin to give him five *louis*, which would enable him to complete the printing of several maps. Four days later, Longchamps fils writes a letter of his own: one of the editors of the *Journal militaire* has promised to serialize the manuscript and pay one *louis* per page, starting in April.[6] However, that will be too late for his suffering family, who depend on Franklin for relief. Having seen Franklin in person, Longchamps fils is confident that he will lend them two or three *louis*, which they will promptly repay in April. In an undated note that was probably enclosed with this letter, Longchamps' daughter joins her brother in imploring Franklin to save their family from ruin and promising that any advance will be repaid.

Dominique Perrin, reminding Franklin that they met during the American's ill-fated mission to Montreal,[7] writes on February 15 from Varennes, Quebec. Perrin had provided Franklin with important information marked *secret*, for which Franklin promised to compensate him. Since that time his business has been ruined by the litigation of a royalist named Richard Daubie, and he can no longer provide for his family. He reminds Franklin of his promise and asks him to send money as well as to open a collection among his friends, especially Thomas Walker,[8] whom Perrin knows well. Franklin should address his response to James Taylor, merchant in New York.[9]

5. A member of BF's circle: XXIX, 328n.

6. The *Journal militaire, dédié à Monsieur frère du Roi* resumed publication on April 15, 1784, after a hiatus of four years: Jean Sgard, ed., *Dictionnaire des journaux, 1600–1789* (2 vols., Paris, 1991), II, 772–3.

7. For BF's part in trying to persuade settlers in Canada to stand with the 13 colonies in the spring of 1776 see XXII, 380–1.

8. Formerly a merchant in Montreal: XXV, 111–12.

9. A duplicate of this letter is at the APS.

Franklin receives many requests for personal interviews. On September 18, Pierre-Antoine-Jean Remond, *maître des eaux et forêts du Berry,*[1] announces that he is delighted to give Franklin a new opportunity to serve his country. Fifteen minutes will suffice to explain his patriotic project, whenever it is convenient. Three days later, Remond sends his regrets that due to a small accident he will be unable to accept Franklin's invitation for the following morning and asks for a new audience on Thursday or Friday. On October 21 Madame Benoist de Frenay seeks Franklin's sage advice on a matter too delicate to discuss by post, involving the unhappy situation of a man of merit. On October 23 the chevalier de Contrepont announces that he wants to talk with Franklin about a subject which he thinks will please him. On November 15 the sieur du Demaine Grandais, a young cleric, begs permission to pay homage to Franklin in person and discuss his plans to become a tutor for American children sent to France by their parents. The Baron de La Courtette[2] writes on December 18 that the kindness Franklin had shown him the previous year and Franklin's association with his Masonic lodge encourage him to ask for help. He is the father of four children, whom he managed to place well: his daughter is at the Royal Abbey of Montmartre and his three sons at different military schools. He is now alone in his misery, wishing for death at the age of 34. Only an audience with Franklin can unburden his heavy heart, dry his tears, and keep him from the grave. On January 7 Paris notary Blossier complains that it has been some time since he requested the honor of conferring with Franklin. Could Franklin please inform him of the place, day, and time for an audience? The widow Denis and her daughter, who met Franklin the previous February, when one of them played the harp, ask for an audience of ten minutes this evening, January 18, or tomorrow morning. Franklin also receives two undated requests in English that were probably written in 1783 at the earliest. John Kiddell, Jr., an Englishman who is passing through Paris on his way home after a tour of Spain, congratulates Franklin on the peace. He asks whether he might pay his respects in

1. Remond was also *capitaine des chasses* for the comte d'Artois. A member of the lodge Thalie in Paris, in 1784 he was instrumental in the creation of Sainte Solange, the first lodge in Bourges, which received its constitutions in 1785. Remond was its first *vénérable:* Le Bihan, *Francs-maçons parisiens,* p. 414; Robert Durandeau *Histoire des francs-maçons en Berry* (Limoges, 1990), pp. 61–2.

2. The representative in Paris of the Commandeurs du Temple, a Carcassonne lodge with which BF had been in correspondence since 1780: XXXIV, 482.

person the next morning, and offers to carry letters to England. William Whitchurch[3] sends a letter recommending the bearer, a young Englishman who desires to "visit the Western Shores" and learn French before embarking. He is one of several Englishmen who wish to emigrate, and hopes to obtain Franklin's advice on the "propriety of the Remove." Whitchurch would consider it a personal honor if Franklin would grant the young man an interview.

On December 6, M. de Rocheplate, residing on the rue de Tournon, begs Franklin for a half hour of his time, whenever it is most convenient, though, if possible, before December 10. In a second letter, he explains that Franklin's "petit mot" offering an appointment for December 8 at noon was not delivered until eleven o'clock on the appointed morning, too late for Rocheplate to make it to Passy in time. Mortified (as he writes) at this development, he begs for another opportunity. On December 18, his third and final letter explains that he is sending Franklin two manuscript works on geometry.

Four Frenchmen seek recommendations. While their letters are undated, we have assigned them to 1783 since such journeys were more likely to be undertaken after the cessation of hostilities. Dabbé, a captain of hussars in the Chamborant regiment, has offered his services to Lafayette and wants Franklin to put in a good word for him based on a recommendation from the baron de Breteuil.[4] Jacques Dutilh, who lives in Nérac, wants to travel to Boston and asks for a letter of recommendation. (On the verso, Franklin wrote "Me Brillon".) The abbés Chalut and Arnoux, Franklin's longtime friends, ask for a recommendation on behalf of Louis Jolly, a Paris merchant from a wealthy family, who has emigrated to America. They also supply Franklin with what appears to be a draft for this recommendation, in which they spell the merchant's name "Joli," explain that he wants to share the good fortune of the Americans, and add that he is currently in Philadelphia. In a third note, written on a Sunday, the abbés ask Franklin to send them the recommendation if he has had the time and goodness to write it.[5] The Prince of Liège writes on behalf of Jean

3. The English engraver: XXII, 22n.
4. Before being appointed by Louis XVI as minister of the king's household in 1783, the baron de Breteuil served as French ambassador in various European capitals; it is less likely that he would have written a recommendation for a French officer during that period. See our annotation of Breteuil's letter of Dec. 26.
5. All three documents are in the hand of Arnoux. On the verso of the draft recommendation BF wrote "Monsieur".

Nicolas Joseph Hankart, who needs recommendations to the leading persons of Philadelphia.[6]

Also probably dating from 1783 is an undated application for citizenship from the abbé Le Poër. The abbé descends from a distinguished noble Irish family. Since he is denied the full rights of a French subject, he would like to become an American citizen instead. Moreover, several members of his family have fought and would fight again for American independence, and one brother plans to emigrate. The abbé would be happy to swear an oath of allegiance, if possible in Franklin's presence.[7]

Finally, we note a brief letter sent by Paris notary Aleaume, who asks Franklin on November 6 to certify two enclosed powers of attorney.

Monseigneur   a mirebeau ce 12. Xbre. 83.

Comme Etant un de vos sujets, ayant Servis dans vos Etats unis de lamerique, sous les ordres du General Wagenton et du Glle. Grenne, dépuis le 10. juillet 1778. jus'qua ce jour, avec honneur & fidelité, dont j'offre le justifier par les Recomandation de mes officiers, j'ose vous assurer avoir Eprouvé tout ce que L'homme peut Eprouver dardue & de disgratieux, tant par le manque des provisions que des habilements, n'i même payé

---

6. Although no letters of recommendation have been located, BF wrote at the bottom of the present letter "to Mr Hillegas to Mr Morris". The author of the present note was probably François-Charles de Velbruck (1719–1784), *prince-évêque* of Liège from 1772 until his death. Known as a proponent of Enlightenment thought, he founded such charitable institutions as the Hôpital général de Saint-Léonard. He died on April 30, 1784, and was succeeded by Constantin-François de Hoensbroeck on Aug. 17, 1784. For both men see *Biographie nationale* (44 vols., Brussels, 1866–1985).

7. In a postscript to the present document, the abbé explains that his name is spelled "Power" in Ireland. He is possibly Francis Power (*c.* 1740–1817), a native of Ireland who was educated and ordained a priest in Paris. He became a canon and later the archdeacon of the diocese of Avignon. Francis' brothers Peter and John served as officers in Dillon's regiment of the Irish Brigade: Richard Hayes, *Biographical Dictionary of Irishmen in France* (Dublin, 1949), p. 270. A Pierre Power (1733–1780) rose to the rank of captain in Dillon's regiment and might have fought at Savannah: Bodinier, *Dictionnaire*.

depuis le 1e. avril 1780. jus'qua ce jour, á la Reserve de quatre mois payé En papier á six mois de datte et dont il a fallû perdre dessus prés de la moitié.[8]

Vous déves Croire quel tout cela me fait deux ans & huit mois de payé En outre la possesion de monnaie que je n'aye point Reçu En outre 200 arpent de terre promis a Ceux Engagé pour toute la Guerre; je n'aye passé En france que par un freleau pour quel affaire de famille. Je suplie vôtre Grandeur, de vouloir Bien avoir Egard aux pauvre malheureux, d'autant plus a plaindre que je Suis Estropié d'une jambe; pour Cet Cause j'ay Été transferé par ordre du Glle Grenne dans le Corps des invalides á philadelpia;[9] auparavant jestois du 1e. Regt de la marilande Compagnie Capitaine pralles[1] Comendé par le Colonel pierre adam.[2] Monseigneur En cecy j'implore vôtre Clemence et vôtre justice, & j'espere que vous voudrés bien avoir Egard á la demende juste et Legitime de Celuy qui Est trés Respectueusement Monseigneur Votre trés humble et trés obeissant Serviteur[3]

BOUTTRET DURIVAULT FILS

Chéz mr. Darivaux president du Grénier á sel á mirebeau En poitoue

8. Complaints about outstanding and depreciated pay were common among Continental Army soldiers throughout the war: Charles Royster, *A Revolutionary People at War: the Continental Army and American Character, 1775–1783* (Chapel Hill, N.C., 1979), pp. 295–8; Stuart D. Brandes, *Warhogs: a History of War Profits in America* (Lexington, Ky., 1997), pp. 36–7.

9. Congress raised the Invalid Corps in June, 1777, to serve in garrisons and as guards of magazines and hospitals. It was also intended to function as a military school. Congress disbanded the corps in May, 1783: *JCC*, VIII, 485, 554–6; Fred A. Berg, *Encyclopedia of Continental Army Units . . .* (Harrisburg, Pa., 1972), pp. 54–5.

1. Edward Prall, captain in the Md. infantry: Francis B. Heitman, *Historical Register of Officers of the Continental Army . . .* (1914; reprint, with addenda by Robert H. Kelby, Baltimore, 1982), p. 634.

2. Peter Adams, lieutenant colonel of the 1st Md. Regiment from Aug. 1, 1779, to Jan. 1, 1781: Berg, *Encyclopedia of Continental Army Units*, p. 64.

3. On Jan. 19, 1784, Bouttret Durivault repeated this request: APS.

Addressed: A Monseigneur / Monseigneur De franquelin / ambassadeur des Etats unis / de L'amerique En Son hotel / A Paris

Notation: Bouttrel du Rivault fils, 12 Decr. 1783.

From the Abbé Girault de Kéroudou

ALS: American Philosophical Society

au College de Louis Legrand, Ce 12. Xbre. 1783./.

Monsieur,

Dans Le recueil de M. Le President Rolland, que J'ay eû L'honneur d'envoyer à votre Excellence,[4] il Se trouve une dissertation sur L'emplois de La Langue française dans Les inscriptions, Les traités, &c. L'autheur desirant y faire Les Changements et Les additions Convenables,[5] me Charge de recourir à vos Lumieres pour Sçavoir si Les deliberations de votre republique, et quelques unes de ses inscriptions, sont en français. Votre zele pour tout Ce qui peut-etre utile aux Sciences, aux Lettres et aux hommes, ne vous permettera pas de me refuser Cette grace. Je vous demande encore Celle d'agreer Le profond respect avec Lequel Je suis, Monsieur, Votre trés hble et obt. Serviteur   GIRAULT DE KEROUDOU,

grand-maitre du College de Louis Legrand.

Notation: Girault de Keroudou 12 Decr. 1783.—

4. Girault de Kéroudou had sent *Recueil de plusieurs des ouvrages de Monsieur le Président Rolland* ... (Paris, 1783), by Rolland d'Erceville: XL, 237–8.

5. Rolland was revising his *Dissertation sur la question de savoir si les inscriptions doivent être rédigées en Latin ou en François* (Paris, 1782), which argued that French inscriptions could be of equal quality to those in Latin. The second edition was published by March 14, 1784, when it was reviewed in the *Jour. de Paris.*

From Luigi Pio   AL: American Philosophical Society

Ce Vendredy 12. Xre. 1783./. Hôtel montmorency
Chaussée d'Antin
Mr. de Pio a l'honneur de presenter ses hommages à Mon-
sieur Franklin, et de lui envoyer le IV. volume de l'Ouvrage de
Mr. filangieri de Naples avec sa lettre aussi.[6]

From Lafayette   ALS: American Philosophical Society

My dear Sir   Paris Saturday Evening [December 13, 1783?][7]
The Inclosed is a Paper I intend to Present to the Several
Ministers, with the Hope it May Give them some favourable
ideas Upon the American trade—[8] But Before I do it, I wish
of Course to Have Your Approbation— Be so kind, My dear
Sir, as to Read it Over, and if You think it May Answer a Good
purpose, I will in My private Capacity Give it to Marechal de
Castries, M. de Vergennes, and M. de Calonne—[9] To Morrow

6. Filangieri's letter is above, Oct. 27.
7. The Saturday before Dec. 18, when Calonne acknowledged receiving his copy of the memoir that Lafayette enclosed here: Idzerda, *Lafayette
Papers*, v, 178.
8. Lafayette had been working on "Observations Sur le Commerce entre la France et les Etats-Unis" since October, when he announced to WTF
his intention to submit "beneficial" ideas on Franco-American trade to the
French government before it had formed a policy. He asked WTF to forward
an enclosed plan of his ideas to Thomas Barclay for his comments, and also
asked for the opinions of WTF, his "friends," and BF (APS). On Nov. 11 Lafayette informed GW that he was "Collecting the Opinions of Every American Merchant Within My reach" for a presentation to the government. The
memoir did not claim to present new ideas or solutions, but merely to summarize American complaints about trading with France: the high duties and
complicated regulations, the lack of long-term credit, the control held by the
farmers general over the tobacco trade, the delay in naming free ports, and
the restrictions on commerce with the French West Indies: Idzerda, *Lafayette
Papers*, v, 164, 168–75, 382–8. BF's copy of the memoir has not been found.
9. On Dec. 26 Lafayette also sent a copy to Robert Morris. The day
before, Calonne, the newly appointed controller general of finances, com-
mended the memoir and assured Lafayette he would report on it to the king,
after consulting with Vergennes. As a result of those discussions, Calonne

about ten in the Morning I Hope Having the Honour to Call upon You in My Way to Versaïlles.

With the Highest Respect I Have the Honour to Be Your obedient Servant and Affectionate friend   LAFAYETTE

for this time Excuse the Scribbling

His excellency B. franklin Esq.

From Menier de Saint Yver

ALS: American Philosophical Society

Monsieur   Paris ce 13. Xbre. 1783.

Votre Excellence a toujours eu la bonté de promettre à M. Schaffer qu'aussitot le retour de M. Barcklay elle engageroit ce Consul a lui rendre service. Veuillés donc bien, Monsieur, puisqu'il est de retour ne pas refuser à m. Schaffer de le faire reclamer par quelqu'un qui puisse au moins nous tirer du precipice où votre silence nous a plongé; ce Service rendu a M. Schaffer est de la plus grande utilité pour moi qui me trouve lié à son Sort dans cette cruelle circonstance, et en le lui rendant vous porterés le Calme dans une famille respectable qui en conservera une eternelle reconnoissance.

Je suis avec le plus profond respect Monsieur de Votre Excellence Le très humble et tres obeissant serviteur[1]

MENIER DE SAINTYVER

---

announced to Lafayette on Jan. 9, 1784, the naming of four free ports and promised measures to address the other American complaints: *Morris Papers*, VIII, 842–4; Idzerda, *Lafayette Papers*, V, 182, 189, 389–91.

1. On Dec. 23, Shaffer had "un ami" (Menier de Saint Yver) write a letter on his behalf to WTF, which Shaffer signed. Too ill with a fever to write, he begged WTF to ask BF to send money for his relief to Beaumont. That afternoon, Beaumont wrote WTF a letter that evidently accompanied Shaffer's request. The amount they needed was three *louis*, which would cover various legal expenses and the recovery of Shaffer's seized goods. (Both letters are at the APS.)

To Vergennes LS:[2] American Philosophical Society

Sir, Passy, 14. Decr 1783.

Permit me to introduce to your Excellency the Bearer Mr Nesbitt a very respectable American Merchant settled at L'Orient. He will himself have the honor of communicating to you the Business he is come to Paris upon, and I request your Excellency will give him a favourable Audience & that support which the nature of his Case seems to merit.[3]

With great Respect & Esteem I am, Sir, Your Excellency's most obedient and most humble Sert., B FRANKLIN

His Exy. Count de Vergennes.—

Endorsed: M De R.[4]

Notations: Franklin / recommandation en faveur de M. Nesbit marchand americain

From John Adams Copy: Massachusetts Historical Society

Sir London Decr: 14th: 1783.

The Day before Yesterday, Mr. Boudinot called upon me, with Dispatches from the President of Congress, his Brother.[5] There were two Letters addressed to the "Ministers" and these I opened but found little or Nothing but Duplicates of Dispatches, receiv'd by you before I left Auteuil.[6]

2. In WTF's hand.

3. Nesbitt was attempting to resolve a dispute over the premium demanded by the French insurers of the *Nancy;* see his letters of Oct. 20 and 27.

4. Gérard de Rayneval.

5. Lewis Boudinot had arrived in Falmouth, England, at the end of September; see his letter to BF, Sept. 29. We do not know why it took so long for him to reach London.

6. One surely was Elias Boudinot's July 15 letter to the peace commissioners (XL, 301–8); the other probably was Boudinot's June 16 letter to them (XL, 178–80).

There are two letters, and one large Packet addressed to you,[7] which I have the Honour to transmit by Mr: Little page.[8]

Mr: Jay and I are waiting, for Advices from your Excellency if this Packet or that by Captn: Jones contains a Commission to treat with Great Britain, it will be necessary that we should return, to Paris, or that you should come to London very soon— I am also very anxious to hear whether it is possible for you to Save Mr: Morris's Bills at Amsterdam from a Protest for Non payment. If it is not, many Individuals will be disappointed, and the Catastrophe to American Credit must come on.

With the greatest Respect, I have the Honour to be, Sir, your most obedt:

His Excellency Benjn: Franklin Esqr:

To Joseph Banks

ALS: British Library; ALS (draft): University of Pennsylvania Library

Dear Sir,   Passy, Dec. 15. 1783

You have probably had enough of my Correspondence on the Subject of the Balloons, yet I cannot forbear sending you Mr Charles's Account of his Voyage,[9] wch contains some Circumstances that are curious & interesting. And perhaps you may, for a Conclusion, have one more Letter from me by him, if

7. On the same day JA wrote the present letter, he wrote to Congress complaining that the dispatches addressed to "The Ministers" contained nothing but duplicates, "wereas a larger Packet addressed to Dr Franklin, leaves room to Suppose that it contains a Commission or other Papers for Us all." He asked that in the future, anything of general importance be addressed to all the commissioners, so that he would be permitted to open it; this would avoid not only "inconveniencies," as had happened in the past, but also the "greater Evil" that the present circumstance might cause: *Adams Papers*, XV, 423.

8. Lewis Littlepage. The date of his arrival is unknown, but on Jan. 15, 1784, in a letter to WTF, he alluded to his "late residence in London" (APS).

9. On Dec. 9, Charles delivered an account of his balloon voyage as part of the opening lecture of his new course on experimental physics. It was published in the *Jour. de Paris* on Dec. 13 and 14. These issues were prob-

he makes the Flight, said to be intended the first fair Wind, from Paris to London. With great Esteem, I am ever, Dear Sir, Your most obedient Servant   B Franklin

Sir Joseph Banks, Bart.

To William Carmichael

ʟs:[1] Henry E. Huntington Library; press copy of ʟs and transcript: National Archives

My dear Friend,   Passy, Dec. 15. 1783.

I am much concern'd to find by your Letter to my Grandson, that you are hurt by my long Silence, and that you ascribe it to a suppos'd Diminution of my Friendship.[2] Believe me, that is by no means the case; but I am too much harassed by a Variety of Correspondence together with Gout and Gravel, which induces me to postpone doing what I often fully intend to do, and particularly Writing, where the urgent Necessity of Business does not seem to require its being done immediately; my sitting too much at the Desk having already almost killed me; besides, since Mr. Jay's Residence here, I imagin'd he might keep you fully informed of what was material for you to know, and I beg you to be assur'd of my constant and sincere Esteem and affection.

---

ably what BF enclosed.

The course was announced in the *Jour. de Paris* on Dec. 6, and it is likely that WTF attended. On what was undoubtedly Dec. 8, 1783, WTF composed a brief letter to Charles offering congratulations, asking to enroll in his course, and requesting permission to bring one or two friends to hear Charles's lecture the following day: WTF to Charles, undated draft, APS.

1. In the hand of L'Air de Lamotte.

2. Carmichael wrote to WTF on Nov. 26, responding to WTF's recent packet enclosing a letter from the president of Congress and other letters that BF had asked him to forward. Carmichael expressed, at some length, his concern that BF harbored an ill opinion of him, saying that he had "*Ministerial* information" to that effect. He asked for copies of *Constitutions des treize Etats-Unis de l'Amérique* and some *Libertas Americana* medals, which several highly placed people had requested; if necessary he would pay for them out of his salary, but as a public servant he expected that he would have received them as a matter of course. APS.

I do not know whether you have been informed that a Mr. Montgomery, who lives at Alicant, took upon himself (for I think he had no Authority) to make Overtures last Winter, in behalf of our States, towards a Treaty with the Emperor of Marocco; In consequence of his Proceedings, I received a Letter in August, from a Person who acquainted me that he was arrived in Spain by the Emperor's Order, and was to come to Paris, there to receive and conduct to Marocco, the Minister of Congress appointed to make that Treaty, intimating at the same time an Expectation of Money to defray his Expences.[3] I communicated the Letter to Mr. Jay. The Conduct of Mr. Montgomery appeared to us very extraordinary and irregular; and the Idea of a Messenger from Marocco coming to Paris to meet and conduct a Minister of Congress, appearing absurd and extravagant, as well as the Demand of Money by a Person unknown, I made no answer to the Letter, and I know not whether Mr. Jay made any to Mr. Montgomery who wrote about the same time. But I have lately received another Letter from the same Person,[4] a Copy of which I enclose, together with my Answer[5] open for your Perusal, and it is submitted to your Discretion whether to forward it or not. The Mr. *Crocco* who writes to me having been as he says at Madrid, you possibly may know more of him than I can do, and judge whether he is really a Person in Credit with the Emperor and sent as he pretends to be; or not rather an *Escroc*, as the French call Cheats and Impostors. I would not be wanting in any thing proper for me to do, towards keeping that Prince in good humour with us, till the Pleasure of Congress is known, and therefore would answer Mr. Crocco if he be in his Employ; but am loth to commit myself in Correspondence with a Fripon. It will be strange if being at Madrid he did not address himself to you. With great & unalterable Regard I am ever, my dear Friend, Yours most affectionately.   B. FRANKLIN

M. Carmichael

3. Crocco to BF, July 15: XL, 310–12.
4. Above, Nov. 25.
5. Immediately below.

To Crocco

Press copy of LS:[6] National Archives

Sir, Passy, Dec. 15. 1783

I have just received the Letter you did me the honour of writing to me the 25th. past. I did indeed receive your former Letter of July,[7] but being totally a Stranger to the mentioned Proceedings of Mr. Montgomery and having no Orders from Congress on the Subject, I knew not how to give you any satisfactory answer, till I should receive farther Information; and I communicated your Letter to Mr. Jay, Minister of the United States for Spain, in whose District Mr. Montgomery is, and who is more at hand than I am for commencing that Negociation. Mr. Jay who is at present in England, has possibly written to you, tho' his Letter may have miscarried, to acquaint you, that Mr. Montgomery had probably no Authority from Congress to take the Step he has done;[8] and that it was not likely that they desiring to make a Treaty with the Emperor, would think of putting his Majesty to the Trouble of sending a Person to Paris to receive and conduct their Minister, since they have Ships, and could easily land him at Cadiz or present him at one of the Emperor's Ports. We have however written to Congress, acquainting them, with what we had been informed of the good and favourable Dispositions of his Imperial Majesty to enter into a Treaty of Amity and Commerce with the United States;[9] and we have no doubt but that as soon as their Affairs are a little settled, which by so severe a War carried on in the Bowels of their Country by one of the most powerful Nations of Europe, have necessarily been much deranged, they will readily manifest equally good Dispositions; and take all the proper Steps to cultivate and secure the Friendship of a Monarch, whose Character, I know, they have long esteemed and respected. I am, Sir, Your most obedient & most humble Servant B FRANKLIN

M Crocco

6. In L'Air de Lamotte's hand.

7. XL, 310–12.

8. We have no record of Jay's having written to Crocco before March 11, 1785, when he informed him that Congress had not given Montgomery any authority to make overtures to the Moroccan emperor for a treaty of commerce: Giunta, *Emerging Nation*, II, 580–1.

9. XL, 605, 621.

To David Rittenhouse

Reprinted from William Temple Franklin, ed., *Memoirs of the Life and Writings of Benjamin Franklin* ... (3 vols., 4to, London, 1817-18), III, 464.

SIR,   Passy, Dec. 15, 1783.

All astronomical news that I receive, I think it my duty to communicate to you. The following is just come to hand, in a letter from the President of the Royal Society, dated at London the 9th instant.[1]

"A miserable comet made its appearance to Mr. Nathan Pigot, in his observatory at Yorkshire, on the 19th past, and the weather has been so hazy in the evenings that it has scarce been observed since. It was on the 19th

	h.	m.	Right Ascen.			North Dec.
"at 11	15	41	0	0		3° 10'
"On the 20th	10	54	40	0	0	4 32

"On the 21st it was seen in the place where it was expected; but the night was too hazy to observe it.

"It appears like a nebula, with a diameter of about two minutes of a degree; the nucleus faint. It is seen with difficulty when the wires of the instrument are illuminated, but is not visible with an open[2] glass." —Mr. Pigot.

"Nov. 29th. It was seen near the chin of Aries, and appeared like a nebulous star: as there was some moon-light, it was difficult to find it.

"Dec. 1st. It was removed near the preceding eye of Aries; but conceiving other astronomers who had fixed instruments,

---

1. Joseph Banks to BF, Dec. 9. Banks's punctuation is scanty and his hand, in places, nearly indecipherable. It is evident from this transcription that either BF rendered the text grammatical when copying it for Rittenhouse or WTF, as was his wont, edited the letter for publication. We relied on this transcription when making our own, published above, but note below one word that was misread. The error was most likely introduced by the individual employed by WTF c. 1817 to prepare copies for the printer. Unfortunately, neither the copy nor the original from which it was made has survived.

2. The word was "opera."

have noted its place, he has not calculated the distance from any known star."—Mr. Herschell.

With great esteem, I have the honor to be, &c.

B. FRANKLIN

To Vergennes[3] LS:[4] Archives du Ministère des affaires étrangères

Sir,   Passy, Dec. 15. 1783.

I understand that the Bishop or Spiritual Person who superintends or governs the Roman Catholic Clergy in the United States of America, resides in London, and is supposed to be under Obligations to that Court, and subject to be influenced by its Ministers. This gives me some uneasiness, and I cannot but wish that one should be appointed to that Office, who is of this Nation and who may reside here among our Friends. I beg your Excellency to think a little of this Matter, and to afford me your Counsels upon it. With the greatest Respect, I am, Sir, Your Excellency's most obedient and most humble Servant[5]

B FRANKLIN

3. This letter appears to be the first time BF consulted Vergennes on a topic he had discussed in July and August with Archbishop Pamphili, the papal nuncio: how the Catholic Church could best minister to its American followers after independence. The memoranda BF sent Pamphili in August included the suggestion that a French ecclesiastic (rather than an American) be named bishop or vicar apostolic for the United States, a suggestion he repeats here: XL, 410–12, 516–18. In October, Pamphili assured the Vatican that he would continue discussions with BF about establishing missions in America until the issue was concluded: Jules A. Baisnée, *France and the Establishment of the American Catholic Hierarchy: the Myth of French Interference (1783–1784)* (Baltimore, 1934), p. 57.

4. In the hand of L'Air de Lamotte. BF added the last six words of the complimentary close before signing.

5. We have no record of a response, but docketing on the present document indicates that a translation was made and sent on Dec. 29 to Marbeuf, the bishop of Autun and minister of ecclesiastical benefices. Marbeuf sent his "Observation" to Vergennes on Jan. 4. He advised that before making any decision about the ecclesiastic superior, Vergennes should examine Pamphili's proposal that the French government establish a mission in America and train 20 students of different ages in colleges and seminaries (at an annual cost of 1,000 *l.t.* per student) who would serve in America

His Excelly. the Count de Vergennes.

Endorsed: M. de R[6]

From Laurent-Jean-Antoine de Leutre[7]

ALS: American Philosophical Society

Or∴ de paris, le 15e. jour du 10e. mois,
T∴ C∴ F∴[8]   5783. [*i.e.,* December 15, 1783]

L'homme justement celebre, le citoyen vertueux, le philosophe aussi humain qu'eclairé qui a donné la liberté à sa patrie, et qui voit couronner ce grand ouvrage par la paix générale, doit être le plus bel ornement d'une fête celebre à l'occasion de cette paix si desirée. Ce sont ces motifs, T.C.F. qui portent les freres de la R∴ L∴ du Contrat Social, M∴ L∴ Ec∴[9] à l'or∴ de paris, à vous inviter à assister au *Te Deum* qu'ils feront célébrer mercredi prochain, et aux travaux maçoniq∴ auxquels ils se livreront ensuite dans leur local, rue Coq-héron. Ces travaux tendroient à leur perfection si vous veniez les éclairer de vos vives lumieres.[1]

Nous avons la faveur d'être par l.n.m.c. et C.p.u.(?), T∴ C∴ F∴ Vos très affectionnés et devoués Serviteurs et freres les membres de la R∴ M∴ L∴ Ec∴   DELEUTRE
Secretaire general
Par Mandement

---

upon graduation. Pamphili also wanted the king to endow a bishop or an apostolic prefect, at the cost of 12,000 *l.t.* per year. Marbeuf emphasized that Vergennes should consult BF before making a final decision. This Jan. 4 letter (AAE) is published in Baisnée, *France and the Establishment of the American Catholic Hierarchy,* pp. 61–2.

6. Gérard de Rayneval.

7. De Leutre (Deleutre) (b. 1746), secretary of the masonic lodge Saint-Jean d'Ecosse du Contrat Social, was a banker and director-general of a porcelain factory in the faubourg Saint-Denis: Le Bihan, *Francs-maçons parisiens.*

8. Très cher frère.

9. Respectable Loge . . . Mère Loge Ecossaise.

1. BF also received two printed invitations to the Te Deum, signed by De Leutre (APS). It was to be sung "dans l'Eglise de Messieurs les Prêtres de

From Madame Sorin[2]   AL: American Philosophical Society

Paris ce 15. xbre. 1783.

Mde. Sorin a l'honneur de faire mille complimens à monsieur franklin et d'Envoyer savoir de Ses nouvelles. Elle lui aurait infiniment d'obligation si il pouvait lui procurer un Exemplaire du Traité de paix des Etâts unis de L'amérique avec l'angleterre et un autre de cette même puissance avec L'Espâgne.

Mde. Sorin ainsi que Mr. et Mde. Roger[3] prient Monsieur franklin d'assurer monsieur son petit fils de leurs civilités Et du désir qu'ils ont de le voir.

M. franklin.

From Thomas Barclay[4]

LS: Archives du Ministère des affaires étrangères; copy: Library of Congress

Sir,   Auteuil 16 Decemr. 1783

I return you the Papers relative to the Attachments laid on the property of the United States by Messrs. Forsters & Puchelberg & Co.[5] and I beg leave to remark that as on the one hand

l'Oratoire de la rue Saint-Honoré, le Mercredi 17 Décembre 1783, à onze heures très-précises du matin."

2. Who spent summers in Passy; see XXXVI, 131n. We now know that her name was Aglaé-Marguerite Blavet du Marais, that she died in 1823 at the age of 91, and that her husband Jean-Louis Sorin de Bonne had died c. July, 1781: E. Ledru, "Notes sur Épernon," *Mémoires de la Société archéologique de Rambouillet*, XX (1908), 288; *Jour. de Paris*, July 25, 1781.

3. Pierre-François Roger du Quéné, a *conseiller au parlement* of Rouen, and his wife, Anne-Marguerite-Charlotte Bourdet, the niece of Mme Sorin: Gérard Fabre, *Joseph Boze, 1745–1826: Portraitiste de l'Ancien Régime à la Restauration* (Paris, 2004), pp. 38–41; Edmond Cleray, "Une amie de Mme Vigée-Lebrun . . . ," *L'Art et les artistes*, XII (1910–11), 67.

4. Barclay had just returned from a three-month trip to Lorient and Nantes, attending to his business affairs: XL, 407n. During that time, Rayneval informed him of Vergennes' Oct. 24 letter to BF: Rayneval to Barclay, Nov. 16, 1783, AAE.

5. Earlier that day, Barclay asked WTF to send them to him; they were Vergennes' letters to BF of Oct. 24 and Dec. 3, with their enclosures. Bar-

I never did mean to bring up a new Mode of arranging such affairs, neither on the other, have I been willing to give up a point which I look'd upon as a National Concern, by pleading it in a Foreign Court as an Affair between two Subjects— I apprehend the Custom of Countries on similar occasions must be well known, and therefore whatever it be, I suppose your Excellency will have no objection to conform to it now.

The demands made by Messrs. Fosters and Puchelberg having arisen before my Arrival in France I need not trouble you with many remarks concerning them, I shall however observe that Congress having directed Mr. Johnson to examine Mr. Puchelberg's account do's not by any means establish the Debt to be due to him before it is Examin'd—[6] My Commission superceded Mr. Johnson's[7] and I am ready to settle the account when ever I am call'd upon, and to Certify whatever Balance appears due, this I offer'd to do at Nantes when the Claim was made in the Name of Mr. Schweighauser[8] but it now stands Transfer'd to that of Puchelberg and indeed I do not know which of them have the demand.— It has been said, that I defended the Cause already in the Court at L'Orient, but this I apprehend is a mistake, for I know of no defence made there, but what Mr. Moylan, who is no Agent of Congress, made in behalf of the Crew, whose property was involved in the Attachments. If any thing farther was done it was without my knowledge, and never shou'd have had my Approbation, as I always thought it a great National Concern, that an Equipment, form'd by a Sovereign Power, shou'd not be defeated by a demand, whether real or pretended, made by a Subject of another in Alliance.—

---

clay also asked WTF for the accounts of Sabatier fils & Després (XXIV, 122–3), which he and Matthew Ridley were to audit that day and which BF had set aside "some time ago": APS.

6. Congress appointed Johnson on Aug. 24, 1781: XXXVII, 657n.

7. Barclay was selected to examine the public accounts on Nov. 18, 1782, and BF notified him of the appointment in February, 1783: XXXVII, 735n; XXXIX, 174.

8. The firm of Schweighauser & Dobrée had requested BF's help in getting their advances reimbursed in the summer of 1782: XXXVII, 450, 657–8.

I have the Honor to be Your Excellencys Most Obedt. Most Hum. servt: THOS BARCLAY

His Excellency Benjn. Franklin Esqr.

To John Paul Jones[9]

Copies: Archives Nationales, Library of Congress[1]

[December 17, 1783]
To the Honorable Captain John Paul-Jones Commodore in the service of the United-States of America.

In pursuance of a Resolution of Congress of the first of November 1783. a Copy wereof is hereunto annexed,[2] I do hereby authorize and direct you to solicit as Agent for payment and satisfaction to the officers and crews citizens or subjects of the said states, for all Prizes taken in Europe ander your Command, and to which they are any wise intitled, and in whose hands soever the Prize-money may be detained.

[LS]   Given at Passy this seventeenth of December 1783.
signed B FRANKLIN

Minister Plenipotentiary from the United-States of America at the Court of France.

---

9. BF prepared this authorization according to the Oct. 29 instructions he received from Congress (above), which enclosed the resolution mentioned here. (BF acknowledged having received the resolution in his Dec. 25 letter to Mifflin, below.) With this document in hand, Jones met with Vergennes and Castries and was presented anew to the king on Dec. 20: Morison, *Jones*, p. 338. He sent the original of the present document to Castries on Feb. 1, 1784, asking for a settlement: Bradford, *Jones Papers*, reel 7, no. 1496.

1. This copy (badly faded, but apparently in Jones's hand) is among TJ's papers: Bradford, *Jones Papers*, reel 7, no. 1491.

2. The Nov. 1 resolution (*JCC*, XXV, 787–8) named Jones as agent to solicit, under BF's direction, prize money for the American officers and crewmen formerly under his command. See *Morris Papers*, VIII, 617–19, 716, 737, 741.

From Guillaume-Pierre-François Delamardelle[3]

ALS: American Philosophical Society

Monsieur   Paris ce 17 Xbre. 1783
  Comme je Crois que vous pouvez Etre instruit de La demeure
de Mr. Barclay, Et que je desirerois de Le voir; ozeroisje vous
prier de m'indiquer sa demeure. On m'a dit qu'il Etoit agent de
L'Etat de virginie, Et Chargé En Cette qualité des interets de
son Pays.[4]
  J'ay L'honeur d'Etre avec La plus haute Estime Et Le plus
grand Respect Monsieur de votre Excellence Et Encore plus de
votre merite personel Le tres humble Et tres obeissant serviteur
                      DELAMARDELLE
                      Procureur Général à St. Domingue
                      actuellement Rüe du maille
                      hotel d'angleterre.

M. franklin ministre Plenipotre. des Etats unis de L'amerique.

Notation: De Lamardelle 17 Dec 1783.—

From Joshua Barney

ALS: American Philosophical Society

Sir   Havre de Grace Decr. 19, 1783
  I have the honor to Acknowledge the Rect. of your letter
of 16th.—[5] The three Barrells and Box seeds I have this day

---

  3. Delamardelle (1732–1813), *procureur général près le conseil supérieur de
Port-au-Prince*, was the author of works on geology and law: Quérard,
France littéraire, under La Mardelle.
  4. Thomas Barclay, appointed agent of the state of Virginia in 1782, had
just returned to his home in Auteuil from a trip to Brittany: XXXVIII, 601;
Roberts and Roberts, *Thomas Barclay*, pp. 110, 130–3, 314n; Barclay to BF,
Dec. 16, above.
  5. Not found, although the substance is known. On Dec. 16, John Paul
Jones informed Barney that BF was sending him by the same post a letter
asking Barney to forward by diligence the articles he had brought: Bradford, *Jones Papers*, reel 7, no. 1490. BF also encouraged the captain to visit,
according to two passages from the now-missing letter quoted in Mary Barney, ed., *A Biographical Memoir of the Late Commodore Joshua Barney . . .*
(Boston, 1832), pp. 145–6: "If you come to Paris, I have a room and bed

shipp'd on bd. a Vessell for Rouen.[6] I hope they will arrive in Good order, the Nuts your Excelly. Speaks of I have None, but will If you think proper bring on my next Voyage a Quantity— I return you my Sincere thanks for your kind offer, but the time of my Stay is so very short I cannot embrace it, my Ship requiring my Attendance.[7] I beg your Excellency to believe that I am with the Greatest respect Your Obt. & Hble Servt. J BARNEY

Excelly. B Franklin

Addressed: A Son Excellence / Monsieur B. Francklin / Ministre Plenipotentiaire des Etats unis / de L Amérique pres la Cour de france / a Passy

Notation: Barney Dec. 19. 1783

From Jean-Baptiste Bonnefoy[8]

ALS: American Philosophical Society

Monsieur   lyon le 19 Xbre. 1783.
    Daignez excuser La liberté que je prens de vous écrire, en faveur du motif qui m'y engage. L'univers vous doit des autels

---

at your service, and shall be glad you would accept of them," and "If in anything I can serve you here, let me know, and I shall do it with pleasure."

6. They would be sent from there to Passy. In a letter from Barney to WTF of Dec. 14, the captain asked for instructions on how best to send the "three Barrells a Large case and two Small ones sent by Mrs. Bache." (He also enclosed a bill from a "poor Widow" who had been hounding him for advice; he asked for BF's opinion, and requested that BF not return the bill.) On Dec. 30, the eve of his departure from Le Havre, Barney wrote WTF acknowledging the dispatches WTF had sent and expressing the hope that "the Barrells & Box of Seeds for your Grandfather" had arrived safely. Both letters are at the APS. For the items sent by the Baches see RB's letter of Nov. 5.

7. Barney's orders were to remain at Le Havre and wait three weeks for BF's dispatches before returning: Barney, *Biographical Memoir,* p. 145.

8. Bonnefoy (Bonnefoi) (1756–1790) was a Lyonnais surgeon. In addition to the works mentioned in the present letter, he also wrote *Analyse raisonnée des rapports des commissaires chargés par le roi de l'examen du*

pour votre sublime découverte des paratonnerres; l'amérique qui vous doit sa liberté aquitera cette dette, et au bas de votre statue sera gravé ce vers devenu immortel:

Eripuit coelo fulmen, sceptrum que tyrannis[9]

Je vois cette nouvelle partie du monde, ayant à peine secoué les chaînes de son esclavage, élever sa tête avec majesté. Tout y dispose à une heureuse révolution; les charmes de la liberté naissante y apèlent de toute part Le comerce, les arts et les sciences dont les progrès ont une si grande influence sur la prosperité des états. Parmi les sciences il en est une que son utilité indispensable ne permet pas d'oublier, c'est La chirurgie: cultivant cette science par état et par gout, mes vœux seraient comblés si je la voyais parvenir à Son dernier degré de perfection; cependant dans l'univers entier il n'y a que la france et l'angleterre qui aient une chirurgie qui est encore bien loins du terme qu'elle doit atteindre; et combien de siècles n'a-t-il pas fallu pour en venir jusques la; combien d'obstacles à vaincre, combien de préjugés à combatre? J'ai conçu un plan dont l'execution doit porter en Douze ans la chirurgie américaine presqu'à son derniers degré de perfection, et voilà l'objet de la lettre que j'ai l'honeur de vous écrire.—

Je suis membre du colège de chirurgie de Lyon, j'y ai soutenu pour mon agrégation une dissertation sur l'aplication de l'électricité à l'art de guérir,[1] dont j'ai eu l'honeur de vous envoyer un exemplaire; je viens de remporter un prix à l'académie de chirurgie de paris sur l'influence des passions de l'ame dans les maladies chirurgicales;[2] j'ai l'honeur d'être conu de MM. Louis, secrétaire de L'académie,[3] peyrilhe auteur de l'histoire

magnétisme animal (Lyon, 1784), which BF owned: Wolf and Hayes, *Library of Benjamin Franklin.*

9. The first line of Turgot's sestet: XXVI, 670–1n.

1. *Mémoire sur l'application de l'électricté à l'art de guérir* (Lyon, 1783).

2. *Mémoire sur l'influence des passions de l'ame dans les maladies chirurgicales* (Lyon, 1783).

3. Antoine Louis (1723–1792), secretary of the Académie royale de chirurgie: Larousse.

de la chirurgie,[4] De Sault,[5] baudeloque,[6] chopart,[7] tous célè-
bres chirurgiens de paris et qui ont été mes professeurs; Mr De
La Martinière premier chirurgien du roi,[8] qui vient de mourir
m'avait fait des ofrès aussi flateuses qu'honorables pour me fixer
à paris; l'amour de ma patrie l'a emporté, et pour me déterminer
à faire ce dernier sacrifice, il ne faudrait rien moins que l'espoir
d'être un jour l'instaurateur de la chirurgie américaine: excusez
cette espèce d'apologie, je l'ai crue nécessaire pour vous prouver
que je n'etais pas un aventurier, et que les seuls motifs qui me
dirigeaient etaient l'amour que j'ai pour la chirurgie, et le zèle
qui m'enflâme pour ses progrès. Si vous croyez que mes idées
puissent être de quelque utilité, j'aurai l'honeur de vous envoyer
le détail du plan que j'ai conçu, et si je suis assez heureux pour
qu'il réponde à mes intentions, l'amérique à qui vous êtes si cher
à tant de titres, vous devra encore la perfection d'une des sciences les plus utiles à l'humanité.[9]

Daignez agréer les sentimens les plus sincères du profond respect avec lequel j'ai l'honeur d'être Monsieur Votre très humble et très obéissant serviteur   BONNEFOY
                                    membre du colège de chirurgie
                                    de lyon maison de
                                    Mr de fétan, rue Sala[?]

Notation: Bonnefoi 19 Decbre. 1783.

4. Surgeon Bernard Peyrilhe (1735–1804) was the author of the second
volume of *Histoire de la chirurgie* (2 vols., Paris, 1774–1780), as well as a
third volume that was never published: *Biographie universelle,* under Peyrilhe and Dujardin.

5. Pierre-Joseph Desault (1744–1796), a member of the academy and a
surgeon at the Hôpital de la Charité: *DBF.*

6. Jean-Louis Baudelocque (1745–1810), a renowned obstetrician. His
Principes sur l'art des accouchements..., first published in 1775, and *L'Art des
accouchements ...*, first published in 1781, became the standard reference
works for French midwives: *DBF.*

7. François Chopart (1743–1795), a member of the academy and chief
surgeon at the Hôpital de la Charité: *DBF.*

8. Germain Pichault de la Martinière: *Almanach royal* for 1783,
pp. 604, 610.

9. BF's response (if sent) has not been located, but he intended to answer;
Bonnefoy's name is on BF's list of letters to write [*c.* Jan. 1?], below.

From Anne d'Estko[1]   ALS: American Philosophical Society

Monseigneur   Le 19. Xbre 1783. à Brzescü en Lithuanie.

Je n'ai nul droit qui puisse m'autoriser à Vous demander une grace, mais je sais par Votre grande reputation jusqu'a quel point Votre Ame èst bienfaisante, et qu'en lui offrant les moyens de faire une bonne action on peut s'adresser à Vous avec confiense: Mon Frere Thadé Koscüuszko[2] passé depuis long tems au service des Etats Unis de l'Amerique, m'a laissé en partant la direction et le soin de ses bien et, de ses terres, comme il n'a pas donné aucun nouvelle depuis son depart, et que le bruit s'est repandû qu'il etoit mort, les Creancier de son Frere Ainé (:qui a dissipé tout son bien:)[3] veuillent s'emparer de ces terres, qui effectivement en cas de la mort du dit mon Frere Thadé Koscüuszko doivent comme de raison apartenir a la succession de son Frere et passer entre les mains de ses Creanciers, dans cette extremité j'ai recours à la protection de V:E: en le supliant de vouloir bien prendre dans son paÿs des informations de l'existence de mon Frere Thadé Koscüuszko et de m'expedier un certificat ministeriale a ce necessaire, qui sera bien respecté dans nos Tribuneaux, et fera taire les Usurpateurs. Je prend la liberté de joindre ici pour

---

1. Anna Barbara Krystyna Estkowa (1741–1814), the elder sister of Tadeusz Kościuszko. When Kościuszko left Poland in 1775 he made Anna's husband, Piotr Estko, his legal representative: James S. Pula, *Thaddeus Kościuszko: the Purest Son of Liberty* (New York, 1999), pp. 22, 30–1, 211–2; Bartłomiej Szyndler, *Tadeusz Kościuszko, 1746–1817* (Warsaw, 1991), p. 438.

2. Tadeusz Andrzej Bonawentura Kościuszko (1746–1817), who was trained in engineering and artillery, sailed to Philadelphia in the summer of 1776. He offered his services to the American army and soon was appointed a colonel of engineers. He served with distinction under Generals Gates and Greene, supervising the construction of major fortifications (including those that contributed to the victory at Saratoga in 1777), and eventually assuming the duties of a cavalry officer. Congress honored him after the war's conclusion with an appointment as brigadier general. Kościuszko was a founding member of the Society of the Cincinnati and a member of the APS. He returned to his native land in the summer of 1784 and became a leading figure there in the struggle for independence. *DAB.*

3. Józef Kościuszko's poor management had brought the family estate to the verge of bankruptcy by 1774: Pula, *Thaddeus Kościuszko*, pp. 30, 211–2; Szyndler, *Tadeusz Kościuszko*, p. 449.

303

l'information de V:E: l'extrait d'une lettre ecrite de Paris par
Mr: le Comte de Murinet a S:A: madame la Princesse Sapieha,[4]
qui a la bonté de s'interesser au sort de mon Frere, cette lettre
auroit sufit pour contaster [constater] l'existence de mon Frere,
d'autant plus que Monsieur le Comte de Murinet etant extremement respecté dans notre paÿs son temoignage auroit été d'un
grand poids, mais comme sa lettre n'est pas signé de son nom
(comme il se pratique ordinairement dans la correspondence
Amical:) ainsi Elle ne peut pas etre recevable aux jugements.

Il n'est pas sans doute necessaire que je cherche à Vous interesser dans cette affaire que Vous trouverez certainement bien
juste et meritant Votre compassion. Je crois avoir assez dit Votre
bon coeur dira le reste. Trés flaté que cette occasion me procure
l'avantage de pouvoir vous presenter mes hommages, que Vos
vertûs et votre grand Nom nous a inspiré; quoique nous sommes les habitants le plus eloignés et le plus ignorés du reste de
l'Univers, nous ne cessons cepandant de partager l'admiration
de l'Europe entiere a cet egard; que n'avons nous pas un Franklin pour nous voir hors de l'opression.

J'ai l'honneur d'etre Monseigneur de Votre Excellence la tres
humble et tres obeissante Servante.

ANNE D'ESTKO NÉE KOSCÜIUSZKO

P.S. Je joint ici la lettre pour mon Frere que je Vous suplie de
faire parvenir a mon Frere.

P.S. Mon adresse est par Varsovie, Brzescü, Lithuanie.

Ou si vous aimez mieux remetre Votre lettre à m: le Comte de
Murinet elle me parviendra surement sous l'envelope de Me. la
Princesse Sapieha, qui m'a permis de m'en servir de son adresse.

4. The extract is of a letter dated Dec. 8, 1781. The comte de Murinais assured the princess that he had made inquiries about Kościuszko.
The engineer was reportedly fine, was currently serving under the comte
de Grasse in Virginia, and had earned great recognition in the American
army. Murinais predicted that he would soon return to his country "avec
des Lauriers Amerique." APS. Murinais forwarded the present letter to BF
on Feb. 25, on Princess Sapieha's behalf; see his letter, below.

From Joseph-Jérôme Le Français de Lalande

ALS: Dartmouth College Library

au College royal le 19 dec. 1783.

Monsieur et illustre confrere

J'ai reçu avec bien de la reconoissance la lettre que votre Excellence a pris la peine de m'ecrire pour m'apprendre les observations de la nouvelle comete;[5] je les communiquerai a l'academie de votre part; mais ce qui m'est personel c'est l'obligation que je vous ai d'avoir daigné vous Souvenir de moi dans cette occasion. Celui qui fait la gloire de l'humanité dans les deux hemispheres est Sur d'exalter l'amour propre de tout autre humain quand il daigne lui donner une marque de consideration ou d'amitié.

Je Suis avec un profond respect et p.l.n.c.d.s.m.[6] Monsieur et tres respectable frere Votre tres humble et tres obeissant Serviteur   LaLande

From John and Rosamond Sargent

AL: American Philosophical Society

London 19th Decem 1783 Ormond Street

Mr. & Mrs. Sargent present Their most affectionate Compliments to Dr. Franklin, & being acquainted by Monsr. Charettier,[7] the Gentleman Mr. S. introduced to His Acquaintance some Time agoe, He was returning to Paris, on the Business of His Mission, could not help seizing the Opportunity to assure The Doctor of Their constant Regard & Devotion—& desiring, if He comes hither, in the Spring, or Summer ensuing, as a Friend of Dr. Price's, flatters Him with,[8] He would give Himself no Trouble to look out for a House, but be pleased to accept of His, which, tho' not like His Hotel, is decent, clean, & commodious,—&

5. See Banks to BF, Dec. 9, and BF to Rittenhouse, Dec. 15. BF's letter to Lalande has not been located.

6. An abbreviation standing for a variant of "Par les noms connus des frères maçons," a phrase the freemasons often used in letters to one another: XXXV, 88. Lalande, a founding member of the Neuf Sœurs, had preceded BF as *vénérable* of the lodge: XXVI, 697; XXIX, 528–9.

7. John Charretié; see his letter of Dec. 28.

8. BF wrote to Price about a possible visit in his letter of Sept. 16, above.

within Seven Doors of Lord Thurlows,—⁹& by the Neighbours preferrd to His,— & is, with His County House, & Equipage, entirely at His Service—and His Wife, & He offer Him with the same *bonne Voluntè, & bon Coeur* as to Their Father—

They are Both very well, & Mrs. Chambers Their Mother, & Their Children the same—Long to see Him & to embrace Him—but, shall be ashamed to converse with Him on the Subject of this Country & it's Government, which is daily sinking deeper & deeper in Disgrace—as You will soon hear—

Adieu Dear Sir.

We have but a few Minutes to write This, But You will consider Us ever Your affectionate

From the Marquis de Vaudreuil¹ and Other Consulship Seekers
ALS: American Philosophical Society

The number of solicitations for American consulships in European ports, sent by either the candidates themselves or people recommending them, began to diminish during the period covered by this volume.² Franklin continued to explain that he had no power to grant such appointments. The question of whether foreign nationals would be permitted to serve as American consuls would not be settled until March 16, 1784, when Congress resolved to restrict such consulships to United States citizens.³

Writing from Paris on September 17, Carrèl, "ancien consul du Roy d'Espagne,"⁴ forwards a *mémoire* from Jean Larrouy, a merchant

9. Edward Thurlow, the former and future lord chancellor; see David Hartley to BF, Dec. 25. Thurlow lived at 45 Great Ormond St.: Henry B. Wheatley, *London, Past and Present: Its History, Associations, and Traditions* . . . (3 vols., London, 1891), II, 617.

1. The celebrated naval officer who commanded the French squadron that in 1782 transported Rochambeau's troops back to France; see XXIX, 180; XXXI, 272; XXXVIII, 70–71, 76–7, 332n, 505n.

2. All the documents described here are in French and at the APS unless otherwise noted.

3. *JCC*, XXVI, 144–5.

4. A Pierre Carrel was vice-consul for Spain at La Rochelle: *Almanach royal* for 1779, p. 505.

in Andaye (Hendaye) who wishes to be named vice-consul there. The enclosed *mémoire* points out that this appointment would be especially useful if the nearby city of Bayonne should be established as a free port.

Tournachon, the deputy from Lyon to the Conseil royal de commerce, reminds Franklin on September 26 that he had both written and visited Passy to discuss the appointment of Aimé Bonnaffons, a Lyon merchant, to be the American consul in Genoa. Franklin had been too ill to receive him when he called, but Franklin's grandson had told him to send a memoir that could be forwarded to the United States. He encloses one.[5]

Thirty-year-old Franz Rudolph von Grossing,[6] who calls himself Grossing de Leidenthal, writes from Gotha on November 10, detailing his qualifications to be named American consul for all the German principalities. Descended from a noble Hungarian family, he was named secretary to Maria Theresa three years ago and at her request was groomed for a diplomatic career by the imperial chancellor and the foreign minister. Joseph II had asked him to draft a policy on tolerance, which was adopted in large part and which von Grossing is currently translating into French. He lost his position because of an envious cabal and has written three works that express his anti-tyrannical sentiments.[7] America could not do better than to take him into its service; he speaks many languages, including English, and is familiar with European courts. He would accept the position for 100 *louis d'or* per year. He currently lives at the court of the duke of Saxe-Gotha, where he is retained as a "Cavalier de conversation," discussing literary matters for two hours a day. He has a violent, tormenting passion to go to America. In a postscript, he adds that he is enclosing a copy of

5. Tournachon's previous letter was written on Aug. 25 (XL, 219). His third and final letter, dated April 7, 1784, enclosed another memoir on behalf of Bonnaffons. APS. (In his three letters Tournachon spelled the candidate's name Bonnaffons, Bonnafons, and Bonnafond, respectively.)

6. Identified in [Carlo] Denina, *La Prusse littéraire sous Frédéric II* (3 vols., 1790–91; reprint, Geneva, 1968), II, 153–4; Constant von Wurzbach, ed., *Biographisches Lexikon des Kaiserthums Oesterreich* . . . (60 vols., Vienna, 1856–91).

7. He names them in French: "Systeme universel de Tolerance et de Religion pour tous les Pays de Monde" (*Allgemeines Toleranʒ und Religions-System für alle Staaten und Völker der Welt* [Leipzig, 1784]), "L'Eglise et L'Etat leur droits, et dévoirs mutuels" (*Die Kirche und der Staat: ihre beyderseitige Pflicht Macht und Gränʒen* [Berlin, 1784]), and "L'Histoire des Papes" (*Papstengeschichte im Grundriss* [Göttingen, 1784]).

a promissory note given by Arendt, a colonel in the American service, to a certain Fritsch of Frankfort.[8] Would Franklin or some other ambassador take charge of satisfying the debt?[9]

On December 15, *capitaine de vaisseau* Georges-René Pléville Le Pelley of Marseille writes what he says is his second letter since the peace soliciting Franklin's help in obtaining a consulship in Marseille for his son-in-law, Luc Laugier.[1] Le Pelley describes his own service in the war under d'Estaing and as adjutant of the French army's *intendant* in Boston, during which time he was assaulted. He also describes the record of his late son, who served with him under d'Estaing on the *Languedoc* in 1778, became a lieutenant, and was captured by the British and released out of consideration for Le Pelley's having saved an English ship in 1770 (for which he received a fine gift from the British nation).[2] Within days of having returned to France after the peace, his son died of a fever. Le Pelley helps Americans whenever possible, within his limited means, and has procured work for them on French merchant ships while he helped find them passage home. An American consul in Marseille would be very useful.

On December 16, the Paris banker Beauregard recommends to Franklin the merchant Louis Berail of Cette (Sète) in Languedoc for the position of American consul in that port. He encloses Berail's undated petition at the candidate's request. It explains that Berail speaks German, Dutch, Italian, and a little English, and for the past three

8. While on a year's leave from the American army Arendt had stayed in an *auberge* run by Fritsch, from whence he wrote to BF in 1779; see XXIX, 501–3; XXXII, 372n.

9. The note, dated Paris, May 23, 1780, acknowledges a debt of 100 rix-dollars, payable in one year. In case of Arendt's death or failure to repay, he grants Fritsch permission to send a copy to BF or some other American ambassador for the purpose of collecting the money, which represents 20 months of salary and other claims on the United States.

After completing his service in America, Arendt returned to France in the fall of 1782, presenting BF with an order from Robert Morris to remit the balance due him. BF did so: XXXVIII, 213.

1. The only other extant letter from Pléville Le Pelley was written in March. It concerned a prize ship that was partially owned by his son-in-law, whose firm, Ginette frères et Luc Laugier, also wrote to BF. See XXXIX, 404–5, 406; Le Pelley is identified on p. 406n.

2. A letter of thanks from the Lords of the Admiralty and a silver service: Christian de La Jonquière, *Les Marins français sous Louis XVI: Guerre d'indépendance américaine* (Issy-les-Moulineaux, France, 1996).

years has served as vice-consul for Sardinia.[3] Franklin also receives an undated petition in excellent English from the candidate's father, Peter Berail. Writing on behalf of Peter Berail & Cie., a firm consisting of himself and his son, he offers their services as consul or commissary at Cette.[4] Berail *père* hopes that Franklin will appoint his son as American agent while they await congressional approval for the consulship. For forty years his firm has been in charge of the English and American trade, including all tobacco from Virginia, and they have served as interpreters for ship captains and for tobacco exporter Samuel Martin.

Finally, we summarize three undated appeals that remain among Franklin's papers but cannot be linked to any other correspondence.

François-Barthélemy Paquet Dubellet hopes to be named the American consul in Boulogne. He is the *procureur* of the *sénéchaussée* of Boulogne-sur-Mer, and is about thirty years old. He has traveled in America and speaks good English. Franklin endorsed his *mémoire* "Recommendé par Made. de Dardoncelle".

Pierre Ferée Darcour, formerly a *capitaine de vaisseau* but now married and established as a merchant in Le Havre, hopes to be named consul there. During his long career at sea he sailed many times to the Americas, particularly Saint-Pierre. He knows the "Ameriquaine" language and writes it fluently.[5]

The baron de la Houze, French minister at Copenhagen,[6] sends a one-sentence note asking that Touton Van Oosterom, a merchant in Bayonne,[7] be named American consul there.

Monsieur   Paris le 19 Xbre. 1783

J'ai eû l'honneur d'envoyer à Votre excellence, le 3e 9bre. dernier, deux Mémoires que M. Pacaud, interprête pour le Roi au Cap francois de l'isle de st. Domingue m'a chargé de vous remettre et par lesquels il sollicite la place de Consul des Etats

3. Louis Berail is listed as vice-consul for Sardinia in the *Almanach royal* for 1783, p. 266. He is also named among the principal merchants of Cette in the *Almanach des marchands* for 1785, p. 156.

4. Hist. Soc. of Pa.

5. BF endorsed this letter "Pierre Ferrée Consulat at Havre".

6. XXXI, 405n.

7. In fact, one of the leading firms of Bayonne: *Almanach des marchands* for 1779, p. 74; Josette Pontet-Fourmigué, *Bayonne: un destin de ville moyenne à l'époque moderne* (Biarritz, 1990), pp. 616–18, 629–30, 634–5, 651. This letter is at the Hist. Soc. of Pa.

unis de l'Amérique dans cette Colonie.[8] Je vous reitere, Monsieur, tout le bien que je vous ai dit de M. Pacaud et je vous prie de vouloir bien les faire parvenir au Congrès. Je serai très reconnoissant de ce que Votre Excellence voudra bien faire pour ce Mr. auquel je m'intéresse beaucoup et qui dans le cours de la derniere guerre a été très utile aux Americains vos Compatriotes qui ont commercé dans cette Partie des Indes occidentales.

J'ai l'honneur d'être avec une Respectueuse consideration De Votre Excellence Le très humble et très obeissant serviteur[9]

LE MIS. DE VAUDREUIL

Lt. Genal. des Armées navales, Rue de Grenelle—

From Samuel Chase

ALS: American Philosophical Society

My Dear Sir   London. 20th December 1783.

I did Myself the Honour of writing You from this City, on the 18 of September, and on the 8 of November.[1] I inclosed Papers on two Subjects, the first concerning the loss of a Ship from the Misconduct of the Commander of a french frigate, the other relating to a young Lady of Annapolis. I took the liberty to request your advice & Assistance. Both my letters were sent in the Dispatches from the Ministry here to the Minister at Paris, and therefore I flattered Myself they would come safe to your Hands. I begin to fear some Accident. I am unwilling to take up any Part of your time, which can be so much more usefully employed but I know not to whom I can apply who can render Me so much good Service and advice. If your Attention cannot be spared to the Consideration of either of the Subjects, I beg the favour of You to inform Me if my letters are received, and the Papers inclosed safe.

8. His earlier letter and the enclosures are missing.

9. BF drafted a note for a reply on a partial sheet of paper that is undated and filed separately at the APS: "That I receiv'd the Memoires, & shall not fail to communicate them to Congress, who I make no doubt will respect the Recommendation of M. le Mis de Vaudreuil if they determine to have a Consul at the Cape."

1. The first is above; the second has not been located.

You will hear of the Dismission of the late Ministry, before this reaches You. Mr Pitt is prime Minister. No other Appointment is fixed. Lord Temple will certainly be one of the Secretaries of State. Lords Camden, Gower, and Thurlow, with the Dukes of Richmond & Rutland, will be Part of the new Arrangement.[2] Lord Shelburne is rejected by all.

I beg You to accept my warmest Wishes for your Health and Happiness.

Your Affectionate and Obedt. Servt   SAM. CHASE.

You will be pleased to direct to Me at Mr Deards. Dover Street. Piccadilly.

Addressed: His Excellency / Benjamin Franklin Esqr / Minister of the united States / of America / Paris—

Notation: Chase Mr. Samuel, London 20 Decr. 1783.—

From John Paul Jones   AL: American Philosophical Society

Paris Decr. 20th. 1783

Captain Paul Jones returns his respectful Compliments to Doctor Franklin and has the honor to accept his kind Invitation for Dinner on Thursday the 25th. Instant.[3]

Addressed: His Excellency / B. Franklin Esquire &c &c / Passy

From Jonathan Williams, Sr.

ALS: American Philosophical Society

Dear sr—   Boston Decr. 20th. 1783—

I am honour'd with your favour of Sept 13th. Inclosing a Bill Drawn in my favr on Doctr. Cooper for 2722 Livres 16 *s.* 8 *d.*

2. For Pitt's cabinet, see Hartley to BF, Dec. 25.

3. This is the first of several responses to BF's invitation to dinner on Dec. 25. None of the actual invitations has been located.

being the Amount of What you have paid for the Education & other expences of his Grand Son,[4] you advice to apply to the Father if in Boston, I hear he is, but he is Shut up & good for nothing, Doctr. Cooper was Sick When I recd your Letter & Still remains at the point of death, but little hope if any of his Serviveing, there has been no time Since I recd your Bill that I Could have presented it, tho' if the Doctr Should die as I Belive he will, I hope the famley will pay it, I dont Expect that Jhnnot will or Can pay it, if I Can Obtain it, I Will place it (agreeable to your desire) on Interest for your Sister,[5] the money I recd for your Bills on Johnnot & Warin amo £171. Stg., my Wife & Aunt Settled before I Got home by her Note of hand, On Interest, which is at present better then any trade that I know off, I offerd aunt any of my Goods at the Cost when I got hom to the amo: of the Bills £171 Stg[6] but She refus'd, & its much the best for her that She did, I must Loose, Goods are So plenty from all parts that they will not fetch the Cost,— Aunt Who now Lives at Cambridge with her daughter Collis,[7] adviced me that there was a Seat that was formely ownd by Mr Oliver now Own'd by mr Andrew Cabot of Beverley, to be Sold, She thinks if you Should prefer Cambridge for a residence this Seat would Suit, you may remember the house it Stands about four miles & ½ from Charlestown ferry, one Miles & ½ from the Bridge, not a mile from the Colledge, has a boutifull prospect, a Garden of rich frute Stables & other Out houses with a hundred & Seventy Acres of Land,[8] I only mention this as Aunt mention'd it to me, I told aunt that I Should be happy to receive any Com-

4. BF's letter is missing. For the bills he had paid on behalf of Samuel Cooper Johonnot, see XL, 59–60, 468–9, 507–8.
5. On Sept. 13, the same day he wrote to Williams, BF informed Jane Mecom that he was making more money available for her: XL, 624.
6. For BF's plan to have Williams offer Mecom goods purchased in England amounting to the total of Winslow Warren's and Gabriel Johonnot's notes see XXXIX, 534n, 604; XL, 625; Van Doren, *Franklin-Mecom*, pp. 228–9.
7. Jane Mecom Collas.
8. The estate that Lieut. Gov. Thomas Oliver (XXI, 299n) abandoned in 1774 was purchased by Cabot in 1779; he sold it to Elbridge Gerry in 1787: Adeline A. Douglass, "Tory Row," in *Cambridge Sketches by Cambridge Authors*, ed. Estelle M. H. Merrill (Cambridge, Mass., 1896), pp. 34–7.

mands from you that you please to give—my Love to your Son
& all you Love, & belive me Ever Your Dutifull Nephew &
most Hble Servant   JONA. WILLIAMS

Addressed: His Excellency Benjamin Franklin Esqr / at Passy /
In / France

From Joshua Barney[9]   ALS: American Philosophical Society

Sir   Havre de Grace Decr 21st. 83.
   Yesterday in Examining Sundry Packages onbd. I found one
Directed to Your Excellency which I had brought onshore. It
was Opened & proved [*to*] be Snuff & Tobacco. I really do not
know who Sent it from America, but suppose you have letters
respecting it it seems that there is a heavy fine of 1200 *l.t.* if
I had been detected Bringing it onshore.[1] It is now With me.
Mr. Limozin[2] tells me it cannot be Sent, therefore beg Your Ex-
cellys. advice in respect to it. And am Sir With due respect, your
Obt. Servt.   J BARNEY

Excelly. *B Franklin*

Addressed: a Son Exellence / Monsieur Le Doctr. Francklin /
Ministre Plenipotentier des Treize Etats / Unis de L'Amerique a
La Cour de France / en Son Hôtel / a Passy

---

9. This is Barney's last extant letter to BF. He received BF's dispatches on
Dec. 30 and weighed anchor the next day in a terrible gale. He arrived at
the mouth of Chesapeake Bay in mid-February, but the bay being almost
entirely frozen, it took another two weeks to reach Annapolis. He arrived
there on March 5 and immediately delivered BF's dispatches to Congress:
Barney to WTF, Dec. 30, 1783 (APS); notation on BF to Mifflin, Dec. 25
(below); *Maryland Jour. and Baltimore Advertiser*, March 5, 1784; Mary Barney, ed., *A Biographical Memoir of the Late Commodore Joshua Barney . . .*
(Boston, 1832), pp. 146–7.
   1. The importation of tobacco was a monopoly of the farmers general,
and smuggling was heavily fined, sometimes on the basis of dubious evidence: XXIII, 44n, 129; XXXVII, 485–6; Idzerda, *Lafayette Papers*, V, 170–1.
   2. Andrew Limozin, American agent at Le Havre, was now Thomas
Barclay's deputy: XL, 262–3; *Morris Papers*, VIII, 133n.

From Bariatinskii LS: American Philosophical Society

Around December 14, Major Pierre-Charles L'Enfant arrived in Paris from Philadelphia[3] on a mission from the Society of the Cincinnati. The society was a fraternal organization of Continental Army officers that had formed the previous spring as the troops were disbanding. Its aims, as stated in its institution (charter), included promoting national unity, maintaining ties of friendship, and providing financial support to members and their families. The society was open to all American officers who met particular standards of service and to generals and colonels in Rochambeau's army. Honorary membership was to be conferred upon men whose stature and distinguished service so merited. Members would receive an "order," initially to be a gold medal, suspended by a blue and white ribbon. In what would prove to be the most controversial provision, membership was to be hereditary, passed on to the eldest son or to worthy "collateral branches" of the family. By November, the society had established chapters in every state.[4]

L'Enfant, after redesigning the order to be a badge in the shape of an eagle,[5] sailed to France to oversee its manufacture and to help organize the French branch of the organization. He carried a letter of introduction from George Washington, president general of the society. He also carried Washington's letters to General Rochambeau, naval officers d'Estaing, de Grasse, Barras, and Destouches, former minister Gérard, and Lafayette, informing them of their election and enclosing copies of the society's institution.[6]

Upon receipt of their letters, Rochambeau wrote to Minister of War Ségur, d'Estaing to Minister of the Marine Castries, and Lafayette to Vergennes, requesting them to urge the king to allow French officers to join the society. The royal council considered the matter on December 18. Louis XVI not only gave his consent, but in a highly unusual ruling that acknowledged Franco-American friend-

3. L'Enfant sailed on the *General Washington* with Capt. Barney (see Morris to BF, Nov. 4). The ship landed at Le Havre on Dec. 8: *Gaz. de France*, Dec. 23, 1783, translated in Idzerda, *Lafayette Papers*, v, 178n. By Dec. 14 he had delivered the letters from GW described below.

4. See Minor Myers, Jr., *Liberty without Anarchy: a History of the Society of the Cincinnati* (Charlottesville, 1983), pp. 23–47, and for the text of the institution, pp. 258–65.

5. The badge is illustrated facing p. 503; see also the List of Illustrations.

6. Asa B. Gardiner, *The Order of the Cincinnati in France . . .* (n.p., 1905), pp. 7–9.

ship he granted the officers license to wear their Cincinnati badges at court. Rochambeau and his colleagues immediately began planning for the establishment of a French branch.[7]

The first public announcement of the society appeared on December 23 in the *Gazette de France*. Although it was published after the royal council had met, the article did not mention the king's approbation. Written by Lafayette a week earlier (December 16) and sent to Vergennes for placement in the paper, the article announced L'Enfant's arrival, stated that the association had been founded by American officers, described the badge (explaining that the "Bald-Eagle" was a species of eagle indigenous to America), and stated that General Washington had deputized Lafayette to sign up officers of the American army in Europe and had conferred upon Rochambeau and other French officers the society's honors.[8]

If Bariatinskii was confused about the nature of the society—having heard, as he says here, that it had been endorsed by Congress—he was not alone. Long after the article appeared on December 23, Franklin would receive requests for assistance with applications for membership from French military officers who erroneously believed that Congress had established the Cincinnati and that Franklin was its representative in France.

Monsieur,   Paris ce 22. Decembre 1783.

Les marques d'amitié et d'honnetteté, que vous m'avez données en toute occasion m'ayant habitué a avoir la plus grande confiance en votre Personne et en votre Complaisance pour moi, je prends la liberté de m'adresser à vous à l'occasion d'une nouvelle qu'on m'a dit pour certaine. Il est question d'une Resolution du Congrès, par laquelle il auroit été decidé de prier le Roy de permettre aux officiers françois, qui ont servi en Amerique d'accepter les marques d'un ordre, qui auroit été crée en memoire de la Revolution arrivée. On m'a ajouté, que cette affaire, ayant été agitée au Conseil du Roy, il y auroit été decidé d'acquiescer à la resolution du Congrès. S'il en est ainsi l'affaire va devenir incessamment publique et tous les détails vont en être imprimés, et

7. Rochambeau and d'Estaing wrote their letters on Dec. 14, and Lafayette wrote on Dec. 16: *ibid.*, 9–13. See also Myers, *Liberty without Anarchy,* pp. 145–8.

8. Lafayette sent the article to Vergennes with his letter of Dec. 16, cited above. An English translation is in Idzerda, *Lafayette Papers*, v, 178n.

comme je voudrois avoir la satisfaction d'en prevenir ma Cour, je vous serois bien sensiblement obligé, Monsieur, si vous me communiquiez tant la lettre du Congrès au Roy que la decision de Sa Majesté à cet égard, si elle est dejà entre vos mains, ainsi que les statuts du nouvel ordre. Je ne crois pas commettre une indiscretion en cette occasion; mais si ma demande en etoit une, je me repose sur votre amitié même, qui saura m'excuser.

J'ai l'honneur d'être avec les sentiments d'Estime et de considération les plus distingués Monsieur, Votre trés humble et trés obéissant serviteur,   PCE. IVAN BARIATINSKOŸ

à Mr. le Docteur franklin à Passy.

To Bariatinskii   AL (draft): American Philosophical Society

[c. December 22, 1783]
I have never before heard of the Resolution of Congress you mention, and I doubt much of its Existence. Nor do I know any thing of the suppos'd Decision in Council at Versailles concerning it.[9] I understand that a Number of the American Officers have agreed to form themselves into a Society for the laudable Purpose among others of relieving their poor Widows & Orphans hereafter, and that they have made certain Rules for the Conduct of the Society; but I have no Copy of those Rules. When I have better Information, I shall communicate it to you with Pleasure.—

From John Dickinson   ALS: Harvard University Library

Sir,   Philadelphia December 22d. 1783
Mr. Vernon[1] proposing to return from a Visit to America thro France, and earnestly desiring to have the Honor of your Acquaintance, I cannot forbear complying with the Wishes of a

9. The decision had been made on Dec. 18; see the headnote to Bariatinskii's letter, above.
1. This must be Henry Vernon (1748–1814) of Hilton Park, Staffordshire, who in late 1783 accompanied Polish poet Tomasz Węgierski on a

Gentleman recommended by his Politeness and his favorable Dispositions towards this Country.

I am with the sincerest Esteem Sir, your most obedient & hble servant   JOHN DICKINSON

His Excellency Benjamin Franklin Esquire

Notation: John Dickinson 22 Decr. 1783.—

From Mercy-Argenteau, with Franklin's Note for a Reply

L: American Philosophical Society

à Paris le 22. Décembre 1783.

L'Ambassadeur de l'Empereur ayant été chargé par sa Cour de recourir à la complaisance de Monsieur Franklin relativement à l'Envoi des deux Lettres ci-jointes à l'adresse de MMrs. le Baron de Beelen et le Professeur Märter, il a l'honneur de Le prier de vouloir bien les faire passer à leur destination par la premiere occasion qui se présentera,[2] L'Ambassadeur se flatte que Monsieur Franklin voudra bien déférer à cette demande, il Lui en aura une

---

journey through Pennsylvania, New Jersey, New York, and New England. As far as we can determine, Vernon did not go to Passy until April, 1785, a few days after meeting JW at a dinner hosted by a mutual friend. Vernon showed JW several letters of introduction to BF that he was carrying. Based on the nature of those letters, JW immediately invited him, his brother-in-law Richard Dawson (with whom he was traveling), and Mr. Arthur (the mutual friend) to dine at Passy the following Saturday. Writing to inform WTF of this, JW described Vernon as "an English Gentleman of Family" and "brother to the famous Lady Grosvenor," who had recently traveled in America: JW to WTF, [April 6 or 13, 1785], APS; John Burke and John Bernard Burke, *A Genealogical and Heraldic Dictionary of the Landed Gentry of Great Britain and Ireland* (2 vols., London, 1846), II, 1478, 1550; Edmund Lodge, *The Peerage of the British Empire . . .* (2nd ed., London, 1833), pp. 120–1; Miecislaus Haiman, *Poland and the American Revolutionary War* (Chicago, 1932), pp. 119–33; Fitzpatrick, *Writings of Washington*, XXVII, 181.

2. Commercial agent Beelen-Bertholff and naturalist Franz Joseph Märter, traveling to America on government missions, had arrived in Philadelphia in September: XXXIX, 445, 474–5, 490–1; XL, 10. The enclosure for Beelen-Bertholff was probably a Dec. 4 letter (received on March 26)

obligation personnelle, et aura l'honneur d'aller lui-même Lui
en faire ses remercimens./.

Endorsed: Put this in French polite.—[3] Mr Franklin will with
Pleasure forward the Letters for Mess. Beelen & Marter, by a
Packet Boat that sails from Havre the 29th. Inst. Mr F. begs
leave to request M. l'Ambassadeur to permit this Pacquet for
Dr Ingenhause, to go by his next Courier

From Monsieur and Madame de Valnais

AL: American Philosophical Society

Paris Decembr. 22d. 1783./.

Mr. & Mrs. de Valnais's most Respectful Compliments to his
Excellency Dtr. Franklin & propose to wait upon him next
thursday agreable to his polite invitation—

Mr. de Valnais Returns his thanks to Mr. Franklin Junr. for
the Letter from Dtr. Cooper, he was So kind as to Send him
which he Receiv'd in good order.

Addressed: A Son Excéllence / Son Excéllence Monsieur /
Franklin, Ministre Plenipotentiaire / des Etats unis de L'amérique auprés / de la Cour de France / A Passi—

From ——— Harrison[4]

AL: American Philosophical Society

Hotel des armes de L'Empire rue D'auphin Paris.
23 Xbre. 83

Mr Harrison presents his respectful Compliments to His Excellency, is sensible of his polite Invitation at same Time is sorry

---

from Paul d'Almasy, governor of the port of Fiume, requesting Va. tobacco seeds for planting in Hungary: Hanns Schlitter, ed., *Die Berichte
des ersten Agenten Österreichs in den Vereinigten Staaten von Amerika Baron
de Beelen-Bertholff* . . . (Vienna, 1891), pp. 317–18.

3. Instructions for L'Air de Lamotte, who wrote the French reply on
Dec. 25, below.

4. The handwriting is unfamiliar to us. We suspect that this is the American merchant George Harrison, who was based in Nantes and met BF in

that an Indisposition that has Kept him confined since his arrival in Paris, prevents his having the Honor to wait on His Excellency on Thursday next.[5]

His Excellency Benjamin Franklin Esqr.

Addressed: A Son Excellence / Monsieur Franklin / en Son hôtel / a Passy

From Jean-Baptiste Le Roy

AL: American Philosophical Society

Tuesday morning [December 23, 1783?][6]

My Dear Doctor give me leave to Send you these two petitions The One for The Woman That I talked to you of and who cries night and Day for a Son who She thinks is dead now, having had no news from him These Seven years.[7] The other is for an Officer who fought in America for your good cause and who is the brother-in Law of The young M. Cassini. Accept my Dear Doctor of my best compliments be So good to Send me The Volue of the Encyclope in which there is the B.

August, 1783, when BF gave him a letter of introduction to Vergennes: XL, 490–1, 509.

5. Christmas day, when BF hosted a dinner party; see John Paul Jones to BF, Dec. 20.

6. The second of the two petitions enclosed in the present letter (both of which are missing) was on behalf of the vicomte de Mory, the brother-in-law of Cassini *fils*, and most likely concerned his desire to enter the Society of the Cincinnati; see Cassini *fils* to BF, Jan. 2, 1784, enclosing a similar if not identical petition. We speculate that the present letter preceded Cassini's and induced BF to send Mory the medal that Cassini acknowledges on Jan. 2. We therefore assign the present letter to the first Tuesday following the French court's acceptance of the Society of the Cincinnati (for which see the headnotes to Bariatinskii to BF, Dec. 22, 1783, and BF to SB, Jan. 26, 1784).

7. For a similar appeal from a desperate mother see XL, 20.

From Joseph Mayo[8]

AL: American Philosophical Society

Hotel de Portugal. Decr. 23. 1783—
Mr. Mayo presents his most respectful Compliments to Dr. Franklin, and is very sorry that a late illness, of which he still feels the effects, will prevent his having the honor of dining with his Excellency on thursday next.—[9]

Addressed: A Monsieur / Monsieur Franklin, Ministre / Plenipotentiare des Etats unis de l'a- / mérique— / à Passy—

From Jonathan Nesbitt

AL: American Philosophical Society

Paris Decr: 23d: 1783—
Mr: Nesbitts most respectful Compliments wait on Doctr Franklin & will do himself the honor to dine with him on Thursday next.—[1] Mr Nesbitt incloses the Letter of Mr. de Vergennes relative to the 22d Article of the Preliminary Treaty—[2]

Notation: Nesbit, Decr. 23. 1784.

Draft Consular Convention between France and the United States

D: Archives du Ministère des affaires étrangères

The Franco-American Treaty of Amity and Commerce of 1778 granted each country the right to appoint consuls, vice-consuls,

---

8. The former classmate of WTF's who came to France in 1780 and had been traveling in Europe. BF gave him a passport in July, 1782, to go to Geneva, but he was back in Paris by the fall of 1783 at the latest: XXXII, 424n; XXXVI, 380; George Fox to WTF, Oct. 7, 1783 (APS).

9. Dec. 25; see John Paul Jones to BF, Dec. 20.

1. Dec. 25; see John Paul Jones to BF, Dec. 20.

2. The enclosure is missing. Nesbitt had already sent BF a copy of Vergennes' letter to him of Oct. 20; see his Oct. 27 letter. As a result of his recent trip to Versailles, he may have obtained a copy of the letter Vergennes wrote on Nov. 15 to the underwriters of the *Nancy*, who had inquired about Article 22. Vergennes informed them that everything beyond the farthest of

agents, and commissaries in the ports of the other. Their powers, privileges, and immunities were to be stipulated in a separate agreement.[3] The present document is a draft of the convention that would be signed by Franklin and Vergennes on July 29, 1784, after years of disputes and delays.[4]

The protracted negotiations began in Philadelphia. In June, 1779, Conrad-Alexandre Gérard, the French minister to the United States, submitted to Congress a plan for regulating the consular service, which Congress referred to committee but never acted on.[5] In September of the following year, Vergennes approached Franklin, hoping he would be authorized to negotiate a consular convention. Franklin had received no such instructions. Because the Americans were unaware of what functions and powers were assigned to consuls in Europe, Franklin suggested that Vergennes send instructions to Gérard's successor, La Luzerne, and authorize him to negotiate with Congress.[6]

In July, 1781, La Luzerne submitted to Congress a draft consular convention prepared by Sartine and Vergennes, and requested that

---

the Canary Islands was included in the term of two months. Therefore, hostilities were presumed to have ceased at Philadelphia on April 4, not March 4. (Gallwey & Co. sent BF copies of this letter on Jan. 22 and 31, below.)

3. This was outlined in Article 31 of the Feb. 6, 1778, treaty (XXV, 624), but was renumbered Article 29 after two articles were dropped by mutual agreement: XXVI, 448–9, 462; XXVII, 330–2.

4. Twelve of the 16 articles remained identical to the ones here; Articles 3, 4, 6, and 8 were slightly revised. For an English translation of the signed version see Giunta, *Emerging Nation*, III, 28–35. The convention would change significantly before being ratified in 1789.

5. *JCC*, XIV, 696, 760.

6. XXXIII, 250–1, 256. BF assured Vergennes that the states were unlikely to contest Congress' authority to negotiate a consular convention, even though it was not among its enumerated powers.

As early as July 20, 1778, the American commissioners had recommended to Congress the appointment of Americans as consuls in France who would support themselves by trade and a moderate commission. The commissioners also enclosed a memorandum titled "Functions of Consuls," which reflected new changes made to the consular office by a royal edict in June. The edict distinguished French consuls from those of other European nations by giving them not just commercial but also extensive judicial and police authority over French subjects abroad: XXVII, 128–9; Wharton, *Diplomatic Correspondence*, II, 652–3; Anne Mézin, *Les Consuls de France au siècle des lumières (1715–1792)* ([Paris, 1998]), pp. 33–44.

the Americans enter into negotiations "with all possible despatch."[7] It took a congressional committee five months to review the French draft and arrive at a counterproposal. That document, produced in January, 1782, contained only a few significant changes. The most contentious issue was the jurisdiction of consuls over citizens of their respective nations at sea and on foreign soil, including the power to prevent their emigration. These issues were covered in Articles 12 through 14 of the French proposal. In revising Article 12, Congress limited the consuls' jurisdiction over their nation's ships and crews to civil cases, whereas the French draft had given them broad police powers over their nationals. Secretary for Foreign Affairs Robert R. Livingston sent the counterproposal to Franklin on January 26, along with congressional authorization for him to enter into a convention with Louis XVI, unless the king wished for that to take place in the United States. According to Congress' instructions, Franklin was to "use his discretion as to the words or arrangement of the convention," while "confining himself to the matter thereof in all respects." Excepted from this prescription was the Article 6 clause, added by Congress, allowing consuls to maintain chapels in their residences. Livingston made it clear that if Franklin substantively altered the convention, it would have to be returned to Philadelphia for signing.[8]

Before acting on his instructions, Franklin wanted to consult the American consul Thomas Barclay, who was traveling and would not get back to France until the end of August. In the meantime, Vergennes, who had known about Congress' instructions since April, was growing impatient. In mid-August he prodded Franklin to begin negotiations on the consular convention. Two weeks later, Barclay returned to Paris.[9]

Barclay reviewed the counterproposal immediately. His only objection was to Article 3, prohibiting consuls and vice-consuls from trading as merchants. He argued that this provision would exclude the most qualified candidates and force Congress to fund the entire consular service itself. Six weeks later Barclay wrote of his concerns

7. *JCC*, XXI, 792–811, 845, 1053. The French proposal is also in Giunta, *Emerging Nation*, III, 8–15. Its authorship is established by Castries to Vergennes, Jan. 31, 1784 (AAE).

8. XXXVI, 484; *JCC*, XXII, 17–28, 43–4, 46–7. The congressional counterproposal is on pp. 47–54. It is also in Giunta, *Emerging Nation*, III, 17–22.

9. XXXVII, 535, 740n; XXXVIII, 35. On Feb. 4, 1782, La Luzerne sent detailed accounts of his negotiations with Congress to Castries and Vergennes. According to the endorsement, Vergennes received it on April 26 (AAE).

to Congress, which, upon taking the matter under consideration, was deeply divided over whether to amend or suspend the convention. It ultimately failed to take any action.[1]

While on the American side the negotiations were hampered by Congress' irresolution, on the French side they became part of the long-standing rivalry between Vergennes and Castries. It was not obvious who should be in charge. The consular service was part of the naval ministry, but treaty negotiations were handled by the foreign ministry. Accordingly, La Luzerne sent an account of his discussions with Congress to both Vergennes and Castries. Vergennes sharply reminded the minister that he was to report to the foreign ministry only.[2]

On February 23, 1783, the king promoted Vergennes to *chef du conseil royal des finances*, effectively making him Castries' superior.[3] Four days later, Vergennes sent word to Franklin that he was ready to focus on the consular convention. There is no record of when the two men discussed the articles, but on April 15 Franklin reported to Livingston that the convention had "not yet been concluded." He called Congress' attention to the importance of Article 3 and urged the delegates to "reconsider" it.[4]

While Franklin waited for a response from Congress, Castries tried to insert himself into the negotiations. On May 29, 1783, he sent Vergennes his critical analysis of the congressional counterproposal. Probably aware of the ongoing talks between Vergennes and Franklin, Castries emphasized that Franklin's instructions restricted him to signing the American proposal without substantial changes. He maintained that La Luzerne should conclude the negotiations in Philadelphia, an option that Congress had kept open in its instructions to Franklin.[5] However, Vergennes had long since decided that he and Franklin would sign the convention at Versailles, without any involvement of the ministry of the marine.[6]

On August 29, just before the United States and France were to sign their definitive peace treaties with England, Vergennes' *premier commis*, Gérard de Rayneval, asked William Temple Franklin to re-

---

1. XXXVIII, 63, 553; Giunta, *Emerging Nation*, II, 55–6; William T. Hutchinson *et al.*, eds., *The Papers of James Madison*, First Series (17 vols., Chicago, London, and Charlottesville, 1962–91), VI, 5, 15–16.
2. Vergennes to La Luzerne, Oct. 14, 1782, AAE.
3. XXXIX, 203n.
4. XXXIX, 225, 470.
5. Castries to Vergennes, with enclosed *mémoire*, May 29, 1783, AAE.
6. Vergennes to La Luzerne, Oct. 14, 1782, AAE.

mind his grandfather of the consular convention, which he wished to see completed.[7] With Vergennes determined to sign at Versailles, and Franklin being constrained by Congress not to sign anything with substantive changes, the two were at an impasse. Finally, in mid-December Franklin received Elias Boudinot's letter of November 1, which, in discussing the economy of employing consuls as diplomatic representatives, tacitly agreed with the position taken by Barclay and Franklin in regard to Article 3.[8] Franklin appears to have taken this comment as an implicit sanction of his position, or at least as an indication that Congress had no objection to revising the convention. Whatever the case, he and Vergennes quickly concluded their negotiations, agreeing on the document published below. On December 24, Vergennes sent a copy of this draft convention to Castries.[9] Although Vergennes asked for the marine minister's comments, his request was surely a formality. In Franklin's view the convention was completed. When writing to Thomas Mifflin the following day, Franklin reported that a fair copy was being prepared for signing.[1]

Castries' reply to Vergennes of January 31, 1784, did not conceal his resentment at having been excluded from the negotiations. He commented on each article and tried again to persuade Vergennes to have La Luzerne reopen discussions with Congress. Even if La Luzerne should not succeed in obtaining a more favorable agreement, he observed, the only disadvantage would be a short delay. Vergennes responded by sending Castries a point-by-point refutation of his criticisms, challenging him to lay the matter before the king.[2] Castries, though pointing out that his department would be the one most affected by the convention, declined to press the matter further.[3]

Franklin and Vergennes appear to have agreed on most articles. Twelve of them remained substantially unchanged from the congressional counterproposal. Franklin convinced Vergennes to omit Article 3 altogether, because, as Vergennes later wrote, Congress would depend for financial reasons on local merchants to serve as American consuls while France would retain the right to prohibit its own agents

7. Gérard de Rayneval to WTF, Aug. 29, 1783, APS.
8. Boudinot to BF, Nov. 1, above.
9. Vergennes to Castries, Dec. 24, 1783, AAE.
1. BF to Mifflin, Dec. 25, below.
2. Castries to Vergennes, Jan. 31, 1784; Vergennes to Castries, Feb. 6, 1784, with enclosed memorandum (both at the AAE). The foreign ministry also prepared a separate memorandum, dated only "février 1784," for submission to the king, detailing the dispute with Castries. AAE.
3. Castries to Vergennes, Feb. 13, 1784, AAE.

from trading.[4] As neither side regarded Article 6 on religious toleration as essential, it was deleted as well. The revised Article 11 (Article 13 of the congressional counterproposal) no longer gave consuls
any criminal jurisdiction, following the example of Congress' change
to Article 12 of La Luzerne's original draft.

[before December 24, 1783]

Projet de convention entre le Roi T.C. et les Etats Unis de
l'Amérique Septentrionale a l'Effet de déterminer et fixer les
fonctions et prérogatives des Consuls, Vice Consuls, Agens
Commissaires respectifs.

Le Roi très Chretien et les 13. Etats Unis de l'Amérique
Septentrionale s'étant accordés mutüellement par l'arte: XXIX.
du traité d'amitié et de commerce conclu entre Eux, la liberté
de tenir dans leurs Etats et ports respectifs, des Consuls, Vice
Consuls, Agens et commissaires et voulant en conséquence dé-
terminer et fixer d'une maniere réciproque et permanente les
Fonctions et prérogatives des dts. [dits] Consuls, Vice Consuls,
Agens et Commissaires, il a été convenu ce qui Suit.

Art: 1er.

Les Consuls et Vice Consuls nommés par le roi T.C. et les Etats
Unis seront tenus de présenter leurs provisions à leur arrivée
dans les Etats respectifs Selon la forme qui s'y trouvera établie.
On leur délivrera sans aucun frais *l'Exequatur* nécessaire à
l'éxercice de leurs fonctions, et sur l'exhibition qu'ils feront du
dt. *Exequatur,* les Gouverneurs, Commandans, Chefs de justice, les Corps, tribunaux ou autres officiers ayant autorité dans
les ports et lieux de leurs consulats les y feront jouir aussi tôt
et sans difficulté des preéminences, autorité et privilèges accordés réciproquemt. sans qu'ils puissent exiger des dts. Consuls et
vice Consuls aucuns droits sous aucunes prétextes quelconques.

4. Foreign ministry memorandum of February, 1784, for submission to
the king, cited above. This memorandum contains the only known account
(brief as it is) of the negotiations. BF explained to President of Congress
Richard Henry Lee on Feb. 8, 1785, that Article 3 had been considered "unnecessary to be stipulated, since either Party would always have the Power
of imposing such Restraints on its own Officers, whenever it should think
fit." APS.

Arte. 2.

Les Consuls respectifs auront la faculté d'établir des Vice-Consuls dans les différens ports et lieux de leur département, où le besoin l'éxigera: on leur délivrera egalement *l'Exequatur* nécessaire à l'exercise de leurs fonctions dans la forme indiquée par l'Arte. précédent, et sur l'Exhibition qu'ils feront du dt. *Exequatur,* ils seront admis et reconnus dans les termes et selon les pouvoirs, autorité et privilèges stipulés par les Art: 1. 4. et 5. de la présente convention.

Art: 3.

Les Consuls respectifs pourront établir des Agens dans les différens ports et lieux de leurs départemts. où le besoin l'éxigera; Ces Agens pourront être choisis parmi les Négocians nationaux ou étrangers, et munis du brevêt de l'un des dits Consuls, ils se renfermeront respectivemt. à rendre aux Commerçans, Navigateurs et batimens respectifs, tous les services possibles, et à informer le Consul ou Vice Consul le plus proche des besoins des dts. Commerçans, Navigateurs et batimens, sans que les dts. Agens puissent autrement participer aux immunités, droits et privilèges attribués aux Consuls et Vice Consuls, et sans pouvoir sous quelque prétexte que ce soit, exiger aucun droit ou émolument quelconque des dts. Commerçans.

article 4.

Les Consuls et vice Consuls, les officiers du Consulat et généralement toutes les personnes attachées aux fonctions consulaires dont la liste sera approuvée et visée par le pouvoir éxecutif du lieu de leur résidence, jouiront respectivement d'une pleine et entière immunité pour leur personne, leurs papiers et leurs maisons.

Ils seront éxemts de toute service personnelle, et offices publics, logemt. de gens de guerre, milice, guet, garde, tutelle, curatelle, ainsi que de tous droits, taxes, impositions, charges quelconques fors les biens fonds dont ils seront proprietaires les quels seront assujettis aux taxes imposées sur les biens de tous autres particuliers.

Ils placeront sur la porte extérieure de leur maison les armes de leur souverain, sans cependant que cette marque distinctive puisse donner le droit d'asile à la de. [dite] maison pour aucun malfaiteur ou Criminel, de manière que le cas arrivant, òu aucun malfaiteur ou Criminel s'y réfugie, il sera rendu sur le champ à la 1ere. requisition et sans difficulté.

article 5.

Dans tous les cas généralement quelconques intéressant la police ou l'administration de la justice, où il sera nécessaire d'avoir une declaration juridique des dts. Consuls et vice Consuls respectifs, les Gouverneur, commandt., Chefs de la justice, les Corps tribunaux òu autres officiers quelconques de leur résidence respective ÿ ayant autorité, seront tenus de les en prèvenir en leur écrivant ou en leur envoyant un officier militaire ou civil pour leur faire connoitre, soit l'objet que l'on se propose, soit la nécessité dans la quelle on se trouve d'aller chéz eux pour leur demander cette déclaration, et les dts. Consuls et vice Consuls seront tenus, de leur côté, de se prêter loyalement à ce qu'on désirera d'eux dans ces occasions.

arte. 6.

Les Consuls et Vice consuls respectifs pourront établir une chancellerie où seront déposés les actes et délibérations consulaires, tous les effets délaissés par deffunts, ou sauvés des naufrages, ainsi que les testamens, obligations, contrats et généralement tous les actes et procédures faits entre leurs nationaux.

Ils pourront en conséquence, commettre à l'éxercice de la de. Chancellerie des personnes capables, les recevoir, leur faire prêter serment, le donner la garde du Sceau, et le droit de sceller les commissions, jugemens et autres actes du Consulat, ainsi que d'y remplir les fonctions de Notaires et Greffiers.

Article 7.

Les consuls et vice consuls respectifs auront le droit exclusif de recevoir dans leur Chancellerie ou à bord des batimens, les declarations et tous les autres actes que les Capitaines, Patrons, équipages, passager et negoçians de leur nation voudront y passer, même leur testament et autres dispositions de dere. [dernière] volonté; et les expéditions des dts. actes duement légalisés par les d. consuls ou vice consuls et munis du sceau de leur consulat feront foy en justice dans tous les tribunaux de france et des Etats Unis.

Ils auront aussi et exclusivement le droit de faire l'inventaire, la liquidation, et de procéder à la vente des effets mobiliers de la succession des Sujets de leur nation qui viendront à mourir dans l'étendüe de leurs consulats, ils y procéderont avec l'assistance de 2. négocians de leur de. nation, à leur choix, et feront déposer, dans leur chancellerie, les effets et papiers des des. Successions, sans qu'aucuns officiers militaires, de justice ou de police du pays puissent les y troubler ou y intervenir de quelque maniere que ce soit, mais les dts. Consuls et vice Consuls ne pourront faire la délivrance des Successions et de leur produit aux heritiers légitimes ou à leurs mandataires, qu'après avoir fait acquitter toutes les dettes que les deffunts auront pû avoir contractées dans le pays par jugement, par actes ou par billets dont l'écriture ou la Signature Seront reconnues et certifiées par deux notables Négocians de la nation des dits deffunts, et dans tous les autres cas le paÿement des dettes ne pourra être ordonné qu'en fournissant par le Créancier, caution suffisante et domiciliée de rendre les sommes induemt. perçües, principal intérets et frais, les quelles cautions cependant demeureront düemt. déchargées après une année en tems de paix et 2. en tems de guerre, si la demande en décharge ne peut être formée avant ces délais contre les héritiers qui se présenteront.

Article 8.

Les Consuls et vice Consuls respectifs recevront les declarations, Consulats ou autre actes consulaires de tous Capitaines et patrons de leur nation respective pour raison d'avaries essuyées à la mer par des voyes d'eau ou de jets de marchandises; et les Capitaines et Patrons remettront à la Chancelerie des dts. Consuls et vice consuls des consulats et autres actes consulaires qu'ils auront faits dans d'autres ports pour les accidens qui leur seront arrivés pendant leur voyage. Si un Sujet du roi T.C. et un habitant des Etats Unis sont intéressés dans la de. cargaison, l'avarie sera reglée par les Tribunaux du Pays, et non par les Consuls ou Vice Consuls. Mais lors qu'il n'y aura d'intéressés que des Sujets de leur propre nation ou des étrangers, le Consul ou le Vice Consul nommeront d'office des Experts de leur de. nation pour régler les dommages ou avaries.

article 9.

Dans le cas où par tempête ou autre accident, des Vaisseaux ou batimens françois échoueront sur les côtes des Etats Unis, et des vaisseaux et bâtimens des Etats Unis échoueront sur les cotes de france, le consul ou le vice Consul le plus proche du Lieu du naufrage pourra faire tout ce qu'il jugera convenable, tant pour sauver le d. vaisseaux ou batiment, son chargement et appartenances, que pour le magazinage et la sûreté des effets sauvés et marchandises. Il pourra en faire l'inventaire sans qu'aucuns des Officiers militaires, des Douanes de justice ou de police du Pays puissent s'y immiscer autrement que pour faciliter aux Consuls et Vice Consuls, Capne. et équipage du vaisseau naufragé ou echoué, tous les secours et faveurs qu'ils leur demanderont, soit pour la célérité et sûreté du sauvetage et des effets sauvés, soit pour éviter tous désordres.

Pour prévenir même toute espèce de conflit et de discussions dans les dts. cas de naufrage, il a été convenu que, lorsqu'il ne se trouvera pas de Consul ou vice Consul pour faire travailler au sauvetage, ou que la résidence du consul ou vice consul ne se trouvera pas sur le lieu du naufrage, sera plus éloignée du dt. lieu que celle du juge territorial competent, ce dernier y fera procéder sur le champ, avec toute la célérité, la sûreté et les précautions prescrites par les loix respectives, sauf au dt. juge territorial à Se retirer, le consul ou vice Consul survenant, et à lui remettre les procédures par lui faites, dont le Consul ou vice Consul lui fera rembourser les frais.

Les marchandises et effets sauvés devront être déposés à la Douane ou autre lieu de sûreté le plus prochain avec l'inventaire qui en aura été dressé par le consul ou vice consul, ou, en leur absence, par le juge qui en aura connu, pour les dts. effets et marchandises, être ensuite délivrés, après le prélévemt. des frais et sans forme de procès, aux propriétaires qui, munis de la main levée du Consul ou Vice Consul le plus proche, les reclameront par eux mêmes ou par leurs mandataires, soit pour réexporter les marchandises, et dans ce cas, elles ne payeront aucune espèce de droit de sortie, soit pour les vendre dans le pays, si elles n'y sont pas prohibées, et, dans ce der. cas, les des. marchandises se trouvant avariées, on leur accordera une modération sur les droits d'entrée, proportionnée au dommage souffert, le quel sera constatté par le procès verbal dressé lors du naufrage ou de l'échouement.

article 10.

Les Consuls et Vice Consuls auront à bord des Batimens de leur nation respective tout pouvoir et jurisdiction en matiere civile. Ils feront exécuter les loix, ordonnances et reglemens respectifs concernt. la navigation à bord des dts. batimens, et à cet effet ils pourront s'y transporter, sans qu'aucun officier ou autre personnes puissent les en empêcher.

Ils pourront faire arrêter tous batiment portant pavillon de leur nation respective, le faire séquestrer et même le renvoyer respectivement des Etats Unis en France et de france dans les Etats Unis, et faire arrêter sans difficulté tout capitaine, patron, matelot ou passager de leur de. Nation respective.

Ils pourront faire arrêter ou détenir dans le pays les matelots ou Deserteurs de leurs nations respectives, ou les renvoyer et faire transporter hors du Pays.[5]

Ils suffira, pour prouver que les Matelots et déserteurs appartiennent à l'une des nations respectives, que leurs noms soyent inscrits sur les registres du vaisseau, ou porté sur le rôle de l'Equipage.

L'une ou l'autre de ces preuves étant ainsi administrée concernant les Matelots et Déserteurs, aucuns tribunaux, juges et Officiers quelconques ne pourront en quelque maniere que ce soit, connoitre des plaintes que les matelots et Déserteurs pourroient former. Mais ils seront au contraire délivrés sur un ordre signé

5. Article 12 of the 1781 French draft convention gave consuls the power to arrest and deport "sailors, deserters and the vagabonds" of their own nation. The 1782 congressional counterproposal deleted vagabonds from the list: Giunta, *Emerging Nation*, III, 13, 21. In his May 29, 1783, letter to Vergennes, cited above, Castries argued for the reinstatement of this power to control unauthorized emigration. But Vergennes' own reasoning—how would a consul determine who was a vagabond?—and "la resistance invincible de M. franklin" preserved the article as revised by Congress: French foreign ministry memorandum of February, 1784, cited above.

par le Consul ou Vice Consul sans qu'on puisse aucunement les détenir, engager ou soustraire.

Et pour parvenir à l'entière exécution des dispositions contenues dans cet art. toutes Personnes ayant autorité seront tenues d'assister les dts. Consuls ou Vice Consuls, et sur un simple réquisitoire signé d'Eux, ils feront detenir et garder dans les prisons à la disposition et aux frais des dts. Consuls ou Vice Consuls les dts. matelots et déserteurs jusqu'à ce qu'ils ayent occasion de les faire sortir du Pays.

Article 11.

Dans le cas où les sujets respectifs auront commis quelque crime contre aucuns habitans du Pays, ils seront justiciables des juges du Pays.

article 12.

Tous les différends et procès entre les sujets du Roi T.C. établis dans les Etats Unis ou entre les Citoyens et sujets des Etats Unis établis en france, et tous les différends et procès concernant le commerce entre les sujets du Roi T.C. et une des parties résidente en france ou ailleurs, et l'autre dans les Etats Unis, ou entre les Citoyens et sujets des Etats Unis, l'une des parties faisant sa résidence dans les Etats Unis ou ailleurs, et l'autre en france, seront terminés par les Consuls respectifs, soit par un renvoy par devant des arbitres, soit par un jugement sommaire et sans frais.

Aucun officier civil ou militaire ne pourra intervenir ou prendre une part quelconque à l'affaire. Les appels seront portés devant les tribunaux de france ou des Etats unis qui devront en connoitre. Les Consuls ou Vice Consuls ne pourront connoitre des disputes ou différends qui s'eleveront entre un sujet du Roi T.C. et un citoyen des Etats Unis, mais les des. disputes et différends seront portés devant les tribunaux dont le défendeur sera justiciable.

Article 13.

L'utilité générale du commerce ayant fait établir en france des tribunaux et des formes particulieres pour accélerer la décision des affres. de commerce, les Négocians des Etats Unis jouiront du bénéfice de ces établissemens en france, et le Congrèz des Etats unis recommendera aux législatures des différens Etats de procurer des avantages équivalents en faveur des Négocians françois pour la promte expédition et décision des affaires de la même nature.

article 14.

Les sujets du Roi T.C. et ceux des Etats Unis qui justifieront être du corps de la nation respective, par le certificât du Consul ou du Vice Consul du district faisant mention de leurs noms, surnoms, et du lieu de leur établissement, comme inscrits dans les régistres du Consulat, ne pourront perdre, pour telle cause que ce soit, dans les domaines et Etats respectifs, la qualité de sujets du pays dont ils sont originaires, conformémt. à l'Art: xi du traité d'amitié et de commerce du 6. fevrier 1778. dont le présent Arte: servira d'interprétation en cas de besoin, et les dts. sujets respectifs jouiront en conséquence de l'exemption de tout service personnel dans le lieu de leur établissement.

article 15.

Si quelqu'autre nation acquiert en vertu d'une convention quelconque, soit en france, soit dans les Etats Unis, un traitement plus favorable relativement aux préeminences, pouvoirs, autorité et privilèges consulaires, les Consuls, Vice Consuls et agens du Roi T.C. ou des Etats unis réciproquement y participeront aux termes stipulés par les Art: II. III. et IV. du Traité d'amitié et de commerce conclu entre le Roi T.C. et les Etats Unis.

Article 16.

Les ratifications de la présente convention seront données en bonne forme et echangées de part et d'autre dans l'espace de six mois ou plus tôt si faire se peut.

    En foy de quoi &ca../.

Notations:[6] Envoyé copie à Mr. le Mal. de Castries le 24. xbre. 1783./. / Rédigé contradictoiremt. avec Mr. franklin./.

---

6. In the hand of Gérard de Rayneval.

To Ingenhousz ALS: Yale University Library

My dear Friend, Passy Dec. 24, 1783
I am greatly indebted to you for Letters.[7] I shall write largely
to you soon. With this I send you some American Papers, more
Letters to Sir Jos. Banks, A Letter to Mr Nairne on Thermometers, & some Catalogues of Seeds.—[8] I have sent the Order to
America for Seeds which your Friend desired, but I fear the Vessel I sent it by is lost, not being arriv'd the 6th of last Month:[9]
Luckily I have a Copy which shall send by a Packet that sails the
29th. Do what you please with my Papers, and among the rest
that of the Wethercock.[1] I am hearty & well, except a Stone in
my Bladder, which however does not yet give me much Pain.

7. BF last answered a group of Ingenhousz' letters on May 16 (XL, 8–13).
Since then, Ingenhousz had written on June 23, Aug. 15, Sept. 1, and
Nov. 19. (The first three are in XL, 216–17, 475–84, 562–3; the fourth is
above.)
   8. On Nov. 19, Ingenhousz acknowledged receiving a copy of BF's first
letter to Banks about balloons. BF must have now enclosed his subsequent
letters of Oct. 8 and Nov. 21 [i.e., 22–25]. We have found no letters to
Nairne about thermometers, but BF sent him a long letter about hygrometers on Oct. 18. We are not certain of which "Catalogues of Seeds" BF sent.
They were either copies of John Bartram's broadside list, one of which
had recently arrived from RB (see XL, 593; RB to BF, Nov. 5, and Joshua
Barney to BF, Dec. 19), or else they were the French translation of that
catalogue, which BF had printed in Paris at some time before April, 1784.
(For the French version, see XL, 593n. The only known explicit reference
to it is in an April 18, 1784, letter from the abbé Nolin to Mme Helvétius:
APS.) We suspect that BF had copies printed because he had received so few
from Bartram and wanted to distribute them. The only element he translated was the title; otherwise, the catalogue listed plant names in Latin,
leaving off the vernacular English names. It is possible that BF could have
had a printer produce these sheets in time to send with the present letter to
Ingenhousz.
   9. The source of this information was probably Capt. Joshua Barney,
who left Philadelphia around Nov. 6. The order of seeds was for Count
Chotek; Ingenhousz had forwarded to BF the count's letter and bill of exchange on Sept. 1 (XL, 562). BF may have entrusted them to John Thaxter,
who left Paris on Sept. 14 to carry the definitive treaty to Philadelphia.
Thaxter did not arrive until Nov. 22: XL, 600; Thaxter to BF, Sept. 20
(above); Adams Correspondence, V, 235n.
   1. "An Attempt to explain the Effects of Lightning on the Vane of the
Steeple of a Church in Cremona . . .": XXXV, 548–9; XXXVII, 504–12.

With the greatest & most sincere Esteem, I am ever, my dear Friend, Yours most affectionately   B FRANKLIN

Is there any dependance on dissolving Remedies for the Stone? Had I not better content myself with some Regimen that may prevent its growing?

From ——— Creuzé   ALS: American Philosophical Society

Monsieur   Poitiers le 24 xbre 1783.
Vos Talens consacrés au bonheur de L'humanité, vous attachent a tous les pays. Vous Estes par vos vertus le citoyen du monde Entiér. Me Serait il permis Monsieur de vous considerér un Seul moment Sous cet unique point de vüe? Pourrais je vous adresser quelques reflexïons touchant la machine aerostatique? Ce n'est point une curiosité puerille qu'il S'agit de Satisfaire. Il faut nous Elevér dans des regions que les hommes n'avaint point parcourües jusqu'a nos jours. Les Sciences Et les arts attendent avec impatience les resultats de L'Experience qui doivent Eclairér leurs procedés Et favorisér leurs progrés.

Nous avons L'art de nous Elevér dans les airs, nous pouvons nous y maintenir dans un certain Equilibre, mais il faudrait un gouvernail aërien pour dirigér la marche Et luy donnér le degré de célérité convenable.

La forme la plus convenable a la machine Est celle d'un batteau. Dans la partie Superieure nous placerons le ballon pour Elevér la machine Et la faire flottér dans les airs. Mais pour luy imprimér un mouvement horizontal plus ou moins acceleré, il faut avoir un reservoir Sur le derriere du Batteau ou l'on fera Successivement Entrér du gaz par le moyen des Soupapes. Ce gaz ne trouvant pas d'autre issüe Se précipitera avec rapidité dans des tuyaux qui aboutiront a la partie anterieure du batteau ou trouvant une issüe, lair inflammable Se dissipera. Mais comme le reservoir En fournira continuellement, il SEtablira un courant dair, dont la direction imprimera au batteau le mouvement horizontal, Et le portera au point desiré. Les tuyaux qui prolongeront le Batteau doivent Estre plus larges vers le reservoir Et diminüér insensiblement jusqua leur Extremité. C'est ainsy que le gaz fera un plus grand Effort pour Sortir Et donnera une vitesse accelerée. On doit Sattendre que le gaz du resérvoir Et celuy des tuyaux feront un double Effort. L'un pour prendre une direction verticalle ce qui Soulevera d'autant la machine, Et L'autre pour Sechapper par les tuyaux placés horizontallement. C'est par une juste combinaison que l'on parviendra a dirigér la marche du Balon qui pourra au Besoin decrire la parabole.[2] On Saisit a Paris mieux Qu'ailleurs de pareilles idées, Et on Execute mieux a Paris que dans nos provinces. Si cette Combinaison avait quelque merite permettés moy, Monsieur, de vous L'offrir comme un justé hommage que je rends a vos talens. Mais Si tout cela n'Etait qu'un Songe, je me reveilleray avec Lidée flatteuse d'avoir conversé un moment avec le Socrate Et le platon de nos jours.

Je Suis avec Respect Monsieur Votre tres humble Et trés obeissant Serviteur   Creuzé
                                                        trésoriér de Bauce

From William Lee Perkins[3]

Two ALS: American Philosophical Society; University of Pennsylvania Library[4]

Sir   Kingston upon Thames Decr. 24th. 1783.
    I have lately received from America a Diploma, constituting my late honoured and dear Father Dr. John Perkins a corresponding member of the *Royal Society* of *Medicine* at *Paris*,

2. Creuzé elaborated on his idea of using air pipes and a steering rudder to direct the motion of balloons in a letter dated Jan. 4, 1784 (APS).
    3. Son of Boston physician John Perkins (IV, 267n), William Lee Perkins (1737–1797) was himself a physician in Boston until the war broke out. He fled to Nova Scotia in 1776, was proscribed in 1778, and moved to England, where he continued to practice medicine: Sabine, *Loyalists;* Colonial Society of Massachusetts, *Medicine in Colonial Massachusetts, 1620–1820* (Charlottesville, 1980), pp. 70n, 72, 83, 97; Peter J. Wallis and R. V. Wallis, *Eighteenth-Century Medics: Subscriptions, Licences, Apprenticeships* (Newcastle Upon Tyne, 1988), p. 465.
    4. The second ALS, marked "Copy," is a duplicate that Perkins sent to BF on Nov. 17, 1784. A notation on the duplicate misdated it Dec. 7, 1783.

which arrived there after his decease and which was transmitted to me.[5]

Recalling to mind the favors and civilities You was pleased formerly to honour me with, resting on the friendship formerly subsisting between You and my Father, and above all relying on that benevolence, which makes so essential a part of Your distinguished Character, I have presumed to commit to Your Patronage the inclosed account of the *Influenza* as I observed it here in England, and to request the favour of your aid of my wishes to lay it before the *Royal Society* of *Medicine* at *Paris*. I have left it unseal'd that it might be subject to Your inspection, previous to its being offered to the Society, in case of Your Approbation.

In this essay to comply with the intentions of the Society, I feel the highest satisfaction in having performed the part of filial duty, by endeavouring to discharge for a parent a part of those obligations, which had he lived to receive the honor done him by the Society, he would most certainly have held himself bound to fulfill.

If the Society should so far approve it as to honor it with a place amongst its publications, and think fit to transfer to me the honor intended for my father, I should receive it as an obligation urging me to activity and zeal in future, in my endeavours to contribute to their salutary and benevolent intentions.

I have only, Sir, to add my most ardent wishes, that to the honors attendant on Your Name throughout the World, there may be continually added all that personal comfort and happiness, which can render life a real blessing.

5. John Perkins had been recommended to the Société royale de médecine by BF, who gave them a copy of Perkins' "A few thoughts on epidemic colds or catarrhal fevers." The paper, written in 1768, was dedicated to BF, who had urged Perkins to study the topic. The medical society published a condensed version (in translation) in 1779, under the title "Extrait d'un Mémoire rédigé par M. Perkins, Médecin de Boston, sur la nature & l'origine des fièvres catharrales épidémiques, & remis à la Société par M. Franklin"; see IV, 267n; XXX, 251. When the next volume of *mémoires* was published, Perkins was listed as one of the society's corresponding members: *Histoire de la Société royale de médecine* for 1777–78 (Paris, 1780), p. 15.

I have the Honour to be Sir, with the most respectful Esteem, Your Excellency's most obedient & most devoted humble Servant   WM. LEE PERKINS

His Excellency B. Franklin Esqr.

From Vergennes   L: American Philosophical Society

à Versles. [Versailles] le 24. Xbre. 1783./.
M. Le C. de Vergennes a l'honneur d'envoyer à Monsieur franklin un paquet pour Mr. le Chever. de La Luzerne.[6] Il le prie de vouloir bien le faire passer à Sa destination par le vaisseau *le Wazington./.*[7]

To Mercy-Argenteau   L:[8] Haus-, Hof- und Staatsarchiv, Austria

Passy ce 25. Xbre. 1783.
M. Franklin a reçu les deux Lettres à l'adresse de Mrs. Le Baron de Beelen et le professeur Marter que Monsieur l'Ambassadeur de l'Empereur lui a fait l'honneur de lui adresser pour faire passer en Amerique.[9] C'est un vrai plaisir pour Mr. Franklin de trouver l'occasion de faire quelque chose qui puisse être agréable à Monsieur l'Ambassadeur et il aura grand soin de les faire partir par le paquet-bot qui est actuellement au Havre et qui doit

6. Vergennes' dispatch no. 53 to La Luzerne, of the same date. Vergennes expressed relief that Congress had denied BF's request to return home; he thought it important that BF stay until the situation with Great Britain was stable, as BF was more sympathetic to France than were his colleagues. As for BF's grandson, Vergennes had found his conduct "uniformément sage et circonspecte," and thought he would be a fine chargé d'affaires in BF's absence. Vergennes would certainly prefer dealing with him than with either Jay or JA. He suggested that La Luzerne recommend WTF to Congress if the occasion arose. AAE. Excerpts of this letter are translated in Giunta, *Emerging Nation,* I, 957–9; they do not include the portions about WTF.
7. The *General Washington.*
8. In the hand of L'Air de Lamotte.
9. The ambassador had sent them on Dec. 22 (above).

mettre à la Voile le 29. de ce mois.[1] Il a aussi recours aux Bontés de Monsieur L'Ambassadeur, pour le prier de vouloir bien permettre que le paquet cy joint pour le Dr. Ingenhauss[2] parte par le premier Courier qu'il enverra à Vienne, il en sera infiniment reconnoissant.—

To Thomas Mifflin

LS, copy, and transcript:[3] National Archives; AL (draft): Library of Congress

Sir,   Passy, Decr. 25th. 1783.

Not having heard of the Appointment of a new Secretary for foreign Affairs, I take the Liberty of addressing this Dispatch directly to your Excellency.[4]

I received by Capt. Barney, a Letter from the late President, directed to the Commissioners, dated Novr 1. with a Set of Instructions dated the 29th of October, a Resolution of the same Date respecting Hamburgh, and another of the 1st Novr, relating to Capt. Paul Jones, all which will be duly regarded.[5]

1. The *General Washington*.
2. BF to Ingenhousz, Dec. 24.
3. The LS is in WTF's hand. The copy was written by L'Air de Lamotte and sent to Congress; it was signed with BF's name by BFB (we believe) and bears BFB's note at the top of the first page: "Duplicate. The Original went by Capt. Barney."

BF's outline for this letter is at the APS (undated). It is a list of topics headed by the word "President." After finishing the list, BF ordered the items by number in the left margin. He deviated from this order somewhat as he drafted the letter. As he wrote about each topic, he lined through it with a vertical stroke. At the bottom of the sheet BF wrote, "separate Letter to Mr Mifflin," an allusion to his personal letter to Mifflin (letter I) of Dec. 26, which included some of these topics. He also reserved two items ("Medal" and "A new Loan here") for the letter he would write to Robert Morris on Dec. 25, the outline of which is on the verso of this sheet. He crossed out one item altogether: "Don't Expect Mr Hartley's Return."

4. Boudinot had informed the American peace commissioners of Mifflin's election as president of Congress in the Nov. 3 addition to his Oct. 27 letter, above. The post of secretary for foreign affairs was still vacant.

5. Congress' Oct. 29 instructions, former president Boudinot's Nov. 1 letter to the commissioners, and his Nov. 1 letter to BF, which enclosed a

Capt. Jones, in passing thro' England, communicated these Papers to Mr. Adams, then at London. Mr. Adams disappointed in not finding among them the Commission we had been made to expect, empowering us to make a Treaty of Commerce with England, wrote to me that he imagined it might be contained in a Packet that was directed to me, and requested to be immediately informed, adding that in Case no such Commission was come he should depart directly for Holland;[6] so I suppose He is now there. Mr Lawrens is gone to England with an Intention of embarking soon for America.[7] Mr Jay is at Bath, but expected here daily.[8] The English Ministers (the Duke of Manchester and Mr Hartley) are both at present in Parliament. As soon as either of them return, we shall endeavour to obtain an additional Article to the Treaty explaining that mentioned in the Instructions.[9]

The Affairs of Ireland are still unsettled. The Parliament and Volunteers are at Variance: the latter are uneasy that in the late Negociations for a Treaty of Commerce between England and America, the British Ministers had made no mention of Ireland, and they seem to desire a separate Treaty of Commerce between America and that Kingdom.[1]

It was certainly disagreable to the English Ministers that all their Treaties for Peace were carried on under the Eye of the French Court. This began to appear towards the Conclusion, when Mr Hartley refused going to Versailles to sign there with the other Powers our Definitive Treaty, and insisted on its being done at Paris, which we in good Humour complied with, but at an earlier Hour, that we might have time to acquaint le

---

letter to the city officials of Hamburg that quoted the congressional resolution, are above. BF had carried out Congress' instructions concerning Jones on Dec. 17; see his letter to Jones of that date, above.

6. JA to BF, Dec. 5. JA's Dec. 14 letter suggested that he and Jay might return to Paris, but BF did not receive that letter until after the new year; see BF to JA, Jan. 3, below.

7. Laurens did not sail for America until June 22, 1784: *Laurens Papers*, XVI, xlv.

8. Jay did not arrive in Paris until late January: *Jay Papers*, III, 492.

9. Probably the seventh item of the Oct. 29 instructions.

1. For recent Irish developments see BF's correspondence with Newenham.

Comte de Vergennes before he was to sign with the Duke of Manchester.[2] The Dutch Definitive was not then ready, and the British Court now insists on finishing it either at London or the Hague.[3] If therefore the Commission to us, which has been so long delayed is still intended, perhaps it will be well to instruct us to treat either here or at London, as we may find most convenient. The Treaty may be conducted even there in Concert and in the Confidence of Communication with the Ministers of our Friends, whose Advice may be of use to us.

With respect to the British Court, we should I think be constantly upon our guard, and impress strongly upon our Minds, that tho' it has made Peace with us, it is not in Truth reconciled either to us or to its Loss of us; but still flatters itself with Hopes that some Change in the Affairs of Europe or some Disunion among ourselves, may afford them an Opportunity of Recovering their Dominion, punishing those who have most offended, and securing our future Dependance. It is easy to see by the general Turn of the Ministerial News-Papers; (light Things indeed as Straws and Feathers, but like them they show which way the Wind blows) and by the malignant Improvement their Ministers make in all the Foreign Courts, of every little Accident or Dissension among us, the Riot of a few Soldiers at Philadelphia, the Resolves of some Town Meetings, the Reluctance to pay Taxes &ca &ca all which are exaggerated to represent our Governments as so many Anarchies, of which the People themselves are weary, the Congress as having lost its Influence being no longer respected: I say it is easy to see from this Conduct that they bear us no Good Will, and that they wish the Reality of what they are pleased to imagine. They have too a numerous Royal Progeny to provide for, some of whom are educated in the Military Line. In these Circumstances we cannot be too careful to preserve the Friendships we have acquired abroad, and the Union we have establish'd at Home, to secure our Credit by a punctual Discharge of our Obligations of every kind, and our Reputation by the Wisdom of our Councils:

2. See XL, 540, 542, 566–8.
3. As Dumas reported on Dec. 11, above.

Since we know not how soon we may have a fresh Occasion for Friends, for Credit and for Reputation.

The extravagant Misrepresentations of our Political State, in foreign Countries, made it appear necessary to give them better Information, which I thought could not be more effectually & authentically done than by publishing a Translation into French, now the most general Language in Europe, of the Book of Constitutions which had been printed by Order of Congress. This I accordingly got well done, and presented two Copies handsomely bound to every foreign Minister here, one for himself, the other more elegant for his Sovereign. It has been well taken, and has afforded Matter of Surprize to many, who had conceived mean Ideas of the State of Civilisation in America, and could not have expected so much Political Knowledge & Sagacity had existed in our Wildernesses.[4] And from all Parts I have the Satisfaction to hear that our Constitutions in general are much admired. I am persuaded that this Step will not only tend to promote the Emigration to our Country of substantial People, from all Parts of Europe, by the numerous Copies I shall disperse, but will facilitate our future Treaties with Foreign Courts, who could not before know what kind of Government and People they had to treat with. As in doing this I have endeavour'd to further the apparent Views of Congress in the first Publication, I hope it may be approved, & the Expence allow'd. I send herewith one of the Copies.[5]

Our Treaties with Denmark & Portugal remain unfinish'd for want of Instructions respecting them from Congress, & a Commission impowering some Minister or Ministers to conclude them.

The Emperor of Morocco, we understand has express'd a Disposition to make a Treaty of Amity and Commerce with the United States. A Mr Montgomery, who is a Merchant settled

4. Among BF's papers is an undated 12-page manuscript in an unknown hand, titled "Observations sur les Constitutions des États-Unis de l'Amérique Septentrionale," that was written in response to the work's recent publication. APS.

5. BF had sent a copy to Robert R. Livingston in July, as soon as it was published; see XXXIX, 376–8; XL, 368, 376–7n.

at Alicant, has been it seems rather forward in proposing a Negociation without Authority for so doing, and has embarrass'd us a little, as may be seen by some Letters I enclose.[6] Perhaps it would be well for the Congress to send a Message to that Prince, expressing their Respect and Regard for him, 'till such time as they may judge it convenient to appoint an Ambassador in form, furnish'd with proper presents, to make a Treaty with him.

The other Barbary States too, seem to require Consideration, if we propose to carry on any Trade in the Mediterranean; but whether the Security of that Trade is of sufficient Importance to be worth purchasing at the Rate of the Tributes usually exacted by those piratical States, is a Matter of doubt, on which I cannot at present form a Judgment.

I shall immediately proceed, in Pursuance of the First Instruction, to take the proper Steps for acquainting his Imperial Majesty of Germany with the Dispositions of Congress, having some Reason to believe the Overture may be acceptable. His Minister here is of late extreamly civil to me, and we are on very good Terms. I have likewise an intimate Friend at that Court.—[7] With respect to other Powers, it seems best not to make Advances at present, but to meet and encourage them when made, which I shall not fail to do, as I have already done those of Sweden, Denmark & Portugal. Possibly Hamburgh, to whom I have forwarded the Letter of Congress, may send a Minister to America, if they wish for a Treaty, to conclude it there. They have no Minister here.[8]

I have lately received a Memorial from the Minister of Denmark, respecting a Ship of that Nation the Providentia, taken by one of our Privateers; and carried into Boston. I inclose a

6. The enclosures (transcribed by Congress and filed with the transcript of the present letter) were Crocco to BF, Nov. 25; BF to Crocco, Dec. 15; and BF to Carmichael, Dec. 15, all above.

7. The minister was the comte de Mercy-Argenteau, the friend, Jan Ingenhousz.

8. Its affairs were handled by a chargé d'affaires, Jean, comte de Diodati-Tronchin, who also represented Mecklenburg-Schwerin and later became TJ's friend: *Repertorium der diplomatischen Vertreter*, III, 182, 244; *Jefferson Papers*, XIII, 439; XXI, 145.

Copy of it,[9] and request to be furnish'd with directions & Informations for the Answer. It may be well to send me a Copy of the Proceedings in the Courts. From a Perusal of the Papers communicated with it, I am satisfied that the Cargo was clearly British Property. We have hitherto enter'd into no Engagements respecting the armed Neutrality, and in Obedience to the fifth Instruction, shall take Care to avoid them hereafter.

The Treaty between this Court and the United States for regulating the Powers, Privileges, &ca of Consuls, is at length compleated, and is transcribing in order to be signed. I hope to transmit a Copy by the next Packet.[1]

I have received the Congress Ratifications of the two Money-Treaties, which will be soon exchanged, when I shall send Copies of them, with that of Sweden.[2]

I have given and shall continue to give Capt. Paul Jones, all the Assistance in my Power, towards recovering the Prize-Money; and I hope it may be soon accomplished. When Mr Jay returns, I shall desire him to make the Enquiry directed in the Fourth Instruction respecting the Expedition under that Commodore, and report thereon to Congress. In the meantime I can answer respecting one of the Questions, that the King paid the whole Expence, and that no Part of it has ever been placed to the Account of Congress. There exists indeed a Demand of one Puchelberg, a Person in the Employ of M. Schweighauser, of about 30,000 Livres, for Provisions and other Things furnish'd to Capt. Landais, after he took the Alliance out of the Hands of Capt. Jones: But as the Ship was at that Time under the Kings Supply, who having borrow'd her for the Expedition when fitted for Sea, & just ready to sail with Mr. Adams, had order'd her to be deliver'd in the same Condition free of all Charges accru'd or accruing by her being in Holland and in L'orient, and as M. Puchelberg had not only no Order from me to furnish

9. Blome to BF, Nov. 21, above. (A transcript is filed with the transcript of the present letter.)

1. See above, [before Dec. 24].

2. Ratifications of the "money treaties" were brought by Capt. Barney; see Morris to BF, Nov. 4, above. For the ratification of the American-Swedish commercial treaty see Boudinot to BF, Nov. 1.

Capt. Landais, but acted contrary to my Orders given to Mr. Schweighauser, and contrary to the Orders of M. Schweighauser himself, I refused to pay his Account, which besides appear'd extravagant, and it has never yet been paid.—[3]

I shall do my best in executing the third Instruction, respecting our Claim upon Denmark. I have written to London, to obtain if possible in Acct of the Sums insured upon the Ships deliver'd up, as such an Account may be some Guide in the Valuation of the Prizes.[4]

A Capt. Williams formerly in the British Service, and employed upon the Lakes, has given me a Paper containing Information of the State of the back Country. As those Informations may possibly be of some Use, I send herewith the Paper.[5]

3. For Puchelberg's claims see Vergennes to BF, Oct. 24 and Dec. 3.

4. For background see XL, 361–3. BF wrote a now-missing letter to William Hodgson on Dec. 26, which Hodgson acknowledged on Jan. 23, below.

5. "Capt. Williams" was Charles Joseph Abram Williamos (né Vullyamoz), a native of Lausanne who served in the British army during the French and Indian War and was deputy to the superintendent of Indian affairs for the Northern Department: *Jefferson Papers*, VIII, 270n. His six-page paper, undated and unsigned (National Archives), concerned the fur trade on the border with Canada. It argued that since the most valuable Indian trading posts and navigable waterways now belonged to the United States, the government should try to exclude British merchants from them in future trade agreements. Thus Britain's share in the fur trade would be limited to the coast of Labrador and the western St. Lawrence River. Williamos probably delivered the paper to BF in mid-December, around the time he requested a passport to go to America: Williamos to WTF, Dec. 16, 1783, APS. BF issued a passport to "Mr. Williams" on Dec. 17, 1783: Anderson Galleries, Inc., *Collection of Peter Gilsey, Part 2* . . . (New York, 1903), p. 118. (Current location unknown.)

Williamos had been a friend of JW's since 1780, when JW tried to help him reclaim his N.Y. estates and establish himself in America. In September, 1780, JW wrote him letters of introduction to Silas Deane and William Carmichael, and it was probably around that time that Williamos sent the undated memo that describes land claims in America and requests BF's advice. BF endorsed it "Mr Charles Williams's Memo. Lands in America": APS. (JW's correspondence with Williamos is at the Yale University Library.)

When Williamos' paper on the fur trade was received by Congress, it was separated from the present letter and its other enclosures and referred to a four-man committee whose members (including TJ) are named in a

Mr. Carmichael has sent me the Accounts of the Money Transactions at Madrid.[6] As soon as Mr. Jay returns, they will be examined.—

Be pleased to present my dutiful Respects to Congress, and assure them of my most faithful Services.

With great Esteem & Regard, I have the honor to be, Sir, Your Excellency's most obedient & most humble Servant.—

B. FRANKLIN

His Excellency Thomas. Mifflin Esqr. President of Congress.

Notation: Letter 25. Decr. 1783 Doct Franklin Read 5 March 1784 Referred to Mr Gerry Mr Jefferson Mr Sherman Mr Read Mr Williamson

To Robert Morris

AL (draft): Library of Congress; incomplete press copy of LS:[7] American Philosophical Society

Sir,   Passy, Dec. 25. 1783.

I have received your Favour of the 30th of September, for which I thank you. My Apprehension that the Union between France & our States might be diminished by Accounts from hence, was occasioned by the extravagant and violent Language held here by a Public Person in public Company, which had that

---

notation on the verso of the last page. The referral of Williamos' paper was not recorded in the *JCC,* and there is no evidence of any further action. For an extensive discussion of Williamos see *Jefferson Papers,* VIII, 270–3; IX, 270.

6. Carmichael had sent some accounts in April (XXXIX, 462–4) but had not yet sent all, much to the dismay of John Jay; see the annotation of Congress' instructions to the American commissioners, Oct. 29, above.

7. In the hand of BFB. Only the final page survives, beginning with "I perfectly agree with you . . ." and ending with BF's signature.

BF wrote an outline of topics to be covered in this letter on the verso of his outline for the letter to Mifflin, immediately above. (See the annotation there.) As in that case, he drew vertical lines through topics as he covered them.

Tendency; and it was natural for me to think his Letters might hold the same Language; in which I was right; for I have since had Letters from Boston informing me of it.[8] Luckily here, and I hope there, it is imputed to the true Cause; a Disorder in the Brain; which tho' not constant has its Fits too frequent. I will not fill my Letter with an Account of those Discourses; Mr Laurens when you see him, can give it to you; I mean of such as he heard in Company with other Persons; for I would not desire him to relate private Conversations. They distress'd me much at the Time, being then at your earnest Instances soliciting for more Aids of Money, the Success of which Solicitation such ungrateful and provoking Language might I fear'd have had a Tendency to prevent.[9] Enough of this at present.—

I have been exceedingly hurt & afflicted by the Difficulty some of your late Bills met with in Holland. As soon as I receiv'd the Letter from Messrs Willink & Co which I inclose,[1] I sent for Mr Grand, who brought me a Sketch of his Account with you, by which it appear'd that the Demands upon us, existing & expected, would more than absorb the Funds in his Hands. We could not indulge the smallest Hope of obtaining farther Assistance here, the Public Finances being in a State of Embarrassment, private Persons full of Distrust occasioned by the late Stoppage of Payment at the Caisse d'Escompte, and Money in general extreamly scarce. But he agreed to do what I propos'd, lend his Credit in the Way of Drawing & Redrawing between Holland and Paris, to gain Time till you could furnish Funds to reimburse Messrs Willinck & Co. I believe he made this Proposition to them by the Return of the Express. I know not why it was not accepted.[2] Mr Grand I suppose will himself give you an Account of all the Transaction, and of his Application to Messrs Couteulx, &c. therefore I need not add more upon this disagreable Subject.

8. The public person is JA. One of the letters warning BF about him was from Samuel Cooper: XXXIX, 561–3.

9. In his outline, BF had written "My fears of Representations arose from Discourses here which laid me under Difficulties."

1. Undoubtedly the bankers' Nov. 30 letter, above. See also BF's reply to them of Dec. 3.

2. Though acceptable in America, this practice was shunned by the Dutch: *Morris Papers*, VIII, 392, 396n.

I have found Difficulties in settling the Account of Salaries with the other Ministers, that have made it impracticable for me to do it. I have therefore, after keeping the Bills[3] that were to have been proportioned among us, long in my hands, given them up to Mr Grand, who finding the same Difficulties will I suppose return them to you. None have come to hand for the two or three last Quarters, and we are indebted to his Kindness for advancing us Money, or we must have run in debt for our Subsistance. He risques in doing this, since he has not for it your Orders.—

There arise frequently contingent Expences for which no Provision has yet been made. In a former Letter to the Secretary for Foreign Affairs I gave a List of them, and desired to know the Pleasure of Congress concerning them.[4] I have only had for Answer, that they were under Consideration, and that he believed House-Rent would not be allowed:[5] but I am still in Uncertainty as to that and the Rest. I wish some Resolutions were taken on this Point of Contingencies, that I may know how to settle my Accounts with Mr Barclay. American Ministers in Europe are too remote from their Constituents, to consult them and take their Orders on every Occasion; as the Ministers here of European Courts can easily do. There seems therefore a Necessity of allowing more to their Discretion, and of giving them a Credit to a certain Amount, on some Banker who may answer their Orders, for which however they should be accountable. I mention this for the sake of other Ministers, (hoping & expecting soon to be discharg'd my self) and also for the Good of the Service.

The Remissness of our People in Paying Taxes is highly blameable, the Unwillingness to pay them is still more so. I see in some Resolutions of Town-Meetings, a Remonstrance against giving Congress a Power to take as they call it, *the People's Money* out of their Pockets tho' only to pay the Interest and Principal of Debts duly contracted. They seem to mistake the Point. Money justly due from the People is their Creditors' Money, and no longer the Money of the People, who, if they withold it, should be compell'd to pay by some Law. All Prop-

3. *I.e.*, bills of exchange.
4. XXXVIII, 61.
5. XXXVIII, 555.

erty indeed, except the Savage's temporary Cabin, his Bow, his Matchcoat, and other little Acquisitions absolutely necessary for his Subsistence, seems to me to be the Creature of public Convention. Hence the Public has the Right of Regulating Descents & all other Conveyances of Property, and even of limiting the Quantity & the Uses of it. All the Property that is necessary to a Man for the Conservation of the Individual & the Propagation of the Species, is his natural Right which none can justly deprive him of: But all Property superfluous to such purposes is the Property of the Publick, who by their Laws have created it, and who may therefore by other Laws dispose of it, whenever the Welfare of the Publick shall demand such Disposition. He that does not like civil Society on these Terms, let him retire & live among Savages.— He can have no right to the Benefits of Society who will not pay his Club towards the Support of it.

The Marquis de la F. who loves to be employ'd in our Affairs, and is often very useful, has lately had several Conversations with the Ministers & Persons concern'd in forming new Regulations respecting the Commerce between our two Countries, which are not yet concluded.[6] I therefore thought it well to communicate to him a Copy of your Letter, which contains so many sensible and just Observations on that Subject. He will make a proper Use of them, and perhaps they may have more Weight as appearing to come from a French man, than they would have if it were known that they were the Observations of an American.[7] I perfectly agree with you in all the Sentiments you have express'd on this Occasion.

You have made no Answer to the Proposition I sent of furnishing Tobacco to the Farmers General.[8] They have since made a Contract with Messrs. Alexander & Williams for the same Purpose;[9] but it is such a One as does not prevent their making another with you, if hereafter it should suit you. I am sorry for the Publick's sake that you are about to quit your Office, but on

6. See Lafayette to BF, [Dec. 13].

7. In a letter to Morris of Dec. 26, Lafayette wrote that he had had extracts of Morris' letter translated into French and would take them to Versailles: *Morris Papers*, VIII, 842–4.

8. XL, 402.

9. See William Alexander to BF, Nov. 6.

personal Considerations I shall congratulate you. For I cannot conceive of a more happy Man, than he who having been long loaded with public Cares, finds himself reliev'd from them, & enjoying private Repose in the Bosom of his Friends & Family.

The Government here has set on foot a new Loan of an Hundred Millions. I enclose the Plan.[1] It is thought very advantageous for the Lenders. You may judge by that how much the Money is Wanted, and how seasonable the Peace was for all concerned.—

If Mr Alexander, who is gone to Virginia, should happen to come to Philadelphia, I beg leave to recommend him to your Civilities, as an old Friend of mine, whom I very much esteem.

With sincere Regard & Attachment, I am ever, Dear Sir, Your most &c

Honble Robt Morris Esqe Superintendant des Finances

From David Hartley

Copy:[2] William L. Clements Library

My Dear friend   Xmas Day 1783 London

Before you receive this you will have heard of a total change of the British Administration. It is not as yet many hours since this event has taken place. The Cabinet is as follows viz

Mr Pitt first Lord of the treasury[3]

Ld Thurlow chancellor	marquis of Carmarthen	Secretaries
Ld Gower President	Lord Sidney	of State[4]
of Council	Ld Howe first Ld of	
D of Rutland	the Admiralty.	
Privy Seal		

1. The enclosure has not been found, but the royal edict of Dec. 1 was printed in the Dec. 16 issue of the *Gaz. de Leyde*.

2. A retained copy, in Hartley's hand and signed by him.

3. Pitt was appointed prime minister on Dec. 19, but could not form a cabinet until the evening of Dec. 23: John Ehrman, *The Younger Pitt* (3 vols., New York and Stanford, Calif., 1969–96), I, 127–31.

4. Francis Osborne, marquess of Carmarthen (XXXIX, 75n), was the new secretary of state for foreign affairs. The secretary of state for the home department was Hartley's close friend Thomas Townshend, who had

It is impossible for me to expect as yet any instructions in my department. In the mean time I beg of you to send me the earliest notice whenever the ratification of our definitive treaty of Peace shall arrive from America, that we may loose no time in bringing that blessed event to a complete termination. I am My Dear friend Ever yours most affectely   D HARTLEY

To Dr Franklin &c &c &c—

To Samuel Cooper

Press copy of ALS and transcript: Library of Congress

Dear Sir,   Passy, Dec. 26. 1783.

I have received your Favour of the 16th October, and am much oblig'd by the Intelligence it contains.— I am happy to hear that your Government has agreed to furnish Congress with the Means of discharging the National Debt. The Obstruction that Measure met with in some of the States, has had very mischievous Effects on this side the Water; it discourag'd the Loan going on in Holland, and thereby occasion'd a Protest of some of Mr Morris's Bills. Nothing can recover our Credit in Europe & our Reputation in its Courts, but an immediate Proof of our Honesty & Prudence by a general Provision in all the States for the punctual Payment of the Interest & the final regular Discharge of the Principal. I hope we shall never deserve, nor any longer appear likely to deserve the Reproof given to an Enthusiastical Knave in Pennsylvania, who being call'd upon for an old Debt, said to his Creditor, *Thou must have a little more Patience: I am not able yet to pay thee.* Give me then your Bond, says the Creditor, & pay me Interest. *No, I cannot do that; I cannot in Conscience either receive or pay Interest, it is against my Principle.* You have then the Conscience of a Rogue, says the Creditor: you tell me it is against your Principle to pay Interest;

---

been named Baron Sydney the previous March. He had filled the same position during the Shelburne administration: XXXVII, 679n; *ODNB*.

and it being against your Interest to pay the Principal, I perceive you do not intend to pay me either one or t'other—[5]

My young Friend, your Grandson, must have had a long Passage, since he was not arrived when you wrote; indeed all the Vessels that left Europe for America about the time he did, have had long Passages, which makes me less uneasy on his Account. I hope he is in your Arms long before this time. His Father never made any Provision here for his Return, that I have heard of; and therefore I have drawn on you for the Ballance of the Account,[6] as you directed. I wrote you a too long Letter some time since, respecting Mr A.'s Calumnies, of which perhaps it was not necessary to take so much Notice.[7]

The Government in England is again disordered. The Lords have rejected the Ministry's Favourite Bill for demolishing the Power of the India Company: the Commons have resented it by some angry Resolutions. And it is just now reported here that the Ministers are dismiss'd and the Parliament dissolv'd. Of this we have yet no certain Advice, but expect it hourly.—[8]

5. BF told a brief version of this story to Jane Mecom in 1772: XIX, 28. He had used it as an aphorism in *Poor Richard Improved, 1753:* IV, 404.

6. The September bill was payable to Jonathan Williams, Sr.; see his letter of Dec. 20, above.

7. BF sent two dispatches to Cooper about JA's "calumnies," both of which are now missing. The first was a private letter, folded into a cover letter to RB, which BF sent to America with JA's secretary John Thaxter in September. (Thaxter left Paris on Sept. 14; see Thaxter to the American Commissioners, Sept. 20.) Though that letter was meant to be confidential, Thaxter learned of its subject and notified JA: *Adams Papers,* XV, 464, 465n. In November, BF entrusted to William Alexander a packet for Cooper that we assume included the testimonials that BF had demanded from JA, Laurens, and Jay (XL, 614–15, 626–8; Laurens to BF, Sept. 21, above.) He addressed this packet to RB, as well, with instructions to forward it to Boston: RB to BF, March 7, 1784 (Yale University Library); RB to BF, June 21, 1784 (APS); Smyth, *Writings,* IX, 487.

8. The House of Lords rejected the India Bill on Dec. 15 and 17; see the annotation of Laurens to BF, Nov. 28. On those same days, the House of Commons passed resolutions condemning the crown's involvement in the Lords' debate: [London] *Public Advertiser,* issues of Dec. 16, 17, and 18; *Gaz. de Leyde,* Dec. 26 (sup.); Cobbett, *Parliamentary History,* XXIV, 196–225. On Dec. 18 the king asked for the resignation of the Fox-North

There are Hopes that the War against the Turks will blow over;[9] the rather, as all Flames are apt to spread, & the late belligerent Powers have all need of a continu'd Peace: This however is not certain, and it behoves us to preserve with Care our Friends and our Credit abroad, & our Union at home, as we know not how soon we may have occasion for all of them.

With great and sincere Esteem, I am ever, my dear Friend, Yours most affectionately   B. FRANKLIN

Revd Dr Cooper.

To Ebenezer Hazard[1]   ALS: Historical Society of Pennsylvania

Sir,   Passy, Dec. 26. 1783.—

I am desired by the General Post Office of Great Britain to recommend to your Consideration a Sketch of an Advertisement respecting the Packet Boats, which they think it may be useful to publish.[2] You will do in it what you think proper. Perhaps you have already done what is necessary. As I was formerly long connected with that Office, & have Friends in it, if I can be of use in forwarding any Arrangements you have to propose for

---

ministry, and Pitt was appointed the following day. (For the new ministry see Hartley to BF, Dec. 25.) Parliament, however, was not dissolved. For a fuller explanation of these events see John Cannon, *The Fox-North Coalition: Crisis of the Constitution, 1782–4* (Cambridge, 1969), pp. 124–55; Namier and Brooke, *House of Commons*, I, 87–8.

9. Kéralio had informed BF of this in a letter of Nov. 30. Under French pressure the Turks accepted Russian annexation of the Crimea, signing a peace treaty with Russia on Dec. 28, 1783 / Jan. 8, 1784: Clive Parry, comp., *The Consolidated Treaty Series* (243 vols., Dobbs Ferry, N.Y., 1969–86), XLIX, 11–15; Alan W. Fisher, *The Russian Annexation of the Crimea, 1772–1783* (Cambridge, 1970), pp. 137–8.

1. Hazard, whom BF had appointed postmaster of New York (XXII, 146–7), was elected postmaster general by Congress on Jan. 28, 1782, in a move that ousted RB: XXXVI, 109, 186, 553–4.

2. See Todd to BF, Nov. 18.

AN ODE

IN IMITATION OF

ALCÆUS.

WHAT conſtitutes a State?
Not high–rais'd battlement or labour'd mound,
Thick wall or moated gate;
Not cities proud with ſpires and turrets crown'd;
Not bays and broad-arm'd ports,
Where, laughing at the ſtorm, rich navies ride;
Not ſtarr'd and ſpangled courts,
Where low-brow'd baſeneſs wafts perfume to pride.
No: — MEN, high-minded MEN,
With pow'rs as far above dull brutes endued
In foreſt, brake, or den,
As beaſts excel cold rocks and brambles rude;
Men, who their *duties* know,
But know their *rights*, and, knowing, dare maintain,
Prevent the long-aim'd blow,
And crush the tyrant while they rend the chain:
Theſe conſtitute a State;
And ſov'reign LAW, *that State's collected Will*,
O'er thrones and globes elate
Sits Empreſs, crowning good, repreſſing ill;
Smit by her ſacred frown
The fiend *Diſcrétion* like a vapour ſinks,
And e'en th' all-dazzling *Crown*
Hides his faint rays, and at her bidding shrinks.

PASSY 1783,
Printed by B. F. BACHE.

Benjamin Franklin Bache's First Broadside

the Benefit of yours, you may command freely Sir, Your most obedient Servant[3]   B FRANKLIN

Ebenezer Hazard Esqr Postmaster General

Addressed: Ebenezer Hazzard Esqr / Post Master General of / the United States / of America.—

Endorsed: Letter Benja. Franklin Decr. 26th. 1783

To Mary Hewson   ALS: Yale University Library

Dear Polly,   Passy, Dec. 26. 1783.
    In reading Mr Viny's Letter when I receiv'd it, I miss'd see-ing yours which was written behind it in a Corner.[4] I thank you much for your kind Offer respecting my Grandson. I was fully resolv'd on sending him in September last, and engag'd Mr Jay, one of my Colleagues then going to England, to take him over in his Company:[5] But when it came to be propos'd to him, he show'd such an Unwillingness to leave me, and Temple such a Fondness for retaining him, that I concluded to keep him till

3. Though Hazard did receive this letter (as witnessed by his endorse-ment), there is no evidence that he answered it. Neither did he acknowledge it when writing a long letter of complaint to the president of Congress at the end of 1784 about the deficiencies of the arrangement; on the contrary, he implied that he had never been consulted about any aspects of the packet service. He had already complained to a previous president when he first read about the arrangement in a New York newspaper in the fall of 1783. To establish the packet service without consultation with Congress, and "in direct violation of their Ordinances," he wrote, showed "high Contempt of their Authority" and was "an Insult offered to their Dignity." Hazard to Richard Henry Lee, Dec. 23, 1784; Hazard to Elias Boudinot, Oct. 14, 1783 (both at the National Archives).

4. Her note was on the verso of Viny's letter, which is published under the date [after Nov. 28].

5. BF also talked to Henry Dagge about escorting BFB. In a note to BF dated only "Saturday morning" (October, 1783?), Dagge wrote that be-cause he had received no word from BF since his visit to Passy, and as he was leaving Paris the next day, he would not "have the pleasure of

I should go over myself. He behaves very well, & we love him very much.

I send herewith two different French Grammars, not knowing which to prefer, Opinions here being divided. Your French Master may take his Choice, and you will present the other to my Godson[6] as my New Year's Gift, with the two Volumes of *Synonymes Françoises*,[7] an excellent Work. They will be left at Mr. Hodgson's, Merchant, in Coleman Street, where you may have them on sending for them. Adieu, my dear Friend. I long to see you and yours, but God only knows when that may happen. I am nevertheless Yours most affectionately   B FRANKLIN

Mrs Hewson

Endorsed: B. F. Dec. 26 /— 83

To Jane Mecom

Reprinted from *The London Magazine*, new series, III (1825), 479.[8]

Dear Sister,   Passy. Dec 26. 1783.

Our Cousin, Mr. Williams, left London in June last, on his return to Boston. He carried some goods for you. I hope he

---

Escorting my young Friend to London." He had just spoken to Walpole, and would soon send BF a memoir about the "Ohio Business." Walpole would also discuss it with BF. APS. Dagge visited BF *c.* the end of September; see Dagge to BF, [Sept. 26] and, for the Walpole Co., the references cited there.

6. William Hewson, Jr.: XIX, 43.

7. BF misspelled the title of Gabriel Girard, *Synonymes françois . . .*, ed. Nicolas Beauzée (2 vols.; Paris, 1769). He had owned a set of these volumes since at least 1781, though it has not been located: XXXVI, 332. The work was reprinted several times in Paris and elsewhere, and a revised edition was published in Paris in 1780.

8. On March 28, 1825, a correspondent signing himself "D W B. Jr." sent to the *London Mag.* copies of eight previously unpublished letters from BF to female family members: one to his mother, one to his daughter, and six to Jane Mecom. The correspondent explained that he had copied them from originals in the possession of BF's family, and knew BF's handwriting well enough to pronounce them genuine. In 2006 the Library Company of Philadelphia acquired a manuscript that appears to be a retained copy of

arrived safe, though I have no Letter from him. I have since sent him a bill of exchange for your account on Dr. Cooper, and signified my desire that the whole might be put to interest to produce a little annual income for you.[9]

I hope you continue to enjoy health, one of the best of God's blessings. He has been pleased to continue mine to me through a long life hitherto, and I feel myself still strong and vigorous. Too sedentary a life, occasioned by an employment that requires much writing, has brought upon me, sometimes the gout, and at length the stone. It has not yet become very painful, and if by the regimen I observe I can prevent its increase, it may, for the little time I can expect to live, be borne with.

I am soliciting leave to come home,[1] which, if I can obtain, we may yet once more see each other before we die.— Till when, I am ever, my dear Sister, Your affectionate Brother,

B. FRANKLIN

the transmittal, including the cover letter and four additional items (three letters from wf to Jane Mecom and one fragment of a letter to Josiah Flagg). The Library Company argues convincingly that the manuscript is in the hand of William Duane, Jr., a son of bfb's widow: *The Annual Report of the Library Company of Philadelphia for the Year 2006* (Philadelphia, 2007), pp. 34–5. The *London Mag.* published these eight letters from bf, plus a ninth from bf to Jane Mecom, in the issues of August, November, and December, 1825. Two of them have not survived in any other form, including the present document. The other, which was overlooked by our predecessors, will be published in the addenda: bf to Jane Mecom, Aug. 19, 1762 in the *London Mag.*, new ser., III (1825), 430.

9. bf here repeats what he had written to Mecom on Sept. 13; see xl, 624–5, and Williams to bf, Dec. 20 (above).

1. See letter (I) to Mifflin, immediately below.

To Thomas Mifflin: Two Letters

(I) AL (incomplete draft):[2] Library of Congress; (II) ALS and transcript: National Archives

I.

Dear Sir,   Passy, Dec. 26[3] 1783.

I congratulate you very sincerely on your Appointment to that very honourable Station, the Presidency of Congress: Every Testimony you receive of the public Sense of your Services and Talents, gives me Pleasure.

I have written to you a long Letter on Business, in my quality of Minister.[4] This is a private Letter, respecting my personal Concerns, which I presume to trouble you with on the Score of our ancient Friendship.

In a Letter of the 12th of March 1781. I stated my Age and Infirmities to the Congress, and requested they would be pleased to recall me, that I might enjoy the little left me of the Evening of Life in Repose and in the Sweet Society of my Friends and Family.[5] I was answered by the then President, that when Peace should be made, if I persisted in the same Request, it should be granted.[6] I acquiesc'd. The Preliminaries were signed in No-

---

2. What survives of this draft is two pages written on the recto and verso of a single sheet. The text, marked up by WTF, was the source for what was published in WTF, *Memoirs*, I, 358–9. WTF made a number of revisions: he underlined certain elements, changed a word, altered several spellings, expanded abbreviations, and provided two citations. He also inserted a closing bracket at the end of the last full sentence on the second page, lined through the remaining text (the beginning of a sentence that obviously continued on a second sheet), and placed a row of asterisks over the deleted line. The *Memoirs* reproduces the asterisks, followed by an explanatory paragraph written by WTF that begins with the word "Some," which WTF wrote as a catchword at the bottom of the sheet.

Subsequent editors of BF's writings published WTF's version but did not include the asterisks. Instead, they supplied a complimentary close and a signature, creating the illusion of a complete letter. We have ignored WTF's interventions in the text presented here.

3. BF originally wrote 24; the 6 was overwritten.

4. Above, Dec. 25.

5. XXXIV, 446–7.

6. XXXV, 174–5.

vember 82, and I then repeated my Petition.[7] A Year is past and I have no Answer. Undoubtedly if the Congress should think my continuing here necessary for the public Service, I ought as a good Citizen to submit to their Judgment and Pleasure; but as they may easily supply my Place to advantage, that cannot be the Case; I suppose therefore that it is merely the multiplicity of more important Affairs that has put my Request out of their Mind: What I would then desire of you is, to put this Matter in Train to be mov'd and answer'd as soon as possible, that I may arrange my Affairs accordingly.

In the Letter above mention'd, to which I beg leave to refer you, I gave a Character of my Grandson Wm. Temple Franklin, and solicited for him the Favour & Protection of Congress.[8] I have nothing to abate of that Character; on the contrary I think him so much improv'd as to be capable of executing with Credit to himself & Advantage to the Public, any Employment in Europe the Congress may think fit to honour him with. He has been seven Years in the Service, and is much esteem'd by all that know him, particularly by the Minister; who, since my new Disorder, the Stone, makes my going to Versailles inconvenient to me, transacts our Business with him in the most obliging & friendly manner. It is natural for me, who love him, to wish to see him settled before I die, in some Employ that may probably be permanent; and I hope you will be so good to me, as to get that Affair likewise moved and carried thro' in his Favour. He has I think this additional Merit to plead, that he has serv'd in my Office as Secretary several Years for the small Salary of 300 Louis a Year, while the Congress gave 1000 a Year to the Secretaries of other Ministers, who had not half the Employ for a Secretary that I had.[9] For it was long before a Consul was sent here, and we had all that Business on our hands, with a great deal of Admiralty Business in examining & condemning Captures taken by our Cruisers, & by the French Cruisers under our Commission; besides the constant Attendance in examining & recording the Acceptances of the Congress Bills

7. XXXVIII, 416–17.

8. XXXIV, 447–8.

9. For Congress' resolution setting secretarial salaries see XXX, 543; for WTF's salary see XXXVIII, 166n.

of Exchange, which has been from the immense Number very fatiguing; with many other extra Affairs, not usually occurring to other Ministers, such as the Care of the Prisoners in England, & the constant Correspondence relating to them, in all which he serv'd me as Secretary, with the Assistance only of a Clerk at low Wages (60 Louis a Year),[1] so that the Saving has been very considerable to the Publick. And it should not be forgotten that tho his Commission as Secretary to the Plenipotentiaries[2]

(Private) To His Excelly. Tho. Mifflin Esqr President of Congress

II.

Sir,   Passy, Dec. 26. 1783.——
If the Congress should think it fit to have a Consul for the United States in London, and do not appoint one of our own Country to that Office, I beg leave to mention the Merits of Mr. William Hodgson, a Merchant of that City, who has always been a zealous Friend of America, was a principal Promoter of the Subscription for the Relief of American Prisoners, and Chairman of the Committee for Dispensing the Money rais'd by that Subscription: He also took the Trouble of applying the Monies I furnished him with, when the Subscription was exhausted; and constantly assisted me in all the Negociations I had with the British Ministers in their Favour, wherein he generally succeeded, being a Man of Weight & Credit, very active, and much esteemed for his Probity & Integrity. These his Services continued steadily during the whole War, seem to entitle him to

1. The clerk in question was L'Air de Lamotte, whose salary for the first half of 1783 was raised to 1,440 *l.t.* (60 *louis*) per year: Account XXVII (xxxii, 4). BF had originally written "50 louis," Lamotte's former salary. A numeral 6 was written over the 5, but we cannot be certain of when that change was made.

2. A clue as to what the remainder of this letter might have contained comes from BF's outline of topics to be covered in letters to Mifflin, for which see the annotation of BF to Mifflin, Dec. 25. The line he numbered 14 covers the topics included thus far: "My Malady Incertitude. Grandson." The line numbered 15, which is reflected in no extant letter to Mifflin or to any other member of Congress, reads: "If not permitted to resign I think of taking a House at Versailles. Sedans." This is our only direct evidence that BF was seriously considering a move. A possible location was proposed to him by Feriet on Jan. 21, below.

the favourable Notice of Congress, when any Occasion offers of doing him Service or Pleasure. With great Respect, I have the honour to be, Sir, Your Excellency's most obedient & most humble Servant   B FRANKLIN

His Excelly. Tho. Mifflin Esqr President of Congress.—

Notation: Letter 26 Decr. 1783 Doctr B. Franklin Read 5 March 1784 Referred to Mr Gerry &c

To Benjamin Rush[3]

Reprinted from *The Pennsylvania Packet, And General Advertiser,* June 29, 1784; copy:[4] Bibliothèque de Genève

Dear Sir,   Passy, near Paris, Dec. 26, 1783.

I do not know who is at present secretary of our philosophical society, and therefore I address to you, who read French, a book lately published here,[5] which gives an account of one of

3. At its meeting on March 19, 1784, the APS acknowledged receiving a letter from BF with "a French treatise on Air Balloons," *i.e.,* the present letter. The society directed Rush to publish it along with "translations of the most interesting parts of the treatise": *Early Proc. of the APS* (Philadelphia, 1884), p. 124. Rush did not publish any translations, to our knowledge, but did submit BF's letter to the *Pa. Packet,* where it appeared following an open letter to the citizens of Philadelphia announcing a subscription to finance the construction of "a large and elegant Air Balloon" 60 feet high and 50 feet in diameter. Some 88 prominent Philadelphians, including Rush, were subscribers. After the list of their names, BF's letter was introduced with this statement: "It may not be amiss to close this detail with the following letter from our ingenious countryman and fellow citizen, now minister from the United States of America, at Paris; being addressed to a former secretary of the American philosophical society in this city."

4. The copy is in a hand we do not recognize but appears to be contemporary. We publish from the newspaper version, as the copy contains several obvious spelling mistakes. Furthermore, as compared to the printed version, it contains differences in capitalization and abbreviations, as well as minor discrepancies in wording. It also includes a line below the signature that identifies the recipient as "Dr Benj. Rush".

5. Barthélemy Faujas de Saint-Fond, *Description des expériences de la machine aérostatique de MM. de Montgolfier* . . . (Paris, 1783). TJ had a copy by April 28, 1784, when he summarized the various experiments: *Jefferson Papers,* VII, 134–7.

the most extraordinary discoveries that this age has produced, by which men are enabled to rise in the air, and travel with the wind. Having been an eye witness twice of this amazing experiment,[6] I thought it my duty to communicate to the society as early as possible the best account that has been published of it, which I now beg leave to do through you, who can easily make an extract and translation of the most material parts for the satisfaction of the society. Never surely was a philosophical experiment so magnificently attended as the last, of which I enclose a print that well represents it. All Paris was out to see it, and all the inhabitants of the neighbouring towns, so that there could hardly be less than half a million of spectators. The flight of these two philosophers, messieurs Charles and Robert, was considerably farther than the distance between Dover and Calais.

I intend the society a considerable and valuable present of books, such as are proper to promote the ends of their institution. The French *Encyclopedie*, is among them.— Be pleased to assure the society of my respects, and believe me to be, with sincere regard, Dear Sir, Your most obedient, humble servant,

B. FRANKLIN

From the Baron de Breteuil[7]

LS: American Philosophical Society

Versailles Le 26. Xbre. 1783.

J'ai reçu, Monsieur, La lettre que vous m'avez fait l'honneur de m'ecrire[8] et par laquelle vous demandez au nom des Parens du Né. [nommé] schaffer détenu dans les Prisons de La Con-

6. BF witnessed manned balloon ascensions on Nov. 21 and Dec. 1; see his letters to Joseph Banks of Nov. 21 [*i.e.*, 22–25] and Dec. 1[–2].

7. Louis-Auguste Le Tonnelier, baron de Breteuil (1730–1807), was a diplomat who between 1760 and 1783 served as French ambassador to Russia, Sweden, the Dutch Republic, the Kingdom of Naples, and the Habsburg Monarchy. In 1783 Louis XVI appointed him minister of the king's household (*la Maison du Roi*), thereby putting him in charge of overseeing the administration of Paris: *DBF*.

8. While this letter has not been found, there is a much edited draft of it among BF's papers, written by Shaffer's lawyer, Beaumont, with a few emendations by WTF. Calling Shaffer a "malheureux étourdi," it states that

DECEMBER 26, 1783

ciergerie, des Ordres du Roi pour le faire passer aux Isles.—
Je vais en Ecrire à M. Lenoir, et je vous prie d'Etre persuadé
d'avance que je ferai tout ce que Les Circonstances pouront
permettre. Mais je ne dois pas vous Laisser ignorer d'abord
qu'on n'envoye plus personne de force aux Isles, et que d'ailleurs
quand les tribunaux Ordinaires ont pris Connoissance d'un délit
quelconque, l'autorité ne peut plus S'en meler, a moins que Les
Juges ne consentent a ne donner aucune suite aux procedures
qu'ils ont commencées.

J'ai l'honneur d'Etre avec un très sincere attachement, Monsieur, votre trés humble et trés obéissant serviteur./.

LE BON. DE BRETEÜIL

M. franklin, Ministre Plenipotentiaire des Etats unis de L'amerique..à Passi.

From Joseph-Mathias Gérard de Rayneval

ALS: American Philosophical Society

A Versailles le 26. Xbre. 1783
Permettez-vous, Monsieur, que je vous recommande le paquet
ci-joint. Je Supose que la fregate le Washington[9] n'est pas encore
parti.

Barclay and BF suggest deporting Shaffer by means of a *lettre de cachet* to
the "isles," where he could hide his remorse and shame. APS.

Though deportation was not generally practiced in France, delinquents
from wealthy or prominent families could request this extralegal punishment; they were sent either to North America or the Caribbean. The families had to pay all expenses: Richard M. Andrews, *Law, magistracy, and
crime in Old Regime Paris, 1735–1789* (1 vol. to date, Cambridge and New
York, 1994–), I, 410n.

9. The *General Washington.* BF received two other requests dated
Dec. 26, 1783, to forward letters in the express he was sending to Capt.
Barney at Le Havre: from "Mr. Carter" (John Barker Church: XL, 263–4)
and from Griffin Greene, who stressed the urgency of his letter's being
sent to Gen. Nathanael Greene (his cousin). Both notes are at the APS.
For Greene's trip to France to sell the *Flora,* in which his extended family
owned a part interest, see Richard K. Showman *et al.,* eds., *The Papers of
General Nathanael Greene* (13 vols., Chapel Hill, N.C., and London, 1976–
2005), I, 107n; XII, 662–4, 677–8; XIII, 240n.

Un de mes amis, Monsieur, desiroit avoir une lettre de recommandation de Votre part pour M. le Dr. Price, et je Serois Sensiblement obligé Si vous vouliez bien me l'accorder. Mon ami
S'appelle de Chateaufort; il va passé quelques mois en angleterre
pour Satisfaire Sa curiosité.[1]

J'ai l'honneur dêtre avec un parfait attachement, Monsieur,
Votre très humble et tres obeissant serviteur   DE RAYNEVAL

From John Jay

ALS: American Philosophical Society; AL (draft): Columbia University
Library

Dear Sir   Bath 26 Decr 1783

Since we parted I have been so much & so long indisposed
as that (except short Letters to Mrs. Jay) I have denied myself
the Pleasure of writing to my Friends. The Kindness you have
shewn us both, has nevertheless not been forgotten, nor has my
Disposition to acknowledge and be influenced by it in the least
abated.

We have lately had a Report here that you was very ill with
the Stone, and some have said that you intended to seek Relief
from an operation. This Report has alarmed your Friends, and
I am anxious to know how far it may be well founded. It would
give me sincere Satisfaction to have it contradicted under your
own Hand—

I decline saying any thing about politics, for obvious Reasons—the public Papers afford you the Means of forming a
Judgment of them especially as your long Experience & knowledge of this Country enable you to see further than ordinary
Observers.

There are many in this Country who speeke of you with
great Respect. The honest Whig Club drink your Health very

1. BF obliged, though the letter has not been located. Ignace-Romain,
chevalier d'Aristay de Chateaufort (1743–1814), was sent to England on a
confidential mission at the end of 1783. When he returned to Paris the following spring he was appointed consul in Charleston: Gérard de Rayneval
to BF, May 15, 1784 (APS); Anne Mézin, *Les Consuls de France au siècle des
lumières (1715–1792)* ([Paris, 1998]), pp. 103–5.

affectionately—there are others who like you as little as the Eagle did the Cat,[2] and probably for the same Reasons. When we meet we will talk these Matters over with less Reserve than I can write— Present my affectionate Compliments to your two Grandsons[3]—and believe me to be with great Esteem & Regard Dear Sir Your obliged & obt. Servt   JOHN JAY

P.S. As we have yet no news of Mr. Thaxter's Arrival, would it not be well to send over Copies of the Treaty?—

His Excellency Doctr. Franklin—

Addressed: His Excellency / Doctr. Franklin / Minister plenipotentiary from the United States / of America at the Court of France— / Passy

Notation: John Jay, Bath 26 Decr. 1782.—

To Elias Boudinot   ALS: Yale University Library

Sir,   Passy, Dec. 27. 1783.—
     Your two Letters to the Commissioners, dated at Princeton the 27th of October & 1st of November, and one to me of the first of November, came duly to Hand; Mr Adams saw the public Letters in England, Capt. Jones having landed with them at Plymouth. We thank you much for the Intelligence they contain. I am now alone here, Mr. Jay being at Bath, with Mr Laurens, and Mr Adams either in England or Holland: But I have written fully to the new President respecting the Instructions, &c. communicated with your Letters.[4] And now, Sir, give me leave to congratulate you on the fortunate Events that have distinguish'd your Presidency, and on your honourable Retreat from it into private Life. The first well-improv'd may make us all happy, and

     2. A fable by BF, in which a cat forces an eagle to release her. BF had told it to his fellow peace commissioners in the fall of 1782: XVII, 3; XXXVIII, 269.
     3. Jay wrote to WTF on Dec. 30, saying that his health was improving and that Samuel Chase had complained to him of not receiving an answer to his letter to BF (as Chase himself reminded BF on Dec. 20, above). APS.
     4. To Mifflin, Dec. 25, above.

the last must make you so: for I can hardly conceive a happier Being than the Man, who, having been long laden with public Cares
and fatigu'd by every-body's Business, is allow'd to retire into
the Bosom of his Family, and enjoy *Otium cum dignitate.*

With great & sincere Respect, I have the honour to be, Sir,
Your most obedient & most humble Servant   B FRANKLIN

Honble. Elias Boudinot Esqr

Endorsed: Dr. B. Franklin Decr 24. 1783

From Jérôme-Marie Champion de Cicé[5]

ALS: Library of Congress

paris le 27. xbre. 1783

J'ay reçu, Monsieur, la lettre que vous m'avez fait l'honneur de
m'ecrire au sujet des Catholiques americains.[6] Vous pouvez etre
Sur en Cette occasion Comme en toute autre de mon empressement à Seconder vos vües tant par rapport à vos Catholiques
dont il est facile d'assurer le Service, qu'en faveur de M. L'abbé
de la Roche que j'estime et aime. J'aurois besoin dans le moment
de quelques ecclaircissements qu'il est sans doute en votre pouvoir de me procurer;[7] je voudrois savoir

5. Champion de Cicé (1753–1810), a liberal and reformer, had been archbishop of Bordeaux since 1781: *DBF*. An English translation of his letter is
published in Jules A. Baisnée, *France and the Establishment of the American
Catholic Hierarchy: the Myth of French Interference (1783–1784)* (Baltimore,
1934), p. 58.

6. This now-missing letter appears to have been similar to the one BF
wrote to Vergennes on Dec. 15. Champion de Cicé described its contents
in a letter to Vergennes written on the same date as the present letter: BF
proposed the appointment of a French ecclesiastic to oversee the Catholic
Church in America. The archbishop urged Vergennes not to miss this opportunity to strengthen the Catholic faith as well as ties between the United
States and France. Before he answered BF, Champion considered it his duty
to seek Vergennes' advice. Vergennes replied on Jan. 8 that he had already
written to the bishop of Autun on this matter: Baisnée, *France and the Establishment of the American Catholic Hierarchy*, pp. 59–61. For the bishop's
response see the annotation of BF to Vergennes, Dec. 15.

7. We have no record of BF's response. On Jan. 31, 1784, La Luzerne,
the French minister in Philadelphia, wrote Vergennes, warning that Ameri-

1° Comment S'est fait jusqua present le Service des Catholiques
2° Si les pouvoirs des pretres Catholiques venoient directement de Rome, ou Si l'Ev. [Evêque] de quebec avoit quelque
jurisdiction en amerique
3° Si la Subsistance des ministre Catholiques est assurée et par
quels moyens.

Ces ecclaircissements me mettront en etat de vous proposer
mes Vües pour l'avenir.

Ne doutez jamais je vous prie du Sincere et Respectueux attachement avec lequel j'ay l'honneur d'etre Monsieur Votre très
humble et très obeissant Serviteur

† J. M. ARCH. DE BORDEAUX

From Samuel Vaughan, Jr.

ALS: American Philosophical Society

Clausthall in the Hartz, 27 Decr. 1783.

My Dear & Honoured Sir,

It has long been my sincerest wish to return you my warmest & best thanks for your kind & affectionate attentions to me
when at Paris,[8] but I refrained troubling you with a letter till I
could entertain you with something new & worthy your attention. Till the present moment I have unfortunately been only in
those spots that you have yourself formerly visited;[9] & if I have
happened to have made any new observation, It is in the miner-
alogical line which cannot so much interest you.

Another Subject is therefore the occasion of my addressing
you at present. It would give me singular satisfaction if you
would be so obliging to send me some Account of Mr Charles's

can Catholics would not be pleased with a foreign bishop. This letter was
received on April 23: Baisnée, *France and the Establishment of the American
Catholic Hierarchy*, pp. 63–7, 79.

8. In June BF provided Vaughan with a letter of introduction to Ingenhousz and possibly with financial support and a passport for his trip to Germany: XL, 96, 443n.

9. BF and John Pringle traveled through Germany from June to August,
1766, visiting Bad Pyrmont, Hanover, Göttingen, Frankfurt, Mainz, and
Cologne: XIII, 314–16, 383–4.

process to raise his Machine,[1] & the Stuffs of which it was made; as the Gazettes, altho' filled with accounts of it, are yet imperfect or confused on both these heads: but the articles which I am most interested to be acquainted with, are the results of Mr Lavoisiers memoirs, viz, the *cheapest* manner to procure Inflammable Air, its cost at Paris, the sort of Inflammable Air he thought best suited the purpose & *their relative Weights*.[2] I should be far from making the above request Sir, was I not perfectly convinced from the notority of the Subject, that all the above must be in Print, & that you have only to request Mr Darcel[3] your under Secretary to inclose & forward them for me, to the care of Baron Reden, Berghauptman,[4] at Clausthall in the Hartz, by the earliest post he conveniently can.

I have had under my examination a Mountain which you have Sir formerly visited, but as perhaps you did not examine it with the same views as myself, I shall take the liberty of mentioning some particulars respecting it.

The Weisner is an Isolated Mountain, as it is the highest in the Country of Hessia,[5] & bears no proportion in this respect to the Hills that are by the side of it. The Entire Top is of Basalt, & under it on every side is found a *Coal originating from Wood;* & the Roof of this immense Coal Mine is Cristals of Basalt. I do

1. Charles's hydrogen balloon, which he launched most recently on Dec. 1: BF to Joseph Banks, Dec. 1[–2].

2. Vaughan was most likely thinking of the memoir Lavoisier read at the public meeting of the Académie des sciences on Nov. 12, described in the *Jour. de Paris* on Nov. 15. It reported on experiments conducted in June (see XL, 78n) which showed that water was not an element, but a compound of dephlogisticated and inflammable air (oxygen and hydrogen), which could be decomposed and recomposed. The memoir also speculated that there might be more than one kind of inflammable air. An extract of the memoir was published in the December issue of the *Jour. de physique;* an expanded version appeared in the *Mémoires* of the Académie des sciences the following year: *Histoire de l'Académie royale des sciences* for 1781 (Paris, 1784), pp. 468–94.

3. Nicolas Darcel was the clerk of Matthew Ridley: XXXVII, 278n.

4. Claus Friedrich von Reden served as superintendent of mines (*i.e.*, the *Berghauptmann*) in Brunswick-Lüneburg: *Neue Deutsche Biographie* (24 vols., Berlin, 1953–2010), XVI, 600.

5. Vaughan is undoubtedly referring to the Wasserkuppe, the highest peak (3,117 feet) in the Rhön mountains within the state of Hesse.

not doubt Sir Joh: Banks having seen Basalt formed by Lava's running into the sea;[6] but merely offer it as a doubt, whether Nature has not in this case two methods of producing the same effect: For, according to his Theory, the Top of this Mountain should have been entirely under Water; which excludes the possibility of Wood being under Basalt, as Forest could not grow there, & that flooded Wood would occupy the highest part of the Sea; & consequently, be beyond the sphere of action of *solid* Basalt. I have some very fine pieces of this Wood, which I procured myself in the Mine, & it is so very perfect, that it bears in the Mine, with the action of Water & Air, the same plants Wood always does when put in a similar situation, & is in the first Stage of Decay. I am a little anxious to know the Species of Wood, which can be determined; & I carry specimens with me in hopes of meeting a Connoisseur of the internal texture of Woods.

As I write in Haste I cannot enlarge on the above subject, or enter on others: however, I hope shortly Sir, to have the honor again to address you or Mr William Franklin, to whom I beg my most affectionate regards.[7]

I was very sorry to hear of your being attacked by the Gout; but as you assisted at the Experiments of Messrs Mongolfier & Charles, you must be of course recovered. My prayers will be ever for your health & happiness, being with the greatest respect, My Dear Sir, Your truly affectionate, devoted, & Obliged hble servt., SAMUEL VAUGHAN JUNR

6. In his celebrated description of Fingal's Cave on the island of Staffa, which he visited in August, 1772, Joseph Banks noted that the cave's basaltic columns had the appearance of cooled-off lava. Banks's description, from his manuscript journal of an expedition to Iceland, became widely known after it was published in Thomas Pennant, *A Tour in Scotland, and Voyage to the Hebrides* . . . (Chester, 1774): Roy A. Rauschenberg, ed., "The Journals of Joseph Banks's Voyage up Great Britain's West Coast to Iceland and to the Orkney Isles, July to October, 1772," APS *Proc.*, CXVII (1973), 206–9; Harold B. Carter, *Sir Joseph Banks, 1743–1820* (London, 1988), pp. 119–20, 124.

7. Vaughan did not write again during this trip, to the best of our knowledge, and did not correspond further about the geology of the Wasserkuppe. However, on the verso of the postscript sheet he drew and annotated a sketch of the mountaintop area, identifying active mines and the site

ps. The Queries I have taken the liberty to lay down Sir at the beginning of this letter respecting Mr Mongolfiers Machine, are not merely from Curiosity. Plans are yet too young to mention, but if they are completed & attended with Success, the result will be of no small importance. The only demur is the Expense of Air, but I think too much cannot be known beforehand; & therefore I should wish also to add one Query to the preceeding ones: What method Mr Charles used to let out his Inflammable Air when he wished to descend.

I beg My Congratulations to Mr Charles, & Comps to all American friends, & the good Abbés at Place Vendome.[8]

Addressed: To / His Excellency Dr Franklin, / Minister Pleni-potentiary from the / United States of America, / at Passy, / near Paris. / *franc* Ffort

Notation: Vaughan Mr. Samuel 27 Decr. 1783.

From John Charretié[9]   AL: American Philosophical Society

28 December 1783
Mr Charretié presents his best respects to his Excellency Dr Franklin he proposed having the honour of waiting upon him but his business at Versailles having prevented him, from whence he is this moment returned, with an express order from

---

where BF had entered with Pringle and "Prof: Hollmann of Gottingen." This was Samuel Christian Hollmann (*ADB*), a naturalist and professor of philosophy and natural theology at the University of Göttingen. Hollmann was a founder of the Königliche Gesellschaft der Wissenschaften at Göttingen, which admitted BF and Pringle as members on July 19, 1766, during their visit to the town. BF reciprocated by sending the academy a copy of the 1769 edition of *Exper. and Obser.*, inscribed: "To the Royal Academy of Sciences at Göttingen As a small Token of his Respect and Duty, This Book is humbly presented by the Author": Beatrice M. Victory, *Benjamin Franklin and Germany* (Philadelphia, 1915), pp. 48–9.

8. The abbés Chalut and Arnoux stayed on the Place Vendôme in the Paris residence of the farmer general Geoffroy Chalut de Vérin: XXX, 250n.

9. A French merchant living in London who, with BF's recommendation, became the French government's agent for representing the interests of French prisoners of war in England: XXXIV, 101, 152.

the Minister[1] to sett out for London on Teusday morning, this renders his going to Passy impossible, he therefore sends the inclosed[2] by a Messenger, and if his Exce has any commands for Mr Sargent or any other person Mr Charretié begs they may be sent by to morrow night to him at Mr Bousie rue du petit Bourbon F. S. G.[3]

Notation: Charretie 28 Dec. 1783.

From the Société Typographique de Lausanne[4]

Printed D with MS insertions:[5] American Philosophical Society

Monsieur   LAUSANNE, le *28e. Xbre 1783.*

NOUS avons l'honneur de vous donner avis, d'une entreprise que nous venons de faire, & qui nous a paru jusqu'à présent, aussi désirée qu'utile au Public. C'est de prendre dans la nouvelle Encyclopédie par ordre de matieres, tout ce qui manque à la premiere Encyclopédie par ordre alphabétique, & d'en former un Supplément à l'usage de tous ceux qui sont possesseurs de cette derniere, dans les formats in-folio, in-4°. & in-8°. L'ouvrage est déja commencé, & avancera rapidement, parce que tout est préparé pour agir. Pour connoître mieux les détails & les conditions de l'entreprise, Nous vous envoyons le Prospectus.[6]

1. Castries.
2. The Dec. 19 letter from John and Rosamond Sargent.
3. Faubourg Saint-Germain.
4. Our usual practice is to spell names in our title lines according to how the writers themselves sign. In this case, we correct the society's typographical error. The previous correspondence from this publishing house concerned BF's failure to pay for its edition of the *Encyclopédie* in octavo, a printed version to which he had subscribed in 1778: XXVII, 594–5; XXXVIII, 297–8; XL, 552–4.
5. The insertions are in the hand of co-director Jean-Pierre Duplan. Because we reproduce them in italic type, we do not preserve the italics in this printed circular, which was set almost entirely in italic, with roman type used to emphasize certain phrases. Small capitals were used for the dateline, signature, and first word; these we preserve.
6. In the four-page printed enclosure, dated Dec. 10 and titled "Prospectus d'un Supplément à l'Encyclopédie alphabétique, extrait de l'Encyclopédie

En attendant l'honneur de vos ordres, nous avons celui d'être parfaitement, M*onsieur* Vos très-humbles & très-obéissants Serviteurs,   LA SOCIÉTÉ TYPOGRAHHIQUE
à Lausanne en Suisse.

Addressed: A Monsieur / Monsieur le Docteur Francklin / à Paris / par Versoix

Notation: La Sociéte typographique de Lausanne 28 Dec. 1783

To John and Rosamond Sargent[7]

ALS: Princeton University Library

Passy, Dec. 29. 1783

You cannot conceive, my dear Friends, how happy your kind Letters make me. To find that thro' all the unpleasant Circumstances that so long have separated us, you still retain your ancient Regard for me, gives me a Pleasure inexpressible. A Thousand Thanks for your hearty Invitation to your House. I am sure I can be no where happier, than with a Family I so much love. Whether I can come over in the Spring, is yet uncertain, but it is very certain that I long exceedingly to see & embrace you all; being ever, my dear Friends, Yours most affectionately

B FRANKLIN

Mr & Mrs Sargent

---

par ordre des matieres," the Sociétés typographiques of Lausanne, Bern, and Neuchâtel announced the opening of a subscription for a supplement to Diderot's *Encyclopédie*, which would consist of selections from the recently launched *Encyclopédie méthodique* (XXXVII, 240–1n) that contained new or revised information. Instead of having to buy the expensive new edition, owners of the old *Encyclopédie* would thus be able to acquire only those parts that corrected Diderot's mistakes or brought the scientific information up to date. Although the prospectus attracted many subscribers, publication of the *Encyclopédie méthodique* proceeded so slowly that this edition of pirated selections was never issued: Robert Darnton, *The Business of Enlightenment: a Publishing History of the* Encyclopédie, *1775–1800* (Cambridge, Mass., and London, 1979), pp. 385–8.

7. In answer to their letter of Dec. 19.

From John Walter[8]   ALS: American Philosophical Society

Sir.   London Decr. 29th. 1783.

As a Gentleman of Science & a Well Wisher to the new erected Empire, I address myself to You on an Improvement, which is now introduc'd into the World, on which a pamphlet is just publish'd,[9] to print with Words entire, instead of single Letters, which will be of the most important Use in the future Conduct of the Press, both for Dispatch, neatness, & Correctness— It is intended to be executed both by an Alphabetical, & numerical Arrangement, which are now inspecting by many Men of Letters, & has had the strong Approbation of Sr. Jos. Banks, the Members of the British Museum &c & has had a very gracious Reception from our Sovereign, to whom it is dedicated by his Permission.—

As no Doubt this Improvement will be equally acceptable to America, if a liberable Encouragement is given, an exact Copy of the Founts, & the Mode of conducting it shall be sent You, which cannot fail of proving acceptable to a Country, where the Arts will no Doubt flourish in an eminent Degree— The numerical Fount will be particularly useful in the dead Languages, as a numerist only is requir'd to know the Subject, the Compositor having Numbers before him, & therefore may be ignorant of what he composes. If any Correspondent of yours should make Application by your Direction, further Particulars may be known, as no doubt will the Writer of this Letter from Sir Your Most Obedt. Servt.   JOHN WALTER

PS. My Address is Queens Square Bloomsbury.

Dr. Benja. Franklin.

---

8. Walter (1739–1812), a coal merchant whose business was ruined during the war, bought from Henry Johnson in 1782 the patent for "logography," a method of printing with casts of complete words instead of individual letters. In 1785 he established a newspaper that was printed logographically; that paper became the *Times* of London: *DNB*. The present overture led to an enthusiastic exchange of letters that continued for many years. Most of it is published in George S. Eddy, "Correspondence Between Dr. Benjamin Franklin and John Walter, Regarding the Logographic Process of Printing," American Antiquarian Society *Proc.*, XXXVIII (1929), 349–63.

9. Henry Johnson, *An Introduction to Logography* . . . (London, 1783).

371

Addressed: Doctor Benja. Franklin. / at / Paris

Notation: John Walter Decr. 29 1784—

From Jonathan Williams, Sr.

ALS: American Philosophical Society

Hond sr—   Boston Decer 29th. 1783—
    I Wrote you a few days ago[1] adviceing that Doctr. Coopers
being Sick provented my presenting your Bill, he is now dead,
he die'd this Day about 12 oClock, I shall endever to git your
Bill answerd, I think the famley will pay it as the Doctr. has left
a good Estate for one of the Cloth we think the death of this
Ameable man is not only a Loss to his famley & Church but to
the public in general—
    I have Cleard your huse agreeable to your Sisters desire, I
expect Aunt with her Children to town Next week to take
Possession & Live there Which I Conclude will be agreeable
to you—[2]
    I Entertaind Some flatering expectations of your Coming to
Boston this fall, now we hope you will Come in the Spring, at
our house we Shall be happy to Se you & your G Son—
    My Wife Joines in duty to you & Love to Billey Belive me
ever Your Dutefull Nephew & most Hble Servant—

                                          JONA. WILLIAMS

Addressed: His Excellency Benjamin Franklin Esqr / at /
Passy / in France

1. On Dec. 20, above.
2. The Unity Street house in Boston had formerly belonged to BF's half
sister Elizabeth Douse. As of 1763, BF arranged for Williams to let the
house and forward the rent payments to Jane Mecom: x, 198n, 356–7, 384;
XXXIV, 202. She moved there with her daughter and son-in-law, Jane and
Peter Collas, and their niece: Van Doren, *Franklin-Mecom*, pp. 225–6, 230.

From Charles-Marguerite-Jean-Baptiste Mercier Dupaty[3]

ALS: American Philosphical Society

Sir   Paris December the 30th. [1783]

I have the honour to send you with a thousand thanks, the book you have been so good as to lend me.[4] I have perused it with satisfaction, notwithstanding I thougt the system of the Author incomplete, sometimes erroneus, often chimerical, and in general treated in a manner rather too superficial. But the importance of the subject, the continual clearness of the style, a good deal of Eloquence, and now and then some happy ideas, impressed if not with the fire at least with the flame of the Love of humanity, have dragged me with some rapidity to the end. I think the reader is often wandering in Heaths, but he always treads on the green and sometimes on the flowers. With pleasure then, shall I read the following volume, and should think myself under a great obligation, if you would send it to me with the two others. Were I not affraid of abusing of your Complaisance, I would beg of you to send me back this one, that I might in a second perusal, embrace at once the whole system.

3. A former advocate-general in the Parlement of Bordeaux, Dupaty became widely known in 1780–82 for his ultimately successful struggle with the Parlement over his admission as its president *à mortier*. Unable to work with the Parlement, however, Dupaty left for Paris in September, 1783. There he embarked on a long-planned study of the criminal codes of foreign nations as the basis for reform in France, for which he solicited support from Miromesnil, Vergennes, and Calonne. It is not known whether Dupaty had met BF during a previous visit to Paris or was introduced in the fall of 1783. He had been a member of the *Neuf Sœurs* since at least 1779, and was made *vénérable* in the spring of 1784; he also frequented Mme Helvétius' salon: *DBF;* William Doyle, "Dupaty (1746–1788): a Career in the Late Enlightenment," *Studies on Voltaire and the Eighteenth Century,* CCXXX (1985), 37–69.

4. Most likely the first volume of Book III of Filangieri's *La scienza della legislazione,* which BF received the previous summer: XL, 297–8, 460. BF must have informed Dupaty that he had just received the second volume; see Luigi Pio to BF, Dec. 12. During a trip to Italy in July, 1785, Dupaty was introduced to Filangieri by means of a letter written by the secretary of the queen of Naples. It characterized the bearer as one of the most esteemed magistrates in France, who greatly admired Filangieri's work and had often discussed it with BF: Doyle, "Dupaty," p. 77.

I shall not be less punctual in restoring your books, than in paying you the tribute of hommage and Veneration, wich must be looked upon as a duty by all those that are animated by the Love of philosophy, Liberty and humanity.

I have the honour to be Sir Your most humble obedient servant   DUPATY.

From the Chevalier Du Ponceau[5]

ALS: American Philosophical Society

Sir   Island of Ré the 30th. Xber. [1783]

I am in the last uneasiness Concerning my Brother's Fate. There is one year Since I receiv'd letters from him. I am afraid he Could be Sick; for I am at a loss how interpret Such a Silence. If by your assistance I could have knowledge of What it is become of him Nothing Could equal my obligations. He Was in the beginning under Secretary in the department of foreign affairs at Philadelphia but Mr. de Livingston having resigned, it is probable that he is now in an other Employement.[6]

I Inclose a Letter for him, under his ancient direction; you'll do me a great favour in Conveying it to him. I assure you that I'll never forget Such a Kindness.

Excuse me Sir, for the Liberty I take in troubling you but my unquietness is Without bound.

I have the honor to be Sir Your most humble & obedient Servant   LE CHR. DU PONCEAU

officier in the regiment of saintonge

5. The chevalier and his sister had each written to BF earlier in 1783, worried about their brother Pierre-Etienne, who had been serving Congress as undersecretary of foreign affairs: XL, 71–2, 583–4.

6. Pierre-Etienne (Peter Stephen) Du Ponceau resigned his position in early June, around the same time as Livingston's resignation was accepted. He remained in Philadelphia for the rest of his life, becoming a prominent member of the bar and winning international acclaim as a scholar of Native American languages. He was elected to the APS in 1791, and eventually served as its president: XL, 72n; *ANB; DAB;* APS List of Members.

Franklin: Certificate for Cripps & May[7]

Copy: Archives Départementales de la Gironde

Passy Trente un Xbre. 1783.

J'ai eu Connoissance de la Lettre de Mrs. Cripps et May dont il Est fait mention, négocians de Charlestown. Je Crois qu'elle Contient Vérité, et Je ne puis qu'espérer que Le placet du Capitaine Conte, Sera favorablement accüeilli. signe B Franklin

From Breteuil

LS: American Philosophical Society

Vlles. 31. Xbre 1783.

Depuis la lettre, Monsieur, que j'ai eu l'honneur de vous ecrire le Vingt Six de ce mois au Sujet du Nommé Schaffer, j'ai eté informé que ce particulier a eté arreté au mois de juillet dernier Comme prevenu d'Escroqueries; que Son procès ayant eté instruit, il a eté Condamné au Carcan et au bannissement,[8] et que Sur L'appel de ce Jugement il a eté transféré dans les prisons de la Conciergerie. L'affaire etant dans cet etat, il Serait Contre toutes les Regles que l'autorité S'en Mêlat. Mais vous pouvez vous adresser à M. le garde des Sceaux[9] pour obtenir des lettres de Remission ou de Commutation de peines. Je Suis bien faché que les Circonstances ne me permettent pas de faire ce que vous auriez desiré.

J'ai l'honneur d'être avec un très Sincere attachement, Monsieur, votre très humble et très obéissant Serviteur.

Le Bon. De Breteüil

7. A South Carolina mercantile firm that owned and outfitted ships, and traded with firms in Bordeaux: xxv, 428; xxix, 178; Idzerda, *Lafayette Papers*, ii, 59.

8. The *carcan*, an iron collar attached to a post where the convict was subjected to public shaming, was one of most common punishments at this time and was often followed by banishment from Paris (if not France). Banished convicts were frequently branded: Richard M. Andrews, *Law, magistracy, and crime in Old Regime Paris, 1735–1789* (1 vol. to date, Cambridge and New York, 1994–), i, 310–16, 410.

9. Armand-Thomas Hue de Miromesnil: xxi, 536n.

M. francklin ministre plenipotentiaire des Etats unis de L'amerique à Passy.

Notation: Le Bn. De Breteuil

From Caffiéri   ALS: American Philosophical Society

Monsieur   De Paris ce 31 Dx 1783
Si je netois pas indisposé, j'aurois l'honneur D'aller vous Souhaiter au renouvellement de cette année tout ce qui peut arriver de plus heureux à un homme de votre merite; privé de ce bonheur permettes moi de vous faire parvenir Les assurances de mon respect.

J'apprens par Les papiers publics que malgré une guerre dispendieuse Les Etats Americains, pour rendre L'autorite Civile Et Le Commerce de plus En plus florissante, Se proposent de faire batir une ville Et un palais pour Le Congrés.[1] Jose Esperer de vos bontés que Si mes foibles Talens peuvent être employés, vous voudres bien vous ressouvenir de moi, et croire que mon empressement et mon zele me rendront peut-être digne de votre chois. Soyez persuadé que je regarderai Comme un des momens les plus Gloirieux de ma vie, ce lui où je Serai asses heureux pour Servir a Eterniser en quel que chose L'Epoque La plus brillante du dix huitieme Siecle.

Je Suis avec Respect Monsieur Votre tres humble Et tres obeïssant Serviteur   CAFFIÉRI

Notation: Caffiery 31 Dec. 1783.

1. Congress resolved on Oct. 7 to erect buildings for "a federal town," the seat of the national government, along the Delaware. Due to opposition from southern delegates, this decision was repealed on Oct. 20, and the following day Congress passed a new resolution to construct two alternate capitals, one on the Delaware and the other on the Potomac: *JCC*, xxv, 654–9, 697–9, 707–14; Lawrence D. Cress, "Whither Columbia? Congressional Residence and the Politics of the New Nation, 1776 to 1787," *W&MQ*, 3rd ser., xxxii (1975), 593–6. A French translation of the Oct. 7 resolution, which mentioned "Edifices" (not a palace), was printed in the *Gaz. de Leyde*, Dec. 16, sup.

From the Chevalier Dubuysson[2]

ALS: American Philosophical Society

Monsieur   moulins En Bourbonnois le 31. Xre. 1783.

M Le marquis de lafayette me fait demander Les papiers que J'ai eu L'honneur de vous faire passer.[3] Je ne scais si c'est pour vous Les Communiquer ou pour vérifier Lui même. Si je Suis susceptible de Lordre des Cincinati en [ce] cas Je vous prie Monsieur, de vouloir bien Les Lui faire passer sur Le champ j'ôse en même tems vous suplier Monsieur, de m'être favorable dans La circonstance présente:

Jai L'honneur d'être avec un profond Respect Monsieur Votre très humble Et très obéissant Serviteur[4]

LE CHEVR. DUBUYSSON
Coel. des Coies. françoises

From John Holker

ALS: American Philosophical Society

Most Worthe friend   Rouen 31 of Decbr 1783

I have not words to express, the Pleaseur I had in Receving your very kind leter, which you was so good as to send me by

---

2. Charles-François Dubuysson served with distinction in the Continental Army from 1776 to 1780, when he was wounded and taken prisoner. Released on parole, in 1781 he was granted leave to return to France. Louis XVI promoted him to the rank of colonel of infantry of the colonies: XXXV, 447–8; XXXVI, 88–9, 217; Asa B. Gardiner, *The Order of the Cincinnati in France* . . . (n.p., 1905), pp. 158–9.

3. Lafayette was in charge of enlisting qualified French officers for the Cincinnati; see the headnote to Bariatinskii to BF, Dec. 22.

4. Another letter about membership in the Cincinnati, undated and unsigned, might have been written as early as December. It describes the service of the late chevalier de Ternay. The writer explains that Ternay had commanded the naval squadron that escorted Rochambeau's fleet (XXXII, 72–3n), had died in service, and was buried in America. Louis XVI had ordered a memorial tablet for his grave. The writer proposes membership for the chevalier's young nephew Charles-Gabriel-Hilaire d'Arsac, the only descendant to carry his name (APS). We suspect the author of this letter to be the father of the candidate, the chevalier's older brother Gabriel d'Arsac, marquis de Ternay (1721–1796). For both

Mr. Lamot,[5] for allthoug I have not seen you for this lage(?) Past, my heart warms when ever I here your Naime mensiend, as does my wife,[6] for She Loves you sincearly. Could wee but have the Pleaseur to Injoy you here, was it but for a few days, it woud make us very happey, you know you promisd us this favor before you quit the Country, & wee air in hopes youl keep your word.

I see somtime past a Relation of David Hartleys,[7] & I praid him to tell him, that youd give him the meeting here in the Spring; If he excepts of the offer I hope youl not faile him, and wee shall strive to make you bouth satisfied with your visit. You have now accomplished all you wanted, & wished for; which does you an Eternel honour, & Really it is heigh time you Injoy your Self, could the wishes of my Wife & me Contribut to your future happeness no one should be more so, which is the Sentements of your Sincear friend My Dr. Sir your Most Obedt & affectionet humble sert   J Holker

ps Our best Complements attend your Son[8] from my wife & Dougter Inlaw,[9] who where very Sencible as well as my Self for his Kind Rememberance, I found the wheels you Mension on Board of an English Vessel,[1] and Claimed by Mr. Garvey your Consil here,[2] who will forward them by the fert occasion by water, but I am affread youl think it long as the Rever wont be Navegable so soon

Notation: Holker Rouen 31. Decr. 1783—

---

men see H. Beauchet-Filleau and Ch. de Chergé, *Dictionnaire historique et généalogique des familles du Poitou* (2nd ed.; 4 vols., Poitiers, 1891), I, 121–2. Ternay's French tombstone was placed on his grave in Newport, R.I., in 1785: Edwin M. Stone, *Our French Allies* ... (Providence, 1884), pp. 340–51.

5. L'Air de Lamotte. The letter BF sent has not been found.

6. Marie-Marguerite Thérèse Ribard Holker (xxx, 436n) was his second wife: *ODNB*, under John Holker.

7. Probably Hartley's cousin Samuel Hartley, a London merchant who had visited France in 1780 (xxv, 579n; xxxiii, 332n, 369–70).

8. WTF.

9. Elisabeth-Julie Quesnel Holker (xxxvi, 618n).

1. Which John Viny had shipped to Rouen aboard the *Friendship;* see Viny to BF, [after Nov. 28], above.

2. Probably Antoine Garvey, a partner in the firm R. & A. Garvey (xxx, 436n; xxxii, 469), who was an American agent in Rouen. Holker

The Abbé André Morellet to William Temple Franklin[3]

ALS: American Philosophical Society

mercredy 31. [December, 1783][4]

Permettes Monsieur que je vous addresse un memoire sur lequel Mr. le cardinal de rohan[5] demande l'avis de vôtre respectable papa. La rigueur de la saison m'empeche d'aller le lui demander moi même. Il s'agit je crois de savoir si ces gens sont connus de vous si vous aves entendu parler de leur affaire s'ils meritent les secours qu'ils demandent. Mr. le cardinal m'a chargé de prendre ces eclaircissemens et de les lui communiquer. Je prendrai cette occasion pour voir si on ne pourra pas finir l'affaire de vôtre ancien domestique qui comme vous saves a essuyé une difficulté qu'il ne dependoit pas tout à fait de mr le cardinal de vaincre parceque la 1ere loi des quinze vint est d'etre parfaitement aveugle.[6] Rappelles moi à cette occasion au souvenir de votre cher papa vous aures bien la complaisance de me renvoyer le memoire. Receves les assurances de mon respectueux attachemens sans autre formule de complimens comme si j'etois quaker et vrai comme les quakers font profession de l'etre   L'ABBÉ MORELLET

---

later recommended him to TJ for a consulship: *Jefferson Papers*, XIV, 62n. Garvey had been second consul of the *Chambre de Commerce* at Rouen in 1778: Guy Richard, "A Propos des Garvey: les gentilshommes commerçants irlandais de Rouen au XVIIIe Siècle," *Annales de Normandie*, XI (1961), 240–2.

3. We publish this letter and Morellet's to WTF of [Jan. 8] because they discuss BF's help in obtaining housing and care for his "ancien domestique" Arbelot, then destitute and nearly blind. Arbelot was BF's valet from March, 1779, to November, 1781: XXIX, 3; XXXIII, 4; XXXVI, 5.

4. Dated by two clues. The allusion to the "rigors of the season" suggests winter, and the only "mercredy 31" that occurred during a winter month between 1781 (when Arbelot left BF's house) and 1785 (when BF left France) was in December, 1783.

5. Louis-René-Edouard, prince de Rohan-Guéménée. In XXVIII, 96n, we stated erroneously that he died in 1757. He lived until 1803. The enclosed memoir has not been found.

6. The Hospice des Quinze-Vingts was a home for the indigent blind in Paris. Its name derived from its capacity of 300 (15 times 20) beds. As grand almoner, Cardinal de Rohan was in charge of all Parisian charitable institutions: Hillairet, *Rues de Paris*, I, 313–14; II, 425–6.

To Madame Brillon[7] ALS (draft): American Philosophical Society

[December, 1783?]

Je vous envoye incluses, les petites Pieces[8] que vous, ma très chere Amie, m'a fait l'honneur de me demander. Celle sur le Jeu des Echecs, doit etre dedieé à vous, la plus belle conseil qu'elle contient, etant copié de votre maniere genereuse & magnanime de jouer, que j'ai si souvent experiencé.

Mon petit Fils a été voir votre Maison. Je suis bien sensible de votre bonté en m'offrant la Preference, mais il le trouve trop magnifique pour nous.—

Avec infiniment d'Estime & d'Affection, je suis, toujours a vous.[9]

B F.

7. After Mme Brillon moved from Passy to Paris in the fall, she did not visit BF or write to him until Feb. 15, 1784. In her letter of that date, below, she justified her silence by pointing out that WTF had come to see her several times and brought news of BF. The present letter must have followed one of these visits. WTF probably relayed Mme Brillon's request for "les petites Pieces" and her offer for BF and his household to move into her residence—an offer that she may have extended after hearing of BF's painful bladder stone, which by early December made it impossible for him to travel.

We publish the draft as BF wrote it, replete with grammatical errors. In a note below, we print WTF's corrected version.

8. An allusion to his bagatelles, which Moritz Meyer, the compositor BF engaged in December, may have started to print. In addition to "La Morale des echecs" (mentioned in the next sentence), BF probably enclosed "La Belle et la Mauvaise Jambe" (xxxiv, 41–6). These were the two bagatelles he mentioned by name in his letter to Mme Brillon of April 8, 1784, as having already been sent to her (APS). No Passy imprint of "The Morals of Chess" has been found, in either English or French: xxix, 751.

9. BF gave this draft to WTF, who corrected the French of the first paragraph and, after reading the second two paragraphs, crossed them out and rewrote them entirely. His hastily rewritten version (with its own mistakes) is as follows: "J'envoye cy inclus, les petites Pieces que ma très chere Amie m'a fait l'honneur de me demander. Celle sur le Jeu des Echecs, doit lui etre dedieé, le plus beau conseil qu'elle contient, etant copié d'après sa maniere genereuse & magnanime de jouer, que j'ai si souvent eprouvée.

"Mon petit fils a été voir l'Hotel que vous avez bien voulu me proposer,

Franklinia alatamaha

From the Abbé de La Roche

ALS: American Philosophical Society

[December, 1783?][1]

Bonjour, cher Papa, je suis toujours estropié, et dans l'impossibilité d'aller vous voir, d'aprendre par moi même des nouvelles de vôtre Santé. Nôtre Dame[2] n'ose point sortir au milieu de cette neige. Elle vous envoye la petite graine de l'Altamaha[3] que lui a demandée Mons. vôtre fils. Auriez vous 3 ou 4 bouteilles de Madère sec ou de Xeres à m'envoyer, vous me feriez grand plaisir. Les habitans d'Auteuil vous embrassent, et vous aiment L. DE LA ROCHE

Mais il le trouve trop magnifique pour des simpples Republicains. Agréez je vous prie mes sinceres Rémerciements pour votre Offre obligeante. Je suis desolé qu'il ne puisse me convenir puisque céla m'auroit approché de vous, très excellente Femme, que j'aime, estime, & respecte de fond de mon Cœur."

1. Dated by two clues: the snow and the mention of Alatamaha seeds. The seeds, offered for the first time by the Bartrams in their 1783 broadside catalogue (see the note below), were probably included in the box of seeds from John Bartram, Jr., that arrived in December with Capt. Barney: XL, 391, 593; RB to BF, Nov. 9, and Barney to BF, Dec. 19, above. The mention of snow suggests either late December, 1783, or early February, 1784, when Paris experienced snow storms.

2. Mme Helvétius.

3. Bartram's 1783 broadside catalogue (XL, 593n) included "Alatamaha" at the end of the list as one of "Three Undescript Shrubs lately from Florida." It had been discovered by his father John Bartram, Sr., and his brother William along the Altamaha River in Georgia during their 1765 trip to Florida. William brought seeds to Philadelphia in January, 1777, and for the first time the botanists saw it in flower. By October, 1784, when the Bartram sons issued their next seed list, they had determined that the plant warranted its own genus, which they named for Franklin. *Franklinia Alatamaha*, item no. 153, was now described as "a beautiful flowering Tree lately found in Florida, seems allied to the Gordonia" (MS list, Hunt Institute for Botanical Research). The following year Humphrey Marshall published the first full description of the tree under that name: *Arbustrum Americanum: the American Grove* . . . (Philadelphia, 1785). See Joel T. Fry, "Bartram's Garden Catalogue of North American Plants, 1783," *Jour. of Garden History*, XVI (1996), 3–16, 48–53, 56–7; William Bartram, *Travels*, ed. Francis Harper (New Haven, 1958), p. 417; Edmund Berkeley and Dorothy Smith Berkeley, *The Life and Travels of John Bartram: from Lake Ontario to the River St. John* (Tallahassee, Fl., 1982), pp. 245–6.

Addressed: A Monsieur / Monsieur franklin / A Passy

Notation: De La Roche

Morellet's Translation of "Reflections upon the Life and Death of Edward Drinker"

AD (draft)[4] and press copy of copy: American Philosophical Society

In May, 1783, an essay about an uncommonly healthy and long-lived Philadelphian appeared in the *Gentleman's Magazine* under the title "Reflections upon the Life and Death of Edward Drinker, of the City of Philadelphia, who died on the 17th of November, 1782, in the 103d Year of his Age. Written by an ingenious literary Gentleman of that City, for the Amusement of a Lady." During the summer and fall it was reprinted in several newspapers in England and America and summarized in at least one French publication.[5] The author, as would be revealed years later, was Benjamin Rush.[6] It is not known how and when Franklin obtained the piece, whether he knew its author to be Rush, and why he wanted a French version. We surmise that sometime in 1783 the abbé Morellet prepared this translation and Franklin's secretary Jean L'Air de Lamotte copied it. The disposition of that fair copy is not known, but Franklin retained a press copy of it along with Morellet's draft.

The piece would have had particular resonance for the American minister. It is likely that he knew Drinker; he certainly knew his great-nephew Henry, a Quaker merchant.[7] Drinker had lived according to the principles of moderation and generosity that Franklin espoused, which may have contributed (as the author suggested) to a life largely free from illness. Finally, from his small plot of land this centenar-

4. In the hand of the abbé Morellet.

5. The earliest newspaper appearance we have located is in the May 20, 1783, issue of the *Public Advertiser*. By mid-summer, a French summary adapted from "les papiers américains" was available in Paris: *Journal politique, ou Gazette des gazettes* (Bouillon), second half of July, 1783, pp. 62–3.

6. It was attributed to Rush in the *American Museum*, II (1787), 73–5, and he included it in his *Essays, Literary, Moral & Philosophical* (Philadelphia, 1798), pp. 295–300.

7. Henry Drinker and Abel James were partners in a mercantile firm. On at least one occasion BF sent DF a letter from London by way of Henry Drinker: IX, 33; XI, 436n; Elaine F. Crane *et al.*, eds., *The Diary of Elizabeth Drinker* (3 vols., Boston, 1991), I, 406.

ian had witnessed the transformation of America. Franklin may have hoped to see this article published in its entirety in the French press. If it did appear, we have not located it.

⟨[1783, in French]: Edward Drinker was born on December 24, 1680, in a small cabin near what is now the corner of Walnut and Second streets in Philadelphia. The area was inhabited by Indians and a few emigrants. His parents came from Beverly, Massachusetts. He went to Boston at the age of 12 and was apprenticed to a cabinetmaker. In 1745 he returned to Philadelphia and remained there for the rest of his life. He was married four times and had 18 children with his first wife. A principled and cheerful man, Drinker enjoyed uncommonly good health, though he lost his eyesight and his teeth decades before his death. His hearing remained sharp, and he maintained his mental acuity until his final year. His habits were wise and temperate and his religious principles were steady. He ate heartily, avoided excessive drinking, and always slept soundly. Drinker witnessed the transformation of a wilderness into an urban civilization and of a colony into a republic. He saw the beginning and the end of the British Empire in Pennsylvania. The subject of seven successive kings, he lived to celebrate American independence.⟩

From the Baronne de Bourdic: Three Letters[8]

(I) AL: American Philosophical Society; (II) ALS: Historical Society of Pennsylvania; (III) AL: American Philosophical Society

I.

a paris le 23[9] hotel de modene rue jacob f S germain [1783]
Monsieur franklin aime a faire le bien: Cest Connû de tout le monde, Cest dapres Cella que Mde La Baronne de Bourdic ose

8. For the baroness and her 1783 visit to Paris see XXXIX, 483–4, where we published the first of five undated letters. We publish here the next three, all written from Paris. We believe them to be in the proper sequence though we cannot ascribe even tentative dates to any but the first.

9. The earliest possible month is July, as she is petitioning BF on behalf of a Frenchman who arrived in Philadelphia on June 11 and wrote to her from there asking this favor.

lui demander une lettre de recommandation pour un de Ses Compatriotes du languedoc pour lequel elle noseroit reclamer Ses bontes Si Son honnetete ne lui etoit pas Connue;[1] elle le Suplie donc de vouloir bien Se preter au desir quelle a de lobliger, elle lassure davance de toute Sa reconnaissance elle ira la lui temoigner et prendre Congè de lui avant de quitter Paris

II.

Sir   paris thé fifteen [1783]

   The first wish I formed upon mŷ arrival at paris was to Sée a man who maŷ verŷ justlŷ bé Considered as the first character of the present age, when once I became acquainted with him, I endeavour'd to See him frequentlŷ even at the risk of becoming troublesome mŷ desire has been accomplished, but Still there remains an unsatisfied wish, and at the verÿ moment, I am about to quitt the citÿ he inhabits, and am perhaps upon the point of abandoning the hopes of ever Seeing him again, I would most willinglŷ Carrŷ awaŷ with me a part of himself, and join the reading of his works, to the grateful remembrance, I Shall ever retain of his obliging Behavior to me, he will therefore greatlŷ add to the obligations I alreadŷ owe him; if he will be so good as to let me know where I Can get them, and if theŷ are not to be had at paris; I flatter mŷself he will furnisch me with them, this is a favour he cannot refuse me in Consideration of the high idea I entertain of him and of the verŷ respectful Sentiments wherewith I have the honor to be his most obedient and most humble Servant   La Baronne de Bourdic

1. The subject of this appeal was most likely Jean-Jacques Coirard, whose undated letter to the baronne de Bourdic is among BF's papers and was probably enclosed with the present note. Coirard introduces himself as a silk manufacturer and merchant from Nîmes, who had gone to Philadelphia to sell his merchandise and possibly to settle there. Knowing no one, he asks the baronne to request of BF a letter of recommendation to city officials. He will be staying with the merchants Lacaze and Mallet (XXX, 88n; XXXVIII, 391) after having sailed to Philadelphia on the *Grand d'Estaing*. APS. That ship arrived in port on June 11, 1783. Another passenger, Jean Hadenbrock, carried letters from BF to RB and Jonathan Williams, Sr., which might have inspired Coirard's request: XXXIX, 495. Coirard is listed in the *Almanach des marchands* for 1779, p. 351.

Addressed: A Son excellence / Monseigner Le docteur / Franklin ministre plenipotentiare / des etats unis / A passÿ

III.

[1783]

Mde La Baronne de Bourdic ira demain a passi pour prendre Congè de Monsieur Franklin et le remercier de Ses honetetes elle lui demande la permission de lui presenter des dames qui ont le plus grand desir de faire Connaissance avec lui; dans le Cas qu'il ne fut pas a passi demain Samedi Mde de Bourdic desireroit le Savoir le matin.

Addressed: A Son excellence / Monsieur Le docteur / Franklin ministre / plenipotentiaire / A passi

From Madame Brillon: Two Letters[2]

(I) and (II) AL: American Philosophical Society

I.

[1783]

Mon aimable papa, il fait si beau que cela me donne l'ésperance de vous débaucher ce soir pour prendre le thé a la maison, venés de bonne heure pour avoir le tems de vous reposér et de retourner doucement avant la nuit; Mr votre fils et Benjamin seront assés aimables pour vous accompagner:

Addressed: A Monsieur / Monsieur Franklin / [*In another hand:*] A Passy

---

On the blank sides of Coirard's letter sheet are mechanical drawings that we assume were made in BF's office. They appear to be parts and views of spinning machines.

2. Because these undated invitations include both of BF's grandsons, they had to have been written after mid-July, 1783, when BFB returned to Passy, and before the Brillon family moved to Paris, which we believe occurred in the fall of 1783. For the move, see the annotation of Mme Brillon to BF, [after Oct. 20].

II.

ce samedi a 7 heures ½ [1783]

Mon bon papa faittes moi l'amitié d'estre chés moi a neuf heures ainsi que mrs vos fils, distes a l'aîné qu'il ne faut point de toillétte que j'aime mieux le voir en chenille que de l'attendre en papillon,[3] qu'enfin je suis obligée de sortir a dix heures; je vous embrasse mon bon papa et vous attends avec grande impatience:

Addressed: A Monsieur / Monsieur Benjamin / Franklin / [*In another hand:*] A Passy

From Alexander Gross

AL: American Philosophical Society

[*c.* 1783]

To his Excelency Dr. Franklin plenepotentary &c &c &c &c

The humb: pettition Of Alexander Gross Native Of Cape Codd in *America* Most humbly Sheweth that your Excelency's pettitioner is Now A hostage in Dunkerque prison—is A Native Of Cape Codd in America his parents Now Live there, is Abt. Twenty Six Years Of Age, Entered A Volentiere About 8 Years Ago in the Americian Servise On the proclamation Of his *Excelincy General* WASHINGTON And Served One Year, the time then Spacefied to Serve in his Excelency's proclamation THAT at The Expiration Of the Said Year the Enemy Appeared in the Jarsey Islands, your Excelency's pettitioner Stayed *Six* weeks Longer At the Request Of *Genl. Sulivan* Then his Com-

---

3. WTF's correspondence in 1783 and 1784 documents his preoccupation with high fashion. From haberdasher P. B. Graft, WTF ordered many pairs of ruffles; Graft also notified him of the latest offerings in waistcoats: Graft to WTF, March 8, June 2, Oct. 23, 1783; July 10 and Aug. 6, 1784. On Sept. 29, 1783, the Paris jeweller Foncier asked WTF to stop by his shop to verify that his new buckles had exactly the right contour. Henry Grand, while on a trip to England, sent fashionable buttons, a patent string for a hat, patterns for waistcoats, fabric for a greatcoat, and six pins; he also requested WTF's measurements before buying a cocked hat, mourning buckles, and leather breeches. WTF reimbursed Ferdinand Grand for some of the shipping costs: Henry Grand to WTF, Oct. 29, Dec. 26, 1783; January, [1784], Jan. 20, 1784; Ferdinand Grand's Statement of Account with WTF, Jan. 26, 1784, to July 25, 1785. All documents are at the APS.

mander, After Was Granted his Discharge. Soon After he went On board Of A Merchant Vessel from Cohasset to the Ise A Cape, On his Return With the Sd. Vessel Which Was Loaded With Rum Coffee & Cotton, was taken by A Letter of Marque Of *Liverpool,* Brought there And Imprisoned. Soon After Was Sent A prisoner to plymouth And sent On board the *Duke* Man Of War,[4] was Often tempted to Enter And Take bounty, Never Did Either, in Consequence Of Which he was kept Close Confined for the Space of Three years And—Nine Months— At Last Found Means to Effect his Escape, And Went to Southamton, there Shiped himself On board of A Sloop bound to Cork in Ireland THIS in hopes to be taken, And Carried A prisoner to America, Or Some Other place from Whence he May Effect his Escape to *America.* When Out in Said Sloop Four Days, Was taken by A private Ship Of Warr, the property Of One Missil Merchant Of Dunkerque. The Commander Of Sd. Sloop Insisted On My Going As Hostage for her for the Sum of 200 Guineas. Intirely Against My Inclination, On My Arival At Dunkerque I was Shut Up in Close prison Where I am Now One Year And Four Months Existing On One Scanty Meal pr. Day, And At present with Less hopes Of Redemption than Ever, Finding the Owner Of Sd. Sloop (I having No Tie On him) Means to Leave Me for Ever, Unredeemed, THEREFORE, Most humbly Crave Your *Excelency's* kind Interposition in My behalf—As the Father—protecter—And Source Of Redress Of All My Just Acting Countrymen in this part Of the world— And Your Excelency's Distressed pettitioner in Duty bound Will Ever PRAY—

Addressed: A Son Exclcy Monsieur Monsr. / Franklin plenepotentery a Lês Estàte / Unie D.'Amerk. / A / Paris

Notation: Gross Mr. Alexander—

4. H.M.S. *Duke* was launched in 1777: David Lyon, *The Sailing Navy List: All the Ships of the Royal Navy Built, Purchased and Captured, 1688–1860* (London, 1993), p. 65.

From Jacques-Louis Joannis[5]

ALS: American Philosophical Society

Monseigneur   [c. 1783]

Il y a environ 3 ans que j'ai eu l'honneur de vous vendre une fonte de gros texte. Je vous témoignai alors le desir de passer en Amérique, Sous vos auspices, pour m'y établir fondeur en Caractere, vous me repondites que les circonstances de la guerre ne vous permettoient pas d'acquiescer à ma demande, mais que Si elles venoient a changer de face vous me faciliteriez volontiers les moyens d'y passer.

Aujourd'hui que la paix vient d'exaucer les voeux de toutes les nations et de rétablir la tranquilité parmi elles, je desirerois que vous me fissiez la grace de me choisir pour diriger en Amerique la fonderie que vous êtes dans l'intention d'y établir. Mon intention est de me fixer dans vos états persuadé que vôtre protection ne manquera pas d'y faire mon bonheur. Je ferai tous mes efforts pour la mériter par mon Zele, mon activité et mon intelligence. J'ai moi-même beaucoup de caractere dont je vous accommoderai avec bien du plaisir s'ils vous plaisent assez pour les reunir à votre fonderie.

JOANNIS
fondeur en Caractere, rue des sept voyes st. hilaire maison de Mr. Claris

A Monseigneur le Docteur Franklin, ministre Plénipotentiaire des Etats unis de L'Amérique

Endorsed: Joannis Fondeur des Caracteres d'Imprimerie

---

5. A typefounder who established himself in Paris in 1775 and produced a specimen book in 1776: Augustin-Martin Lottin, *Catalogue chronologique des libraires et des libraires-imprimeurs de Paris* (Paris, 1789), p. 242 of 2nd pagination. BF purchased two boxes of *gros texte* ("great text") from Joannis in 1778: XXVII, 3; XXXIV, 321n.

Analysis of Loyalists[6]

d: Library of Congress

[1783?]

Two hundred & eighty eight persons called Loyalists, & specified by Name in the Morning Post, classed in the following Manner.—

Persons residing in Great Britain	32.
Deceased Persons	34.

APOSTATES, that is to say, persons who had conformed to the American Government, & voluntarily taken the necessary Oaths, among whom also are divers who had been Demagogues & Leaders of the People, & who had REFORMED in hopes of saving their Estates after the capture of Charles Town by Sr Henry Clinton & who are now desiros of being re-reformed for the same benefit— } 139.

PERSONS of doubtful Principles, vizt, who, from the beginning, were endeavoring to play a safe Game, & take the strongest side, as Occasion might offer . . . . 12.

PERSONS whose Names are unknown & others who are known to be of no weight or importance; the greatest part of whom would probably come, properly, under the title of Apostates . . . . 71.

288.

American true Loyalists . . . . 000.

288.

Analysis of Loyalists.

6. This undated satire on classifications of Loyalists, found among BF's papers, remains to some degree mysterious. We believe the text to be in the hand of Henry Laurens, Jr. (who adopted his father's idiosyncratic spellings), and "Analysis of Loyalists," written on the verso, to be in the hand of Laurens himself. The *Laurens Papers* editors found no trace of this piece, and our search of newspapers yielded no definitive clues. Whatever its origins and date, its sentiments conform to the views exchanged by Laurens and BF in the spring of 1783: XXXIX, 298, 358, 430–1; see also 230–4.

389

From Jean-Baptiste Le Roy: Four Letters[7]

(I) and (II) ALS: American Philosophical Society; (III) and (IV) AL: American Philosophical Society

I.

ce Dimanche matin [1783?]

Mon Illustre Docteur j'ai été hier au soir chez vous pour avoir lhonneur de vous voir et malheureusement je n'ai pas eu celui de vous trouver. Je voulois vous demander si vous pouvez nous faire l'honneur de venir mardy avec Monsieur Votre petit Fils prendre du Thé l'après midy et voir partir un ballon. M. Le Prince de Bariatinskoÿ s'y trouvera et vous savez combien il aime à vous voir. J'espere Mon Illustre Docteur que vous m'accorderez ma requête. Vous savez combien je vous suis passionnément attaché pour la vie   Le Roy

Addressed: a Monsieur / Monsieur Franklin

II.

mardy matin [1783?]

J'ai été désolé hier Mon Illustre Docteur de n'avoir pas pu aller passer la soirée avec vous comme je vous l'avois promis. Mais il falloit voir si mes ballons étoient en bon état et combien ils prenoient de tems à remplir et tout cela m'a mené beaucoup plus tard que je ne croyois et tellement que bien malgré moi je n'ai pu avoir l'honneur de vous voir. Et pour comble de malheur il fait si mauvais tems aujourdhui. Le Baromètre est si bas que j'ai contremandé les Personnes que j'avois engagée. J'ai l'honneur de vous proposer deux choses en conséquence pour me dédommager de ce que j'ai perdu hier. L'une de nous faire l'honneur de venir prendre du Thé avec nous ou de nous en donner. Un petit mot de reponse s'il vous plait et ayez la bonte mon Illustre Docteur de faire mille remercimens de nos parts a Monsieur Votre petit fils de ses offres obligeantes pour notre The que nous le prions de nous confirmer pour les premiers jours où le tems sera remis où je compte bien que vous nous conserverez la même bonne volonté de venir voir partir des ballons.

7. We assume that these four undated notes were written in the second half of 1783, when private balloon experiments became fashionable and when BF became friendly with the Russian minister, Bariatinskii.

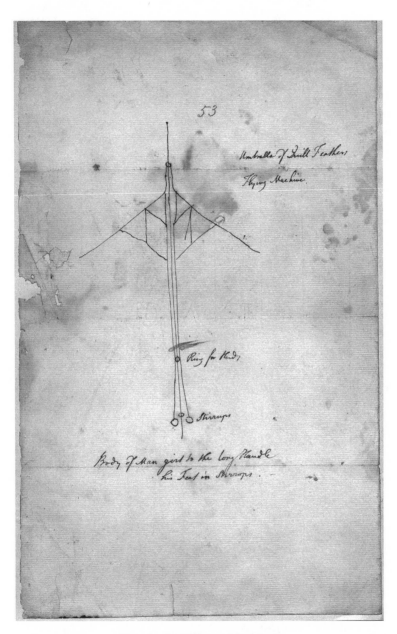

Sketch of a "Flying Machine"

Recevez Mon Illustre Docteur les sinceres assurrances des sentimens d'attachement que je vous ai voués pour la vie

LE ROY

Addressed: a Monsieur / Monsieur Franklin

Endorsed: Le Roi

III.

ce Jeudy matin [1783?]

J'envoye vous demander Mon Illustre Docteur si vous pourrez nous faire lhonneur de venir prendre du Thé samedy et voir partir un Ballon ou des ballons. Des Dames que Mde. Le Roy a engagé à s'y trouver l'ayant prié de remettre à samedy ce petit Passetems Physique j'ai lhonneur de vous souhaiter bien le bonjour.

P.S. Je ne sais Mon Illustre Docteur si ce n'est pas le Jour que vous donnez à Mde. Brion mais vous pourriez y aller après. Un petit mot de reponse s'il vous plait car je remettrois, la Fête ne vaudroit rien sans vous.

IV.

ce Jeudy matin [1783?]

Le Prince Bariatinskoÿ Mon Illustre Docteur m'a mandé que vous diniez chez lui aujourdhui et m'a engagé à y dîner avec vous. J'envoye vous demander si vous pouvez me faire l'amitié de me mener et en cas que vous m'accordiez ma demande à quelle heure vous comptez partir. J'ai l'honneur de vous souhaiter bien le bon Jour. Jespere que votre goutte va de mieux en mieux ou plutot s'en va de plus en plus.

From the Comte de Mailly[8]   L: American Philosophical Society

[1783]

M. Le Maréchal de Mailly, ayant sçû que, Monsieur francklin, désireroit connoître Le plan et la Situation du Port-Vendre.

8. The military commander of Roussillon in the eastern Pyrenees (*DBF,* under Haucourt), who since 1773 was responsible for enlarging and deepening the harbor of Port-Vendres and augmenting its fortifications. In 1783

Il a crû pouvoir lui en Envoyer quelques Exemplaires,[9] et Il désire qu'ils puisse Lui plaire Ét luy paraître de quelque utilité Respective./.

Notation: Le Mal. de Mailly—

To [Mary Hewson]   ALS: American Philosophical Society

Passy, Jan 1. 1784.—
Health and Prosperity, and many happy Years, to my dear Friend, and to her Children, for whom I send the three enclos'd little Books.[1]   B FRANKLIN

Let me know if you have not the compleat Year.—[2]

Endorsed: Passy Jan 1 — 84 44

Mailly commissioned the architect Charles de Wailly to design four bronze reliefs for the base of a newly erected obelisk placed at the mouth of the harbor. They commemorated American independence, free trade, the French navy, and the abolition of slavery in France: Sylvia Pressouyre, "Un ensemble néo-classique a Port-Vendres," *Les Monuments historiques de la France,* new ser., IX (1963), 199–222. We suspect that the present letter was written in 1783, when Mailly must have been promoting trade with the United States and was probably involved in the campaign to have the French government choose Port-Vendres as a free port for American shipping: Gilbert Larguier, "Port-Vendres: une fondation d'inspiration maçonnique," in *Les Lumières en Roussillon au XVIIIe siècle: hommes, idées, lieux,* ed. Larguier (Canet, France, 2008), p. 197. For the competition in the first half of 1783 among French cities to be selected a free port see XXXIX, 104–7; XL, 6–7.

9. The enclosures have not been found, but they may have been the engravings of Wailly's view and plan of Port-Vendres that were produced around 1780 and 1781 (printed in Pressouyre, "Un ensemble néo-classique a Port-Vendres," 206–7).

1. The October, November, and December issues of *L'Ami des enfans.* Berquin ceased publication of the series at the end of 1783.

2. BF had evidently lost track of what he had already sent Hewson, which were the books for January through August. She answered that she lacked September: XXXIX, 504; XL, 588; Hewson to BF, April 2, 1784 (APS).

List of Letters to Write[3]

AD:[4] American Philosophical Society

[*c.* January 1, 1784?]

Lettres à ecrire
Chev. de Keralio[5]
M. de Breteuil[6]
Mr. le Chancelier
Mr Chase
M. de Vergennes[7]
Mr Todd[8]
    Quy. what is become of the Post-Office Negn
Chevr d'Osmont[9]

---

3. BF occasionally apologized to his friends for being a poor correspondent; see his Dec. 24 letter to Ingenhousz, for example. This list, which he compiled in at least three stages, using different inks, may have been written around the New Year. It contains names of people to whom he owed responses, and names of people and topics that indicate letters that he himself wished to write. Because BF believed that he would soon receive Congress' permission to return to America, this uncharacteristic effort at organization may have been an attempt to tie up loose ends.

Only one entry is crossed out: "Mr Chase," to whom BF wrote on Jan. 6, 1784. We identify below the letters to which we believe BF was planning to respond. Unless otherwise noted, those responses have not been found.

BF wrote this list next to, and curving around, a crude sketch of what appears to be a kind of balloon.

4. On the verso of this sheet, along the left margin, BF wrote a geometric sequence of 32 numbers beginning with one and multiplying each time by two, ending with 2,121,883,648. This was the same sequence he employed in his calculation of descendants of knights of the Cincinnati carried down to the ninth generation; see BF to SB, Jan. 26. Elsewhere on the sheet BF took the penultimate number in the sequence and divided it by 12.

5. Kéralio's most recent letter was dated Nov. 30.

6. Breteuil wrote on Dec. 26 and 31 regarding the case against John Shaffer. In the latter, Breteuil suggested that BF ask Miromesnil for help. In addition to being *garde des sceaux*, Miromesnil served as chancellor, so the following entry might refer to him: XXI, 536n.

7. On Jan. 12, BF responded to Vergennes' letter of Dec. 3.

8. Anthony Todd's letter of Nov. 18 required no answer. BF evidently wanted to inquire about the progress of the postal-service contract negotiations.

9. We summarize the Dec. 9 letter from the chevalier d'Osmont and his sister in the headnote to Bouttret Durivault's letter of Dec. 12.

c. JANUARY 1, 1784?

M. Lamy[1]
Made Chaumont
Bonnefoy[2]
Hambourgh[3]
R Peters Esqr[4]
Turin[5]
Miss Davies[6]
Amelia Barry——[7]
M. Le Noir[8]
New Stove[9]
Dr Ingenhausz[1]

From Frédéric-Samuel Ostervald

ALS: American Philosophical Society

Monsieur,   Neuchatel le 1r de 1784
Puisje me flatter que votre Excellence ne désaprouvera pas la
liberté que je prends de lui renouveller aujourdhui l'expression

1. Lamy's letters of Nov. 4 and Dec. 24 are summarized in the headnote
to Maupin's letter of Jan. 13.
2. Bonnefoy wrote on Dec. 19.
3. BF copied the address of the Hamburg government on a dinner invitation from the Jays of Feb. 3; see our annotation there.
4. Richard Peters wrote two letters in December, 1780: XXXIV, 165–6.
On Oct. 7, 1785, he complained of not having received a letter from BF
since 1779 (APS).
5. Most likely a reference to BF's election to the Accademia Reale delle
Scienze in Turin, announced in Gian Francesco Cigna's letter of July 28,
1783. BF did not reply until July 5, 1785: XL, 409–10.
6. Mary Ann Davies wrote on Oct. 17.
7. The most recent letter from Amelia Barry was dated Feb. 21, 1783:
XXXIX, 192–4. BF wrote her a now-missing response on Sept. 20, 1784:
Barry to BF, Dec. 10, 1784 (APS).
8. Lenoir wrote on Dec. 4.
9. The subject of Lenoir's letter. BF finally wrote "Description of a new
Stove" on his voyage home in the summer of 1785: see the annotation of
Lenoir to BF, Dec. 4.
1. BF wrote to Ingenhousz on Jan. 16, but did not respond fully to the
backlog of Ingenhousz' letters until April 29, 1785 (Library of Congress).

de mon hommage le plus respectueux, & de reclamer les bontés qu'Elle voulut bien me marquer lorsque j'eus l'honneur de le lui présenter moi meme il y a environ trois ans.[2] Une circonstance particuliere semble même m'y autoriser aujourdhui. Votre Excellence possêde dans sa bibliotêque un Exemplaire de nos Descriptions des Arts & métiers, in Quartò.[3] Mais j'ai lieu de craindre que par l'effet des Ordres donnés il y a quelque tems sur les frontieres parraport à la Librairie étrangère & à cause de la proscription particuliere, qu'éprouve notre travail—Elle n'ait pas receu les derniers volumes que nous en avons publiés & qui s'etendent jusques au Dixneuvieme, inclusivement, le Vingtieme occuppant actuellement nos presses.[4] Je supplie donc Votre Excellence, de vouloir m'apprendre quels sont ceux de ces mêmes volumes qui lui manquent, a fin que je puisse les lui procurer, étant persuadé que si le paquet qui les renfermera porte l'addresse respectable dont je le décorerai, il surmontera tous les obstacles qu'il pourroit rencontrer sur la route.

Lors que ces mêmes volumes seront parvenus à Vôtre Excellence, Elle pourra s'assurer, que vû la lenteur avec laquelle les membres de l'académie des Sciences de Paris publient de nouveaux Cayers des Arts in folio, nous aurons bientot réimprimé

2. This is consistent with what Ostervald wrote in his previous letter, of Feb. 6, 1783, where he recalled meeting with BF two years earlier. As we indicate there, the only meeting of which we have evidence is the one in April, 1780: XXXIX, 138–41. The present letter was forwarded through Morellet, who sent it under cover of a letter to WTF on a "jeudi" that was probably Jan. 8; it is below, under that date.

3. BF was a subscriber to the revised and expanded quarto edition of the Académie des sciences' *Descriptions des arts et métiers* published by the Société typographique de Neuchâtel (STN): X, 261, 393; XXXII, 300; XXXIX, 139n.

4. On June 12, 1783, Vergennes decreed that all books imported into France had to pass inspection by the *chambre syndicale* of the booksellers' guild at Paris before distribution to their final destinations. This policy doomed the STN's profitable trade in pirated editions. BF may not have received vol. 19 of the *Descriptions* (the set he bequeathed to the Library Company does not include it), and vol. 20 was never published: Robert Darnton, *The Literary Underground of the Old Regime* (Cambridge, Mass., 1982), pp. 191–3; Wolf and Hayes, *Library of Benjamin Franklin*, p. 62; Arthur H. Cole and George B. Watts, *The Handicrafts of France as recorded in the* Descriptions des Arts et Métiers, *1761–1788* (Boston, 1952), pp. 36–7.

& commenté tous ceux qui ont parû jusques ici. Mais me seroit il permis sans indiscretion & de lui presenter dans ce moment une idée, que ses lumieres & son Zêle pour les progrès des Sciences & des arts sauront apprécier. Lors que notre Édition in quartò commença à paroitre, le premier volume fut dédié, comme juste, au roi de Prusse, notre souverain; Ensuite & considérant qu'un ouvrage de ce genre appartient également à tous les peuples policés, nous avons demandé & obtenû la permission d'en dédier des volumes successivement à S.M. l'Impératrice de Russie, et de même à S.M. le roi de Dannemarck, à S.M le roi de Pologne & tout récemment à S.M. le roi de Suede. Cela étant ne nous seroit il point permis d'aspirer à lhonneur de consacrer aussi l'un de nos volumes au Corps si respectable qui gouverne les Etats unis de l'amérique, & qui sans doute, ne verroit pas avec indifference cette occasion de répandre des connoissances utiles & même nécessaires chès les peuples qui habitent ces heureuses & libres contrées. Nous oserions donner cette glorieuse destination à notre Vingtieme volume actuellement sous presse & qui réunit les Descriptions de divers arts rélatifs à la Navigation. Telles seroient mes vues & mes desirs. Je les soumets rèspecteusement à la décision de Votre Excellence.

Mais outre cet objet je prendrai la libertè de lui en présenter un autre qui dans son genre ne pourroit qu'être utile a ses compatriotes. Nous avons imprimé la ste. Bible avec les refflexions & les Arguments d'ostervald en deux formats. L'un en deux volumes folio, orné de belles gravures, avec une carte de la Terre Sainte, & l'exemplaire coute £18. L'autre en un gros volume 8o. très bien exécuté, dont le prix est de £6. Quoi que l'un & l'autre Soyent très modiques nous les diminuerions encor si l'on en prenoit un certain nombre d'Exemplaires.[5]

Je me borne pour le coup à ces deux articles, en Suppliant Votre Excellence de me faire eprouver de nouveau ses bontés par une favorable réponse, & de recevoir avec tous mes voeux pour sa precieuse conservation, l'assurance du profond respect

---

5. A year earlier, when discussing with Morellet the low prices of English-language books published in London, BF had used as an example a Bible printed in 12° that sold for only 14 s. Morellet reported this to Ostervald, who hoped to compete in the American market: XXXIX, 140n; Medlin, *Morellet*, I, 470.

avec lequel j'ai l'honneur d'être Monsieur De Votre Excellence
le très humble & très obèissant serviteur

LE BANNERET D'OSTERVALD

Notation: Le Banneret d'osterval 1784.—

From Bache & Shee   Two ALS:[6] American Philosophical Society

Sir   Philadelphia 2d January 1784
Tho' hitherto, we have not taken the liberty of addressing
your Excellency; we have requested Mr. W. T. Franklin, to acknowledge how sensibly we are obliged by your attention to
the interest of our house, as well as the many advantages we
have derived from your friendly recommendations,[7] a continu-

6. Both in the hand of John Shee. The one we do not publish is
marked "2d".
7. The most recent instance concerned Saxony. The previous spring, BF
had recommended RB's firm to Saxon minister Schönfeld, who had given
BF a list of his country's manufactures: XXXIX, 311–12n. WTF forwarded
that list to Bache & Shee with a letter (now missing) requesting on Schönfeld's behalf that it be published. We speculate that WTF wrote that letter in
late July, when BF was providing Saxony's newly appointed commissioner
of commerce with letters of introduction, and sent it to Philadelphia with
Capt. Barney, who arrived on Sept. 9: XL, 350–1, 375, 376, 444n. Bache &
Shee had it by Sept. 22, when they announced to the public that a newly
arrived price list of Saxon manufactures and raw materials, along with pat-
tern cards, could be examined in their store, as well as a price list of Prussian textiles (for which see XL, 363n). Their advertisement ran in various
Philadelphia newspapers throughout October; it is quoted in William E.
Lingelbach, "Saxon-American Relations, 1778–1828," *American Hist.
Rev.*, XVII (1911–12), 521–2n.
    Bache & Shee answered WTF on Nov. 1 (APS), enclosing the newspaper
announcement and explaining that it would have been too costly to publish the list itself. Like other American merchants they were experiencing
"almost insuperable difficulties" in establishing commercial relationships
outside England, being ignorant of the customary terms and not knowing
whom to contact. Wishing to import some of the Saxon cloth, and hoping
that their relationship to BF would induce manufacturers to extend credit,
Bache & Shee sent WTF open letters addressed to unnamed manufacturers in Döbeln and Budissin (Bautzen), asking WTF to insert the names of
suitable trading partners and forward the letters. If the manufacturers did

ance of which we flatter ourselves we shall merit, by evincing upon every occasion the utmost attention and deference— We cannot Sufficiently thank your Excellency for the recent instance of your goodness in preventing the return of the bill we drew on Mr. Williams,[8] such circumstances being peculiarly injurious to mercantile reputation.

We now enclose, for your reimbursment the two following drafts on Messrs. Le Couteulx & Co. Paris.

John Browns, on said house at 20 days st.　　　15,000 *l.t.*[9]
Our own draft on ditto at 30 do.　　　　　　　　10,000
　　　　　　　　　　　　　　　　　　　　　　　25,000

making together 25000. *l.t.*

We have taken the liberty of drawing on those Gentlemen before they have advised us of thier being in Cash, for us, from the circumstance of thier house in Cadiz, having made Insurance for us, on a Vessel that was lost, & as the loss became due the 3rd. of last October and we had directed our proportion of it upwards 20000 *l.t.* to be placed to our Credit with thier Parisian house, we cannot but conclude it has been done long 'ere this, tho' we are yet without advice shou'd any untoward circumstance have delayed it of which no doubt we shall soon be acquainted; we will immediately replace the sum we have now drawn for; observing only, that shou'd our bill, in the pres-

---

not want to "become exporters," could WTF ask BF to identify a mercantile house in Hamburg that could handle these orders or at least serve as an insurer? A French translation of a letter from Bache & Shee to a manufacturer in Döbeln, and a copy of their letter (in English) to a Hamburg mercantile house, both dated Nov. 3, are at the APS. They are in the hand of L'Air de Lamotte.

RB sent WTF the Nov. 1 letter from Bache & Shee with the abovementioned enclosures under cover of a personal letter dated Nov. 5 (APS). He sent duplicates by another conveyance on Nov. 9 (APS). A copy of Bache & Shee's letter to WTF has been located in the state archive of Saxony, which indicates that BF probably gave it to Schönfeld: Lingelbach, "Saxon-American Relations, 1778–1828," p. 522n.

8. Bache & Shee's bill on JW arrived at a time when he was experiencing acute financial difficulties. BF paid the bill to prevent it from being protested: XL, 112, 318, 417.

9. Brown's bill of exchange, dated Jan. 2, 1784, was to be paid to the order of Bache & Shee. On the verso, the firm endorsed it to BF. APS.

ent instance, be refused, the trouble & expence of protest may be avoided. Our Mr. R B, being in the Country, from whence probably he may not return in time to write by this packet; we have the pleasure of informing of the good health of the family, subscribing ourselves with every sentiment of respect and esteem Your Excellency's Most Obliged hum Servts.

BACHE & SHEE

His Excellency Benjn. Franklin Esqr

Endorsed: Bache & Shee Jan 2. 1784—

From Marie-Françoise-Dominique Brouttin Mollien de Sombres[1]

ALS: Historical Society of Pennsylvania

Monsieur   paris 2. jv. 1784. rue des gravilliers.

Jai l'honneur de vous adresser le memoire de M. morel de dunkerque[2] duquel jai eu celui de vous parler chez M Cadet de Vaux lorsque vous y vinte diner; tendant à obtenir le Consulat des états unis a dunkerque.

M. thommas barclay a du vous en remettre aussi un pour lui?[3] Vous y veré Monsieur quil a toujours et sa famille rendu beaucoup de Service au américains; et que cest a juste titre quil Sollicite cette place, quil attens de vos bontés. Je joins aupré de vous monsieur, mes prierres aux Siennes. C'est mon parent, je vous aurai la plus grande aubligation de ce que vous voudré bien faire pour lui, je vous assure que vous ne pouvez faire un meillêur choix.

1. The wife of a former captain of a French infantry regiment, Gaspard-Antoine-Louis de Mollien de Sombres: Charles Thierry-Mieg, *La Succession de Jean Thierry de Venise: histoire de la famille Thierry* (Paris, 1894), p. 243. This is her second extant letter; her 1778 appeal is summarized in XXVII, 104.

2. This petition, in a secretarial hand and signed by Benjamin Morel Dufaux, is almost identical to the one he sent BF on Oct. 11, described in annotation to that letter. The chief difference is that this version does not mention Silas Deane.

3. A third copy of Morel Dufaux's memoir, which also omits Deane's name, is at the APS. No cover letter has been located.

J'apprendrai avec [*plaisir*] si vous acceuillé sa demande?[4] Jai l'honneur d'etre avec toute la veneration qui vous est due Monsieur Votre tres humble et tres obeissante servante

BROUTTIN, MOLLIEN DE SOMBRES

From Jacques-Dominique de Cassini fils[5]

ALS: American Philosophical Society

Monsieur   ce 2 janvier 1784

La Medaille que vous avez eu La bonté de donner au Vicomte de Mory mon beau frere en consideration de ses Services en Amerique a été pour lui la plus pretieuse recompense de ses travaux militaires.[6]

Ses premieres Campagnes, Ses premieres armes, ont été pour la defense de L'amerique. Cinq Campagnes, Quatre Sieges, un Combat Naval Et deux blessures, voila les premieres epoques de sa vie, Elles seront eternellement liées avec celle de la brillante revolution qu'a operé le courage de vos illustres compatriotes.

C'est a ces titres, Monsieur, Exprimés plus au long dans le memoire cy joint[7] que j'ose vous faire Une demande dont le

4. On Jan. 18 Mme Brouttin inquired whether BF had received the memoir and asked for a response. On Feb. 21 she informed BF that she had called at Passy but had not found him at home; she still hoped for a reply and another opportunity to meet with him. Both letters are at the APS.

5. An astronomer like his famous father, César-François Cassini de Thury (XXIX, 323n; XL, 405n), Cassini was designated to succeed him as director of the Paris observatory from the time the position was created in 1771. He received the official appointment after his father's death in September, 1784. Since 1773 Cassini had been married to Claude-Marie-Louise de La Myre-Mory, whose brother is the subject of the present letter: *Dictionary of Scientific Biography*.

6. André-Jérôme de La Myre (Mire), vicomte de Mory, joined d'Estaing's fleet in 1778, was wounded in the naval battle off Grenada in 1779, and fought at the siege of Savannah. He was promoted to the rank of captain in 1781. The medal BF gave him was probably a *Libertas Americana*. La Myre realized the ambition described here and became a member of the French branch of the Cincinnati: Bodinier, *Dictionnaire;* Ludovic de Contenson, *La Société des Cincinnati de France et la guerre d'Amérique, 1778–1783* (Paris, 1934), p. 203.

7. Not found.

succèz feroit le bonheur et la gloire de la famille de mon beau frere, et rejailliroit même Sur la mienne.

Si les etats unis accordant L'ordre de *Cincinnatus* aux generaux et Colonels de L'armée francoise, avoient La deference d'y admettre quelques autres officiers de grade inferieur, j'ose vous prier avec instance, Monsieur, de vouloir bien mettre au nombre de ceux qui seront favorisés de cette grace, Le Vicomte de Mory mon beau frere. Je ne crois pas qu'il y ait beaucoup d'officiers françois qui dans un age aussi Tendre ayent rassemblé des titres plus dignes d'être distingués.

Je vous avoue qu'en mon particulier je mettrai le plus grand prix a cette faveur pour mon beau frere, regardant comme une nouvelle et veritable gloire pour le Nom de Cassini de pouvoir Un jour se dire lié a celui d'un defenseur des Etats unis et d'un Chevalier de l'ordre de Cincinnatus. Vous ne pouvez donc douter, Monsieur, de ma reconnoissance eternelle, ainsi que du respect et de la profonde Veneration avec lesquels je Serai toute ma vie Votre trés humble Et trés obeissant serviteur

> De Cassini fils
> Directeur en Survivance de l'observatoire Royal
> Et membre de L'academie Royale des Sciences

Notation: De Cassini, 2 Janr. 1784.

From Ingenhousz

ALS: American Philosophical Society

Dear Friend   Vienna Jan. 2. 1784

You will have recieved my lettre dated Nov. 19th. with a parcel to mr le Begue Containing papers for the press. Count choteck inquired again whether his bill of exchange has been forwarded by you to America. I told him you have probably had no time to write me about it, but that I make no doubt but the commission is sent to America. From the inclosed notification you will see that we are about making an air balloon if we can get a sum adequate to the expenses, and if we can get a perfect knowledge of every thing belonging to the stucture and management of the machine. The *proces verbal* of the first aerial navigation,[8] you was so good to send me, arrived one or two days before it appeared in the news papers, but unlukkely it came one day after the Emperour went to Italy.

One of us, a young man, well versed in many branches of natural philosophy and in mechaniks, will undertake a journey to Paris in the beginning of february, on purpose to instruct him self in every article concerning the balloons and air voyages so as to be able to make one and to goe up with it—[9] This our undertaking supposes, that at this time nothing will be kept secret about the whole affair. But, as from all the printed accounts, it is allmost impossible to get a thorough knowledge of the Construction and menagement of the balloons, you would oblige me greately, if you would inform me by a line of answer, whether Mr. Montgolfier, Pilatre the Rosier, or Charles would be willing to show the balloon, to explain its structure, and to give all necessary instructions about it, so that one can imitate the machine and goe up with it. I Should want the answer about the end of this month, as the Gentleman of our society will set out or not, according to such an answer. If they keep secrets, it would be useless to goe to Paris and return with doubts and confusion.

I can not look upon those balloons but as one of the greatest discoveries of natural philosophy; a discovery bigg with the most important consequences and capable of giving a new turn to human Society, of overturning the whole art of conducting wars. If they can conduct the balloons in the same way as they doe ships, who could an army subsist when the ennemy can throw fire and destruction upon their stores and magazines at any time? Who can an armed fleet attack any seacoast town, when the people of the country can swarm in the clouds and then fire upon it in the middel of the night? Doe not you

8. Above, under the date of Nov. 21.

9. Alois Joseph Franz Xaver von Widmanstetter (1754–1849), a book printer from Graz who had recently invited Ingenhousz to witness several experiments with a small balloon. Widmanstetter did not ultimately go to Paris, and his plan of constructing a larger balloon appears to have remained unrealized: Otto Nirenstein, *Luftfahrt im alten Wien* (Vienna, 1917), pp. 9–10; Constant von Wurzbach, ed., *Biographisches Lexikon des Kaiserthums Oesterreich* (60 vols., Vienna, 1856–91); Norman Beale and Elaine Beale, *Echoes of Ingen Housz* (East Knoyle, Eng., 2011), p. 349.

think that this discovery will make an end of all wars, and thus force monarks to perpetual peace or to fight their own quarrels among themself in a duel? We may find thus the greatest tirants to be the greatest cowards, and thus reduced to the necessity of involving no more their subjects in those miseries, which are too frequently brought on them by the misconduct of their souverains. They would be punish'd themselfs by their own follies.

The German edition of my book,[1] now under the press these two years at Paris, is allready sold out, and the original edition is not yet publish'd. This is in the highest degree vexing. I wish I could come over to Paris next summer myself.

I believe it is national jalousie, which make the English look upon the air balloons with so much indifference.

I got a few days ago three parcels of american Newspapers and the pensylvania almanack, which you did send me a year and a half ago.[2] It was kept all that time in the Custom hous at Vienna, tho I had inquired about it. I complained immediately of this misconduct to the ministry, and they gave me the satisfaction of reprimanding the custom hous officers and of establishing such new regulations as will very likely put a stop to such negligence in those transactions.

As I suspected this misconduct to exist, I have, a long while ago, sollicited from Count Mercy to wrap a cover over each parcel directed to me, to seal it, and direct it *A Monsieur de Spielman chevalier de l'ordre de Saint Etienne, conseilier aulique de cours et d'etat.*[3] This gentleman recieving first all the state papers recieves then my parcels among them, and sends them to me directly.

It seems to me as if the air navigators conciel still their art, for mr. Charles pretens that his Globe, with which he went up, was filled with *Inflammable air,* which I think impossible considering the immense Capacity of the balloon. He says that when on the ground the cloath of his balloon follded together and buried

1. *Vermischte Schriften physisch-medizinischen Inhalts* . . . (Vienna, 1782).
2. BF had sent Ingenhousz the German-language publications in June, 1782: XXXV, 547.
3. Baron Anton Spielmann (1738–1813) was privy councillor to Joseph II: Constant von Wurzbach, *Biographisches Lexikon des Kaiserthums Oesterreich* (60 vols., Vienna, 1856–91).

under it his compagnon. This shows that the balloon was then emptyed of air. And yet he extended it immediately again and went up at 1524 toises. He certainly had no inflammable air at hands at the place. Thus it seems to me, that he had only rarifyed the air within, either by burning spirit of wine, straw or some other combustible; and that they have endeavoured to blind fold the spectators on purpose to make them fail in their attempt to imitate them. What is your opinion about this affair?

Pray let me have a line of answer as soon as possible.

I am very respectfully dear friend Your most obedient humble servant   J. INGEN HOUSZ

I begg to be excused to send this parcel of penny post lettres at your charge. They are about the balloon an ought to be answered immediately. You will be so good as to fill up the direction of *mr. Charles,* and that of mr. *le Roy,* who lives, I believe, Rue de Seine.[4]

to Benj. Franklin ministre plenipot. of the united States of America at Passy

From Gabriel-Louis Galissard de Marignac[5]

ALS: American Philosophical Society

Monsieur,   Genève ce 2e. Janvier 1784

J'ai reçu le 31e. de Xbre. la lettre, dont vous m'avès honoré le 22e;[6] La satisfaction, que vous y témoignés, le contentement, que vous avés de Bache, ont été un baume pour mon cœur, qui ne desiroit rien tant que de repondre à vôtre bienveuillance;

4. On the same day as the present letter, Ingenhousz wrote to Charles, Le Roy, and Lebègue de Presle about balloons: Beale and Beale, *Echoes of Ingen Housz,* pp. 349, 563–4.

5. BFB's former tutor, who had last seen BFB in early July. (For BFB's departure from Geneva see XL, 267n.) Marignac's July 28 bill for 790 *l.t.* 19 *s.* was paid on BF's order on Sept. 28. His final bill, for 480 *l.t.,* was dated Jan. 5. Payment was issued on March 1: Account XVII (XXVI, 3).

6. Not found, but to judge by Marignac's enthusiasm, it must have contained a gift. BF also sent an end-of-year gift to Mme Cramer in Geneva; see her letter of Feb. 12.

soyès assuré, Monsieur, que je conserverai toute ma vie un souvenir respectueux & reconnoissant de vos bontés; Cette nouvelle année ne sauroit ajouter aux vœux, que je fais continuellement pour vôtre bonheur, & pour la durée d'une vie aussi honorable à nôtre siècle, que précieuse à l'humanité. C'est avec ces Sentimens que j'ai l'honneur d'être avec la Consideration la plus distinguée Monsieur Vôtre trés humble & trés obéissant serviteur

G. L. DE MARIGNAC

Je profiterai au premier jour avec la plus vive gratitude de vôtre dernière marque de bonté.

Notation: Marignac 2 Janvr. 1784.

To John Adams

ALS: Massachusetts Historical Society

Sir   Passy, Jan. 3. 1784.
I received the Letter you did me the Honour of writing to me by Capt. Jones, and immediately answer'd it, acquainting you that my Packets contain'd no Commission, nor any Mention of one.[7] I have just receiv'd another Letter from you, dated the 14th past, with a Number of Dispatches, but they are Duplicates only and as old as July; they contain nothing of the Commission neither, except the Vote that directs the making it out, which is dated in May.[8] It seems to be forgotten. It was by no means possible for me to save Mr Morris's Bills. I was in hopes that if you had gone to Amsterdam you might have done something towards it. With great Respect, I have the Honour to be, Sir, Your Excellency's most obedt & most humble Servant

B FRANKLIN

His Excelly. John Adams Esqr.

7. JA's letter was dated Dec. 5 and BF answered on Dec. 10; both are above.
8. The resolution was passed on May 1: XL, 178–9.

From John Shaffer

ALS: Historical Society of Pennsylvania

Sir   Paris ce 4 Janvier 84./.

Was theire ever an Example of aney person in Life to be abandoned as I am, you may be asured it is with great Reluctance that I persist in adressing my Self to you, in my last[9] I took the liberty of asking you what Mr Barclay had Concluded to do for me, as Mr Barclay before his departure Refered me to you for an Answer of what you had Concluded upon at your last meating with Mr Beaumont, do Not Keep me aney longer in Suspence I beg of you, if I am to Expect my Judment in Parlement that I may make my defence, my Reporteuer is Not as yet Nominated but Expect he will hourorly when I hope you will Not abandon me in the Absance Of Mr. Barclay, I have Not as yet Seen Mr Beaumont, wich Gives me Pain, as to my Situation Mr Beaumont has Certainly gave you a tableau.

I imbrace the Opertuenety of wishng you an agreable and happe New year.

I have the honour to be with Profound Respect your Exelencys Most Obedent and very humble Servant   J Schaffer

ps I am in the most Cruel situation in life and live upon the blacke bread of the Prison this 15 days

His Excelency Docter Franklin

---

9. Most likely a similar letter (undated) in which Shaffer asked BF about Barclay and made an appeal for "what Ever Small Sum" BF thought proper: Shaffer to BF, [before Jan. 4, 1784], APS.

[Thomas Mifflin] to the American Peace Commissioners[1]

Press copy of copy: American Philosophical Society; copy:[2] William L. Clements Library; press copy of copy: Massachusetts Historical Society

Gentlemen,   Annapolis Jany. 5. 1784. In Congress

I am directed to inform you[3] "that the definitive Treaty after a very long Passage arrived during an Adjournment of Congress from Princeton to this Place. No more than seven States are yet assembled. These are unanimously desirous to ratify the Treaty and the measure will be taken up as soon as nine States are assembled.[4] In the mean while as the weather is severe and travelling extreamly difficult from a heavy fall of Snow, it is to be feared that the Ratification may not arrive in the time limited for the Exchange,[5] and that inconveniences may arise unless the time for exchanging the Ratification should be extended."

I am with the highest Esteem & Respect Gentlemen, Your obedient humble Servt.—

1. BF assumed at first that this letter was from Charles Thomson, as the MS he received (now missing) was unsigned but in Thomson's hand: BF to Thomson, March 9, 1784 (National Archives). Thomson later informed him that the letter was from Mifflin, who had accidentally sealed it before signing: Thomson to BF, Aug. 13, 1784, in Smith, *Letters*, XXI, 771. BF called it a letter from Thomson when sending copies to his colleagues: BF to Hartley, March 11, 1784 (Library of Congress); BF to JA, March 15, 1784 (Mass. Hist. Soc.).

2. Made by Hartley from the copy (now missing) that BF sent him on March 11. Hartley erroneously indicated that it was signed by Thomson. The surviving press copies, made from two different copies by L'Air de Lamotte, left the signature line blank.

3. The quotation marks that follow are puzzling; the entire text, including this initial phrase, was approved by Congress on Jan. 5. The committee that drafted this letter for Mifflin's signature had been authorized to do so on Jan. 3: *JCC*, XXVI, 4–5, 8.

4. The assembled states were Massachusetts, Rhode Island, Pennsylvania, Delaware, Maryland, Virginia, and North Carolina. Nine were needed for ratification: *JCC*, XXV, 836–7. A motion to authorize seven states to ratify the treaty was debated in late December but never put to a vote, and a compromise motion to ratify tentatively was referred to committee on Jan. 2: Smith, *Letters*, XXI, 235n; *Jefferson Papers*, VI, 424–6, 439–42.

5. The treaty specified a time limit of six months, which would make the deadline March 3: XL, 574.

JANUARY 5, 1784

The Honorable John Adams, Benjamin Franklin, John Jay &
Henry Laurens.

To Samuel Chase   AL (draft): American Philosophical Society

Dear Sir,   Passy, Jan. 6. 1784—
   I duly Receiv'd your Letter of the 18th. of September, with
the Papers that accompanied it; but being at that time afflicted
with two painful Disorders, the Gout and Gravel, I could not
then give any Attention to Business; and before my Recovery,
the Letters and Paper were both most unaccountably missing.
I spent Hours from time to time in searching for them, and
delay'd writing in continual Hopes of finding them, which I was
not able to do till within these few Days, when on removing a
writing Press in my Closet, I discover'd that they had fallen and
lay conceal'd behind it.—
   I had deliver'd the Letter you enclos'd to the Marquis de la
Fayette,[6] and as the Court was then at Fontainbleau, and I could
not follow it by reason of my Illness, I requested him to sound
Mr le Marquis de Castries on the Subject of the Loss of your
Ship. He did so, and the Result of the Conversation was, that
if you thought fit to prosecute the Matter, you should present a
Memorial, upon which he might regularly take the Affair into
Consideration.[7] You mentioned your coming to Paris before
finishing your other Business in case I should think there was
a Probability of obtaining Compensation either from the Prop-

6. This was a letter from either Chase himself or his fellow Marylander
James McHenry, Lafayette's former aide-de-camp and frequent correspondent. McHenry was concerned, along with Chase, in trying to help Ann Le
Vacher de Vaubrun (for whom see Chase to BF, Sept. 18). From the surviving correspondence, it is clear that he asked Lafayette to exert his influence
to help her case. When writing to McHenry on Dec. 26, 1783, Lafayette
alluded to previous letters detailing his efforts and added that though he
thought there was "little to be Got," he would continue to pursue the affair:
Idzerda, *Lafayette Papers*, v, 185.
   7. This meeting, concerning the loss of the *Matilda*, had to have taken
place before Dec. 26, as Lafayette mentioned it in his letter of that date,
cited above.

erty of the Captain[8] or the Generosity of the Prince. I have not yet been able to learn any thing of the Captain's Circumstances, and as clear Proof of his Delinquency must precede an Application to the King, and perhaps the Protest of Capt. Belt will hardly be thought sufficient Testimony, and other Evidences corroborating cannot be obtained but with great Expense & Loss of Time, and the Chicanery practis'd in the Courts here to procure Delay is immense and endless, on these Considerations I cannot advise your coming hither for the Purpose of such a Prosecution, to the Prejudice of your other Affairs; tho' I shall be happy to see you when it may be convenient to you; and when you are here, we will take the Advice of some judicious Persons, and if it appears possible for me to serve your Cause I shall do it with great Pleasure.—

Mr de Rochambeau was not in Town, but I forwarded Mr Carrol's Letter to him. I have written as you desired to Brest,[9] and as soon as I receive an Answer I will communicate it to you. I am not enough acquainted with the French Laws or Customs to inform you what Claims the Widow of M. le Vaché may have on his Property. I only think I have heard, that Marriages by a Protestant Minister are not deemed valid. I will make Enquiry.—*

I shall be glad to hear that you have succeeded in Recovering the Publick Money; and that you continue to enjoy your Health; being with sincere & great Esteem, Dear Sir,

Honble Samll Chase Esqr

* Since writing the above I am inform'd that if celebrated in a Protestant Country according to the Laws of that Country, they are deem'd valid here. As are also the Marriages of Protestants here, if in the Chapel of a Protestant Ambassador.—[1]

8. Chevalier de Quemy.

9. Chase made this request on Sept. 18. BF's letter to Sané has not been located.

1. Protestant marriages performed in France were void until the Edict of Toleration of 1787, although courts had begun to validate Protestant inheritance through legal subterfuges for at least a decade. Protestant marriages performed abroad (or within the diplomatic jurisdiction of a Protestant power in France, as BF describes) were recognized under French civil law even before 1787: David D. Bien, "Catholic Magistrates and Protestant Marriage in the French Enlightenment," *French Hist. Studies*, II (1962),

To John Jay

ALS: Mrs. Marion Brawley, Oakley, South Carolina (1959); press copy of ALS, copy, and incomplete copy: Library of Congress

Dear Sir,   Passy, Jan. 6. 1784—

I received your kind Letter of the 26th past, and immediately sent the inclosed to Mrs Jay,[2] whom I saw a few days since with the Children, all perfectly well. It is a happy Thing that the little ones are so finely past the Small Pox, and I congratulate you upon it most cordially.—[3]

It is true, as you have heard, that I have the Stone, but not that I have had Thoughts of being cut for it. It is as yet very tolerable. It gives me no Pain, but when in a Carriage on the Pavement, or when I make some sudden quick Movement. If I can prevent its growing larger, which I hope to do by abstemious Living and gentle Exercise, I can go on pretty comfortably with it to the End of my Journey, which can now be at no great distance. I am chearful, enjoy the Company of my Friends, sleep well, have sufficient Appetite, and my Stomach performs well its Functions. The latter is very material to the Preservation of Health; I therefore take no Drugs lest I should disorder it. You may judge that my Disease is not very grievous, since I am more afraid of the Medicines than of the Malady.—

It gives me Pleasure to learn from you that my Friends still retain their Regard for me. I long to see them again, but I doubt I shall hardly accomplish it. If our Commission for the Treaty

---

409–421; Margaret Maxwell, "The Division in the Ranks of Protestants in Eighteenth Century France," *Church History,* XXVII (1958), 114.

2. John Jay's Dec. 26 letter to his wife: *Jay Papers,* III, 536–7.

3. At the end of November, Sarah Jay, learning that "the famous Inoculator, Dr. Sutton" was in Paris, had her young daughters inoculated, hoping that her husband would approve. He did. Maria was not yet two years old (XL, 322), and Ann was born on Aug. 13 while the family was staying with BF at Passy (XL, 180n). Both girls developed high fevers and a mild outbreak of pox, but were out of danger by mid-December. The Dr. Sutton in question may have been Daniel (*ODNB*), a prominent member of the family well known for its inoculation clinics in England and Europe: *Jay Papers,* III, 480, 521–2, 531–2; Hervé Bazin, *The Eradication of Smallpox* . . . (San Diego, San Francisco, and New York, 2000), pp. 16–18.

of Commerce were arriv'd, and we were at Liberty to treat in England, I might then come over to you, supposing the English Ministry dispos'd to enter into such a Treaty. But no late Letters from the Congress make any Mention of it. They continue however with every Dispatch to send a Copy of the Minute which directs the Commission to be prepared,[4] as if it was thought we might act upon that, at least so far as to make the Convention for a Year. I send you enclos'd one of those authenticated Copies. It may serve as Ground for proposing a Conference with one of the new Ministers, in which you might discover whether they really intend a Treaty or not. If not, we can inform the Congress, and save them the Trouble of preparing the Plan.—

I have, as you observe, some Enemies in England, but they are my Enemies as *an American;* I have also two or three in America, who are my Enemies as *a Minister:* but I thank God there are not in the whole World any who are my Enemies as *a Man;* for by his Grace thro' a long Life I have been enabled so to conduct myself, that there does not exist a human Being who can justly say, Ben Franklin has wrong'd me. This, my Friend, is in old Age a comfortable Reflection. You too have, or may have, your Enemies: But let not that render you unhappy. If you make a right use of them they will do you more Good than Harm. They point out to us our Faults;[5] they put us upon our guard;[6] and help us to live more correctly.

Three Copies of the Definitive Treaty have been sent, and I suppose we may soon expect the Ratification. I have just receiv'd a Letter from Mr Hartley, acquainting me with the Change of Ministry, and requesting to have "the earliest Notice whenever the Ratification shall arrive, that we may lose no time in bringing that blessed Event to a complete Termination."[7] I imagine you will see him when you return to London. He seems to speak as if *his* Commission was likely to continue.

4. See BF to JA, Jan. 3. The minute is in *JCC,* XXIV, 321.
5. As Poor Richard had observed in 1756, "Love your Enemies, for they tell you your Faults": VI, 321. See also XXXV, 473.
6. A point he made to his sister in 1767: XIV, 73.
7. Above, Dec. 25.

My Grandsons are sensible of the Honour of your Remembrance, and join their respectful Compliments and best Wishes with those of, Dear Sir, Your affectionate humble Servant

B. FRANKLIN

His Excelly. John Jay Esqr

Endorsed: Dr Franklin 6 Jan. 1784 recd. 15 Jan. 1784

Remarks concerning the Savages of North America

Printed at Passy, [1784]; AD (draft): Library of Congress; two copies: Library of Congress; incomplete press copy of copy: American Philosophical Society

In the fall and winter of 1783–84, when Franklin's diplomatic responsibilities were at an ebb, he was confined to his house by painful ailments, and he was hoping for permission to leave France, he seems to have spent much of his time reflecting on the differences among peoples and nations, and considering how to characterize the nation he had helped to create. During these dark months he labored over three remarkably different pieces that, in various ways, contrasted America—or what he wanted America to be—with the culture of Old World Europe. All three were translated into French, but he circulated only two, in the form of printed pamphlets: "Remarks concerning the Savages of North America" and "Information to Those Who Would Remove to America" (published at the end of this volume). The third piece, written in the form of a private letter to his daughter, was suppressed on the advice of the abbé Morellet. Its critique of the French aristocracy was too blunt.[8]

Neither of the two printed essays can be dated with any precision. "Remarks" had to have been written well before January 7, when the duc de La Rochefoucauld sent Franklin his French translation. (His cover letter is below.) The only other clue to the timing of its composition is a tenuous one: a crude pencil sketch on the verso of page 6 of the draft, depicting a manned hot-air balloon tethered to the ground with ropes. If contemporary with the draft, the drawing

8. See BF to Sarah Bache, Jan. 26 (below).

indicates that Franklin was working on "Remarks" during Montgolfier's first manned balloon trials in October.[9]

"Remarks" and "Information," which were both produced in
English and French editions, were not printed until sometime around
March.[1] This was the period when Franklin was printing, as keepsakes for his friends, the shorter *jeu d'esprits* that he had written over
the years of his residence at Passy and now gathered under the title
"Bagatelles." "Remarks" and "Information" were included in that
collection.[2] Unlike the other bagatelles, however, which were only
distributed to his circle of intimates, Franklin intended "Information," and probably also "Remarks," for a wider audience.

The first surviving references to these pamphlets are to the English versions. "Information" was ready by March 9, when Franklin
sent a copy to Congress.[3] On March 10, the abbé Morellet sent both
"Information" and "Remarks" to Lord Shelburne.[4] In May, without
Franklin's knowledge, John Stockdale in London published the pair
as *Two Tracts . . . by Dr. Benjamin Franklin,* thereby attaching his
name to pieces that had been issued anonymously.[5] Two months later,

9. In the sketch, the basket suspended below the balloon holds a tiny figure wearing a cap, arms outstretched, evidently stoking the fire. Montgolfier conducted his first manned balloon trials in just this way: his aeronaut
was lifted a short distance into the air under very controlled conditions. See
the annotation of Le Roy to BF, [Oct. 19?].

1. Facsimiles of the English and French imprints of "Remarks concerning the Savages of North America" are in *The Bagatelles from Passy* (New
York, 1967), pp. [157]–80.

2. BF wrote as much to Mme Brillon on April 8, 1784, after sending her
the French versions of "Remarks" and "Information" (APS). Only two
examples of the collected bagatelles survive, one at the Yale University Library, the other at the Bibliothèque nationale. The Yale copy contains the
English and French versions of both essays. The copy at the BN contains
only the French versions.

3. See the headnote to "Information to Those Who Would Remove to
America," [before March].

4. Morellet noted in his letter that this was how BF had occupied his leisure time since the peace. He added that BF was now expecting his recall:
Medlin, *Morellet,* I, 508.

5. When BF learned of the publication, he wrote to Benjamin Vaughan
that he would "rather [my name] had been omitted." At that point, he had
heard only that "Information" had been published: BF to Vaughan, July 26,
1784 (Library of Congress). *Two Tracts* proved so popular that it went
through three editions before the end of 1784.

a Passy imprint of "Remarks" was given to Birmingham printers Pearson and Rollason, probably by Joseph Priestley. They reissued it with a prefatory "Advertisement" that attributed the essay to Franklin. A reviewer concurred that the style was certainly his.[6] In the fall of 1784 Jacques-Pierre Brissot de Warville translated the pieces and published them in his *Journal du Licée de Londres*. Although the pamphlets were "sans date & sans nom d'Auteur," he wrote, they had surely come from the pen of "le politique profond & le Phisicien célèbre dont s'honore l'Amérique."[7]

Franklin's French edition of "Information," entitled "Avis à ceux qui voudraient s'en aller en Amérique," was printed by early March, around the same time as the English; see the headnote to that piece. The earliest reference to his French edition of "Remarks" is a month later: when Mme Brillon requested a copy of "Avis," he sent her both "Avis" and "Remarques sur la politesse des sauvages de l'Amérique septentrionale."[8] His note to her of April 8 constitutes the sole surviving record of his having given "Remarks," in either French or English, to anyone. That same month, however, the French version appeared in the *Correspondance littéraire*, where the editor noted that it had been translated from Franklin's English by the duc de La Rochefoucauld.[9]

Three manuscript versions of Franklin's text survive, all undated:[10] his eleven-page draft and two contemporary copies of it made by Ben-

6. The advertisement stated: "A gentleman who has just received from France a copy of the following 'Remarks,' written by Dr. Franklin, and printed by himself, for his amusement, at his own house at Passey, near Paris, having favoured the publishers with it; they re-print the same, being sensible that the most trifling miscellaneous productions of that distinguished author, will be agreeable to the public." Paul L. Ford suggested that Joseph Priestley was the pamphlet's source, as Pearson and Rollason published his works: *Franklin Bibliography* . . . (Brooklyn, N.Y., 1889), p. 171. The review appeared in the *Monthly Review*, LXXI (1784), 70.

7. Brissot printed "Information" (whose title he translated as "Avis à ceux qui voudroient émigrer en Amérique") in the October issue. "Remarks" ("Remarques sur les Sauvages de l'Amérique Septentrionale") appeared in November: *Journal du Licée de Londres*, I (1784), 229–42, 290–302. The short-lived journal was published monthly during 1784: Jean Sgard, ed., *Dictionnaire des journaux, 1600–1789* (2 vols., Paris, 1991), II, 659–60.

8. Mme Brillon to BF, [April] 4, 1784; BF to Mme Brillon, April 8, 1784 (both at the APS).

9. [Friedrich Melchior Baron von Grimm *et al.*, eds.], *Correspondance littéraire, philosophique et critique de Grimm et de Diderot, depuis 1753 jusqu'en 1790* (15 vols., Paris, 1829–31), XII, 93–103.

10. We do not publish the French text, as it was not primarily the work of

jamin Franklin Bache. One of the copies is nearly perfect; this may have been the one given to the translator. The other (from which the press copy was made)[1] has several mistakes that Franklin corrected. He also made further revisions. The printed text includes those revisions, as well as two final wording changes that were not marked on this copy. They are noted in annotation, below.

We reproduce the text as printed on the Passy press because it reflects Franklin's final revisions, and because it was the version that he made public. It is marred, however, by innumerable discrepancies that were introduced by the compositor: changes in punctuation, the rendering of contractions and ampersands, the use of italics, and the use of hyphens. The compositor was almost certainly Moritz Meyer, a Saxon printer with only a rudimentary knowledge of English, who worked for Franklin from December, 1783, until May, 1784.[2] That the compositor was a nonnative speaker is suggested by the nature of the occasional misspellings. That Franklin himself did not set the type is indicated by, among other things, the hyphenization of "North-America" throughout "Remarks" and "Information." Franklin never hyphenated this name, nor was it hyphenated in any of Benny Bache's copies. In our own title line, above, we render the name of this piece as Franklin did.

"Remarks" is in some ways the most enigmatic of the pamphlets Franklin printed at Passy. Whereas his purpose in distributing "Information" is well documented, his papers are silent as to "Remarks." We have scant evidence of where he sent it, have found no acknowledgments of its receipt, and, with the one exception noted below, have found no reactions to it by any of his friends.

An unidentified British reader of *Two Tracts* took "Remarks" to be a "ludicrous" attempt to neutralize the stories of Indian savagery that were deterring potential emigrants from settling the American frontier, as recommended in "Information to Those Who Would Remove

---

BF. The degree to which he suggested alterations is impossible to gauge, as La Rochefoucauld's manuscript is missing. It must have been at La Rochefoucauld's suggestion, however, that "la politesse" was added to the title. For the French text, see *The Bagatelles from Passy*.

1. This press copy was taken before BF corrected and emended the text.

2. For Meyer, see the annotation of Rufin and Meyer to BF, Oct. 31, above. It is possible that he was assisted by BFB, whom he may have been tutoring in the arts of composition and printing. BFB printed his first broadside in late December, 1783; it is reproduced facing p. 354. See also the List of Illustrations.

to America."³ The doctor's good friend Cabanis, on the other hand, writing an appreciation of Franklin after his death, saw "Remarks" as an expression of the American minister's belief in simplicity as the root of happiness, a belief that had been informed by firsthand observations of Indian tribes. Franklin viewed the Indians' "mœurs" as superior to "les nôtres" in several ways, wrote Cabanis; living under the freedom they enjoyed had brought them greater happiness than that of "nations civilisées."⁴ These reactions reflected two common stereotypes of America. Both of these contemporaries failed to see in the essay what seems so evident to modern readers, the satire on the parochialism and hypocrisy of every nation's view of itself and others.

[before January 7, 1784]
REMARKS
CONCERNING THE SAVAGES
OF NORTH-AMERICA.

SAVAGES we call them, because their manners differ from ours, which we think the Perfection of Civility; they think the same of theirs.

Perhaps if we could examine the manners of different Nations with Impartiality, we should find no People so rude as to be without Rules of Politeness; nor any so polite as not to have some remains of Rudeness.

The Indian Men, when young, are Hunters and Warriors; when old, Counsellors; for all their Government is by the Counsel or Advice of the Sages; there is no Force, there are no Prisons, no Officers to compel Obedience, or inflict Punishment. Hence they generally study Oratory; the best Speaker having the most Influence. The Indian Women till the Ground, dress the Food, nurse and bring up the Children, & preserve & hand down to Posterity the Memory of Public Transactions. These Employments of Men and Women are accounted natural and honorable. Having few Artificial Wants, they have abundance of Leisure for Improvement by Conversation. Our laborious manner of Life compared with theirs, they esteem slavish and base; and the

3. *Public Advertiser,* Oct. 7, 1784.
4. Cabanis himself considered this view naive: *Œuvres complètes de Cabanis* (5 vols., Paris, 1823–25), V, 245–6.

Learning on which we value ourselves; they regard as frivolous and useless. An Instance of this occurred at the Treaty of Lancaster in Pennsylvania, Anno 1744, between the Government of Virginia & the Six Nations.[5] After the principal Business was settled, the Commissioners from Virginia acquainted the Indians by a Speech, that there was at Williamsburg a College with a Fund for Educating Indian Youth, and that if the Chiefs of the Six-Nations[6] would send down half a dozen of their sons[7] to that College, the Government would take Care that they should be well provided for, and instructed in all the Learning of the white People. It is one of the Indian Rules of Politeness not to answer a public Proposition the same day that it is made; they think it would be treating it as a light Matter; and that they show it Respect by taking time to consider it, as of a Matter important. They therefore deferred their Answer till the day following; when their Speaker began by expressing their deep Sense of the Kindness of the Virginia Government, in making them that Offer; for we know, says he, that you highly esteem the kind of Learning taught in those Colleges, and that the Maintenance of our Young Men while with you, would be very expensive to you. We are convinced therefore that you mean to do us Good by your Proposal, and we thank you heartily. But you who are wise must know, that different Nations have different Conceptions of things; and you will therefore not take it amiss, if our Ideas of this Kind of Education happen not to be the same with yours. We have had some Experience of it: Several of our Young People were formerly brought up at the Colleges of the Northern Provinces; they were instructed in all your Sciences; but when they came back to us they were bad Runners, ignorant of every means of living in the Woods, unable to bear either Cold or Hunger, knew neither how to build a Cabin, take a Deer, or

5. From here until the end of the paragraph, BF presents a fuller version of a story that he had related to Peter Collinson in a letter of May 9, 1753. Both versions differ from the official record; see IV, 482–3.

6. BF did not hyphenate "Six Nations," and he added "Chiefs of the" after the fair copies were made.

7. BF's draft and both fair copies have "young Lads" here. The French translation renders this "jeunes garçons", leading us to think that La Rochefoucauld was working from one of BFB's copies.

kill an Enemy, spoke our Language imperfectly; were therefore neither fit for Hunters, Warriors, or Counsellors; they were totally good for nothing. We are however not the less obliged by your kind Offer, tho' we decline accepting it; and to show our grateful Sense of it, if the Gentlemen of Virginia will send us a dozen of their Sons, we will take great Care of their Education, instruct them in all we know, and make *Men* of them.

Having frequent Occasions to hold public Councils, they have acquired great Order and Decency in conducting them. The old Men sit in the foremost Ranks, the Warriors in the next, and the Women and Children in the hindmost. The Business of the Women is to take exact notice of what passes, imprint it in their Memories, for they have no Writing, and communicate it to their Children. They are the Records of the Council, and they preserve Tradition of the Stipulations in Treaties a hundred Years back, which when we compare with our Writings we always find exact.[8] He that would speak, rises. The rest observe a profound Silence. When he has finish'd and sits down, they leave him five or six Minutes to recollect, that if he has omitted any thing he intended to say, or has any thing to add, he may rise again and deliver it. To interrupt another, even in common Conversation, is reckoned highly indecent. How different this is from the Conduct of a polite British House of Commons, where scarce a day passes without some Confusion that makes the Speaker hoarse in calling *to order;* and how different from the mode of Conversation in many polite Companies of Europe, where if you do not deliver your Sentence with great Rapidity, you are cut off in the middle of it by the impatient Loquacity of those you converse with, & never suffer'd to finish it.

The Politeness of these Savages in Conversation is indeed carried to excess, since it does not permit them to contradict, or deny the Truth of what is asserted in their Presence. By this means they indeed avoid Disputes, but then it becomes difficult to know their Minds, or what Impression you make upon them. The Missionaries who have attempted to convert them to

8. The role of women in memorizing tribal history is also related in a textual note to "The Captivity of William Henry": XV, 152n. BF's possible authorship of that piece is discussed in XV, 145–8, where a similarity to "Remarks" is discussed.

Christianity, all complain of this as one of the great Difficulties of their Mission. The Indians hear with Patience the Truths of the Gospel explained to them, and give their usual Tokens of Assent and Approbation: you would think they were convinced. No such Matter. It is mere Civility.

A Suedish Minister having assembled the Chiefs of the Sasquehanah Indians, made a Sermon to them, acquainting them with the principal historical Facts on which our Religion is founded, such as the Fall of our first Parents by Eating an Apple, the Coming of Christ to repair the Mischief, his Miracles and Suffering, &c. When he had finished, an Indian Orator stood up to thank him. What you have told us, says he, is all very good. It is indeed bad to eat Apples. It is better to make them all into Cyder. We are much obliged by your Kindness in coming so far to tell us those things which you have heard from your Mothers. In return I will tell you some of those we have heard from ours.

In the Beginning our Fathers had only the Flesh of Animals to subsist on, and if their Hunting was unsuccessful, they were starving. Two of our young Hunters having killed a Deer, made a Fire in the Woods to broil some Parts of it. When they were about to satisfy their Hunger, they beheld a beautiful young Woman descend from the Clouds, and seat herself on that Hill which you see yonder among the blue Mountains. They said to each other, it is a Spirit that perhaps has smelt our broiling Venison, & wishes to eat of it: let us offer some to her. They presented her with the Tongue: She was pleased with the Taste of it, & said, your Kindness shall be rewarded. Come to this Place after thirteen Moons, and you shall find something that will be of great Benefit in nourishing you and your Children to the latest Generations. They did so, and to their Surprise found Plants they had never seen before, but which from that ancient time have been constantly cultivated among us to our great Advantage. Where her right Hand had touch'd the Ground, they found Maize; where her left Hand had touch'd it, they found Kidney-beans; and where her Backside had sat on it, they found Tobacco.[9] The good Missionary, disgusted with this idle Tale,

9. This corn myth varies from the one in the "Captivity": XV, 151–2. BF learned of it from Conrad Weiser and Lewis Evans, who marked the hill on

said, what I delivered to you were sacred Truths; but what you tell me is mere Fable, Fiction & Falsehood. The Indian offended, reply'd, my Brother, it seems your Friends have not done you Justice in your Education; they have not well instructed you in the Rules of common Civility. You saw that we who understand and practise those Rules, believed all your Stories; why do you refuse to believe ours?[10]

When any of them come into our Towns, our People are apt to croud round them, gaze upon them, and incommode them where they desire to be private; this they esteem great Rudeness, and the Effect of want of Instruction in the Rules of Civility and good Manners. We have, say they, as much Curiosity as you, and when you come into our Towns we wish for Opportunities of looking at you; but for this purpose we hide ourselves behind Bushes where you are to pass, and never intrude ourselves into your Company.

Their Manner of entring one anothers Villages has likewise its Rules. It is reckon'd uncivil in travelling Strangers to enter a Village abruptly, without giving Notice of their Approach. Therefore as soon as they arrive within hearing, they stop and hollow, remaining there till invited to enter. Two old Men usually come out to them, and lead them in. There is in every Village a vacant Dwelling, called the Strangers House. Here they are placed, while the old Men go round from Hut to Hut acquainting the Inhabitants that Strangers are arrived who are probably hungry and weary; and every one sends them what he can spare of Victuals and Skins to repose on. When the Strangers are refresh'd, Pipes & Tobacco are brought; and then, but not before, Conversation begins, with Enquiries who they are, whither bound, what News, &c. and it usually ends with Of-

his 1749 *Map of Pensilvania, New-Jersey, New-York, And the Three Delaware Counties* (III, 392n) as "Onwgaréxnu M[ountain]. Where Indian Corn, Tobacco, Squashes, and Pompions were first found by the Natives, according to their traditions": J. A. Leo Lemay, *The Life of Benjamin Franklin* (3 vols., Philadelphia, 2006–9), II, 483.

10. The same rhetorical question was posed in almost identical terms in "Captivity": xv, 157.

fers of Service, if the Strangers have Occasion of Guides or any Necessaries for continuing their Journey; and nothing is exacted for the Entertainment.

The same Hospitality, esteemed among them as a principal Virtue, is practiced by private Persons; of which *Conrad Weiser,* our Interpreter, gave me the following Instance. He had been naturaliz'd among the Six-Nations, and spoke well the Mohock Language. In going thro' the Indian Country, to carry a Message from our Governor to the Council at *Onondaga,* he call'd at the Habitation of *Canassetego,*[1] an old Acquaintance, who embraced him, spread Furs for him to sit on, placed before him some boiled Beans and Venison, and mixed some Rum and Water for his Drink. When he was well refresh'd, and had lit his Pipe, Canassetego began to converse with him, ask'd how he had fared the many Years since they had seen each other, whence he then came, what occasioned the Journey, &c. &c. Conrad answered all his Questions; and when the Discourse began to flag, the Indian, to continue it, said, Conrad, you have liv'd long among the white People, and know something of their Customs; I have been sometimes at Albany, and have observed that once in seven Days, they shut up their Shops and assemble all in the great House; tell me, what is it for? what do they do there? They meet there, says Conrad, to hear & learn *good things.* I do not doubt, says the Indian, that they tell you so; they have told me the same; but I doubt the Truth of what they say, & I will tell you my Reasons. I went lately to Albany to sell my Skins, & buy Blankets, Knives, Powder, Rum, &c. You know I used generally to deal with Hans Hanson; but I was a little inclined this time to try some other Merchants. However I called first upon Hans, and ask'd him what he would give for Beaver; He said he could not give more than four Shillings a Pound; but, says he, I cannot talk on Business now; this is the Day when we meet together to learn *good things,* and I am going to the Meeting. So I thought to myself since I cannot do any Business to day, I may as well go to the Meeting too; and I went with him. There stood

---

1. Canassatego was a chief of the Onondaga: xv, 149n.

up a Man in black, and began to talk to the People very angrily. I did not understand what he said; but perceiving that he looked much at me, & at Hanson, I imagined he was angry at seeing me there; so I went out, sat down near the House, struck Fire & lit my Pipe; waiting till the Meeting should break up. I thought too, that the Man had mentioned something of Beaver, and I suspected it might be the Subject of their Meeting. So when they came out I accosted any [my]² Merchant; well Hans, says I, I hope you have agreed to give more than four Shillings a Pound. No, says he, I cannot give so much. I cannot give more than three Shillings and six Pence. I then spoke to several other Dealers, but they all sung the same Song, three & six Pence, three & six Pence. This made it clear to me that my Suspicion was right; and that whatever they pretended of Meeting to learn *good things,* the real Purpose was to consult, how to cheat Indians in the Price of Beaver. Consider but a little, Conrad, and you must be of my Opinion. If they met so often to learn *good things,* they would certainly have learnt some before this time. But they are still ignorant. You know our Practice. If a white Man in travelling thro' our Country, enters one of our Cabins, we all treat him as I treat you; we dry him if he is wet, we warm him if he is cold, and give him Meat & Drink that he may allay his Thirst and Hunger, & we spread soft Furs for him to rest & sleep on: We demand nothing in return*.³ But if I go into a white Man's House at Albany, and ask for Victuals & Drink, they say, where is your Money? and if I have none, they say, Get out, you Indian

2. "Any" was a typographical error; Stockdale corrected it in his London reprint.

3. *Note in text:* "**It is remarkable that in all Ages and Countries, Hospitality has been allowed as the Virtue of those, whom the civiliz'd were pleased to call Barbarians; the Greeks celebrated the Scythians for it. The Saracens possess'd it eminently; and it is to this day the reigning Virtue of the wild Arabs. S. Paul too, in the Relation of his Voyage & Shipwreck, on the Island of Melita, says,* The Barbarous People shew'd us no little Kindness; for they kindled a Fire, and received us every one, because of the present Rain & because of the Cold."

In the draft, the quotation is identified as coming from "Acts ch. 27." It is actually from Acts of the Apostles 28:2.

Dog. You see they have not yet learnt those little *good things,* that we need no Meetings to be instructed in, because our Mothers taught them to us when we were Children. And therefore, it is impossible their Meetings, should be as they say for any such purpose, or have any such Effect; they are only to contrive *the Cheating of Indians in the Price of Beaver.*

To David Hartley   Copy:[4] William L. Clements Library

My Dear friend   Passy Jan 7 1784
   I have this moment recd your favour of the 25th past acquainting me with the change in administration. I am sure that in reforming the Constitution wch is sometimes talked of, it wd not be better to make your great offices of State hereditary, than to suffer the inconvenience of such frequent & total changes. Much Faction & Cabal wd be prevented, by having a hereditary first Ld of the Treasury, a hereditary Ld Chancellor, Privy Seal President of the council, Secretary of State, first Ld of the Admiralty &c &c &c— It will not be said that the Duties of these offices being important, we cannot trust to nature for the chance of requisite talents, since we have an hereditary set of judges in the last resort, the House of Peers; an hereditary King, and in a certain German university an hereditary professor of Mathematics.— We have not yet heard of the arrival of our Express in America who carried the definitive treaty. He sailed the 26 of September.[5] As soon as the Ratification arrives I shall immediately send you word of it.
   With great Esteem I am ever My Dear friend Yours most affectely   B FRANKLIN

To D Hartley Esqr.

   4. In Hartley's hand.
   5. BF would soon learn of Thaxter's arrival from a letter Jay wrote to WTF on Dec. 30, 1783. Jay, in Bath, had learned the news from a private source (APS).

From the Duc de La Rochefoucauld

AL: American Philosophical Society

Paris 7 jer. 1784.

Le Duc de la Rochefoucauld fait bien des Complimens à Monsieur Franklyn et à L'honneur de lui présenter la traduction de ses remarques sur les Sauvages⁶ qu'il a cherché a rendre le moins imparfaite qui lui a été possible; il est bien faché que le mauvais tems l'empêche d'aller la lui présenter lui même et savoir de ses nouvelles dont il demande souvent à Mons. l'Abbé Rochon.

Toute la famille lui fait bien des Complimens.

From Jean-Baptiste Le Roy

ALS: American Philosophical Society

mercredy matin [January 7, 1784]⁷

Vous êtes trop bon mon Illustre Docteur de penser comme cela à moi. Lobservation que vous m'avez envoyée est vraiment Intéressante.⁸ Je Suis tout à fait honteux que vos Voeux pour moi ayent prévenus ceux que Je voulois Vous porter pour votre conservation au Comble de la gloire, où vous étes arrivé, il n'y en a point d'autres à vous faire. La rigueur de la saison et un dérangement d'estomac et de santé m'ont empêché d'aller vous voir de cette année et auparavant J'ai été Si occupé que cela ne m'a pas eté possible mais Je compte bien m'en dédommager au premier moment. J'ai toûjours votre lettre de M. Banks⁹ que J'aurai L'honneur de vous reporter.

6. "Remarks concerning the Savages of North America," [before Jan. 7], above.

7. Dated on the basis of the New Year's greetings in the first paragraph, the reference to the forthcoming balloon experiment in Lyon (which occurred in January, 1784), and Le Roy's reference to the tenth of the month as being in the future. The only possible Wednesday is Jan. 7.

8. Not found.

9. Joseph Banks to BF, Dec. 9. One result of BF's having sent the letter to Le Roy was that Banks's admission of the importance of the balloon

Argant Un Jeune homme que J'ai eu Lhonneur de vous présenter cet automne et qui est actuellement à Londres[1] mande ici qu'au milieu de tout ce qu'il voit et qu'il entend il lui paroît que les anglois n'attachent pas une grande Importance à la découverte des ballons et que vraisemblablement ils ne S'occuperont pas beaucoup de les perfectionner. Cependant J'ai reçu il n'y a pas Longtems une lettre d'un Médecin de mes amis homme de beaucoup d'esprit qui demeure à Liverpool et qui me marque qu'on ne parle que des ballons et qu'une Société Philosophique de Manchester dont il est a fait partir un glóbe, Je crois de dix pieds de Diamètre, qui a parcouru plus de 40 milles en l'air avant de tomber.[2] Quant au continent Je ne Sais Mon Illustre Docteur si vous avez appris que le ballon de Lyon de 100 pieds de haut sur 100 de Diamètre ne Sera prêt et ne doit partir que le 10 de ce mois c'est au moins ce que me mande un homme de mes amis qui doit etre de L'embarcation. La manière dont il sexprime mèrite d'être rapportée *Le ballon ne pourra être prêt que Le 10 ainsi* NE

---

experiments was widely circulated. In an article about balloons published in the *Mercure de France* at the end of December, the author gloated that Banks's letter to BF was nothing less than an honorable apology to the French by the president of the Royal Society for having accused them of being preoccupied with useless things: *Mercure de France (Jour. politique de Bruxelles)*, Dec. 27, 1783, pp. 174–5.

1. Ami Argand had been in London since late October, 1783, and through Jean-André Deluc had been invited to give a demonstration of a balloon before George III. On Nov. 25, at Windsor Castle, Argand inflated a two-foot hydrogen balloon, which the king dangled before his family, stationed in windows above, and then released: *Morning Post and Daily Advertiser* (Nov. 27, 1783); John J. Wolfe, *Brandy, Balloons, & Lamps: Ami Argand, 1750–1803* (Carbondale and Edwardsville, Ill., 1999), p. 10; Barthélemy Faujas de Saint-Fond, *Première suite de la description des expériences aérostatiques de MM. de Montgolfier . . .* (Paris, 1784), pp. 191–2.

2. *Parker's Gen. Advertiser and Morning Intelligencer* (Dec. 26, 1783) reported a balloon experiment in Manchester on Dec. 23. Due to the hazy weather, the balloon disappeared from view within minutes and was found later that day 45 miles away. The article did not mention any involvement of the Manchester Literary and Philosophical Society.

NOUS ATTENDEZ QUE LE 14 comme Si ces Messrs avoient parole du Vent de les conduire ici directement. Au reste cette Navigation Aërienne Sera nombreuse car ils Seront dans la machine tout au moins cinq.[3] La foule y est même pour S'embarquer mais beaucoup d'appellés peu d'Elus. Vous Savez Mon Illustre Docteur que L'Académie est chargée par Le Gouvernement de travailler à perfectionner les ballons et qu'elle a nomme des commissaires pour S'occuper particulierement de cet objet.[4] Comme Je Suis du nombre cela m'a fait réfléchir plus profondément Sur les moyens de Les diriger et La possibilité m'en paroit aujourdhui aussi démontrée que celle de preserver les edifices de la Foudre me parut prouvée Lorsque J'eus lu votre Sublime Idée Sur les moyens d'y parvenir. Il y a plus. J'ai fait un calcul avec un homme de mes amis duquel il résulte qu'un ballon des mêmes dimensions que celui de MM Charles et Robert et rempli du même air inflammable portant deux hommes ne produit une résistance au mouvement qu'on veut lui imprimer que d'une quantite telle que ces deux hommes peuvent par leur action lui imprimer un mouvement de 3600 toi par Heure[5] mais Je vous en dirai davantage demain matin Mon Illustre Docteur que Je

3. After numerous setbacks, accidents, and failed attempts, the balloon *Le Flesselles*, 126 feet high and 102 feet in diameter, ascended from Lyon on Jan. 19, 1784. It carried seven passengers, including its designer, Joseph Montgolfier: Faujas de Saint-Fond, *Première suite*, pp. 67–76; Gillispie, *Montgolfier Brothers*, pp. 69–79.

4. During its session on Dec. 23, 1783, the Académie des sciences received the report on balloons from the commission appointed in July (XL, 395). They also established a new nine-member commission on flying machines, which included Le Roy, Condorcet, Lavoisier, Bossut, Tillet, Brisson, La Rochefoucauld, Berthollet, and Coulomb: *Procès-verbaux*, CII (1783), 236. Four days later the new commission met and agreed on four main areas of research: first, identifying a lighter, less permeable, and more resilient fabric; second, finding a light and inexpensive gas; third, developing a mechanism to control the machine's ascent and descent without discarding gas or ballast; and fourth, determining an effective method of steering the machine: Antoine-Laurent Lavoisier, *Œuvres* (6 vols., Paris, 1862–93), III, 741–4.

5. At the bottom of the page BF performed a series of calculations related to Le Roy's theory.

compte avoir Lhonneur de vous voir Vers les Onze heures et demie. Recevez en attendant tous mes Voeux Les plus Sincères pour votre Santé et pour votre Conservation et Les assurrances de tous les Sentimens d'attachement que Je vous ai Voués pour la vie   LE ROY

mille et mille complimens Je vous prie Mon Illustre Docteur a Monsieur William Franklin

Morellet to William Temple Franklin

ALS: American Philosophical Society

Monsieur   jeudy [January 8, 1784][6]
   Le mauvais tems me prive depuis bien longtems du plaisir de voir et votre respectable papa et vous.[7] J'en attens la fin avec bien de l'impatience. J'ai recû votre reponse au sujet de l'affaire que m'avoit confiée mr. le cardinal de rohan et je la lui ai communiquée. Il remercie Mr. votre pere de cet eclaircissement. J'ai pris cette occasion de lui rappeller les promesses qu'il a faites au pauvre arbelot. Mais cette promesse il l'a executée autant qu'il etoit en lui. Les provisions de d'arbelot sont signées. Il ne lui manque que d'etre tout à fait aveugle et il a porté un certificat par lequel il conste qu'il ne l'est pas entierement. Les reglemens sont si formels là dessus qu'il n'est pas possible au cardinal de vaincre cet obstacle. Le sujet est examiné avec beaucoup de rigueur par le conseil et il ne depend pas du grand aumonier *to inforce* son admission. Il falloit qu'arbelot après avoir vecû quelque tems loin

6. A week and a day after Morellet's previous letter to WTF of Wednesday, [Dec.] 31, above. This would have allowed time for WTF to respond and for Morellet to visit Cardinal de Rohan.
7. We do not know how long it had been, but Morellet had been obliged to decline on behalf of his entire family a dinner invitation that the Franklins had issued in November. In an undated note probably written on Nov. 17, 1783, he informed WTF that his family was out of town and he had a bad cold: Morellet to WTF, [Nov. 17, 1783], in Medlin, *Morellet*, 1, 497–8.

de paris et de ses environs envoyat un certificat d'un chirurgien juré sur lequel on lui auroit accordé la pension en attendant la place. Je lui expliquerai tout cela pour vous en epargner la peine et je ne perdrai pas de vüe cette affaire qui vous interesse.[8] Voicy encore une demande à mr vôtre pere mais qui n'est pas bien importune ni difficile à accorder. Les entrepreneurs de la societé typographique de neufchatel qui executent en 4to une collection des arts demandent la permission d'en dedier le 20e vol. à mr. franklin[9] obtenes son consentement pour cela et je les en instruirai. Je vous prie de croire au tendre et respectueux attachement dont je fais profession pour vous et pour Mr votre pere

L'ABBÉ MORELLET

Addressed: A Monsieur / Monsieur Franklin le fils / A Passy

From Jean-Baptiste-Charles Lucas Despeintreaux[1]

ALS: American Philosophical Society

⟨Paris, January 9, 1784, in French: Until now, I had always thought I would spend the rest of my days in France, despite the negative aspects of the regime. The revolution carried out by your brave citizens has inspired me. Word of your actions and

8. BF's concern for Arbelot was well known among his friends. Long after BF had returned to America, Le Veillard informed him of the need to provide a new recommendation for the servant: Le Veillard to BF, March 13, 1787, APS.

9. See the letter from Frédéric-Samuel Ostervald of Jan. 1, above.

1. This appeal was successful. Two days later BF granted Despeintreaux an audience, talked with him about America, and promised to provide him with a letter of recommendation when he was was ready to leave. On March 20, after he had sold part of his estate, Despeintreaux returned to Passy and BF wrote a letter of introduction to the Baches for him and his future wife, Anna Emily Sebin. The couple embarked for Philadelphia via London in mid-May, and on Aug. 10, 1784, they were married at St. Joseph's Church in Philadelphia: —— Lucas to BF, June 30, 1785; Despeintreaux to BF, July 28 [*i.e.*, 18?], 1788, both at the APS; Francis T. Furey, ed., "Father Farmer's Marriage Register, 1758–1786," *Records of the American Catholic Hist. Soc.*, II (1889), 311.

those of your countrymen, and of your austerity and simplicity, induce me to want to live among such men. Your country's moderate climate, fertile lands, and vast tracts in comparison to the number of inhabitants, make me hope to share in these benefits and contribute to the general prosperity. I am determined to establish myself there as soon as possible, if my means are sufficient. Knowing how busy you are, I nonetheless hope that you will grant me an audience and offer your advice.

My name is Jean-Baptiste-Charles Lucas. I am French, twenty-five years old, and live in Pont-Audemer, Normandy, where I was born. I am a lawyer at the Royal Bailliage; my father, who died last year, was *premier conseiller* there for more than thirty years. I am related to the majority of bourgeois notables in my town, and both my father and mother were descended from nobles. The family inheritance is now divided between my mother, me, my four brothers, and one sister. My own share is worth about fifteen thousand francs. It is with this modest sum that I hope to live a free life in your country. I fear you will tell me that the sum is insufficient.

I have heard that there is much uncultivated land in America which one can obtain from the government on the promise of clearing it. Having enough money to emigrate, I would like to establish myself on a small holding and cultivate enough land to sustain myself modestly, with the aid of slaves or servants. You may perhaps think this a romantic dream; it is not. Since my youth, I have spent six months of each year in the country, which I have always loved, and was sorry not to have been born the son of a laborer. I would be eager to live the rural life in your country, where there is neither *dîme*[2] nor feudalism, nor the kind of scorn for countryfolk that exists here.

If I were certain of being able to depart, I would provide you with certificates attesting to my background. I await your response, telling me whether my fortune is sufficient to emigrate

2. The *dîme* was a tax levied by the Catholic and Protestant Churches on crops and farm products. Under feudal law, peasants also paid fees to the seigneur in addition to their labor: Joël Cornette, *Histoire de la France: absolutisme et lumières, 1652–1783* (Paris, 1993), p. 237; Pierre-François Boncerf, *Les Inconvéniens des droits féodaux* (London, 1776), p. 6.

and establish myself in your country. I beg you to give me an audience; I came to Paris expressly to see you, and I cannot stay long.⟩

From Dumas

ALS: Library of Congress; AL (draft): Nationaal Archief

Monsieur   Lahaie 9e. Janv. 1784.

La Dépeche ci-jointe³ étoit prête à partir pour l'Orient, sous couvert de Mrs. Barclay, Moylan & Ce. afin d'être acheminée au Congrès par le Paquebot du Port-Louis, ou autrement, lorsque la réflexion, que son contenu interessant pourroit vous être agréable, m'a fait prendre le parti de la faire passer par vos mains, avec priere de vouloir bien, après l'avoir lue, la fermer, & lui donner cours comme ci-dessus, le plutôt le mieux.

Je saisis cette occasion de vous présenter les voeux que je fais pour votre conservation & prospérité, non seulement à l'occasion de ce renouvellement, mais tous les jours de l'année; étant pour toujours avec le plus respectueux dévouement, De Votre Excellence Le très-humble & très-obéissant serviteur

C. W. F. DUMAS

Paris à Son Excellence Mr. Franklin, Min. Pl. des E.U.

3. His dispatch no. 37 of Dec. 18–Jan. 8. That letter is missing, but the postscripts dated Jan. 15 and Jan. 16, which Dumas sent in subsequent letters, are at the National Archives, with a wrapper sheet bearing BF's notation, "For the Committee of Foreign Affairs", and a notation by Congress indicating that the dispatch was received on May 14. According to Congress' "List of letters received from Mr. Dumas" (National Archives), he enclosed papers marked A, B, C, D, and E. Translations of the two postscripts and enclosure D are published in *Diplomatic Correspondence of the United States*, VII, 27–9. Dumas may also have sent at this time a long Dec. 1, 1783, memoir to the president of Congress describing the workings of the Dutch government: *ibid.*, VII, 3–27. A copy in Dumas' hand is among BF's papers at the APS, as is a press copy taken from a copy made by L'Air de Lamotte.

From Stephen Hopkins and James Manning[4]

LS: American Philosophical Society; ALS (draft):[5] Brown University Library

Sir   Providence State of Rhode Island 9th Jany 1784

Influenced by your Promptitude in promoting the great Interests of Society, and especially by your predilection of Your native Country, discovered by that early and decided Part which you took in its Favour, and which has been Continued by Such unparalleled Success through a Life protracted far beyond the Common Bounds marked out for Man; by your Interestedness in promoting American Literature, so greatly indebted to your inventive Genius for that enviable Point of Light in which it is viewed by Some, at least, of the Nations of Europe; together with your long Residence at, and Interest with the Court of France,—

The Corporation of the College at Providence in the State of Rhode Island, at their Meeting on the 7th. of January 1784 voted unanimously, to request your Assistance in presenting the inclosed Address to his *most Christian Majesty,* soliciting his Patronage of this College by establishing a Professor of the French Language and History therein, and presenting such Books in the French Language, or other Benefactions thereto as shall be most agreeable to that Munificent Monarch.[6]

4. The first chancellor and president, respectively, of Rhode Island College, later Brown University. For Hopkins, whom BF knew, see XI, 357. The Rev. James Manning (1738–1791) was a Baptist clergyman: *ANB.*

5. In the hand of James Manning.

6. The corporation had decided to embark on this course of action in September, 1783, and asked their congressman, David Howell, to enlist the support of La Luzerne. Howell did not speak to La Luzerne until *c.* Feb. 20, when the minister agreed to send the present letter and its enclosure with his own diplomatic dispatches. Howell could not have expected it to receive a positive reception, however. La Luzerne was furious at states like Rhode Island for being so recalcitrant in agreeing to Congress' plan to tax citizens in order to repay the debt to France, which required unanimous ratification (XL, 65n). On March 12 he reported to Vergennes what he described as the "incohérence" of the federal system and advised him to alert BF to the king's displeasure. BF could help his country, La Luzerne wrote, if he would convey frankly what was being said about the federal system and the Americans' resistance to meeting their obligations (AAE). For more

Encouraged by his generous Proffer of important literary Favours to Yale College in Connecticut, which, we are Assured from Authentic Information, the Corporation of that College thought proper to decline,[7] we take the Liberty to make this application.— Inclosed is a Copy of the Address to his Majesty for your Perusal.[8] Secure of your Concurrence in every Measure which promises to add Permanence to that Union, So happily formed between France & the United States of America, the Corporation have only to request your Assistance in having this Address properly introduced, and your prevalent Influence with the King of France in gaining its Object, Together with the Favour of a Line to advise us of its Success.

With the highest Sentiments of Esteem, in behalf of the Corporation, we are Sir, Your most obedient and most humble Servants—   STEP HOPKINS Chancr.
                                                        JAMES MANNING Prest:

His Excellency Benjamin Franklin Esqr

---

background on the college's request see Walter C. Bronson, *The History of Brown University, 1764–1914* (Providence, 1914), pp. 66–8, 76–80; Reuben A. Guild, *Life, Times and Correspondence of James Manning . . .* (Boston, 1864), pp. 298–9, 301.

7. The "authentic" source reported, altogether inaccurately, that the king had offered to endow a professorship in French and give Yale College a library of 2,000 volumes of the best French authors: Joseph Brown to Vioménil, Dec. 12, 1782 (Brown University Library). This rumor may have stemmed from a proposal to Yale made by Silas Deane in 1778. Arguing for the importance of French instruction, Deane offered to tap wealthy European aristocrats to underwrite a French professor, perhaps from Geneva. The Yale officers returned a lukewarm reply and never made a decision: *Deane Papers*, II, 476; Franklin B. Dexter, ed., *The Literary Diary of Ezra Stiles, D.D., LL.D., President of Yale College* (3 vols., New York, 1901), II, 296, 297–8, 304n.

8. The address to Louis XVI, dated Jan. 9, 1784, was signed by Hopkins and Manning. It remains among BF's papers at the APS, along with the copy (also signed). Making the case for the importance of knowing French, so vital to future commercial enterprises, the officers ask for books and a professor, which they themselves cannot afford. In exchange they promise everlasting gratitude, "firmly believing that whatever tends to make Men wiser, better, and happier, will meet with your royal Assistance and Encouragement." The petition is published in Guild, *Life, Times and Correspondence of James Manning*, pp. 301–3.

From Edward Nathaniel Bancroft

ALS: American Philosophical Society

Dear Doctor,   January. 10.[–*c.* 14]⁹ 1784

I had the honour of writing you Sometime ago a few lines,[1] which I hope you received. As I never forget my good friends, although they may be at many other parts of the world; I am glad of embracing every opportunity of enquiring after their health & happiness & as I have a very great regard for your's, on account of the great friendship that has subsisted for many years between my dear Papa & you, who loves you as much as if you was his father. I Shall therefore have the honour & esteem for all gentlemen that are or, ever may be in his confidence & friendship & as I am Sure all those who chuses him in theirs will never repent & that they will find him that great & Sage man, although in a private Station, ever ready as far in his power lays to Serve mankind in general, & his country's friends & to whom he has rendered many great Services & there is no doubt on it, sir, but you are better acquainted with them than I am, or that my feeble capacity or years are able to describe & though I meet with attention & kindness from every one who has the happiness of Knowing him, but I must beg pardon for intruding on your time in the worthy praises of my dear Papa & who is one of the best fathers to his Children & whose heart must ever flow with love & gratitude more & more to Such a one & as also must the hearts of those who have the happiness of the protection & friendship of so great & ingenius a man as our dear friend & country-man, Doctor Franklin, who I hope will except of my humble & best respects concluding with wishing you & also to Mr. Wilm. Franklin & other of your family this & many other happy new years with the blessing of heaven attend you all & America.

I remain with the greatest respect & esteem Dear Doctor Your most obedient humble Servant

EDWRD. NATHEL. BANCROFT

9. As implied by the boy's final postscript, squeezed into the space at the bottom of the last page.

1. Above, Nov. 19.

JANUARY 10[–*c.* 14], 1784

No. 6 Duke Street. St. *James's*

P.S. Etant a la maison pour y passer les vacances avec Maman, elle m'a commandée de vous faire ses respects & de vous souhaiter une bonne & heureuse année accompagnee de plusieurs autres ainsi qu'à Mr. votre fils & elle a grand plaisir a vous informer qu'elle a eu plusieurs fois des nouvelles de son mari qui est en bonne Santé a Philadelphie & qu'il conte d'aller à Princetown dans quelques jours, & ensuite de retourner a Carolina & delà à Philadelphie & ensuite de venir en France[2] comme il a des affaires avec Mr. le Prince de Luxembourg[3] & il ne manquera pas d'aller voir tous ses bons amis a Paris & a Passy & marque a maman qu'il accomplira tout ça dans cinq ou Six mois & S'il plait a dieu nous aurons le bonheur de le voir içi à Londres que nous attendons impatiemment. Mon frere & mes Sœurs vous font bien leurs respects dont les dernieres sont retablis de la petite verole qu'elles ont eu tres favorablement & n'en sont point marqués du tout mais nous devons ce bonheur a l'inoculation car celle qui l'a eu la premiere naturellemant ne l'eut pas si bien que les autres & maintenant, dieu merci! ils Se portent tous bien ainsi qui ma chere Maman qu'il y a environ trois mois quelle est accouchée d'une petite fille qui paroit jouir d'une assez bonne santé.[4] Monsieur Comme je ne vous ecris pas bien souvent Je suis bien

2. In addition to delivering dispatches from the American commissioners to Congress and pursuing his own business interests, during this trip Bancroft also reported on American affairs to the British government and secretly corresponded with Silas Deane: XL, 161n and the sources cited there; Thomas J. Schaeper, *Edward Bancroft: Scientist, Author, Spy* (New Haven and London, 2011), pp. 230–5.

3. Bancroft represented the prince of Luxembourg, who had outfitted the frigate *South Carolina*, in his claims against the state of South Carolina. His mission to Charleston on Luxembourg's behalf ended in failure when he was outwitted by Alexander Gillon, former captain of the warship: *Deane Papers*, V, 212; James A. Lewis, *Neptune's Militia: the Frigate South Carolina during the American Revolution* (Kent, Ohio, and London, 1999), pp. 113–15; Schaeper, *Edward Bancroft*, pp. 232–5.

4. Edward's siblings included Samuel Forrester (1775–1799), Maria Frances (1777–1853), Julia Louisa (1779–1851), John Paul (1780–1786), and Catherine Penelope (1781–1866). His infant sister, Sophia, died of smallpox the following April: information kindly provided by Professor Thomas Schaeper, St. Bonaventure University. See Schaeper, *Edward Bancroft*, pp. 83, 239, 242, 244, 264.

content de vous faire voir mes progres, depuis Six mois que nous sommes en pension, dans la langue angloise. C'est pourquoi j'ai pris la liberté de vous ecrire en ces deux langues.

Monsr., Maman vous prie de faire Ses compliments à Mde. Jay, à Mr. & Mde. Chaumont & toute sa famille & les miens aussi, s'il vous plait.

Vous aurez la bonté d'envoyer ce paquet de lettres aux personnes a qui elles sont adressées & vous obligerai beaucoup celle qui a l'honneur d'etre du nombre de vos amies.

E. N. B & P. Bancroft[5]

To Docr. Franklin

N.B. Mama recd. a letter from Papa the 14 insnt. who was well at Philadelphia the 28 of Novber. & was going to Set out the next morning to New york with Mr Holker to See General Washington & the Governors of that City & Jersey to Celebrate the Definive Treaty, where there was to be great joy & feasting &c &c.

Addressed: A / Son Excellnce. Dr. Franklin / Ambassr. Des Etats unis / D'Amerique / A Passy

From Jean-Charles-Julien Luce de Lancival[6]

ALS: American Philosophical Society

Monsieur   paris le 11 Janvier 1784

Quoique je n'aye l'avantage de vous connoitre que de nom, avantage dont je ne puis me prévaloir, puisqu'il m'est commun avec tous les peuples de l'Europe, je dirois presque du monde entier, je prends la liberté de vous envoyer le foible essais dune Muse encore au berceau.[7] C'est etre temeraire, je l'avoue, et jai besoin

5. The boy also signed for his mother, Penelope.

6. French poet and playwright (b. 1764), who at this time was a student at the Collège Louis-le-Grand. He gained recognition during this period for his Latin poems, one of which he enclosed with the present letter. In 1786 he was appointed professor of rhetoric at the Collège de Navarre: *Biographie universelle; Larousse.*

7. *De pace carmen* (Paris, 1784). BF's copy is at the Library Company of Philadelphia. BF wrote an answer to the present letter on this sheet. Dated Passy, March 8, 1784, it reads: "Sir, I receiv'd the Letter you did me the

d'indulgence mais c'est a un grand homme que je m'adresse. . . .
parmi les defauts de ma piece (car je n'ose me flatter qu'elle en
soit exempte) jen reconnois un essentiel que tout le monde ap-
percevra aisement et qui n'echapera qu a vous seul, cest que dans
un Sujet ou vous avez eu tant de part, je me sois si peu etendu sur
votre Eloge, mais outre qu'il n'y a personne qui ne sente qu'en
louant, qu'en felicitant Les Americains c'est franklin que j'ai
Loué, que j'ai felicite, qu'aurois-je pu dire qui ne fut infiniment
au dessous de ce que tout le monde pense et de ce que vous meritez? L'admiration est un sentiment qu'on ne peut pas toujours
exprimer. Fiere d'avoir Seulement pu prononcer une fois le nom
de franklin, ce nom qui vaut seul un Eloge, ma muse s'est ar-
reteé tout a coup et a tressailli de joie. Que seroit-ce donc si vous
daigniez sourire a ses jeunes efforts? J'ose l'esperer, Monsieur, et
si mon bonheur veut que l'ouvrage ne vous deplaise point, vous
mettrez le comble a ma joie en communiquant un Exemplaire à
votre digne Cooperateur a l'immortel Wagincsthon.

Jai l'honneur d'etre avec le plus profond respect Monsieur
Votre très humble et très obeissant serviteur

L'ABBÉ LUCE DE LANCIVAL
en philosophie au college de Louis le grand

Notation: Luce de Lancival 11. Janr. 1784.——

To von Blome

ALS (draft):[8] Reproduced in Charles Hamilton Auction Catalogue No. 49
(May 6, 1971), Lot 162.

At Passy, this 12th of January, 1784.——
The Underwritten Minister Plenipotentiary from the United
States of America to the Court of France, acknowledges the
Receipt of the official Representation *sent* to him the 21st of No-

---

Honour of writing to me, accompanied by your Poem *de Pace*. My Friends
who are better Judges than I am, find it excellent. I am very sensible of the
honour you have done me in it, and beg you would accept my thankful Acknowledgements." We assume that this text was translated into French before being sent.

8. At the top of the sheet is a note by WTF: "Rough Draught of an Official Note, from Dr. Franklin to Baron de Blome; *being entirely in his own*

vember by his Excellency the Baron de Blome, Envoy Extraordinary from his Danish Majesty at the same Court, respecting the Capture of a Vessel called the Providence, by the American Privateer Hendrick, together with the original Papers accompanying the said Representation; Having perused the said Papers, he returns them as desired; and he has forwarded the Representation to his Sovereign the Congress,[9] who he doubts not will in Respect to his Danish Majesty take the same into immediate Consideration, and do therein what shall be just & right. In the mean time an Extract of a Letter from the American Secretary for Foreign Affairs, respecting the same Capture, & the Discharge of the Ship, is herewith communicated to his Excellency, who will therein find express'd the Disposition prevalent in the Government of America to maintain a good Understanding with the Court of Denmark.[1]   B FRANKLIN

To Vergennes

LS:[2] Archives du Ministère des affaires étrangères; AL (draft): Library of Congress

Sir,   Passy, Jany. 12. 1784.
I duly received the Letters your Excellency did me the honor of writing to me the 24 of Octr., and the 3d of December past, respecting the Arrest of our Arms & Ammunition by the sieur Puchelberg, accompany'd by Copies of the Letters of M. Le Marquis de Castries and M. Chardon, and a Paper of the said

---

hand writing. Given to James Wolff Esqe- by the Doctor's Grandson, W. T. Franklin London 21st Jany. 1815."

9. BF enclosed it in his Dec. 25 letter to Thomas Mifflin.

1. Presumably a section of Robert R. Livingston's letter of March 26, 1783: XXXIX, 395–6. On March 16, 1784, after receiving BF's letter to Mifflin of Dec. 25, Congress resolved to forward an extract of that letter and a copy of Blome's letter of Nov. 21 to Mass. governor John Hancock, with a request that Hancock send copies of the admiralty court proceedings. Mifflin wrote to Hancock on March 26: Smith, *Letters,* XXI, 459. An official copy of that March 16 resolution reached BF, who had it copied (DS, signed by Charles Thomson, Hist. Soc. of Pa.; press copy of copy, APS).

2. In WTF's hand. BF added the end of the complimentary close before signing.

Puchelberg. The long Absence of Mr Barclay, who had in his Hands some of my Papers relating to that Affair, and my Indisposition since, have occasioned the Delay in answering. I communicated the Letters as you advised to Mr Barclay, and I inclose the Letter I thereupon received from him.[3] To which I would add a few Observations, after stating truly to your Excellency the Fact respecting the Furniture made by Puchelberg, which he has placed in false Lights & egregiously misrepresented.

When his Majesty in 1779 was pleased to order a small Squadron to be equipped at his Expence and put under the Command of Capt. Jones, M. De Sartine, then Minister of the Marine, in a Letter to me requested that I would strengthen the Squadron by ordering the Alliance to join it; which I did immediately.[4] She made the Cruize accordingly in which the Baltic Fleet was attacked, and the Ships that convoy'd it taken.[5] The Ship arrived with the Squadron in Holland & afterwards at L'Orient.[6] His Majesty was pleased to order, as M. De Chaumont[7] informed me, that the Expences of her Relache in Holland and at L'Orient should be defray'd, and the Ship deliver'd in the same Condition fit for Sea, as she was received. Accordingly she was in the Course of receiving her daily Provisions and necessaries from Messrs. Gourlade & Moilan, whom M. de Chaumont had appointed to supply her at the Kings Expence, when Capt. Landais, who had quitted her in Holland[8] came to L'Orient, intrigu'd with the Crew, got possession again of the Ship in the Absence of Capt. Jones,[9] and apply'd for a Continuance of Supplies to this Puchelberg, who was a Commis or Agent

3. Barclay to BF, Dec. 16, written shortly after his return from Brittany. At the time of the present letter Barclay was no longer in Paris. He left for London on Dec. 30 for what he expected to be a three-week trip. In fact, he did not return until April: Roberts and Roberts, *Thomas Barclay,* pp. 136–8.
4. XXIX, 382–3, 405.
5. The cruise began in August, 1779, and culminated in the Battle off Flamborough Head: XXX, 154–5, 452–8, 477–8.
6. Jones's squadron was in Holland by early October, and the *Alliance* was at Lorient by mid-February, 1780: XXX, 442; XXXI, 482.
7. Le Ray de Chaumont was in charge of the arrangements for the squadron: XXXIII, 19.
8. Landais left the ship on Oct. 22, 1779: XXX, 580–1ñ.
9. On June 13, 1780: XXXII, 519–20.

for Mr. Schweighausser, and being fond of the Business took it out of the Hands of Messrs. Gourlade & Moylan. Mr. Schweighauser who seem'd to doubt the Regularity of the Proceeding, wrote to me desiring to know if I approved of it. As soon as I was fully acquainted with the Circumstances I forbid it, by a Letter to M. Schweighauser, as bringing on us an unneccessary Expence,[1] and I have his Letters informing me that he had accordingly order'd Puchelberg to desist but that he had nevertheless continued.[2] The Account was afterwards sent to me by M. Schweighauser, amounting to 31,668 *l.t.* which I refused to pay, not only because the Articles were furnished contrary to my Orders, but because the Necessaries were furnish'd in unnecessary Quantities, and there were many Superfluities, and at extravagant Prices, so that I could not with any Face propose to the Minister of the Marine that such Supplies should be at the Expence of his Majesty.[3] He urged a general Order he had received from the Naval Board at Boston, to supply Landais; and I therefore referr'd him to that Board for Payment. He it seems apply'd to Congress and they order'd Mr Johnson to enquire into the Claim, which he declined.[4] I suppose that M. Schweighauser may have refused to allow the Acct. to Puchelberg, because he acted contrary to Orders, and Puchelberg hopes to obtain it, by arresting our Magazine. The United States received no particular Advantage from the Cruize of their Ship; 180 Prisoners taken as I understood by her when separate from the Squadron, were deliver'd with the rest, about 500, to the Kings Ambassador in Holland, and exchang'd for his Subjects, not a single American Prisoner in England being set at Liberty by that means as was expected.[5] If in consideration of this, and that

1. Schweighauser wrote on June 20, 1780, and BF replied on June 24: XXXII, 586–7.

2. An extract of Schweighauser's July 15, 1780, letter is in XXXIII, 77.

3. BF refused to accept the bills on Aug. 9, 1780: XXXIII, 171.

4. BF referred Schweighauser to the navy board on Aug. 10, 1780. On Aug. 24, 1781, in response to Schweighauser's appeal, Congress authorized Joshua Johnson to examine the account, but he refused to do so: XXXIII, 7–8, 171–4; XXXVII, 657–8; Schweighauser to the President of Congress, Nov. 30, 1780 (National Archives).

5. BF and Jones expected that prisoners taken by American ships would be exchanged for Americans: XXX, 69; XXXI, 150.

Puchelberg's Supply lessen'd the Expence at L'Orient, which his Majesty had had the Goodness to order, it should be thought proper for this Governt. still to discharge as much of his Demand as Appears just for reasonable Necessaries, I certainly can make no Objection. But I by no means propose it.— I am afraid of taking up too much of your Excellency's Time, but I thought it necessary to justify our Government & myself from the Reflection[6] contained in Mr. Puchelberg's Paper, which seems to have had too much Weight with M. le Ms. De Castries. For otherwise I should only have observed in a few Words the apparent Impropriety, as it seems to me, of arresting the Goods of a State for a Debt, supposing it just, due to a Private Person, since there are many other more decent Modes of Application for Payment. If the Law admits of such a Proceeding in France, I cannot expect a Law should be dispens'd with for us on this Occasion; but I apprehend Inconveniences may arise from it. An Ally at War cannot venture to order the Purchase of Arms Ammunition or Cloathing here for their Troops, without incurring the Risque of having an Expedition perhaps ruined by Delay, since the Enemy may easily hire some petty Merchant here to arrest the Goods on Pretence of a Debt from the State, and the Season be over, before the Cause can be determined. With us I think such a Process would not have been supported. The King lately sent a Ship to America to fetch away the Cannon &ca. left by General Rochambeau. If some Merchant who had supply'd, perhaps extravagantly, the Captain of one of his Majesty's Ships with Provisions &ca. which Captn. had gone away without paying for them, should have presum'd to attach those Military Stores and hold them 'till his Demand was comply'd with, I am certain his Action would be dismiss'd, and that he would incur Censure from the Government for his Insolence.

There is in my Opinion still less Foundation for the Claim of the Sieurs Foster. A Ship belonging to Cork laden by them with Wine from Bordeaux was taken & brought into France by the Alliance Capt. Landais.[7] She had two Pass-Ports, one from the King of England, the other from his Majesty. The English

6. BF had written "Reflections" in the draft.
7. The *Three Friends*, captured on June 28, 1779: XXX, 12n.

Pass-port *required* and *commanded* all the Kings Officers and Commanders of armed Vessels to let the said Ship pass without Hindrance or Molestation, and requested[8] the same of his Friends and Allies. That from the King of France was simply a Command to his own Subjects, *without any Request to those of his Allies.* Consequently Landais thought he had a Right to make Prize of her, and indeed he could not well have answer'd it to his Officers and Men if he had not brought her in. The American Commissioners here were likewise of Opinion that she was good Prize. Nevertheless in Respect to the Kings Pass-port, we made no Opposition to the Reclamation of the Sieurs Fosters, with which they had reason to be contented, because it was their own Fault that their Ship was brought into Port. Damages I believe are never allow'd, but for detaining a Vessel without apparent just Cause, which was not their Case. They should have taken Care to obtain a more perfect Pass-port, or have got one also from us as others did without Difficulty on showing us that they had one from the King. Many Years have past, and I do not remember to have heard of their making any such Claim, till they or their Friends had purchased a large Parcel of our Sugars, and then it was made use of to delay Payment. These Claims have indeed had that Effect greatly to our Damage. Mr. Barclay is exceedingly embarrass'd by that Delay and very uneasy that it is not hitherto removed.[9] Thinking the Affair more particularly appertaining to him I was unwilling to meddle with it, but have been obliged to comply with his earnest Instances.

Your Excellency may be assured that upon a proper Application of Messrs. Forster to the Congress, & of M. Puchelberg to the Naval Board of Boston by whose Orders to Mr. Schweighauser he pretended to justify his Supply of Capt. Landais, their respective Claims will be duly consider'd, and whatever Justice

8. This word should probably have been italicized, as it was in BF's draft.

9. The embarrassment was financial. Robert Morris had drawn bills on Ferdinand Grand above and beyond the funds in hand, and ordered Barclay to pay the prize proceeds to Grand to help offset the overdraft. The cargoes of the prizes included 1,200 hogsheads of sugar. The net proceeds of the sale of the prizes, held on Jan. 17, 1783, amounted to 562,387 *l.t.* 16 *s.* 8 *d.:* XXXIX, 161, 423; XL, 407; *Morris Papers,* VI, 625, VIII, 10, 11; Roberts and Roberts, *Thomas Barclay,* p. 313; Account XXVII (XXXII, 4).

may be due to them readily obtained. I therefore hope and request that their forcible Arrest of the Property of the United States will be taken off by Authority of Government, and Mr. Barclay put in Possession of it.

With great and sincere Respect, I am Sir, Your Excellency's most obedient and most humble Sert.[1]   B. FRANKLIN

His Excellency Count de Vergennes.

Endorsed: M de R

From François-Simon Defay-Boutheroue[2]

ALS: American Philosophical Society

Monsieur,   à orléans le 12 janvier 1784

L'accueil dont votre excellence honore ceux qui cultivent les sciences, m'enhardit à vous supplier d'agréer un exemplaire d'un ouvrage de ma Composition, intitulé *La nature considérée dans plusieurs de ses opérations, ou Mémoires et observations sur diverses parties de l'histoire naturelle,*[3] et d'en faire passer un autre à l'illustre sociéte de philadelphie, que vous présidés si dignement. Le bien que les ouvrages périodiques, et notamment le Mercure de france, le journal enciclopedique, et le journal de l'orléanois, viennent de dire de cet ouvrage, au commencement de ce mois,

1. To accompany this letter, BF made extracts of three letters that are now missing: Schweighauser to BF, July 15, 1780; Gourlade & Moylan to BF, July 10, 1780; and Schweighauser to BF, Sept. 7, 1780. (His draft of those extracts remains with the draft of the present letter.) L'Air de Lamotte copied them for inclusion in the present letter to Vergennes. They are filed at the AAE with Barclay's letter to BF of Dec. 16, 1783, which BF enclosed here, but which the AAE filed under its own date. For the extracts see XXXIII, 54, 77, 261.

2. A merchant and scientist (1739–1820) who in 1789 was elected as deputy of the third estate to the Estates General: *DBF;* Adolphe Robert *et al.,* eds., *Dictionnaire des parlementaires français* ... (5 vols., 1889–1891; reprint, Geneva, 2000), II, 290.

3. The book, published in Paris in 1783, carried the additional subtitle "Avec la minéralogie de l'Orléanois." The day after Defay wrote the present letter, a long and favorable review appeared in the *Jour. de Paris.* (The review in the *Mercure de France,* which he mentions below, appeared on Jan. 3, pp. 26–31.) The copies Defay sent to BF have not been located.

m'a déterminé à vous supplier de m'accorder cette grace. Je ne dissimulerai point à votre excellence combien je tiendrois a honneur que la Savante Societé daignat m'associer à ses travaux, si elle trouvoit dans mon ouvrage quelque chose qui pût fixer son attention; cependant, dans le cas ou cette composition ne vous parôitroit pas mériter cet honneur, je vous supplie néanmoins de l'agréer comme un hommage de mes sentimens respectueux.

Puis-je espérer, Monsieur, que votre excellence me fera savoir si je ne me suis pas trop flatté en espérant qu'elle daignera permettre que je lui fasse passer ces deux exemplaires?

Je suis avec respect, Monsieur, de votre excellence Le très-humble et très-obeissant serviteur

DE FAŸ

de la Société Royale des Sciences de Montpellier et de la Société de phisique d'histoire naturelle et des arts d'orléans, demeurant rue Sainte Catherine à orléans

Endorsed: Mons de Fay 1784

From John Shaffer

ALS: American Philosophical Society

Sir   Paris 12 January '84./.
You was Kind Enough to honour me with your Protection in Righting to Monr Breteuel to have me sent to america wich has made an Impretion upon my gratitude wich I canot *Express*,[4] the last line you honoured me with you Say you will Not medle aney farther with my affairs,[5] to Whom Sir Can I adress my self to but you who is our Protecteur *Natural*, Monr. Beaumont assured me that you will Not abandon me affter the letter you Rote to Mr. Breteuel, wich indusses me to take the liberty of adressing my Self to you onst *more*,

It is you and Only you Sir by Righting a line to Mr Rosambo President of the Tournelle, and to Mr. Degars de Courcells my Raporteuer,[6] wich will be Sufcient to draw me

4. Shaffer also sent a note of thanks to WTF on Jan. 8: APS.
5. Not found.
6. The Tournelle was the criminal appeals chamber of the Parlement. Louis Le Peletier de Rosambo, one of the presidents of the Grand Chambre, was the judge in this case, according to Menier de Saint Yver's letter

out of the, gouffre in wich I have Plunged my self into by my inConsequence.

Monr. Beaumont who has taken my Cause To heart desires to have a Moments interview with your Exelency, if it is agreable to Morrow morning he will do him Self the honour to wait upon you. If you Should be engaged, if Mr Temple(?) your Nevew has a moment to Spare it will answer the same End—

I have the honour to be with Profound Respt sir your Most Obedent and Very humble servant   J. SCHAFFER

P.S. the adress of my Raporteuer Rue Hautefeuille Conseiller au Parlement

His Exelency Docter Franklin

From Jean-Jacques Lafreté

ALS: University of Pennsylvania Library

Paris le 13. janvier 1784.

Il y à longtems, mon Cher Papa que je n'ai eû le plaisir de vous voir, Je ne suis plus de ce monde depuis la perte affreuse que j'ay faite, et J'evite autant que je peux les occasions de montrer

---

described below. Augustin-Jean-Antoine de Gars de Courcelles (b. 1751) was councillor at the *première chambre des enquêtes: Almanach royal* for 1784, pp. 299, 310; Joël Félix, *Les Magistrats du parlement de Paris (1771–1790): Dictionnaire biographique et généalogique* (Paris, 1990), pp. 179–80; see also Richard M. Andrews, *Law, magistracy, and crime in Old Regime Paris, 1735–1789* (1 vol. to date, Cambridge and New York, 1994), I, 81, 89.

Menier de Saint Yver sent a similar appeal to BF on Jan. 12. His and Shaffer's release was entirely in BF's hands, he wrote, and BF's silence had been interpreted as tacit confirmation of the clockmaker Couture's deposition. Another appeal, undated, came from the baron de Lauriol-Vissec, writing from the Hôtel de Turin, rue des Grands Augustins. Admitting that he is unknown to BF, he nonetheless hopes that his letter will convince BF to help Shaffer, who is "plus malheureux que coupable" (a phrase BF had seen before: from Menier de Saint Yver, Nov. 28, above; from Shaffer, Sept. 12: XL, 619). Shaffer and his two "compagnons d'infortune" are to be judged the following week at the Parlement, and it is essential that the sentence delivered at the Châtelet be overturned. Both letters are at the APS.

ma triste figure.[7] Cependant dès que le tems sera un peu plus traittable J'irai vous faire une petite visitte à Passy.

Voici une lettre que j'ai recû, d'un de mes amis qui est négociant à cétte en Languedoc, il est actif et intelligent. Il scait L'anglois parfaitement, et a de plus la plus grande envie d'Etre consul des américains Dans le dit Port.[8] Si cela dépend de Mr. Lejai, comme vous me l'avéz dit autrefois, et qu'il soit encore à Nantes, vous me feriéz plaisir de m'envoyer une lettre de recommandation pour lui en faveur de Mr. Philippe Aribert.[9] Je puis vous assûrer que vous ne scauriéz faire un meilleur choix.—

Trouvéz bon que je fasse mille complimens à Monsieur votre fils, et que je vous présente mon cher Papa l'hommage du Respectueux attachement avec lequel je serai toute ma vie, votre Très humble et trés obeissant serviteur.   LAFRETÉ

From ——— Maupin[1] and Other Offerers of Goods and Schemes

ALS: American Philosophical Society

The offers that Franklin receives during the period covered by this volume can be divided into three broad categories.[2] The first includes authors who send copies of their works, some in the hope of winning

7. Lafreté's wife had died the previous spring: XXXIX, 101n.

8. The letter was from Philippe Aribert, writing to Lafreté from Sette on Dec. 28, 1783. Aribert asks him to request of BF a letter to Mr. Jay in Nantes, who is in charge of naming consuls. BF has already been told by a Dutch friend of JA's that Aribert speaks and writes English well, knows commerce, and could be very useful to the "insurgents." He would serve without salary. Hist. Soc. of Pa. Aribert was probably a member of the wealthy mercantile family of Montpellier of that name: Pierre Clerc, *Dictionnaire de biographie héraultaise: des origines à nos jours . . .* (2 vols., Montpellier, 2006), I, 85.

9. Both Lafreté and Aribert were confused about the name of the American consul, Thomas Barclay.

1. Former *valet de chambre* of Queen Marie Leszczyńska, wife of Louis XV, and author of numerous books and pamphlets on viticulture who sought to prove that it was possible to grow quality wine on the outskirts of Paris: *Nouvelle Biographie;* Quérard, *France littéraire.*

2. Unless otherwise indicated, all the documents summarized here are in French and are at the APS.

Franklin's support for the projects described therein. Among these individuals is the viticulturist Maupin, whose letter is printed below. The second class consists of entrepreneurs who propose the establishment of various manufactures in the United States. The third group comprises merchants who offer goods or seek to open trade relations. Miscellaneous offers that do not fall within these groups are summarized at the end.

On November 4 Monsieur Lamy, writing from Paris, begs Franklin to accept a copy of his work.[3] He had wanted to present it in person, but did not know how. On December 24, having received no response, he informs Franklin that he had sent a pamphlet to him and to the comte d'Estaing on the fourth of November. Its subject was the chevalier d'Assas and the Auvergne regiment, part of which served under Washington.[4]

On November 16 Carré de Malberg,[5] writing from Varennes in Argonne, sends Franklin an announcement (now missing) of a book that offers a new approach to an old but unjustly forgotten subject. The same day, the abbé Wavran writes from Hesdin in northern France. In January, 1782, he had sent Franklin several notebooks containing his thoughts on particular aspects of physics. He had planned to mail the rest of his work a few months later, but an attack of the quartan fever disrupted his plans. In addition, his work turned out to be much longer than anticipated, and he will not be able to

---

3. *Precis historique sur le regiment d'Auvergne, depuis sa création jusqu'à présent. Précédé d'une epitre aux manes du brave chevalier d'Assas; par M. Lamy, ancien soldat au regiment* (Clostercamp, 1783); BF's copy is at the Hist. Soc. of Pa.

4. Nicholas-Louis d'Assas (1733–1760) gained posthumous fame for his bravery at the battle of Clostercamp during the Seven Years' War: *DBF.*

Several miscellaneous words and phrases were written on blank sections of this letter. At the top of the letter, BF wrote "BFarinelli". On the verso, in what we believe to be BFB's hand, are three words that appear to be penmanship practice: "Chapter", "Reputation", and "Commander". Below them are the Latin proverbs "In nomine domini incipit omne malum" (In the name of God begins all evil) and "Nullum magnum ingenium sine mixtura dementiæ" (No great intellect has been without a touch of madness). The latter is a quote from Seneca's "De Tranquillitate Animi," where it is attributed to Aristotle: Seneca, *Four Dialogues,* ed. C. D. N. Costa (Warminster, Eng., 1994), pp. 96–7.

5. Jean-Baptiste-Louis Carré de Malberg (1749–1835) had served in the royal *gendarmes écossais* until 1770, then as *avocat* in the Parlement of Nancy, and since 1779 as *maîtrise des eaux et forêts* for the prince de Condé: *DBF.*

present it until next spring.[6] A few months ago he wrote to Condorcet challenging Nollet's theory of electricity, on the basis of Franklin's experiments and some of his own. Condorcet has not answered, and Wavran wonders whether he is a follower of Nollet, and might be the author of some notes in a work on the history of electricity that defend Nollet's theory and attack Franklin's. He asks for Franklin's protection.

On December 13, Théodore-Henri-Joseph Lefebvre, *avocat* at Lille, sends a copy of a speech he delivered during that day's municipal ceremony publicizing the peace, in compliance with the royal ordinance of November 3. It is printed in a seven-page pamphlet dated December 13, which also contains an account of the ceremony and the text of the royal ordinance, titled *Procès-Verbal de la Publication de la Paix, a Lille*. Lefebvre's discourse extolled the American Revolution and the French king.[7]

Writing from Lyon on January 7, d'Auberteuil de Fréminville congratulates Franklin on American independence. Recalling the times he dined with Franklin and discussed diplomacy and physics, he asks permission to send his new observations on phosphorous as well as a treatise on diplomacy that he composed in his leisure time.

Four entrepreneurs try to convince Franklin of their ability to establish industries in the newly independent United States. François Giordana writes fom Turin on October 22 to remind Franklin of the letter he had written on September 3, forwarded by a friend in Lyon on September 12, seeking information on establishing a silk manufactory.[8] Having received no response, Giordana repeats his offer, which will again be transmitted by his friend.

On January 17 Charles Grosett writes in English from Brunswick, proposing to emigrate with a hundred Protestant workers and set up a textile factory whose products will be equal in quality and price to the French and English competition. The workers are all sober and industrious but require support for the passage and their expenses for the first six months. Counting the £5,000 worth of raw materials to

6. A bound manuscript by C. L. B. Wavran titled "Essai de phisique, presenté a son excellence Monseigneur le docteur Franklin" is at the APS. It contains chapters on topics from electricity to earthquakes. The author may be the same abbé Wavran (d. 1799) who served as *curé* of the church Saint-Michel in Etaples, near Hesdin, from 1776 to 1793: Pierre Baudelicque, *Histoire d'Etaples des origines à nos jours* (2 vols., Saint-Josse-sur-Mer, 1993), I, 245, 278.

7. The printed enclosure is at the APS.

8. His first letter is summarized in XL, 29.

begin production, initial outlays for the entire factory will not exceed £8,000, a moderate advance compared to the sums private individuals commonly invest in similar enterprises in England. If Franklin is interested, he should pay for Grosett and the chief manufacturer to come to Paris to discuss the details. Grosett would then demonstrate an entirely man-powered machine of his own invention that can apply whatever force is required to work a mill, engine, or forge by means of geometrical principles.

Mazue writes from Marseille on February 27. Since his letter of the previous March 24 did not merit a reply,[9] he now proposes a scheme that will benefit America and put his depreciated American money to good use. He has long wanted to establish a vineyard on a dry, rocky hillside with sandy soil that is unsuitable for any other crop. He is confident of being able to produce a wine equal to the *vin ordinaire* of Europe. He will also cultivate an olive grove, almost as important. These two projects will require only a few acres of land, which he could buy with the paper money issued by Congress. If his project should fail, he will restore the land to its previous owner, acknowledging his gratitude.

One undated, unsigned proposal was probably made after the declaration of the peace. This four-page memoir proposes to establish a foundry in the United States. Foundries will stimulate population growth, clear forests, and attract and employ new colonists. A foundry would produce useful merchandise made of glass, pottery, iron, steel, and other materials that currently have to be imported at great expense. All the raw materials are available in America in abundance and good quality. Thirty families from Europe, containing a hundred trained workers, would be sufficient to carry out this project. The authors have 150,000 *l.t.*, which would cover transportation and housing for the workers and their families, land, and construction of the factories, but they need Congress to provide the following: a credit of 100,000 *l.t.* for livestock and food, a land grant of 50,000 acres of wood, free use of a ship for transportation, and guarantees that the contracts between the entrepreneurs and the thirty families would remain valid in the United States.[1]

Other merchants and firms offer to export particular goods to the United States or ask Franklin's help in opening trade relations. On October 10, Isidore Lefebvre de Revel fils writes that because he was not admitted to see Franklin when he called at Passy he is sending a memoir written by his father, who lives in Naples and has connec-

9. The letter is summarized in XXXIX, 15.
1. BF endorsed this "Memoire about Iron Works".

tions with the government there. The memoir concerns the trading voyages to America being planned by Neapolitan merchants with the help of their government. In order to encourage this trade, they seek Franklin's assurance that the Neapolitan flag will be welcomed in all United States ports.[2] The son writes again on November 21 to remind Franklin of the memoir and request a reply.

John George Hoffmann of Hirschberg reminds Franklin on October 10, in English, of the letter he wrote to the American commissioners in 1777 about exporting linen, and the answer he received from Silas Deane dated January 13, 1778, written on behalf of Franklin, Deane, and Lee.[3] Now that peace has been declared, he recalls the commissioners' promise to recommend him to American merchants or to provide the names of some good firms. He also would like to be named the agent of a consortium or single American mercantile firm for buying and sending goods from the Silesian linen factories. He has just been elected president of the regional merchants' association and is informed that the Prussian king wants to send envoys or ambassadors to America to establish trade connections and negotiate a treaty of commerce. Would such overtures be welcome to the Americans and serve a mutual purpose?

John Gottfried Braumüller of Berlin, who a few months earlier had offered his services as a commission merchant,[4] writes again on October 14, in German. In a conversation with a local councillor about trade with America, particularly in regard to Virginia tobacco, the official stated that there was a potential for profit. Braumüller would have loved to have been in the position to offer some concrete proposals, but he could not do so without Franklin's authorization. He assures Franklin of his eagerness to serve the United States.

N. Lavallée, a merchant in Orléans, writes on November 4. Having heard from friends that considerable amounts of iron made in Berry are being shipped to America, he asks Franklin for the address of the suppliers. He would be able to furnish one million pieces of

2. The memoir is missing, but it appears that the son also gave BF a letter he had received from his father, dated Aug. 28, which enclosed the memoir and explained it; the father's letter and the son's Oct. 10 letter to BF are among BF's papers at the Hist. Soc. of Pa. The father's Aug. 28 letter makes clear that the memoir was written at the request of John Francis Edward Acton (*ODNB*), one of the chief ministers of King Ferdinand IV of Naples. It also alludes to Meuricoffre's earlier discussion with BF about appointing a consul: XL, 25n.
3. *Deane Papers*, II, 327.
4. His letter of Aug. 2 is summarized in XL, 26.

iron made in Berry by next July and asks if Franklin could provide him with passports to avoid customs duties.

On December 30, Theodoor Van Moorsel & Co. in Ostend offers to sell the United States cannons of excellent quality, made of Swedish iron.[5]

Five undated requests either allude to the reopening of British-American trade or contain an implicit expectation of increased French-American commerce, which leads us to assign them to the year 1783. An implicit inquiry is contained in a brief memorandum listing the particulars of two ships sailing under English colors, loaded with salt and bound for Virginia "if they can possibly get in, under cover of English Clearances": the brig *Jeany*, Capt. Charles Smith, and the *Five Brothers*, Capt. J. Paten.[6] François Romand & fils, a family business in Lyon, wants to send one of the sons to Boston and asks Franklin for a letter of recommendation to the best firms there. He will carry merchandise worth around 80,000 *l.t.*, but the main purpose of the trip is to establish contacts with American merchants. Veuve Gaspard Mollien et fils aîné, merchants and *commissaires de la marine* of the States General in Calais, seek a letter of recommendation from Franklin that would encourage American vessels in Calais to engage their services as business agents. They can provide both professional and personal references and speak and write English.[7] An unknown correspondent asks Franklin on behalf of a French firm to name a port in the United States where it can establish a branch and for advice on what to export to America. A list of questions sent to Ferdinand Grand from his associate in Madrid, the marquis d'Yranda, concerns the opening of trade relations between Spanish ports and Charleston. Grand copied the list and presented it to Franklin, who endorsed it "Marquis D'Aranda Questions to Mr G."[8]

Finally, we summarize letters that do not fit into the three main categories. On October 3 Coulougnac de Coste Belle, writing from Nantes, gratefully acknowledges the receipt of *Constitutions des treize États-Unis de l'Amérique*, which Franklin conveyed through Jonathan Williams, Jr., apparently in return for Coulougnac's lengthy critique

5. Van Moorsel had earlier expressed his desire to be appointed American consul at Ostend and Antwerp: XXXIX, 184–5.

6. This small sheet of paper (Hist. Soc. of Pa.) comes with no letter of explanation.

7. BF endorsed this letter "Agent or Consul Calais".

8. Library of Congress.

of the American political system.[9] Although he claims to be happy to discover that American laws generally conform to the plan he had sent, Coulougnac still finds much to criticize, for instance the lack of a standing army. In the six years he has been trading with them, Coulougnac has noted that Americans are handicapped by their tendency to be concerned only with the present moment. But he approves of Americans in general, and the proof of that is that his credit lies in their hands. He leaves for Philadelphia in less than three months with his wife, children, and goods. There he will be the principal in the firm of Coulougnac, Savary & Cie., while his Nantais firm will operate independently. He requests letters of recommendation and suggests that he be named consul or commercial agent in charge of trade with France, a task he will fulfill to the satisfaction of both nations.

Wanting to be useful to the United States, the chevalier de Sugny offers on October 25 to raise a corps of Frenchmen who could be put to work in America in any way Franklin thinks best. This plan has the endorsement of his sovereign. Sugny will personally choose men who are strong and courageous, used to hard work, and equipped with all sorts of skills. They could be employed as a group or individually. If Franklin approves of this plan, the chevalier will tailor it to his needs. Sugny has already had great success with a similar commission under the maréchal de Belle Isle.[1] His former superiors, especially the Marshals de Broglie and Ségur, can attest to his abilities. Sugny writes again on November 17 to ask whether Franklin received his first letter and what his reaction to the project was. He writes from Montbrison en Forest, near Lyon.[2]

Desfours l'aîné, who signs himself as a captain of cavalry,[3] also wants permission to share a plan with Franklin. Writing from Lyon

9. For a summary of his earlier letter, dated Sept. 10, and biographical information see XL, 30–1. The current letter is at the Hist. Soc. of Pa.

1. Charles-Louis-Auguste Fouquet, duc de Belle-Isle, maréchal de France (1684–1761), became *secrétaire d'Etat* for the department of war in 1758 and initiated numerous reforms in the organization and training of the French army: *DBF*.

2. On Feb. 12, 1785, the author's cousin, the marquis de Ponçins, reminded BF of this inquiry, identifying the writer as the chevalier de Montorcier de Sugny, former captain in the Flanders regiment, then in his sixties (APS). Such an individual is listed as Montorcier in the *Etat militaire* for 1767, pp. 184–5.

3. In the *Etat militaire* for 1782, p. 348 (the last listing we find for him), he holds the rank of *sous-lieutenant*. His Sept. 25 letter is at the Hist. Soc. of Pa.

on September 25, he claims that his scheme will make the United States one of the most powerful countries in the world. It is easily executed, and he is sure Franklin will approve. If his project can be of use, it would fulfill all his ambitions, and if not, at least he will have the consolation of having tried to help an ally. He writes again on November 10, imparting a sense of urgency and promising to send the plan if Franklin will only respond.

On a more modest scale, a Parisian by the name of Lasson invites Franklin on December 23 to the opening of his basketry shop three days hence. It will offer a variety of goods, including furniture, tea boxes, and looms, all made of straw. He signs as "ancien officier des chasses de feu Monseigneur Le Prince de Conty".

Also writing from Paris, one Gombert tells Franklin on January 24 that he has discovered a secret method for curing and preventing toothaches. He made this discovery by chance, but for the past three years he has practiced it on his family, who have not suffered the least pain since. Although neither a doctor nor surgeon he is not a charlatan, and he is not afraid to prove the validity of his method in a way that will leave no doubt, even among the greatest of philosophes. Of course, his invention might put dentists out of work, but should one not consider the greater good?

On February 10 Jeannotas, the owner of a newly opened residential hotel, informs Franklin that he named it after a great general whose virtues equal his talents. He hopes to attract American customers who will rally, he hopes, under the banner of one of their heroes. He asks Franklin to forward to Philadelphia the enclosed advertisements (now missing), thereby lending another famous American name to the endeavor. This might seem beneath Franklin, but Jeannotas believes that the hands that secured the fate of an empire can surely help a simple individual.

In an undated letter written after the declaration of the peace, an Italian admirer from Carrara, the comte François Antoine del Medico, wants to ensure that the heroic exploits and sacrifices of the American Revolution are properly memorialized as an inspiration to future generations. He offers Franklin white marble from his quarry as well as the services of his brother, an able sculptor, if Franklin would be so kind to send them a design for a great monument. He identifies himself as the Prussian chargé d'affaires in Italy, serving at the court of Naples,[4] and gives as his address the chamberlain of the duc de Modène.

4. He is listed in *Repertorium der diplomatischen Vertreter*, III, 249, as Francesco conte del Medico.

Finally, we take note of three undated memoirs in French, written by the English inventor and *mécanicien* James Milne, who had come to France in 1779 and established a cotton-spinning factory in partnership with François Perret.[5] After that factory closed in November, 1783, because of financial failure, Milne went to Paris to petition for a royal privilege. The three memoirs in question, which Milne probably brought to Franklin in person, are copies of his petitions and may well date from early 1784.[6] The one titled "Mémoire" is seven pages long and addressed "au gouvernement." Milne recalls his government-funded construction in 1780 of a cotton-carding machine that was approved by the Academy of Sciences. He relates the history of the Neuville factory, blaming his partner Perret for the financial problems, about which he had known nothing. He states that in October, 1783, an official inspection of his manufactory concluded that the three machines of his invention—a cotton-carding machine, a roving machine, and a spinning machine that produced threads of varying thicknesses—were producing superior products. Milne begs for government protection. The "Second Mémoire" proposes to introduce into France five new inventions: an improved flour sieve that will yield healthier loaves, a water-powered wool-carding machine that can do the work of thirty people, a spinning machine that can do the work of twenty and spin threads of varying thicknesses superior to anything spun by hand, a cotton-cleaning machine that will be especially useful in the West Indies, and a machine that cleans and mills rice. The carding and spinning machines will be of particular importance to France, he writes, as the cloth produced from this yarn will be better and cheaper than that made in England, and France will become America's favored trading partner. Franklin endorsed this: "Memoire of Milne, Mecanicien Anglois." The "Dernier Mémoire" is addressed to the *contrôleur général*. Because of the bankruptcy and

5. Milne had requested an audience with BF in 1780; see XXXII, 395–6, for a discussion of his introduction of this technology into France and the success of the petitions described here.

6. Milne probably came to see BF in early 1784, and may have drawn the sketches of spinning machines that are described in the annotation of the baronne de Bourdic's letters published under [1783?]. We wonder whether he sounded out BF on the possibility of relocating to America if the French government refused to back him. Milne did go to Georgia in 1787 and spent two years working with cotton growers. In 1789, he convinced GW of the potential for growing cotton in Georgia and South Carolina. That same year Pennsylvania's Society for the Encouragement of Manufactures commissioned TJ to ship to America some of the Milne factory carding and spinning machines: *Jefferson Papers*, XIV, 546; XV, 476–7.

death of his partner Perret, and the seizure of the assets of his other partner, d'Hauteroche, Milne has abandoned the Neuville manufactory and come to Paris to seek justice. He asserts his ownership of the machinery as well as his claim to the inventions, requests a government inspection, and asks for a *privilège du roi* and a government pension.[7]

Monsieur   Paris le 13. janvier 1784

Je crois avoir quelqu'interêt a honorer la science, et surtout celle de l'invention, mais quelque puisse etre mon respect pour un savant d'ont la reputation a passée depuis longtems et avec tant d'eclat, du nouveau Monde dans l'Ancien, c'est a lhomme d'Etat et au digne Representant d'une grande Nation que j'ai l'honneur de preter la parole et d'adresser mon livre.[8]

Vous n'y trouverez pas, Monsieur, mais vous y verrez que j'ai trouvé une nouvelle methode plus simple, plus économique et plus parfaite pour planter et cultiver la vigne: vous y verrez encore que mes inventions et mes nouveaux procedes pour la manipulation et la fermentation des vins, ont la double proprieté de les rendre beaucoup meilleurs et d'une plus longue durée.

Toutes ces inventions, Monsieur, que je crois pouvoir vous presenter comme le seul code general de la Vigne et des vins pour les matieres auxquelles elles se rapportent, ne conviennent pas moins a l'Amerique qu'a l'Europe, et j'espere que ce ne sera pas un savant tel que vous, qui mettra la chose en doute; ainsi, Monsieur, en travaillant pour un Monde, j'ai travaillé pour l'autre, et plus encore, en quelque sorte, pour le Nouveau ou, a cet egard, tout est encore a faire, que pour l'ancien, ou tout est fait et a défaire. Il y a plus, Monsieur, c'est qu'en travaillant pour ce dernier, mon intention a eté de travailler en même tems, pour

7. The *contrôleur général* was Calonne. In October, 1785, he granted Milne, his father, and his brother a site at La Muette in Passy, and the financial backing to establish this factory. For a fuller account of the Milnes in France see J. R. Harris, *Industrial Espionage and Technology Transfer: Britain and France in the Eighteenth Century* (Aldershot, Eng., 1998), pp. 363–5, 369, 374–7.

8. Maupin published several books in 1783 and 1784. The only works of his that have been identified as belonging to BF's library are pamphlets, now at the Hist. Soc. of Pa.: *Eclaircissemens concernant plusieurs points de la théorie et de la manipulation des vins . . .* (Paris, 1783), and *Avis de l'auteur sur la nouvelle édition de la richesse des vignobles* (Paris, 1783?).

l'autre, et je m'en suis expliqué assez clairement, dans l'ouvrage que j'ai donné avant celui que j'ai l'honneur de vous faire passer.

Ne croyez cependant pas, Monsieur, que je vous fasse cette remarque en vue d'aucun interêt pécuniaire. Comme je ne demande point l'or de mon pays, je ne demande point non plus celui des Nations etrangeres; quoique, dans ma maniere de voir, je croye y avoir encore plus de droit; mais, lorsque je suis assez heureux pour leur rendre les plus grands services, je voudrois, au moins qu'elles regardassent ces services comme des bienfaits, et qu'elles daignassent me le temoigner. J'ose dire plus, Monsieur, c'est qu'elles y ont interêt, et je me flate que si vous me faites l'honneur de lire mon livre, vous en serez persuadé.

J'ai l'honneur d'estre avec un profond respect, Monsieur, Votre tres humble et tres obeissant serviteur

MAUPIN

rue du pont aux choux, au petit hotel de poitou

P.S. Je pense, Monsieur, que le plus grand honneur que pussent m'accorder les Etats unis seroit de donner a mes inventions le meme eclat et la meme publicité que l'on donne en france a l'idée du balon aerostatique.

Notation: Maupin 13 Janvr. 1784.

To Daniel Lathrop Coit[9]

Printed invitation with MS insertions:[1] Johns Hopkins University Library

[January 14, 1784]

DR. FRANKLIN requests the honour of Mr. *Coit's* Company at Dinner on *Sunday* the *18. Inst*

9. Daniel Lathrop Coit (1754–1833), a merchant of Norwich, Conn., sailed to England in May, 1783, and went to Paris at the end of October. He witnessed the Dec. 1 manned balloon ascension (which he described in a letter published in the *Norwich Packet*, Feb. 26, 1784) and the Dec. 14 illuminations in honor of the peace. While in Paris he also met Lafayette. What survives of his diary of the trip does not extend beyond December: William C. Gilman, *A Memoir of Daniel Lathrop Coit of Norwich, Connecticut, 1754–1833* (Norwich, Conn., 1907), pp. 6–25, 67; Daniel Lathrop Coit, "Diary of a trip to Europe," Conn. Hist. Soc.

1. L'Air de Lamotte filled in the invitation and WTF supplied the address. An earlier example of this invitation is illustrated in XXXIX, facing p. 409.

Passy, *Jany. 14 1784.*

The favour of an Answer is desired.

Addressed: A Monsieur / Monsieur Coit. chez / Mr. Carter[2] /
Hotel d'Angleterre / Rue des Filles St Thomas.

Endorsed: Doctr. Franklin's Billet to Dine

Thomas Mifflin to the American Peace Commissioners

Press copies of copies:[3] South Carolina Historical Society, American
Philosophical Society; copies: Massachusetts Historical Society, National Archives

Gentlemen, Annapolis 14th. Jany. 1784.—
This day, nine States being represented in Congress, Vizt:
Massachusetts, Rhode Island, Connecticut, Pennsylvania, Delaware, Maryland, Virginia, North Carolina and South Carolina,
together with one Member from New-Hampshire, and one Member from New-Jersey,[4] The Treaty of Peace was ratified by the
unanimous Vote of the Members;[5] This being done, Congress
by an unanimous Vote, ordered a Proclamation to be issued, enjoining the strict and faithful Observance thereof, and published
an earnest Recommendation to the several States in the very
Words of the 5th. Article—[6] They have likewise resolved, that

2. John Carter (John Barker Church): XXXVIII, 546n; XL, 264n.
3. The two copies from which these press copies were made are in the
hand of L'Air de Lamotte, as is the copy at the Mass. Hist. Soc., which is
endorsed by JA.
4. Nine states were required for ratification, but each state had to have
two delegates present in order to be represented. That condition was not
met until Jan. 14, when S.C. delegate Richard Beresford, who had been
ill in Philadelphia, arrived in Annapolis: Smith, *Letters,* XXI, xxv; *JCC,*
XXVI, 22; Edmund C. Burnett, *The Continental Congress* (New York, 1941),
pp. 591–3.
5. See *JCC,* XXVI, 22–9. The ratification and proclamation (mentioned
below), drafted by TJ in December, are also in *Jefferson Papers,* VI, 456–65.
6. The proclamation is in *JCC,* XXVI, 29–30. Pursuant to Article 5 of
the treaty (XL, 572–3), Congress issued a recommendation to the state legislatures that they provide for the restitution of estates, rights, and properties confiscated from British subjects and from persons resident in areas

the Ratification of the Definitive Treaty of Peace between the United States & Great Britain, be transmitted, with all possible Dispatch, under the Care of a faithful Person, to our Ministers in France, who have negotiated the Treaty; to be exchanged; and have appointed Colonel Josiah Harmar to that Service.[7] He will have the Honor of delivering to you the Ratification; together with Copies of the Proclamation of Congress and of their Recommendation to the States conformably to the 5th. Article.[8]

I take the Liberty of recommending Colonel Harmar to you as a brave and deserving Officer and am, with the highest Respect & Esteem, Gentlemen, Your obedient, and most humble Servant. (signed) THOMAS MIFFLIN.

[*In Franklin's hand:*] To their Excellencies John Adams, B. Franklin, John Jay, & Henry Laurens Esquires.

From Cadet de Vaux

L: American Philosophical Society

Ce 14 Janvier 1784

Mr Cadet De Vaux a l'honneur de presenter son respect à Monsieur Frankelin, et il le previent que la farine de Maïs est actuellement a Paris; il se propose sous le bon plaisir de Monsieur Frankelin de lui faire parvenir cette Farine a Passy par la voiture de l'homme qui apporte les eaux.

Notation: Cadet de vaux 14 Janvr. 1784.

---

possessed by the British between Nov. 30, 1782, and Jan. 14, 1784, who had not borne arms against the United States: *JCC,* XXVI, 30–31.

7. *JCC,* XXVI, 29. Josiah Harmar of Pennsylvania (*ANB*), who had achieved the rank of brevet colonel in the army by 1783, was at this time serving as Mifflin's private secretary: Dwight L. Smith, "Josiah Harmar, Diplomatic Courier," *PMHB,* LXXXVII (1963), 420–30. For his Jan. 14 instructions from Mifflin see Smith, *Letters,* XXI, 274–5; an extract in BF's hand is at the APS.

8. Copies of the proclamation and recommendation, in the hand of Charles Thomson, are among BF's papers at the APS. No copies of the ratification have been located among the papers of the American peace commissioners, though the copy that Hartley retained (in the hand of his secretary) is at the Clements Library: Smith, "Josiah Harmar, Diplomatic Courier," p. 30.

From Charles-Eléonor Dufriche de Valazé[9]

ALS: American Philosophical Society

à paris hotel d'orléans Rue du parc Royal Le 14 jer 1784.
Monsieur

J'ai l'honneur de vous demander une Entrevue, pour avoir celui de vous remettre un Exemplaire du livre intitulé loix pénales que je viens de dédier à Monsieur frere du Roi.[1] Je vous prierai d'En faire passer un Exemplaire au Congrès d'amérique. J'ai la glorieuse Espérance de Contribuer à la perfection des loix de ce pays.

Je suis avec un profond Respect, Monsieur, Votre très humble Et très obéissant serviteur   DUFRICHE DE VALAZÉ

From Ingenhousz

ALS: American Philosophical Society

Dear friend   Vienna Jan. 14 January 1784

This lettre will be delivred to you by the *Countesse de Fries*,[2] a lady, to whose family I am obliged for their constant kindness and civitilities towards me. Her Husband, one of the richest and the most respectable men of Europe, establish'd here in the most extensive banking business, a protestant and a Republican, being a Swish born; being very desirous of knowing you and of being known by you, has desired me to send an introductory lettre to you for his lady, who is now at Lions and intends to come back to Vienna by the way of Paris.

9. The former infantry officer and lawyer who warned BF in 1779 against the evils of luxury and hereditary nobility in the new American republic: XXXI, 234–5.

1. *Loix pénales* (Alençon, 1784). Dufriche reiterated his request for an interview on Feb. 10, his dedication to the public good overcoming his mortification at receiving no response from BF. He enclosed one copy of the book, hoping that if BF read it he would agree to send a second copy to Congress (APS). BF's copy of *Loix pénales* is at the APS.

2. Anne d'Escherny was the daughter of Jean-François d'Escherny of Neuchâtel, who served as consul at Lyon for the king of Poland. In 1764 she married the wealthy banker and industrialist Johann Fries (1719–1785), who became a count in 1783: P. G. M. Dickson, *Finance and Government under Maria Theresia, 1740–1780* (2 vols., Oxford, 1987) I, 172–7; Lüthy, *Banque protestante*, II, 236n.

I hope you will be so good as to show her that good countenance, you have allways bestowed on those, who were recommended to you by Your affectionate friend[3]   J. INGEN HOUSZ

Addressed: a Son Excellence / Monsieur Benj. Franklin / Ministre plenipot. des Etats unies / de l'Amerique / a Passy

Endorsed: Jan 14. 84

From Sir Edward Newenham

ALS: American Philosophical Society

My Dear Sir—   Carlow 14 Janry: 1784
    Can a few Lines compensate the trouble of opening this Letter? It is to convey the sentiments of a whole family in wishing you & your Worthy Grandson many returns of the present Season—you have not, in the Extensive Dominions from the Bay of Fundy to the Missisippi, more sincere, warm or Impartial friends than Lady Newenham & the Colonels of the Liberty Volunteers;[4] it is with pleasure I reflect, that I declared these Sentiments in the days of adversity; it was then that I decided in favor of Virtue, & reprobated the Conduct of British Tyrany;[5] In pleading for the rights of America, I met many Severe oppositions, but as truth gained Grownd, I Surmounted the first difficulties, & our first Victory was gained by the Address against the American War, & then refusing to receive the Hannoverians, in full confidence that if we received them, every Soldier in Ireland would have been sent to America, & that would have added 6000 more to your opponents;[6] Ireland, particular-

3. On the verso is a cartoon-like sketch of a smiling man and woman receiving a treatment from one of Mesmer's *baquets* (tubs), which will be discussed in vol. 42.
    4. Newenham, colonel of Dublin's Liberty Volunteers (see XXXVIII, 188n), may be referring to himself and his eldest son, Edward, who in 1782 was listed as captain: Thomas Mac Nevin, *The History of the Volunteers of 1782* (New York, 1845), p. 113.
    5. *E.g.*, XXXIII, 274–5, 503.
    6. In late October, 1775, Newenham attended a meeting of freeholders and freemen in Dublin that issued an address deploring the "civil war" in America and asking George III to "heal the breach." By mid-November

ily the Cities of Corke & Dublin, deserve very warm returns in National connection & friendship from the United States of America, & I hope in the Course of Trade an Union of sentiments will appear—

I have been very uneasy in my mind for this time past, on reading the accounts of dissentions upon disbanding the Army, without the troops having received their arrears; though his Excellency General Washingtons answers to the Addresses lessens my fears,[7] yet I cannot divest myself of anxiety, when I imagine some thousand of Soldiers are dispersed through the Country dissatisfied, & more so at this important Period, when it requires the most peaceable & the most unanimous Connections between all parts of the New Empire, to form their Police, arrange their Laws, regulate their Commerce & Establish a System for permanent Legislation, and to have these matters regulated as soon as possible, for it might happen, in the Course of human Events, that the Politics of the European Powers might change, & involve the United States in a War, before they had recruited their Strength; discontented Soldiers would then be a dangerous Class of men;— Pardon these Ideas, for they arize from the warmest attachment to your Cause—a Cause that has been Crowned with Success by perseverance & Unanimity, & must, now, be Supported by wisdom & disinterested Virtue—

The foggy Air of the Metropolis induced me to quit it during the recess of our Assembly[8] (miscalled a Representation of the People) and take the Diversion of Shooting during the hard frosts we have had these some days; Wild fowl were never Known to be in Such plenty or so good, but the Number of Peo-

---

the address had gathered nearly 3,000 signatures. Newenham then took a lead role in the House of Commons against sending Irish troops to America and replacing them with foreign mercenaries. Parliament resolved that it would send 4,000 Irish soldiers to America while refusing the admission of Hessian mercenaries on Irish soil: James Kelly, *Sir Edward Newenham MP, 1734–1814: Defender of the Protestant Constitution* (Dublin, 2004), pp. 120–1; David Dickson, *New Foundations: Ireland, 1660–1800* (rev. ed., Dublin and Portland, Ore., 2000), p. 158.

7. See XXXIX, 394–5; XL, 301–8.
8. The legislature adjourned on Dec. 22, 1783, until Jan. 26, 1784: *The Journals of the House of Commons of the Kingdom of Ireland . . .* (31 vols., Dublin, 1782–94), XXI, 409.

ple now permitted to Carry arms, renders it sometimes dangerous to Sport near a town or Village—

All the Electors of this Kingdom, except the Counties of Waterford, Carlow, Louth & Kildare, are in motion for obtaining Petitions & addresses in respect to a more Equal Representation; those 4 Counties are mere Boroughs, & their owners are perfectly inimical to every System of oeconomy or Reform; however we have better hopes, now, than ever we had, if the young Minister Mr Pitt remains in *power* as he inherits the Principles of a Reform from his father; and Richmond has given it under his hand;[9] our greatest difficulty, then, will be how to liquidate the Compensation money; for we must purchase the acquiescence of the Borough Mongers; many Boroughs are included in marriage settlements; some are entailed upon minors, others divided among females; it will require the greatest abilities & Judgement to form an adequate Bill, as we have so many Enemies, naturaly & interestledly, inimical to the measure— Should the 28 remaining Counties, & the 8 free Cities & towns join in the same mode of petitioning, even our present Venal Parliament must yield to the Voice of Justice & Right;—

These changes in the British Ministry injure & impoverish us; we Scarce become acquainted with the Character & plans of one Vice-roy, before he is Superseded;[1] another comes & he bribes another Squadron of Corruptable Ruffians, & Each Vice-roy gets 3000 pound for a service of Plate; Each secretary gets a Doceuer, or a sine Cure employment, & we are overrun with a Swarm of Black Locusts, who accompany the *Vice* King to the Land of Canaan; if I find a proper Spirit at our next meeting I will agitate these matters—our Crown & Civil officers are

9. The Duke of Richmond, Charles Lennox (*ODNB*), had been a supporter of the American cause and in 1783 published a pamphlet on parliamentary reform responding to questions raised by the Irish Volunteers in their circular letter of July 19. He served in Pitt's cabinet as master-general of the ordnance and was initially a close adviser to the prime minister. See XL, 337–42; *ODNB; Proceedings Relative to the Ulster Assembly of Volunteer Delegates* . . . (Belfast, 1783), pp. 21–5, 49–63; John Ehrman, *The Younger Pitt* (3 vols., New York and Stanford, Calif., 1969–96), I, 130, 139, 185–6.

1. Robert Henley, the viceroy (lord lieutenant), was replaced with Charles Manners (1754–1787) on Feb. 11: *ODNB*.

dogs, let who will be Miller; they compliment Every L: Liewtenant, let his Character & Connections be what they may—

As I mentioned in a former part of my Letter, I find by this days post, that the City of Waterford has resolved against a reform;[2] I Suspected it, as the Tyrone Interest[3] is predominant there; is it not astonishing that the Tyrone Interest should Carry such a Sway? Whether their Characters are already Known to you, I cannot Say, but I can assure you, that in the main & almost all the Collateral Branches united, they cannot produce two Men of tolerable good Sence;—

We are in anxious expectation of the proceedings in the British house of Faction on the 12th Instant;[4] we are *told*, that a new arrangement is to take place here, but as that never happened amidst all former Changes (except in one or two Employments) I doubt it—though I am confident some Changes in the Revenue Department would be of service to our Trade—

We could not find a Merchant in our whole City of Abilities & Spirit to Stand Candidate, so we have two blundering Aldermen battling for it— Warren was a poor Deputy Guager, & I took him into my office as a Clerk, & afterwards made him Cashier, while I was Collector; I got him made a freeman of the City of Dublin & then Sherriff & Alderman; immediately after, he shewed his Gratitude & opposed my Election for the County of Dublin, to the utter Surprize of Every body, as we never had the Smallest dispute; he will Carry this Election, as the Independant Interest have no Object—it is realy astonishing, that in Such a City, we should not find a Single Man of worth & abilities to Stand forward;—[5]

2. By a vote of 54 to 84: *Dublin Evening Post*, Jan. 13, 1784.

3. George de la Poer Beresford (1735–1800), 2nd Earl of Tyrone, and his family connections: Edith M. Johnston-Liik, *History of the Irish Parliament, 1692–1800* ... (6 vols., Belfast, 2002), III, 156–8.

4. Parliament had reassembled on Jan. 12 following the appointment of Pitt as the new prime minister, for which see David Hartley to BF, Dec. 25.

5. Nathaniel Warren (1737–1796) did indeed win this parliamentary by-election. He had served as sheriff in 1773 and become an alderman in 1775 before opposing Newenham's first successful run for parliament in 1776:

My Eldest Son & I have some thoughts of Visiting the Continent of America in the Course of the present year, when I shall hope for Letters of Introduction from your Excellency & your friends— Lady Newenham & all my family, Join me in the warmest Sentiments of respect to you & yours—

I have the Honor, to be, with the Highest Respect your Excellencys most Obt: & Obliged Humble Sert

EDWARD NEWENHAM

Addressed: His Excellency Benj: Franklin / Minister Plenipotentiary / from the United States / Passy

From Charles Thomson   ALS: American Philosophical Society

Dear Sir,   Annapolis 14 Jany 1784

I have received Your letter of 13 Septr. with the papers enclosed[6] and have taken Steps to procure the Intelligence wanted. I have written to our old friend Reuben Haines who I take to be the person meant by Mr Heintz a brewer in Market Street with whom Marggrander is said to have lived to obtain the necessary certificates respecting him[7] and have directed enquiries to be made respecting the other gentlemen mentioned. As soon as I receive answers to my letters I will forward them. The memorial from David & Anne Barry I have delivered to the delegates for North Carolina together with the paper respecting the Grenville claim.[8] The letter from Mr De Bernardi I communicated to Con-

Johnston-Liik, *History of the Irish Parliament*, VI, 505–6; Kelly, *Sir Edward Newenham*, p. 124.

6. See XL, 625–6.

7. BF had forwarded to Thomson the Aug. 10 letter he had received from Du Pont de Nemours, inquiring about a certain Marggrander who was employed by "Heintz": XL, 456–7. Thomson wrote to Haines on Jan. 1: Smith, *Letters*, XXI, 254–5.

8. BF had forwarded to Thomson a now-missing petition claiming a substantial tract of property in North Carolina on behalf, apparently, of the 6th Earl of Coventry, devisee of the 3rd Earl Granville. George II had granted the land in 1744 to the 2nd Earl Granville, a descendant of one of the original Carolina proprietors. The N.C. state legislature, to whom Gov. Alexander Martin referred the claim in April, 1784, took no action. Lord Coventry, after failing to win a suit against the grantees of the state in

gress, who did not think proper to take any measures thereon.[1] The ports of the United States are open to all foreigners and the Several States are ready to receive any men of science or abilities who may be willing to settle among them, but the Sovereign body of the Union do not seem to think it necessary to give any particular encouragement to any nation or to any individual.

This day the definitive treaty was ratified and the ratification is entrusted to the care of col J. Harmar who is the Presidents private Secretary and whom I beg leave to recommend to your particular notice and attention.

I am with the greatest respect Dear Sir Your affectionate Friend and humble Servt   CHA THOMSON

Addressed: The honble B. Franklin / Minister plenipotenty of the United States / of America / Passy near / Paris

Endorsed: Cha. Thomson Esqr.—Jan. 14 1784

Thomas Mifflin to the American Peace Commissioners

Copy: National Archives

Gentlemen,   Annapolis January 15th.[2] 1784
    This day nine States being represented in Congress viz. Massachusets, Rhode Island, Connecticut, Pennsylvania, Dela-

---

federal court in 1806, appealed to the Supreme Court, which dismissed the case in 1817: Henry G. Connor, "The Granville Estate and North Carolina," *University of Pa. Law Rev.*, LXII (1914), 671–97; Herbert A. Johnson *et al.*, eds., *The Papers of John Marshall* (12 vols., Chapel Hill, N.C., 1974–2006), VI, 400–1; Walter Clark, ed., *The State Records of North Carolina* (26 vols., Goldsboro, N.C., 1886–1907), XVII, 43.

At the same time that Gov. Martin laid the Granville claim before the state legislature, he also transmitted the memorial of David and Ann Barry (XL, 626n), and the appeal that BF had written to him in August, 1782, regarding the confiscated property of Edward Bridgen (XXXVII, 703): Clark, ed., *The State Records of North Carolina*, XVII, 43.

1. Bernardi's July 5 petition, offering to supply America with Italian men of arts and letters, including himself (XL, 626n), was tabled by Congress on Dec. 18, 1783: *JCC*, XXV, 816, 817n.

2. The dateline of this copy is problematic. There can be no doubt that the letter was written on Jan. 15, but its opening phrase "This day" refers to

ware, Maryland, Virginia, North Carolina and South Carolina, together with one Member from New Jersey and One from New Hampshire, The Treaty of Peace was ratified by the unanimous Vote of the Members. This being done, Congress by an unanimous vote ordered a proclamation to be issued enjoyning the strict and faithful Observance thereof; and published an earnest recommendation to the several States in the very words of the fifth Article—[3] They have likewise resolved, "That a triplicate of the ratification of the definitive Treaty be sent to our Ministers plenipotentiaries by Lieutenant Colonel David S. Franks" who has directions to proceed with all possible dispatch to Paris—[4] We are in hope that Colonel Harmar who is charged with the first instrument of the ratification, and who left this place yesterday, in order to take his passage in the L'Orient Packet at New York, will arrive at Paris before the 3d of March or if he should not, that Colonel Franks may be so fortunate as to effect it—[5] A Duplicate was sent last Evening to the Care of Mr. Morris at Philadelphia to be forwarded by him—[6]

---

the day before. The first two sentences, in fact, were copied verbatim from Mifflin's Jan. 14 letter, above; surely, the secretary should have changed the first word to "Yesterday." When BF and Jay acknowledged receiving the present letter, they referred to its date as Jan. 14: BF and Jay to Mifflin, April 16, 1784 (National Archives).

3. Up to this point, the text had been copied from Mifflin's letter of Jan. 14; see the previous note.

4. The resolution instructed Franks to sail "from any port eastward of Philadelphia, for France or any port in the channel, in which neither of the instruments of the ratification, already forwarded, may be sent, provided such vessel shall sail before the 3 day of February next." *JCC*, XXVI, 34–5.

5. Harmar boarded the *Courier de l'Amérique* at New York on Jan. 19, but due to weather and various mishaps the ship did not sail for France until Feb. 21. Franks, also in New York, sailed for London around the same time on the British ship *Edward: Morris Papers*, IX, 81n; Dwight L. Smith, "Josiah Harmar, Diplomatic Courier," *PMHB*, LXXXVII (1963), 424–5. The deadline for exchanging ratified copies was March 3.

6. Morris, in turn, entrusted it to Capt. Samuel Gerrish on Feb. 2, with instructions to forward it from New York or Boston: *Morris Papers*, IX, 79.

I beg leave to recommend Colonel Franks to you as a very deserving Citizen and am with the greatest Respect and esteem. Gentlemen Your Obedient Servant[7]   THOMAS MIFFLIN

The Honorable Benjamin Franklin John Adams and John Jay Esqrs.

From William Carmichael   ALS: Library of Congress

Dear Sir   Madrid 15th. Jany.[–February 4] 1784
I recd. on the 4th instant the Letter which your Excy did me the honor to write me the 15th Ulto., The kind assurances which it contains of your constant esteem and affection have removed from my mind an uneasiness which had oppressed it for a long time— Until I was led to think that by some means or other your friendship for me was diminished, It was always a consolation for me to reflect amidst the disagreements & chagrins which I met with here or elsewhere, that I preserved the good opinion of a man whose good opinion I ever regarded as the best sheild against detraction or envy.

I never expected regular returns from you in the way of correspondence, I knew the multiplicity of your Occupations, and therefore whenever I received a letter from your Excy. I esteemed it as a favor and an honor— Your Silence was not the first motive of my apprehension that I had lost your Confidence— In the course of the Summer I was asked by a person of high rank who has always shown a very great regard for me whether I had any cause to think that your sentiments with respect to me were changed— I replied in the negative— He then told me *confidentially* that he had been informed that there was a coldness on your part and advised me in a friendly manner to endeavour to remove the occasion of it, If any in reality existed. Conscious of having nothing to reproach myself with respect to Your Excy. that could deprive me of your Esteem, I deter-

7. On Jan. 23, Mifflin asked Annapolis merchant Charles Wallace to send a copy of the present letter to his business partner Joshua Johnson in London, to be forwarded to Ferdinand Grand's address: Smith, *Letters*, XXI, 283n.

mined to leave to time and Circumstances the clearing up of my conduct, however affecting it might be to me to suffer in Silence what I considered a great Misfortune.

When Mr Jay wrote to me to come to Paris, it was painful for me to have the reasons which I had to refuse acceeding to his proposition, because I was persuaded that I should be able in a very short conversation to reestablish myself in your good opinion—[8] When I found that this court had determined to receive a Minister from the United States in a public Character I expected Mr Jay would have immediately come hither— The Same reasons would not then have subsisted for my residence At this Court, and I was resolved in quitting it to have quitted Also my political carreer— A Friendly expression in a Letter from your Grandson & the small hope I entertained of seeing you shortly After Mr Jays resignation, of which I recd the first information from the Cte de Florida Blanca[9] induced me to hazard opening myself to him— I am happy that I did So, since it has procured me such obliging and Friendly Assurances from your Excy. while at the Same time it Affords me an opportunity of explaining candidly the source of what has been a great Affliction to me— I hope your Excellency will pardon the length of this Detail, It contains the only complaint I ever made against you & I am persuaded it will be the Last—

The Mr Montgomery who occasioned your Excellency the correspondence of which you have done me the honor to send me Copies is not unknown to Mr Jay—[1] On that Gentlemans departure from this Country, he addressed me on acct of a Law Suit he had before the council of war here, In which it was requisite that I should interfere to prove that he had taken the

8. Jay's first letter instructing Carmichael to come to Paris was dated July 1, 1783. For their ongoing dispute see the annotation of Congress' instructions to the peace commissioners, Oct. 29.

9. Jay informed Carmichael in a letter of Sept. 20, 1783, that he was resigning his post. He asked Carmichael to pay the rent on his house in Spain, give up the lease, and dismiss the porter (Columbia University Library).

1. Their correspondence dates back to late 1781, at least, when Robert Montgomery applied for a consulship: Jay to Montgomery, Dec. 31, 1781, a copy of which was enclosed in an undated letter from Montgomery to Jay (National Archives).

Oaths of Fidelity to the United States— For this purpose he put into my hands a certificate signed by your Excellency—[2] This rendered it my Duty to afford him all the assistance in my power— I did so, he had lost his cause before the same Tribunal, He gained it by a revision of the Sentence—

In one of the Letters from him to which this Affair gave rise He informed me that an Ambassador from Morrocco had put into Alicant— In my answer I desired him as an American to be as usefull as he could to that Personage, because hereafter he might be of service to us—[3] I heard no more on this subject until Several months After, when he inclosed me a copy of a very singular Letter, which he had taken the Liberty to write to the Emperor, not by the Ambassador abovementioned, but by some Other who had afterwards been in that Post,[4] advising me at the Same time of his having transmitted to your Excy & Mr Jay a copy of this & of the Answer he had recd to it—[5] I wrote him expressing my surprize that he should have taken such a Step without having the Smallest authority that I knew of for that purpose, I at the same time requested him to send me copies of the answers he might receive from Paris. My Letter I beleive offended him, for he hath not written to me since— In the month of July Mr Harrison advised me of the arrival of Gacomo Franco Croco at Cadiz, as also that he had applied to him for Money— I advised him to treat the man civilly, but to make no advance whatever— In Augt. last Mr Croco waited upon me at Sn. Ildefonso— I received him with Politeness, made use of

2. See xxx, 602–3. The copy of that oath of allegiance shows its being attested by Arthur Lee and JA: xxvi, 242–3n; xxx, 217n.

3. Following a meeting with Moroccan ambassador Muhammad ibn 'Abd al-Malik in the fall of 1782, Montgomery wrote to Carmichael asking whether it would be appropriate to approach the diplomat about a possible commercial treaty between Morocco and the United States. He claimed to have received Carmichael's approval with further instructions on the subject: Priscilla H. Roberts and James N. Tull, "Moroccan Sultan Sidi Muhammad Ibn Abdallah's Diplomatic Initiatives Toward the United States, 1777–1786," APS *Proc.*, CXLIII (1999), 246–7; Roberts and Roberts, *Thomas Barclay*, p. 200.

4. Montgomery's Jan. 4, 1783, letter to the sultan of Morocco (see XL, 311n) mentions that it would be delivered by a Sidi Mustafa Belgasnachi.

5. Not found.

General Expressions of the Desire of the States to cultivate the Emperors Friendship, but Added that I believed they had not given the necessary powers to any one in Europe to conclude a Treaty— He told me that he had written to your Excellency from Cadiz & expected your Answer— I soon discovered that he had come to Spain on a particular commission not I beleive of a political nature, for I saw him once or twice in the Minister of State's Antichamber & remarked that he was treated with little Attention— In public he generally appeared in Low company— He told me that he had a Letter from the Emperor to Congress which he had left at Cadiz— This circumstance appeared to me Somewhat Singular, as he had before mentioned to me his design of Proceeding to Paris when he had finished his business here & should have an answer to the Letter he had written to your Excellency. He left Sn. Ildefonso a short time Afterwards & I have not seen or heard from him since— This Sir is all that I know on the Subject. I was much hurt & vexed by the forwardness & imprudence of Mr Montgomery who in other respects is a very worthy man & has been useful to many of our Countrymen since the Commencement of the Late War—

I find myself in a very disagreable situation here, owing to a total want of intelligence from Congress— I have recd but two public Letters in 15 months— The one dated Septr 1782 the Other in May 1783— The last advised me that my Conduct Was fully approved of—[6] I have no cypher and therefore am constrained to employ private Conveyances for Letters which I do not wish to submit to the inspection of Others— Safe opportunities do not often occur— This causes me an apprehension of irregularity in my American Correspondence which causes me great Uneasiness— Almost all the Intelligence I receive comes thro' the Channel of Public Prints. Thus having matters but of Little importance on which to address the Minister, I have few occasions of seeing him, for mere visits of Compliment must be tiresome to a Man, whose time is occupied by so many important Affairs— In short the Silence of Congress, the irregularity of remittances as well from the Public as from

6. Livingston to Carmichael, Sept. 12, 1782, and May 7, 1783: Wharton, *Diplomatic Correspondence*, V, 725–6; VI, 408–9.

those who have the care of my property in America have almost entirely disgusted me with my present carreer and incline me to desire to return to my Native Country— I hope that Congress hath proceeded to the Nomination of a Minister to this Court on receiving Mr Jays resignation— I informed them that the Spanish Minister plenipotentiary would not proceed to America until it was known here that one had been appointed. You will probably see at Paris Mr Musquiz— The Polite Attentions which I receive from his Father the Minister of Finance, induce me to request your Excellencys particular Notice of the Son.[7] The Bank established by the Protection of the Ct de Florida Blanca[8] has been conducted with such activity & prudence that it has been able to give in nine months a dividend of more than five pr. Ct. to the Accionists— The influx of Money expected soon from Spanish America begins already to lessen the Depretiation on the paper money, which will probably be on par when The Specie arrives, as your Excellency knows that this paper bears an Interest of four pr. cent, Those who keep their cash in their Coffers will prefer it to Specie— The Sum in the Latter which is expected is said to amt. to upwards of twenty million of Dollars, exclusive of the other produce of the Country— I cannot ask your Excellency to give yourself the Trouble of writing to me, but I hope if you should receive any information from America that may be interesting or usefull to me, My Namesake[9] will supply what the multiplicity of your Occupations will not permit you to do— I beg your Excy to have the goodness to mention me in a proper Manner to all who do me the honor to remember me, I flatter myself that the Marquis de la Fayette, The Cts D Estaing & Montmorin are of the Number. Indeed if

7. Carmichael informed Livingston on Aug. 30, 1783, that Charles III had chosen as the Spanish minister to the United States the marqués de Múzquiz, who was currently in London: Wharton, *Diplomatic Correspondence*, VI, 667. The nomination was subsequently canceled. Ignacio de Múzquiz y Clemente, marqués de Múzquiz (1759–1813), was the son of finance minister Miguel de Múzquiz y Goyeneche, conde de Gausa: Didier Ozanam, *Les Diplomates espagnols du XVIIIe siècle: introduction et répertoire biographique (1700–1808)* (Madrid and Bordeaux, 1998), pp. 361–2.
8. The Banco de San Carlos: XXXVIII, 22n.
9. WTF.

I have their good opinion, I can promise myself the satisfaction of not being forgot by Others.

With the highest respect & most Affectionate regard I have the honor to be Your Excellencys Most Obliged & Humble Sert   WM. CARMICHAEL

P.S.   Madrid 4th Feby 1784

I have kept the preceeding letter by me in daily expectation of sending it by a Gentleman recommended Me by Mr Adams who purposed setting out Post for Paris— Finding however that he has business to terminate which may still detain him some time here— I venture it by the common conveyance— I beg you will be pleased to inform Mr Grand that I have written him twice since the Month of August & have no acknowledgement of the receipt of my Letters— By the Gentleman Above mentioned I shall have the honor to send your Excellency two Spanish productions which the Ct de Campomanes now at the head of the Council of Castile gave me for you— I wish that your Excellency would send me the French Translation of our Constitutions to present him in your name— The kind notice that this Eminent Patriot has taken of me ever since my arrival here calls for my warmest gratitude. He has placed a medal which the Ct. de Montmorin gave me, struck to commemorate our Independance in the Collection of the Medals of the Academy of history— With the highest respect & the most Affectionate regard I have the honor to be Your Excellencys Most Obliged & Most Humble Sert   WM. CARMICHAEL

From Dumas   ALS:[1] Library of Congress

Monsieur   La haie 15e. Janv. 1784.

Je n'ai qu'un instant de reste pour vous informer, que Mr. Adams est arrivé de Londres,[2] & reparti hier pour Amster-

1. The bottom half of the sheet, beneath the signature, is missing. As a consequence, only a small portion of the address (written on the verso) is visible.

2. JA had received word from his Dutch bankers on Dec. 29 that Morris had sent them new drafts totaling 750,000 ƒ., which they would have to

dam d'où je l'espere de retour dans peu de jours. J'espere aussi que l'incluse arrivera assez à temps pour être acheminée s'il se peut avec ma précédente au Congrès.[3]

Je suis avec mon respectueux dévouement, De votre Excellence le très-humble & très-obéissant serviteur,

C. W. F. DUMAS

A Son Excellence Mr. Franklin M.P. des E.U.

From Charles Thomson   ALS: American Philosophical Society

Dear Sir   Annapolis 15 Jany 1784

Yesterday nine States being for the first time since October last represented, Congress immediately took up and ratified the definitive treaty with the unanimous consent not only of all the states represented but of *every* individual Member in Congress. And that it might reach you with the greatest dispatch they immediately sent off col J Harmar with the ratification by the way of New York, there being no vessel sailing from this bay. They also sent a duplicate to be forwarded by Mr Morris, and this day from an earnest desire that it may if possible arrive in due time they have determined to send lieut col D S. Franks with a triplicate to take the chance of a vessel from some of the eastern ports.

I wrote a few lines by Col Harmar[4] to inform you that I had received your favour of the 13 Sept with the papers enclosed and have taken steps to obtain the information desired. I have written to Mr R Haines respecting Mr Marggrander. And have directed enquiries to be made respecting Charles Francis D'Averton and Gabriel Vigeral.[5] The memorial of Doct D Barry & Wife

---

protest for insufficient funds. JA and JQA set out for Holland on Jan. 2, 1784, reaching The Hague on Jan. 12: *Adams Correspondence*, v, 316n; *Adams Papers*, XV, 432–6, 438.

3. Doubtless the Jan. 15 postscript to his dispatch no. 37; see the annotation of Dumas to BF, Jan. 9.

4. Above, Jan. 14. See the annotation there for Marggrander, whom he mentions immediately below.

5. For the inquiries BF forwarded, concerning these two Frenchmen who had served the United States but whose families had not heard from them for several years, see XL, 625n and the references there. Thomson sent

I have communicated to the delegates of North Carolina, but apprehend if matters are as stated in their memorial they have only to send an Agent with proper powers to obtain the object of their wishes. As to the paper stating the Granville claim I have also communicated it to the North-Carolina delegates, but apprehend that is a business which must be settled with the government of the States as the claim of Mr Lotbinier must be with the government of the state where his lands lie.[6] The demand on Baron Steuben is only proper for an Attorney at Law, and by no means a state Matter and therefore I must beg leave to decline meddling with it.—[7]

I have the satisfaction to inform you that a disposition begins to prevail in the states to comply with the acquisitions of Congress and to grant funds for the regular payment of the interest and discharge of the principal of the debts contracted by the war.[8] I make no doubt but the creditors in Europe are anxious and uneasy at the backwardness of the States. But whoever consults the history of Nations will find that taxation is among the late Acts of government, that in governments which have been long established it is not without great difficulty that permanent funds are introduced and even in the oldest governments new taxes often occasion great uneasiness. Considering therefore that in the United States every thing is new and unusual instead of being surprized at the backwardness of the people in this respect, it is rather a matter of wonder that they have made so great a progress and have discovered such a facility in getting the better of that aversion to taxes which is so universally prevalent. For my own part I have a great confidence in the good

English translations of the inquiries to Michael Hillegas on Dec. 30: Smith, *Letters*, XXI, 245–6.

6. Thomson had mentioned the Barrys and the Granville claim in his letter of Jan. 14; see the annotation there. For the claims of Michel-Alain Chartier de Lotbinière to two seigneuries near Lake Champlain, which BF forwarded to Thomson, see, in particular, XXXIX, 398–9, 401.

7. See XL, 626n.

8. Thomson's optimism was misplaced as remittances from the states continued to be inadequate even to service the foreign debt: Jack N. Rakove, *The Beginnings of National Politics: an Interpretive History of the Continental Congress* (New York, 1979), p. 339.

sense of my country men in general, nor can I admit a doubt but that they will speedily fall upon measures to do justice to all the public creditors. Though you and I have lived to see a great work accomplished, yet much still remains to be done to secure the happiness of this Country. May that Almighty Being who has thus far conducted us safely through many scenes of difficulty and distress inspire the people of these United States with wisdom to improve the opportunity now afforded of becoming a happy nation.—

I need not recommend col Franks to your notice as you are already acquainted with him.[9] He has great merit for the early part he took & the sacrifices he has made in the late controversy & for his steady adherence to our cause.

I long for the pleasure of seeing you, but forego that pleasure with the more ease as I am sensible you are usefully employed in a work which is of great importance to our Country. I need not assure you that I am with the most perfect esteem & respect Dear Sir Your affectionate old friend   CHA THOMSON

Doct B. Franklin

Endorsed: Cha. Thomson Esqr to B F. Jan. 15. 1784

From Jean-Georges Treuttel

ALS: American Philosophical Society

Monsieur,   Strasbourg le 15. Janvr. 1784.

Votre Excellence est déjà instruite de l'Almanac Américain qui a été entrepris à Berlin:[1] je m'empresse d'avoir l'honneur d'être le premier à Vous en présenter un & à Vous en faire hommage au nom du libraire entrepreneur le Sr. Spener qui est de mes amis. La beauté, Monsieur, dont il a exécuté ce petit ouvrage, sans enchérir sur le prix, qui n'est que de trois Livres,

9. Franks carried letters from Morris to BF and Jay in 1781; see XXXV, 255, 266; XXXVI, 23.

1. *Historisch-genealogischer Calender oder Jahrbuch der merkwürdigsten neuen Welt-Begebenheiten,* compiled by Johann Karl Philipp Spener. In May, 1783, when Spener asked BF for help with the illustrations, Treuttel offered to serve as an intermediary: XL, 68–71, 108.

mérite, ce me semble les suffrages du Public, mais si Votre Excellence daigne lui faire la grace de mettre ce petit ouvrage sous Sa protection, ce sera certainement le plus grand accueil qui pourra lui arriver, & dont l'effet pourroit pénétrer jusqu'aux vastes pays même dont la révolution étonnante a fourni la matiere.

Etant chargé, Monsieur, du dépôt de cet Almanac pour mes environs & la france, je Suis à même de pouvoir satisfaire incessamment à Vos ordres y relatifs, & serai enchanté s'il plaira à Votre Excellence à m'en honorer. Dommage que la traduction françoise n'en a pas eu lieu, le traducteur tombé malade, en a fait lever l'entreprise après qu'il y en eut même cinq à six feuilles d'imprimées.

Monsieur Gérard,[2] ayant eu la bonté de m'offrir son entremise pour l'expédition de ce volume, j'en profite d'autant plus que sous la grace de Ses auspices j'ose mieux espérer d'obtenir celle de Votre approbation.

J'ai l'honneur d'être avec la considération la plus respectueuse Monsieur De Votre Excellence Le très-humble & très-obéissant Serviteur   TREUTTEL
                    Libraire cidevant Bauer & Treuttel.

From Vergennes

LS: Library of Congress; draft: Archives du Ministère des affaires étrangères

A Versailles le 15. Janvier 1784.

J'ai l'honneur, Monsieur, de vous envoyer en original une lettre qui m'a été ecrite par un Sr. Schaffer[3] qui se dit Lieutenant Colonel de la Milice des Etats Unis, et qui est actuellement détenu dans les prisons de la Conciergerie dans l'attente du Jugement d'un procès criminel qui s'instruit contre lui au Chatelet de Paris. Il paroit, Monsieur, que vous avez connoissance de cette affaire, Je ne puis que m'en remettre au jugement que vous

2. Most likely Conrad-Alexandre Gérard, who since 1781 had served as the *préteur royal* of Strasbourg: *DBF*.

3. BF had L'Air de Lamotte make a copy of this Dec. 28 letter (APS) before returning it to Vergennes. For its contents see BF's reply of Jan. 17.

croirez devoir porter sur les raisons que ce particulier allégue en sa faveur. Je vous prie de vouloir bien en me renvoyant sa lettre, me faire part de ce que vous en pensez.

J'ai l'honneur d'être très sincerement, Monsieur, votre très humble et très obéissant serviteur   DE VERGENNES

M. Franklin.

From Jonathan Williams, Sr.

ALS: American Philosophical Society

Hond sr—   Boston Janry 15th. 1784—
I hope you Will excuse me, for the Liberty I take in advice-ing you, of the Town of Franklin, & how it Came to be thus Named, a part of the people of Wrentham Wh. Town was too Large, a parish of 40 years Standing prefer'd a petition to the General Court 1778 at the Very time, that we or they, heard that you was Assassinated, in Commeration [commemoration] of Doctr Franklin the people Where Unanimous, in Nameing there Town by the Name of Franklin, Whos Name & Per-son they highly Esteemd,[4] the Town or people are Now about Boulding a New Meeting House,[5] & I find they would Bould a Stepel if they had a prospect of Gitting a Bell. I happn'd to be in Compeny with two of the most Respectable & of the Com-mette, they Expressd a Wish that Doctr Franklin Would pre-sent them a Bell, as it would be Recd by the Town from him in prefrence to anybody in the World— I find the house is to be, 60 foot Long, 42 foot Wide, about 26 foot high. Franklin Town is 25 Miles from Boston in the Way to providence—as

4. The petition to set off the western portion of Wrentham as a separate town did not specify a name. The Mass. General Court, which received that petition, at first suggested Exeter, but the name was changed to Frank-lin by the time the town was incorporated on March 2, 1778: Mortimer Blake, *A History of the Town of Franklin, Mass.* . . . (Franklin, Mass., 1879), pp. 40–3.

5. In April, 1784, the town voted £200 towards building a new meeting-house, but that decision was overturned the following year. Plans for a new meetinghouse were finally settled at the end of 1787, and the building was completed in 1789: *ibid.*, pp. 90–2.

I dont know Whether you Will think proper to take Notice of this Letter therefore I Shall Say Nothing about it—[6]

We are all Well my Love to Billey I am as Ever Your Dutifull Nephew   JONA WILLIAMS

NB I am told that your Bill on the Late doctr Cooper Will be paid out of his Estate

Addressed: His Excellency Benjamin Franklin Esqr. / at Passy / In / France

To Ingenhousz

ALS: New York Public Library; copy: Library of Congress

Dear Friend,   Passy, Jan. 16. 1784

I have this Day received your Favour of the 2d Instant. Every Information in my Power respecting the Balloons I sent you just before Christmas,[7] contain'd in Copies of my Letters to Sir Joseph Banks. There is no Secret in the Affair, and I make no doubt that a Person coming from you would easily obtain a Sight of the different Balloons of Mongolfier & Charles, with all the Instructions wanted; and if you undertake to make one, I think it extreamly proper and necessary to send an ingenious Man here for that purpose. Otherwise for want of Attention to some particular Circumstance, or of being acquainted with it, the Experiment might miscarry, which being in an Affair of so much public Expectation, would have bad Consequences, draw upon you a great deal of Censure, and affect your Reputation. It is a serious thing to draw out from their Affairs all the Inhabitants of a great City & its Environs, and a Disappointment makes them angry. At Bourdeaux lately, a Person who pretended to send up a Balloon & had received Money of many People, not being able to make it rise, the Populace were so exasperated that they pull'd down his House, and had like to have kill'd him.—

6. BF's answer has not been located, but Jane Mecom read it before writing to BF on Oct. 21. She saw that he intended to donate to the town of Franklin books for a parish library rather than a bell, "hopeing the Franklins will Prefer Sense to Sound": Van Doren, *Franklin-Mecom*, pp. 231–2.

7. BF to Ingenhousz, Dec. 24.

It appears as you observe, to be a Discovery of great Importance; and what may possibly give a new Turn to human Affairs. Convincing Sovereigns of the Folly of Wars, may perhaps be one Effect of it: since it will be impracticable for the most potent of them to guard his Dominions. Five Thousand Balloons capable of raising two Men each, would not cost more than Five Ships of the Line: And where is the Prince who can afford so to cover his Country with Troops for its Defense, as that Ten Thousand Men descending from the Clouds, might not in many Places do an infinite deal of Mischief, before a Force could be brought together to repel them?— It is a pity that any national Jealousy, should, as you imagine it may, have prevented the English from prosecuting the Experiment, since they are such ingenious Mechanicians, that in their Hands it might have made a more rapid Progress towards Perfection, & all the Utility it is capable of affording. The Balloon of Messrs Charles & Robert, was really fill'd with inflammable Air. The Quantity being great it was expensive, & tedious in filling, requiring two or three Days & Nights constant Labour. It had a *Soupape* near the Top, which they could open by pulling a String and thereby let out some Air when they had a mind to descend; and they discharg'd some of their Ballast of Sand, when they would rise again. A great deal of Air must have been let out when they landed, so that the loose Part might envelope one of them; yet the Car being lightned by that one getting out of it, there was enough left to carry up the other rapidly. They had no Fire with them. That is us'd only in Messrs Mongolfier's Globe, which is open at Bottom, and Straw constantly burnt to keep it up. This kind is sooner & cheaper fill'd; but must be much bigger to carry up the same Weight; since Air rarify'd by Heat is only twice as light as common Air, & inflammable Air ten times lighter. M. de Morveau a famous Chemist at Dijon, has found an inflammable Air that will cost only a 25th part of the Price of what is made by Oil of Vitriol pour'd on Iron Filings. They say it is made from Sea Coal. Its comparative Weight is not mentioned.—[8]

8. In the *Jour. de Paris* of Jan. 7, 1784, Louis-Bernard Guyton, *dit* Guyton-Morveau, announced the opening of a subscription in Dijon for the

I dispatch'd your Letters by the petit Poste to day as soon as I receiv'd them.—[9]

As the Pacquet of German Papers & Almanacs were 18 Months in getting to your hands,[1] I begin to fear for my last Packet, since it was trusted to the same Conveyance, being sent to the Ambassadors, who promis'd to take care of it. I therefore send a Copy of my Letter with this per Post, but I cannot copy the other Papers (they being too long) so as to go by this Courier.— Nor can I now add farther but that I am, as ever, my dear Friend, Yours most affectionately   B FRANKLIN

I have still some Letters of yours to answer.—

Dr. Ingenhausz

Addressed:[2] A Monsieur / Monsieur Le Dr. Ingenhauss / Medecin de Sa Majesté Imperiale / à *Vienne* / en *Autriche.*

construction and launch of a balloon, to be elevated by an unspecified and inexpensive type of inflammable gas. He later revealed that the substance was hydrogen distilled from potatoes: *DBF;* Barthélemy Faujas de Saint-Fond, *Premiere suite de la description des expériences aérostatiques de MM. de Montgolfier* ... (Paris, 1784), pp. 246–7.

9. BF's account of postage shows payments on Jan. 17 and 18 for sending a letter and a packet, respectively, for Ingenhousz: Account XXV (XXXII, 3).

1. As Ingenhousz complained in his letter of Jan. 2.

2. The address was added by L'Air de Lamotte.

From Pierre-Charles L'Enfant, the Chevalier de Villefranche, and the Chevalier de Rochefontaine[3]

AL: American Philosophical Society

[c. January 16, 1784][4]

Mrs. L'Enfant, de Villefranche et de Rochefontaine Se sont presentés pour assurer Monsieur le Docteur franklin de leurs devoirs respectueux, à leur arrivée d'amerique—

3. The wording of this note, written on a half-sheet of paper, leads us to suspect that L'Enfant had not yet called on BF, though he had been in Paris since the middle of December; see the headnote to Bariatinskii's Dec. 22 letter. If that is the case, then he and his companions, French engineers newly arrived from Philadelphia, may have called on BF to discuss the French branch of the Society of the Cincinnati. Genton de Villefranche had gone to America in 1777 with Du Coudray. He rose in rank from captain to lieutenant-colonel of engineers: Bodinier, *Dictionnaire*. For Béchet de Rochefontaine see XXXI, 11n. Both officers remained in the United States until at least the end of November, when they secured debt certificates from the treasury and an advance of back pay from Robert Morris: *Morris Papers*, VIII, 751, 752–3n, 781, 785.

4. On either Jan. 16 or 19 (the evidence is conflicting), Rochambeau hosted the first official meeting of the French chapter of the Society of the Cincinnati, which all three men attended. The newly manufactured eagle badges were distributed on this occasion: Asa B. Gardiner, *The Order of the Cincinnati in France . . .* (n.p., 1905), pp. 14–16. It was reported that d'Estaing refused to accept his badge until naval officers were admitted to the society. Whether or not this is true, there was widespread dissatisfaction among French naval officers about their being excluded and d'Estaing had written GW a letter of protest on Dec. 25, 1783. The society changed its policy to include naval officers at its next meeting in May, 1784: Minor Myers, Jr., *Liberty without Anarchy: a History of the Society of the Cincinnati* (Charlottesville, 1983), pp. 62, 149–51; *Gaz. de Leyde*, Feb. 20, 1784, sup.; Edgar E. Hume, ed., *General Washington's Correspondence concerning The Society of the Cincinnati* (Baltimore, 1941), p. 148; Bachaumont, *Mémoires secrets*, XXV, 89.

To Vergennes

LS:[5] Archives du Ministère des affaires étrangères; press copy of LS: Library of Congress

Sir   Passy. Jany. 17th. 1784

I received the Letter your Excellency did me the honour of writing to me the 15th. Instant, inclosing one from a certain Schaffer, who calls himself Lieutenant Colonel of the Continental Militia, requesting that you would cause to be restored to him a Bill of Exchange for 60 Dollars, that has my Name on it, and which, with his other Papers, has been seiz'd & deposited in the *Greffe criminel du Chatelet;* and complaining that neither the Consul nor myself afford him any Protection;[6] and you are pleased to desire my Sentiments on the Affair. This same Schaffer has been in Paris now about three Years; but this is the first time I have heard any mention of his military Character: He brought a little Money with him, as I understood, to purchase Goods. But he soon fell into the hands of a Set of Sharpers, and being a young Man of very weak Understanding, having neither Good Sense enough to be an honest Man, nor Wit enough for a Rogue though with a strong Inclination, they first cheated him, (as he complained to me,) and then join'd with him to cheat others. For this purpose they got his Name inserted in the Al-

---

5. In the hand of BFB. BF added the complimentary close before signing.

6. Shaffer's letter to Vergennes, dated Dec. 28, 1783, fills three dense pages. It begins: "Je suis étranger, je suis américain, cette double qualité me donne quelques droits à votre puissante Protection." Writing from the Conciergerie, where he is detained for reasons he does not understand, he states that he has been abandoned by both the minister plenipotentiary and consul of the United States. Not understanding French well, he complains of having been interrogated many times without an interpreter, which is surely against the law of nations. He is the son of a wealthy and respectable family; in fact, he himself is "riche," owning three houses in Philadelphia and much land. He details a record of service in the American militia, and mentions that his brother is a member of Congress. His treatment has been monstrous and cruel; French authorities seem to be out to frame him. Vergennes is his last hope, and he asks for his help in reclaiming the bill of exchange for 60 dollars, signed by BF, that was seized along with his other papers. If Vergennes wishes, Shaffer can explain why BF and Barclay have refused him help. (A copy in L'Air de Lamotte's hand is at the APS.)

manack Royal of 1782, & 1783 among the Bankers, under the Title of *John Schaffer & Compagnie, Commissionaires des Etats Unis de l'Amerique, rue des Fossés St. Marcel,* to which Title they had not the smallest Pretence; but it served to give them some Credit with the honest but ignorant Shopkeepers of Paris, with whose Complaints of our *Commissionaire's* not Paying I have been frequently troubled. It is by this running in Debt & by borrowing where he could, that he has for sometime subsisted: and I understand it that for some of these *Escroqueries* that he is now in Prison. When he was there the first time, about two Years ago, not having then so bad an Opinion of him, I interested myself in his Favour, endeavoured to accommodate his Affairs, & lent him some Money in his Distress; which he has never repaid; and yet on various Pretences of Sickness and Misery has obtained more from me lately; but I am now quite tired of him; as is also Mr. Barclay; and if I have refused to make Use of any Interest I may be supposed to have, to screen him from Punishment, it is because I think it prostituting the Interest of a Minister to employ it in Protection of Knaves; and I am really ashamed to appear in his favour, and afraid that my doing it would tend to lessen the weight of any Application I might hereafter have occasion to make in behalf of an honester Man. The Bill he mentions is I suppose one of the Loan-Office Interest Bills sent to him by his Brother thro' the hands of Mr. Barclay, which I accepted, & it will be paid when presented to Mr Grand. I make no Objection to its being deliver'd up to him, tho' the Creditors perhaps who prosecute him may, for whose Use probably his Effects have been seized.

The Account he gives of his Riches, is, I believe altogether as fictitious, as his Characters of *Lieut. Colonel, & Commissionaire des Etats Unis;* but that his Father & Brother-in-law are respected Persons in Pensilvania, is true, Mr. Barclay has some Knowledge of them; for their Sakes, if the Punishment of the *Carcan,* which I hear is intended for him, could be commuted for one less *fletrissant,* a longer Banishment, or the like, I should be glad; & if your Excellency can obtain this for him without too much Trouble, I shall in their Behalf acknowledge it as a Favour. With great Respect, I am, Sir, Your Excellency's most obedient & most humble Servant   B. FRANKLIN

P.S. I return the Letter enclos'd. I take it to be written by one Beaumont his Advocate.

His Excellency the Count de Vergennes

From John Charretié   LS: American Philosophical Society

Monsieur   Londres, le 17. Janvier 1784.

Je suplie Votre Excellence de vouloir bien recevoir mes excuses si je n'ai point eu l'honneur de vous aller faire ma cour à Passy pendant le séjour momentané que j'ai fait à Paris et à Versailles. Les ordres du Ministre ont causé mon départ précipité sans me permettre cette satisfaction dont j'etois si jaloux. A mon arrivée ici, je n'ai point manqué de faire tenir à Monsieur Sargent la lettre dont vous aviez bien voulu me charger.[7]

Comblé des bontés de Votre Excellence, permettez, Monsieur, que j'ose encore les implorer aujourd'hui en vous suppliant de m'honorer de votre puissante recommandation auprès de M Le Maréchal de Castries. Je viens d'avoir l'honneur de faire passer à ce Ministre un Etat de mes dépenses personnelles ici pendant les trois années d'exercice de ma commission. Un modique traitement annuel de Douze Cent Livres m'a réduit à la nécessité de recourir à mes amis pour être en etat de servir mon Roi et mon païs, ce que j'ai toujours fait avec le plus vrai Zèle, mais je reste endetté d'une somme de Douze mille Livres tournois montant de ce même Etat et dont la rentrée est pour moi de la plus grande importance. Je sais combien M Le Maréchal est juste, et comme je sais aussi, Monsieur, combien il a d'estime et d'attachement pour la personne de Votre Excellence, je suis sûr qu'honoré de votre appui, mon remboursement ne souffrira aucune difficulté. Vous me rendrez un service très-essentiel et dont je conserverai, ainsi que de vos bontés passées, la plus sincère et la plus vive reconnoissance.

Je ne crois pas avoir besoin, Monsieur, de renouveller à Votre Excellence l'offre de mes services en ce païs-ci. Puisque vous

7. For Charretié's visit see his Dec. 28 letter. He doubtless carried back to London BF's letter to John and Rosamond Sargent dated Dec. 29.

connoissez mon cœur, vous savez que je m'estimerai toujours heureux de pouvoir vous temoigner mon Zèle.

Je suis avec un profond respect Monsieur De Votre Excellence Le très-humble très-obéissant et très-dévoué serviteur

JN. CHARRETIÉ
Chargé de la rentrée des Prisoniers
françois répandus en Angleterre

Au Caffé de la Nouvelle York. Sweeting's Alley à Londres.

Addressed: A son Excéllence. / Monsieur Le Dr. Franklin. / Ministre Plénipotentiere des Etats / Unis de L'Amerique à La Cour de / France. / a Passy.

Notation: Charne John, London 17 Janvr. 1784

From Robert Morris

LS: American Philosophical Society; copy: Library of Congress

Sir   Philada January 17th. 1784

Colo Harmar the Bearer of this Letter is just arrived from Annapolis charged with the Definitive Treaty Ratified by Congress with which he is to proceed for Paris in order to deliver the same to the Ministers who negotiated the Treaty, that the Ratifications may be exchanged— Congress have directed me to supply Colo Harmar with Money to defray his Necessary Expences,[8] In Consequence of this Order I have advanced him Two Hundred Spanish Dollars here and now write to Mr. Grand Requesting that he may Supply such farther sum as you shall agree may be proper & necessary for the above purpose—[9] I suppose His Excellency the President of Congress has Recommended Colo Harmar to your Notice— He has been a brave and deserving officer which alone will procure him your favorable Attention.

8. Congress' resolution and Mifflin's letter to Morris, both dated Jan. 14, are in *JCC*, XXVI, 29, and *Morris Papers*, IX, 29.

9. A copy of his Jan. 17 letter to Grand is at the Library of Congress: *Morris Papers*, IX, 958.

I am Your Excellencys Most obedt & very humble servt.

ROBT MORRIS

His Excellency Benjamin Franklin Esqre Minister Plenipotentiary &a. Passy

Addressed: His Excellency / Benjamin Franklin Esqre / Minister Plenipotentiary &a / Paris

From the Vicomte de Toustain-Richebourg[1]

ALS: American Philosophical Society

paris 17 jer. 1784. Rue neuve st. Gilles, au marais.
Monsieur

La société patriotique-Bretonne formée dans la presqu'île de Rhuis, unie sous les auspices de Leurs altesses Royales MONSIEUR et MADAME au premier musée françois,[2] et de la quelle j'ay l'honneur d'être membre et inspecteur-correspondant, m'accorde la flatteuse commission de vous donner avis des hommages rendus dans sa solemnité du 17 7bre dernier aux grandes qualités militaires, civiles et patriotiques de Son excellence Monsieur le General Wasington, ainsi qu'aux éminentes vertus et lumieres de Son excellence Monsieur l'Ambassadeur Franklin. Ces deux illustres noms ont été proclamés et inscrits avec toute la distinction qui leur est due. M. le Cte de Sérent,[3] ancien

1. An officer and author who applied to BF for a military commission in America in April, 1778: XXVI, 29–30.

2. The Breton society evidently took its inspiration from the Parisian club *Lycée françois,* also known after its patron as *Museé de Monsieur.* Both salons offered their members, including women, access to newspapers, journals, and books, as well as a venue to hear lectures and discuss politics. Among the society's members were the comtesse de Genlis (XXXVII, 471n), the baronne de Bourdic (XXXIX, 483–4), and the comtesse de Beauharnois (XXX, 387n): Vivian R. Gruder, *The Notables and the Nation: the Political Schooling of the French, 1787–1788* (Cambridge, Mass., and London, 2007), pp. 201–2; Bachaumont, *Mémoires secrets,* XXVI, 61.

3. Armand-Sigismonde-Félicité-Marie, comte de Sérent, a military officer and governor of Presqu'île de Rhuis, was the society's founder: Jean-François-Eugène Robinet, Adolphe Robert, and Julien Le Chaplain, eds., *Dictionnaire historique et biographique de la Révolution et de l'Empire, 1789–1815* (2 vols., Paris, [1899]); Bachaumont, *Mémoires secrets,* XXVI, 60.

commissaire de la noblesse de Bretagne, a rempli dignement á cette occasion les fonctions d'Orateur. Je suis avec un profond respect Monsieur Votre tres-humble et tres-obéissant serviteur

LE VICOMTE DE TOUSTAIN-RICHEBOURG
major de cavalerie, ancien commissaire
de la noblesse aux états de Bretagne,
associé de plusieurs academies.

A Son excellence Monsieur le Docteur Francklin ambassadeur des Etats-unis d'Amerique auprès de Sa majesté Tres-chrétienne.

Notation: Toutain, Richebourg 17 Janr. 1784.

From Anton Georg Eckhardt[4]

Partial copy:[5] American Philosophical Society

[January 18, 1784]
Comme j'ai pu remarquer, Monsieur, par les Papiers publics votre attention pour la Decouverte si distingué de Monsieur Montgolfier (que je languis infiniment de connoitre), Je puis vous informer que depuis les Experiences que nous avons faites ici les premiers de la Machine Aerostatique qui ont eu le plus desirable Succés (par le procedé même de Monsieur Montgolfier c'est à dire au moyen de la Rarefaction de l'air) nous pensons avoir trouvé un objet qui pourroit lui etre d'utilité, C'est un *Poile* dont le feu se renouvelle et se nourrit de lui même et a cette Proportion de Chaleur qu'on puisse le desirer (même assez forte pour fondre l'Argent et le Cuivre) et cela par la flamme d'une matiere qui est extremement legere et a bon marché et meme tellement qu'elle ne revient pas a la moitié des frais du Chauffage ordinaire, et dont on peut ainsi prendre provision avec soi dans la Machine Aérienne pour une bonne espace de temps. Nous avons encore formé des Idées sur la Construction la plus favorable de cette Machine pour voguer dans les Airs, et

4. A Dutch inventor whom BF had known for many years: XXXII, 247n.
5. The postscript only, copied by BFB. BF sent the original and its enclosures to Le Roy on Feb. 25; the cover letter is below.

les Aides qu'on pourroit y adapter pour la diriger et nous serions charmés de les Communiquer a Mr. Montgolfier si vous nous le conseillez, desirant infiniment d'etre utile a cet Homme de Genie si distingué et d'aider a la perfection d'une Decouverte qui pourroit devenir assurement de la plus grande Utilité pour le public.

Parmi les Idées qui nous sont venues Monsieur sur son Utilité Je ne puis laisser de vous confier celle ci, qu'elle pourroit assurement servir à decouvrir des Terres inconnues jusqu'a ce jour en l'employant avec les vaisseaux qui vont a leur decouverte; quand on pourroit, etant arrivé a telle hauteur ou l'on presumeroit pouvoir se trouver des Terres, s'elever alors avec un Ballon auquel on pourroit attacher une Corde, et alors s'elever a la plus grande hauteur; l'on pourroit voir avec des Instrumens d'observation à une très grande distance s'il se trouve des Terres et au moyen d'une Boussole noter leurs directions et situations, quand on pourroit toujours facilement retourner au vaisseau en retirant la sus dite corde soit au Ballon ou sur le Vaisseau dans le cas qu'on n'eut pas encore imaginé de diriger le Ballon a volonté. Les Ballons Aerostatiques peuvent etre encore employés à plusieurs Usages les plus Utiles, et c'est une invention de la plus grande Utilité qui fait assurement le plus grand Honneur a son Auteur.

In Franklin's hand: Postscript of a Letter from Mr Eckhardt of Utrecht dated Jan 18. 1784 to B Franklin

From François-Louis Teissèdre de Fleury

AL: American Philosophical Society

à paris Le 18e. janvier 1784.

Mr. de fleury desesperé de partir de paris, sans avoir L'honneur de préndre Congé, de Mr. Le docteur franklin, à L'honneur de L'assurèr de son Respèct. Il le prie de vouloir bien Rénfermèr dans son prémiér paquèt pour Le congrès; Les Léttres qu'il prènd La Libertè de lui adressèr pour les faire parvenir en amérique.[6] Comme elles sont tres importantes pour Luy, il Le

6. These letters most likely concerned the efforts by Fleury and other French officers to obtain compensation from Congress for their wartime service. Joshua Barney was carrying to La Luzerne an earlier package of

prie de vouloir bien Les Rénfermer dans Le prémièr paquèt quil énvera en amérique, il Luy sera infinimént obligè.

Addressed: a son excéllénce / Monsieur Le docteur franklin. / Ministre plenipotentiaire / des états unis à La Cour de / france / à passy.

Notation: De Fleury

From Samuel Chase

ALS: American Philosophical Society

Dear Sir.   London. 19 Jany. 1784.

On Fryday last I had the Honour to receive your letter of the 6th. Inst., for which be pleased to accept my thanks. The temporary loss of the Papers gives Me no other Concern, that what arises from the Remembrance that your Illness was the Cause of the Accident. I am glad to hear of your Recovery, & sincerely wish You may never again be afflicted with the Gout, Gravel, or any other painful Disorder.

I am not very sanguine in my Expectations of Compensation for the loss of the Ship, in which I was considerably interested. Mr. Jay having been so kind as to promise his Assistance not only to Me, but to Mrs. le Vachè, that he may be informed of the Circumstances in both Cases, I take the liberty to request You to deliver him my letter of 18 of September with the protest of Capt. Belt, & any Papers relative to the Widow of M. le Vachè. If on Consideration Mr. Jay shall think it adviseable to present a Memorial, he will take the trouble to prepare one,[7] and

---

letters on this subject from Fleury and other veterans, which arrived by March 14. Congress considered Fleury's continued appeals on Dec. 16: *Morris Papers*, IX, 186–7; *JCC*, XXVII, 692.

7. Jay did so, and it was endorsed by Lafayette; see Idzerda, *Lafayette Papers*, V, 436, where the document is calendared and a citation given to its location in the Fonds de la Marine. Among BF's papers at the APS are four more documents concerning this incident that Chase must have brought with him to London: the deposition of John Dorsey, acting partner of Dorsey, Wheeler & Co., owners of the *Matilda* (Jan. 18, 1783); the deposition of Michael McNamarre, captain of marines on the *Matilda* (Jan. 13, 1783); the protest of Charles Harrison, captain of the *Jolly Tar* (Oct. 24,

your friendly Interposition & Influence with M. le Marquiss de Castries, & the Marquiss de la Fayette will ever be thankfully remembered and acknowledged by Me.

I have, at present, but little prospect of obtaining the Bank Stock. I intend to return to Maryland in February or March[8] and therefore must relinquish the Pleasure I had proposed to Myself of paying my Respects to You at Paris.—

I most cordially wish You the greatest of all human Blessings, Mens sana in Corpore sano[9] farewell, and beleive Me to be at all times Dear Sir, With Great Respect Your Affectionate Friend & Obedient Servant   SAML. CHASE

From Herman Heyman, Jr.

ALS: American Philosophical Society

Sir!   Bremen the 19 Januari 1784

I had the satisfaction to lay before Your Excellency by the Letter I took the Liberty to address your Excellency the 31 July last[1] a Plan of a Glass-manufactori which I intended to Establish in one of the United Provinces of Nord America for Your

---

1782); and the deposition of Joseph Smith, a passenger on the *Jolly Tar* (Jan. 13, 1783).

8. Those intentions were frustrated by prolonged litigation. In February, when Chase finally engaged the trustees in discussions, he found Grove and the executors of (then-deceased) Osgood Hanbury willing to yield, but Russell—who insisted on compensation for his own confiscated property as a condition to settlement—opposed. Russell filed a Chancery suit against Chase, Grove, and the Bank of England. Chase finally returned to Maryland in August, leaving the case in the hands of his solicitors. It was not resolved until 1804, when Maryland recovered most of its appreciated stock and reinvested dividends, and Chase (then a U.S. Supreme Court justice) received a hefty commission: James Haw et al., *Stormy Patriot: the Life of Samuel Chase* (Baltimore, 1980), pp. 123–4, 127–9; Jacob M. Price, "The Maryland Bank Stock Case: British-American Financial and Political Relations before and after the American Revolution," in *Law, Society, and Politics in Early Maryland*, ed. Aubrey C. Land et al. (Baltimore and London, 1977), pp. 10–31.

9. A healthy mind in a healthy body: Juvenal, *Satire X*, line 356.

1. XL, 420–2.

Consideration; and beg'd most Humbly from your Excellency the Favor to grant me your Skilful Advise on that head, but am hetherto deprived of the honour to Receive any Reply from Your Excellency. But this does not prevent me to Venture again to Address your Excellency a Second Letter, flattering myself that what ever concerns the Prosperity and Extension of your good Country will be agreeabel received from your Excellency; and there fore have the honour to inform you that three other Gentlemen with me Considered most Earnestly on that Plan all the time since, and taking every things back and forwards find that it can't but be very advantageous as well to your good Country as likewise to the Concerners to Errect a Glass-Manufactory in some part of the United states, and we Chused Maryland to be the properest Country for it; beeing a spot of Land where by all the Description we Read it groes the most plenty of Wood, one of my three Friends Mr John Fried Amelong who had the Manage of a Glass Manufactory here in Germany will go himself in the Spring by the first Vessell over to Baltimore and take the Direction of the intended Establishing Glas Manufactory, he Carries besides him 80 more Families all Experienced to our Purpose in the Vessell for Baltimore.[2]

I can't but Expect that our Ardent wishes to encrease our Connection with the United states can't but be satisfactory to Your Excellency and this gives me the Agreeabel Aspects that you'll grant us your Kind Assistance and Protection in our Undertaking, and inform us to who our Friend Mr Amelong must make his first Aplication at Baltimore, or in the State of Marriland, to Errect the Manufactory, and to receive some part of Land fit for the Establishment directed, and your Excellence Opinion would

2. Johann Friedrich Amelung (XL, 421n) left Germany with 68 workers and family members in late spring, and arrived in Baltimore on Aug. 31. Fourteen more workers followed shortly afterward. Amelung purchased a glassworks in Frederick County, Md., acquired additional tracts of land and more equipment, built houses for his workers, established a school, and expanded the operation into the New Bremen Glassmanufactory, the largest in the states. Although its products were considered superior, the enterprise was beset by problems and the owners declared bankruptcy in 1796: Dwight P. Lanmon and Arlene M. Palmer, "John Frederick Amelung and the New Bremen Glassmanufactory," *Journal of Glass Studies*, XVIII (1976), 9–10, 24–38, 135.

be the best Guide for us if we may Expect that Government will grant us every Assistance And give Certain Priviledges, and a part of Land at rent to it, or if we must Purchase the latter and perhaps not find the Reception to fullfil our wishes, and according as such Considerabel undertaking merits, I can't but expect it by what I Know that the Congress wishes are to enlarge and Populate the United States, and I am assured Our small Transport, or may I call it establishing Colonie, will give both Pleasure to the Congress and Honnor to us, as they are all People of the best Conduct Virtue and Understanding, and not like many others which enter in America beeing Rejected in Germany, I shall therefore most Humbly beg from your Excellency the Favor to grant our Mr Amelong some of the best Letters of Introduction & Recommandation for the States of Mariland[3] that he may meet a Agreeabel Reception and not be detained at his Arrival to bring our Speculation to an Accomplishment and Perfection; and through this exposed to a very Considerabel loss by mentaining the many Families without Emploiing them to our Intent[ion].

Give me leave to assure your Excellency of my most devoted Respects and of my Sincere Regard with which I have the Honnor to Remain Sir your most Obedt humbl Servt

HERMAN HEYMAN JR

Addressed: His Excellency Benjamin Frank- / lin, Ambassadeur of the 13 United States / of Nord America & the Court of france / residing / at / Paris

3. In his *Remarks on Manufactures, Principally on the New Established Glass-House, near Frederick-Town, in the State of Maryland* (1787), Amelung wrote that he carried letters of recommendation from BF, JA, and Thomas Barclay to President of Congress Thomas Mifflin, several prominent Md. officials, and many leading merchants. If BF wrote such a letter, it has not been located: Lanmon and Palmer, "John Frederick Amelung and the New Bremen Glassmanufactory," pp. 24, 135.

From the Baron de Feriet ALS: American Philosophical Society

Versailles Le 21 janvier 1784

Je crois, Monsieur, avoir trouvè ici Deux maisons entières qui pouraient Vous convenir;[4] elles ont toutes deux des jardins, mais L'une rèunit a ce qu'il me semble, tous Les avantages et les agrè-mens qu'il est possible de se procurer a versailles; elle est neuve, et n'a point ètè occuppèe quoiqu'elle soit bâtie depuis quelque tems; Les embellissemens ne sont pas même entierement achevés; tout est boisè, Vernissé, et Si bien appropriè, qu'il n'y faut point d'autres meubles que des fauteuils et des lits; on m'a assuré qu'on comptait y mettre pour vint mille francs de glaces, ce qui en fera un vrai bijou. Outre cela il y a un logement si ènorme, que Vous, et tout Votre monde parfaitement Logè, vous pourés encore disposer de quelques appartemens dans Le cas ou Vous auriés quelques amis a Loger. Plusieurs terrasses forment un jardin assès considèrable; il n'est sèparé que par un mur d'un terrein très grand couvert d'une plouse très agrèable pour se promener; ce terrein ètant un des plus èlevés de Versailles, on y jouit de la vue la plus agrèable qu'on puisse avoir ici; il communique au jardin de cette maison par une porte dont Vous auriès La clef, et ce serait pour Vous une promenade d'autant plus agréable, que Vous seriés sur de n'y rencontrer que ceux que Vous Voudriès bien y mener avec Vous. La maison a pour Vue, Le jardin d'un côté, et L'avenue de st. cloud de L'autre. La distance de là, au château, est un peu forte; voila le seul inconvé-nient que j'y trouve, mais il me parait balancè par un trop grand nombre d'avantages, pour qu'il puisse faire quelqu' impression sur Vous; beaucoup de personnes attachèes au chateau ont des Logemens plus èloignés; dans les quartiers plus rapprochès, il serait impossible de trouver de jardins; ayant la facilité de faire de L'èxercice et de prendre L'air sans sortir de chéz Vous, Vous vous promenerés plus souvent que Si vous ètiés obligè pour cela de sortir, et de courrir les risques de rencontrer a chaque pas Une foule d'importuns dont la bonne ville de Versailles est aussi bien pourvue qu'aucune autre du royaume; vous serés habituel-lement dans un meilleur air, et en supposant que Vos porteurs

4. Feriet (XL, 19) evidently knew that BF was considering a move to Ver-sailles; see the annotation of BF to Mifflin, Dec. 26, letter (I).

ne puissent pas vous porter tout d'une traite dans les endroits ou vous voudrés aller, il ne sera pas bien malheureux que dans le milieu de vos courses Les plus èloignées, ils fassent une pause d'une minute; Vous Serès plus souvent chèz Vous que dehors, et rien ne me parait plus convenable qu'un local vaste, agrèable, Sain, et bien situé. Comme je crains, Monsieur, que cette maison ne soit pas long-tems Vacante, Si vous croyés qu'elle puisse vous convenir, vous pouriés charger monsieur Votre fils d'aller La voir Lorsqu'il viendra a versailles. S'il voulait me le mander La veille, ou quelques jours avant, je L'attendrais chèz moy, et en même tems je lui ferais Voir une collection de chaises a porteur, dans le nombre desquelles il en trouverait surement une qui Vous conviendrait; il y en a de toutes les façons et de tous Les prix, parcequ'elles sont D'hazard.

Je Desire bien, Monsieur, pouvoir Vous trouver ici ce qui vous en rendrait le sèjour agreable. Si je suis assés heureux pour ne pas Vous être tout-a-fait inutile, vous ne m'en devrés assurément aucun remerciement; ici plus qu'ailleurs Les hommes n'ont en vue que Leur intérêt personnel; Si a cet ègard je n'ay point èchappé a La corruption gènèrale, il me reste au moins assès de bonne foi pour vous avouer que je travaille a mon bonheur en cherchant a vous faciliter Les moyens de Vous fixer dans La ville que j'habite.

Toute ma famille me charge, Monsieur, de La rappeller a votre souvenir; ne nous oubliès pas, je vous prie, prés de monsieur votre fils; puissions nous tous, vous renouveller dans vingt ans Les vœux que nous formons pour votre bonheur dans ce renouvellement d'annèe.

Agrèés, je vous prie, Les assurance de L'attachement tendre et respectueux avec Lequel j'ay L'honneur D'être Monsieur Votre très humble et très obeissant serviteur   LE BON. DE FERIET

Il y a huit jours que j'ay remis a Mde. La duchesse de Villeroy, quelques verres D'harmonica montés, et parlant aussi parfaitement avec des touches qu'avec les doigts.[5]

---

5. In 1775 the duchesse de Villeroi devised a plan to add keys to BF's armonica. She gave a copy to JW, who passed it on to BF: XXII, 49. The plan is now missing.

Je joins ici mon adresse dans le cas ou mr Votre fils l'aye per-
due, parceque sans cela il trouveroit difficilement mon Logement
rue des bourdonnois Maison de Mr. Ris,
entre la rue St. honoré, et la rue royale.

Notation: De Feriet 21 Janr. 1784

From David Gallwey & Co.

ALS: Archives du Ministère des affaires étrangères

Nantes ce 22 Jany 1784

Mr: Barclay Consul General laid before your Excellency le
Comte de Vergennes letter to the underwriters on the american
ship Nancy Capn. Sewell saild from Philadelphia for L'orient the
16. March 1783. In Consequence of said letter of which annexed
is Coppy[6] The underwriters have summond us at the Court of
Admiralty to pay the premio of insurance at Twenty five per
cent pretending the hostilities ceased only the 4 April in the
american seas—

We are apprehensive the juges will pronounce on Mr. De
Vergennes Letter. We Therefore request your Excellency will
honour us with the result of your Conferance with the minister
on this Subject or let us Know when we may expect your decision to put a stop to the expence of a Process at law of which at
all events a decision can be only given by the Council in Case
you & Mr. De Vergennes shou'd differ in opinion.

We have the honor to be very respectfully Your Excellencys
Most faithfull & obedient Servants   DAVID GALLWEY & CO

His Excellency, Benjamin Franklyn Esqr. Ambassador of the
united states of America at the Court of France

Notation:[7] M de R

6. The enclosure is missing, but for Vergennes' Nov. 15, 1783, letter to
the French underwriters of the *Nancy* see the annotation of Nesbitt to BF,
Dec. 23, above.

7. In Vergennes' hand. BF, or more likely WTF on his behalf, must have
conveyed the present letter to Vergennes, who turned it over to Gérard de
Rayneval.

From Dumas

ALS: Library of Congress; AL (draft): Nationaal Archief

Monsieur   Lahaie 23e.[–27] Janvier[8] 1784

Dans l'espérance que vous avez bien reçu, & eu la bonté d'acheminer mes précédentes pour le Congrès, & notamment mon No. 37 du 18e. Dec. au 8e. Janv., & mon Postcrit du 15e., en voici un autre & dernier du 16e., que vous voudrez bien lire, fermer & acheminer pareillement.[9] Je suis avec tout le respectueux dévouement qui vous est connu, De Votre Excellence Le très humble & très obéissant serviteur   C. W. F. DUMAS

S.E. Mr. Adams est à Amsterdam. Dès que vous saurez, Monsieur, que le Traité définitif avec cette republ. a été signé, ou va l'être entre les Plénipo: hollandois & le Duc de Dorset,[1] je vous serai fort obligé de me le faire écrire promptement par Mr. Votre Petit fils, que je prie d'agréer mes complimens, & de vouloir bien m'informer du bon état de votre santé.

P.S. du 27e. Janv. L'arrivée de Mr. Adams, & l'honneur qu'il m'a fait de me demander pour lui tenir compagnie, est cause que cette Lettre ne peut partir qu'aujourd'hui.

Passy à S.E. Mr. Franklin M.P. des E.U.

Endorsed: Reçu Jan. 31. 1784

From William Hodgson   ALS: American Philosophical Society

Dear sir—   London 23 Jany— 1784

I recd your favor of the 26th Ultimo & have been endeavouring all in my Power ever Since to find out the Value of the two

---

8. Dumas mistakenly wrote "Juin". BF crossed it out and wrote "Janvier".
9. See the annotation of Dumas to BF, Jan. 9.
1. Pitt's new government abandoned Fox's plans to make concessions in the final Anglo-Dutch treaty in order to obtain an alliance with the Netherlands. After minor alterations were made to the preliminary treaty, the final treaty was signed on May 20, 1784: Nicholas Tarling, *Anglo-Dutch Rivalry in the Malay World, 1780–1824* (Cambridge and St. Lucia, Australia, 1962), pp. 10–11. John Frederick Sackville, Duke of Dorset, was appointed

Ships you mention,[2] but hitherto I have not been able to succeed, I find these Ships were released by the Court of Denmark, but so long a Time has elapsed, that those who did the Insurance cannot easily turn to the Acc't indeed the Union had only a trifling Sum done upon her. She belonged to Atkinson the Contractor[3] so that she was laden as I presume for Goverment Acc't, I have been so hostile to A— all the War, that I fear much I shall have great Difficulty in procuring the Value, but I will try every possible method— The other I hope I shall be able to procure from Liverpool to which place she belonged, I shou'd suppose these Ships from their Size & general Idea of Cargoes for such a Voyage coud not be worth less than from 10 to 15 thousand pounds per Ship— I return you my best thanks for your intended Kindness in respect to the Consulship & remain allways Dr sir Your Affectionate Friend & very Hble Servant   WILLIAM HODGSON

To His Ex. B. Franklin Esqr

Addressed: To / His Excellency Benj Franklin Esqr / Minister Plenipotentiary from the United / States of America / a / Paris

Notation: Wm. Hodgson— 23 Jany 1784.—

---

ambassador to the French court in December, 1783, and arrived on Jan. 13: *ODNB*, under Sackville; *Repertorium der diplomatischen Vertreter*, III, 162; Jeremy Black, *British Foreign Policy in an Age of Revolutions, 1783–1793* (Cambridge, New York, and Oakleigh, Australia, 1994), p. 22. Dumas was asking BF for news of the signing because the negotiations were being conducted in France.

2. In their instructions to the American commissioners of Oct. 29, above, Congress ordered BF to pursue the matter of obtaining restitution for the *Union* and *Betsy,* prizes taken during the cruise of John Paul Jones's squadron in 1779 and then turned over to the British by Denmark (XXXI, 261–5). BF's letter to Hodgson has not been located.

3. Doubtless Richard Atkinson (XXII, 301n), a major provisions contractor during the American war: Namier and Brooke, *House of Commons,* II, 32.

From Jean-Antoine Houdon[4]

LS: American Philosophical Society

Monsieur   [before January 24, 1784][5]

J'ai l'honneur de vous prévenir que je dois couler une statüe en bronze: Si cette opération d'un moment peut intérresser votre goût et votre curiosité; je vous prie de me faire celui de vous rendre à onze heures précises du matin 24 de ce mois au lieu indiqué par l'adresse ci-incluse.[6]

4. This generic invitation is the first extant letter from Houdon to BF. The two must have met in 1779, when Houdon's celebrated bust of BF was exhibited at the Salon and BF presented a copy to the Loge des Neuf Sœurs, of which he was then *vénérable* and Houdon was a newly elected member: XXX, frontispiece, xxxi, lxiv–lxv, 231, 238n. According to WTF, Houdon gave BF four copies of the bust, though no evidence survives of when those gifts were made: WTF to Caffiéri, April 3, 1785, APS.

Charles C. Sellers and other scholars have claimed that Houdon was not formally introduced to BF until the fall of 1783, based on a letter of Nov. 8, 1783, from Houdon to an unnamed correspondent, in which the sculptor alludes to the recipient's having recently "presented" him to BF (APS). For a discussion of the sculptor's relationship to BF during this period see Sellers, *Franklin in Portraiture*, pp. 304–16; Jack Hinton, Melissa Meighan, and Andrew Lins, *Encountering Genius: Houdon's Portraits of Benjamin Franklin* (Philadelphia, 2011), pp. 26–37, 70–3.

5. The day Houdon attempted to cast a bronze statue of Diana in one piece, rather than casting individual parts to be assembled by welding, as he had previously done. To his great disappointment, the experiment failed: Guilhem Scherf, *Houdon: Diane chasseresse* (Paris, 2000), p. 24.

Houdon discussed this rarely used casting technique with BF and others shortly before writing the Nov. 8 letter cited above. In that letter, he informed his correspondent that the comte de Buffon had offered to take BF a copy of the "livre en question Sur la fonte de Louis quinze." Suspecting that Buffon might delay, however, Houdon offered to lend BF his own copy, and asked the correspondent to deliver it. The work was undoubtedly Pierre-Jean Mariette, *Description des travaux qui ont précédé, accompagné et suivi la fonte en bronze d'un seul jet de la statue équestre de Louis XV, dit le Bien-Aimé* . . . (Paris, 1768), which detailed the painstaking process of casting Edme Bouchardon's equestrian statue of Louis XV in one piece in 1758. Because Houdon's letter remains among BF's papers, we assume that it was given to BF at the time the volume was delivered.

6. The enclosure is missing. Houdon's atelier at Nos. 197 and 199, rue du Faubourg-Saint-Honoré was in the same building complex as the du Roule foundry where Bouchardon's statue had been cast: Hillairet, *Rues de Paris*, I, 510; Geneviève Bresc-Bautier, "Fonderie et ateliers du Roule," in *Rue du*

J'ai l'honneur d être Monsieur Votre très humble et très obeïssant serviteur./.[7]   HOUDON

From John Adams   AL (draft): Massachusetts Historical Society

Sir   The Hague Jan. 24. 1784.
Desirous of doing all in my Power, to Save Mr Morriss Bills,
I determined to go to Amsterdam, and accordingly, Sett off, the
Beginning of this Month from London, in a Season too rigorous
for Pleasure.—[8] At Harwich we were obliged to wait Several
Days for fair Weather, which when it arrived brought Us little
Comfort as it was very cold And the Wind exactly against Us.
The Packetts were obliged to put to Sea and I embarked in one
of them. We were more than Three Days in advancing Thirty
three Leagues with, So unsteady a Course, and Such a tossing
Vessell that We could not keep a fire, the Weather very cold and
the Passengers all very Seasick. As We could not, on Account of
the great Quantities of Ice upon the Coast, reach Helvoet [Hel-
levoetsluis], We were put on Shore on the Island of Goree [Goe-
ree], where We got a Boors Wagon to carry our Baggage and
We walked about Six Miles to the Town of Goree. Not finding
Iceboats here We were obliged to go in open Boors Waggons
across the Island to Middle Harness [Middelharnis]. Here We
were detained Several Days in very bad Lodgings unable to
find Boats to carry Us over the Arm of the Sea to Helvoet. At
Length Iceboats appeared, and We embarked amidst a Waste of
Ice which passed in and out every day with the Tide, and by the
Force of Oars, & Boat hooks Sometimes rowing, in the Water,
and sometimes dragging on the Ice, which would now & then

Faubourg-Saint-Honoré, ed. Béatrice de Andia and Dominique Fernandès
(Paris, 1994), p. 373.
    7. BF appears not to have accepted this invitation, but WTF evidently did
attend. He met there the comte de Diesbach (*DBF*), to whom he sent a copy
of *Constitutions des treize Etats-Unis de l'Amérique* later in the day: Diesbach
to WTF, Jan. 24 and May 5, 1784, APS.
    8. Dumas wrote of JA's arrival in his Jan. 15 letter to BF, above; see the
annotation there.

498

break & let Us down, in the Course of the Day We got over, and thought ourselves lucky, as the last Boat which passed got stuck in the Ice and was carried out with the tide and brought in again, So that they were out from 9 in the Morning to one O Clock the next night before they reached the opposite Shore. We could not reach Helvoet, but landed on the Dyke about two Miles from it, and took Boors Waggons again for the Brille [Brielle], which We reached at Night. Next Morning We took Ice Boats again to cross another Water obstructed with Ice as before, and then a Third the Maese [Maas], which We found Sufficiently frozen to walk over on the Ice. Another Boors Waggon carried Us to Delft, and from thence a Coach to the Hague. After the Rest of a day or two I went to Amsterdam. Our Bankers had applied to the Regency, and I offered to enter into any reasonable Contract, and to pledge the Faith of the United States for the Performance of it, but all in vain. The Gentlemen of the Regency, Seemed very desirous of doing Something for Us, if they could. But as usual, they are so afraid of making a Precedent, and that other Powers, as much distressed for money as We, would take Advantage and demand the Same favour, that they dare not, and our Bankers were advised to take back their Application, to avoid a certain decision against Us.— Yesterday I returnd to the Hague.

I Should look back with less Chagrin, upon the disagreable Passage from London, if We had Succeeded, in obtaining the Object of it, but I find I am here only to be a Witness that American Credit in this Republick is dead, never to rise again, at least untill the United States Shall all agree upon Some Plan of Revenue, and make it certain that Interest and Principal will be paid. There has Scarcely an Obligation been Sold Since the News of the Mutiny of Soldiers in Philadelphia[9] and the diversity of Sentiments among the States about the Plan of Impost.

I have no Information from Congress or Mr Morris, but am told by our Bankers there are Bills to the Amount of Thirteen hundred Thousand Guilders which must be Sent back, a terrible

9. Which Boudinot had described to the America commissioners: XL, 302–4.

disappointment to great Numbers of People! Some of the Bills became payable, the Beginning of March, and the Rest being much the greatest Part in May.

At Amsterdam I recd the Honour of yours of the 3 of this Month.

Dr Franklin.

From Samuel Bird[1]   ALS: American Philosophical Society

Sir   Andely Januy. the 24. 1784

Having the honour of your Protection to establish the fabrication of woolen Cloth in the United states of North america (and the same time I gave You the patterns of Cloth, Cazimear, Ratteen, &c which I manufactur'd in france) For the completeing of the same, and according to my promis, I take the liberty to give you a detail of what I am Capable of performing in that branch, Likwise giving you a Small account of my Life, and how I Came to be in france.

I am a Native of England 30 Years of age, serv'd Seven Years apprentiship to learn the art of making & dressing all sorts of broad Cloth in one of the most renowned manufactures in England, For my further experience I worked in all the Counties in England remarkable for making of Cloth, Wiltshire, Yorkshire, Worstershire, Somerset Shire, Devonshire, And Gloucestershire, of whom I am a Native, I had the Conducting of Several manufactures in these Counties, & in London Likwise, where I was pressed for the Kings Service but having a natural dislike to the American war, I made my escape & Came to france (notwith Standing in geting away I was wounded in the thigh) and by the good protection of the governer of Calis I was Soon

1. Possibly the same Samuel Bird who from 1787 to his unexpected death in 1797 directed a Spanish cloth factory, the Royal Factory of Saint Nicholas in Guadalaxara, transforming it into a profitable enterprise: James Clayburn La Force, Jr., *The Development of the Spanish Textile Industry, 1750–1800* (Berkeley, Calif., 1965), 40n, 44n, 82.

placed In the manufacture Royal at Andely[2] which is now five
Years, the master gave me the Command of all notwithstanding I Could not speake one word of french; I got sum English
tools and set to work, taking to pieces the utensiles & Changing
them to my liking, & Shewing the people by Signs my manner
of working. In one Years time my master told me I had Saved
him 12000 Livers.

Since I had the honour of Seeing [*you*] I have finished a machine to row the Cloth (that is to bring the wool on the Cloth
with teasils to form the dress, in English this machine is Call'd,
gigmill, and is turn'd by water) I have presented it to the Coun-
cel of paris and expects every day their answer.

I am Capable of Constructing & Conducting this gigmill in
the highest perfection, A piece of Superfine Cloth 30 Yards to
Row it by hand will Cost about 1 *l.t.* 10 *s.* and by the gigmill
about 3 *s.* and Cours Cloth in proportion the Soldiers Cloth at
9 *d.* the piece, this gigmill was first adopted by the English government to Clothe their Soldiers at a Less expence. I Should be
Sorry to assert a thing I Could not perform, I flatter my Self
capable to undertake the establishing of a manufacture for all
sorts of broad Cloth. Cazimear, Ratteen &c. in the highest perfection. Can dye nearly all sorts of Colours in the wool (except
woad blue). For grain Colours and Coulours Commonly dyed
in the piece Can dye Scarlet, Crimsons, Roas, Cherry Coulor,
Saxon greens, Saxon blues, Grays, buff Coulors, Black, the
Whitening of Cloth with or without brimston. The art of Manufacturing & Preparation for the double Coulor Cloth give Instructions for the Building of the mills, and Conduct it from the
Beginning to the Ending, Teaching the People the most Shortest methwood of working. Can make the Stones for Naping
mills, and mak no doubt of puting them to work notwithstanding I have not undertaken as Yeat that piece of work (except the
making of the Stones) I have an ernes desire to be established
with my Country people, that I my be Profitable to them and my

2. The royal manufacture in Petit-Andely. Since 1755 the owner was
Louis Flavigni: Brossard de Ruville, *Histoire de la ville des Andelis et de ses
dépendances* (2 vols., Les Andelis, France, 1863–64), I, 273–5.

self. And should I be so happy as to succeed, Shall rest under the greatest Obligation to Your honour.

If the Congress will undertake it, it may be more to my Advantage & much more to my Satisfaction, if not any Gentleman or Gentlemen that will undertake it I am at their Command, by paying my passage and a Salary sufficient to Live genteelly, the place I possess is 60 pound per Year Sterling, but if I may take the Liberty I shall Leave all to Your Discretion & wise Conduct.

From Your Most Obedient and Humble Servant

SAML. BIRD.

Should you honour me with a Line at any time Direct
A Monsieur
Monsieur Bird Contre maître de La Manufacture Royale au petit Andely, aux Andelis Normande

From John Paul Jones   ALS: American Philosophical Society

Sir,   Paris Jany. 26th. 1784

I have the honor to transmit you herewith a peice written in America against the Cincinnati[3] and a News Paper containing the Institution of that Society.—[4] I pray you when you write on

3. Cassius [Aedanus Burke], *Considerations on the Society or Order of Cincinnati; Lately Instituted By the Major-Generals, Brigadier-Generals, and Other Officers of the American Army.* . . . The pamphlet was first published in Charleston in October, 1783, and was widely reprinted thereafter, galvanizing public opinion against the society: Minor Myers, Jr., *Liberty without Anarchy: a History of the Society of the Cincinnati* (Charlottesville, 1983), pp. 49–55. The Philadelphia reprint was advertised for sale on Nov. 4 in the *Pa. Evening Post,* in time for Jones to have purchased one before embarking on the *General Washington* the following week.

4. The society's institution, or charter, was adopted on May 13, 1783, and began circulating in the American press the following fall. Shortly before Jones's departure it was reprinted in the Nov. 5 issue of the *Freeman's Journal* (Philadelphia). See Myers, *Liberty without Anarchy,* pp. 24–7, 66n, and for the text of the institution, 258–65.

Society of the Cincinnati Eagle Insignia, Obverse

that Subject to Monsieur Gerard[5] to present to him my respectful Compliments. I am affectionately Sir Your most obedient
and most humble Servant[6]   J PAUL JONES

His Excellincy B. Franklin Esqr. &c &c.

Notation: Paul Jones, Jany. 26. 1784.—

To Sarah Bache

Transcript, AL (draft), and press copy of LS:[7] Library of Congress

Franklin had been aware of the Society of the Cincinnati since at least
mid-December, when Pierre-Charles L'Enfant arrived in Paris to deliver George Washington's letters and begin the work of establishing
a French branch.[8] A week after L'Enfant's arrival, however, Franklin

5. Conrad-Alexandre Gérard, the former French minister to the United
States, was one of the seven French honorary members chosen at the society's founding meeting. GW's letter to him, carried to France by L'Enfant, is
in Fitzpatrick, *Writings of Washington*, XXVII, 210. We have not been able
to discover why BF intended to write to him about the Cincinnati, nor have
we found any record of that letter.

6. Also on Jan. 26, Jones sent BF a brief, unsigned note accepting a dinner invitation for "Friday next," Jan. 30. Dartmouth College Library.

7. The transcript, made *c.* 1817 for WTF, *Memoirs*, II, 46-50, includes
revisions by BF that postdate the other extant versions. The evolution of
this text appears to be as follows. The LS is in the hand of BFB. BF corrected
and emended it before signing, and before the press copy was made. BF's
subsequent revisions were made on a MS that is now lost (perhaps the LS
itself?). The transcript incorporates all the emendations visible on the press
copy, as well as some two dozen other changes, including the addition of
one entire sentence. When Morellet eventually published his translation,
which included everything but the final two paragraphs, his French text
incorporated all those changes. We therefore conclude that they came from
BF's pen. As for the final two paragraphs, for which no translation exists,
we can only assume that the discrepancies with the press copy reflect BF's
own choices, though it is possible that WTF might have altered some of
the words—just as he deleted a word on the transcript we publish (noted
below).

8. For background on the information in this paragraph, see Bariatinskii
to BF, Dec. 22, and BF's reply of [*c.* Dec. 22].

still knew nothing specific about the organization and was unable to answer the questions sent to him by his Russian counterpart, Bariatinskii. Too ill to travel as of early December, the American minister was isolated at Passy. Even Vergennes, whom he would normally have seen at the weekly meetings of the diplomatic corps, was more fully informed, having received a copy of the society's institution (or charter) from Lafayette.

Franklin's papers give almost no indication of who might have visited him during the severe winter months and provided him with authoritative information about the society.[9] Whatever he learned, he kept his opinions private. Other Americans registered their concerns in letters to one another and to Congress, but Franklin, whose diplomatic status required more delicacy, did not. In March, Lafayette would inform George Washington that "Most of the Americans Here are indecently Violent Against our Association. . . . Doctor Franklin Said little. But Jay, Adams, and all the others warmly Blame the Army."[1]

Franklin does not appear to have seen the Cincinnati's institution until January 26, when he received it from John Paul Jones, himself not yet a member.[2] Jones also enclosed a pamphlet by Judge Aedanus Burke opposing the society, which had been published in Charleston in the fall and was widely reprinted thereafter. Burke called on his fellow citizens to mount a vigorous opposition before it was too late, arguing that the organization was "a deep laid contrivance to beget, and perpetuate family grandeur in an aristocratic Nobility, to terminate at last in monarchical tyranny."[3]

On January 26, evidently prompted by what he had read, Franklin conceived a satire informed by his long-held views and his recent reading of a work on Chinese culture. He would not dwell on

9. The only such evidence is L'Enfant *et al.* to BF, [*c.* Jan. 16].

1. Idzerda, *Lafayette Papers*, V, 209. For the concerns of Matthew Ridley (who wrote to JA at The Hague), JA (who fumed about the disregard of the Articles of Confederation), and John Jay, see *Adams Papers*, XV, 437, 468-9; *Jay Papers*, III, 557, 559-60.

2. See Jones's letter, immediately above. He petitioned for membership before leaving Philadelphia: W. W. Abbot *et al.*, eds., *The Papers of George Washington*, Confederation Series (6 vols., Charlottesville and London, 1992—97), I, 296.

3. Cassius [*i.e.*, Aedanus Burke], *Considerations on the Society or Order of Cincinnati; Lately Instituted By the Major-Generals, Brigadier-Generals, and other Officers of the American Army* . . . (Philadelphia, 1783), p. 14.

the transgression against the Articles of Confederation, the focus of many of his colleagues, nor would he predict the extreme consequences that Burke foretold. Instead, with characteristic humor, he would show that the Cincinnati's attempt to transplant the customs of European nobility to an American setting exposed the fundamental absurdity of all such distinctions and practices. By addressing this letter to his only daughter (with whom he never corresponded about politics), leavening it with family lore, and feigning at the outset that his opinion "cannot be of much importance," Franklin cloaked what was intended to be a public essay in a fictional veneer of privacy.

Franklin never sent this "letter" to Philadelphia. He showed it to no one apart from his grandsons until, around the beginning of March, he sent it to the abbé Morellet to translate into French. Morellet did so, but counseled him against making it public. Franklin acknowledged the prudence of this advice and assured Morellet that the piece would not be made public during his lifetime.[4]

Franklin's ostensible letter to his daughter, so often quoted in our time, remained all but unknown in his. Morellet's partial translation was published in Paris within months of Franklin's death,[5] but the full text in English was not made public until 1817, when William Temple Franklin included it in his edition of Franklin's writings.

Passy Jany: 26: 1784

My dear Child.

Your care in sending me the news-papers is very agreeable to me. I received by Captn. Barney those relating to the *Cincinnati*. My opinion of the institution cannot be of much importance. I only wonder that when the united wisdom of our nation had, in the Articles of Confederation, manifested their dislike of establishing ranks of nobility, by authority either of the Congress or of any particular state,[6] a number of private persons should think proper to distinguish themselves and their posterity, from their fellow citizens, and form an order of hereditary Knights, in direct opposition to the solemnly declared sense of their country.

---

4. Morellet to BF, and BF's reply, both of March 16, 1784. In July, BF shared sections with the comte de Mirabeau, who included them without attribution in his *Considérations sur l'ordre de Cincinnatus, ou imitation d'un pamphlet anglo-américain* (London, 1784). The story of these various translations will be covered in forthcoming volumes.

5. *Jour. de la Société de 1789*, issue of July 24, 1790.

6. Article VI of the Articles of Confederation: *JCC*, XIX, 216.

I imagine it must be likewise contrary to the good sense of most of those drawn into it, by the persuasion of its projectors, who have been too much struck with the ribbands and crosses they have seen hanging, to the button holes of foreign officers. And I suppose those who disapprove of it have not hitherto given it much opposition, from a principle somewhat like that of your good mother, relating to punctilious persons who are always exacting little observances of respect, that "*if People can be pleased with small matters, it is pity but they should have them*". In this view, perhaps I should not myself, if my advice had been asked, have objected to their wearing their ribband and badge themselves according to their fancy, though I certainly should to the entailing it as an honour on their posterity. For, honour worthily obtained, as that for example of our officers, is in its nature a personal thing, and incommunicable to any but those who had some share in obtaining it. Thus among the Chinese, the most antient, and from long experience the wisest of nations, honour does not *descend*, but *ascends*. If a man from his learning, his wisdom, or his valour, is promoted by the emperor to the rank of Mandarin, his parents are immediately entitled to all the same ceremonies of respect from the people, that are established as due to the Mandarin himself; on the supposition, that it must have been owing to the education, instruction and good example afforded him by his parents that he was rendered capable of serving the public.[7] This *ascending* honour is therefore useful to the state, as it encourages parents to give their children a good and virtuous education. But the *descending honour*, to a posterity who could have no share in obtaining it, is not only groundless and absurd, but often hurtful to that posterity, since it is apt to make them proud, disdaining to be employed in useful arts, and thence falling into poverty, and all the meannesses, servility and wretchedness attending it; which is the present case with much of what is called the *Noblesse* in Europe. Or if, to keep up the dignity of the family, estates are entailed entire

7. BF had been studying the fourth volume of *Mémoires concernant l'histoire . . . des Chinois* (for which see above, p. 37). The Chinese practices that he here relates are discussed on pp. 134, 137, and 147.

on the eldest male heir, another pest to industry and improvement of the country is introduced, which will be followed by all the odious mixture of pride, and beggary, and idleness that have half depopulated and decultivated Spain; occasioning continual extinction of families by the discouragements of marriage, and neglect in the improvement of estates. I wish therefore that the Cincinnati if they must go on with their project, would direct the badges of their order to be worn by their fathers and mothers, instead of handing them down to their children. It would be a good precident and might have good effects. It would also be a kind of obedience to the fourth commandment, in which God enjoins us to *honour* our father and mother, but has no where directed us to honour our children. And certainly no mode of honouring those immediate authors of our being can be more effectual, than that of doing praise worthy actions, which reflect honour on those who gave us our education; or more becoming than that of manifesting by some public expression or token, that it is to their instruction and example we ascribe the merit of those actions.

But the absurdity of descending honours is not a mere matter of philosophical opinion, it is capable of mathematical demonstration. A man's son, for instance, is but half of his family, the other half belonging to the family of his wife. His son too, marrying into another family, his share in the Grand son is but a fourth; in the great grandson by the same process it is but an eighth. In the next generation a sixteenth; the next a thirty second; the next a sixty fourth; the next an hundred and twenty eighth; the next a two hundred and fifty sixth; and the next a five hundred and twelfth. Thus in nine generations which will not require more than 300 years, (no very great antiquity for a family) our present Chevalier of the Order of Cincinnatus's share in the then existing knight will be but a 512th part; which, allowing the present certain fidelity of American wives to be insured down through all those nine generations, is so small a consideration, that methinks no reasonable man would hazard, for the sake of it, the disagreeable consequences of the jealousy, envy, and ill will of his countrymen.

Let us go back with our calculation from this young noble,

the 512th. part of the present Knight, through his nine generations till we return to the year of the institution. He must have
had a father and mother, they are two; each of them had a father
and mother, they are four. Those of the next preceeding generation will be eight; the next sixteen, the next thirty two; the next
sixty four; the next One hundred and twenty eight; the next two
hundred and fifty six; and the ninth in this retrocession five hundred and twelve, who must be now existing and all contribute
their proportion of this future Chevalier de Cincinnatus. These,
with the rest, make together as follows.[8]

$$
\begin{array}{r}
2 \\
4 \\
8 \\
16 \\
32 \\
64 \\
128 \\
256 \\
512 \\
\hline
\end{array}
$$

Total $\overline{1022}$

One thousand and twenty two men and women contributors
to the formation of one knight. And if we are to have a thousand
of these future knights there must be now and hereafter existing
one million and twenty two thousand fathers and mothers who
are to contribute to their production, unless a part of the number
are employed in making more knights than one. Let us strike
off then the 22000 on the supposition of this double employ
and then consider whether after a reasonable estimation of the
number of rogues and fools, and Royalists[1] and scoundrels, and

8. In the draft, BF experimented with, and then crossed out, a slightly
different table. He listed the number of progenitors of each member of the
society going back generations, beginning with the ninth. In the *Poor Richard* for 1751, BF had calculated the number of a nobleman's ancestors back 21
generations, to the Norman Conquest: IV, 97-8.

1. In the transcript from which we print, "Royalists" is lined through.
This was presumably done by WTF, who omitted the word from his edition
of BF's writings. The word was present in BF's draft and in the LS, and we
therefore preserve it here.

prostitutes, that are mixed with and help to make up necessarily their million of predecessors, posterity will have much reason to boast of the noble blood of the then existing set of chevaliers of Cincinnatus. The future genealogists too of these Chevaliers in proving the lineal descent of their honour through so many generations, (even supposing honour capable in its nature of descending,) will only prove the small share of this honour which can be justly claimed by any one of them, since the above simple procession arithmetic makes it quite plain and clear, that in proportion as the antiquity of the family shall augment, the right to the honour of the ancestor will diminish; and a few generations more would reduce it to something so small as to be very near an absolute nullity.[2] I hope therefore that the order will drop this part of their project, and content themselves as the Knights of the Garter, Bath, Thistle, St Louis, and other orders of Europe do, with a life enjoyment of their little badge and ribband, and let the distinction die with those who have merited it. This I imagine will give no offence. For my own part, I shall think it a convenience when I go into a company where there may be faces unknown to me, if I discover, by this badge, the persons who merit some particular expression of my respect; and it will save modest virtue the trouble of calling for our regard, by awkward round about intimations of having been heretofore employed as officers in the continental service.

The gentleman who made the voyage to France to provide the ribbands and medals; has executed his commission. To me they seem tolerably done; but all such things are criticised. Some find fault with the Latin, as wanting classical elegance and correctness; and since our nine universities were not able to furnish better Latin, it was pity, they say, that the mottos had not been in English.[3] Others object to the Title, as not properly as-

2. This sentence was added after the LS was made, and appears in the French translation.

3. The "medals" (badges) featured abbreviations of two of the society's Latin mottos: on the obverse, "Omnia Relinquit Servare Rempublicam" (He left everything to serve the republic); on the reverse, "Virtutis Praemium" (Reward of Valor). The various workshops involved in crafting the earliest medals rendered and abbreviated the mottos in different ways: Minor Myers, Jr., *Insignia of The Society of the Cincinnati* (Washington, D.C., 1998),

sumable by any but General Washington, and a few others who served without pay. Others object to the bald eagle, as looking too much like a *Dindon* or turkey. For my own part I wish the bald eagle had not been chosen as the representative of our country. He is a bird of bad moral character. He does not get his living honestly. You may have seen him perched on some dead tree, where, too lazy to fish for himself, he watches the labour of the fishing hawk; and when that diligent bird has at length taken a fish, and is bearing it to his nest for the support of his mate and young ones, the bald eagle pursues him, and takes it from him. With all this injustice, he is never in good case, but like those among men who live by sharping and robbing he is generally poor and often very lousy. Besides he is a rank coward: the little *king bird* not bigger than a sparrow attacks him boldly and drives him out of the district. He is therefore by no means a proper emblem for the brave and honest Cincinnati of America, who have driven all the *king birds* from our country, though exactly fit for that order of knights which the French call *Chevaliers d'Industrie*.[4] I am on this account not displeased that the figure is not known as a bald eagle, but looks more like a turkey. For in truth, the turkey is in comparison a much more respectable bird, and withal a true original native of America. Eagles have been found in all countries, but the turkey was peculiar to ours, the first of the species seen in Europe being brought to France by the Jesuits from Canada, and served up at the wedding table of Charles the ninth. He is besides, (though a little vain and silly tis true, but not the worse emblem for that) a bird of courage, and would not hesitate to attack a grenadier of the British guards who should presume to invade his farm yard with a red coat on.

I shall not enter into the criticisms made upon their Latin. The gallant officers of America may not have the merit of be-

pp. 15–16, 37–8, 41–9. The nine universities were Harvard, Dartmouth, Yale, William and Mary, the colleges of Rhode Island (now Brown) and New Jersey (now Princeton), King's College (now Columbia), Queen's College (now Rutgers), and the University of the State of Pa. (now the University of Pa.).

4. A French term for an adventurer, crook, or swindler.

ing great scholars, but they undoubtedly merit much as brave soldiers from their country, which should therefore not leave them merely to *fame* for their *virtutis premium*, which is one of their Latin mottos. Their *esto perpetua*,[5] another, is an excellent wish, if they meant it for their country; bad, if intended for their order. The states should not only restore to them the *omnia* of their first motto,*[6] which many of them have left and lost, but pay them justly, and reward them generously. They should not be suffered to remain with all their new created chivalry *entirely* in the situation of the gentleman in the story, which their *omnia reliquit* reminds me of. You know every thing makes me recollect some story. He had built a very fine house and thereby much impaired his fortune. He had a pride however in showing it to his acquaintance. One of them after viewing it all, remarked a motto over the door, ŌIA VANITAS. What says he is the meaning of this ŌIA? 'tis a word I don't understand. I will tell you said the gentleman: I had a mind to have the motto cut on a piece of smooth marble, but there was not room for it between the ornaments, to be put in characters large enough to be read. I therefore made use of a contraction antiently very common in Latin manuscripts whereby the *m*'s and *n*'s in words are omitted, and the omission noted by a little dash above, which you may see there, so that this word is OMNIA, OMNIA VANITAS. O. says his friend, I now comprehend the meaning of your motto, it relates to your edifice; and signifies, that if you have abridged your *omnia* you have nevertheless left your VANITAS legible at full length.

I am as ever Your affectionate father

BF

5. The society's third motto: May It Last Forever.
6. [*Footnote in text:*] "**Omnia reliquit servare Rempublicam.*"

From Feriet

AL: Library of Congress

Versailles le 27 janvier 1784

J'ay vû, Monsieur, Le Sr. Rollin[7] qui a èté très incommodé de sables et de graviers; comme il n'a point ète sondé, et qu'il prètend cette opération fort dangereuse, il n'est point sur S'il avait La pierre en gros ou en détail, mais ce qu'il y a de certain, c'est qu'il est extrêmement soulagé, qu'il peut vacquer Librement a ses affaires et a son service, et que le remède qu'il a pris ne L'a incommodé D'aucune manière; il consiste dans un demi verre de jus d'oignon le matin deux heures avant de manger, et gros comme une olive de savon de naples qu'il avalait a chaque repas au moment de se mettre a table. Il m'a dit, Monsieur, que si le jus D'oignon Vous répugait, vous pouviez Le mêler avec ègale quantité de bouillon. Quant au savon, il prennait La précaution de le bien pétrir avec les mains dans plusieurs eaux, avant que d'en faire des pillulles, il prétend cette précaution nècessaire. Il m'a fort assuré que pendant tout le tems qu'il a fait usage de ce remède, sa poitrine et son estomac n'en ont pas ressenti La moindre incommodité. Si j'avais oublié quelque dètail qui puisse Vous intéresser, je vous prie, Monsieur, de Vouloir bien me le faire dire,[8] et D'être persuadé de tout le plaisir que j'aurai toujours a faire quelque chose qui vous soit agrèable, et a vous donner des preuves de L'attachement sincère et du respect avec lequel j'ay Lhonneur D'être, Monsieur, Votre très humble et très obéissant serviteur   DEF

7. Rollin was a *valet de chambre* in the household of the king's sister-in-law; he was the *feutier*, in charge of tending fires: *Almanach de Versailles* for 1784, p. 182.

8. BF may indeed have asked for further details. Preserved among his papers are two versions of a MS titled "Remede dont fait usage à Versailles de S. Rollin attaché au Service de Madame": the original, which we assume is in Rollin's own hand (Library of Congress), and a press copy of a copy made by L'Air de Lamotte (APS). It is a careful set of instructions, more comprehensive than Feriet's summary, and specifies that beef, veal, chicken, and three white onions should form the ingredients of the prescribed bouillon, which is to be poured over a crust of bread. M. Rollin, who is about the same age and size as M. Franklin, has used this remedy for two months; the results have convinced him that the stone is dissolving.

mille complimens, je vous prie, a Monsieur votre fils; Lorsqu'il viendra ici, je lui ferai voir trois chaises a porteur que j'ay trouvées chèz des particuliers; elles sont fort belles, et presque neuves, mais elles sont depuis 18, jusqu'a 22 Louis, on ne peut en trouver de bonnes qui soyent d'un moindre prix.

From David Hartley

ALS: Library of Congress; copy: William L. Clements Library

Dear Sir   London Jan 28 1784

I am requested by Mr Dempster whom you must probably know by Parliamentary reputation[9] to introduce to your acquaintance the bearer of this letter Dr Ross who proposes to settle in America as a Physician.[1] I have no other acquaintance with him than thro Mr Dempster's means but he appears by his conversation to be very ingenious and well informed. Tho a young man (about 34) he has been a great traveller having passed several years in various parts of the East Indies and Turky. He proposes with your permission to take your advice with respect to his proposed settlement as a practising Physician in America. Mr Dempster has given me a very high character for understanding & abilities wch as far as I have experienced

9. The Scottish M.P. George Dempster (1732–1818) had been a champion of the American colonies and an opponent of Lord North: *ODNB;* Namier and Brooke, *House of Commons,* II, 313–17. He arranged for Dr. Ross (see below) to receive a letter of introduction to GW, as well as the present letter to BF: W. W. Abbot *et al.,* eds., *The Papers of George Washington,* Confederation Series (6 vols., Charlottesville and London, 1992–97), I, 74–5.

1. Dr. Andrew Ross also carried a letter of recommendation from William Strahan (below, Feb. 1). BF in turn provided Ross with a letter of recommendation to Benjamin Rush, dated March 12, 1784 (Yale University Library). Ross helped found the College of Physicians in 1787 and was elected to the APS on July 15, 1791. He returned to his native Scotland around 1798/99, and died in Dundee in 1822: *Trans. of the College of Physicians of Philadelphia,* 3rd ser., XXXI (1909), 374, 391; *Early Proc. of the APS* (Philadelphia, 1884), p. 195; John T. Rutt, ed., *The Theological and Miscellaneous Works of Joseph Priestley* (25 vols., [London, 1817–32]), XVII, 132; *Monthly Mag. and British Register,* LIV (1822–23), first pagination, 576.

his conversation he appears entitled to. As such I beg leave to transmitt Mr Dempsters recommendation to you.[2]— I thank you for yours of the 7th Inst. & for your political parable, and think very seriously (as I know you do) of the moral of your fable. I shall be very glad to hear of the arrival of the ratification from America, and upon the first notification from you, will apply for the exchange of the british ratification. Pray remember me to Mr & Mrs Jay Mr W T Franklin & all friends.

Ever yours most affectely   D HARTLEY

To Dr Franklin &c &c &c

Endorsed: D Hartley Esq to B F. Jan. 28. 1784

From John Coakley Lettsom

ALS: American Philosophical Society

Honoured Friend   London Jan. 28. 1784.

I write this at the request of my friend & Countryman Thornton, a Student of medicine, & a young gentleman of fortune from Tortola;[3] who has, like every other person of sentiment &

2. Not found.

3. The future architect and inventor William Thornton (1759–1828) studied medicine at the University of Edinburgh before going in the fall of 1783 to London, where he studied art as well as medicine and came under the guardianship of Lettsom, a distant relative. He went to Paris to continue his studies and stayed until early August. In Paris he cultivated an interest in natural history and geology, and got to know Faujas de Saint-Fond and his associates. Faujas enlisted Thornton to join his expedition to Scotland in the fall of 1784: *ANB;* C. M. Harris *et al.*, eds., *Papers of William Thornton* (1 vol. to date, Charlottesville and London, 1995–), I, xxxiv–xli, 14; Thornton to TJ, Jan. 9, 1821 (Library of Congress); Paolo Andreani, *Diario di viaggio di un gentiluomo milanese, Parigi-Londra 1784* (Milan, 1975), p. 79.

Thornton recorded two occasions on which he and BF discussed science at Passy. One conversation had to do with the survival of toads in unlikely conditions: XXXVII, 100n. Another time, the young man brought to Passy a bottle made of lava glass, which he believed to be one of the first ever made. BF tested its "electric power, & he concluded it to be about thirty times more electric than common Glass. These bottles tho' much lighter were also

ambition, a fond desire to know Dr. Franklin, & I have taken the liberty to request his delivery of this letter— I think he will make a distinguished character; he has at present too much sail, but age will give him ballast: I shall recommend him to lodge, if convenient, with our friend Mr. Le Sue le chirurgien,[4] to perfect himself in the language & in his Art.

I purpose soon to make an elegant edition, if paper & type can do it, of Dr. Fothergill's life, in which I mean to add some Anecdotes of the Doctors more particular & honourable acquaintance, with portraits elegantly engraved. I hope Dr. Franklin will forgive me for placing him in this situation, in the company of Dr. Cleghorn, Dr. Cuming, Dr. Russell & Peter Collinson—[5] I have in my possession a striking medallion of Dr. Franklin, which I mean to have engraved, under which will be placed the four lines, which are inscribed under the head prefixed to our late amiable friend Dr. Dubourg's edition of Les Œuvres de Franklin.[6] I have not any authentic early anecdotes, but recent ones will furnish many great and striking outlines.

Whatever freedoms I may have taken with the most distinguished character in Europe, I hope Dr. Franklin will attribute

---

much stronger than common green glass": "Some Account of Lettsom's Island," undated, William Thornton Papers, Library of Congress, fol. 2827. Thornton doubtless obtained his bottle from Faujas, who had recently announced in the press that he had been the first to make such vessels. That claim was disputed by Balthazar-Georges Sage, who insisted that his former student Chaptal had been the first. The dispute, aired at length in the pages of the *Jour. de Paris*, continued through the spring of 1784: issues of Jan. 2, Feb. 19 sup., Feb. 21, Feb. 27 sup., Feb. 29, April 8, 1784.

4. Jean-Joseph Sue père: XL, 55–6n.

5. Lettsom's *Memoirs of John Fothergill, M.D. &c.*, which was not published until 1786, expanded his earlier *Some Account of the Late John Fothergill* (1783): XXXV, 479n. The additional material included biographical sketches of the physicians George Cleghorn, William Cuming, and Alexander Russell, as well as the naturalist Peter Collinson. BF's sketch did not appear, as BF never revised the preliminary draft that Lettsom sent him, for his review, on March 1, 1785 (APS).

6. This engraving was published in *Memoirs of John Fothergill, M.D. &c.* following p. 164. It was made by James Heath (*ODNB*, under Heath family) after a fur-cap Nini medallion. For the quatrain composed by Barbeu-Dubourg for the engraving in his *Œuvres de M. Franklin* see XX, frontispiece, xvii; XXI, 100–1, 193–4.

my conduct to that sincere respect with which I ever Subscribe
myself his Admirer & obliged friend   J. C. Lettsom

Addressed: Benjn. Franklin

Notation: Lettsom 28 Jan. 84.

From Erik Magnus Staël von Holstein[7]

l: American Philosophical Society

Jeudi ce 29 Jan 1784.
L'Ambassadeur de Suede a l honneur de faire bien des compliments à Monsieur de franklin. Il est faché de ne pas pouvoir
avoir l'honneur de profiter de son invitation pour demain mais il
aura celui de passer chez monsieur de franklin un des jours de la
semaine prochaine pour echanger des Ratifications.[8]

Notation: L'Ambassadeur de Suede 29. Jan. 1784.

From ———— Lucet[9]

al: Library of Congress

hôtel de Soubise 30. Jer. 1784.
Lucet Sre. des commandements de Mgr. Le Pce. de Soubise a
L'honneur d'assurer Monsieur Francklin de ses devoirs, et de
luy envoier un Paquet Pour luy qui est Venu Sous l'envelope du
Prince, et qu'il a Prefferé d'envoier a Passy a la demeure connüe
de Monsieur Francklin, qu'a L'hôtel de M. Le Rai de Chaumont
qu'il ne connait Pas.

---

7. Appointed Swedish minister at the French court in May, 1783 (xl,
159n), Staël von Holstein was promoted to ambassador the following November: *Repertorium der diplomatischen Vertreter*, iii, 408.

8. The exchange of ratifications took place on Feb. 6: Staël von Holstein
to Rosencrone, Feb. 6, 1784 (Svenska Riksarkivet); copy courtesy of Jane
Fitzgerald, National Archives.

9. The secretary of the royal hunting preserve governed by the prince
de Soubise: *Almanach royal* for 1784, pp. 460–1.

From David Gallwey & Co.

ALS: American Philosophical Society

Nantes 31 Jany. 1784

We had the honour to address your excelency the 22d. inst. on the Subject of an insurance we effected by order & for account of Messr. Jonathan Nesbitt & Co. of L'orient on the american ship Nancy Capn. Sewel parted from Philadelphia for Lorient the 16. of March 1783. arrived safe, the Conditions of the Policy are that sd. ship arriving without risk of capture the Premio woud be five per cent. if the contrary Twenty five, its evident from the 22d. art. of the Treaty of Peace between the kings of France and Great Britain that hostilities were to have ceased in all the Seas to the Nortwhard of the Canaries whether in the Ocean or Mediteranean on the 3d. March. which is plainly demonstrated by the inclosed authentick coppy of a sentence pronouncd by the Admiralty Court of Tortola in the cause of the Brigg. Justine Capne. Michateau captur'd on the 4th. day of March 1783. at 4 ô clock A.M, in 30 Degrees 40 minutes north latitude & given up to her owners.[1] Notwithstanding these proofs produced at the Court of admiralty sentence has been given against us to pay by Provision & in cash Twenty Five per Cent to the underwriters in consequence of the Comte de Vergennes letter of the 15th. November;[2] we have enter'd an appeal but are obliged to pay the money.

If your Excellency is not pleased to interfare & obtain a quick decision of this question from the minister, this Lawsuit may continue for a number of years & the Proprietors of this Ship lye out of a Considerable Sum.

1. The enclosure was an official French translation of the Tortola admiralty court sentence of April 19, 1783, and of BF's statement about Article 22 of the preliminary treaty (XXXIX, 172). These were entered into the records of the Nantes admiralty on Dec. 2, 1783, at the request of David Gallwey & Co., and attested on Jan. 11, 1784.

2. Among BF's papers at the APS is a copy of Vergennes to the underwriters of the *Nancy*, dated Nov. 15, 1783, written on the verso of a copy of the admiralty court's sentence. The court met on Jan. 26, 1784, and on Jan. 30 the defendants were notified that they had one week to pay the full premium, with interest. According to Nesbitt's letter of Jan. 31, immediately below, this document was enclosed in the present letter.

We have the highest Confidence that your Excellency will take this affair into consideration & obtain a quick decision on it.

We have the honor to be Your Excellencys Most Obedient & most devoted humble Servs.   DD: GALLWEY & CO.

His Excellency Benjamin Franklyn Esqr. Minister Plenipotentiary of the united States of America at the Court of France

From Jonathan Nesbitt   ALS: American Philosophical Society

Sir   Nantes. Janry 31st. 1784

A few days before my departure from Paris I had the honor to inclose your Excellency a Letter from Mr Cormier relative to the Insurance on the Ship Nancy Captain Shewell.—[3] On my arrival here yesterday I found that the Court of Admiralty had given Sentence against me on the authority of the Comte de Vergennes' Letter[4] only, without paying, in my oppinion, a proper attention to the twenty second Article of the Preliminary Treaty, nor to your Excellencys Letter explaining that Article,—nor to the Sentence of the Court of Admiralty of Tortola,[5] which entirely Coincides with your oppinion, & which proves clearly that had the Nancy been Captured on her passage from Philadelphia to L'Orient she would undoubtedly have been restored; nor in short to any other Paper that could be laid before

3. Nesbitt's cover letter has not been located. The enclosure was the ALS he had received from J. (G.?) Cormier, written from Nantes on Jan. 10. Cormier reported that the settlement of the premium for the *Nancy* would be on the first court docket. He had requested that sentencing be postponed so that Nesbitt could get the question settled by the ministers, but considering the letter from Vergennes that the underwriters had produced, it was almost certain that Nesbitt would be condemned to pay the higher premium. Nesbitt would need a strong endorsement from BF if the case was to be decided in his favor. APS.

4. For the substance of this letter see the annotation of Nesbitt to BF, Dec. 23.

5. BF's declaration on Article 22 and the Tortola admiralty court's decision were entered into evidence at Nantes; see the letter from Gallwey & Co. immediately above.

them, or Argument that could be made use of in support of our Plea.— According to the advice of all my friends I have ordered an appeal from the Sentence, but this does not prevent my being under the Necessity of immediately paying the full premium (such it seems are the Laws here) which is particularly distressing, as my adversarys are thereby enabled to Plead against me with my funds in their hands.— Mr. Gallwey, to whom I take the liberty to refer your Excellency for further particulars, will inclose you a Copy of the Comte de Vergennes Letter to the Underwriters on the Nancy, also Copy of the Sentence of the Court of Admiralty of this place & that of the Court of Admiralty of Tortolla, to which I have little to add, only once more to request your Excellency's Protection in this affair, which is not only of the greatest Consequence to me, but to the Americans in general, as the fate of a number of similar Actions may depend on the final determination of the present;—

I have the honor to remain with Sentiments of the highest respect & Esteem. Sir Your most Obedt: Servt:

JONATN: NESBITT

From Daniel Roberdeau   ALS: American Philosophical Society

London Leaden-hall Street No. 49 [January, 1784][6]
Dear Sir

I arrived here in September last,[7] with a purpose of visiting France and of paying my respects and offering my Congratulations on the restoration of Peace, and to you for the honor you have acquired in this business, as I cannot now do it personally permit the offering in this mode with my best wishes for a continuance of your health and strength of which I have

6. Roberdeau wrote on Feb. 2, below, that he sent this letter "a few days ago."

7. Roberdeau was in England visiting relatives and reestablishing his business connections. The address he gives, above, is the business address of Charles Pearce-Hall, the husband of his cousin Elizabeth Cunyngham: *ANB;* Roberdeau Buchanan, *Genealogy of the Roberdeau Family . . .* (Washington, D.C., 1876), pp. 34, 38, 89, 104.

heard, from your Colleagues,[8] with great pleasure, and that every blessing may attend you.

As I have forgot Mr. Grand's address allow me the liberty of sending a letter for him enclosed, also open that you may know the business and do me the service I require of which I will receive information in Philadelphia and your permission to draw for the money in question, if the bill of Excha. sent to Mr. Grand should be paid, in which case perhaps the money had better remain in his hands and that he give me authority to draw wc. would save you trouble. I mention the pleasure of hearing from you in Philada. because the success of an address to me here would be very uncertain as I am on the wing to depart, but without the use of a Balloon, which I shall leave to my ingenious Countrymen the French, as a better suited to their lively tempers.

I am with great respect and Esteem Dear Sir Yr. most obedient & very humble Servt.   DANIEL ROBERDEAU

Addressed: His Excellence / Benjaman Franklin Esqr. Doctor of Laws / and Minister Plenepotentiary at the Court / of France for No. America / Passe / Paris

To Dumas   ALS: Historical Society of Pennsylvania

Dear Sir,   Passy, Feb. 1. 1784—
I receiv'd duly yours of the 23d past, as well as those therein mentioned, with the Enclosed for the Office of Foreign Affairs, all of which except the last are forwarded, and that will go next Wednesday.— I thank you for the Opportunity given me of seeing the Intelligence they contain. I sent you 5 or 6 Weeks since, a Packet containing some fresh American Newspapers. You do not mention receiving them. They went by a Person whose Name I have forgot: He had formerly been in the

---

8. John Jay and JA left Paris for Britain in October, 1783: BF to Hartley, Oct. 8 and 16, both above. Laurens had left for England in August of the same year: XL, 444.

House of Messrs de Neuvfville. I wrote at the same time a few Lines.—⁹ I am ever, Dear Sir, Your faithful humble Servant

B FRANKLIN

P.S. I condole with you on the Loss of the Ship mention'd in the enclos'd Newspaper—¹

M. Dumas—

From Jacques Finck: Proposed Agreement

AD: American Philosophical Society

When Jacques Finck was hired as maître d'hôtel in January, 1783, he and Franklin made the following agreement: after three months, during which Finck would get a sense of what the family expected and what the expenditures were likely to be, he would no longer receive an annual salary and be reimbursed for itemized monthly statements. Instead, Finck would receive a fixed amount from which he would supply the basic tableware and kitchen equipment, provide dinners for a set rate per person, and be responsible for paying the cook and kitchen boy their wages. Franklin would henceforth be responsible only for procuring wine and liquor, wood for the fireplaces, and candles and lamp oil.[2]

This new arrangement was never implemented. For the duration of 1783, Finck continued to submit monthly statements that itemized the purchase of all foodstuffs, beverages, general household supplies, and, occasionally, the services of a tradesperson. The wages of the cook and kitchen boy were also included.[3] William Temple Franklin verified Finck's monthly totals and arranged for payment. On the bottom of each monthly account, Temple wrote some variation on "received by" and Finck signed.

At the beginning of 1784, Franklin tried again to implement a system in which Finck would manage and feed the household on a fixed

9. Not found. The bearer of the packet was named Chouquet: Dumas to BF, Feb. 5 and Feb. 12, below.
1. More than 300 men were lost when the Dutch ship of the line *Erfprins* foundered near Massachusetts: XL, 155n; *Adams Papers*, XIV, 497n.
2. XXXVIII, 530–1.
3. Summaries of these items, under Account XXXI, are in the Editorial Headnotes on Accounts in vols. 38 through 41.

budget. The document published below is, we believe, the agreement that was settled on for the year 1784, though many questions remain unanswered.

Franklin's extant papers include about a dozen items relating to Finck and his accounts, all but one of them undated and some as yet inexplicable.[4] At the least, they indicate that Temple and the maître d'hôtel argued over a period of years about what was expected and how much it would cost. The documents include two similar versions in Finck's hand of an agreement, one of them undated and with his annual stipend left blank, the other (published here) dated and with the sum and payment schedule specified; a heavily emended draft contract in Temple's hand that is substantially different in form and content from all other extant versions of agreements with Finck; several individual sheets of Temple's notes and calculations, figuring the average costs of meals for family members and servants; an indignant letter from Finck rejecting a now-missing offer and insisting that he could not do the job for less than 20,000 *l.t.* a year;[5] a sheet in an unknown hand listing four sample menus that could serve five people at a cost of 12 *l.t.* per head; and a copy, in the hand of one of Ferdinand Grand's clerks, of an undated account submitted by Finck, annotated with explanatory notes, showing that between 1783 (when Finck hired his nephew, whose wages were as yet upaid) and the present time, he was still owed 2,335 *l.t.* 10 *s.* The picture that emerges from these items is not altogether coherent, especially in light of the letter Finck wrote to Thomas Jefferson *circa* September 1785, shortly after Franklin had left France. Finck petitioned Jefferson to intercede with Congress to see that he received the money that Franklin owed him. In support of his narrative, which described Temple as being in charge of the house and the chief cause of his problems, he enclosed a copy of what he claimed was his agreement with Franklin— an undated document that is nearly identical in wording to the text published below except for the financial arrangement, which is completely different: Finck engages to "fournir la maison" for 1,700 *livres* per month (which works out to 20,400 *livres* per year).[6] Both L'Air de Lamotte and Chaumont wrote to Franklin in Philadelphia, informing him that Finck claimed to be owed money and that he had cheated

4. All these sheets, unless otherwise noted, are filed together at the APS under the title "Accounts and Agreements between Franklin and Jacques Finck [1783–1784]."

5. Filed with a large group of "Miscellaneous Notes" at the APS.

6. Finck to TJ, undated (Library of Congress). The letter is summarized under the date [1787?] in *Jefferson Papers*, XII, 485–6.

many of his suppliers, who were now clamoring for payment. Franklin replied that Finck had been reimbursed for all his "just claims," and that he and Temple had full receipts. He had always suspected Finck of being dishonest, and "so it proves."[7]

The convention published below has to have been the one implemented on February 1, 1784, as the agreement calls for Finck to receive an annual sum of 20,000 *l.t.*, payable in four quarterly sums of 5,000 *l.t.* Finck received the first of those quarterly payments on March 16, 1784, for having engaged to pay "toute la Depense de la Maison de M. Franklin (excepté les Vins Exes. [Extraordinaires], Liqueurs et Bieres,) depuis le 1r Fevr Jusqu'au dernier Jour d'Avril inclusivement."[8] The undated documents described above suggest that this arrangement must have been the result of significant negotiation. It is possible that Finck and Temple initially discussed a monthly stipend,[9] and that Finck proposed the terms he cited in his letter to Jefferson. If so, Temple must have offered a smaller stipend, eliciting Finck's angry letter insisting on no less than 20,000 *l.t.* per year—the sum that was finally accepted.

The "nouvelle arrangement," as Temple and Finck called it, did not last beyond the first quarter. Franklin's accounts indicate that between May, 1784, and the time Franklin left France, Finck was reimbursed each month according to the itemized receipts he submitted.[1]

For all the information about groceries that is available from Finck's itemized household bills, and for all the calculations of how

7. Le Ray de Chaumont to BF, Aug. 10, 1785; L'Air de Lamotte to WTF, Sept. 27[–Oct. 18], 1785; BF to Chaumont, Oct. 20, 1785; all at the APS.

8. Receipt written by WTF and signed by Finck on March 16, 1784. This receipt also lists 900 *l.t.* for Finck's wages, tips, etc., from Jan. 1, 1783, through Feb. 1, 1784, when "par mon Nouvelle Arrangement mes Gages n'ont plus lieux." It is among the sheets making up Account XXXI (XXXVIII, 3).

9. Several of the miscellaneous items relating to Finck's accounts reflect attempts to calculate average monthly expenses. On one of them, WTF calculated the cost of meals per month as follows: 720 *l.t.* to feed five masters, 240 *l.t.* to feed seven servants, and four dinners for 20 people at 100 *l.t.* per dinner, for a total of 1,360 *l.t.* He then calculated what Finck would receive annually if his monthly stipend were set at 1,500 *l.t.*, 1,600 *l.t.*, or 1,700 *l.t.*

1. His payments are recorded in Account XVII (XXVI, 3), and itemized bills survive for February and March, 1785 (University of Pa. Library). After April, 1784—the end of the first quarter of the new arrangement— L'Air de Lamotte tabulated actual monthly payments to the butcher, grocer, fruit seller, poultry supplier, and wood supplier, from early 1783 to April, 1784: BF's collection of miscellaneous bills and business memoranda

much the meals would cost, only one document in this archive describes the meals themselves. The following specifications are from Temple's working draft of a contract with Finck. For Franklin's table of five people,[2] *déjeuner* would consist of bread, butter, sugar, honey, coffee, and, once a week, chocolate. Dinners were to consist of a roast of either beef, veal, or mutton, a platter of chicken or game, two side dishes, two platters of vegetables, one platter of pastry with hors d'oeuvres of butter, radishes, and pickles, and the following items for dessert: fresh fruit (two kinds in winter and four in summer), two kinds of stewed fruits, a cheese platter with biscuits and sweets, and ice cream once a week in winter and twice a week in summer. As for the servants, Finck would agree to feed them well. They would receive breakfast, dinner, and a supper that was simple but ample.[3]

[February 1, 1784]

Convention à laquelle le Sieur finck S'oblige de faire la dépenses de la maison de Monsieur franklin pour tout ce qui Concerne la bouche en general telle quelle est Conposé au jourdhuy de cinq maitre et de neuf domestiques, et fournira en outre de la depenses ordinaire, au desire de Monsieur franklin, une table

---

(APS). Finck's narrative of his employment, as told to TJ in the 1785 letter cited above, presents an entirely different picture. He claims that he continued in his arrangement, receiving 1,700 *l.t.* per month, for six months, after which he broke the contract because he was losing too much money. The undated statement of his expenses, mentioned above, conforms to this story and might have been submitted to Ferdinand Grand around the same time. One of Finck's explanatory notes on that statement says that during the six-month period in question, more guests came to dinner than he expected, including two visitors named Franck and Bellefy(?) who, with their servants, lived and dined in the house for two and a half months.

2. The fifth person, besides BF, WTF, BFB, and L'Air de Lamotte, was Bob Alexander (XXXVI, 640), son of William Alexander, who lived with the family from late September, 1783, until December, 1784, when he went to London to study law. We know little of what he did at Passy, other than that JW expected that he would assist with paperwork and BFB enjoyed his company: JW to William Alexander, Oct. 4, 1783 (Yale University Library); BFB's journal.

3. WTF's draft contract specifies seven servants, whereas the agreement with Finck published here lists nine. WTF had calculated that seven could be fed well for 8 *l.t.* per day, if Finck took advantage of the leftover food from BF's table. The daily allowance for the masters' meals, by contrast, was one *louis*, or 24 *l.t.*, per day.

de 20 a 24 Couverts par Semaines, et une fois par moi ces meme vingt quatre couverts sera a deux services tel que la dignité de Monsieur franklin lexige et tel que le dt. finck a toujours servie de puis quil a L'honneur de lui appartenir, tout fois dans cet arrengement il ne Sera pas chargé de fournir les vin extraordinaire et les liquers ni de la bierre, en cas de repas de ceremonie, le dt. finck Se chargera de décorer les table avec tout la magnificence que les Circonstance lexigeront et come il a faites par le passé

Comme l'Etat actuel de tout ce qui est necessaire pour le service de la maison et dont le dt. finck est chargé, nest pas Suffisant, il ÿ Sera ajouté par Monsieur franklin vingt quatre Couvert dargent et six Cuillieur a Ragout et le dt. finck Se chargera de fournire le surplus comme linge batterie de cuissine faÿance verrerie &ca. qui lui Seront rendües en cas que les convention ne Subsistent plus, aux Condition détaille cÿ dessus, le dt. finck S'engage de fournir la maison pour la sommes de 20000 *l.t.* qui lui seron payé en quatre payement, savoir le 1er. mars 1784 5000 le 1er. juin 5000 le 1er. 7bre. 5000 et le 15 janvier 1785—5000

faite a pasÿ le premier fevrier 1784

From John Shaffer

ALS: American Philosophical Society

Sir   Paris the 1 febuary 1784./.

I have the honour to inform you that the house of Parlement has Rendered Me *Justis* on thursday Last,[4] I was Judged at liberty and *Discharged* of Every accusation, And Conducted to With all the honours of war to the Grand Stairs of Parlement, in order to have the Right to persue those who have bean the Ocation of my Disgrace.[5]

4. Jan. 29.
5. This may refer to the customary public announcement of an *absolution*, a complete acquittal, by court criers. *Absolution* nullified all charges against the defendant, whose name was erased from the jail register, and it entitled the defendant to sue for damages against the plaintiff: Richard M. Andrews, *Law, magistracy, and crime in Old Regime Paris, 1735–1789* (1 vol. to date, Cambridge and New York, 1994–), I, 473–4.

My inosance is Now proved theirefore I hope my Country-man will Contribute towards having my arrest Pupleshed in or-der to prove to the puplick my inosance, before my Departure.

I hav the honour to be with Profound Respect sir your hum-ble servant[6]   J. SCHAFFER

From William Strahan   ALS: American Philosophical Society

Dear Sir   London Febry 1. 1784.

I wrote to you in August last in answer to your very kind Note of July 29th. inclosing a Line to you from Mrs. Bache, which I then forgot to return to you, but which I now inclose. This Let-ter I sent by the common Post which I hope came safe to hand, tho' I have not had the Pleasure of hearing from you since.[7]

I therein acknowleged, and beg leave to repeat my warmest Acknowlegements for the very friendly and effectual Patronage you and your good Family on the other Side of the Water af-forded my poor helpless and singularly distressed Kins woman,[8] than whom none can be more grateful, or more deserving this great Kindness you have shewn her. By this time I dare say you are convinced that the high Character I presumed to give you of her was in no Shape exaggerated, and that she is really the worthy and accomplishd young Woman I represented her to be. Her late Letters to me are all full of the strongest Expressions of Gratitude for Mrs. Bache's continued Goodness to her.

6. The following day, Feb. 2, Beaumont wrote to BF with the same de-scription of Shaffer's honorable release at 8 A.M. the previous Thursday, and news that the court chose to disregard the spurious comments attrib-uted to WTF. Confident that BF's good opinion of Shaffer has been restored, the lawyer asks for money to help his client rehabilitate his good name. John Paul Jones has promised to contribute; his example will doubtless be imitated by other compatriots. Beaumont admits to being humiliated by his poor reception at Passy, but expects that BF will now help Shaffer return to America. APS.

7. BF's July 29 letter is in XL, 413–14; we suggest there that the letter from SB was probably hers of June 1. Strahan's August reply has not been found.

8. Sally Beckwith, whose school SB described in her June 1 letter.

Notwithstanding what you told me in your last, I cannot, nor will I renounce, all Hope of seeing you again, and that soon too. You have so many Friends here whom you must love, because they love you, and whom you must therefore be anxiously eager to see, that I judge it needless to add any other Inducement, tho' I could mention many, which I dare say will readily occur to yourself. In short, I am clearly for your spending the rest of your Days here, where you know you may have every Comfort and Amusement this World can afford, and where you can most easily and most perfectly enjoy yourself in your own way. I earnestly request you will give all due Attention to this Advice, which I wish to impress upon you (without the Assistance of Madeira) with all possible Earnestness. One Argument only will I now add more. I hear, and with real Concern I hear it, that you are affected with the Gout, &c. I need not tell you, that is the best medical Assistance this World affords. And now I will not tease you more upon this Subject till I have the Happiness of hearing from you again.

My worthy Friend Dr. Ross is the Bearer of this Letter, has promised to deliver it into your own Hands.[9] If he has the Honour of seeing you he has promised to give me the Satisfaction of telling me so, and of informing me of your Health and Welfare, and upon his Report I can surely depend. He has already spent much time in the East, in quality of Physician to our Army there, but the Air of that Country by no means agreeing with his Constitution, he was obliged to return home, without a Nabob's Fortune, for the Recovery of his Health and is now determined to follow his Profession in North America, where I have no doubt his Singular Skill and Humanity will (as soon as he becomes a little known) surely meet with the Encouragement they deserve. Wherever he goes, you well know, your Recommendation will be of the greatest Service to him. He is a Man of Sense and Observation, as well as of strict Veracity, so that you will find him well informed and most agreeable. In short, I will rest all my Credit with you, as a Man incapable of deceiving you, if you do not find Dr Ross such as I describe him to be, and of course *highly* deserving your Countenance.

9. For Andrew Ross see Hartley to BF, Jan. 28.

We are still in the greatest political Confusion here. After several Adjournments we the H. of C. meet again tomorrow; but I do not hear that any Conciliation, so much wanted, is likely to take place. What this will end as it is impossible for me to say, but it is not probable we [*go?*] on many Days longer in our present Situation.[1]

My Family[2] are all in their ordinary, and will all be very happy to see you once more in this still most agreeable Country: I remain with [unalterable?] Esteem and Affection Dear Sir, Your most obliged and faithful humble Servant

WILL. STRAHAN

The Frost is now so intense here this Morning, that there is no getting [*obscured by ink blots:* any Pen?] to write

From Daniel Roberdeau ALS: American Philosophical Society

Dear Sir   London Feby. 2d. 1784

Mr. Vanderhorst with his Daughter[3] are on an excursion to Paris, and their return will be most favorable for remittance, if you should, in consiquence of my Letter and a bill of Exchange enclosed to you a few days ago,[4] have it in your power, you'll oblige me to send by Mr. Vanderhorst who is directed in that

1. Strahan had been in the House of Commons since 1774. The change of ministry in December had resulted in a fresh political crisis, with Fox's supporters in Parliament challenging the legitimacy of Pitt's ministry, which was not expected to endure. The standoff in Parliament continued until mid-March: Namier and Brooke, *House of Commons*, III, 489; David Hartley to BF, Dec. 25, above; John Ehrman, *The Younger Pitt* (3 vols., New York and Stanford, Calif., 1969–96), I, 133–4, 138–42.

2. His wife, Margaret; his daughter, Margaret Spottiswoode; and his two sons, George and Andrew: IV, 224n; X, 137n, 169n.

3. The merchant Elias Vanderhorst (1738–1816), born in Charleston, S.C., immigrated to Bristol in the early 1770s and served as American consul there from 1792 to 1815. Vanderhorst had five daughters who survived to adulthood; we do not know which of them accompanied him on this trip: information kindly provided by Graham Tratt, Bristol Record Office, Eng. See also *Laurens Papers*, XVI, 139n, 140–41n.

4. The letter is published under the date of [January].

case to pay the money, or transmit the seal to my Son[5] whom I have left in Bristol for twelve months to learn the Art of refining of Sugar as I intend to establish that branch superadded to my dististillery, deranged during the late troubles, on my return to America.

Mr. Vanderhorst is a Gentleman of Character from South Carolina, and he and his Daughter desire attention all that you'll be pleased to show to them will oblige Dear Sir Yr. most obedt. & very hume. Serv.   DANIEL ROBERDEAU

Addressed: His Excellency / Doctor Benjaman Franklin / Minister Plenepotentiary at the Court of / France / Passe / Paris / Mr. Vanderhorst

From John and Sarah Jay   AL:[6] American Philosophical Society

Chaillot 3d. Febry.— [1784][7]

Mr. & Mrs. Jay request the honor of Dr. Franklin's Company at Dinner at 3 o'Clock on Saturday the 7th. Inst.—

Addressed: His Excellency Dr. Franklin / Passy—[8]

5. Isaac Roberdeau (1763–1829) went to England with his father and spent four years there. He became a topographer and surveyor, and is best known as L'Enfant's assistant in laying out Washington, D.C.: *ANB;* Roberdeau Buchanan, *Genealogy of the Roberdeau Family . . .* (Washington, D.C., 1876), pp. 34, 101, 104–22.

6. In the hand of Sarah Jay.

7. The only year during the Jays' stay in France that Feb. 7 fell on a Saturday. John Jay had only just returned from England; he rejoined his family at the end of January: *Jay Papers,* III, 492.

8. On a blank section of the sheet BF wrote "[*deleted:* To] The honourable the Burgomasters and Senate of the Free Imperial City of Hamburgh", interlining "The honourable" and correcting the spelling of Hamburgh. He was making the address conform to what appeared on the address line of Congress' Nov. 1 letter to the city officials, which Boudinot had asked him to forward while enclosing a second copy for BF's own files: Boudinot to BF, Nov. 1. For the address line BF was copying, see Smith, *Letters,* XXI, 133n.

From Henry Laurens

ALS: Library of Congress; copy: University of South Carolina Library

Dear Sir.   No 18. Fludyer Street Westminster 3d febry 1784.

I ask your pardon for having so long delayed an acknowledgement of your favor of the 6th. December. first occasioned
by a purpose of writing by Mr. Jay, whose departure was uncertain & I happned to be abroad when he was so good as to call
upon me at Bath to take leave. Immediately after he left us, I was
seized by a violent Cough lately attended by severe attacks from
the Gout in my head, & these by perhaps a little laziness which
deprived me of all disposition to business, at this moment I attempt to pay my respects under much pain & uneasiness.

I thank you Sir, for the Letters, meaning the two anonymous
& two from Mr. de Neufville's House— Upon a dispassionate
comparison I cannot perceive any likeness in the Characters in-
ducing a belief that the former & the latter are the performance
of the same hand, or to say the least, there is not near so great a
similarity as appears upon comparing the habitual emendations
of particular, or rather many, words in the supposed Culprit's
former Letters with those which stand in the two anonymos
marked Bruxelles. But alas! an investigation is now of little moment, since that Man,[9] remains incontrovertibly convicted of
Crimes, more heinous than would be that of writing an anonymous Letter with a view of putting an injured person upon his
guard against a flattering deceitful friend. The Major includes
the Minor. I have heard nothing concerning Jenings except seeing a Letter to a Gentleman in which he speaks of his mild vin-
dicatory answer,[1] as if he had actually made a reply, but I cant
learn that any person has seen it. This is very consistent with
his Love of duplicity & darkness. Let him rest; his Associate &
Sole countenancer shall hear from me.[2]

My Son who will have the honor of presenting this,[3] will also

9. Edmund Jenings.
1. Jenings' pamphlet *A Full Manifestation*.
2. Laurens wrote to JA on the same date as the present letter, demanding
two letters of his that JA had opened: *Laurens Papers*, XVI, 379–80.
3. Henry Laurens, Jr., was going to Le Vigan to accompany his aunt and
sister to England: *Laurens Papers*, XVI, 379.

deliver a Packet containing Mr. President Boudinot's Letter &
the documents accompanying it which you were pleased to indulge me with. These Papers have afforded information & much
satisfaction to some of our most judicious friends but I have not
been tempted to a Publication. The Young Man will also deliver
you some of the latest News Papers, you will thence learn something of the quantity & drift of inflamable air on this side & of
the number of Political Balloons which have been played off in
a House very near me since the Calends of December, but notwithstanding even the Vote of last Night,[4] I would as soon hazard an opinion upon the Wind of next Tuesday, as adventure to
say on whose side success will appear in the event of the present
struggle for Place & Power,[5] much wiser Men are equally cau-
tious. A majority of the House of Commons is evidently on one
side, while the bulk of their Constituents are provoked to declare their sentiments very openly on the other, but holding the
Purse strings is an advantage which in present circumstances
may be found irresistible & render an appeal to that bulk much
too hazardos. Be this as it may 'tis no great concern of mine,
'tis more in my Province to remark that the predictions which
were sometime the dernier hope of our Enemies have taken an
inverted course; the United States of America are not by their
Independence involved in Anarchy nor are their Inhabitants
cutting each others throats; Nor, if we can rely on those who
are the most feeling Judges of the fact, are those States more
dependent for Trade & Commerce with the British West India
Islands than these are upon the former, for supplies of every
kind essential to their existence as valuable Colonies.

Mr. Trumbull who left Boston the middle of December[6] assures me those people called Loyalists lately gone from New

4. A vote in favor of a resolution offered by Thomas William Coke (xx,
104n) stating that the continuation of the Pitt ministry would be detrimental to the country: *Laurens Papers*, XVI, 382n; Namier and Brooke, *House of
Commons*, II, 234–5.

5. Between Pitt and Fox. The tide was beginning to turn in Pitt's favor:
John Ehrman, *The Younger Pitt* (3 vols., New York and Stanford, Calif.,
1969–96), I, 138–42.

6. After spending almost two years in the United States, Trumbull returned to London to study with Benjamin West: Theodore Sizer, ed., *The*

York to Nova Scotia, furnish a vast demand upon the New England States for Lumber & other articles for building & subsistence, creating a New & very gainful Commerce to our Eastern Countrymen— These reflections lead me Sir, to apply to you as our Minister for information of the present allowable intercourse in Trade between France, the French West India Islands & our United States, respecting free Ports in the former & Commerce to & from the Islands. I think it necessary I should be acquainted with the true state at this conjuncture especially as Mr. Adams not long since contradicted my opinion founded upon information which I had received or understood in conversation with you at Passy. His assertion that France would not admit American Vessels to be carriers between her Islands & the United States may possibly be well grounded & I may have been under a mistake, but the Policy of the declaration & upon the Authority which he quoted, jarred against my Ideas of propriety. Silence may upon such occasions be preserved without violation to Candor.

I hardly dare to ask if by late Remitances from our Constituents you are in Cash for assisting a quandam Colleague now growing very poor & retaining an ancient stubbornness against letting the World know it.

This Kingdom is indebted to me two thousand Eight hundred & some Seventy Pounds Sterling for provisions for their Army drawn from my Plantations under Sequestration in S. Carolina an Authentic Account of which by their own Officers I delivered in to the Treasury in September last but I have no hopes of their paying me a farthing.[7] I may also say they owe me about £2500. Sterling for Indigo seized near three Years since on board a Neutral Ship, which is kept in the Court of Admiralty, the Judge delaying or refusing to condemn or acquit it.[8] I am told the best to be expected is, that the full value will be swal-

Autobiography of Colonel John Trumbull, Patriot-Artist, 1756–1843 (New Haven and London, 1953; reprint, New York, 1970), pp. 80–5.

7. Payment was refused in May, 1784: *Laurens Papers*, XVI, 335, 436–7, 456.

8. The case of the indigo seized in 1780 was not resolved until 1787: *Laurens Papers*, XV, 408n, 505–6n; XVI, 109n.

lowed, by pilferage Storage Court & proctor's Charges, these things with a failure of Remitances from America, are against me, & 'tis a little affecting to think my Employers have made no provision for a decent & safe conduct home again. Should they have any Money on this side to spare for their Servants I shall be glad to touch a small part of it; if I could recover my own, I would spare them, knowing they are poor also.

Miss Laurens joins in best Compliments to your self & Mr. Franklin & I have the honor to be With sincere affection & Esteem Sir Your Obedient & Most humble servant

HENRY LAURENS

His Excellency Benjamin Franklin Esquire Minister Plenipotentiary from the United States of America at the Court of France at Passy.

To John Adams

ALS: Massachusetts Historical Society

Sir,   Passy, Feb. 5. 1784

I received the Letter you did me the Honour of writing to me the 24th past. You have had a terrible Passage indeed, taking it all together from London to Amsterdam. The Season has been, and continues, uncommonly severe, and you must have suffered much. It is a Pity that the good Purpose of your Voyage, to save if possible the Credit of Mr Morris's Bills could not be accomplished, by your obtaining a Loan from the Regency. I do not wonder at their declining it, nor at the Stop you mention as put to the general Loan by the News of the Diversity of Sentiments among the States about the Plan of Impost. I hope these mischievous Events will at length convince our People of the Truth of what I long since wrote to them, that *the Foundation of Credit abroad must be laid at home.*[9] When the States have not Faith enough in a Congress of their own chusing, to trust it with Money for the Payment of their common Debt, how can they expect that that Congress should meet with Credit when it wants to borrow more Money for their Use from Strangers?

9. XXXVIII, 489.

Your Excellency saw in England the Instructions brought to us by Capt. Jones from the Congress, and which you forwarded to me.[1] Expecting your & Mr Jay's speedy Return hither, I took no Step in consequence of them. Mr Jay is now return'd. And we are both desirous of knowing whether it is your Intention to join us again here, in order to execute those Instructions; because in that Case we should wait your Arrival.

I have the honour to be, Your Excellency's most obedient & most humble Servant B. FRANKLIN

His Excellency John Adams, Esqr.

Endorsed: Dr Franklin Feb 5 ansd 11. 1784.

From Cadet de Vaux ALS: American Philosophical Society

Monsieur. Ce 6 [*i.e.*, 5][2] fevrier 1784

Votre poele-cheminée est construit; c'est pour la Seconde fois, la forte Gelée que nous eumes, le mois dernier, l'ayant réduit en poussiere, malgrés le feu qu'on avait entretenu dans l'attelier pour le faire Secher.

Je vous prie de Vouloir bien, ainsi que vous avés eu la bontè de nous le promettre, prendre un jour pour Venir chés le poelier, voir si on a bien Exécuté le plan, afin de rectifier les défauts avant qu'il soit séché.

Mon frere, l'Inspecteur Général des ponts et chaussées,[3] ose vous Supplier de lui faire l'honneur de diner chés lui ce jour là; et J'Espere que vous voudrés bien ne pas nous priver de la Satisfaction de vous posseder encore en famille.

Me permettrés vous de vous proposer le lundi 9 ou le mercredi 11 de ce mois, ou tel autre Jour de la Semaine prochaine, Excepté le mardi.

J'aurais l'honneur d'aller vous prendre, à Passy, le jour que

1. JA's covering letter is above, Dec. 5. Boudinot forwarded Congress' Oct. 29 instructions in his letter to the commissioners of Nov. 1.
2. This letter elicited BF's of Feb. 5, below.
3. Jean Cadet de Limay (1732–1802), an engineer, became *inspecteur général* in 1777: *DBF.*

vous voudrés bien m'Indiquer, a 11 heures, pour Etre chés le poelier entre midi et une heure, et de là revenir diner chés mon frere.

Je Suis avec un profond respect Monsieur, Votre très humble et tres obèissant Serviteur CADET DE VAUX

Rue des Gravilliers

To Cadet de Vaux LS:[4] Bibliothèque Municipale, Nantes

Passy, le 5. Fev. 1784.

Malgré tout le desir que J'ai, Monsieur, de faire quelque Chose qui puisse vous etre agreable ainsi qu'a M. Votre Frere,— Il m'est absolument impossible de faire le voyage de Paris dans Ce moment cy; ma Maladie, et la saison rigoureuse, sont des obstacles insurmontables pour moi—

J'ai moi meme fait executer un Poele Cheminée propre a bruler le Charbon de Terre, & telle que M. le Noir a paru desirer que Je fis connoitre dans ce Pays cy.[5] Je serai charmé de vous le montrer, quand vos Affaires vous permettrons de venir a Passy: Je ne puis encore en faire un Usage habituel faute de Charbon de Terre.— Si vous pouvez m'en procurer vous me ferez grand Plaisir.—

J'ai recu dans le Tems—La Farine de Bled de Turquie, que vous avez eu la complaisance de me faire venir—et pour laquelle Je vous suis redevable.—[6] Je vous envoye par le Porteur un

4. In WTF's hand.

5. See Lenoir to BF, Dec. 4, and Cadet's letter immediately above. We have not been able to determine what BF was offering to show Cadet. It is possible that he had brought to France the vase stove made in England in 1771, which he carried back to America and used during the winter of 1775: "Description of a new Stove for burning of Pitcoal . . . ," in Smyth, *Writings*, IX, 459–60. If BF did have this stove at Passy, however, it is curious that he had not shown it to Cadet earlier.

6. Cadet de Vaux had recently sent BF corn flour (here called "Bled de Turquie"); see his letter of Jan. 14. We suspect that Cadet, who had consulted BF on American breadmaking the previous spring (see XXXIX, 355), had asked him to prepare a sample loaf using corn meal, which was being explored as a superior source of nutrition for people as well as animals. An

FEBRUARY 5, 1784

Echantillon de Pain fait en Partie avec cette Farine,—mais Je crois qu'il seroit possible de le faire meilleur: Je vous envoye la Recette pour le faire[7]—si vous jugez a propos d'en faire faire l'Essaye a l'Ecole de Boulangerie—

J'ai l'honneur d'etre, avec un sincere Attachement, Monsieur votre très humble & très obeissant Serviteur.— B. FRANKLIN

M. Cadet de Vaux

Notation: Franklin

Recipe for Making Bread of Corn Flour Mixed with Wheat Flour

D:[8] American Philosophical Society

[*c.* February 5, 1784][9]

Pour faire du Pain avec la Farine de Maïs, mêlée avec la Farine de Blé.

La Farine de Maïs demande plus de tems pour bien cuire, que la Farine de Blé; C'est pourquoi si on les mêle à froid, et qu'on les fasse fermenter et cuire ensemble, la Partie de Blé sera suffisamment cuite, lorsque la Partie de Maïs sera encore crue.

Pour parer à cet Inconvenient, Nous faisons bouillir un Pot d'eau dans lequel on jette un peu de Sel et pendant que l'eau bout, nous Jetons dedans avec une main un peu de Farine de

---

article in the December, 1783, *Jour. de physique* claimed that corn was the most nutritious of all grains, described its ease of cultivation, and called on experts in "l'Art de la Boulangerie" to perfect the technique of making bread with corn flour: *Jour. de physique* XXIII, part II, 447–52. Around this time the Royal Academy of Bordeaux issued a prize question calling for a study of corn and its uses. They awarded the prize on Aug. 24, 1784, to Parmentier, co-director with Cadet de Vaux of the Ecole de Boulangerie, for a study published the following year as *Maïs, ou Blé de Turquie . . .* (Bordeaux, 1785). The bread recipes in Parmentier's book also mixed corn and wheat flours, but would have yielded loaves far lighter than the one BF made.

7. Immediately below.

8. In the hand of L'Air de Lamotte, with emendations by WTF.

9. This appears to be a draft of the recipe BF sent to Cadet de Vaux on Feb. 5, immediately above.

Maïs, et avec l'autre nous la remuons dans l'eau bouillante qu'on laisse sur le feu; et cette operation doit être repetée avec un peu de Farine à chaque fois, Jusqu'a ce que la masse devienne si épaisse qu'on ait peine à la remuer avec le Baton. Ensuite, après l'avoir laissée quelque tems encore sur le feu, Jusqu'a ce que la derniere Poignée ait bouilli, on l'ôte, et on verse la Masse dans la Huche, où on doit la bien mêler et pétrir avec une Quantité de Farine de Blé, suffisante pour former une Pate propre a faire le Pain, et du Levain, ou de la Levure de Biere, pour la faire lever; et après le tems nécessaire on la met en Pains, et ensuite au Four.

Notation by Benjamin Franklin Bache: Pour faire du Pain avec un Melange de Farine de Maïs et de Bled.

From Dumas

ALS: American Philosophical Society; AL (draft): Nationaal Archief

Monsieur,   Lahaie 5e. Fevr. 1784

Le Sr. Chouquet,[1] après avoir charrié plus d'un mois avec lui le paquet du 17e. Dec. que vous aviez eu la bonté de lui remettre pour moi, me l'a enfin envoyé de Dunkerque par Amsterdam, d'où je l'ai reçu il y a quelques jours. Heureusement les Dépeches de Mr. Van Berckel à L.H.P.[2] ne nous avoient pas laissé ignorer si longtemps le contenu des papiers qu'il renfermoit. Je me recommande toujours à votre bonté, Monsieur, pour me faire parvenir la connoissance prompte de ce qui doit se passer incessamment, à ce que l'on suppose ici, entre le Duc de Dorset & les Plenipo: hollandois au sujet de la conversion des Préliminaires en Traité définitif, comme aussi de l'état de votre santé, pour laquelle je fais assidument les voeux que me dicte le respectueux attachement avec lequel je suis, De Votre Excellence Le très-humble & très obéissant serviteur   C. W. F. DUMAS

1. A former employee of de Neufville & fils: BF to Dumas, Feb. 1, above.
2. Berckel is Pieter Johan van Berckel, the Dutch minister in Philadelphia, while L.H.P. stands for "Leurs Hautes Puissances," an honorific title for the States General of the Netherlands.

Quand vous aurez lu, Monsieur, l'incluse pour le Congrès,[3] Mr. votre P. Fils, que j'embrasse cordialement, voudra bien la fermer & expédier promptement pour sa destination.

Passy à Son Excellence Mr. Franklin M. Pl.

Addressed: à Son Excellence / Monsieur Franklin Esqr., Ministre / Plenipo: des Etats Unis d'Amerique / à Passy./. / pres Paris./. / France

From the Chevalier de Failly[4]

ALS: American Philosophical Society

Monsieur   a Rouen Le 5e. fevrier 1784

La Liberté des Braves americains vos Dignes Compatriotes Est Louvre de votre Excellence; puissies vous jouir Long tems dans La Santé La plus parfaite, et La plus Constente prosperité du fruit de vos travaux à jamais mémorable. Ce Sont Les veux Bien Sinceres que je feray Pour vous dans tous Les tems de ma vie, et que je vous prie D'agreer a Ce Renouvellement D'année; vous avés Sçu Bon gré, Monsieur a tous Les officiers françois qui Secondent vos vues patriotiques ont Contribué à La Reussitte de vos projets vastes, et Glorieux, j'ay Servy Sous Les Drapeaux americains avec autant de zelle que Desinteressement Dans la Campagne de 1777 sous Les ordres du general Gates aux affaires de Stile Water, et a La prise du general Bourgoinne, et Tout Lhiver au Camp de val forge Sous Les ordres du général Waginsthon, et a la division Du marquis de la fayette, En 1778 j'ay Servy a la Retraite des anglois qui Evaquoit Philadelphie, et au Combats de Mountmot En gersay Le 28: juin, ou j'ay Eu mon Cheval blessé Sous Moy au poitraille, j'ay été au Siege de Rode Islande jour et Nuit; L'honnorable Congrès m'a Donné une Commission de Lieut Colonel du 21 aout et une de Colonel du 17: 8bre. 1777. jour de La prise du general Bourgoinne,

3. Doubtless Dumas' Feb. 1[–4] letter to the Department for Foreign Affairs: *Diplomatic Correspondence of the United States,* VII, 29–33.
4. Identified in XXXIII, 90n.

j'ay aussy un Certificat du genal Gates. Jose Supliér votre Excé-
lence de M'accorder Sa protection, pour etre admis a lhonneur
de Cette Noble assossiation.[5] Je ne Sesseray tant que je vivray
de faire des veux pour votre Excellence.

J'ay lhonneur detre avec un tres profont Respect Monsieur
Votre tres humble et tres obeissant serviteur

LE CHER. DE FAILLY
Capne. Comdt. au Regt. D'anjou Et
Colonel au Service des etats unis d'amerique

From Thomas Mifflin
ALS: American Philosophical Society

Sir   Annapolis 5 Februy 1784
Lt Colonel Murnan has requested me to give him a Letter of
Introduction to your Excellency; which he supposes will assist
him in his military Pursuits—[6] I have seen many Certificates
from General Washington[7] General Howe & other Officers under whom he has served; & have made a particular Enquiry into
his Conduct, during the late War: And it with much Pleasure I
now recommend him to you as a very deserving Officer.

I am with the greatest Respect & Attachment Your Excellencys Obedient & humble Serv   THOMAS MIFFLIN

Addressed: The Honorable / Benjamin Franklin / Passy

Endorsed: Thos Mifflin Esq 5 Feby. 84 Recomn. of Col Harmar

5. The Society of the Cincinnati.

6. Jean-Bernard-Bourg Gauthier de Murnan (1748–1797), an engineer
in the Continental Army who had been promoted to lieutenant colonel the
previous September and who had just resigned his commission. He was initially unsuccessful in obtaining a post in the French army, but during the
French Revolution became *général de brigade provisoire: JCC,* XXVI, 63–4;
Bodinier, *Dictionnaire,* under Gauthier.

7. GW's certificate, lauding Murnan's services, was dated May 24, 1783:
Fitzpatrick, *Writings of Washington,* XXVI, 452–3.

From the Comte de Barbançon[8]

ALS: American Philosophical Society

Monsieur,   A Paris ce 8. fevrier 1784.

Je regrette infiniment que la saison rigoureuse ou nous sommes me prive d'aller moi même vous prier d'agréer les assurances de ma reconnoissance. Vous avez bien voulu me faire passer par Caillot la lettre du Sr. Bertram;[9] nous vous sommes redevables, Monsieur, de nouvelles richesses vegetales.

Vous m'aviés flatté, la derniere fois que j'eus l'honneur de vous voir chez vous, que je pourrois vous être utile pour procurer à vos amis quelques espéces naturelles à notre climat, et dont vous ne jouissés pas encore à Philadelphie, je serais si jaloux de trouver une occasion de pouvoir vous être bon à quelque chose, que vous me permettrez, Monsieur, d'insister sur cet article.

J'ai l'honneur d'être Monsieur Votre très humble et très obéissant serviteur   LE CTE. DE BARBANÇON

Notation: Barbançon le Cte. De 8 Fevr. 1784.

From the Comtesse de Chinon[1]

L:[2] American Philosophical Society

[before February 9, 1784][3]

Made. la Comtesse de Chinon prie Monsieur franklin ministre des Etats unis de vouloir bien lui faire l'honneur de venir au Bal

---

8. Officer and amateur botanist: XXXVII, 230.

9. John Bartram, Jr., whose packet was forwarded by RB on Sept. 8: XL, 593.

1. The former Rosalie Rochechouart, who in 1782, at the age of 12, married the 15-year-old comte de Chinon, the grandson of the maréchal de Richelieu. Immediately after the wedding, the comte left with his tutor for a tour of Europe and did not return until 1788 or 1789: Henriette-Lucie Dillon, marquise de La Tour du Pin Gouvernet, *Memoirs of Madame de La Tour du Pin*, ed. and trans. Felice Harcourt (London, 1969), p. 93.

2. BF's name and title were inserted by another hand into what was evidently a generic invitation.

3. During BF's stay in France, Feb. 9 fell on a Monday in 1778 and 1784. In 1778, the comtesse was not yet married.

que lui donneront M. et Mde. la Marechale de Richelieu dans leur hotel de Lundi Neuf fevrier, Lequel commencera a quatre heures après midy et finira a dix.

Addressed: A Monsieur / Monsieur franklin Ministre / des Etats unis / A Passy/.

From Beaumont

ALS: American Philosophical Society

Son Excéllance,   Paris Ce 9. fevrier 1784./.

En Conséquence de Notre Entrevuë de Samedy dernier,[4] nous nous Sommes Transportés chéz Mr. le Lieutenant criminel: Nous avons prié ce magistrat de Vous Envoyer directement La Traite de 60. Dollars pour en Vériffier la Signature.[5]

Le Sr. Schaffer Se flatte que Vôtre Excéllance repondera Sans délais à Mr. le Lt. criminel, en lui donnant Toute Satisfaction Sur la Validité de la Signature, et même Engagera Ce Magistrat à ne Remettre la ditte Traite qu'a lui *Seul, Schaffer;* attendû que cet objet est la Seule ressource qu'il ait pour le Moment, et qu'avéc cet argent il pourra lever une Expédition de L'arrêt du parlement Sans le quel il ne peut Se montrer dans Sa Patrie. Avèc L'arrèt du parlement à la main le Sr. Schaffer est persuadé que sous vos auspices tous Ses honorables Compatriotes se Cottiseront pour lui faciliter un prompt Retour dans son Pays.

4. Feb. 7.

5. Beaumont had been trying to obtain this bill of exchange for the better part of a week, but Bachois de Villefort would not release it without BF's permission. The *lieutenant criminel* first sent BF a copy of the bill, explaining that it was among the seized possessions that Shaffer was now reclaiming and asking whether BF would agree to its being returned. (That letter is undated, but we assume that it was after Feb. 2, when Beaumont wrote to BF with the news of Shaffer's release and mentioned nothing about this difficulty; see the annotation of Shaffer to BF, Feb. 1, above.) Beaumont wrote to BF on a "Jeudy Cinq heures du Soir," probably Feb. 5, saying that he had just seen Bachois, and that the *lieutenant criminel* would not release the bill of exchange until BF verified that the signature on it was genuine: Bachois de Villefort to BF, [after Feb. 2, 1784?]; Beaumont to BF, [Feb. 5, 1784?], both at the APS.

Je suis avèc Respèct de Son Excéllance Le très humble Et très obt. Serviteur.   DE BEAUMONT

Notation: De Beaumont 9. Fevr. 1784—

From John and Angelica "Carter" [*i.e.*, Church][6]

AL: American Philosophical Society

Tuesday Feby 10 [1784]
Mr & Mrs Carter Request Dr. Franklin to do them the Honor to dine with them on Saturday next.
The Favor of an Answer is desired.

From Ingenhousz

ALS: American Philosophical Society

Dear friend.   Vienna febr. 10th. 1784
This will be delivred to you by my Good friend the Prelate or Abbé *Nekrep* president of the oriental College at Vienna,[7] a Gentleman much estimed here, a very good scholar and philosopher.

He goes for a few weeks to Paris in pursuet of knowledge regarding his profession, and as his particular pride is to know you, I take the liberty to recommend him to your acquaintance.

I recieved your lettre of the 23th of jan.[8] and have recieved allso a Satisfactory answer of mr. le Roy.

Mr. *Nekrep* was one of our philosophical Society for constructing the balloon, of which nothing will be done, because the Nobility has not furnish'd us with money enough to bear the expenses. However I feel myself reather happy that the undertaking was not encouraged; because I foresaw to many dif-

---

6. The son-in-law and daughter of Philip Schuyler. BF had learned the husband's true name, John Barker Church, in October: XXXVIII, 546; XL, 263–4.

7. Johann von Gott Nekrep (1738–1784) was director of the Oriental Academy (Orientalische Academie): Constant von Wurzbach, *Biographisches Lexikon des Kaiserthums Oesterreich* (36 vols., Vienna, 1856–91).

8. Not found.

ficulties, danger of miscarrying in the execution, and after great peine, care and trouble to find at last my reputation in danger. Your answer has Confirm'd me in the resolution of giving it up.

As Abbé *Nekrep* will only Stay a few weeks at Paris, you may give him, when he sets out, what ever you may have at that time to send to me, a lettre, a pamphlet, american news papers &c.

I have also given him an introductory lettre to Mr. le Begue and Le Roy.

I am with great respect Yours obedient humble serv. and affectionate friend   J. INGEN HOUSZ

It gives me peine to be informed that you labour under a Stone in the bladder. However, as it gives very little trouble, you have the best change [chance] that it is one of that sort, which will not produce much peine.

There is indeed very little to be depended upon true lithontriptics or dissolvents of the Stone as yet: tho we doe not dispare to find out such a remedie. Those which have given the greatest relief are *lixivium alcalinum* or Soap lie, quick lime water, and Soap. Doctor Chitticks medecine was soap lie.[9] Sir John Pringle had Some Confidence in it, but prescribed oftenner, Spanish Soap made up in pills and taken two or three times a day at a dose of 20 grains or a scrupul, increasing the Dose to three dragmas or half an ounce a day, and even more if the stomach could bear it. It has often the effect of diminishing the symptoms and preventing the growth of the Stone. I saw several times a very singular effect of water impregnated with fixed air by Parker's machine. They trink of it at least a pint a day. This water is only an artificial seltzer water, and this last may be taken instead of it. It is very innocent and can doe no harm if it does no good. I publish'd a pamphlet upon it during my last journay being in London. It was a latin translation of Dr. Hulme. You have a Copy of it which I presented to you. The titel is *Nova tuta faci-*

9. Chittick, a Bath physician, became known in the early 1760s for his secret remedy to dissolve stones. In 1763, apothecary Alexander Blackrie performed chemical analyses and identified the ingredients, publishing them in the *Scots Magazine*. In 1771 Blackrie published his method of preparing and administering the remedy: George W. Corner and Willard E. Goodwin, "Benjamin Franklin's Bladder Stone," *Journal of the History of Medicine and Allied Sciences*, VIII (1953), 362.

lisque methodus curandi calculum podagram, destruendi vermes. . . .
It is printed at Leyden 1778.[1]

I would not advise you to change materialy your diet as for eating and drinking, so that your appetite or digestion may be hurt by it. In your age nothing is more essential than to keep up the good disposition of the stomach.

a Mr. Franklin a Passy[2]

Addressed: a Son Excellence / Mr. B. Franklin. Ministre Plenipot. des / Etats unis de l'Amerique à la Cour de France / a Passy

Endorsed: Feb. 10. 84

From John Adams   AL (draft): Massachusetts Historical Society

Sir   The Hague Feb. 11. 1784

Last night I received your obliging Favour of the fifth of this Month.

Your Excellencys Sentiment, "that the Foundation of Credit abroad must be laid at Home" is perfectly just, and accords with the General Sentiment of the Money Lenders, Undertakers and Brokers in this Country, whose Universal Cry is "We should choose to see Some certain Method agreed on and established, for the Payment of Interest before We adventure farther in the American Loan."

I am glad to hear of Mr Jays Safe return, to Paris and hope his Health is confirmed.— As the Instructions may be executed by any one or more, of the Ministers for the Peace, residing at the Court of Versailles, it Seems to me to be more for the Benefit of the publick Service, that I Should remain here for Sometime, rather than go to Paris. I have not given over all Endeavours to obtain the Money for the Bills, although the best Friends We

1. Ingenhousz had written about this method, and the pamphlet he translated, a year earlier; see XXXIX, 91–2.

2. Ingenhousz had initially addressed this letter to Le Roy, but crossed out his name. Le Roy's name and address were likewise crossed out on the address sheet.

have inform me, there is no hope at all from the Publick. We are endeavouring to discover if it is possible by any new Plan of a Loan, to obtain the Money of the Undertakers. Yet by all I can learn I despair of Obtaining it, with out agreeing to Terms so disadvantageous as to be little better than the final Protest of the Bills.— Indeed it is Still improbable that I can obtain it, upon any Terms at all.— Money is Scarce as well as our Credit feeble. The Loan of the East India Company, warranted by the States of Holland, does not fill, a Case unknown in this Country.

Your Excellency with Mr Jay, may proceed to execute those Instructions without me, and I hereby intreat that you would without waiting at all for me. It is not likely there will be any difference of Opinion between your Excellencies, concerning any of those Instructions, in which Case alone it would be necessary for me to attend, if Mr Laurens does not.

It is probable We may soon learn Something from Congress in Answer to our Letter with the definitive Treaty[3] which will determine whether it is necessary I should join you, at Paris or not.— It would be very inconvenient to me, in the present tender State of my Health to make a Journey to Paris without a necessity, at least untill this formidable Winter breaks up, although I should be ambitious enough of the Honour of joining in the Execution of those orders.

I wish your Excellencies an happy Year and much Pleasure in the Enjoyment of Peace, as well as Success in your Negotiations, whether joined or not by your most obedient and most humble sert

Dr Franklin

From ——— de l'Auréole, with Franklin's Note for a Reply, and Other Applicants for Emigration

ALS: American Philosophical Society

The relentless stream of letters from people throughout Europe and Great Britain who sought Franklin's help in immigrating to the

3. XL, 600–6.

United States finally induced him, in the winter of 1783–84, to write "Information to Those Who Would Remove to America," which was intended to answer all such queries.[4] We summarize here the unsolicited letters and petitions that "pestered" Franklin, as he put it, during the months covered by the present volume.[5] We also include the undated appeals that have defied our efforts to locate them more precisely, ascribing them to the year 1783, after the armistice was declared. We group the dated applications by nationality, and the undated applications by type.[6]

English men and women seek Franklin's assistance from either residences abroad or their native country. Richard Holmes writes from Naples on October 18, on behalf of himself and his Italian partner, Domenick Romero. Masters of dyeing and weaving fine cloth, they had been co-directors of a Neapolitan woolen manufactory that was forced to close because of the financial misfortunes of its owner, a merchant. They have no families, and seek passage to Philadelphia, where they believe their skills will be useful. Walter Brown writes from Newcastle upon Tyne on November 17, wondering whether Franklin received his previous letter (now missing), which he entrusted to Henry Laurens. He knows the linen manufactory "from the Seed to the Needle"; this knowledge will certainly be useful in America. Having lost his fortune because of his American sympathies, he wishes to emigrate. He has twenty-one lawfully conceived children, the eldest of whom served in the American Navy. The five youngest are named after the "Worthys of America." (He specifies only three of them: Washington, Franklin, and Laurens.)

Miss E. Stubbs, living at Versailles with the comtesse d'Harville,[7] writes a series of letters championing the case of a young Parisian physician named d'Avelange, with whom—it is gradually revealed—she is in love. On September 16, she attests to the doctor's superior talents and morals, explaining that he cured her of melancholy shortly after

4. It is below, under the date [before March, 1784].

5. The two exceptions are the letters from John Curwen, Oct. 23, and Lucas Despeintreaux, Jan. 9, which are published. Both men went to Pennsylvania. We know that BF encouraged Despeintreaux to emigrate, and we suspect that Curwen might have received similar encouragement.

6. All these documents are at the APS. The letters from English men and women are written in English. All others are in French, unless otherwise noted.

7. Marie-Henriette-Augustine-Renée dal Pozzo de La Trousse, wife of army general Louis-Auguste de Jouvenel d'Harville des Ursins, comte d'Harville and marquis de Trainel: *DBF*.

she arrived from England. She also writes that she is enclosing a letter from him. The letter from d'Avelange is dated September 17: he is thirty-three years old, the youngest of twelve children, and descends from a noble family. He has no fortune, speaks French, German, Italian, and Latin, and holds tolerant religious beliefs. He wishes to settle in America and hopes that Franklin might recommend him. On October 1, Miss Stubbs sends an agonized message begging for an answer to her letter. On October 14 she acknowledges Franklin's reply (now missing): his remarks were "perfectly just" and his advice "extremely prudent." He was kind enough to say that he would "take a pleasure in rendering service to a Man of merit." If he did so, Franklin would make two people happy, as Dr. d'Avelange, once he is established, plans to marry Miss Stubbs, and they will start a family.

Most of the would-be emigrants are French. A theology student at Embrun, the abbé de Solas, writes on September 27, pointing out that he is the first cousin of the chevalier de Chefdebien, who served as an officer in America and is known to Franklin. Now in his final year of study for the priesthood, the abbé realizes that it is not his calling. His family is not wealthy and he cannot afford further education. He wants to emigrate and will take whatever post Franklin would be good enough to obtain for him.

A third-year medical student named Rousset writes on September 29 from Paris. His parents plan to take him out of school, as they can no longer afford to support him. He hopes to go to America under Franklin's patronage and gain experience in medicine, surgery, and obstetrics. He has received numerous honors and won several first prizes, including one in botany from the Collège de pharmacie, which was presented on September 1 by Lieutenant of Police Lenoir. Since there is no one who surpasses Franklin in doing good, will he help Rousset to complete his education? If so, Rousset would be for some time completely at Franklin's disposal.

Charvet l'aîné, from Serrières, writes a long letter on October 4 about the possibility of raising silkworms in America. He is thirty-three years old and from a poor family. He cultivates mulberries in his native Vivarais, where silk production is a major industry, but longs to put his expertise into practice on a large scale. He is also interested in viticulture.

On October 15, Vigneron de la Jousselandière of Beauvoir-sur-Mer implores Franklin's protection.[8] His health requires him to live in a warm climate. He wants to buy large tracts of land, preferably in Virginia, and settle there with his followers, who number more than

8. He does not mention his earlier letters, for which see XXX, 35–6.

six hundred. He worries that these people would soon wish to set up homesteads of their own. What American law would ensure their fidelity? If they were to leave, he would have to use slave labor.

A Paris glassmaker named Sutter, who lives chez Monsieur de Brossard,[9] writes a brief letter on October 29. He has heard rumors that Franklin wants to find master glassmakers to work in Philadelphia. He offers his services, and believes he could convince several co-workers to accompany him.

Nirmont, writing on November 4, explains that he had come to Paris two years ago on the promise of a position that never materialized. He has heard that Franklin frequently finds places in America for young Frenchmen, and begs to be one of them. If he finds work in America, he will be able to send aid to his impoverished mother.

From La Rochelle on November 8 comes a letter from Lacour, who offers his expertise in earthenware and ceramic design. Hoping to settle in Philadelphia, he wants to know if he would be welcomed there, if he could find all the workers he would need, what would be his chances of success, and whether he would be compensated while waiting for his operation to become profitable.

Uncertain as to whether the United States has a policy of religious tolerance or whether it has an established religion, Hardy, a Catholic priest and principal of a *collège* in Ervy in the diocese of Sens, writes on December 20.[1] His desire to emigrate comes not from any secret ambition or dissatisfaction with his present situation. His one desire is to be useful to a nation he loves and respects, which had long been enslaved and now is free. He imagines that ecclesiastics are rare in America, and offers his services as either a priest or an educator. Before leaving France, he would like the assurances of Franklin's protection and of an advantageous placement by Congress.

Lagarde, a young surgeon who has been practicing in Paris since 1780, writes to Franklin on January 24 after having failed to find him at home two days earlier. Lagarde details his training and experience

9. The Brossard family of Normandy had for centuries specialized in the manufacture of "grand verre," including windows and mirrors: James Barrelet, *La Verrerie en France de l'époque gallo-romaine à nos jours* (Paris, 1953), pp. 47, 171–2.

1. Hardy is listed as one of four "Chanoines à l'Autel St. Pierre & St. Paul" in the diocese of Sens in *France ecclésiastique* for 1783, p. 250. He was probably Jean-Baptiste-Etienne Hardy, who still served as a priest in Sens at the beginning of the nineteenth century: Alype-Jean Noirot, *Le Département de l'Yonne comme diocèse, 1790–1843* (5 vols., Auxerre, 1979–82), I, 79, 118.

in military hospitals, first in Metz, then in Dunkirk, and now in Paris, where Calonne has paid his expenses and he has been learning the theories of M. Baudelocque. His prospects now seem uncertain, and he has decided to offer his talents to America. He asks for an appointment.

Writing from Saint-Malo in Brittany on January 27, Mallet de la Brossière, a forty-one-year-old physician, has been in government service for thirteen years, with little to show for it. While stationed with the Royal Navy at Brest, he was sent to Tunis to cure the bey's son-in-law of a serious illness.[2] In 1776 he was posted to Juda (Ouidah), where he spent the war years forgotten by his government, his health deteriorating in the dangerous climate. His hopes for compensation or at least a pension after his return were cruelly disappointed. M. Poissonnier[3] can vouch for Mallet's respectability and professional expertise. Since his own fatherland has rejected him, why shouldn't Mallet look for a new one? He requests to be put in charge of a military hospital, as he had been in France, and to be given a free passage to the United States. If this is possible, all he needs are recommendations from Franklin and Poissonnier. He signs as "Med. de la faculté de Montpellier."

Writing from Champigny sur Marne on February 3, the comtesse de Waldner tells Franklin how much she regrets not having seen him before she left Passy.[4] Noting the kindness he had shown her in the past, she recommends Loiseau from Tours, a relative of one of her servants, who is well educated and wishes to settle in America with what fortune he possesses. The comtesse takes a great interest in this family, and Franklin would oblige her infinitely if he offered the young man his protection.

2. Julien Mallet de la Brossière was elected to the Société royale de médecine in 1777. Shortly thereafter the society published his account of treating two scorpion-bite victims in Tunis: *Histoire et mémoires de la Société royale de médecine* for 1777–78 (Paris, 1780), pp. 38, 315–17. His full name is given in Hélène Berlan and Étienne Thévenin, *Médecins et société en France du XVIe siècle à nos jours* (Toulouse, 2005), pp. 85–6.

3. The physician and counselor of state whom BF had met more than ten years earlier. His most recent extant letter invited BF to one of his lectures: XIX, 328n; XX, 314; XXXVI, 572–3.

4. Henriette-Louise de Waldner de Freundstein (1754–1803) descended from an illustrious Alsatian family. She was well known in French aristocratic circles, socialized with the royal family, and participated in the cultural and literary life of Paris during her occasional visits. She supported Mesmer's experiments in animal magnetism, and in June, 1784, was invited to Versailles to witness an ascension of a hot air balloon: Suzanne Burkard, ed., *Mémoires de la Baronne d'Oberkirch sur la cour de Louis XVI et la société française avant 1789* ([Paris], 1970), pp. 11–22, 35, 168, 301–9, 333, 355.

Duhamel Deschenaix from Saint-Malo was captured by the British and robbed of all his fortune as he was returning from eight years in the East Indies. He writes on February 28, seeking advice on emigrating and help in procuring either land or a means of honest employment once in America.

Two citizens of Geneva (as they sign themselves), A. Barthold and C. Vaucher, write from Paris on November 4. Their own government is crumbling under despotism, and they implore Franklin to offer them protection in emigrating to America. They lack the funds to pay their own transportation and hope Franklin will arrange a passage at no cost.

An evangelical Lutheran pastor, signing himself Joh. Georg. Mono, writes in Latin on November 18 from Leiselheim, Germany. He recommends the skills of his son, Joh. Jac. Fridericus, who is well educated in trigonometry, architecture, French, and penmanship, a sample of which in French and German is included. He hopes that Franklin will either hire his son as an assistant or recommend him to Congress, and will arrange his free passage to America.

The appeals summarized below are the residue of undated applications that we have been unable to ascribe to any particular time. We place them under the tentative date [1783?] on the assumption that would-be emigrants were likely to seek passage to America after the armistice was declared.

Captain Frederic Guillaume Ferdinand de Brandenstein writes from Wüstenstein in Franconia,[5] addressing Franklin as the president of Congress. The news of America, which has reached far and wide, has inspired the hopes of several noble families to emigrate under the protection of the United States government. Having neither first-hand knowledge nor a faithful description of the situation and rights of new settlers, they wish to pose the following questions: Will new settlers be accepted or not? Will they be able to make their own arrangements or are there set conditions? If the former, whom should they contact?

Several letters come from military men, past and present. Pierre-Simon Girard,[6] an *ingénieur architecte,* sends a memoir detailing his

5. Friedrich Wilhelm Ferdinand von Brandenstein (1754–1818), a military officer, amateur engraver, and owner of a publishing house: *Allgemeines Künstlerlexikon* (71 vols. to date, Munich, Leipzig, and Berlin, 1992–), XIII, 611.

6. Girard (1765–1836), who did not emigrate, participated in Napoleon's expedition to Egypt and was in charge of planning and constructing the Ourcq canal: *DBF.*

career. After completing his education he became a professor at the Ecole des ponts et chaussées. Under the duc de Choiseul he trained military engineers, and then, under the comte d'Artois, trained officers of the Swiss Guard. Since leaving the military he has practiced architecture, constructing buildings that are still standing. He now wishes to follow the advice of several French officers and establish himself with his family in the United States, where he hopes to focus on civilian rather than military projects.[7]

Lemerre, a nineteen-year-old soldier from Lyon, anticipates that his second letter may annoy Franklin, who on November 16 sent him a negative reply.[8] Lemerre is determined to go to America and enter the military service there; his family has given him permission, and he has the opportunity to leave with a group of merchants the following month. Despite the peace, and the orders Franklin received from Congress not to send any more officers, he begs for a letter of recommendation. He is prepared to come to Paris and discuss this in person.

The chevalier de Valori,[9] twenty-eight years old, is the youngest of six children born into a family with no money. After attending the Ecole militaire he joined the *gardes du corps du roi*, but his family could not afford to procure him a promotion in a cavalry regiment. His father, who served in the military for forty-three years, died when Valori was a child, and the great-uncle who cared for him immediately after his father's death, the marquis de Valori,[1] was a lieutenant general of the king's army, a member of the Order of Saint Louis, and an ambassador to Prussia. Valori can no longer afford his military commission and has resigned, though with his reputation for good conduct intact. He asks Franklin to help him obtain employment and lands in the United States of America.

The combination of honest parents and failed fortunes was a theme sounded in many of the applications Franklin received. Among the undated letters, twenty-eight-year-old Guillaume Chemisard explains that his financial ventures failed three years ago. He plans to

7. BF endorsed this memoir, "Le Sieur Girard Ingenieur."

8. BF's letter has not been located.

9. Possibly the François-Florent, comte de Valori (Valory), who gained renown in 1791 as one of the *gardes-du-corps* who accompanied the royal family during their flight to Varennes. Biographical sketches of him differ substantially in the details of his early life. One that conforms to the information given in this letter, listing his year of birth as 1755, is found in Alphonse Mahul, ed., *Annuaire nécrologique* . . . (6 vols., Paris, 1821–26), III, 210–13.

1. Louis-Gui-Henri, marquis de Valori (1692–1774): Larousse.

emigrate, and begs an audience to gain Franklin's protection and approval. Heraut, in Paris, is eager to escape his current state of poverty and misfortune. He cannot afford the passage, but hears that America is looking for *sujets*. He has worked for an attorney and a notary; if Franklin thinks he could find work using these skills, would the minister sponsor him? He wishes to make this sacrifice for his family, and without Franklin's help his future is hopeless. He desires a response as soon as possible.

Several applicants have manufacturing experience. François Perrault, from the Norman town of L'Aigle, hopes to open a business in America, based on his familiarity with different types of manufactures. As he is visiting Paris, he asks for a brief audience to discuss his plans. Jean-Baptiste Tournemelle, a twenty-nine-year-old master gunsmith in Paris, seeks a free passage to Boston, where he would make use of his talents. He could be useful even during the crossing, and will pray ceaselessly for Franklin's well-being.[2]

Caquery de Mezancy, an "ancien gentilhomme" who had worked in the glass industry and comes from a well-known family,[3] reminds Franklin that he had called a month earlier to discuss his *mémoire*, which requested help on behalf of a group of artisans who wished to establish a glassworks in America.[4] Franklin had assured him that once in America they would have no trouble finding a partner who would furnish all necessary funds; he also indicated that they would receive free passage on an American ship. Mezancy asks Franklin to

2. BF endorsed this letter "Tournemelle Arquebusier," and L'Air de Lamotte added, "Demandant son passage franc pour aller a Boston exercer son talent."

3. They had been prominent glassmakers in Normandy since the fourteenth century: James Barrelet, *La Verrerie en France de l'époque gallo-romaine à nos jours* (Paris, 1953), p. 172.

4. An earlier letter and the *mémoire* to which he alludes, both undated, are at the Hist. Soc. of Pa. In the letter, Caqueray and five other Normandy glassmakers (members of the Caqueray family and Le Vaillant family, for which see Barrelet, *La Verrerie en France*, p. 177), ask BF for an audience so that they can present their plan to emigrate to America. They want to establish a glass manufactory specializing in plate glass and bottles; this would benefit the United States by employing a large number of people and providing new trade opportunities. The *mémoire*, which is unsigned, refers to current problems in the glassmaking industry that are exacerbated by the "guerre actuelle." Appended is a detailed account of the expenses of a typical glasshouse in France and the daily rate of production that could be expected from such an operation.

alert them as soon as this ship arrives by writing to Montécot, *avocat au parlement.*[5]

Two men who are honest and talented, but neglect to give their names, wish to establish a silk manufactory in America. One is thirty-three, the other thirty-five; they have very intelligent wives, and three children of an age to work. Moreover, they are confident that other workers from their region will be glad to follow them. They know all aspects of the trade, from cultivating mulberry trees to constructing looms. Their silk thread is of such a superior quality that they have received enticing offers to work in the Dutch East Indies and in the Cévennes mountains, in Languedoc. They know that with Franklin's protection they will succeed in any region in the United States.

Two men living in Bordeaux, also unnamed, wish to go to Philadelphia. One has made a small fortune manufacturing goods that are consumed in Brittany, Normandy, Flanders, and the French West Indies. He asks for nothing but Congress' protection and permission to establish a manufactory in Philadelphia. The second is motivated by a pure love of liberty. He has been a medical doctor and surgeon for twenty-two years, and offers his services as chief surgeon to the American army. Having been a professor of anatomy and surgery for the past ten years at the hospital in Bordeaux and at the Collège royal de France, he could teach those subjects at a public *collège* during times of peace. Medicine is not his only skill. He also can offer Congress his knowledge of all aspects of wine growing.[6]

Another unnamed Frenchman, young, educated, and from an honest family, offers his talents to benefit America. He asks Franklin to name the day and hour when he could come to get advice and discuss his plans.

Finally, we summarize a note evidently written by the sieur Ducher, who reminds Franklin that on the recommendation of the chevalier de Chastellux, Franklin had promised to provide him with letters of recommendation for Philadelphia and Boston. On the bottom of this note Franklin wrote, "He would settle there."[7]

5. A lawyer known for promoting the projects of others: XXVI, 170n. His address is given as rue du Hazard Richelieu, maison de M. Brador.

6. BF endorsed this *mémoire*, "Proposal to go & make Wine in America."

7. Possibly G. J. A. Ducher, an *avocat au Parlement de Paris* from 1773 to 1783. Ducher sailed to America on Nov. 22, 1783, was appointed vice-consul in Portsmouth, N.H., in 1785, and was transferred to Wilmington, Del., the following year. After his return to France in the early 1790s he was

Monsieur   Lyon, ce 11 février 1784
   J'ai appris que vous faisiez travailler des ouvriers à l'imprimerie
en Amérique. Je suis correcteur des épreuves à l'imprimerie de
la ville à Lyon. Si je pouvois me rendre utile par mon petit talent, auprez de vous; j'aurois deux avantages: celui de servir un
savant; et celui de m'éloigner d'un climat qui m'est funeste à tous
égards . . . . Pour vous, Monsieur, vous n'en n'auriez point d'autre,
que celui qu'éprouve un homme bienfaisant qui se fait un plaisir
de faire des heureux . . . . Oui, Monsieur, vous pourriez par ce
moyen rendre une famille heureuse, le pere, la mere, et l'enfant. Je
suis persuadé que ce seul motif est capable de vous inspirer le dessein de m'employer: attendu que vous trouveriez dans moi un sujet
docile, exact à son devoir, plein de zele et de bonne-volonté; et qui
travaille par goût et par honneur, plus que par intérêt, quoique je
n'aie rien autre en ce monde que mon travail qui m'aide à subsister.
   Si vous ne pouviez pas m'employer à la correction des
épreuves . . . . je pourrois m'offrir encore pour enseigner le Latin, et donner l'éducation aux jeunes gens, telle qu'on la donne
dans les Colleges: ce qui seroit encore plus selon mon goût et
mes desirs, y ayant plus d'occasions pour satisfaire à l'envie que
j'ai toujours eu de communiquer les bonnes idées et les beaux
sentimens que j'ai reçu, soit de mes parents, soit des personnes
respectables que j'ai fréquenté en différentes occasions . . . j'ai
des méthodes particulieres pour faciliter les études . . . . . . etc.
   Mais, si je dois parler hautement, ainsi que tout honnête-
homme doit faire, sur les sentimens de mon cœur; je dois d'autant plus me taire sur les qualités de l'esprit, quoique celles-ci me
soient autant nécessaires dans les différents emplois auxquels je
pourrois être occupé . . . . si votre bonté vous porte à m'écrire et
à vouloir agir en ma faveur, vous pourriez prendre des informations de moi, en vous adressant à Mr. PROST DE ROYER, auteur
du Dictionnaire de jurisprudence,[8] pour lequel je travaille . . . .

---

influential in shaping French commercial policies: Anne Mézin, *Les Consuls
de France au siècle des lumières (1715–1792)* ([Paris, 1998]), pp. 255–6; Frederick L. Nussbaum, *Commercial Policy in the French Revolution: a Study of
the Career of G. J. A. Ducher* (Washington, D.C., 1923), pp. 11–119.
   8. French jurist who sought BF's advice on the sections of his *Dictionnaire de jurisprudence* dealing with the United States: XXXVIII, 562–3.

Il demeure actuellement dans la *maison des Célestins, quai de saône*. Mais en ceci, il y aurait deux précautions à prendre, pour ne pas me nuire en voulant me rendre service . . . 1°. ce seroit de s'informer de moi sous un autre prétexte que celui de vouloir me faire partir . . . parce que les Messieurs qui m'occupent, pourroient se formaliser de mon projet, et m'exclure du bénéfice qu'ils me procurent . . . . 2°. ce seroit encore de ne pas me faire quitter ma place sans auparavant être bien assuré d'une autre; sans quoi je pourrois me trouver sur le pavé.

Je ne sais si vous me trouverez trop hardi et téméraire, de vous écrire ainsi; mais votre Renommée, et l'envie de me transporter avec ma famille dans un pays où j'imagine de pouvoir faire un meilleur sort à ma femme et à mon enfant, me permettent bien des choses, et m'excusent sur lés défauts qui peuvent se rencontrer dans ma Lettre . . . .

J'espere tout de votre humanité; et je me flatte que vous daignerez me faire une Réponse à l'adresse de sieur *De L'auréole correcteur de l'imprimerie de la ville, à Lyon, aux halles de la grenette, Recommandée à Mr. Balanche*[9] . . . .

Je suis, avec tout le Respect et toute la considération possible, Monsieur, Votre Très humble et très obéissant serviteur

De L'Auréole

Addressed: A Monsieur / Monsieur Le Docteur Francklin / Ministre plénipotentiaire / des états-unis de l'Amérique / septentrionale / A Passy

Endorsed: You have been misinformed. I do not employ any Persons in America in the Business you mention, and believe it would be difficult for one who is a Stranger to the Language to find Employment there in that Business—

Notation: L'aureole 11 Fevr. 1784

9. Possibly a partner in the Lyon printing house Ballanche et Barret: Aimé Vingtrinier, *Histoire de l'imprimerie à Lyon de l'origine jusqu'a nos jours* (Lyon, 1894), p. 429.

From John MacMahon[1]   AL: American Philosophical Society

feby the 11th. 1784
Doctor MacMahon presents his best respects to the Honourable
Dr. Franklin, and is very Sorry that a pre'engagement hinders
him from accepting the honour of his kind invitation for to
morrow.

Addressed: A Monsieur / Monsieur Franklin Ministre / Plenipotentiaire des Etats Unis / de l'Amerique Septentrionale /
à Passy

To Henry Laurens

ALS: South Carolina Historical Society; incomplete copy: Library of
Congress

Dear Sir,   Passy, Feb. 12. 1784.
I received your Favour of the 3d Inst. by your Son, with
the News papers for which I thank you. The Disorders of that
Government whose Constitution has been so much praised; are
come to a height that threatens some violent Convulsion, if not
a Dissolution; and its Physicians do not seem even to guess at
the Cause of the Disease, and therefore prescribe insufficient
Remedies, such as *Place Bills, More equal Representation, More
frequent Elections,* &c &c. In my humble Opinion the Malady
consists in the *enormous Salaries, Emoluments, & Patronage*
of great Offices. *Ambition,* and *Avarice,* are separately strong
Passions. When they are united in pursuit of the same Object,
they are too strong to be govern'd by common Prudence, or
influenc'd by Publick Spirit & Love of Country; they drive
Men irresistably into Factions, Cabals, Dissention & violent
Divisions, always mischievous to public Counsels, destructive

1. One other letter from Dr. MacMahon survives from the period of this
volume, addressed to WTF on Dec. 25, 1783. It enclosed a letter that a certain Nantes merchant (whom he calls M. Nanty) had written to MacMahon's friend George Woulfe, who forwarded it in hopes that BF could be
of assistance. MacMahon says that he had told BF about the "poor man's"
situation "several months ago." APS.

to the Peace of Society, and sometimes fatal to its Existence. As long as the immense Profits of those Offices subsist, Members of the shortest and most equally chosen Parliament will have them in View, and contend for them, and their Contentions will have all the same ruinous Consequences.— To me then there seems to be but one effectual Remedy, and that not likely to be adopted by so corrupt a Nation, which is, to abolish all those Profits, and make every Place of *Honour* a Place of *Burthen*. By that Means the Effect of one of the Passions above-mentioned would be taken away, and something would be added to counteract the other. Thus the Number of Competitors for great Offices would be diminished, and the Efforts of those who still would obtain them, moderated.

Thank God we have now less Connection with the Affairs of these People; and are more at Liberty to take Care of our own, which I hope we shall manage better.

You desire Information respecting the Commerce that will be allow'd us with the French Islands. That Affair is still under Consideration here, the Ministers are working upon it, and endeavouring to obtain Light from the Merchants, but have not yet compleated their System. All I have hitherto learnt, is, that we are to have two Free Ports, L'Orient & Bayonne, added to Dunkirk and Marseilles;[2] That our Vessels will be allow'd to carry Lumber and Provisions to their Islands, except Flour, which is reserv'd in favour of the Merchants of Bourdeaux, that Article being necessary to fill their outward-bound Ships; & that we may carry from the Islands, Rum, Mollasses, Coffee, and a certain Proportion of Sugar not yet ascertained, but which may be suppos'd equal to our Consumption, tho' not in such Quantities as to make us Carriers of their Sugars to Foreign Markets, which would hurt their own Merchants & Navigation. Tobago & St Lucie are likewise to be Free Ports. These are said to be the Outlines; but there may yet be Changes, perhaps more to our Advantage, & perhaps less.

With Regard to Money-Matters, you will have heard before this time, that we have been oblig'd to suffer some of Mr M.'s[3]

2. When the edict was issued on May 14, a fifth port, St. Jean-de Luz (near Bayonne), was added: XXXIX, 106.

3. Robert Morris.

Bills drawn on Holland to be protested for want of Funds, and no Bills have arriv'd for our Salaries since June last;[4] Mr Grand however has advanc'd for me, tho' at his own Risque, being without Orders, and he will no doubt do the same for you, as it would dishonour our Employers if we were left to run in debt for Subsistence. If therefore you shall think fit to draw on Mr Grand for the Sum you want, I believe he would pay it without Difficulty; but should he make any, I will chearfully add my Credit to yours for removing it. I would have settled the Point with him before writing, but I have long been unable to go to Paris, and I have been disappointed in my Expectation of seeing him at Passy.

We have a terrible Winter here, such another in this Country is not remembred by any Man living. The Snow has lain thick upon the Ground ever since Christmas; and the Frost constant.

My Grandson joins in best Compliments to yourself & Miss Laurens: With sincere Esteem & Affection, I have the Honour to be Dear Sir, Your most obedient & most humble Servant

B. FRANKLIN

His Excelly. Henry Laurens, Esqr

Endorsed: B. Franklin Esqr 12 febry 1784 Recd. 24th Answd 27th

From Catherine de Wesselow Cramer[5]

ALS: American Philosophical Society

Genève le 12 février 1784.

Le dérangement de ma santé & l'espérance d'aller à Paris, m'ont empêchée, Monsieur, d'avoir l'honneur de vous écrire plutôt, & de vous remercier de la marque d'attention que vous avez bien voulu me donner:[6] mais mon voyage devenant chaque jour plus incertain, je ne puis tarder davantage à vous dire combien ce

4. For the bills of exchange to pay salaries see XL, 115–16, 631.
5. The mother of BFB's friend and former schoolmate Gabriel. Mme Cramer looked after BFB during his stay in Geneva: XXX, 248n.
6. BF's letter enclosing the gift has not been found, but from a letter that BFB sent Gabriel on Jan. 19, answering his friend's now-missing letter of Jan. 13, we deduce that the gift was a tea set and that it had been the cause

que vous me mandez de votre petit fils me cause de satisfaction. J'étais sûre que vous seriez très content de son coeur & de son bon sens; mais je me flattais moins sur le chapître des études. Le bonheur de vivre avec vous, & le desir de vous plaire, sont faits pour développer promptement ses talens. Veuilles, Monsieur, lui faire mille amities de ma part, & agréer le respect & les sentimens avec lesquels je suis Monsieur votre très humble & très obéïssante servante   C. CRAMER NÉE DE WESSELOW

From Dumas   ALS: American Philosophical Society

Monsieur,   Lahaie 12e. fevr. 1784

L'anxiété d'une Mere, Madame de Hogendorp, pour son fils qui se trouvoit sur le Vaisseau péri près du Cape Anne, ne lui permettant pas d'attendre que les Glaces laissent nos Passes ouvertes, elle espere avec moi que V. Exc. pardonnera la liberté que je prends de faire passer par vos mains l'incluse pour Mr. Van Berckel à Philadelphie, & que le Paquebot, qui part ce mois de Port-Louis pour N. York, pourra encore l'emporter.[7]

Le St—r. [Stadhouder] a écrit à ceux de Zélde. une Lettre de Maître à Valet sur la Jurisdiction milite. [militaire], laquelle y a mis le feu aux Etoupes.[8] Cela fait penser à Pharaon, qui s'obstine en dépit des plaies.[9]

---

of some confusion. BFB explained (in French) that his grandfather's letter to Gabriel's mother must have been badly translated: the words "*Tea China*" meant "*la Porcelaine pour prendre le Thé.*" Hence, the porcelain was intended for "ta Maman." APS.

7. Hogendorp (XXXIX, 586–7n) survived the shipwreck of the *Erfprins:* XL, 155n. His mother was the former Carolina Wilhelmina van Haren: *NNBW,* II, 587. We have found no trace of the enclosure or of BF's forwarding it.

8. This may refer to a dispute between the States of Zeeland and the stadholder about jurisdiction over military officers serving in the province. Dumas sent a March 20 report on the latter stages of the dispute as an enclosure to his April 10 letter to the Department of Foreign Affairs: *Diplomatic Correspondence of the United States,* VII, 37–40. For the tense situation at the time see Simon Schama, *Patriots and Liberators: Revolution in the Netherlands, 1780–1813* (New York, 1977), pp. 86–7.

9. Exodus 4:21–12:32.

Nous ne savons encore rien ici de ce qui se passe à Paris entre les Plénipo: Anglois & Hollandois.

Voici une Lettre que Mr. Adams a remise à mes soins pour Votre Exce.[1]

L'intéret que je prends à votre santé, Monsieur, me suggere de vous communiquer un remede, dont je sais que plusieurs personnes en ce pays, entre autres Mr. Van Berckel le Plenipo:, se servent, avec succès, pour diminuer & déraciner peu à peu, sans danger, la Goute. Ils prennent assidument, depuis 2 ou 3 ans, trois petites cuillerées à thé par jour de graine de moutarde.

Je suis avec le plus sincere respect De Votre Excellence Le très-humble & très-obéissant serviteur   C. W. F. DUMAS

Je suis très reconnoissant de votre faveur du 1er. Courant. J'ai déjà accusé à votre Exce. la reception du paquet par le Sr. Chouquet.

Passy à Son Excellence Mr. Franklin

From Robert Morris

LS and L:[2] American Philosophical Society; LS: Independence National Historical Park; copy: Library of Congress

Dr: Sir,   Office of Finance 12th. Febry. 1784—

Three Days ago, I received in a Letter of the first of December from Messrs. Wilhelm and Jan Willink Nicolaas and Jacob Van Staphorst De la Lande and Finje at Amsterdam a Copy of their Letter to you of the thirtieth of November. Enclosed you have Copy of my answer of this Date.[3] I flatter myself that you

1. Doubtless JA to BF, Feb. 11.

2. Morris sent four versions of this letter; the one published here (Feinstone Collection) is marked "fourth." The only one now in a collection of BF's papers is the L, marked "first," which Morris neglected to sign. We privilege one of the signed versions; the other LS is published in *Morris Papers*, IX, 104–6.

3. Morris had not yet received BF's letter of Dec. 25, which also enclosed a copy of the bankers' letter. In his reply to them, Morris explained that he had been unaware of the decline in subscriptions to the loan until late 1783. He calculated that his overdrafts should not exceed 500,000 ƒ. and

will not have suffered the public Credit to be ruined for Want of an Engagement to the Amount of so small a Sum as might be necessary to avoid the Danger to which it was exposed, and I wait in the Anxious Expectation of hearing from you what Arrangements have been taken on this Subject, as I wish to conform my Measures to them. If contrary to my Expectations, some unforeseen Causes should have induced you to decline that so necessary Engagement I hope this Letter may arrive in Season and induce you to do it. You will observe that a Copy of this Letter is transmitted to the Houses in Amsterdam, but I have not sent Copy of the enclosed Letters to Mr. Grand and Mr. Barclay which are left open for your Perusal.[4] I have not Time now to go particularly into the Estimation of their Accounts, but I am almost perswaded that there is (between them) and ought to be in the Hands of the former (before this Time) about half a Million Livres belonging to the United States.[5] But in the present Exigency I shall not reckon on this Sum, nor on the second Expedition of five hundred Hogsheads of Tobacco which are, I presume, before this Hour arrived at Amsterdam. I shall calculate on a Deficiency of five hundred thousand Guilders, and prepare Remittance as fast as proper Articles can be purchased to that Amount; because the Surplus may be well disposed of to answer the Interest of the Dutch Loan which falls due in June next. If therefore you can adopt any Measures by which, in circuitous Negotiations, the Time of Payment can be prolonged you may rely on the Arrival of such Remittances in the Months of June and July, at farthest, as shall fully answer

promised to send remittances as soon as the weather permitted: *Morris Papers*, VIII, 394–5n; IX, 108–11.

4. In these letters of Feb. 12 Morris requested Barclay's and Grand's assistance in whatever measures were necessary to save his bills from protest, and asked that Barclay settle the account of the United States with Grand: *Morris Papers*, IX, 101–4, 106–7.

5. Morris expected that Barclay would have obtained the release of the attachments on the *Alliance*'s prize proceeds, and also would have deposited with Grand the money from the sale of the *Duc de Lauzun*. These sums would be reduced by Barclay's public expenditures, and the remainder would amount to the total Morris gives here. Morris, however, was unaware that the attachments were still in force: *Morris Papers*, VIII, 660; IX, 102; BF to Vergennes, Jan. 12, above.

the Sums which may then fall due, and as I have told the Gentlemen in Amsterdam the Advices which I may receive will govern the Direction of those Remittances. I shall give immediate Orders for the Purchase of one thousand Hogsheads of Tobacco, and as that Amount is compleated I shall extend it according as Circumstances may require. The Season has been so intemperate that the Navigation of the Chesapeak is to this Hour shut up by the Ice, but that cannot last much longer, and therefore I have good Hopes that some capital Shippments may depart before the first of April; and, should the Urgency of the Case require it, I can draw at long Sight on the Consignees, and transmit the Bills, which will enable a farther Negotiation if necessary. The Means of making Remittances are now, thank God, in my Power; for the Amount of Taxes exceeds that of the Expenditures, which last are reduced almost to Nothing, and as the Revival of Commerce must encrease the Means of paying Taxes, I have no other Solicitude for the Event than what arises from the Want of Time to make due Arrangements. This Want I perswade myself you will remedy, if you have not already provided against it. And you may rely that any Engagements you may think it necessary to take, shall be most punctually complied with by me—

With Unfeigned Esteem and Respect I have the Honor to be Your Excellency's most obedient & humble Servant

ROBT MORRIS

P.S. Since writing the above it occurs to me, that there is (particularly on the present Occasion) a Propriety in transmitting to you the best Account in my Power of the Situation of things, as to the Funding of our public Debt. I say the best in *my Power,* for I know not what is done Southward of Virginia, No Mail having come from thence in upwards of six weeks; by Reason of the Inclemency of the Weather, which greatly impedes our Intelligence from every Quarter. New Hampshire, Massachusetts, New Jersey, Pennsylvania, Delaware, Maryland, and Virginia have adopted the Plan recommended by Congress.[6] I am assured that New York & Connecticutt will adopt it very speedily;

6. For the funding plan passed by Congress on April 18, 1783, see *Morris Papers,* VII, 523–5.

and I am told (on good Authority) that Rhode Island will come in so soon as the Example of the other States is communicated.[7] It is in Consequence of my Conviction that the Plan will soon be agreed to by all, that I have published an Advertisement of the Ninth Instant Copy whereof is enclosed—[8]

His Excellency Benjamin Franklin Esqr. Minister Plenipotentiary of the United States—

fourth

From Cadet de Vaux
ALS: American Philosophical Society

Monsieur   ce 13 fevr 1784

M.M. Quinquet et lange, auteurs de la lampe[9] dont J'ai eu l'honneur de vous Parler, desirent avoir l'Avantage de la Sou-

7. When Connecticut ratified in May, 1784, all the states had assented to the plan except Rhode Island, which ratified in 1786, and New York, which never ratified on terms acceptable to Congress. Without the agreement of New York, the plan never took effect: *Morris Papers*, VII, 525; IX, 105–6n.

8. The Feb. 9 advertisement assumed that all the states would ratify the 1783 impost and solicited bids for furnishing sums in Europe to pay the debts of the United States in Amsterdam and Paris. BF received both a MS in the hand of Morris' secretary and a copy of the printed notice as it appeared in the *Pa. Packet*, Feb. 12, 1784.

9. In fact, Antoine-Arnoult Quinquet and Ambroise-Bonaventure Lange (L'Ange) had adopted the basic elements of Ami Argand's design of an oil lamp, for which see Le Roy's letter of [Oct. 26?]. Quinquet, Lange, and Argand had discussed Argand's invention while working together on Montgolfier's balloon in the fall of 1783. After Argand left for London to obtain a patent and have the lamp manufactured, Quinquet and Lange assembled their version and began to market it. On Feb. 18, the *Jour. de Paris* ran an article about the device, praising the men for having improved the lamp of a "Physicien étranger, M. A. . . ." and noting where it could be ordered. On Feb. 21 the Frenchmen presented it to the Académie des sciences. The lamp generated much publicity and quickly became known as "lampe à la Quinquet" or simply "Quinquet," despite continued disputes between Argand and his rivals about who could claim to be its inventor: *DBF*, under Lange; Académie des sciences, *Procès-verbaux*, CIII (1784), 37; John J. Wolfe, *Brandy, Balloons, & Lamps: Ami Argand, 1750–1803* (Carbondale and Edwardsville, Ill., 1999), pp. 2, 7, 21–5, 48–50.

mettre à vos lumieres; ils S'Estimeront heureux Si leur dècouverte mérite votre approbation.

Je Suis avec un profond respect Monsieur Votre très humble et très obéissant Serviteur CADET DE VAUX

From Robert Morris

Three LS: Yale University Library, American Philosophical Society, Historical Society of Pennsylvania; copies: Harvard University Library, Library of Congress

Dr. Sir, Office of Finance 13th. Febry. 1784—

I have written to you, under Yesterday's Date, on a very interesting Subject; and I will now add Something farther which I did not chuse to place in that Letter, as a Copy of it is transmitted to the Houses in Holland. And first I will give you an Account of my Situation, as accurately as possible, in order that (seeing the whole State of my Engagements, and the means of fulfilling them) you may rest at Ease under the Operation I have requested, and which I must now most strongly Urge and intreat you to engage in.

My present actual Engagements are threefold Viz. 1st. General Engagements for the public Service not yet Satisfied, including therein the Notes issued by me which remain in Circulation. 2ly. My Bills of Exchange unpaid. And 3ly. My Debts to the National Bank.

The first of these it is difficult to ascertain with Exactness For I take into the Account all Payments to be made for past Services and the like, and I set against it sundry Sums to be received and the public Goods which are yet to arrive. It cannot be expected therefore that any great Precision will take Place in this Estimate but from the clearest Insight I have, the Amount is rather under than over one hundred thousand Dollars.

The Second Stands thus. I drew for a Million of Guilders of which calculating to the Extent, not more than one half remains unprovided for, as I have observed in My Letter of Yesterday. This half may be considered as of the Value of two hundred thousand Dollars. Besides this Sum, I have drawn three Bills of two hundred and fifty thousand Guilders each, and one of one hundred thousand Guilders, for which I have received three hundred and forty thousand Dollars; but as I have agreed that those Bills shall not be protested they are not to be carried to the Account of Bills of Exchange.[1]

My Debt to the National Bank is the above Sum of three hundred and forty thousand Dollars obtained from them by Discounting Notes received for the Bills of Exchange and which Notes they will continue on Interest, untill taken up by my Payments here, or by Monies raised on the Drafts of the Parties who gave them, should My Bills be eventually paid in Europe.[2]

In this Calculation you will perceive that I make no mention of any Monies which I suppose to be in the Hands of Mr. Grand, because (for the greater Certainty) I will on the present Occasion consider them as equal to answer for Contingencies only. And on the other Hand, I will not calculate the Interest to arise on Monies borrowed in Europe, because altho that object may be Stated as of the Value of from one hundred and fifty to two hundred thousand Dollars, yet to answer it I place 1st. the general System for funding the public Debts, and 2ly. Whatever small Sums may arise on the Dutch Loan, supposing it to have no Success worth counting on for other Purposes.—

Hence therefore we will state the Account as of the first of the present Month thus

Balance due for past Services . . . . Dollars 100.000
Due for Bills of Exchange drawn 200.000
Due to the national Bank 340.000
                                                            640.000
Add for Contingencies 10.000
                                            Dollars—650.000.

We come now to the Means of making Payment, after rejecting all Hope of any material Aid from the Dutch Loan. And

1. For the reasons behind Morris' overdraft of the Dutch loan and his plan to insure American credit against the possible protest of his bills, see *Morris Papers*, VIII, 387–97.
2. The discounted notes were from Morris and three of his business associates: *Morris Papers*, VII, 798–9, 819n.

they are as follows— The Taxes for the last four Months, ending the thirty first of January, amounting to somewhat more
than two hundred thousand Dollars. Towards these Taxes, the
States of Delaware, North Carolina and Georgia have as yet
paid Nothing, neither is there any Thing paid by the State of
South Carolina within the Account of those Months. The States
of New Hampshire Connecticutt New York Maryland and Virginia have paid very little, in Proportion to their present Ability,
and the other four States will all by the Extention of Peace and
Commerce, be in better Circumstances for Revenue than they
were before.

From the States of New York Maryland Virginia and South
Carolina, I expect to derive very considerable Releif; particularly from the first, by a proposed Sale of confiscated Lands.
However, I shall (after deducting from the probable Increase of
the Revenue, so much as may pay the current Expenditures) calculate the Surplus, and the proposed Sales of Lands, as amounting to no more than two hundred and fifty thousand Dollars,
by the End of next September. This, then will place the Sum
unprovided for at the amount of four hundred thousand Dollars
and the Fund to pay it at fifty thousand Dollars per Month—
That Fund will discharge the first Article above mentioned, by
the End of March, And the next Thing to be provided for is
the two hundred thousand, to answer Bills of Exchange drawn.
The intended Provision for that Object is as follows, I shall borrow immediately one hundred thousand Dollars of the Bank,
and direct Purchases of Tobacco and Rice partly with Cash,
partly on Credit and partly by Bills drawn on me.[3] By this
Means, I can with that one hundred thousand Dollars, have the
Purchases made in all March and April, so that the Shippments
to the required Amount of two hundred thousand Dollars will
take Place Some in March, some in April, and all of them I hope
by the End of May. The Taxes during April and May, will pay
the Purchases on Credit, and the Bills drawn on me; and the
Taxes in June and July, will pay the hundred thousand Dollars

3. Morris had devised the scheme to purchase tobacco and rice in late
1783 but abandoned the plan after only one shipment: *Morris Papers*, VIII,
848, 849; IX, 278–9, 500n.

due to the Bank. By the End of September therefore I may calculate on a full Discharge of all these Debts.

If the Loan should meet with Success, my Releif will be more speedy; but you will see, Sir, from this Detail, what is most important to you, Viz that the Funds will be placed in Europe during the Months of June and July, to pay the half Million of Guilders which I desire you provide for. I suppose the Mode of circuitous Negotiations to be very familiar with your Bankers, but I would hint at the following as practicable. Suppose the Houses in Amsterdam to draw in the Month of March on Mr. Grand at sixty Days Sight. Mr. Grand might in May draw on a good House in London for his full Reimbursement and the House in London might (in like Manner) reimburse on Messrs. Le Couteulx & Co:, by which Time the Remittances would arrive. Or the Time might be still farther extended, if the House in London should reimburse on Messrs. Wilhelm and Jan Willink, and they on Messrs. Le Couteulx.— Or the last Bills might perhaps be drawn on Mr. Grand instead of Messrs. Le Couteulx. However, supposing that the Credit of those Gentlemen might be useful, I have requested them to aid your Operations, should you think proper to ask their Aid.[4]

And now my dear Sir, let me before I close this Letter, entreat of you most earnestly, that the public Credit just begining to revive, be not totally lost for Want of an Effort which is but Nothing in Comparison with what we have already experienced, and passed thro, with Success.—

With very sincere Esteem & Respect I am Your most obedt. & humble Servant   Robt Morris

His Excellency Benjamin Franklin Esqr. Minister Plenipotentiary of the United States—

---

4. Morris had written Grand and Le Couteulx & Cie. the previous day about assisting BF: *Morris Papers*, IX, 106–7, 107–8.

To Creuzé   AL (draft): American Philosophical Society

Sir,   Passy, Feb. 14. 1784
    I received the three several Letters you did me the honour of
writing to me on the Subject of the Aerostatic Machines, and
the means of directing their Motion.[5] The Academy of Sciences having appointed a Committee to consider that Subject, I
thought I could not better dispose of your Papers than by communicating them to that learned Body, especially as I have too
much Business on my hands to permit my giving that Attention
to the Examination of your ingenious Project which its Importance demands. I have the honour to be, Sir,

From William Carmichael   ALS: Library of Congress

Dear Sir   Madrid 14th Feby 1784
    I had the honor to address your Excellency the 2d of this
month by Post;[6] Mr Barry a gentleman recommended to me by
Mr Adams[7] affords me an occasion of forwarding to you two
publications which the Ct de Campomanes and the Abbe Ga-
varra desired me to present to you in their Names— I am still
without news from America; this & other disagreable circumstances of a private nature prey upon my Spirits & make me desirous to quit the Country & the carreer in which I am in at present— The court seems to think that We are not very desirous to
form a Treaty with this Nation— Perhaps their opinion origi-
nates from a recollection of their past conduct with respect to
us— My principal business is to conciliate good will & weaken
or remove prejudice— Bills from Congress come to hand from
time to time— Some of which Mr Morris has advised me of—
The Others I am at a loss what to do with, but having no instructions to the Contrary, I cannot refuse accepting them—

    5. Two of these letters are extant, and remain among BF's papers; see
Creuzé to BF, Dec. 24.
    6. Carmichael was mistaken; he means his letter of Jan. 15, which he
kept until Feb. 4 in hopes of sending it by the Mr. Barry he names here.
    7. JA wrote to Carmichael on June 18, 1783, to introduce this Mr. Barry:
Adams Papers, XV, 161–2, 458n.

I should be glad to know your Sentiments thereon— I see by the Dutch Papers that Mr Adams is returned to Holland, pray Doth Mr Jay remain in England? I meant to have sent him some Accts & papers by Mr Barry, but cannot get the business finally closed as I expected owing to my bad State of health, which has confined me to the house in a great measure for more than a fortnight past.[8] With the proper compliments to all who may do me the honor to remember me I have the honor to be With the highest respect & regard Your Excellencys Most Obedt. & Humble Sert.   WM. CARMICHAEL

To Henry Laurens   ALS: American Philosophical Society

Dear Sir,   Passy Feb. 15. 1784.
    Since mine of the 12th, I have had an Interview with Mr Grand; and on my acquainting him with your Situation, and proposing to him to furnish you with such a Sum as you might have occasion for, he most readily agreed to it, saying you had only to draw upon him, and your Bills would be honoured. I seize with Pleasure the first Opportunity to inform you of this, being with sincere Esteem & Affection, Dear Sir, Your most obedient & most humble Servant   B. FRANKLIN

I regret with you that our Employers should have forgotten or neglected to contrive Means of decent Return for their Ministers.

His Excelly H. Laurens, Esqr.

Endorsed: Benja. Franklin Esqr 15th febry 1784 Recd. 24th. Answd. 27th.

---

8. By Feb. 16 Carmichael had received Jay's letter of Jan. 28, enclosing instructions from Congress and ordering him to come to Paris. He left Madrid on March 3 and arrived in Paris on March 27: *Jay Papers*, III, 554n, 555–6.

From Madame Brillon AL: American Philosophical Society

ce 15 Février a paris [1784][9]
Je vous ai promis mon bon papa de vous écrire lors de mon depart de passy et jusqu'ici je ne l'ai pas encore fait, parceque monsieur votre fils m'a donné quelquefois de vos nouvélles, d'autres
fois j'en ai envoyé sçavoir, d'autres fois encore j'ai éspéré que le
temp deviendroit moins dur et que je pourrois vous allér voir;
je crains a la longue que vous ne me soupçoniés d'oubly (ce seroit injuste) mais je veux mesme me méttre a l'abri du soupçon
en vous disant mon bon ami que je vous regrétte et vous aime,
comme je vous aimai, comme je vous aimerai toujours; et qu'au
milieu du bonheur qui m'environne (car je suis heureuse) il n'est
point de jours ou je ne pense a vous et a mes bons voisins le
veillard, ou je ne désire le printems qui doit tous nous réunirs,
ce sera vérs le milieu d'avril que j'irai vous rejoindres, que la
nature sera belle alors! Et combien l'amitié l'embéllira encore
a mes yeux! Adieu l'ami chéri de mon coeur aimés moi, pensés
a moi, et distes vous a chacuns des instans ou vous y penserés,
surement óh surement elle pense aussi a moi:

Recevés l'hommage tendre de tous les miens, et embrassés la
bonne maman le veillard, sa fille la jolie voisine caillot, et distes
je vous en prie mon bon papa mille choses amicales de ma part
au grand voisin,[1] au pére caillot et a mrs vos fils:

Addressed: A Monsieur / Monsieur Franklin / ambassadeur des
états unis / de l'amérique / a Passy

From Saint-Olympe ALS: American Philosophical Society

Monsieur L'ambassadeur   á La martinique Le 15. fer. 1784
M. de Lestrade medecin du Roi à la martinique a fait depuis
nombre d'années L'utile découverte d'un remede Contre la
pierre. Après avoir multiplié ses expériences sur un grand nombre de sujets atteints de Ce mal, & arrivé à Ce dégré de Convic-

9. The first February after the Brillons had moved to Paris. Her farewell
letter from Passy is above, [after Oct. 20].
1. Le Veillard.

tion qui peut seule authoriser un médecin à qualifier un remede de *spécifique*. M. de Lestrade a employé divers moyens de le rendre transportable au dela des mers sans que Sa qualité put être alterée. Ses divers essais ont eu le succès qu'il en attendait. Il a rendu par là Commun aux deux hemispheres L'usage d'un trésor dont la nature n'avait rendu dépositaire que Cette partie de notre amérique. Que manquait-il à la gloire de m. de Lestrade? L'honneur de prolonger Les jours précieux du restaurateur de la liberté dans le nouveau monde, du Citoyen le plus utile à l'humanité. Je n'ai pas parlé à m. de Lestrade du besoin que vous auriés de son *spécifique* pour vous débarasser de votre gravelle sans le voir animé du desir d'opérer votre guérison; il partagera avec notre isle la reconnaissance du monde entier. Pressé de vous faire jouir des avantages de son *spécifique* m. de Lestrade vous en envoye deux traitemens avant de L'avoir soumis à L'examen de la faculté de médecine de paris. Si votre excellence veut en faire un premier essay sur un malade attaqué de la pierre, le nom du malade, ne fera que grossir la longue liste de Ceux que Ce remede a délivré de leurs meaux. Le mémoire qui accompagne Ce remede & dont votre excellence pourra prendre Lecture,[2] n'est que le résultat des experiénces faites ici, & particulierement sur les habitations de ma famille. M. de Lestrade se propose de le présenter incessament à la faculté de paris, & après avoir rempli Ce point de forme il rependra en europe & en amerique des traitemens de son spécifique.

Je suis trop glorieux Monsieur L'ambassadeur, des bontés dont votre excellence m'á honoré durant mon séjour à paris pour les jamais perdre de vue; mais j'avoue que le sentiment de la Reconnaissance n'est pas le seul qui m'ait fait saisir L'occasion d'être utile à votre excellence; la gloire de bien mériter de L'humanité en Concourrant à prolonger la vie de son plus ferme soutien a aussi puissament agi sur mon Cœur. J'espere à mon retour à paris à la fin de L'année ou lorsque j'aurai l'honneur de voir votre excellence en amérique[3] apprendre d'elle même l'heureux effet de mes soins à lui procurer le specifique de m. de Lestrade.

2. Not found.
3. The chevalier was in Paris by Feb. 25, 1785, and dined frequently with the Franklins and Adamses. JA's daughter, Abigail, reported that he was

Je suis avec une Respectueuse vénération Monsieur L'ambassadeur Votre très humble & très obeissant serviteur

St. Olympe

To William Strahan

ALS: Yale University Library; two copies: Library of Congress

Dear Sir, Passy, Feb. 16. 1784.

I received and read with Pleasure your kind Letter of the first Inst. as it inform'd me of the Welfare of you and yours. I am glad the Accounts you have from your Kinswoman at Philadelphia are agreable, and I shall be happy if any Recommendations from me can be serviceable to Dr Ross or any other Friend of yours going to America.—

Your Arguments persuading me to come once more to England, are very powerful. To be sure I long to see again my Friends there, whom I love abundantly: but there are Difficulties & Objections of several kinds which at present I do not see how to get over.—

I lament with you the political Disorders England at present labours under. Your Papers are full of strange Accounts of Anarchy & Confusion in America, of which we know nothing; while your own Affairs are really in a Situation deplorable. In my humble Opinion the Root of the Evil lies, not so much in too long—or too unequally chosen Parliaments, as in the enormous Salaries, Emoluments, and Patronage of your Great Offices; and that you will never be at rest till they are all abolish'd, and every Place of *Honour* made, at the same time, instead of a Place of *Profit*, a Place of *Expence* & *Burthen*. *Ambition* and *Avarice* are each of them strong Passions, and when they are united in the same Persons, and have the same Objects in view for their Gratification, they are too strong for Public Spirit & Love of

---

writing about trade between the French West Indies and the United States, and according to JQA, he was planning a trip to America: Taylor, *J. Q. Adams Diary*, I, 226, 227, 232; [Caroline A. Smith de Windt, ed.], *Journal and Correspondence of Miss Adams, Daughter of John Adams* . . . (2 vols., New York and London, 1841–42), I, 50–1.

Country, and are apt to produce the most violent Factions and Contentions. They should therefore be separated, and made to act one against the other. Those Places, to speak in our own old Stile,[4] (*Brother Type*) may be *for the Good of the* CHAPEL, but they are bad for the *Master*, as they create constant Quarrels that hinder the Business. For example, here are near two Months that your Government has been employ'd in *getting its Form to Press;* which is not yet fit to *work on*, every Page of it being *squabbled*, and the whole ready to *fall into Pye*. The Founts too must be very scanty, or strangely *out of Sorts*, since your *Compositors* cannot find either *Upper-* or *Lower-Case* Letters sufficient to set the Word ADMINISTRATION, but are forc'd to be continually *Turning for them.*— However, to return to common (tho' perhaps too saucy) Language, don't despair; you have still one Resource left, and that not a bad one since it may re-unite the Empire. We have some Remains of Affection for you, and shall always be ready to receive and take care of you in case of Distress. So, if you have not Sense and Virtue enough left to govern yourselves, e'en dissolve your present old crazy Constitution, *and send Members to Congress.*

You will say my *Advice* smells of *Madeira*. You are right. This foolish Letter is mere Chit-chat *between ourselves*, over the *second* Bottle: If therefore you show it to any body (except our indulgent Friends Dagge & Lady Strachan)[5] I will positively *Solless*[6] you.

Yours ever most affectionately   B F

Wm Strahan Esqr

4. BF here begins a critique of the political deadlock in England, employing the specialized language of printers.

5. Henry Dagge had been married to Lady Strachan (as she continued to be called), the widow of Sir John Strachan, since 1760: XVII, 32; William Page, ed., *A History of Hampshire and the Isle of Wight* (5 vols., London, 1990–12), V, 95; *The Daily Advertiser*, July 13, 1773.

6. More commonly spelled "solace": punishment for the nonpayment of a penalty for breaching printers' laws or customs.

From ———— de Roucelle

ALS: American Philosophical Society

Monsieur   Paris ce mardy 16 fevrier 1784
    La perte cruelle que nous venons d'Eprouver en la personne,
de M. Macquer, mon Beau Pere;[7] L'affliction ou nous plonge cet
Evénement aussi affreux que terrible me laisse a peine La Force
et les facultés nécéssaires pour vous l'apprendre. Les premiers
jours de tristesse Ecoulés, j'aurai, Monsieur, L'honneur de vous
aller voir et vous porter Les derniéres intentions d'un mourant
en Faveur d'un de ses Alliés auquel il vouloit beaucoup de bien.
C'est un Sujet a tous égards du plus méritant et qu'il esperoit
pouvoir vous présenter Lui même. Mais La mort injuste et bar-
bare ayant tranché le fil de ses beaux jours, je suis responsable de
ses derniéres volontés. C'est un devoir Sacré pour moy et que je
remplirai de toutes maniéres avec un zele égal. J'ose me flatter,
Monsieur, que le Souvenir d'un mortel aussi recommandable
par ses vertus et ses talents que par son nom, vous est et vous
Sera toujours trop cher pour rien refuser à sa mémoire.
    J'ai L'honneur d'Etre avec un respect et une Considération
des plus distingués, Monsieur Votre trés humbl et trés obéissant
Serviteur   DE ROUCELLE
                                  gendre de Mr. Macquer

La premiere fois que j'aurai l'honneur de vous voir j'aurai Celui de vous faire part des intention de M. Macquer et de vous
présenter ce Sujet pour lequel il S'intéréssoit Si vivement

Addressed: A Monsieur / Monsieur Le Docteur / Franklin En
Sa maison / a Passy Paris

From Thomas Barclay   LS: American Philosophical Society

Sir   London 17th. Februy. 1784
    In pursuance of your Excellencys desire a search has been
made by Mr. Hodgson, for a precident relative to the Capture of
Vessels situated in the same manner with that of Mr. Nesbitts;

    7. Chemist Pierre-Joseph Macquer had died the previous day: *Dictio-
nary of Scientific Biography.* BF had known him since at least 1769: XVII, 109.

but none can be found— A Tryal however is soon expected to come on in the Courts here which will determine the point in England, and Mr. Hodgson promises to furnish you with the particulars of the decision.—

I am detain'd here procuring Copies of sundry Accounts and Memorandums from Mr. Deane which are highly necessary for explanation of the Public account and which may hold me ten days longer.—[8]

I am happy in informing you that the last Dutch Mail brings strong assurances that Mr. Morris's Bills on the Negociaters of the Loan in Holland will be Paid,[9] and remain with the greatest respect, Sir Your Excellencys Most Obedient Most Humb. Servt.   THOS BARCLAY

His Excellency Benjn. Franklin Esqr.

From Jean-Baptiste Le Roy

ALS: American Philosophical Society

ce 18 Fèvrier [1784][1]

J'ai reçu Mon Illustre Docteur le pacquet Sur les ballons[2] que vous avez eûe la bonté de m'envoyer je les examinerai et en ferai l'usage que vous désirez. Je vous envoye un pacquet que Je comptois vous porter depuis Long-tems mais que la rigueur de la Saison m'a empêché de vous aller remettre Mais bien malgré moi Je vous assurre. Je compte m'en dédommager au premier moment. Car le temps me paroît enfin Se détendre et nous ramener une Saison moins rigoureuse. Adieu Mon Illustre Docteur recevez Mille Sincères assurrances de tous les Sentimens d'attachement que Je vous ai voués pour la vie

LE ROY

8. Barclay fell ill shortly after writing this letter and did not return until April 11: Roberts and Roberts, *Thomas Barclay*, p. 138.

9. JA was in the Netherlands to try to save Morris' bills from being protested; he announced his success to BF on Feb. 20, below.

1. The year is established by the references to balloons and the exceptionally harsh winter.

2. Possibly material sent by Creuzé; see BF's letter to him of Feb. 14.

Addressed: A Monsieur / Monsieur Franklin / en son hôtel / à Passy

From Jonathan Nesbitt & Co.

ALS: American Philosophical Society

Sir.   L'Orient Febry. 18th 1784—
We receiv'd in Course the honor of your Excellencys Letter of the 11th: Inst: & Yesterday forwarded those which accompany'd it by the Packet for New York.—³ We paid for Postage Sixty one Livres fifteen Sols which we have Charged to your Account:—had we thought ourselves at liberty we should have kept them for Captain Conyngham who will Sail on the 21st: Inst:⁴ which would have saved so much.— With the greatest Respect we have the honor to remain— Your Excellencys most Obedt. & very humble Servts:—

JONATN: NESBITT & CO:

The Packet Saild yesterday with a very favorable Wind—

John Adams to Franklin and John Jay⁵

AL (draft): Massachusetts Historical Society

Gentlemen   The Hague Feb. 20. 1784
The Day before Yesterday the Baron de Thuilemeyer⁶ the Envoy to their High Mightinesses, from the King of Prussia, did me the Honour of a Visit, but as I had Company, he stayed but a short time; As I accompanied him to the Door, he told me,

---

3. BF's letter is missing, but his postage accounts for that day show his sending to Nesbitt a packet containing dispatches for America: Account XXV (XXXII, 3).
4. The *Hannibal*, Capt. Conyngham (XXXV, 182n), reached Philadelphia by early May: *Independent Gazetteer*, May 8, 1784.
5. This letter was forwarded by Dumas. His covering letter of Feb. 20 (now missing) is noted in his letterbook: Nationaal Archief.
6. Friedrich Wilhelm von Thulemeier: XXXIX, 84n.

that he had Something to Say to me from the King, and desird me to name an Hour, when he might call upon me again. I told him his Hour should be mine, and that I would return his Visit at any hour he should choose the next day; But he choose to call upon me and mentioned Eleven in the Morning. Accordingly Yesterday he came, and told me "that the King who honoured him with a Personal Correspondence, and who was acquainted with my Character by Reputation, had directed him to make me a Visit, and to observe to me, that as his Subjects had occasion for our Tobacco and perhaps other Things, and as We had Occasion for Silesia Linnens, and perhaps other Productions of his Dominions, he thought an Arrangement might be made between his Majesty and the United States, which would be beneficial on both Sides," and the Baron desired to know my Sentiments of it.[7]

I Answered him "that I was very Sensible of the Honour done me by his Majesty, but that I had Singly no Authority to treat, or enter into Conferences officially upon the subject. That Congress had been pleased to confer upon their late Ministers at the Peace, Authority to enter into Conferences. That I could do

7. The previous spring, Frederick II had instructed Goltz, his minister at Versailles, to approach BF on the same subject. BF forwarded to America the lists he received of Prussian products suitable for export to the United States: XL, 363. On Nov. 17 Frederick directed Goltz to follow up on these conversations. The minister replied on Dec. 2 that BF still had received no response from America, but was enthusiastic about direct trade with Prussia. On Feb. 15, 1784, Goltz reported that BF, unable to leave Passy, had sent word through WTF that he still had nothing specific to communicate. When pressed by Goltz to explain Congress' lack of interest, WTF replied that there was at present no secretary for foreign affairs and that Congress was preoccupied with domestic issues. WTF added that even his grandfather, who had requested his recall three months earlier, had not yet received an answer.

Frederick, in the meantime, had learned that "a certain Adams" had been sent to Holland. On Feb. 9 he instructed Thulemeier to sound out JA about the possibility of an arrangement whereby Americans would buy linen from the Prussians and sell them Va. tobacco. Thulemeier's report to the king about his Feb. 19 meeting with JA conforms to JA's account in this letter and in his March 9 letter to Congress (*Adams Papers*, XVI, 77–9): Friedrich Kapp, *Friedrich der Grosse und die Vereinigten Staaten von Amerika* (Leipzig, 1871), pp. 96–9.

nothing but in Concurrence with Mr Franklin and Mr Jay who were at Paris: but I thought I could answer for the good Dispositions of those Ministers as well as my own for forming an Arrangement between the two Powers, which might be beneficial to both.— That I would write to you, Gentlemen an account of what had passed between Us."[8] He desired that I would, and said he would, write by the first Post to the King, and enquire if his Majesty had any Thing in particular to propose, would inform him of my Answer, and wait his further Orders, which probably he should receive, as soon as I should have an Answer from Paris.—

I have at last obtained Some better hopes of Saving Mr Morris's Bills which become payable in this Month & March but have as yet nothing like Certainty of Saving those in May. And if fresh Bills appear, which I very much fear, We must fail at last.— However, I have agreed to open a new Loan, and must stay here to Sign the Instruments & Obligations, having obtaind a Promise, of Money to Save the Bills in March, So that I Shall not be able to join you Gentlemen, for sometime.[9]

I Suppose We may make the Treaty with Holland or that with Sweeden, in general the Model of one with Prussia. If you think any alterations necessary, they may be proposed to the King either by the Baron de Goltz or de Thuilemeyer. Meantime I think it would be proper for you Gentlemen to write to Congress for a Commission to treat & conclude for I take it for granted that no Power can conclude with Us, without any other full Power than our Instructions.

Their Excellencies Benjamin Franklin & John Jay Esqrs.

8. JA here wrote but deleted, "But that it was possible you might have already announced to the Baron de Goltz, the. That I should be".
9. JA procured a loan of 2,000,000 f. on March 9: *Adams Correspondence,* V, 316n.

From David Hartley

Reprinted from William Temple Franklin, ed., *The Private Correspondence of Benjamin Franklin* . . . (3rd ed.; 2 vols., London, 1818), II, 412–13; ALS (draft):[1] William L. Clements Library

My dear Friend,   London, Feb. 23, 1784.

I have met with a report from America, that congress has come to some resolution respecting the commerce with Great Britain, which is to depend conditionally upon the proceedings of the British parliament by the 1st of February, 1784.[2] As they have known that the act of the last session of parliament was to terminate on the 20th of December, 1783, it was reasonable to conclude that some proceedings would have taken place in parliament before the 1st of February, 1784. This doubtless was the intention of the last session, by the limit given to the bill. However, in consequence of the late changes, all these considerations have been postponed, by the prolongation of the late bill until the 20th of April.[3] If therefore it has been the design of congress, to wait for some act of the British parliament respecting American commerce, I hope they will remain in the same sentiments, notwithstanding the delay which has happened from the change of the ministry, that all things may remain open between the parties for mutually beneficial and amicable intercourse. I will send you the earliest notice of any steps which may be taken here. I expect daily to hear of the ratifications of the peace from you. Pray remember me kindly to Mr. Jay and family, to Mr. W. T. Franklin, and to Messrs. Adams and son, if at Paris. I am ever your most affectionate friend,

D. HARTLEY.

1. Dated Feb. 20, and lacking the final sentence.

2. In his reply of March 11 (Library of Congress), BF told Hartley that he knew of no such resolution.

3. In early May, 1783, the British Parliament passed a bill authorizing George III to regulate American trade. Based on this authority, the king issued three Orders in Council dated May 14, June 6, and July 2: XXXIX, 479n; XL, 34, 146, 288–9. Just after Parliament extended the royal authority until April 20, 1784, the king, on Dec. 26, 1783, issued another order: *London Gaz.*, Dec. 23–27, Dec. 29, 1783.

To Jean-Baptiste Le Roy

Copy:[4] American Philosophical Society

My dear Friend   Passy Feb. 25. 1784
    Enclosed I send you a Letter and sundry Papers I lately recd
from Mr. Eckhardt of Utrecht,[5] a most ingenious Mechanician
whom I first knew in London. You will see what he desires, and
what Answer I have made him.[6] If you can do him any Service,
I need not pray you to do it, because you have a Pleasure in assisting Genius: Show if you please what he says of the Balloons,
to Mr. Montgolfier. I long to see you, being ever Yours most
affectionately   (signed) B. Franklin

Mr. Le Roy.—

Copy

From Sextius-Alexandre-François Miollis[7]

ALS: American Philosophical Society

Monsieur   a aix en provence Le 25 fevrier 1784.
    Venant d'etre informé par Les papiers publics des marques
de decoration de l'ordre de cincinatus qui ont été accordées a
quelques uns des oficiers français qui ont Servis dans Les etats
unis; je prend La liberté de m'adresser a votre excellence pour
reclamer auprés de votre justice Les memes honneurs; ce Seroit
Le dedomagement Le plus Satisfaisant que je pusse recevoir de
la Situation triste et afligeante dans laquelle m'a reduit La Bles-
sure que j'ay Reçue au Siege d'york en virginie. J'ay essayé de
la faire connoitre dans Le memoire que je vous prie d'avoir la

    4. In WTF's hand.
    5. The letter was dated Jan. 18; no copy of it or its enclosures has been
found. BF had BFB make a copy of the postscript concerning balloons, which
is published above.
    6. BF's reply has not been found.
    7. A lieutenant in the Soissonnais regiment (1759–1828) whose griev-
ous facial injury did not prevent him from having a distinguished military
career, culminating in his promotion to *général de division* in 1799: Bodinier,
Dictionnaire.

bonté de faire parvenir a Son excellence le general Washington president de cette Societé, et j'ose presumer de votre humanité que le Sort d'une malheureuse victime de la guerre vous interessera, et vous engagera a apuyer ma demande.

J'ay L'honneur d'etre avec le Respect Le plus profond Monsieur Votre tres humble et tres obeissant Serviteur [8]
MIOLLIS
ofer: au regiment de Soissonnois

Notation: Miollis 25 Fevr. 1784.—

From the Comte de Murinais[9]

ALS: American Philosophical Society

Monsieur   a Paris le 25 fevrier 1784

Me. La Princesse Sapieha vien de M'adresser la lettre Cy jointe,[1] en me priant de vouloir bien lui faire passer la reponse qu'elle Espere que votre Exellence voudra bien lui faire. Il est question D'assurer l'existance d'un Gentilhomme Polonois qui a passé en amerique pour y Servir dans les troupes des Etats unis.

8. Miollis renewed his request on Dec. 2, assuming that his first letter had failed to reach BF. He provides more details about his injury, which deprived him of three-quarters of his jaw and the use of one eye. Recognition of his sacrifices by the Society of the Cincinnati would help alleviate the pains and deprivations he has suffered for the past three years: APS. He did become a member of the French chapter of the society: Ludovic de Contenson, *La Société des Cincinnati de France et la guerre d'Amérique, 1778–1783* (Paris, 1934), p. 225.

9. Antonin-Victor-Augustin Auberjon, comte de Murinais (1731–1797), maréchal de camp in the French army, had served on a diplomatic mission to Poland a decade earlier: Adolphe Robert *et al.*, eds., *Dictionnaire des parlementaires français* . . . (5 vols., 1889–91; reprint, Geneva, 2000), IV, 463; Mieczislaus Haiman, *Kosciuszko in the American Revolution* (New York, 1943), p. 120.

1. The princess, wife of the grand chancellor of Lithuania, was known to BF, though their meeting (which most likely took place in February, 1778) is not documented. What does survive is a record of missed appointments: XXV, 647, 659. The letter she asked the comte de Murinais to forward to BF was from Anne d'Estko (above, Dec. 19).

Ce Gentilhomme Nommé Cosciuscko Existoit encore apres L'affaire D'yorc, et j'ay pu par le temoignage de Mes Compatriotes françois faire assurer Ces parents de la bonne reputation Dont il jouissoit. Mais dans Ce Moment Cy, il me Semble que le temoignage De votre Exellence Sur son Existance devient absolument necessaire au bonheur, et a la tranquillité De Sa famille.

Si votre Exellence avoit besoin D'Ecrire en amerique pour Donner Cette atestation d'une Maniere plus precise, je la Suplirois toujour de M'adresser un Mot de reponse pour que Madame La Princesse Sapieha ne put pas Douter de mon Empressement a Executer Ses ordres.

J'ai Lhonneur D'Etre avec les Sentiments de la Consideration La plus Distinguée De Votre Excellence Le tres humble et tres obeissant Serviteur   LE CTE. DE MURINAIS
Mal. de Camp, et inspecteur rue Ste. avoye au Marais A Paris.

From John Trumbull

ALS: American Philosophical Society

Sir.   London February 25th. 1784.

Mr Vanderhurst of Bristol[2] inform'd me yesterday that your Excellency had express'd great concern at the relation which He gave you of the State in which I left Doctr Cooper of Boston.— and that you was anxious to be inform'd with certainty.

The enclos'd paragraph cut from a Boston paper of the 5th. of January, which I receiv'd this evening, gives the melancholy confirmation of what we had heard several Days from report.—& leaves no doubt that America has lost that truly eminent Character.[3]

It would be arrogant in me to offer you consolation; but I may join you in lamenting the death of a friend whom you so justly esteem'd.

2. For Vanderhorst's return to London see Roberdeau to BF, Feb. 26.
3. The *Boston Gaz.* of Jan. 5, 1784, described Samuel Cooper's final illness, death, and funeral.

I have the Honor to be with the warmest sentiments of Respect. Your Excellency's most Obedient Humble servant.

JNO. TRUMBULL

His Excelly. B. Franklin Esqr.

Addressed: His Excellency / Benjamin Franklin Esquire / Ambassador of the United States of America / at Versailles / Passy

From Félix Vicq d'Azyr

LS: American Philosophical Society

Monsieur!   ce 25 fevrier 1784

La Société royale de medecine m'a Chargé de vous addresser ces billets pour Sa prochaine Séance publique dont elle vous prie de disposer. Cette assemblée aura Lieu mardi prochain deux de mars.[4] La Compagnie Se Souvient qu'elle a été privée de votre presence dans Sa derniere Séance publique,[5] Circonstance qui augmente encore Le desir quelle a de vous voir assister a celle cy. Nous avons aussi Lhonneur d'y inviter Monsieur votre petit fils. Je dois y Lire Les éloges de Mrs Guillaume hunter et Sanchez[6] et votre presence Seroit un grand encouragement pour moi.

4. At the meeting on March 2, the society awarded gold medals to doctors from Germany, Holland, and England, noting that all of them attended. New prize questions about epidemics were announced, papers were read, and the meeting ended with the eulogies that Vicq mentions below: *Jour. de Paris,* March 4, 5, and 9. The two tickets that he enclosed remain among BF's papers; they specify that the meeting would begin at precisely 4:30, at the Pavillon de l'Infante at the Louvre (APS). BF sent his regrets on March 1, explaining that the stone made it too painful to travel (Académie de Medicine).

5. BF was too ill to attend the Aug. 26, 1783, meeting: XL, 495.

6. The English physician and anatomist William Hunter, whom BF knew, had died on March 30, 1783: XVIII, 192; *ODNB.* Portuguese physician and educator António Nuñes Ribeiro Sanches, former court physician in Russia, had died in Paris in October: Larousse; *Jour. de Paris* of Oct. 16, 1783; Georges Dulac, "Science et politique: les réseaux du Dr. António Ribeiro Sanches (1699–1783)," *Cahiers du monde russe,* XLIII (2002), 251–73.

Jai lhonneur detre avec un profond respect Monsieur Votre tres humble et tres obeissant Serviteur   Vɪᴄǫ ᴅ'ᴀᴢʏʀ

M franklin.

To Vergennes[7]

ʟꜱ:[8] Archives du Ministère des affaires étrangères; ᴀʟ (draft):[9] American Philosophical Society

Sir,   Passy, Feby. 26. 1784

Mr. Williams[1] desiring no farther Surseance against the Bulk of his Creditors with whom he has amicably arranged his Affairs, and to whom he proposes to do exact Justice, I the more willingly join my Request with his, that he may be secured against the small Number remaining, who aim at forcing him to favour them to the Prejudice of the others.—[2] I am with great Respect, Sir, Your Excellency's most obedient & most humble Servant.   B Fʀᴀɴᴋʟɪɴ

7. For ʙꜰ's previous intercession with Vergennes about the financial difficulties of his great-nephew, see xʟ, 112, 506. As noted there, ᴊᴡ had received two successive *arrêts de surséance*, the second of which was due to expire on March 6. The funds he had expected to receive from America had not arrived; hence, this new appeal.

8. In ᴡᴛꜰ's hand.

9. In a corner at the bottom of the sheet, for reasons we have not discovered, ʙꜰ listed under the heading "Doctors" the surnames of seven American clergymen, which he then lined through: "Biles Mather Cooper Eliot Langdon Stiles Rogers." These were doctors of divinity Mather Byles, Samuel Mather, Samuel Cooper, Andrew Eliot, Samuel Langdon, Ezra Stiles, and John Rodgers. We know that ʙꜰ had recommended Byles, Eliot, Cooper, Stiles, and Rodgers for their doctorates: xɪɪ, 199n; xɪᴠ, 218–19; xᴠ, 286n, 290.

1. ᴊᴡ, who was then with ʙꜰ at Passy, had recently moved his family from Nantes to his father-in-law's home in Saint-Germain, intending to use that house as his base while coordinating the delivery of American tobacco to the farmers general under the terms of the contract approved by Vergennes in October (for which see the annotation of Alexander to ʙꜰ, Nov. 6): ᴊᴡ to Alexander John Alexander, Dec. 6, 1783; ᴊᴡ to William Bingham, Jan. 29, 1784 (both at Yale University Library).

2. ᴊᴡ brought to Versailles the present letter along with his own letter to Vergennes of Feb. 26, requesting a renewal of his *lettres de surséance*

His Exy. Count de Vergennes.—

Notation: rep

From Ginet & Meirieu

ALS: American Philosophical Society

Monsieur   Paris Le 26 fevrier 1784
  Il nous a eté Remis de Bordeaux, une Traite de 670..12/ Ti-
rée par Mr. Jean Bonfield de la de. [dite] Ville, le 27. Janvier
dernier, pble. au 20 fevrier ct. à l'ordre de Mr. Jean David Sur
Vous; Comme Son échéance aproche, et que n'etant pas Vizée,
Monsieur Grand ne Voudroit pas la payer, nous prenons La li-
berté, de Vous la Remettre cy Inclus, avec priere de Vouloir Bien
l'honnorer de Votre acceptation,[3] et nous la Renvoyer ensuite.
Permettés, Monsieur, que nous profitions de cette occasion
pour Vous Temoigner·la parfaite Consideration avec laquelle
Nous avons l'honneur d'être Très parfaitement Monsieur Vos
Très-humbles et Très obbeïssants serviteurs
                              GINET & MEIRIEU
                  Negts. Rue st. Denis à la Ville
                  d'Strasbourg prés la Rue Gréneta

Notation: Giner & Meirieu 26 Fevr. 1784.—

---

so that he could forestall a pending crisis with a small group of his creditors. His letter enclosed two supporting documents. The first was a memoir
explaining that these creditors (whom he names) had threatened him with
arrest if he did not repay them in full immediately, which he cannot do. All
other creditors had agreed to alternative arrangements. He seeks a renewal
of *lettres de surséance* for eight months, but only for the named merchants.
(This memoir, signed by jw, is in the hand of L'Air de Lamotte.) The second enclosure was a nine-page schedule listing the creditors, forming a
majority, who had agreed to an extended repayment plan, along with the
amounts he would disburse to each between March 31, 1784, and Sept. 30,
1785. All these documents are at the AAE.
  jw was unable to see either Vergennes or Gérard de Rayneval, his *premier commis.* On Feb. 27 he wrote to wtf asking him to pursue his appeal,
and if possible also to obtain a safe-conduct pass for six months. He hoped
that wtf would have the *sauf conduit* in hand when they saw one another
on March 2. APS.
  3. bf must have accepted the bill, as Grand paid it on Feb. 29: Account
XXVII (xxxii, 4).

From Daniel Roberdeau   ALS: American Philosophical Society

Dear Sir   Gravesend Feby. 26th. 1784
I am honored by your favor of the 13th.[4] and much obliged
by your attention to Mr. Vanderhorst and his Daughter which
he speaks of with great satisfaction and thankfulness;[5] Also for
your care in forwarding to Mr. Grand my letter, but more particularly for your condescending notice of my son and attention to his improvement in the art of refining as practised in the
neighbourhood of Paris after he leaves Bristol, this is greatly
kind, and has occasioned in me a desire to hear further of the
"new principles" in the art of refining at Bercy.[6] If you could
gratify me herein at your leisure by informing me at Philada.
wherein the excellence of the new principles consists, and
whether I could get my son introduced as a workman at Bercy
for a few months you'll greatly obliged me. I am further obliged
by your kind wishes for a prosperous voyage to me, on which I
have set out as you'll see by my dating from this place.[7] Wishing

4. Missing.
5. BF signed a passport for Vanderhorst on Feb. 12, made out for him and
"Mlle. sa Fille, Citoyens des dits Etats, allant en Angleterre": Vanderhorst
Papers, Bristol Record Office. WTF evidently forwarded the passport and
BF's letter to Roberdeau under cover of a letter to Vanderhorst. On Feb. 15
Vanderhorst replied, promising to carry out BF's "commands" and thank-
ing him for "the Model of the Grate which Mr. F. is so good as to promise
by Mr. Laurens." He would be leaving Paris the following night: Vanderhorst to WTF, Feb. 15, 1784, APS.
   The passport for Vanderhorst is the first known dated example of the
type illustrated in Randolph G. Adams, *The Passports Printed by Benjamin Franklin at his Passy Press* (Ann Arbor, 1925), facing p. [5]. This may
have been the last passport form printed at Passy, as BF used it until at least
May 1, 1785, when he issued one to Dr. Thomas Ruston (Yale University
Library).
   6. Frères Boucherie of Bordeaux built an experimental facility at Bercy
in 1776 that yielded a 40 percent increase over older sugar-refining methods. In early 1783, they were awarded the concession to refine sugar on
Martinique for 12 years and, in contrast to historic French trade policy, to
sell as much as 3,000,000 *livres* per year to the Americans: Jean Tarrade,
*Le Commerce Colonial de la France à la fin de l'Ancien Régime: l'évolution du
régime de "l'Exclusif" de 1763 à 1789* (2 vols., Paris, 1972), II, 510–12.
   7. Roberdeau's voyage was not straightforward. His first ship sprang
a leak and was forced to stop in the Azores; the crew of the second ship

you the fullest measure of comfort and hapiness. I am Dear Sir Yr. most obt. & obliged hume. Serv.   DANIEL ROBERDEAU

Addressed: His Excellency / Doctor Benjamin Franklin / Minister Plenepotentiary for the United States / of North America / Passy / Paris / [*note by John Warder:*][8] London 27 Feby. 84 forwarded by thy friend JNO. WARDER

From Michel-René Hilliard d'Auberteuil

ALS: American Philosophical Society

Monsieur   Paris le 27e. fevrier 1784.
    Permettez moi de me rapeller au Souvenir de votre excellence en lui envoyant un mémoire sur une matiere très importante, et qui ne vous est point étrangere.[9]

---

staged an unsuccessful mutiny. He arrived in Philadelphia in mid-July: *Virginia Jour.*, July 29, 1784.

8. John Warder (1751–1828), son of Philadelphia merchant Jeremiah Warder (VI, 440; XV, 267–8n), served as his father's agent in London during the war: Elaine F. Crane *et al.*, eds., *The Diary of Elizabeth Drinker* (3 vols., Boston, 1991), III, 2226.

9. The work that Hilliard enclosed remains a mystery. We wonder whether it could have been his *Nouveau compte rendu, ou tableau historique des finances d'Angleterre, depuis le regne de Guillaume III, jusqu'en 1784* (London [*i.e.*, Paris], 1784), an 80-page booklet printed by Couturier, quai des Augustins. It was advertised to the public in the *Jour. de Paris* on June 9, 1784. BF's copy is at the Hist. Soc. of Pa.

Hilliard applied for permission to publish this work in August, 1783, during a time when Controller General Calonne was curtailing publications about government taxes and finances. No response has been located. Hilliard then appended it to the two volumes he had written of *Histoire de l'administration de Lord North . . .* , which he sought permission to publish in December, 1783. (That work was based, in part, on a book that BF had lent him: XXXVIII, 20.) *Histoire de l'administration de Lord North* was prohibited in January, 1784, but was finally allowed on March 1, three days after Hilliard wrote the present letter: Joël Félix, *Finances et politique au siècle des Lumières: le ministère L'Averdy, 1763–1768* (Paris, 1999), pp. 28–9. The author declared it the first complete, accurate history of "la Guerre de l'Amérique" (pp. ix–x). The *Nouveau compte rendu, ou tableau historique des finances d'Angleterre* appeared at the end of the work with its own title page and pagination, as in the separate publication.

De Monville imprimeur de l'accademie française[1] remettra sur ma lettre, aux ordres de Votre Excellence la quantité d'exemplaires qu'elle voudra envoyer en Amerique. Je suis avec un profond respect Monsieur, de votre Excellence Le très humble & très obéissant serviteur HILLIARD D'AUBERTEUIL

P.S. Cette matiere sera plus profondément discutée dans d'autres mémoires qui suivront. D

Notation: Hillard d'Aubreteuil 27e Fev. 1784

From Henry Laurens

ALS: Library of Congress; copy: University of South Carolina Library

No. 18. Fludyer Street
Dear Sir.   Westminster 28th. [*i.e.*, 27][2] February 1784.
Accept my grateful thanks for the Contents of two Letters which you have honored me with under the 12th. & 15th. Inst.

Your interposition with Mr. Grand for obtaining a supply of Money on my Account has impressed my heart with feelings which will never wear out, altho I have at present hopes of getting through without stretching beyond the Balance standing properly to my Credit in his Books; but tho' I called upon our friend the day before I last left Paris & writ to him by my Son the 3d. Inst. requesting an account of that Balance in order to compare with my own minutes & for avoiding mistakes, I have not heard from him on the subject;[3] should he remain silent at the return of the next Mail, I may presume to draw for pretty

1. Antoine Guénard de Monville (or Demonville) had been the printer of the Académie française since 1774: Paul Delalain, *Les Libraires & imprimeurs de l'Académie française de 1634 à 1793: notices biographiques* (Paris, 1907), pp. 102–6. Hilliard was not a member of the academy, and to our knowledge, Guénard de Monville did not print any of his works.

2. The letter is dated Feb. 27 on the letterbook copy, and when Laurens endorsed BF's letter of Feb. 15 (to which this is the response) he wrote that he answered on Feb. 27. Internal evidence points to that date as well.

3. Grand wrote to Laurens on Feb. 23, informing him that 8,974 *l.t.* 13 *s.* was at his disposal: *Laurens Papers*, XVI, 396n.

nearly the Amount of what appears to me to be due. I wish to avoid blended Accounts.

By writing to you as in my last[4] I meant to take time by the forelock & to avail my self in case of need had there been remitances lodged in your hands for supplying the American Ministers according to the late regulations by Congress, but if I am driven to the necessity of borrowing, certain friends here have engaged me to give them the preference, & as I am persuaded Mr. Grand has had his full share of that sort of indulgence, he will not be offended by my determination against oppressing his good nature.

I had heard that some, indeed all, of Mr. M's late Bills on Holland were in course to be protested, but was informed a day or two ago, that means had been devised for paying off the whole, by a Loan from a Society of Moravians or some other Religionists, the terms of Treaty unknown;[5] whether to rejoice or to be sad at this event I have not yet Resolved. Dishonor to our Country would grieve me, on the other hand I foresee that dishonor & with accumulated weight, inevitable, unless we shall avert the Calamity by prudent conduct henceforward, or shall receive such a Check as will effectually restrain our drawing the Pen at random & compel us to resort to the only proper measures for supporting our Credit & our Union with dignity. Of the former I have slender hopes, nor will we believe or fear the Check while under repeated menaces our wanton draughts continue to be paid. 'Tis lamentable to see a whole Nation a fine promising young Nation too, treading in the steps of a thoughtless profligate Planter running in debt for principal & Interest & principal created for imaginary discharge of Interest until his Creditors divest him of his Estate real & personal & turn himself & family out of Doors. Or do our Governors & Finance-managers reason upon the principles of old Gaillard of Santé. You ask me said the old Man to his Neighbors, how I can sleep under such a load of debt? poh! poh! ask Paul Jenys & the rest of my Credi-

4. Above, Feb. 3.
5. Actually, it was JA who came to the rescue of "Mr. M's" (*i.e.*, Morris') bills by arranging a new loan with the Dutch consortium; see his letters of Jan. 24, Feb. 11, and Feb. 20.

tors how they can sleep. But Paul Jenys soon found his land & Negroes.[6]

Your strictures & observations on the disorders of this Country & the sources of them appear to me to be very judicios, but tho' it be a subject for thankfulness that we have less connexion with its affairs than we formerly had, 'tis to be regreted that we continue to practice too many of the old bad Customs which we had learned in that connexion, I have nevertheless hopes, that there will come a time when we shall manage better, but we must smart first & probably suffer under the pain of some convulsions.

I must refer you to the Newspapers & pamphlets contained in a Packet which Mr. [*blank in MS*] Chollet[7] will do me the favor to deliver, for the present state of Politics in this latitude. You will perceive the Majority, or the Managers of the Majority, have by gradual steps brought their affair to a crisis. The House of Commons will have the King's answer to their Address Reported to day, debates & probably strong Resolutions will ensue, or possibly nothing more than an abrupt or as the present stile is, a *temperate* adjournment to Monday, if Mr. Chollet stays long enough to take the Paper of to morrow Morning with him you may from thence form a judgement of what will be the final Issue—most Men at this moment think a dissolution.[8] I wish as earnestly as any body for an Administration permanent efficient &c &c—in whom I may repose confidence of being paid my Two Thousand Eight hundred & odd Pounds. Resolved on my part to demand a categorical answer whether they will or will

6. In the 1730s planter Frederick Gaillard was forced to sell his land and slaves to pay off his many creditors, including Paul Jenys and Laurens' father, John: Clara A. Langley, *South Carolina Deed Abstracts, 1719–1772* (4 vols., Easley, S.C., 1983–4), I, 340.

7. Samuel Chollet, a merchant who was in partnership in London with Laurens' friend and business associate James Bourdieu (XXXVII, 528n, 710): *Laurens Papers*, VIII, 220n, 423n; XVI, 360n.

8. When George III did not respond to its resolution of Feb. 2 (see our annotation of Laurens to BF, Feb. 3), the House of Commons adopted a resolution on Feb. 20, this one offered by Thomas Powys, urging the crown to heed the sentiments of the House. The king answered on Feb. 27 that he would not dismiss his ministers. Parliament was not dissolved until March 25: A. Aspinall, ed., *The Later Correspondence of George III* (5 vols., Cambridge, 1962–70), I, 37–8; John Cannon, *The Fox-North Coalition:*

not pay me, I will not walk up their 78. Stone steps[9] twice more upon this occasion.

I am very thankful to you Sir, for communicating the commercial Plan in embrio. Glad to find I had neither alleged nor intimated any thing extraordinary respecting it. I have detail'd without names your present information, to Gentlemen here who Interest themselves in the happiness of both Countries. A large meeting of Merchants & West India proprietors are at this moment assembled, to deliberate on the Trade between the British Islands & the United States, you will perceive from the contents of Mr. Edwards's Pamphlet[1] that the West India Planters & Plantation holders are not a little alarmed. I am promised the result of the meeting some time this Evening, if it reaches me in time you shall be informed in a PS.[2] but 'tis boldly asserted here by certain persons, instructed as I apprehend by the late Ministry & encouraged perhaps by the impolitic droppings of a friend, that there is no power at present subsisting on the part of America to treat for Commerce with Great Britain, I can only reply that I believe 'tis a mistake, & hope to be soon fully informed. Mean time the United States seem to have at length felt the effect of the Proclama: of 2d July 1783.[3] No doubt that of [blank in MS] Decem will be a provoking aggravation.[4] Let our people determine to act wisely & these conjurers will soon

---

Crisis of the Constitution, 1782–4 (Cambridge, 1969), pp. 196–8; *Laurens Papers*, XVI, 398n, 422n.

9. To the Treasury building: *Laurens Papers*, XVI, 398n. See also Laurens to BF, Feb. 3.

1. Bryan Edwards, *Thoughts on the Late Proceedings of Government, Respecting the Trade of the West India Islands with the United States of North America* (London, 1784).

2. Laurens enclosed a copy of Benjamin Vaughan's notes from the Feb. 27 meeting, which was addressed by Secretary of State Thomas Townshend, Baron Sydney. Interspersed in the notes are Laurens' own brief comments disparaging various points raised at the meeting. For the text of the notes see *Laurens Papers*, XVI, 400–1.

3. Restricting American trade with the British West Indies to British subjects using British vessels; see XL, 289n.

4. On Dec. 26 the king ordered, among other things, the continuation of the restrictions he imposed July 2: *London Gaz.*, Dec. 23–27, 1783. See also our annotation of Hartley's letter of Feb. 23.

be compelled to act with more wisdom & with a little more sincerity than we have experienced from them in the last eleven Months, or as many Years.

We have felt the Frost as bitterly here as you describe it to have been in France, I have been a fellow sufferer with you under its severity, confined by Gout in my Head & Side, four Weeks, the present open Weather, I hope will affect you as I feel it. But notwithstanding disparity of Years I believe you are the hailest Man. Fifteen Months confined sedentary living[5] to a person who had been accustomed to free Air & much exercise, has broken down the Constitution, I am scarcely ever quite & never 48 hours together tolerably well, 'tis no matter the approaching *End* will be Rest & Health, the thoughts therefore on that approach are not troublesome. Knowing not when the event may happen, I am in the course of duly preparing for embarkation to America. As soon as my Son & the other part of the family shall arrive from the South of France I shall fix on a Vessel for Cheasapeke or Delaware hoping to be at Sea early in April which is not far off. If there are any services in my power which you may wish to command you may depend Sir upon my most zealos endeavors. I don't love many words of profession therefore after presenting My Daughters united Compliments & good wishes to your self & Mr. Franklin I conclude with assurances of being one of those friends who never maintaining your infallibility will ever love you for your merits & never forsake your defence should there be need.   HENRY LAURENS.

His Excellency Benjamin Franklin Esquire Passy.

From Jean Rousseau   ALS: American Philosophical Society

Sir   London the 27th: feby. 1784.

Your kind & precious present, is at last arrived: I have cast my eyes upon, & was mightily pleased, with the contents of this valuable book.[6] Be So good honoured Sir, to accept my most

5. During his imprisonment in the Tower of London.
6. Most likely a copy of the *Constitutions des treize Etats-Unis de l'Amérique.*

hearty thanks, for this extraordinary & Singular favour. I Shall Study his contents, with the greatest pleasure: his fiery & noble maxims, not only proves the framers and makers of those laws, to be true Legislators, but Showes in the Same time, the Manliness of the whole Nation, by the Sanction of the Inhabitants, & their mutual approbation.

As soon as time permits, I will endeavour to fulfill a Small part of my engagements towards your Excellency, for which I beg patience and Indulgence; then even the Small part of the whole, is by far beyond my poor Intellects.

After recommanding my Self to Your powerfull protection, give me leave to Suscribe my Self with the greatest respect Sir of your Excellency's The most humble servant

JOHN ROUSSEAU

Notation: Rousseau Mr. John, London 27 Feby. 1784.

Franklin and John Jay to John Adams

LS:[7] Massachusetts Historical Society

Sir   Passy, 28 Feby. 1784.

We had the honor of receiving your Favour of the 20th. Inst, and are persuaded that the Communication of the Friendly Disposition of his Prussian Majesty made to you by the Baron de Thuilemeyer will give great Pleasure to Congress. The Respect with which the Reputation of that great Prince has impress'd the United States, early induced them to consider his Friendship as a desirable Object;[8] and we are happy in being authorised to assure his Majesty that they will most chearfully enter into such a Commercial Treaty with him as being founded on Principles of Reciprocity may be productive of equal Benefits to both Countries. Altho' we have no Commission to conclude such a Treaty, yet our Instructions from Congress[9] enable us

7. In WTF's hand. BF completed the complimentary close before signing.
8. In 1777, both Congress and the commissioners had expressed interest in cultivating the friendship of King Frederick II: XXIII, 98, 327, 473–4, 591–2, 621; XXIV, 73, 515; XXV, 35–6, 227.
9. Above, Oct. 29.

to join with the King's Minister in preparing a Draft of such Treaty, which being sent to Congress, they would, together with a Commission to conclude the Treaty, give us pointed Instructions on the Subject, and much time might be thereby saved. If you are of this Opinion, and his Majesty should be pleased to approve such a Measure, we think the Articles may be discuss'd between you and the Baron in the first Instance, on the Principles which govern in the Treaties you mention, both of which have been approved and ratified.[1] That being done, we might confer together, & write a joint Letter to Congress on the Subject; we shall nevertheless make this Communication a part of our next Dispatch to Congress.

We have the honor to be, Sir, Your Excellency's most obedient & most humble Servants   B. FRANKLIN
                                                                                                                          JOHN JAY

His Excellency John Adams Esqr.

Endorsed: M M. Franklin & Jay 28. Feb. 1784

From the Comte Biberstein Trembinski[2]

ALS: American Philosophical Society

Monsieur   au Havre en Normandie le 28 fevrier 1784:
Je viens de recevoir incluse dans celle du Duc de Rochefoucauld la lettre dont Votre Excellence a bien Voulû m'honorer pour le President du Congrés des Etats Unies.[3] Je brule de de-

---

1. JA showed this letter to Thulemeier on March 8, and Thulemeier communicated its contents to the king. In response, Frederick authorized Thulemeier to begin negotiations with JA for a treaty of commerce: *Adams Papers*, XVI, 77–9, 90–1.

2. Probably Franz, judging by the signature. He and his brother Adam were both Galician counts: Ernst Heinrich Kneschke, ed., *Neues allgemeines Deutsches Adels-Lexicon* (9 vols., Leipzig, 1859), I, 410.

3. BF's letter to Congress has not been found. It was solicited by the duc de La Rochefoucauld. In an unsigned, undated note (APS), the duke's secretary (XXIX, 258) asked BF to introduce the count as a nobleman who came recommended by the Polish minister and the French ambassador at

sir de voir l'Amerique ce Monument de l'amour de la Patrie, de Valeur, et de la Vertue, et de conoitre ce peuple de héros. Si le hasard ebauche un gouvernement c'est la raison seul qui le perfectionne. Je ne doute nullement que par les Principes que les Etats adopteront pour leurs Constitution Politique, Votre Grande Republique deviendra le Model de tous les Païs qui aspireront a un Gouvernement heureux, comme Elle l'est deja pour ceux qui gemissant sous le joug d'un gouvernement arbitraire chercheront a rentrer dans le droit naturel de toutte Société primitive. Il ne me reste qu'une crainte, que l'etat de ma Santée ne m'empeche point d'entreprendre ce Voyage. En ce Cas la seule chose qui pouroit m'en dedomager cela seroit l'honneur de Vous Connoitre de prés et la permission que je Vous demande de Vous ecrire. Double avantages que je devrai a Mr. le Duc de Rochefoucauld et a Votre Condescendances.

J'ai l'honneur d'etre avec la Consideration la plus distingué Monsieur de Votre Excellence le tres humble tres obeissant Serviteur   FR Comte Biberstein Trembinski

SE: Mr: franklin. Ministre Plenipotencier de la ReP: des Provinces Unies de l'amerique a: Passÿ.

From ———— Deviller   ALS: American Philosophical Society

Rüe des Martires Montmartre No 12
Monsieur   ce 28 fevrier 1784

Il se présente pour entrer a Mon service un nommé Campo qui dit avoir eu l'honneur de vous servir deux ans en qualité de valet de chambre officier.[4] Comme jai pour usage de ne jamais prendre de domestique sans au préalable avoir l'attache des Maitres d'ou il sortents, Oseraije vous prier de me dire la verité

Constantinople (Stanisław Pichelstein and the comte de Saint-Priest, respectively: *Repertorium der diplomatischen Vertreter*, III, 142, 315).

4. Campo-de-Arbe served as BF's maître d'hôtel for about a year before being replaced in June, 1782. In early 1783 he asked BF for a recommendation: XXXIX, 134–5.

sur le Compte de cet homme s'il est fidel, point yvrogne ny dé-
bauché. Je vous en aurai la plus grande obligation et si votre reponse ne repond pas a mes voeus(?) je ne vous Comprometterai
surement pas et je lui donnerai quelques raisons vagues pour
qu'il ne puisse pas se douter que ce puisse estre votre reponse
qui m'ayé empesché de le prendre. Pardon de la painne que je
prend la liberté de vous donner mais c'est un service qui se rend
ordinnairement entre gens honnestes. Je vous prie en attendant
d'estre bien persuadé de la reconnoissance respectueuse avec la
qu'elle je suis Monsieur Votre tres humble et tres obeissant serviteur   DEVILLER

Jai oublié d'avoir l'honneur de vous demander s'il n'etoit pas
Marié

Notation: DeViller 28 Fevr. 1784.

From John Shaffer   ALS: American Philosophical Society

Sir   ce 28 fr. 84./
    This moment I have Obtained the Expetion of the Arrest
of Parlement Rendered in my feavour, wich will Prove to you
my inosance and the Cruel Maner in wich I have bean Treated,
Theirefore I hope you will be Kind Enough to Comunicate The
inclosed arrest,⁵ to all my Countryman before my Departure
and ingage them to assist me, So that I may Return to my Native Country *Decently,* Mr Beaumont will inform you of my
intentions,
    I have the honour to be with Respect your Exelencys Most
Obedent & Very humble servant   J. SCHAFFER

    I Expect to leave Paris in a few days for Philadelpha

5. Missing.

596

Information to Those Who Would Remove to America

Printed at Passy, [1784]; AD (draft):[6] Yale University Library; copy: Library of Congress

When Franklin sent this pamphlet to Secretary of Congress Charles Thomson on March 9, he explained it as follows: "I am pestered continually with Numbers of Letters from People in different Parts of Europe, who would go to settle in America; but who manifest very extravagant Expectations, such as I can by no means encourage; and who appear otherwise to be very improper Persons. To save myself Trouble I have just printed some Copies of the enclosed little Piece, which I purpose to send hereafter in Answer to such Letters."[7]

Franklin may have thought about producing a general reply to the proliferating appeals from prospective emigrants as early as the spring of 1783.[8] He did not have the leisure to write it, however, until after the final peace negotiations were concluded. His labored draft suggests that the essay was written over a period of time: words and phrases were carefully weighed, new thoughts were interlined, and one entire passage, written on a separate slip of paper, was pasted in the appropriate location. When it was finished, Benjamin Franklin Bache attempted to produce a fair copy, making many errors that were carefully corrected by his grandfather.[9] Benny's copying tasks allowed Franklin to instruct him in the English language as well as penmanship, areas in which he was making steady improvements.

"Information to Those Who Would Remove to America" was one of two essays printed at Passy around early March, 1784. The other was "Remarks concerning the Savages of North America,"

6. The draft is untitled, but on the verso BF wrote "Information respecting America / 1784." (Below it, WTF later wrote and initialled, "This was written by Dr. Franklin and is the original Rough Draft in his own hand Writing.") By the time BFB prepared the fair copy, the final title had been established. Facsimiles of the English imprint and its French counterpart are in *The Bagatelles from Passy* (New York, 1967), pp. 109–23, 131–42.

7. BF to Charles Thomson, March 9, 1784 (National Archives).

8. See XXXIX, 39–41. BF also commented on the unrealistic expectations of many emigrants in a letter to RB and SB of July 27, 1783: XL, 392.

9. Evidently unaware of BF's rules of capitalization, for example, the boy neglected to observe them. He missed several phrases that had been written in the margin, and, not infrequently, he misspelled words. Having spoken French for so long while in boarding school, he instinctively put the "u" in "gouvernment," for example, and, still struggling to master the irregularities of English, he put an extra "p" in "coppy."

published above under the date [before January 7]. Neither essay can be dated precisely. Both were translated, and pamphlets were issued in both French and English. In the case of "Remarks," a letter from the translator gives some indication of when the essay was composed. No such letter survives for "Information," and the translator's identity is still unknown.[1] A drawing on the verso of page 10 of the draft suggests that Franklin was composing it during the late fall of 1783,[2] but he labeled the completed draft "1784". In the absence of any other clues, we place the essay at the end of the present volume. Though it was probably finished long before the end of February, it cannot have been completed much later, as the printed pamphlet was ready for distribution by March 9.

We follow the same textual policy here that we apply to "Remarks," publishing the English text as it was issued from the Passy press. As with "Remarks," Franklin made final wording changes that are not marked on either of the surviving manuscripts. We noted in the headnote to "Remarks" that the compositor introduced typographical errors and various kinds of minor alterations; the same is true of this text.

The first page of the English pamphlet is reproduced as the frontispiece of this volume. Its French counterpart, "Avis à ceux qui voudraient s'en aller en Amérique," included a charming title page that sets it apart from all other pamphlets printed by Franklin at Passy.[3] The title itself, broken into four lines, was set in four different fonts, including fancy italic. The center of the page was decorated with an

1. La Rochefoucauld translated "Remarks," and BF may have asked him to translate "Information," as well. Another candidate is the abbé Morellet, who translated BF's letter on the Society of the Cincinnati (BF to SB, Jan. 26, above).

2. The drawing is of the grate stove BF was designing around that time; see Le Noir to BF, Dec. 4, and the facing illustration. For more information see the List of Illustrations.

3. The imprints of "Avis" and "Remarques" required two additional pages of text, as French typically runs longer than the equivalent English. Because extra pages, in the form of folded sheets, were added in multiples of four, this would have left two blank pages. BF took the opportunity to set title pages for both French imprints. The title page of "Remarques," by contrast to "Avis," was starkly unadorned, the title being set in block capitals. Both title pages can be seen in *The Bagatelles from Passy;* they are also reproduced in Luther S. Livingston, *Franklin and His Press at Passy* (New York, 1914), facing p. 46 and between pp. 50 and 51. For general information on the printing of these pamphlets see the headnote to "Remarks concerning the Savages of North America," [before Jan. 7].

ornament of flowers and leaves, and at the bottom of the page, below a rule, the year of publication, 1784, was set in roman numerals. Franklin's French-language description of life in the United States was elegantly dressed.

The French edition must have been printed around the same time as the English. Scarcely a week after sending "Information" to Charles Thomson, Franklin received an appeal from an unknown Frenchman recommending an unnamed younger person seeking help. "I have no Orders or Authority to encourage any Persons to go to America, by promising Lands or other Favours from the Government there," he answered. "The enclos'd printed paper will give such an Account of that Country as may perhaps convince your Friend that he had better stay where he is."[4]

It is not known how many copies of "Information" Franklin printed, nor do we know how many were left in the hands of his successor, Thomas Jefferson. In 1788, however, having no copies of what he described to one potential emigrant as the "petite brochure de M. Franklin," Jefferson commissioned new ones. Without a private press at his disposal, however, he was obliged to pay for the reprinting.[5]

[before March, 1784]
INFORMATION
TO THOSE
WHO WOULD REMOVE
TO AMERICA.

MANY Persons in Europe having directly or by Letters, express'd to the Writer of this, who is well acquainted with North-America, their Desire of transporting and establishing themselves in that Country; but who appear to him to have formed thro' Ignorance, mistaken Ideas & Expectations of what is to be obtained there; he thinks it may be useful, and prevent inconvenient, expensive & fruitless Removals and Voyages of improper Persons, if he gives some clearer & truer Notions of that Part of the World than appear to have hitherto prevailed.

4. BF's March 19 draft for a reply to a letter from Milet l'aîné, March 12, 1784 (APS).

5. In July, 1788, when sending a pamphlet to a certain Gallimard, TJ wrote "No person is better qualified than [Franklin] to give advice on this subject." For the reprint, TJ used a translation that had been published by Mazzei: *Jefferson Papers*, XII, 586–7; XIII, 430–2.

He finds it is imagined by Numbers that the Inhabitants of North-America are rich, capable of rewarding, and dispos'd to reward all sorts of Ingenuity; that they are at the same time ignorant of all the Sciences; & consequently that strangers possessing Talents in the Belles-Letters, fine Arts, &c. must be highly esteemed, and so well paid as to become easily rich themselves; that there are also abundance of profitable Offices to be disposed of, which the Natives are not qualified to fill; and that having few Persons of Family among them, Strangers of Birth must be greatly respected and of course easily obtain the best of those Offices, which will make all their Fortunes: that the Governments too, to encourage Emigrations from Europe, not only pay the expence of personal Transportation, but give Lands gratis to Strangers, with Negroes to work for them, Utensils of Husbandry, & Stocks of Cattle. These are all wild Imaginations;[6] and those who go to America with Expectations founded upon them, will surely find themselves disappointed.

The Truth is, that tho' there are in that Country few People so miserable as the Poor of Europe, there are also very few that in Europe would be called rich: it is rather a general happy Mediocrity that prevails. There are few great Proprietors of the Soil,[7] and few Tenants; most People cultivate their own Lands, or follow some Handicraft or Merchandise; very few rich enough to live idly upon their Rents or Incomes; or to pay the high Prices given in Europe, for Paintings, Statues, Architecture and the other Works of Art that are more curious than useful. Hence the natural Geniuses that have arisen in America, with such Talents, have uniformly quitted that Country for Europe, where they can be more suitably rewarded. It is true that Letters and mathematical Knowledge are in Esteem there, but they are at the same time more common than is apprehended; there being already existing nine Colleges or Universities, viz. four in New-England, and one in each of the Provinces of New-York, New-Jersey, Pensilvania, Maryland and Virginia, all furnish'd with learned Professors; besides a number of smaller Academies: These educate many of their Youth in

6. BF had originally drafted "These Imaginations have little Foundation."

7. BF substituted this phrase for "Landlords," which he originally wrote.

the Languages and those Sciences that qualify Men for the Professions of Divinity, Law or Physick. Strangers indeed are by no means excluded from exercising those Professions, and the quick Increase of Inhabitants every where gives them a Chance of Employ, which they have in common with the Natives. Of civil Offices or Employments there are few; no superfluous Ones as in Europe; and it is a Rule establish'd in some of the States, that no Office should be so profitable as to make it desirable. The 36 Article of the Constitution of Pensilvania, runs expresly in these Words: *As every Freeman, to preserve his Independence, (if he has not a sufficient Estate) ought to have some Profession, Calling, Trade or Farm, whereby he may honestly subsist, there can be no Necessity for, nor Use in, establishing Offices of Profit; the usual Effects of which are Dependance and Servility, unbecoming Freemen, in the Possessors and Expectants; Faction, Contention, Corruption, and Disorder among the People.*[8] *Wherefore whenever an Office, thro' Increase of Fees or otherwise, becomes so profitable as to occasion many to apply for it, the Profits ought to be lessened by the Legislature.*

These Ideas prevailing more or less in all the United States, it cannot be worth any Man's while, who has a means of Living at home, to expatriate himself in hopes of obtaining a profitable civil Office in America; and as to military Offices, they are at an End with the War; the Armies being disbanded. Much less is it adviseable for a Person to go thither who has no other Quality to recommend him but his Birth. In Europe it has indeed its Value, but it is a Commodity that cannot be carried to a worse Market than to that of America, where People do not enquire concerning a Stranger, *What* IS *he?* but *What can he* DO*?* If he has any useful Art, he is welcome; and if he exercises it & behaves well, he will be respected by all that know him; but a mere Man of Quality, who on that Account wants to live upon the Public, by some Office or Salary, will be despis'd and disregarded. The Husbandman is in honor there, & even the Mechanic, because

8. BF here omitted "But if any man is called into public service, to the prejudice of his private affairs, he has a right to a reasonable compensation": *The Constitution of the Common-wealth of Pennsylvania . . .* (Philadelphia, 1776), p. 27. He had discussed this passage with John Baynes in August, 1783: XL, 526–7.

their Employments are useful. The People have a Saying, that God Almighty is himself a Mechanic, the greatest in the Universe; and he is respected and admired more for the Variety, Ingenuity and Utility of his Handiworks, than for the Antiquity of his Family. They are pleas'd with the Observation of a Negro, and frequently mention it, that *Boccarorra* (meaning the Whiteman) make de Blackman workee, make de Horse workee, make de Ox workee, make ebery ting workee; only de Hog. He de Hog, no workee; he eat, he drink, he walk about, he go to sleep when he please, *he libb like a Gentleman.*[9] According to these Opinions of the Americans, one of them would think himself more oblig'd to a Genealogist, who could prove for him that his Ancestors & Relations for ten Generations had been Ploughmen, Smiths, Carpenters, Turners, Weavers, Tanners, or even Shoemakers, & consequently that they were useful Members of Society; than if he could only prove that they were Gentlemen, doing nothing of value, but living idly on the Labour of others, mere *Fruges consumere nati**,[1] and otherwise *good* for *nothing*, till by their Death, their Estates like the Carcase of the Negro's Gentleman-Hog, come to be *cut up.*

With Regard to Encouragements for Strangers from Government, they are really only what are derived from good Laws & Liberty. Strangers are welcome because there is room enough for them all, and therefore the old Inhabitants are not jealous of them; the Laws protect them sufficiently, so that they have no

---

9. BF wrote this passage about the "Observation of a Negro" on a separate slip of paper and marked the place for its insertion with a cross. He deleted a final sentence: "He no good for noting till he dead; den he berry good—*to cut up.*"

1. Born to consume the fruits of the earth: Horace, *Epistles*, book 1, epistle 2, line 27.

Footnote in text: "*There are a Number of us born / Merely to eat up the Corn. Watts." BF is quoting from memory Isaac Watts's paraphrase of Horace published in *Reliquiæ Juveniles: Miscellaneous Thoughts in Prose and Verse* ... (London, 1734), p. 61: "There are a Number of us creep / Into this World, to eat and sleep; / And know no Reason why they're born, / But merely to consume the Corn, / Devour the Cattle, Fowl and Fish, / And leave behind an empty Dish."

need of the Patronage of great Men; and every one will enjoy securely the Profits of his Industry. But if he does not bring a Fortune with him, he must work and be industrious to live. One or two Years Residence give him all the Rights of a Citizen; but the Government does not at present, whatever it may have done in former times, hire People to become Settlers, by Paying their Passages, giving Land, Negroes, Utensils, Stock, or any other kind of Emolument whatsoever. In short America is the Land of Labour, and by no means what the English call *Lubberland*, and the French *Pays de Cocagne*, where the Streets are said to be pav'd with half-peck Loaves, the Houses til'd with Pancakes, and where the Fowls fly about ready roasted, crying, *Come eat me*!

Who then are the kind of Persons to whom an Emigration to America may be advantageous? and what are the Advantages they may reasonably expect?

Land being cheap[2] in that Country, from the vast Forests still void of Inhabitants, and not likely to be occupied in an Age to come, insomuch that the Propriety of an hundred Acres of fertile Soil full of Wood may be obtained near the Frontiers in many Places for eight or ten Guineas,[3] hearty young labouring Men, who understand the Husbandry of Corn and Cattle, which is nearly the same in that Country as in Europe, may easily establish themselves there. A little Money sav'd of the good Wages they receive there while they work for others, enables them to buy the Land and begin their Plantation, in which they are assisted by the Good Will of their Neighbours and some Credit. Multitudes of poor People from England, Ireland, Scotland and Germany, have by this means in a few Years become wealthy Farmers, who in their own Countries, where all the Lands are fully occupied, and the Wages of Labour low, could never have emerged from the mean Condition wherein they were born.

From the Salubrity of the Air, the Healthiness of the Climate, the Plenty of good Provisions, and the Encouragement to early Marriages, by the certainty of Subsistance in cultivating the

---

2. BF here deleted, "and easy to be obtained."
3. BF originally wrote, "Louis d'or."

Earth, the Increase of Inhabitants by natural Generation is very rapid in America, and becomes still more so by the Accession of Strangers; hence there is a continual Demand for more Artisans of all the necessary and useful kinds, to supply those Cultivators of the Earth with Houses, and with Furniture & Utensils of the grosser Sorts which cannot so well be brought from Europe. Tolerably good Workmen in any of those mechanic Arts, are sure to find Employ, and to be well paid for their Work, there being no Restraints preventing Strangers from exercising any Art they understand, nor any Permission necessary. If they are poor, they begin first as Servants or Journeymen; and if they are sober, industrious & frugal, they soon become Masters, establish themselves in Business, marry, raise Families, and become respectable Citizens.

Also,[4] Persons of moderate Fortunes and Capitals, who having a Number of Children to provide for, are desirous of bringing them up to Industry, and to secure Estates for their Posterity, have Opportunities of doing it in America, which Europe does not afford. There they may be taught & practice profitable mechanic Arts withut [without][5] incurring Disgrace on that Account; but on the contrary acquiring Respect by such Abilities. There small Capitals laid out in Lands, which daily become more valuable by the Increase of People, afford a solid Prospect of ample Fortunes thereafter for those Children. The Writer of this has known several Instances of large Tracts of Land, bought on what was then the Frontier of Pensilvania, for ten Pounds per hundred Acres, which, after twenty Years, when the Settlements had been extended far beyond them, sold readily, without any Improvement made upon them, for three Pounds per Acre. The Acre in America is the same with the English Acre or the Acre of Normandy.[6]

4. In both the draft and the copy, this word was "Lastly." BF must have changed it at the last minute.

5. This is the first of a series of typographical errors that we correct, in brackets, based on the MSS.

6. It appears from the draft that BF paused at this point. In the margin he wrote and crossed out notes for additional subjects to be covered: "Facility of obtaining Trades. Manners.— Examples. / Industry. Ind[ustr]y supports Virtue.— Religion."

   Those who desire to understand the State of Government in
America, would do well to read the Constitutions of the several
States, and the Articles of Confederation that bind the whole together for general Purposes under the Direction of one Assembly called the Congress. These Constitutions have been printed
by Order of Congress in America; two Editions of them have
also been printed in London, and a good Translation of them
into French has lately been published at Paris.

   Several of the Princes of Europe having of late Years, from
an Opinion of Advantage to arise by producing all Commodities & Manufactures within their own Dominions, so as to diminish or render useless their Importations, have endeavoured
to entice Workmen from other Countries, by high Salaries,
Privileges, &c. Many Persons pretending to be skilled in various
great Manufactures, imagining that America must be in Want of
them, and that the Congress would probably be dispos'd to imitate the Princes above mentioned, have proposed to go over, on
Condition of having their Passages paid, Lands given, Salaries
appointed, exclusive Privileges for Terms of Years, &c. Such
persons on reading the Articles of Confederation will find that
the Congress have no Power committed to them, or Money put
into their Hands, for such purposes; and that if any such Encouragement is given, it must be by the Government of some
separate State. This however has rarely been done in America;
and when it has been done it has rarely succeeded, so as to establish a Manufacture which the Country was not yet so ripe
for as to encourage private Persons to set it up; Labour being
generally too dear there, & Hands difficult to be kept together,
every one desiring to be a Master, and the Cheapness of Land
enclining many to leave Trades for Agriculture. Some indeed
have met with Success, and are carried on to Advantage; but
they are generally such as require only a few Hands, or wherein
great Part of the Work is perform'd by Machines. Goods[7] that
are bulky, & of so small Value as not well to bear the Expence
of Freight, may often be made cheaper in the Country than they
can be imported; and the Manufacture of such Goods will be

---

   7. "Goods" appears twice in this sentence. In the draft and the copy, the
word is "things."

profitable wherever there is a sufficient Demand. The Farmers in America produce indeed a good deal of Wool & Flax; and none is exported, it is all work'd up; but it is in the Way of Domestic Manufacture for the Use of the Family. The buying up Quantities of Wool & Flax with the Design to employ Spinners, Weavers, &c. and form great Establishments, producing Quantities of Linen and Woollen Goods for Sale, has been several times attempted in different Provinces; but those Projects have generally failed, Goods of equal Value being imported cheaper. And when the Governments have being [been] solicited to support such Schemes oy [by] Encouragements, in Money, or by imposing Duties an [on] Importation of such Goods, it has been generally refused, on this Principle, that if the Country is ripe for the Manufacture, it may be carried on by private Persons to Advantage; and if not, it is a Folly to think of forceing [forcing] Nature. Great Establishments of Manufacture, require great Numbers of Poor to do the Work for small Wages; these Poor are to be found in Europe, but will not be found in America, till the Lands are all taken up and cultivated, and the excess of People who cannot get Land, want Employment. The Manufacture of Silk, they sey [say], is natural in France, as that of Cloth in England, because each Country produces in Plenty the first Material: But if England will have a Manufacture of Silk as well as that of Cloth, and France one of Cloth as well as that of Silk, these unnatural Operations must be supported by mutual Prohibitions or high Duties on the Importation of each others Goods, by which means the Workmen are enabled to tax the home-Consumer by greater Prices, while the higher Wages they receive makes them neither happier nor richer, since they only drink more and work less. Therefore the Governments in America do nothing to encourage such Projects. The People by this Means are not impos'd on, either by the Merchant or Mechanic; if the Merchant demands too much Profit on imported Shoes, they buy of the Shoemaker: And if he asks to [too] high a Price, they take them of the Merchant: thus the two Professions are Checks on each other. The Shoemaker however has on the whole a considerable Profit upon his Labour in America, beyond what he had in Europe, as he can add to his Price a Sum nearly equal to all the Expences of Freight & Commission, Risque or Insurance, &c. necessarily charged by the Merchant. And the Case is the same with the Workmen in every other Mechanic Art. Hence it is that Artisans generally live better and more easily in America than in Europe, and such as are good œconomists make a comfortable Provision for Age, & for their Children. Such may therefore remove with Advantage to America.

In the old longsettled Countries of Europe, all Arts, Trades, Professions, Farms, &c. are so full that it is difficult for a poor Man who has Children, to place them where they may gain, or learn to gain a decent Livelihood. The Artisans, who fear creating future Rivals in Business, refuse to take Apprentices, but upon Conditions of Money, Maintenance or the like, which the Parents are unable to comply with. Hence the Youth are dragg'd up in Ignorance of every gainful Art, and oblig'd to become Soldiers or Servants or Thieves, for a Subsistance. In America the rapid Increase of Inhabitants takes away that Fear of Rivalship, & Artisans willingly receive Apprentices from the hope of Profit by their Labour during the Remainder of the Time stipulated after they shall be instructed. Hence it is easy for poor Families to get their Children instructed; for the Artisans are so desirous of Apprentices, that many of them will even give Money to the Parents to have Boys from ten to fifteen Years of Age bound Apprentices to them till the Age of twenty one; and many poor Parents have by that means, on their Arrival in the Country, raised Money enough to buy Land sufficient to establish themselves, and subsist the rest of their Family by Agriculture. These Contracts for Apprentices are made before a Magistrate, who regulates the Agreement according to Reason and Justice; and having in view the Formation of a future useful Citizen, obliges the Master to engage by a written Indenture, not only that during the time of Service stipulated, the Apprentice shall be duly provided with Meat, Drink, Apparel, washing & Lodging, and at its Expiration with a compleat new suit of Clothes, but also that he shall be taught to read, write & cast Accompts, & that he shall be well instructed in the Art or Profession of his Master, or some other, by which he may afterwards gain a Livelihood, and be able in his turn to raise a Family. A Copy of this Indenture is given to the Apprentice or his Friends, & the Magistrate keeps a Record of it, to which

Recourse may be had, in case of Failure by the Master in any Point of Performance. This Desire among the Masters to have more Hands employ'd in working for them, induces them to pay the Passages of young Persons, of both Sexes, who on their Arrival agree to serve them one, two, three or four Years; those who have already learnt a Trade agreeing for a shorter Term in Proportion to their Skill and the consequent immediate Value of their Service; and those who have none, agreeing for a longer Term, in Consideration of being taught an Art their Poverty would not permit them to acquire in their own Country.

The almost general Mediocrity of Fortune that prevails in America, obliging its People to follow some Business for Subsistance, those Vices that arise usually from Idleness are in a great Measure prevented. Industry and constant Employment are great Preservatives of the Morals and Virtue of a Nation. Hence bad Examples to Youth are more rare in America, which must be a comfortable Consideration to Parents. To this may be truly added, that serious Religion under its various Denominations, is not only tolerated but respected and practised. Atheism is unknown there, Infidelity rare & secret, so that Persons may live to a great Age in that Country without having their Piety shock'd by meeting with either an Atheist or an Infidel. And the Divine Being seems to have manifested his Approbation of the mutual Forbearance and Kindness with which the different Sects treat each other, by the remarkable Prosperity with which he has been pleased to favour the whole Country.

Index

Compiled by Philipp Ziesche.

(Semicolons separate subentries; colons separate divisions within subentries. A volume and page reference in parentheses following a main entry refers to an individual's first identification in this edition.)

Abby (Jay family slave), 5

'Abd al-Malik, Muhammad ibn (Moroccan ambassador), 468

Académie française, 588

Académie royale de chirurgie, 98n, 301, 302n

Académie royale des belles-lettres, sciences et arts de Bordeaux, 536n

Académie royale des sciences, xxx, xxxi, lvii, 14n, 37n, 125n, 126n, 172, 203, 210n, 212, 248n, 305, 366n, 395, 426, 453, 563n, 568

Accademia Reale delle Scienze (Turin), 394

Acton, John Francis Edward, 449n

Adams, Abigail (John and Abigail's daughter), 571n

Adams, John: travels to England, lvi, 107, 137–8, 165, 169n, 247, 339, 363, 520: Holland, lvi, 262, 271, 339, 363, 471–2, 495, 498–500, 533, 569, 575n; and Thaxter, 25n, 46, 351n: Hartley, 107, 143, 579: Fox, 107n: *Alliance*, 143n, 343: consortium of Dutch bankers, 247, 254n, 262, 271, 289, 405, 471–2n, 498, 499–500, 533, 575n, 589n: Littlepage, 289: Laurens, 346: R. Montgomery, 468n: Roberdeau, 520: Dumas, 560, 576n; BF demands certificate from, refuting accusations, 26n, 351n: fears may damage Franco-American relations, 54, 345–6: questions mental stability of, 264, 346: writes to Cooper about accusations by, 351; criticizes French government, BF, 27, 54, 345–6, 351: Society of the Cincinnati, 504; health of, 73, 545;

stays in Barclay's house, 73n, 107n, 264n, 288; essay by BF erroneously attributed to, 77; Pownall sends memorial to, 80; letters, endorsements, notations in hand of, 158, 456n; Price wants to meet, 164; forwards letters, dispatches, 169n, 261, 271, 289, 405, 534; Jones delivers congressional dispatches to, 169n, 261, 271, 289, 339, 363, 534; Mather sends *Dying Legacy* to, 199n; Knox recommends Platt to, 232n; Laurens-Jenings dispute, 234–5, 263, 530; inquires about BF's health, 235, 264: whether BF received commission to conclude commercial treaty with Britain, 261–2, 271, 289, 339, 405; receives book for BF from Fitch, 250n; L. Boudinot delivers dispatches to, 288, 405; complains that congressional dispatches should be addressed to all commissioners, 289n; believed to be less sympathetic to France than BF, 337n; Vergennes would prefer dealing with WTF than with, 337n; introduces Barry to Carmichael, 471, 568; said to have recommended Amelung, 491n; attempts to raise new loan in Holland, 499, 533, 544–5, 575n, 578; reports that news of mutiny, failure to collect taxes, pay debts has damaged American credit in Holland, 499, 533, 544; American trade with French West Indies, 532; asked about plans to return to Paris, 534; asks BF, Jay to execute congressional instructions without him, 544, 545: to request commission for

Hartley, David (XXI, 511): assured that reports of American disunion are false, lvi, 138; and British-American commercial treaty, lvi, lvii, lviii, 47, 64, 84, 151–2, 411: signing of definitive peace treaty, 339–40: ratification of peace treaty, 350, 407n, 411, 423, 457n, 514, 579; drinks to BF's health, 23; visits half-sister at Bath, 40–1, 143; delivers peace treaty to British government, 40n; returns to England, 40n; discusses postwar relations between U.S., Britain, 41, 72–4; proposes temporary, non-reciprocal trade agreement, 41, 72, 137–8: naval alliance between Britain, U.S., 73n; sends greetings to peace commissioners, 41, 72–4: flannel, 142–3, 175; forwards packet to Hewson, 51–2, 239; asked by commissioners about Irish-American trade, 64; concerned about reports of American disunion, 72–3, 138: congressional resolution on trade with Britain, 579; and Fox, 72n, 73n, 107n: Jay, 84, 143, 411, 514, 579: JA, 107, 143, 579; inquires about JA's health, 73; recommends Scrope, 96, 138n; approves of BF's article on rights of noncombatants, 107; delays return to Paris, 143, 165, 339; BF does not expect return of, 338n; reports on change in British ministry, 349–50, 411, 423, 579; invited by Holker to meet BF in Rouen, 378; introduces Ross, 513–14; letters from, 40–1, 71–4, 96, 142–3, 349–50, 513–14, 579; letters to, 83–4, 107–8, 137–8, 423

Hartley, Mary (David's half-sister), 40–1, 83, 138, 143

Hartley, Samuel (London merchant, XXV, 579n; XXXI, 354n), 378

Hartley, Travers (Irish politician), 227n

Hartley, Winchcombe Henry (David's half-brother), 138, 143

Harvard College, 76n, 80n, 509–10, 600

Harville, Louis-Auguste de Jouvenel d'Harville des Ursins, marquis de Trainel, comte d', 546n

Harville, Marie-Henriette-Augustine-Renée dal Pozzo de La Trousse, comtesse d', 546

Harwood, Nicholas, 20n

Hauteroche, ———— d', 454

Hazard, Ebenezer (postmaster general): BF forwards advertisement for packet boat service to, 352; criticizes packet boat service, 353n; letter to, 352–3

Hazelhurst, Isaac, Sr. (merchant, XXXIII, 463n), 95

Heath, James, 515nn

Hédouin de Pons-Ludon, Joseph-Antoine, 278

Helvétius, Anne-Catherine de Ligniville d'Autricourt (XXVI, 429n): invites BF, WTF to dinner, 58–9; corresponds with BF through Cabanis, 58n; observes mourning periods for her siblings, 58n; and French translation of Bartram's seed catalogue, 333n; salon of, 373n; sends Alatamaha seeds, 381; letter from, 58–9

Hendrick (privateer), 213, 437

Henley, Robert, Earl of Northington (lord lieutenant of Ireland), 192n, 227n, 461

Heraut, ————, 552

Hernon, Lt. ————, 33

Herries, Robert, 123

Herries & Co. (London banking firm), 12, 13n

Herschel, William, 196, 197, 269, 294

Hervey, Frederick Augustus (Earl of Bristol and Bishop of Derby), 133–4

Hervey, George William, Earl of Bristol, 134

Hewson, Elizabeth (Mary's daughter), 354, 392

Hewson, Mary (Polly) Stevenson (VIII, 122n): BF sends books to, 51, 354, 392: may entrust BFB to, 52, 239; Hartley forwards packet to, 51–2, 239; requests French grammar, 239; and Viny, 239, 353; letters from, 51–2, 239; letters to, 353–4, 392

Hewson, Thomas (Mary's son), 52, 239, 354, 392

Hewson, William (Mary's son), 52, 239, 354, 392

Sweden. *See* Gustavus III; Treaty of Amity and Commerce, Swedish-American

Sydney, Thomas Townshend, Baron, 349, 591n

Sykes, H. (scientific instrument dealer), 118

Synonymes françois (Girard), 354

Tahon, J., 275–6

Taxes: Americans' reluctance to pay, criticized by BF, lvi, 347–8, 533, 544: by Morris, 57, 566: by JA, 499, 544; difficulty of imposing, in U.S., 57, 340, 347–8, 431n, 473, 544, 566: Thomson claims is universal, 473

Taylor, James (N.Y. merchant), 280

Ternay, Charles-Louis d'Arsac, chevalier de, 377n

Ternay, Gabriel d'Arsac, marquis de, 377–8n

Terrible (prize), 50n

Thalie, Masonic Lodge of, 281n

Thaxter, John, Jr. (JA's secretary, XXXI, 274n): carries peace treaty, dispatches to Congress, 25–6, 46, 147n, 165, 168, 333n, 363, 423; encloses note to Thévenard, 25–6; arrives at New York, 46n, 423n; may have carried Chotek's order for seeds, 333n; carries, discloses confidential letter from BF to Cooper, 351n; letter from, 25–6

Theodoor Van Moorsel & Co., 450

Thévenard, Antoine-Jean-Marie de (Lorient port commandant, XXX, 87n), 25–6

Thieriot, Philipp, 98, 397n

Thomson, Charles (secretary of Congress, VII, 266n): recommends I. Norris, 45–6: Harmar, 464: Franks, 474; and Curwen, 139n; as secretary of Congress, 147n, 154n, 158, 457n; and congressional commission of statue of GW, 159n; believed to be author of letter by Mifflin, 407n; sent "Information," 413, 597; BF forwards inquiries, petitions to, 463, 472–3; makes inquiry for Du Pont de Nemours, 463, 472; forwards petitions, 463–4, 472–

3; BF forwards Du Pont de Nemours' letter to, 463n; claims Congress will not encourage immigrants, 464; makes inquiry concerning Averton, Vigeral, 472; argues all governments have difficulties imposing taxes, 473; declines to pursue claim against Steuben, 473; believes states will contribute to pay national debt, 473–4; letters from, 45–6, 463–4, 472–4

Thornton, John, 238

Thornton, William, 514–15

Thoughts on the Late Proceedings of Government . . . (Edwards), 591

Three Friends (ship), 440–1

Thulemeier, Friedrich Wilhelm von (Prussian envoy to Netherlands), 576–8, 593–4

Thurlow, Edward, Baron (XXVI, 543n), 306, 311, 349

Thurn. *See* Goëzmann de Thurn

Tillet, Mathieu (botanist, XXIX, 275n), 426n

Toaldo, Giuseppe, abbé, 188n

Tobacco: farmers general make contract with Alexander, JW for delivery of, 180n, 348, 584n; as payment of American debt owed to farmers general, 180n, 348: of Dutch loan, 246, 561, 562, 566; farmers general's monopoly on trade in, 286n, 313n; Berail & Cie. handle import of, at Cette, 309; Barney inquires about package of, 313; Almasy requests from Beelen-Bertholff, 318n; Prussian demand for, 449, 577

Tobago, 557

Todd, Anthony (X, 217n): BF sends plan for packet boat service to, lviii, 85–7, 116–17: asks WTF to draft letter to, 71, 85n, 86n: comments on advertisements for packet boats by, 153, 200; responds to BF's proposal for French, British packet boats to U.S., lviii, 22–3, 116–17; and Maddison, 21; drafts, sends advertisements for packet boat service, 22, 24, 116–17, 200; drinks to BF's health with Hartley, 23; inquires about French packet boats, 23;

677